Attachment
in the
Preschool Years

THE JOHN D. AND CATHERINE T. MACARTHUR FOUNDATION
Series on Mental Health and Development

Attachment
in the
Preschool Years

Theory, Research, and
Intervention

EDITED BY
Mark T. Greenberg, Dante Cicchetti, and
E. Mark Cummings

The University of Chicago Press

Chicago and London

The University of Chicago Press, Chicago 60637
The University of Chicago Press, Ltd., London

The University of Chicago Press gratefully acknowledges a subvention from
the John D. and Catherine T. MacArthur Foundation in partial support of the
costs of production of this volume.

Library of Congress Cataloging-in-Publication Data

Attachment in the preschool years : theory, research, and intervention /
    [edited by} Mark T. Greenberg, Dante Ciccetti, E. Mark Cummings.
        p.   cm. — (The John D. and Catherine T. MacArthur Foundation
    series on mental health and development)
    Includes bibliographical references.
    ISBN: 0-226-30629-1 (cloth)
    ISBN: 0-226-30630-5 (paperback)
    1. Attachment behavior in children.   2. Child psychopathology.
I. Greenberg, Mark T.   II. Ciccetti, Dante.   III. Cummings, E. Mark.
IV. Series.
BF723.A75A87   1990
155.42´38–dc20   89-49657
                                                          CIP

⊗ The paper used in this publication meets the minimum requirements of the
American National Standard for Information Sciences—Permanence of Paper
for Printed Library Materials, ANSI Z39.48—1984.

Contents

Contributors

J. LAWRENCE ABER, PH.D., Department of Psychology, Barnard College, Columbia University, 3009 Broadway, New York, N.Y. 10027

MARY D. SALTER AINSWORTH, PH.D., Professor Emeritus, Department of Psychology, Gilmer Hall, University of Virginia, Charlottesville, Va. 22903

AMY J. L. BAKER, PH.D., Department of Psychology, Barnard College, Columbia University, 3009 Broadway, New York, N.Y. 10027

INGE BRETHERTON, PH.D., Department of Child Study, University of Wisconsin, Madison, Wis. 53705

JUDE CASSIDY, PH.D., Psychology Department, Pennsylvania State University, State College, Pa. 16802

DANTE CICCHETTI, PH.D., Departments of Psychology and Psychiatry, Director, Mt. Hope Family Center, University of Rochester, 187 Edinburgh Street, Rochester, N.Y. 14608

E. MARK CUMMINGS, PH.D., Department of Psychology, West Virginia University, Morgantown, W. Va. 26506-6040

M. ANN EASTERBROOKS, Ph.D., Department of Child Study, Tufts University, Medford, Mass. 02155

ROBERT N. EMDE, M.D., Department of Psychiatry, University of Colorado Health Sciences, 4200 East Ninth Avenue, Denver, Colo. 80262

WENDY A. GOLDBERG, PH.D., Program in Social Ecology, University of California, Irvine, Calif. 92717

MARK T. GREENBERG, PH.D., Department of Psychology, NI-25, University of Washington, Seattle, Wash. 98195

ERIK HESSE, Department of Psychology, University of California, Berkeley, Calif. 94720

ALICIA F. LIEBERMAN, PH.D., Department of Psychiatry, University of California, San Francisco, and Senior Psychologist, Infant-Parent Program, San Francisco General Hospital, 1001 Potrero Avenue, San Francisco, Calif. 94110

MARY MAIN, PH.D., Department of Psychology, University of California, Berkeley, Calif. 94720

ROBERT S. MARVIN, PH.D., Director, Pediatric Psychology, Children's Rehabilitation Center, University of Virginia, 2270 Ivy Road, Charlottesville, Va. 22901

CHRISTINE MASLIN-COLE, PH.D., Department of Human Development and Family Studies, Gifford Building, Room 119, Colorado State University, Fort Collins, Colo. 80523

JEREE H. PAWL, PH.D., Clinical Program, Department of Psychiatry, University of California, San Francisco, and Director, Infant-Parent Program, San Francisco General Hospital, 1001 Potrero Avenue, San Francisco, Calif. 94110

DOREEN RIDGEWAY, PH.D., Department of Psychology, State University of New York, Stonybrook, N.Y.

KAREN SCHNEIDER-ROSEN, PH.D., Department of Psychology, Boston College, Chestnut Hill, Mass. 02167

JUDITH SOLOMON, PH.D., Center for the Family in Transition, Corte Madera, Calif. 94925

MATTHEW L. SPELTZ, PH.D., Psychiatry and Behavioral Sciences, Mailstop ZC-10, University of Washington School of Medicine, Seattle, Wash. 98195

SUSAN SPIEKER, PH.D., Parent and Child Nursing, MJ-10, University of Washington, Seattle, Wash. 98195

ROBERT B. STEWART, PH.D., Department of Psychology, Oakland University, Rochester, Minn. 48063

Preface

THE THIRD PHASE OF ATTACHMENT RESEARCH

THIS BOOK indicates that attachment research has now entered its third phase. It often happens with productive initiatives in science that early creative surges are followed by crises, seeming to some like dead-ends, which in turn are revitalized by new approaches and new creative surges. I believe this has happened with attachment. Surely one of our generation's major research areas in social development, the attachment initiative began with the theoretical works of John Bowlby. While based on a psychoanalytic theoretical tradition, particularly stemming from the so-called British Object Relations School, Bowlby's theory so challenged basic tenets for psychoanalysts and other clinicians that it was found difficult to apply. Moreover, the array of behavioral concepts borrowed from ethology seemed difficult to link either to the clinical concepts of individual experience or to the developmental concepts coming from normative experiments and their generalization. Thus, human attachment theory, soon after its inception, was in jeopardy of being relegated to bookshelves as an interesting philosophical corpus. But this did not happen. Instead, it was revitalized for science by Mary Ainsworth, who along with her colleagues created an experimental research paradigm to study attachment theory in infancy. The elaboration of the Strange-Situation assessment for studying individual differences in behavioral patterns of attachment was a landmark achievement. It initiated a second creative phase.

Patterns of secure or insecure attachment in the 1-year-old assessed in the Strange Situation were predictively linked to earlier patterns of sensitivity and responsiveness of mothers observed in the home and also to significant aspects of developmental adaptation in the first and second years of life. Moreover, Ainsworth trained and inspired an entire generation of students and colleagues who engaged in productive research. But again (although others may see it differently), I believe a form of crisis supervened which threatened a dead-end. The field of attachment research was in jeopardy of becoming "paradigm-based." To the interested outsider, it seemed that too much time and energy was being spent in debating the pros and cons of Strange-Situation classification systems applied at 12 and 18 months of age and in discussing whether various modifications of the Strange-Situation procedure did or did not invalidate research results. Classifications of attachment patterns, while generating interesting correlates with respect to individual differences, were in danger of becoming anchored to one experimental paradigm in late infancy, reified accordingly, and thus in danger of becoming ignored by the larger world of developmental researchers.

The third phase of attachment research is represented by this volume. It responds to this seeming dead-end and, in my view, may have created initiatives nearly as dramatic as those of the first two phases. I am pleased that our MacArthur Research Network has provided strong incentives for those initiatives.

The John D. and Catherine T. MacArthur Research Network on the Transition from Infancy to Early Childhood was formed to promote new collaborative approaches to research. Its rationale was both procedural and conceptual. Procedurally, the idea was to network scientists who were engaged in programmatic research and to fund their activities for communications, workshops, and collaborative pilot research. Opportunities were sought to link data bases, to make use of shared methods, and to forge new approaches and ways of thinking through interdisciplinary collaboration. Conceptually, our rationale focused on the transition from infancy to early childhood (roughly the age period from 1 to 4 years) where more work needed to be done in order to understand developmental transformations in socioemotional, cognitive-representational, and linguistic domains. We made the case that more knowledge was needed during this transition age when important developments such as language onset, early moral internalization, socialization of emotions, self-awareness emergence, and the consolidation of representational intelligence took place. Two decades of prior early child development research had focused on infancy, and the "transition age" beyond it had been neglected.

It was in this context that our transition network provided incentives for the attachment working group represented in this volume. The age period of our research network required the assessment of attachment beyond where the Strange-Situation paradigm was deemed appropriate. As a consequence, the working group addressed new issues of both a methodological and conceptual sort. The results of responses to these issues are striking.

New assessment approaches are evolving to address the more complex behavior of the late toddler and preschool ages. As discussed in this volume, these include dimensional approaches to attachment security-insecurity and approaches involving new situations for assessment, including more naturalistic and story-based situations.

But the creative initiatives in response to the challenges of the transition from infancy to early childhood go beyond the methodological. Attachment research has been advanced in three conceptual domains. These include those

Introduction

HISTORY OF A COLLABORATION IN THE STUDY OF ATTACHMENT

Mark T. Greenberg, Dante Cicchetti,

and E. Mark Cummings

ALMOST TWENTY years ago, John Bowlby published the first three volumes of his theory of the nature and development of human attachment relationships. During the past two decades the investigation of infant-parent attachment has attracted widespread interest in developmental and clinical psychology as well as in allied fields, for example, psychiatry, pediatrics, nursing, social work, and education. Beginning with Ainsworth's pioneering studies in Uganda and Baltimore (Ainsworth 1967; Ainsworth, Blehar, Waters, & Wall 1978), the empirical investigation of the development of the attachment system during infancy has proved highly productive. Numerous books have been published on the topic, and countless professional articles have been expounding the importance of studying attachment relations in infancy. These investigations have provided both theoretical validation of the construct of attachment as well as a wealth of information on its normative development and the emergence of individual differences (Bretherton & Waters 1985).

From its inception, Bowlby considered attachment to be a construct of importance across the life span. However, with the exception of a few isolated reports (Greenberg & Marvin 1979; Maccoby & Feldman 1972; Main, Kaplan, & Cassidy 1985; Marvin 1972, 1977), there have been almost no investigations on the development of parent-child attachment after infancy. Although this major gap in our knowledge may seem surprising, it occurred due to a variety of factors. First, most attachment research was conducted by investigators who specialized in the study of infancy. Second, in general, the study of social development during the preschool years was neglected in the last two decades (Maccoby 1984). Third, and contrary to the theory itself, many investigators believed that the study of attachment was only a stage salient issue during infancy. Finally, there was a great deal of speculation that observational methods, which were clearly the method of choice during infancy, would not be valid for studying attachment in early childhood and beyond. The outcome of these factors was that until quite recently there was a meager knowledge base, an absence of conceptual models, and little methodological expertise in studying attachment relationships in early childhood.

Recently, numerous theorists (Ainsworth 1985; Bowlby 1979; Bretherton 1985; Lamb, Thompson, Gardner, Charnov & Estes 1984) have called for the expansion of attachment research and conceptualization during the preschool years. At present only a few widely scattered empirical reports have appeared, and the field has lacked conceptual definition. The purpose of the present volume is to begin to define the field of attachment in the preschool-age period. This volume presents conceptual, empirical, and clinical investigations that have recently been conducted by a group of researchers and clinicians, most of whom have been working collaboratively under the sponsorship of the John D. and Catherine T. MacArthur Foundation.

THE MACARTHUR WORKING GROUP ON ATTACHMENT

In 1983, the MacArthur Working Group on the study of Attachment in the Transition Period (early childhood) was formed. Chaired by Mark Greenberg, the group was comprised of investigators within the MacArthur network as well as a number of outside consultants. The first meeting was held in Seattle, and similar meetings have been held twice yearly for five subsequent years. The working group was a unique experience for its participants in a number of ways. In contrast to typical conferences, the meetings of the working group were small, had open agendas, contained no formal presentations, and produced no immediate products. Instead, they consisted of relatively free-flowing discussions in which hunches, speculations, and tangents were encouraged, and the participants would spend hours viewing and reviewing videotapes in order to decipher their meaning.

Another unique aspect of the working group was its multidisciplinary composition: the participants included professionals from developmental psychology, child psychiatry, clinical psychology, nursing, and education. The group included some members who had no previous connection with one another and some who were quite skeptical regarding the construct of attachment or the feasibility of studying attachment in early childhood. Further, numerous theoretical perspectives were represented. Some investigators had previous experience in attachment research; others held worldviews aligned with behaviorism, social learning theory, ecological psychology, object relations, and family systems theory. In addition, the participants brought experience with a wide range of children and families. These included normative groups, specialized populations, including preterm, deaf, developmentally delayed, physically handicapped, and maltreated children as well as children in high social risk families and those with parents who had serious mental disorders. The representation of a wide range of disciplinary and theoretical perspectives affected the process of the working group in a number of ways. First, it required the development of a common ground of understanding and as a result revealed the dilemma of vague models and unstated and unclear assumptions. The outcome of these discussions revealed a need for greater rigor and clearer explication of the defining features of the attachment construct as well as specification of its boundaries. Second, it leads to a substantial cross-fertilization of ideas. We believe that these benefits are represented in the various chapters of this volume.

The third unique aspect of the working group was its timing. Although a few isolated investigations on normative changes in attachment behavior in early childhood had been reported, the field was at its inception. In synchrony, but without foreknowledge of the formation of the working group, a number of its members had begun independent investigations of attachment relations in this age group with a variety of populations. Thus, the timing was opportune to attempt to tackle collaboratively both theoretical/conceptual and methodological/empirical aspects of the phenomena. The discussions were marked by a hesitancy to foreclose prematurely on ideas and a shared recognition that at present we understand little of the complexity of the attachment process. In summary, the unusual mix of participants, open structure of the agenda, small size, and continuity over time has combined to create a dynamic and truly integrative set of achievements. This volume is the first product of this effort, although other publications deriving from both collaborative and independent projects are forthcoming. Of particular interest is a newly devised classification system for individual differences in 3–4-year-old children that is in its final stages of completion (Cassidy, Marvin, with the MacArthur Working Group on Attachment 1989).

Overview of Volume

The volume is divided into four sections that consider theory, normative research, developmental psychopathology, and clinical application. Part I provides a series of theoretical contributions that span a variety of important topics. In the lead chapter Cicchetti, Cummings, Greenberg, and Marvin provide a broad overview of theoretical and methodological issues that confront the study of attachment in the preschool years. In doing so, they present a guiding theoretical framework for the study of attachment postinfancy and illustrate the necessary integration of concepts from normative developmental thinking, the study of individual differences, and developmental psychopathology.

Given the preschool child's rapidly expanding social understanding and social network, it becomes necessary both to conceptualize the attachment construct in accordance with these developmental transformations and to understand the relationship between the attachment construct and other developing systems of skills. Marvin and Stewart begin with a presentation and comprehensive overview of important features of systems theory and family systems theory. They then proceed to demonstrate how both attachment theory and family systems theory share many assumptions and to illustrate ways in which these theories can move to a higher order of integration that considers both dyadic relationships as well as the operation of larger-order family systems interaction. A further understanding of the internal world of the developing child is presented by Cassidy, who reviews the literature on the theoretical and methodological aspects of the self during early childhood. Cassidy highlights the interrelationships between the representational aspects of attachment and evaluative aspects of the self and reviews research illustrating the importance of this linkage.

As increasing refinements have occurred in the study of infant attachment and as the populations that have been studied have broadened from normative samples to high-risk groups, a number of researchers have identified an additional classificatory group of insecure infants that have been termed "disorganized/disoriented." In a contribution that provides important methodological and theoretical advances, Main and Solomon detail the criteria for identifying infants characterized as "disorganized/disoriented." In a companion chapter, Main and Hesse present new findings on the relationship between the security of attachment in adult caregivers, its relationship to unresolved mourning, and the occurrence of disorganization of attachment in infants of such caregivers.

Part II contains contributions on normative issues in attachment during the preschool years. In Chapter 6, Schneider-Rosen highlights the need for appropriate developmental theorizing in considering both the assessment and measurement of attachment postinfancy. In a presentation of new findings from a longitudinal project, Easterbrooks and Goldberg raise issues regarding the concordance between quality of attachment to different caregivers and the potential importance of concordance to predicting continuity/discontinuity across developmental transformations.

Recently, numerous theorists have emphasized that understanding the child's internal working model of attachment figures becomes increasingly important during the preschool years. In a study of 3-year-olds, Bretherton, Ridgeway, and Cassidy present findings on the relationship between attachment behavior and a new method of assessing internal working models through the use of a doll-story paradigm. A second-stage salient issue during toddlerhood is the development of independent motivation. Maslin-Cole and Spieker (Chap. 8) conceptualize a variety of possible models that might exist between attachment security and motivation and then present findings from two collaborative projects that empirically assess these models.

Given Bowlby's original interest and theorizing, it is not surprising that attachment theory and research has much to contribute to an understanding of developmental psychopathology (see Chap. 1). In Part III, two contributions focus on the theoretical and empirical aspects of this developing subarea of attachment research. Utilizing findings from children of psychiatrically depressed caregivers, Cummings raises both conceptual and methodological issues regarding the assessment of attachment security in young children. Cummings proposes an additional method of scoring attachment quality using a scale assessing the continuum of felt security and illustrates its use with children of depressed mothers. In Chapter 11, Cummings and Cicchetti comprehensively review factors contributing to the etiology of depression. In considering the multiple factors involved, they present a new model in which quality of attachment plays a central role in the emergence of depression.

In the final section, two contributions illustrate how a developmental understanding of attachment relations can be successfully utilized in conceptualization and treatment of young children. In a fascinating contribution, Lieberman and Pawl describe three different patterns of disorders in the secure-base behavior of toddlers. Illustrating their presentation with case studies, the authors present case conceptualizations of the possible etiology of such patterns, their developmental meaning, and issues in their treatment. Lieberman and Pawl also draw attention to the potential for successful integration of theorizing based on attachment theory with those based on developmental psychoanalysis. Disorders of conduct and other related externalizing behavior disorders provide the bulk of child referrals for treatment and parent counseling in the preschool years. At present, most treatment and outcome research has been provided by proponents of social learning theory, operant psychology, or psychoanalytic theory. In Chapter 13, Speltz highlights the potential use of developmental attachment theory both in conceptualization of the etiology and symptoms of noncompliance and its treatment. By considering the presenting problems and their underlying causes to be a reflection of dyadic processes that are ineffective in meeting the security needs as well as other stage salient needs of the child, Speltz illustrates the potential of integrating attachment formulations with those stemming from social learning theory.

In the final chapter, the interface between clinical research and service is highlighted. Aber and Baker describe the program of the Center for Toddler Development at Barnard College which attempts to integrate clinical teaching, research, and education service/practice in the study of attachment in toddlers. In doing so, they describe the development of a new approach for observing attachment in preschool educational settings and provide initial findings on its validity.

Finally, Mary Ainsworth contributes an epilogue that provides further integration and elaboration of themes presented in the volume.

Acknowledgments

We would like to thank the John D. and Catherine T. MacArthur Foundation for their vision to support collaborative efforts such as our own. The foundation's support to the Research Network on the Transition from Infancy to Childhood has provided unusual opportunities for professional growth and scientific exploration in an atmosphere of open communication and collective action. It is a rare professional experience, and we are appreciative of the opportunities it has afforded us. We also thank Dr. Robert Emde, the network director, for his long-term support of the Working Group on Attachment and of the group's meetings that have been instrumental in the development of this volume. He has helped us steer a course that has provided both broad and unstructured discussion as well as the accomplishment of goal-oriented outcomes. We are appreciative of the assistance of Joan Deming, the network administrator (at the University of Colorado Department of Psychiatry), for technical assistance with coordination and funding. We are also grateful to Kathryn Barnard who served as the principal investigator at the Seattle node of the network and also as a participant in the Working Group. Her support was instrumental in both the funding and hosting of the meetings, and her broad vision for the study of early social development in normal and risk circumstances provided a larger perspective from which to view the importance of attachment processes. We are also grateful to the Child Development and Mental Retardation Center (CDMRC) which provided facilities and technical support, and to the Department of Psychology at the University of Washington for its assistance to Mark Greenberg. We wish to thank Victoria Gill for her superb secretarial assistance. We would also like to acknowledge the members and guests of the Working Group who have provided important contributions to its present and future accomplishments. MacArthur Network members of the Working Group included Mary Ainsworth, Kathryn Barnard, Margie Beeghly, Cathy Booth, Inge Bretherton, Dante Cicchetti, Keith Crnic, Mark Cummings, Ann Easterbrooks, Mark Greenberg, Robert Harmon, and Susan Spieker. Guest consultants included Leila Beckwith (1984–1989), Vicki Carlson (1985), Robert S. Marvin (1984–1989), Matthew Speltz (1984–1987), William Friedrich (1984), Mary Main (1985), Karen Grossman (1985), Jude Cassidy (1986–1987), Jay Belsky (1987), Wanda Bronson (1987). MacArthur Postdoctoral Fellows and graduate student participants included Christine Maslin-Cole (1984–1985), Doreen Ridgeway (1986–1988), Heather Carmichael-Olson (1984–1987), Nancy Slough (1984–1987), Colleen Morisset (1986–1989), and Janet Purcell (1987–89).

Finally, on a less formal note, each of us has acknowledgments of a personal nature. Mark Greenberg would like to thank Christa Turksma, his wife, for her patience and support. Dante Cicchetti extends his appreciation to his grandmother, Josephine Butch, his friend, Heidi Mitke, and his mentor, Alan Sroufe, for their encouragement, inspiration, guidance, and affectionate concern. Mark Cummings wishes to thank his wife, Jennifer, and his son, Charlie, for their affection and support.

We believe that this volume will make a unique contribution to the field in a number of ways. It is the first such volume to focus on attachment in the toddler-preschool period (18 months–5 years of age). Although a number of independent researchers recently have been conducting studies in this area, there has been a need to integrate and synthesize this work both to define the field of inquiry and to examine its present strengths and weaknesses. As such, we are hopeful that these contributions will have significant impact on stimulating future research. Throughout this volume, we have attempted to create a balance between theoretical, empirical, and clinical application as well as between more basic and applied research. We are optimistic that this selection of original works will appeal to the theorists, researchers, and practitioners from psychology, psychiatry, and allied disciplines.

REFERENCES

Ainsworth, M. D. S. (1967). *Infancy in Uganda: Infant care and the growth of love.* Baltimore: Johns Hopkins University Press.

Ainsworth, M. D. S. (1985). Attachments across the life span. *Bulletin of the New York Academy of Medicine* 61, 792–812.

Ainsworth, M. D. S.; Blehar, M. C.; Waters, E.; & Wall, S. (1978). *Patterns of attachment: A psychological study of the strange situation.* Hillsdale, N.J.: Erlbaum.

Bowlby, J. ([1969]/1982). *Attachment and loss: Vol. 1. Attachment.* New York: Basic Books.

Bowlby, J. (1979). *The making and breaking of affectional bonds.* London: Tavistock.

Bretherton, I. (1985). Attachment theory: Retrospect and prospect. In I. Bretherton & E. Waters (eds.), *Growing points of attachment theory and research. Monographs of the Society for Research in Child Development* 50 (1–2, Serial No. 209), 3–35.

Bretherton, I., & Waters, E. (eds.), (1985). *Growing points of attachment theory and research. Monographs of the Society for Research in Child Development* 50 (1–2, Serial No. 209).

Cassidy, J., & Marvin, R. S., in collaboration with the MacArthur Working Group on Attachment (1989). Attachment organization in three- and four-year-olds: Coding guidelines. Unpublished manuscript, University of Virginia and Pennsylvania State University.

Greenberg, M. T., & Marvin, R. S. (1979). Attachment patterns in profoundly deaf preschool children. *Merrill-Palmer Quarterly* 25, 265–279.

Lamb, M.; Thompson, R.; Gardner, W.; Charnov, E.; & Estes, D. (1984). Security of infantile attachment as assessed in the strange situation: Its study and biological interpretation. *Behavioral and Brain Sciences* 7, 124–147.

Maccoby, E. (1984). Socialization and developmental change. *Child Development* 55, 317–328.

Maccoby, E. E., & Feldman, S. S. (1972). *Mother-attachment and stranger reactions in the third year of life. Monographs of the Society for Research in Child Development* 37 (1, Serial No. 146).

Main, M.; Kaplan, N.; & Cassidy, J. C. (1985). Security in infancy, childhood and adulthood: A move to the level of representation. In I. Bretherton and E. Waters (eds.), *Growing points of attachment theory and research. Monographs of the Society for Research in Child Development* 50 (1–2, Serial No. 209), 66–104.

Marvin, R. S. (1972). Attachment and cooperative behavior in two-, three-, and four-year-olds. Unpublished doctoral dissertation, University of Chicago.

Marvin, R. S. (1977). A ethological-cognitive model for the attentuation of mother-child attachment behavior. In T. Alloway, L. Krames, & P. Pliner (eds.), *Advances in the study of communication and affect: Vol. 3. Attachment Behavior* (pp. 25–60). New York: Plenum.

PART ONE

Theoretical Issues

1 · An Organizational Perspective on Attachment beyond Infancy

IMPLICATIONS FOR THEORY, MEASUREMENT, AND RESEARCH

Dante Cicchetti, E. Mark Cummings,

Mark T. Greenberg, and Robert S. Marvin

ATTACHMENT IS A vital process in human ontogeny, not only because it enhances the likelihood of survival in infancy but also because it optimizes adaptive personality development across the life span (Bowlby [1969] 1982, 1977a, 1977b). Attachment researchers primarily have focused their investigations on the elucidation of attachment processes in infancy and on the developmental sequelae of secure and insecure infant-caregiver attachments. In keeping with Bowlby's perspective, rather than only construing attachment as a developmental task that must be successfully resolved in infancy and which then decreases in importance, we conceptualize attachment as remaining critical to the child's continual adaptation, even though it changes in organization as the child develops throughout the preschool period (see Greenspan & Porges 1984; Sroufe 1979a; Stern 1985).

Once an attachment develops, it continues to undergo transformations and reintegrations with subsequent accomplishments such as emerging autonomy and entrance into the peer world. Thus, children are continually renegotiating the balance between being connected to others and being independent and autonomous as they encounter each new developmental phase. In other words, we believe that attachment, as is the case with other developmental issues, is a life-span task that requires continual coordination and integration as individuals adapt to their environment.

In fact, the investigation of attachment during the period of infancy has recently become the wellspring for an emerging literature focused on attachment processes throughout the life course (Ainsworth 1985, 1989; Bretherton 1985; Hinde & Stevenson-Hinde 1987; Main, Kaplan, & Cassidy 1985; Skolnick 1986; Sroufe & Fleeson 1986). As a logical extension of this research on the development of individual differences in attachment patterns during infancy, there has been a growing interest in the transformation, devel-

The writing of this chapter was supported by a grant to the authors from the John D. and Catherine T. MacArthur Foundation Network on Early Childhood. We are grateful to Douglas Barnett, Nathan Fox, Michael Lynch, Sheree Toth, Brian Vaughn, and Jennifer White for providing us with feedback on several drafts of this manuscript. We would also like to thank Sara Campbell and Victoria Gill for typing this chapter.

3

opment, function, course, and sequelae of good and poor quality attachments across the life span (see, e.g., Ainsworth 1985; Greenberg, Siegel, & Leitch 1983; Hartup & Lempers 1973; Kobak & Sceery 1988; Kotler & Omodei 1988; Maccoby & Feldman 1972; Marvin 1977; Main, Kaplan, & Cassidy 1985; Skolnick, in press; Weiss 1982). Moreover, researchers are paying increased attention to discovering the intergenerational continuities and discontinuities in the formation of relationships (Egeland, Jacobvitz, & Sroufe 1988; Main & Goldwyn 1984; Rutter, Quinton, & Liddle 1983; Ricks 1985; Rutter 1989; Sroufe & Fleeson 1986, 1988).

GOALS OF THIS CHAPTER

It is our belief that the need to understand the developmental transformations of attachment processes in the preschool years has become increasingly critical. A long overdue and important field of theoretical, empirical, and clinical study is emerging, as evidenced by the breadth of work in this volume and in other sources. At present, however, this area of research lacks a coherent set of defining features, goals, and empirical techniques for investigation. It is our intention to begin this process by presenting broadstroke discussions of topics that we feel must be addressed in order to delineate future directions of inquiry.

In this chapter, we discuss the developmental issues that have necessitated the study of attachment beyond the period of infancy. As the focus of this volume is on the transition from infancy through the preschool and early school-age years, we largely center our discussion on this period of development. We underscore the importance of formulating a theoretical framework to guide research on attachment beyond infancy. We pay particular attention to the central theoretical and empirical aspects that must be considered in the development of such a framework. This is especially important because it is necessary to keep the construct of attachment separate from other systems that undergo change during the preschool period (Hinde 1982). Subsequently, we discuss issues in the measurement of attachment during the postinfancy period. In our penultimate section, we examine attachment and developmental psychopathology, paying particular attention to clinical issues and to how the study of attachment in deviant populations can enhance our knowledge of the development of attachment in normal populations. Finally, we suggest future research directions in the development of attachment during the preschool years and beyond.

DEVELOPMENTAL ISSUES THAT NECESSITATE THE
STUDY OF ATTACHMENT BEYOND INFANCY

Several major theoretical and empirical advances have augmented our understanding of attachment processes during the preschool years. Especially during the past decade, increased attention has been focused on the study of the transition period from infancy through early childhood (Cicchetti & Beeghly, in press; Kagan & Lamb 1988). Based largely on work in the area of cognition, social-cognition, and language, a number of investigators have demonstrated that very young normal and atypical children do exhibit some ability to infer the percepts, thought processes, and emotions of others (Beeghly & Cicchetti 1987; Bretherton & Beeghly 1982; Bretherton, McNew, & Beeghly-Smith 1981; Cicchetti & Beeghly 1987; Kagan 1981; Lempers, Flavell, & Flavell 1977; Shatz & Gelman 1973). Concomitantly, research on the development of self-system processes has illustrated that autonomy *and* connection are both salient developmental tasks for the preschooler (Connell, in press; Mahler, Pine, & Bergman 1975).

Furthermore, research suggesting possible links between insecure attachment in infancy and subsequent child behavior problems (Crowell & Feldman 1988; Erickson, Sroufe, & Egeland 1985; Lewis, Feiring, McGuffog, & Jaskir 1984) highlights the need to examine pathways to later adaptation and maladaptation. Because most developmentalists no longer expect children necessarily to be permanently scarred by their negative early experiences nor to be continuously innoculated from environmental insults by their positive ones, it is now acknowledged that early experience is not necessarily more consequential than later experience (Sroufe 1988). Since changes in life circumstances can bring about changes in relational processes (Lamb, 1987; Vaughn, Egeland, Sroufe, & Waters 1979), researchers have recognized that it is essential to examine the changing organization and integration of the attachment system in concert with its contemporaneous relationship to other developmental issues. For example, Sroufe (1983) notes that the quality of adaptation manifested by preschool children is influenced as much by how their parents manage the aggressive impulses and feelings that children exhibit during the transition from infancy to the preschool period as by the quality of their early care.

Interest in attachment during the preschool years has been enhanced by the concept of internal working models of attachment figures and of the self (Bowlby [1969] 1982, 1980; Bretherton 1985, 1987). Through assessment of this representational construct, the investigation of attachment processes can occur beyond the level of observing mother-child interactions. Bowlby's notions about internal working models were greatly influenced by the writing of object relations theorists (Greenberg & Mitchell 1983). Mental representations of self and other are core theoretical constructs within object relations theory and bear close resemblance to the internal working models of attachment theory. Consequently, there now exists a potent construct for organizing the vast ontogenetic changes that occur within a variety of developmental domains during the preschool years with the transformations that take place within the attachment system.

Through the notion of internal working models, the construct of attachment continues to possess much integrative power. Potentially, attachment theorists may be able to link traditionally disparate disciplines and sub-disciplines of thought (e.g., psychoanalysis [both ego psychology and object relations], social learning theory, mainstream developmental psychology, evolutionary biology, neurophysiology, and cognitive science) into a coherent theoretical framework (Ainsworth 1969; Bowlby [1969] 1982; Bretherton 1985, 1987).

A critical question that must be addressed empirically is whether child-parent attachment is a significant developmental issue beyond infancy and, if so, in what ways it remains important. Historically, a number of theories of development have stated that crucial, new developmental issues do emerge during the preschool period; however, they have not discussed how they are influenced by the quality of the attachment relationship. For example, Hartmann, Kris, and Lowenstein ([1949] 1964) proposed that the manner in which young children learn to control their bodily functions serves as a prototype for the development of self-determination in interaction with signi-ficant people in their lives and that, if their mothers encourage this self-determination and control, a great sense of achievement results. Anna Freud (1965) likewise focused on control, self-determination, interpersonal conflict, decreased dependency, and increased self-reliance in discussing the important "developmental lines" during the preschool period.

Mahler and her colleagues (1975) proposed phases in the development of "separation-individuation" during toddlerhood. Her model focused on chil-dren's increasing sense of separateness from mother, their ambivalence re-garding this increased sense of autonomy, and the roles the development of motor skills, cognition, and language play in children's decreasing needs for mother's physical presence. Erikson (1950) proposed that "Autonomy versus Shame and Doubt" was a central developmental issue for this period, and that parents must present children with firm outer limits and freedom of expression and control in order to allow the children to develop a sense of autonomy. Erikson (1950) stressed the importance of "mutual regulation" between par-ent and child during this period, a concept somewhat similar to Bowlby's ([1969] 1982) notion of a "goal-corrected partnership" between children and their attachment figures which will be discussed later in this chapter.

Likewise, psychoanalytic and social learning theorists, emphasizing dif-ferent mechanisms, have focused on issues of increased independence, self-control, parental limit setting, identification, and socialization (internaliza-tion of behavioral norms) as salient issues during this developmental period (see Bandura 1978; Gewirtz 1972; Goslin 1969; Maccoby & Masters 1970; Richters & Waters, in press). Similarly, developmental researchers studying the patterns of parenting have stressed that, during the latter half of the second year and throughout the third, parents must deal with children's strivings for autonomy and competence while setting limits and rules and providing clarity and firmness in their instructions (Baumrind 1971).

Thus, existing theoretical orientations tend to posit new developmental issues during the preschool years, but usually do not emphasize further developments in the attachment relationship between child and parent. On the basis of these theories, one might conclude that attachment remains a central issue only in one of the following senses: (1) if the attachment figure continues to reinforce "dependency" on the child's part (social learning theory); (2) because the attachment becomes stabilized and consolidated, its major relevance becomes its effect on later developmental tasks (most psychoanalytic models); or (3) that successful negotiation of later developmental tasks can feed back and alter the earlier resolution and stabilization of the attachment relationship (Erikson 1950). Thus, the implications of the theories seems to be that attachment, in the main, should not continue to be conceived as an autonomous area of study, with its own further developmental changes and significant effects on the child's development and relationships.

Although the answer to the question, "Is attachment a major developmental issue beyond infancy?" remains, in part, an empirical one, there are a number of lines of converging evidence that suggest that attachment does remain an important and fruitful area of inquiry. First, the biological function of attachment—namely, the protection of children from danger while they develop the skills to protect themselves—continues to play a paramount role during the preschool and early school-age years (as well as into adulthood). Preschoolers are certainly *not* yet able to protect themselves from most sources of danger. Furthermore, the fact that they do begin to spend more time away from their attachment figure implies that they must be recognizing their attachment behavior in important ways to allow this increased distance.

Second, not all problems in attachment necessarily have their roots in infancy (Cicchetti & Schneider-Rosen 1986; Cummings & Cicchetti, this vol; Greenberg & Speltz 1988; Mahler et al. 1975). That is, insecure attachments may not appear until beyond the infancy period. For example, a previously secure child may become insecure due to the birth of a new sibling, a traumatic event, or to changes in family circumstances. Moreover, as attachment networks begin to develop, insecure attachments also may form between children and other attachment figures during the preschool period (e.g., other adult caregivers, siblings, etc.). This suggests that there are important attachment issues which emerge in the postinfancy transition period.

Third, studies of the stability of attachment provide evidence that, for certain children, the quality of their attachments changes in predictable ways during the postinfancy years (Crockenberg 1981; Vaughn et al. 1979). It is conceivable that these shifts in attachment quality occur, in part, as a result of changes in the differentiation and integration of other developmental domains (e.g., cognition and symbolization) that lead to new organizations of attachment being the most optimal in terms of survival strategies (see Main et al., 1985; Schneider-Rosen, Braunwald, Carlson, & Cicchetti 1985). Changes in social-cognitive abilities also occur during the preschool period (e.g., perspective-taking skills and communication skills). These increased skills allow the attachment between adult and child to become "closer" or more interpersonally meshed at the same time that the child's need for proximity attentuates (e.g., Marvin 1977; Marvin & Greenberg 1982; Serafica 1978). Moreover, these enhanced developments also pave the way for the child's manifestation of greater independence.

For these and for other reasons, we believe that attachment is an important developmental issue and organizational construct beyond infancy. We do not mean to minimize the importance of other developmental issues which we also conceive as life-span tasks (see, e.g., Kegan's [1982] point that separation and individuation are clearly lifelong issues). Rather, we are arguing that the child-parent attachment continues to develop and to change in ways that are significant for the child's survival, security, and adaptation and that it merits investigation in its own right.

Implications of the Processes Underlying Developmental Change for the Investigation of Attachments during the Preschool Period.

To date, much of the research on attachment beyond infancy has been characterized either by continued application of variables and measures developed in the study of infant attachment or by those developed in the study of older children in different or in sometimes contradictory theoretical frameworks. What is needed is to develop measures of the attachment system which are derived from, or consistent with, attachment theory, yet reflect the new skills, developmental tasks, and physical-social environment of the growing child.

An important issue is what Bowlby (1973) calls "natural clues of danger," and other culturally and individually learned clues. What are the various clues that activate attachment behavior in preschoolers? Also, what are the developmental changes in what the child can accept as "safety" when such danger is perceived? And what are the similarities and differences in the manner in which securely and insecurely attached children appraise and cope with these clues?

Based on children's increased social-cognitive and affective perspective-taking abilities at this age (Hesse & Cicchetti 1982; Marvin & Greenberg 1982; Selman 1980), it is not at all surprising that children begin to monitor not only their own safety but also that of others with whom they have affectional bonds. Clinical evidence suggests that at approximately 4 years of age children begin to manifest two new concerns: (1) fears and concerns about monsters, things under the bed, in the closet, etc.; and (2) concerns for the safety of other family members (e.g., warning family members to be careful, avoid dangers, etc.).

Data from the few epidemiological studies that exist on the behavior problems of childhood document that the peaks in fears and phobias, as well as in nightmares, occur during the preschool and early school-age period (Earls 1980; Graham 1977; MacFarlane, Allen, & Honzik 1954). Obviously, these new stressors elicit attachment behavior in new ways as well. Although it may be tempting to take these symptom peaks "at face value" (i.e., as making normative sense given children's levels of cognitive and social-cognitive development), at times it may be necessary to look "beneath the surface" to uncover other possible underlying attachment issues. In this regard, we recall the example of a 5-year-old boy who refused to remain in his kindergarten class. Each day, after his mother brought him to school, he ran away and went back home. This ritual continued for several weeks before it was brought to the attention of the school psychologist. Although it could appear that this child's behavior is an example of a separation anxiety disorder or of a school phobia, clinical investigation revealed that the boy was severely physically abused by his father. The father's business ventures caused him to travel, and it was learned that he had told the boy to "be the man of the house when I'm out of town." Interpreted within a broader attachment framework, we can see how the boy went home to carry out his father's wishes—to be the mother's caregiver rather than fulfilling his own security issues. That is, preschool children begin to increase their own "felt security" by protecting the security of their attachment figures as well.

A second issue for the study of attachment beyond infancy is the assessment of how the unfolding of *other* developmental systems impacts upon the operation of the attachment system, even though these new systems may not be conceived of as predominantly related to attachment. For example, during the preschool years more proficient locomotion develops. Increased facility of locomotion should lead to many changes in how both children and adults organize their attachment/caregiving behavior. Longitudinal studies of both normal and locomotor-impaired (e.g., cerebral palsy, Down's syndrome) children would be illuminating here (see Cicchetti & Schneider-Rosen 1984; Cicchetti & Sroufe 1978; Decarie 1969).

In addition, representational processes undergo rapid development during the transition from infancy through the preschool years. Further studies of the effects which increased communicative and negotiating abilities have on the organization of the attachment system and of how quality of attachment influences language development would be extremely useful (Bretherton 1984; Bretherton, Bates, Benigni, Camaioni, & Volterra 1979; Cicchetti & Beeghly 1987; Gersten, Coster, Schneider-Rosen, Carlson, & Cicchetti 1986; Greenberg & Marvin 1979).

As a final example of the emergence of another developmental process with potentially important implications for attachment, the development of self-knowledge and self-understanding (Damon & Hart 1982; Lewis & Brooks-Gunn 1979) burgeons during the postinfancy period. Because representational models of attachment figures and of the self develop in an independent, yet interactive fashion (Bowlby 1980; Cicchetti & Schneider-Rosen 1986), studies that examine the effects of self-system changes upon the development of attachment behavior and vice versa during the postinfancy period would make important contributions to achieving a fuller understanding of the organization of the attachment system (Cassidy, this vol.; Cicchetti, Beeghly, Carlson, & Toth, in press; Connell, in press). As children mature and their experience base expands, they develop more complex and differentiated models of self, of others, and of relationships, which Bretherton (1985, 1987) describes as a multilayer hierarchical network of representation.

For example, during the preschool years, children can assume new roles in relation to the attachment system. They can become attachment figures to younger siblings (Stewart & Marvin 1984) or serve some attachment function to adults (e.g., by forming a controlling-caregiver type attachment; see Main et al. 1985). Moreover, entry into the peer system becomes a critical developmental issue during the preschool period. Although peer relations constitute a *different* type of relationship than that characteristic of the affectional attachment system, the consensus is that secure attachment relationships facilitate the development of competent peer relations (Hartup 1983; Sroufe 1979a, 1983).

Along with the newly emerging competencies that enable them to find additional ways to derive protection and security, children also may be faced with new vulnerabilities that may arise as a result of these more advanced skills. For example, as noted above during the preschool and early school-age period, children become increasingly adept at taking the perspective of other individuals and of developing the ability to assume a variety of social roles (Watson, in press; Watson & Fischer 1980). Concurrent with these cognitive, affective, and social transformations, children may be more likely to adopt readily any inappropriate roles that may be socialized by the adults in their lives (e.g., parents, relatives, daycare teachers, etc.). One striking example of this may be the high percentage of disorganized/disoriented caretaker relationships manifested by maltreated youngsters (Carlson, Cicchetti, Barnett, & Braunwald 1989).

Along with the variety of major transformations and advances emerging within children's socioemotional, social-cognitive, and cognitive/linguistic (i.e., representational) skills during the preschool and early school-age period, the social world of children broadens and expands during this period, as do the social expectations that adults have for them (Damon 1977, 1983). Unquestionably, the affectional attachment system continues to play a major organizing role in the developmental process. Even though other types of relationships develop during the postinfancy period that are not attachments (Ainsworth 1985, 1989; Hinde 1982), and other developmental issues emerge and grow in ascendance (e.g., autonomy and other self-system processes, peer relationships, etc.), the child's attachment relationships continue to remain of essential importance. In the next section, we discuss the need to develop a guiding theoretical framework which is broad and integrative enough to incorporate the vast developmental changes that occur in the attachment system, both alone and in interaction with other developmental systems, throughout the preschool period.

The Need for a Guiding Theoretical Framework

In order to conceptualize adequately the construct of attachment as it undergoes the developmental transformations discussed earlier, it is necessary to have a guiding theoretical framework. Such a framework should preserve the essential features of the attachment system, such as (1) its functional significance which is protection, (2) its predictable behavioral outcome which is proximity, (3) and its internal subjective "set goal" which is felt security. However, as the attachment construct is increasingly utilized across the life span, it will be necessary to refine its conceptualization and operation in relation to the skills and issues of different developmental phases. As such, it is necessary to conceptualize attachment as a life-span task which undergoes physical, ecological, perceptual, and representational changes that dramatically alter its form and organization. If we fail to view attachment as a continuously developing organizational system, then we will inevitably restrict ourselves to both the construct and methods derived from the empirical work on infant attachment. Further, by adopting infancy constructs without revision or without elaborating the model in developmentally appropriate ways, we risk reifying attachment as a construct specific to infancy. This is not to say that the development of individual differences that have been found in infancy are not robust or that infancy may not be a particularly sensitive period for the formation of lasting individual differences. Rather, we think that the quality of attachment developed in infancy forms some sort of lasting foundation for future intimate relations. However, it is important to emphasize that if attachment is to be a truly developmental construct, it is necessary to conceive of its form and processes as undergoing rule-governed transformations through the life span.

For example, throughout childhood the attachment system serves to protect children from danger, to facilitate their exploration of the environment, to play a role in regulating physical proximity, and to provide a sense of security and trust. However, the manner in which protection occurs, proximity is regulated, and security is derived will be transformed as the child develops.

We think that there are at least six main issues to be considered in the development of a theoretical framework. These components are not necessarily unique to the preschool years, but by considering their contribution to the theoretical perspective, it becomes clear that they play significant roles in the operation and/or conceptualization of the attachment system during this phase of life.

1. The organization of behavior in context. The study of attachment during the preschool years requires an organizational approach (Ainsworth, Blehar, Waters, & Wall 1978; Sroufe & Waters 1977). Just as the infant's tendency to seek proximity to its caregiver cannot adequately be conceptualized without considering how it is organized with the infant's exploratory and fear/wariness behavioral systems, most aspects of the attachment behavior of preschool children will be best understood in relation to other behavior systems, developmental changes in those systems, alterations in the behavior of their attachment figures, and developmental advances in the children's own competencies.

As has been well-explicated in the study of infant attachment (Ainsworth 1973; Bretherton & Ainsworth 1974; Sroufe and Waters 1977), attachment behaviors are so designated because they have the predictable outcome of proximity and/or contact with discriminated others. Further, a given behavior (e.g., crying, approaching, smiling) may serve multiple systems or have multiple meanings depending upon the situational context (Werner & Kaplan 1963). Behaviors are defined as serving the attachment system by virtue of their meaning in specific behavioral contexts. Thus, an organizational, systemic model of attachment defines its component behaviors by their predictable function rather than by their morphology. The value of a behavioral systems approach has been demonstrated in its ability to (a) provide a flexible framework for understanding the function of behaviors (Bischof 1975; Bretherton 1980), (b) conceptually organize the ongoing stream of behavior and behavior systems in context (Bischof 1975; Bretherton & Ainsworth 1974; Cicchetti & Serafica 1981; Greenberg & Marvin 1982), and (c) show consistency in the manifestation of the attachment system across both environmental context and time (Sroufe & Waters 1977).

In adopting a developmental perspective, there are at least three changes that occur in the organization of the attachment system. First, during the preschool years there are changes in the spatial, temporal, and relationship contexts in which the attachment system operates (e.g., separations due to increased time in peer and school contexts, additions of other siblings to the family, and so forth). This will be elaborated below in the discussion of social-cognitive changes and expansion of the secure-base construct.

Second, as the child's perceptual, cognitive-representational, communicative, and social abilities rapidly develop, there is an expansion in the types of behaviors that serve the attachment system, changes in the form of some behaviors that previously served this system, and changes in how the entire system is organized. For example, with increasing age more distal behaviors (smiling and greeting) may have the same functional significance as approach and contact did during infancy (Serafica 1978). Similarly, in certain contexts, for example, oblique approaches to the caregiver upon reunion, behaviors that appear to be serving other functions such as asking the caregiver to tie the child's shoe, may well be clearly functioning as attachment behaviors.

Third, there are alterations in the balance and dynamic interactions among the attachment behavior system and other behavioral systems, for example, fear/wariness, play/exploration, and sociability. For example, Greenberg and Marvin (1982) illustrated the decreased coupling of the attachment and wary behavior systems and corresponding increased coupling of the wary and sociable systems in preschoolers' behavior with strangers.

2. The promise of an evolutionary perspective. Very few studies of attachment beyond infancy have actively used an evolutionary perspective. Because this viewpoint had such a major influence upon the early development of the attachment paradigm, we believe that it could be equally influential in guiding research on attachment during the preschool period. For example, Marvin (1977) utilized an evolutionary perspective to extend Bowlby's ([1969] 1982) notion that the biological function of attachment behavior is protection of the decreasingly helpless child from danger. Marvin suggested that an evolutionary viewpoint provides a framework for thinking about the attenuation of attachment *behavior* (e.g., seeking proximity to mother) beyond infancy. Specifically, evolutionary theory suggests that we should search for those skills in children that make them increasingly more involved in maintaining their own protection. These skills would include directly protective behaviors such as running, appeasement gestures, developing the ability to fight, and skill at anticipating and (thus) avoiding dangers. They would also include more indirect skills, such as those that allow children to become integrated into a larger peer group where there is protection in numbers and in the presence of older, wiser, and stronger individuals who are not their major attachment figures. We should be able to predict, or at least to find, complementary developmental changes in which children's tendencies to remain close to mother, and to display attachment behavior, ought to attenuate as they develop these skills and new relationships (Marvin 1977).

As a corollary, a comparative perspective is also of great potential importance to attachment research. Bowlby ([1969] 1982) derived important components of his basic model of attachment from the results of primate studies, and we believe that research on primates can also be useful for the study of attachment in preschoolers. Briefly, Marvin (1977) has noted that primate studies indicate that young primates develop through three major phases in their relationships with their mothers between birth and adolescence. Each phase is characterized by a unique organization of attachment behavior, caregiving behavior, motor and communicative skills of the young, and degree of autonomous interaction into the larger group "independent" of mother. Each organization "makes sense" in that the structure of mother-offspring involvement at each point in development is adapted to the degree to which youngsters have developed the motor, cognitive, and communicative skills which allow them autonomous integration into the larger troop. In higher primates, as this integration becomes complete, the mother-offspring relationship changes from one based largely on protection to one resembling a cooperative "friendship."

We think a case can be made that humans progress through a similar series of phases, with basically the same sequence of organization among these behavior systems (see Cicchetti & Schneider-Rosen 1986; Marvin 1977). Piaget's stages of sensorimotor, preoperational, and concrete operational thinking may provide an interesting parallel in humans to the three developmental stages identified in the primate studies. We think that it is worth investigating whether infancy, the preschool period, and the latency period are characterized by some of the same developmental and interpersonal organizations that have been found in the primate studies.

Finally, we believe that several constructs drawn from sociobiology may be useful in studying attachment beyond infancy. As one example, Trivers's (1974) notion of "parent-offspring conflict" could be useful. This conflict is demonstrated in most mammalian species and in many human families when mother becomes pregnant again after her older offspring have reached an age where the likelihood of survival is more certain. For a period of time, it becomes to the mother's advantage to invest somewhat less in her older offspring, and to the older offspring's advantage to demand higher degrees of investment from the mother than is her wont. Within a sociobiological perspective, conflict is the inevitable result. The necessary "give-and-take" and capitulation that must ensue to bring about a harmonious, reciprocally rewarding relationship has striking parallels to the processes underlying the formation in humans of a "goal-corrected partnership" (Bowlby [1969] 1982; Marvin 1977).

3. The development of the goal-corrected partnership. In the first volume of *Attachment and Loss,* Bowlby ([1969] 1982) presented a brief outline of a developmental theory of attachment beyond infancy. Marvin and his coworkers (e.g., Marvin 1977; Marvin & Greenberg 1982; Stewart & Marvin 1984) have expanded this theory somewhat and have presented supporting data. Although the theory requires further elaboration and empirical verification, it holds promise in that it is conceptually continuous with the theory of attachment in infancy, presents a *descriptive model of developmental change* rather than a model that merely predicts certain developmental *outcomes,* and is consistent with conclusions emerging from recent developmental studies, especially in the areas of social-cognitive and communicative development.

Basically, the theory posits that it is the developmental task of young children to form a "goal-corrected partnership" with their attachment figures. While this partnership is enacted across the wide range of interactions which constitute the child-parent relationship (see Hinde 1976), it is highly probable that it first develops in the context of attachment-caregiving interactions. Subsequently, a goal-corrected partnership can be seen developing in relationships with others beyond the attachment figures.

The construct of a "goal-corrected partnership" follows from Bowlby's third phase in the development of attachment—the phase of "goal-corrected proximity-seeking." When a baby has developed to the point where *both* mother and infant are able to gain and to maintain proximity and contact with each other in a goal-corrected manner, it becomes logically possible for *both* to operate under a shared set of goals and plans. As a simple example, mother and baby can share a plan for immediate physical contact when the baby is approached by a large dog while playing at some distance from mother in the park. As the child's communicative skills improve, it also becomes easier for both members of the dyad to communicate their goals and plans to one another, and to attempt indirectly to change one another's behavior by directly affecting one another's goals and plans. For example, if mother is preparing dinner and the youngster indicates a wish for physical contact, mother may communicate a plan that the child wait to be held until after she has finished the dinner preparation. If the plan is accepted and then carried out, the dyad can be viewed as operating under a single set of goals and plans, or as acting as a true "partnership." Note that at this point children need not be able to *recognize* that they and mother are operating under a single set of goals/plans. They only need to be able to delay or to inhibit the execution of their attachment behavior and to accommodate to mother's suggestion that they wait. At this point it is only the mother who can attempt purposefully to establish a shared plan or partnership (Marvin 1972, 1977).

Bowlby ([1969] 1982) goes on to suggest that when children become able cognitively to represent their mother's goals and plans to themselves, to distinguish their mothers' plans from their own, and to execute plans in order to bring mother's goals and/or plans more into alignment with their own, they have then achieved a "goal-corrected partnership." Marvin (1972, 1977) has extended the concept of the partnership by examining its implication for the attachment relationship. According to Marvin, the relationship between mother and child (or at least the attachment-caregiving aspect of their relationship) can change from one based solely on physical proximity and contact to one based, in addition, on the ability to share mutually regulated goals and other *internal* states (see Bretherton & Beeghly 1982; Cicchetti & Beeghly 1987). *Both* mother and child now realize that their relationship continues whether or not they are in physical proximity to one another because shared internal states do not require physical proximity. This presents an intriguing paradox, in that at the very same time the children achieve the ability to have a much "closer" relationship with their attachment figure, they require much less physical proximity to their attachment figure (Mahler et al. 1975; Marvin 1972).

Although this very brief outline of the goal-corrected partnership has necessarily omitted many important issues, one point that should be mentioned is particularly relevant to material covered in later chapters of this book. This is the point that whenever two goal-corrected systems are closely coupled, conflict between opposing goals and plans is inevitable (Bowlby [1969] 1982). With respect to attachment interactions during the preschool years, this is certainly true. Marvin (1977) and Marvin and Greenberg (1982) have demonstrated that resolving conflict concerning an upcoming separation and constructing an agreed-upon, shared plan for separation and reunion is associated with low levels of both attachment behavior and conflict upon reunion between mothers and their 4-year-old children. In dyads where this shared plan is *not* constructed, reunion is much more likely to be characterized by anger and overly controlling behavior on the part of the child. Thus, conflict and conflict resolution concerning attachment interactions is a core issue in the maintenance of this goal-corrected partnership and should prove to be an exciting area of research.

4. The ontogeny of working models of attachment relationships. The focus on behavioral *organization and patterns* remains central to the study of attachment beyond infancy because such patterns serve as the primary basis for making inferences about internal events relevant to attachment behavior. As children's behavior and information-processing skills increase in complexity, attachment theory and research will necessarily place greater emphasis on the identification of the attitudes, feelings, ideas, goals, and plans of both the child and the mother concerning their own behavior and internal events. This focus will become important for clinical, as well as normative, developmental research. Relatively few studies of attachment in infancy have made reference to these internal events. This omission is understandable because the vast majority of studies on attachment processes in infancy have been sensorimotor in nature. However, several recent papers (e.g., Bretherton 1985, 1987; Cicchetti & Aber 1986; Main et al. 1985) have discussed these internal events using one of the central notions in the theory of attachment (Bowlby [1969] 1982, 1973), the concept of "working models."

Bowlby describes working models as an individual's conscious and unconscious mental representations, "of the world and of himself in it, with the aid of which he perceives events, forecasts the future, and constructs his plans" (Bowlby 1973, p. 203). Two of the most important parts of these working models are (1) children's conceptions of their attachment figures, their whereabouts, and likely response to the child's behavior; and (2) children's conceptions of how acceptable or unacceptable they are in the eyes of their attachment figures (i.e., their self-image). A third, and largely unexplored, component is childrens' conceptions of their attachment figures' plans and range of caregiving behaviors. It would be of interest to assess how such conceptions affect the way children plan their own attachment behavior (see Marvin & Greenberg 1982).

These working models are constructed out of children's interactions with their caregivers, children's own actions, and the feedback they receive from these actions. They consist of something closer to an "event schemata" (e.g., Mandler 1983) than to a static "picture." They include affective, "appraising" components as well as cognitive components (Bretherton 1985; Bowlby [1969] 1982, 1973). As such, there will be wide variations across individuals in working models, and how accurately individuals' working models reflect their own experience as well as cognitive, linguistic, and behavioral skills. Finally, these internal working models, once organized, tend to operate outside conscious awareness and to resist dramatic change (Bowlby 1980). Changes that occur during childhood will usually be in response to changing (concrete) experiences, while during and after adolescence "formal operations" may enable individuals to alter somewhat their working models through sophisticated thought processes and psychotherapy (Bowlby 1988a; Egeland et al. 1988; Guidano & Liotti 1983; Hunter & Kilstrom 1979; Main & Goldwyn 1984; Main et al. 1985).

There are at least three important issues which must be explored to understand children's working models of their attachment relations: the changing ontogenetic *structure* of working models; the *content* and *operation* of those models; and the role of the attachment figure in the development, maintenance, and functioning of the model. Although there has been little research on this topic (however, see Marvin 1972, 1977), it is likely that structural ontogenetic changes in working models will parallel changes in cognitive structures. If this is true, then working models throughout the preschool years should not be conceptualized as structurally similar. The working models of *very young* preschoolers will be "sensorimotor" in nature and will consist of set goals for the degree of proximity/contact and terminating conditions for attachment behavior. At this point in ontogenesis, children's working models are structured in terms of their own developing ability to perceive internal states and the *behavior* of themselves and their attachment figure. As yet, there is little or no conception of mother's internal states. Paralleling the development of the goal-corrected partnership, structural changes in children's working models of attachment interactions during the remainder of the preschool years consist first of an increased ability to represent internally sequences of behaviors (e.g., interactions between mother and self), and later of an ability simultaneously to represent to themselves two distinct points of view and the degree of match or mismatch between them. As discussed by Main et al. (1985), Bretherton (1985, 1987), and Cassidy (this vol.), the *content* of preschooler's working models of their attachment relations should reflect the patterns of attachment interactions which take place between them, as constrained by the child's cognitive and social-cognitive structures as discussed above.

Finally, the organizational perspective on development traditionally has emphasized the importance of studying the changing integration and organization of cognition, affect, and behavior (Cicchetti & Sroufe 1978; Sroufe 1979b; Sroufe & Waters 1976, 1977). Main et al.'s (1985) empirical elaboration of Bowlby's concept of internal working models as guides to cognition (attention, memory), behavior (reunion responses, coping responses), and affect (sadness, anger) in attachment-related situations appears to be the type of unifying construct that would permit the study of the organization of cognition, behavior, and affect over time and across developmental stages.

5. Expansion of the secure-base construct. The secure-base construct characterizes the interplay of the attachment and exploratory behavior systems (Ainsworth 1974). As a result of the security or trust that children derive from either the actual physical presence or the internalized working model of the attachment figure, children are able to explore and to learn, free of an overly anxious concern about the accessibility of the figure.

In infancy, the secure base construct has been operationalized as the dynamic balance between exploration of the environment and seeking physical proximity and/or contact with attachment figure(s). Individual differences in attachment patterns observed in the Strange Situation have been related to the use of secure-base behavior in the home environment (Ainsworth et al. 1978). With increasing age, there are changes in the distance that children will travel from the parent as well as in the time spent at a distance from the mother and, most important, in the organizing, activating, and terminating conditions of the attachment system (Anderson 1972; Rheingold & Eckerman 1970).

During the preschool years there are a number of developmental transformations that preserve the functioning of the attachment system while requiring an expansion of the secure-base construct. These developments include children's increasing cognitive abilities to represent and anticipate the dynamic moment-to-moment changes in the organization of physical proximity, to utilize internal talk to regulate one's felt security (e.g., "I'm okay, I'm okay"), to utilize communicative strategies in the service of continuing distal contact with the caregiver, and the increasing desire for independent mastery and individuation. This is not to say that actual physical proximity is replaced but, instead, that its role is supplemented by the use of newly developed strategies, some of which are externally observable and others which are internalized actions that may not be open to direct observation. As implied in Bowlby's notion of the partnership phase of attachment, the set-goal which regulates the interplay of the attachment and exploratory systems during this phase represents not only some organization of physical proximity but also of the meshing of representational plans and goals of the dyad (Marvin 1977). From an organizational standpoint, the sense of felt security is now regulated by physical proximity and by these higher level cognitive and communicative skills of which the child is now capable. These new skills play an increasing role in children's ability to develop and to maintain independent action from their caregivers for extended periods of time and thus fulfill the function of "guidance" of the child's activities. Research is needed to elucidate developmental changes in secure-base behavior such as the changing durations and distances of separation, changes in the type of contact, and in the circumstances that activate attachment behavior. Except in times of stress or distress, however, the use of observable secure base behaviors may become increasingly infrequent and thus may require supplementary or alternate methods of assessment.

6. Family systems perspective. Research in infant- and child-parent attachment is clearly organizational and systemic in nature. This is evidenced by theory and research which integrates various subsystems within the child (e.g., fear, wary and exploratory systems, emotions and cognitive processes, behavioral patterns, and inferred "working models"), the child-and-attachment-figure-as-dyad, and the development of attachment in the context of the existing cultural environment (Ainsworth 1967, 1977; Grossmann, Grossmann, Spangler, Suess, & Unzner 1985; Minuchin 1985; Miyake, Chen, & Campos 1985; Sagi, Lamb, Lewkowicz, Shoham, Dvir, & Estes 1985). For obvious reasons relating to issues of conceptual and methodological complexity, there is one especially important context for the development of attachment which has received very little attention—the child's *family*!

Attachment interactions do not usually occur within the isolated context of the infant-mother dyad but rather within the larger context of mother, father, siblings, and often even extended family members. This is probably *especially* true during the developmental period to which this book is addressed, a period during which children are active in expanding their social networks well beyond the boundaries of their relationship with the mother. First, attachment interactions are often activated by circumstances within this larger context. For example, a youngster's attachment system may be activated by a threat from an older sibling, or by mother focusing her attention on that sibling or even her spouse. Second, stable patterns of attachment interactions often include more family members than just mother and child. For example, older siblings are often called upon by the family to "substitute" for a busy primary attachment figure. Moreover, young children who are fearful of open conflict between their parents often successfully divert their parents' attention from their conflict by displaying attachment behaviors at high intensity (Cummings, Zahn-Waxler, & Radke-Yarrow 1981). Third, attachment interactions tend to affect more family members than just mother and child. For example, family therapists have long known that an overly close attachment between child and mother is often associated with unresolved spouse conflict, lack of involvement between father and child, "infantilization" of the child, isolation of the family as a whole from a friendship network, and psychosomatic symptoms in the child. Likewise, recent work (Goodman & Rosenberg 1987; Rosenberg 1987) has demonstrated that children who witness violence in the home are highly likely to develop a myriad of emotional and social-cognitive difficulties. For example, children who are exposed to interparental violence may develop problematic coping and interpersonal problem-solving strategies that may be maladaptive (Cummings & Cummings 1988) or interfere with their relationships with family members (e.g., parents, siblings) and peers or with their school performance (Goodman & Rosenberg 1987). Certainly all of these patterns are prime "targets" for attachment researchers.

While there has been research published on child-father attachment (Lamb 1981), sibling attachment (Stewart and Marvin, 1984), and the seductive mother-son relationship and the quality of the later relationship between mother and *daughter* (Sroufe, Jacobvitz, Mangelsdorf, DeAngelo, & Ward 1985), there has been essentially no research on attachment that reflects an overriding family perspective. This is due largely to the lack of a conceptual framework that expands attachment theory to a family systems level. Marvin and Stewart (this vol.) present such a framework, one they claim to be consistent with current attachment theory. However useful this particular framework proves to be, there is little question that a family systems model of the development of, and individual differences in, the organization of attachment is necessary for a full understanding of intimate relationships.

Finally, in developing any theoretical framework, it is necessary to define carefully the constructs in a manner that provides conceptual and operational criteria of both inclusion and exclusion. As we have pointed out earlier, the attachment relationship is not synonymous with the caregiver-child relationship. Attachment interactions are part of the caregiver-child relationship, not the whole relationship (Bretherton 1980; Hinde 1976, 1979; Sroufe 1988; Stern 1985). They are one dimension of such a relationship, and other types of interactions (e.g., play, teaching) may or may not be shared by the same person.

Although it is important to demonstrate where there are interrelationships between the attachment system and other aspects of the parent-child relationship, it is important to keep other components of relationships theoretically distinct from the attachment system. There is a great need for care here and a potential for obfuscation of the attachment construct (Bretherton 1985). Thus, in the above guiding framework, the attachment construct has been carefully delimited to those issues concerning protection, security and trust, and the organization of physical proximity and contact. In this regard, the constructs of attachment and separation-individuation (Mahler et al. 1975) may not be isomorphic, and all separation-individuation issues may not concern the attachment system. Similarly, other distinctions within the parent-child relationship should be carefully considered. For example, although parental responsivity and sensitivity to a child's signals may underly both secure attachment relations and other abilities such as the parent's role as a language teacher or disciplinarian (Bretherton et al. 1979), the child's mastery motivation (Maslin-Cole & Spieker, this vol.), and the development of problem-solving skills (Matas, Arend, & Sroufe, 1978), they are not equivalent.

Issues in Measurement

An important issue for research on attachment in the preschool period is the development of measurement schemes to assess the nature and quality of attachment relationships (Greenberg in collaboration with the MacArthur Working Group on Attachment 1984). An implicit assumption of attachment theory is that bonds formed in infancy will persist into the toddler and preschool years; one goal of research, consequently, is to examine stability and change in attachment relationships. Further, as noted earlier, in the preschool period children may also form attachments to siblings, grandparents, day-care caregivers, and others as their network of social relationships expands (Berndt & Perry 1986; Cummings 1980; Stewart & Marvin 1984). Another goal thus is to develop methods to assess attachments other than parent-child attachments (Ainsworth 1985).

The transition between infancy and school-age is a period of great transformation, and the changes we mentioned above have implications for the measurement of attachment. First, because proximity seeking will no longer be useful as the nearly exclusive index of attachment, assessment of verbal interaction across a distance, nonverbal cues and signals, and internalized representations of attachment figures become necessary. Second, behavioral-cognitive-emotional systems mediating attachment change significantly during this period. Thus, another important goal is to study behavior, social cognitions, language, representation, and capacities for social expression and interaction as they relate to changes in the attachment system (Schneider-Rosen, this vol.). Third, as children expand their network of social attachments in the preschool period, a family systems approach that includes relationships beyond the mother-child dyad, for example, father- or sibling-child attachments, is necessary to complete description of the role of attachment in development (Easterbrooks & Goldberg, this vol.; Marvin & Stewart, this vol.). Fourth, advances in children's language and representational capabilities make the direct assessment of internal working models (Bowlby [1969] 1982; Bretherton 1985) possible for the first time at preschool age. Further, since preschooler's attachments may, through representation, transcend specific contexts and situations, measurement of their internal working models may be an important component of comprehensive assessment (Bretherton et al., this vol; Cassidy, this vol.). Fifth, multimethod assessment may improve the measurement of attachment in the preschool years. According to attachment theory, attachment behavioral systems should be ascendant in any stress context (Bowlby [1969] 1982); consequently, it should be possible to assess attachment in a variety of settings. Further, observation of interaction in different stress settings and in settings introducing varying levels of stress (e.g., low, moderate, high) may provide optimal characterization of the functioning of attachment (Greenberg in collaboration with the MacArthur Working Group on Attachment 1984). While stress is not essential to the observation of attachment processes, the attachment system should be more salient and ascendant in relation to other systems in stress contexts. The risk of confusing attachment systems with other parent-child systems is certainly heightened when behavior is observed in nonstressful contexts. In naturalistic home settings, relatively long periods of observation are probably necessary to assess attachment patterns adequately, and behavior in relatively stressful situations in the home should still be the most useful indicator of the functioning of the attachment relationship. Finally, although development of procedures and/or coding schemes to assess attachment is an important goal, it is properly viewed as only a first step in the measurement of attachment in the preschool years. Critical follow-ups for any new system are tests of their reliability, stability, and validity. Demonstrating that attachment classification predicts children's behavior in other settings or contexts is not, in itself, an adequate test of validity. The most significant demonstration will be that responding in laboratory contexts is predicted by attachment behavior in the home. Currently, several such studies are in progress in laboratories across the country. In the remainder of this section we consider recent work relevant to these issues in the measurement of attachment in the preschool years.

1. The Strange Situation as an index of attachment in preschoolers. Although the Strange Situation has proven quite useful for measurement of attachment in infancy, it is not necessarily the case that it remains the most appropriate context for the measurement of attachment in the preschool years. For example, if the Strange Situation fails to stress children even minimally, then it cannot, according to the tenets of attachment theory, serve as an adequate context for the measurement of attachment. The procedure may require modification for older children, and schemes for interpreting organizational patterns in the Strange Situation must certainly change consistent with developmental reorganizations and transformations. This issue ultimately is an empirical question. Current evidence suggests that the Strange Situation, and separation-reunion situations generally, *are* useful in the measurement of attachment at least until school age.

However, there has been some controversy in the literature regarding the use of separation-reunions and specifically the Strange Situation with children older than 24 months of age. In three studies, two cross-sectional (Lieberman 1977; Feldman & Ingham 1975) and one longitudinal (Maccoby & Feldman 1972), the fact that outright distress was not the modal response to separation led these researchers to reject such situations as useful or valid in studying attachment postinfancy. However, two major conceptual difficulties in these projects call into question the validity of this conclusion. First, in all three studies, frequency counts of behavior codes used in studying infants were utilized to assess attachment in preschoolers, and thus little account was taken of the changing motor, cognitive, or communicative abilities of the child or dyad. Second, these studies did not assess attachment from the organizational perspective and did not attempt either to characterize the organization of behavioral systems during the situation or to focus on the patterning of responses of the toddler upon reunion with the caregiver.

In contrast, a variety of studies have documented the value of laboratory-based separation-reunion contexts in assessing attachment (Cassidy 1988, this vol.; Crittenden 1985, 1988; Greenberg & Marvin 1979; Main et al. 1985; Marvin 1972; 1977; Radke-Yarrow, Cummings, Kuczynski, & Chapman 1985). In addition, reviews of videotapes from ongoing studies by a number of contributors to this volume (Bretherton, Cassidy, Cicchetti, Cummings, Greenberg, Main, Marvin, and Spieker) have convinced us that there is great richness and diversity in dyadic responses in such situations. Thus, the Strange Situation or other similar situations *do* appear to provide important information on how children and caregivers organize proximity and contact during the preschool years. However, it is critical that researchers focus on the development of coding systems that are developmentally appropriate; rather than focusing on crying and intense physical contact alone, it is necessary to assess the way in which a variety of behaviors which serve the attachment system, including conversation, are organized to maintain and regulate proximity and contact. Thus, it is our belief that it is not the Strange Situation which is invalid but instead the developmentally inadequate coding and classification systems which have sometimes been utilized.

To date, several developmentally sensistive coding schemes for coding Strange-Situation behavior beyond infancy have been developed. Schneider-Rosen and her colleagues (1985) proposed a revision of Ainsworth's scheme for scoring attachments in the Strange Situation at 1 year that can be used at 18 and 24 months (see also Schneider-Rosen, this vol.). In grouping children into *A*, *B*, or *C* classifications, this sytem takes into account the developmental reorganizations that occur *within* the attachment behavioral system as well as *between* the attachment, exploration, affiliation, and fear/wariness behavioral systems. The goal is an age-appropriate scoring system for use with the Strange Situation that includes consideration of children's emerging repertoire of more advanced modes of responding. This approach has proven to be reliable and has been validated in several studies of 18- and 24-month-old maltreated and lower-SES disadvantaged youngsters (Gersten et al. 1986; Schneider-Rosen & Cicchetti 1984; Schneider-Rosen et al. 1985).

Starting from the premise that older children will (*a*) not necessarily experience separation/reunion the same as infants and (*b*) not necessarily use the same set of behaviors as infants to work toward the goal of the attachment system, Aber and Baker (this vol.) created a new code specifically for 19–24-

month-olds seen in their modified attachment paradigm. They measured age-
and context-specific manifestations of the child's expectations of maternal
availability and responsivity across the entire paradigm. From their code they
derived four independent variables—the child's (1) secure communication
with the mother over the course of the entire paradigm, (2) flexible attention
deployment over the course of the entire paradigm, (3) separation insecurity,
and (4) reunion rejection. By measuring across-episode security and reunion
rejection/avoidance separately, Aber and Baker were able to examine the
interrelationship among these different aspects of the attachment system.
Their initial results reveal a number of ways in which developmental advances
around 18 months might effect the conceptualization and measurement of the
attachment system in toddlerhood. For example, across-episode attentional
processes emerged as a useful age- and context-specific measure of a toddler's
internal working model. In addition, the gender-specific pattern of correlations between toddler attachment and later competency highlight the need to
consider such relationships in the context of other emerging issues important
in toddlerhood.

Cassidy and Marvin in collaboration with the MacArthur Working Group
on Attachment (1989) have proposed a system to classify and rate organizations of attachment behavioral systems in 3- and 4-year-olds in the Strange
Situation (Ainsworth & Wittig 1969) or similar separation-reunion protocols
in laboratory contexts. Secure, insecure/avoidant, insecure/ambivalent, and
insecure/disorganized-controlling groups are specified within this system.
Further, a seven-point avoidance scale and a nine-point security scale are included. This system has been used by the MacArthur Working Group on
Attachment in collaborative assessments of diverse and difficult-to-classify
Strange-Situation sessions involving 3- and 4-year-olds. Validation of this
new system is ongoing in the laboratories of several of the contributors to this
volume (Cassidy, Cicchetti, Cummings, Easterbrooks, Greenberg, Marvin,
Spieker) and includes samples ranging across a variety of socioeconomic
strata and diagnostic conditions (e.g., maltreated preschoolers, offspring of
parents with a mood disorder, "high-risk" offspring of adolescent mothers
drawn from the lower SES, etc.).

Finally, Main and Cassidy (1985) have proposed a reliable and valid
scheme for assessing the quality of attachment in young school-aged children.
These classifications are based on the reunion behavior of parents and children following short and/or prolonged separations in a strange laboratory
environment.

2. Multimethod indices of attachment in the transition period. The
Strange Situation provides an eminently valuable, but nonetheless limited,
glimpse of the attachment behavioral system. Main et al. (1985) have pioneered the use of multiple contexts for assessing attachment-related functions
in 6-year-olds, including observations of mother-child interaction and inter-

views regarding children's separation anxiety and their responses to a family picture. Analyses revealed that such measures correlated significantly with behavior in separation-reunion contexts but also accounted for independent variance in attachment.

The MacArthur Working Group on Attachment has made several propositions regarding the conceptualization and measurement of attachment (Greenberg in collaboration with the MacArthur Working Group on Attachment 1984), and over the past several years has continued to consider this issue in small group meetings. Guiding themes in this work include: (*a*) attachment is organized to particular individuals and is not a static personality trait (Ainsworth et al. 1978; Sroufe & Waters 1977); (*b*) correlative changes and individual differences in the attachment-related behavior, cognitions (attributions, expectancies), and language of caregivers should be assessed; and (*c*) the relationship between quality of attachment and interpersonal plans and other partnership issues should also be examined. Furthermore, differing developmental tasks, capabilities, and interests in the postinfancy period and a need to develop more than one situation to validity assess attachment at *all* ages suggests that multiple measures are needed. A focal point with regard to the last issue is that while separation has almost always been used as the context for measuring attachment, it is only one of a variety of stress contexts that could activate and thus yield insights into the attachment behavioral system. Using more than one high-stress situation might increase the reliability of classifications of attachments or allow for more refined and complete characterizations of the child's use of the parent as a secure base. In particular, the use of stress contexts when the caregiver is present allows for study of how the parent serves as a source of security and a moderator of children's negative emotion. Further, the use of multiple contexts of varying levels of stress provides a more complete characterization of the extent of the caregiver's role as a source of security for the child in a range of everyday contexts.

The MacArthur Working Group on Attachment has recently proposed separate "pilot" protocols for 18–36-month- and 36–60-month-old children. These protocols provide initial guidelines for using a variety of laboratory contexts to assess attachment under varying levels of stress and with attachment figures both present and absent. The scenario for the former include (*a*) *semi-structured* or *unstructured free play* (low stress)—the primary purpose is to assess children's exploration of the environment and the degree to which the mother supports the child's experience (Beeghly & Cicchetti 1987); (*b*) a standard *modified version of the Strange Situation* (high stress); (*c*) the *Cookie Task* (moderate stress) (Marvin 1972, 1977)—this task assesses the ability of the dyad to directly and indirectly work out joint plans in which the child must delay gratification in receiving a cookie; and (*d*) *Emotional Conflict Situations* (high stress)—this task presents children with another ecologically valid stress context likely to involve the attachment system, in which the child is faced with anger or emotional conflict between other individuals using procedures developed by Cummings (1987).

The 36–60-month scenario also includes semistructured or unstructured free play, emotional conflict situations, and separation-reunion situations. In addition, cooperation and planning tasks that are developmentally more advanced than the Cookie Task are proposed, including an *Etch-a-Sketch* task and a *Waiting Task* (Carmichael-Olson 1986). Further, projective tests are proposed to assess aspects of children's internal working models around issues of separation. For this purpose, Slough and Greenberg (1986) have developed a variation of the *Separation Anxiety Task* originally developed by Hansburg (1972) and modified by Kaplan and Main (see Main et al. 1985).

These suggestions for multimethod assessment of attachment in 2–5-year-olds were originally made entirely on theoretical grounds. Recent work, however, suggests the possible utility of several of these procedures. For example, following from Bowlby's ([1969] 1982) and Marvin's (1972, 1977) ideas regarding the partnership phase of attachment, Carmichael-Olson (1986) found that the ability of 4-year-old children to cope effectively with the support of their mothers in their home environment while waiting for an attractive present was significantly related to the quality of attachment as assessed at 12 months. Greenberg, Slough, Carmichael-Olson, and Crnic (1988) studied attachment processes in the same sample at 5 years of age using a multimethod approach including a separation-reunion, a joint planning (waiting) task in which the child and parent had conflicting goals, and an assessment of the child's internal working model utilizing a modified version of the Separation Anxiety Test (Slough & Greenberg 1986). Reunion sequences were scored utilizing the classification system developed by Main and Cassidy (1985). Results indicated highly significant relationships between both the rating (one- to nine-point scale) and classification of security upon reunion at age 5 and the child and dyad's ability to cope during a laboratory version of the waiting task.

A next step for research is the integration of responses from several task situations in a comprehensive assessment of the attachment behavioral system. Since discrete behaviors mediating the attachment system change as a function of context, to be productive this analysis must focus on an organizational or higher-order characterization of patterns. An important task is to examine relationships between response to separation-reunion and response to emotional conflict.

3. Assessment of internal working models during the preschool period. Thus far, researchers have inferred internal working models of attachment relationships either directly by observations of children's behavior or indirectly based upon children's responses to projective tests.

Much of the recent work by Main and her colleagues (Main & Solomon 1986, this vol.; Main et al. 1985) is directly relevant to the assessment of internal working models. Main has begun to develop empirical research techniques for assessing children's and adults' "internal working models" of attachment figures. Based on Main's reconceptualization of individual differences in attachment relationships as individual differences in "internal working models" or "mental representations of attachment relationships," these new techniques focus upon the assessment of attachment through language and other representational processes. For instance, Main has developed several scoring techniques to code children's verbal and affective responses to the Klagsbrun-Bowlby adaptation of the Hansburg Separation Anxiety Test (Klagsbrun & Bowlby 1976; see Kaplan, unpublished, for a full description of the scoring procedures). This test is composed of six photographs of young children experiencing separations from the parent, ranging from mildest (e.g., parents saying goodnight) to severest (e.g., parents leaving for two weeks). Children are told that "parents worry sometimes about what children think when they have to go away for a little while," and then are asked after each picture to "tell us what you think a child your age would feel and what a child your age would do when parents go away for a little while."

Children's verbal-affective responses to the six pictures are scored for "emotional openness." High scores on this scale indicate that children could maintain "an easy balance between self-exposure and self containment," that children could imagine the pictured child as experiencing appropriate negative affect (e.g., lonely, sad, fearful, angry) which seemed appropriate because they offered reasons for these emotions. Low scores for emotional openness indicated a variety of insecure responses, ranging from silence or inability to express feelings spontaneously, to denial, and to marked disorganization of response.

Children's response to the most stressful separation (parents leaving for two weeks) were coded for children's expressed strategies to cope constructively with the separation. High scores indicated that children attempted to persuade their parents actively not to leave, expressed negative affect directly to the parent, or found an alternative attachment figure with whom to stay. Middle scores were given to children who distracted themselves through play, and low scores to children who answered "I don't know," were completely silent, or gave a response that would in reality decrease the availability of the attachment figure (see Main et al. 1985).

In a follow-up study of thirty-nine children, Main and colleagues (1985) found that children who were classified as securely attached to mother in infancy, based upon behavior in the Strange Situation, were rated as more emotionally open and more constructively coping based upon verbal-affective responses to the Klagsbrun-Bowlby Separation Anxiety Test at 6 years of age. The significant relationship between early security with mother and later constructive coping and emotional openness about separations was not replicated with father, perhaps suggesting a "hierarchy" of internal working models of attachment figures over the infancy period and that the internal representations of parents' accessibility guide children's attempts to cope with real-life separations (and presumably other attachment-related experiences) later in childhood. Along similar lines, using a modified version of the Separation Anxiety Test in a study of 5-year-olds, Slough (1988) has also reported significant concurrent relationships between the child's emotional openness and style of coping in the Separation Anxiety Test and independent ratings and classifications of security upon reunion after a short laboratory separation from their mothers (Slough & Greenberg, in press).

Main and her colleagues have also developed a method for assessing adults' overall internal working models of their attachment figures which focuses especially on their relationships with their parents. The Berkeley Adult Attachment interview (George, Kaplan, & Main 1985) probes for adults' verbal descriptions of early attachment relationships and experiences, supportive and contradictory memories, and current evaluations of early attachment relationships and experiences. Main reports a significant relationship between the security of the adult's internal working model of attachment relationships (as assessed by this procedure) and the security of the infant's attachment to them for both mothers and fathers ($p.<001$ and $p.<05$, respectively) (see Main et al. 1985).

4. Category and continuum schemes for classification. The use of continua for rating attachment also has been proposed in several recent papers (Aber & Baker, this vol.; Crittenden 1985; Cummings, this vol.; Main et al., 1985). Classification on a continuum can extend and refine the measurement of attachment (see Cummings, this vol., for more on this issue). First of all, not all attachments may fit "prototypes"; however, regardless of behavioral patterning of the attachment relationship, the security that children derive from the attachment relationship can be assessed. Second, even when attachments are classifiable in terms of a prototype, there may be significant differences in felt security among relationships receiving the same classification. Third, when classification decisions require judgments on the borderline between categories, the use of a security continuum can reduce the potential error of measurement (Stevens 1951). For example, when a child is on the borderline between an *A* and *B* classification, a category-based decision makes the difference between a judgment of secure and insecure, but a decision for the same child based upon a security continuum involves only the difference between two close points on a continuum.

Rather than being an alternative, however, classification in terms of a security continuum can best be conceptualized as a compliment to pattern classification; prediction should be optimal when both systems are combined. Pattern classification, because it describes behavioral dispositions, may be particularly useful in predicting the styles of affectional relationships and the *form* taken by developmental difficulties (e.g., behavior problem vs. anxiety disorder), whereas security ratings, because they describe level of disturbance, may best predict risk for developmental difficulty and the *extent* of later problems.

5. *Q*-sort methodology. Waters and Deane (1985) have developed a *Q*-sort for assessing the quality of attachment relationships in toddlers. Their attachment *Q*-set is comprised of 100 statements that they claim permit raters to describe youngsters' internal working models of attachment as inferred from their observable behavior in context (e.g., the home, the school). Waters and Deane (1985) have utilized this measure for children between 12 and 36 months. They have trained both parents and independent coders to achieve high levels of interrater agreement. In addition, Waters and Deane (1985) have produced evidence that the *Q*-sort is a psychometrically robust measure. Aber and Baker (this vol.) also make a compelling argument for employing the *Q*-sort methodology to assess security of attachment and present validity data on an adaptation of the Waters and Deane items and procedures used by child-care staff with children ages 18–31 months old.

Measurement advances such as these are critical if the progress made in understanding attachment across the life span and its role in normal and psychopathological development is to continue.

ATTACHMENT AND DEVELOPMENTAL PSYCHOPATHOLOGY

Within the past decade, there has been a burgeoning interest in the domain of developmental psychopathology (Bowlby 1988b; Cicchetti 1984, 1990; Rutter & Garmezy 1983; Sroufe & Rutter 1984; Zigler & Glick 1986). Researchers and theoreticians working in several of the disciplines which comprise developmental psychopathology have enhanced our knowledge about the processes underlying many normal domains of ontogenesis. Concomitantly, there has been an influx of theoretical and empirical work focusing on the clinical problems of infancy and the preschool years (Belsky & Nezworski 1988; Cicchetti & Aber 1986; Cicchetti & Beeghly 1987; Greenberg & Speltz 1988; Greenspan 1981; Sroufe 1983; Stern 1985; Trad 1986; Tronick & Field 1986).

The Developmental Psychopathology Perspective

Developmental psychopathology, which stresses the importance of understanding the relations betwen normal and pathological development, has emerged as a logical extension of the outgrowth of thinking that emphasized that the developmental approach could be applied to any unit of behavior or discipline and to all cultures or populations, normal or otherwise deviant (Werner 1948). From this developmental worldview (Pepper 1942), *any* psychopathology can be conceptualized as a distortion in the normal ontogenetic process. Moreover, the study of psychopathology from a developmental perspective is believed to contribute to our understanding of both normal and abnormal ontogenesis (Cicchetti, 1990; Rutter & Garmezy 1983; Rutter 1986; Sroufe & Rutter 1984). This viewpoint contrasts sharply with the symptom-based classification system espoused in the DSM-III-R (American Psychiatric Association 1987) and with the paucity of "developmental disorders" found in that nosology. We believe that other than autism and the organic forms of mental retardation, the vast majority of the disorders of the early years of life can best be characterized as transactional "relational psychopathologies"—that is, as problems that have occurred as the result of a dysfunction in the parent-child-family environment transactional system (see Sameroff & Chandler 1975; Sroufe & Fleeson 1986).

Links between Developmental Psychopathology and Attachment Theory

Within the DSM-III-R (American Psychiatric Association 1987), attachment disorders are conceived as occurring for the first time either during infancy or early childhood. Thus, even in an adevelopmental classification system such as the DSM-III-R, the fact that attachment disorders may occur across the life span is acknowledged. The DSM-III-R (American Psychiatric Association 1987) nosology is congruent with the theoretical framework of Erikson (1950) who likewise believed that attachment problems could occur at any point during the life cycle. Conversely, it is possible to develop a secure working model of attachment relationships even if one's working model initially was insecure. However, following Waddington's (1957) epigenetic landscape model, even though change in a working model is theoretically always possible, it is greatly constrained by the branching pathways previously taken (see Cicchetti & Schneider-Rosen 1986; Sroufe 1986).

In addition to the possibility of having an attachment disorder per se, a number of psychopathological conditions have attachment or relational problems as sequelae, including depression and manic depression (Cummings & Cicchetti, this vol.; Kraepelin [1921] 1987), schizophrenia (Bleuler [1911] 1950; Vaughn & Leff 1976), and antisocial disorders (Bowlby 1944; Cleckley 1937). Moreover, an insecure attachment relationship with a significant other, regardless of when the attachment problem occurs during ontogenesis, may be a risk factor for the development of psychopathology. Bowlby ([1969] 1982, 1977a, 1977b, 1980, 1988a, 1988b) has argued that an insecure attachment may render individuals more likely to respond adversely to stress and hence be more vulnerable to pathological breakdowns. As Bates, Maslin, and Frankel (1985), Lewis et al. (1984), and Sroufe (1983; Erickson et al. 1985) have shown, not all insecurely attached youngsters develop later behavioral problems or fail to resolve successfully the stage-salient issues of their developmental period. During the preschool period, several pathological conditions "emerge" for the first time during ontogeny—most notably, childhood borderline disorders, attention deficit disorders, and childhood depression (American Psychiatric Association 1987; Bemporad, Smith, Hanson, & Cicchetti

1982; Cicchetti & Aber 1986; Kovacs, Feinberg, Crouse-Novak, Paulaus-kas, & Finkelstein 1984). Likewise, epidemiological studies suggest that be-havior problems are prevalent during the preschool period (Greenberg & Speltz 1988; Speltz, this vol.). As is the case for adult disorders, the problems that occur during the preschool years are often accompanied by relational difficulties. For example, Bemporad et al. (1982) have speculated that the particular nature of the relational pathology of the childhood borderline syndrome, a condition associated with severe problems in the separation-individuation process (Cicchetti & Olsen 1990a), may be the pathognomonic symptom of this disorder.

Spurred in part by major advances in the understanding of normal on-togenetic domains during the early years of life, a number of researchers have focused their attention on prospective longitudinal studies, many of which have been conducted within an attachment theory framework (Bates et al. 1985; Crowell & Feldman 1988; Erickson et al. 1985; Lewis et al. 1984; Sroufe 1979a, 1983). Such studies have been helpful in elucidating the orga-nization of development in high-risk groups of youngsters and on uncovering the links between the quality of early adaptation and later outcome. One of the major goals of these endeavors has been to identify nascent and/or incipient psychopathology and to prevent such disturbances from undermining the adaptive developmental process (see, e.g., Cicchetti & Toth 1987; Cicchetti, Toth, Bush, & Gillespie 1988; Greenspan, Wieder, Lieberman, Nover, Lau-rie, & Robinson 1987; Provence & Naylor 1983).

Proponents of attachment theory have claimed that many types of psycho-pathology may be brought about by deviations in the development of the at-tachment behavioral system or, less commonly, by failure of its ontogenesis (Bowlby 1977a, 1977b; Guidano & Liotti 1983). In addition, advocates of the attachment theory perspective have argued that there are strong causal rela-tionships between the experience of individuals with their parents and the later capacity to form and to sustain affectional bonds (Bowlby 1944, 1977a, 1977b, 1988a, 1988b; Rutter 1979; Sroufe 1979a; Sroufe & Fleeson 1986, 1988; Sroufe & Rutter 1984). Furthermore, a number of problems have been implicated to be associated with poor quality early parent-child relations, in-cluding marital difficulties, the transmission of dysfunctional parenting, per-sonality disorders, neurotic symptoms, and severe psychopathology (Belsky 1984; Bowlby 1977a, 1977b, 1988a, 1988b; Henderson 1974; Rutter et al. 1983; Rutter, 1989; Sroufe & Fleeson 1986; Winnicott 1965).

Developmental psychopathologists studying attachment are interested not only in investigating relationship disorders but also in uncovering the proto-types of, or precursors to, what may later become a relational disorder. More-over, they focus on charting the course of individual differences in adaptation, both normal and psychopathological. Additionally, they are concerned with identifying the circumstances that render certain individuals vulnerable and others protected with respect to life's vicissitudes. Finally, developmental psychopathologists seek to ascertain the factors underlying the capacity of the organism to utilize environmental resources (e.g., social supports) in an adaptive fashion.

Although developmental psychologists have broken much new ground, major gaps exist in our knowledge about attachment formation and dissolution. Specifically, we possess rudimentary information about attachment relationships in clinically disordered populations. This state of affairs is curious, especially since Bowlby's original formulations of the importance of the attachment relationship emerged from observations of high-risk and clinical populations of youngsters (Bowlby 1944, 1958, [1969] 1982; Rutter 1979). Likewise, object-relations theorists have relied on clinical material to develop their theoretical notions on the etiology of relationships gone awry (Greenberg & Mitchell 1983). Clearly, a great deal of work remains to be done. However, several researchers have begun to study the development of attachment relationships in high-risk groups of youngsters (Crittenden 1988; Cummings & Cicchetti, this vol.; Egeland & Sroufe 1981; Radke-Yarrow et al. 1985; Schneider-Rosen et al. 1985; Spieker & Booth 1988) and to sketch out the role of attachment dysfunction in the emergence of behavior problems (Bates et al. 1985; Lewis et al. 1984; Sroufe 1983). In the following section, research conducted on the attachment development of two high-risk groups of children will be presented.

The Development of Attachment in High-Risk Children

One high-risk group of children whose attachment relationship development has been studied is maltreated children. Studies in the area of child maltreatment, akin to the early nonhuman primate studies of Harlow and his colleagues (e.g., Ruppenthal, Arling, Harlow, Sackett, & Suomi 1976), have demonstrated that maltreated youngsters do form attachments despite receiving inadequate care. As predicted by the Bowlby-Ainsworth theory, the quality of these relationships is poor. Specifically, the vast majority of maltreated youngsters form insecure attachments with their maltreating caregivers (Crittenden 1988; Egeland & Sroufe 1981; Schneider-Rosen et al. 1985); moreover, from 18 months onward, there is a striking tendency for these relationships to be anxious avoidant in nature (Schneider-Rosen et al. 1985). Likewise, studies of both maltreated infants/toddlers and of the offspring of parents with a major depressive disorder (i.e., depressive and manic-depressive disease) have revealed that maternal unpredictability is strongly associated with the formation of disorganized/disoriented type D attachment relationships (Carlson, Cicchetti, Barnett, & Braunwald 1989; Cummings & Cicchetti, this vol.).

In a reanalysis of the Strange Situations of a sample of 12-month-old maltreated infants, Carlson, Cicchetti, and their colleagues (1989) found a preponderance of disorganized/disoriented attachments (82%). From what is known of the caregiving environments of maltreated children, there are several explanations for the high preponderance of *D* attachments in maltreated infants. First, the lives of maltreated infants are characterized by varieties of inconsistent care (Cicchetti & Rizley 1981; Crittenden 1981; Egeland & Sroufe 1981; Garbarino & Gilliam 1980). Studies have linked insensitive overstimulation to avoidant attachment, and insensitive understimulation to resistant attachment (Belsky, Rovine, & Taylor 1984; Crittenden 1985; Lyons-Ruth, Connell, Zoll, & Stahl 1987). Combinations of these insensitive styles could lead to combined responses such as the blending of contradictory features often seen in disorganized/disoriented attachments (e.g., strong proximity seeking followed immediately by strong avoidance; see Main & Solomon, this vol.).

Second, Main and Hesse (this vol.) have suggested that it is the interjection of *fear* into the experience of otherwise adequate caregiving that is essential to developing a disorganized/disoriented attachment. Fear must certainly be a common experience for physically and emotionally abused children. It is also probable that there are frightening aspects of emotional and physical neglect. As Main and Hesse have described, the concurrent activation of the fear/wariness and attachment behavioral systems produce strong conflicting motivations to approach the caregivers for comfort and to retreat from them to safety. Proximity seeking mixed with avoidance results as infants attempt to balance their conflicting approach and avoidance tendencies. Freezing, dazing, and stilling may be the result of overloading, when approach tendencies equal the avoidance tendencies causing them to mutually inhibit one another (Main & Solomon 1986).

The phenomenon of parent-child role reversal suggests another important link between child maltreatment and the disorganized/disoriented attachment pattern. One of the most constantly observed characteristics of abused/neglected children is that they seem to have reversed roles with their caregivers (Dean, Malik, Richards, & Stringer 1986; Morris & Gould 1963). In the parent-child relationships of maltreated children, the children appear to be the sensitive, nurturing members of the dyad. Hence, the role reversal of caregiving behaviors which has been documented in 6-year-olds who were classified as type *D* at 12 months (Main et al. 1985) provides a new perspective on understanding the etiology of this feature in abused and neglected children. The parentification of the maltreated child may be better understood as a specific manifestation of a more general developmental course of an underlying disorganized attachment relationship. Thus, knowledge about attachment relationships in maltreatment cases may prove to be important for prevention and intervention purposes (Cicchetti, Toth, & Bush 1988).

A similar pattern of attachment behavior has been noted in another high-risk group of children—the offspring of affective disordered parents. Given the cyclical nature of an affective disorder and its concomitant effect upon maternal contingent responsiveness (Cicchetti & Aber 1986; Cummings & Cicchetti, this vol.; Trad 1986; Tronick & Field 1986), the increased percentage of avoidant/resistant (A/C) attachments, a subtype of the disorganized/disoriented category, in the offspring of mothers with an affective disorder by Radke-Yarrow and her colleagues (1985) is not surprising. In a related vein, Gilbreath and Cicchetti (in preparation) have found a greater percentage of mood disorders in a large sample (N=200) of maltreating mothers compared to a demographically matched group of nonmaltreating mothers from the lower SES. It is conceivable that depression could have independently contributed to the development of disorganized/disoriented attachment in some of the infants in the Carlson et al. (1989) study.

It also is important to note that research conducted on high-risk or psychopathological populations can inform us about attachment in normal development. For example, Belsky and Vondra (1989) have illustrated how the study of maltreating parents can greatly inform our understanding of the normal parenting process. More generally, we believe that studies of "experiments of nature" (see Bronfenbrenner 1979) can enhance our knowledge about normal development, including relationship formation.

Advantages of the Developmental Psychopathology Approach to Attachment Research

A significant contribution that the developmental psychopathology approach can bring to the study of attachment is specifying the nature of the relation among developmental domains (e.g., biological, cognitive, linguistic, social, and emotional development) and delimiting the effect that deviant experiences and pathological processes have upon the stage-salient issues of the preschool years (e.g., autonomy, communication, and peer relations—see Greenspan 1981; Sroufe 1979a) as well as on the continuing life-span non–stage-salient issues of the preschool period (such as attachment). For example, studies of the organization of the attachment system in atypical populations can provide evidence concerning the nature of the relation between affect and cognition (Thompson, Cicchetti, Lamb, & Malkin 1985), as well as on the interrelations between attachment and self-development (Cicchetti & Beeghly 1987; Schneider-Rosen & Cicchetti 1984) and between attachment and communication (Gersten et al. 1986). More specifically, Cicchetti, Beeghly, et al. (in press) have demonstrated that toddlers who are securely attached at 24 months use more internal state language at 30 months than do insecurely attached youngsters. Maltreated youngsters, the vast majority of whom are insecurely attached, employ significantly less internal state language than do matched comparison toddlers. A lack of integration among the interlocking social, emotional, cognitive, and linguistic domains may be conceived as pathological development (Kaplan 1966), while a similar organization and hierarchical integration of these domains in high-risk youngsters may denote healthy development in the face of adversity.

The developmental psychopathology perspective allows for the possibility that the same ontogenetic pathway may bifurcate to become several distinct and discrete psychopathological disorders (known as the *principle of multifinality*) and that quite divergent early pathways of adaptation may lead to the same final common psychopathological outcome (known as the *principle of equifinality* [see Bertalanffy 1968; Weiss 1969]). Carlson et al. (1989) and Cummings and Cicchetti (this vol.) have provided models that can account for the etiology and the developmental sequelae of secure and insecure attachments in maltreated and depressed children, respectively.

Related to this, Schneider-Rosen et al. (1985) have drawn the important distinction between adaptation and competence in studies of attachment in maltreated youngsters. Specifically, maltreated children become increasingly avoidant of their caregivers within the context of a disorganized/disoriented attachment relationship; however, though avoidance of the caregiver makes adaptive sense in this case, it is not necessarily a competent solution. That is, the use of an alternate pathway to achieve a desired outcome may render the maltreated child vulnerable to psychopathology. Indeed, maltreated youngsters have been shown to have impaired self-systems, deviant communicative development, and disturbed peer relationships (Cicchetti & Olsen 1990b). Given that maltreated children have major difficulties with autonomy, communication, and peer relations—the major stage-salient issues of the preschool period—it is hard to argue convincingly that their avoidant relationship stance with caregivers engenders a competent developmental outcome. Because many children reared in pathological environments, and/or children who themselves are psychiatrically disturbed, may be forced to take alternate developmental routes, it is important that prospective longitudinal studies be carried out in order to ascertain their veridical consequences.

Finally, research on attachment in psychopathological populations provides the opportunity to answer important questions about the organization of normal development. For example, although there has been little empirical confirmation of the relations between the quality of attachment and communicative competence in middle-class youngsters (Bates, Bretherton, Beeghly, & McNew 1982; Bretherton et al. 1979), research with high-risk youngsters provides compelling confirmation that there are socioemotional contributions to linguistic development (Beeghly & Cicchetti 1987; Coster, Gersten, Beeghly, & Cicchetti 1989; Gersten et al. 1986; Greenberg & Marvin 1979). Consequently, strict biological interpretations of language growth no longer stand uncontested as the sole theoretical explanations for the ontogenesis of communication skills (Cicchetti 1989).

Clinical Implications of a Developmental
Psychopathological Approach to Attachment

A developmental scheme is also necessary for tracing the roots, etiology, and nature of maladaptation so that treatment interventions may be appropriately timed and guided (Cicchetti, Toth, & Bush 1988). For example, there are disturbances in internal-state language usage in maltreated children that are associated with insecure attachments (Cicchetti & Beeghly 1987). Therapies enhancing recognition of, and verbalization about, personal emotions should help such children develop better impulse control and self-regulation (Cicchetti, Toth, et al. 1988). Because the child's "overcontrolled" stance may serve as an adaptive coping strategy, care needs to be taken when attempting to intervene. For example, the therapist must insure that the environment is able to tolerate more open verbal expression before attempting to modify the child's mode of expression/interaction. Altering the child's management of affect without assuring that primary caretakers are able to accept and support modifications would be a disservice.

Similarly, Greenberg and Speltz (1988) have argued cogently that many child behavior problems of the preschool years are a function of a faulty parent-child "goal-corrected" partnership (Bowlby [1969] 1982; Marvin 1977). Greenberg and Speltz (1988) stated that these behavior problems may occur through a variety of developmental pathways. First, there could be parents who always indulge their children in the sense that the children have complete control over the goal-corrected planning process. Consequently, these children do not learn to negotiate or to compromise. The second, and by far the largest group of behavior problem children are those in which the parents arbitrarily control the interactions and give the children minimal input in the planning process. As a result, Greenberg and Speltz (1988) contended that the children manifest negative, aggressive, controlling behaviors in reaction. Speltz (this vol.) has proposed ways of intervening with these problem relationships from an attachment theory perspective (see also Bowlby 1988a and Lieberman & Pawl, this vol., for an example of how attachment theory can guide the treatment process).

In order to apply attachment theory in clinical situations, it is necessary to possess a strong body of knowledge of the range of appropriate attachment behavior at different points in development. Before this can be successful in a normative sense, we must obtain a good descriptive literature on the changes and variations in attachment behavior across contexts. Subsequently, we must demonstrate that there is a relationship between behavior problems and certain types of attachment patterns. Epidemiological studies that validate parent-teacher and self-reported behavior problems against home and laboratory behavior are sorely needed in this regard.

Summary and Conclusion

Over the past several years, great advances have been made in the understanding of attachment relationships beyond infancy. As with the research on the causes and consequences of secure and insecure attachments in infants, work that extends the study of attachment into older age groups holds great promise for elucidating the organization of development in normal and abnormal populations. In the future, theoreticians, researchers, and clinicians must address a number of critical issues to insure that the important progress that has been made continues and reaps fruition. We close this chapter by making a series of recommendations that we believe will contribute to the attainment of this goal.

1. There must be ongoing construct validation of the measures that have been devised to assess quality of attachment in preschool and school-aged children.

As we have illustrated, a flurry of research activity has occurred in the area of measure development. The Attachment Working Group of the MacArthur Foundation has advocated the use of multiple measures of attachment under a variety of stress conditions (Greenberg in collaboration with the MacArthur Working Group on Attachment 1984). As attachment becomes progressively representational in nature (Bretherton 1985, 1987; Main et al. 1985), the reliance on single measures and on overt behaviors alone becomes increasingly untenable. Winnicott's (1965) work on the "false self" is but one example of why a focus on behavior is not enough. The appearance of social and personal display rules (Ekman, Friesen, & Ellsworth 1972; Saarni 1978, 1979) and mechanisms of defense (Freud, 1946) provide additional reasons for researchers to develop a psychometrically robust battery for assessing the quality of attachment during the preschool and early school-age years. In this way, we will be able to improve the valid positive and valid negative hit rate for attachment classifications while minimizing false positive and false negative assignments.

Because attachments can change over time, work on the temporal stability of these assessments is essential. Moreover, research guided by a priori theoretical predictions must be conducted to determine the components of the nomological network (Campbell & Fiske 1959; Cronbach & Meehl 1955). Furthermore, because the organization of attachment behavior changes as a function of context (Sroufe & Waters 1977), it is necessary to conduct research on attachment during the postinfancy years in multiple settings (e.g., home, school, laboratory, outdoors). The Q-sort technique devised by Waters and his colleagues (Waters & Deane 1985) should be an especially promising measurement technique for implementing such work. Finally, because individuals may have different working models with different attachment figures

(Bretherton 1985; Main et al. 1985), it is important that researchers assess children's relations with multiple caregivers (e.g., mother, father, siblings, grandparents, teachers, etc.). Much more needs to be learned about discordant working models. For example, How do children form an integrative working model of relationships when several models exist with different caregivers? Or, Can a discordant working model (e.g., a secure model with a grandparent and an insecure model with both parents) serve as a buffering or protective factor for a child who has primarily formed insecure working models of attachment figures?

2. Continued work must be done on the development and validation of measures to assess attachment in adolescents and adults.

Several measures have appeared in recent years that assess adolescents' and adults' recollections about their childhood relationships with parents and peers (Epstein 1983; George et al. 1985) or their concurrent relationships with peers and parents (Armsden & Greenberg 1987; Greenberg et al. 1983). These measures have begun to be validated against the quality of current mother-child relationships (Main & Goldwyn 1984; Main & Hesse, this vol.; Main et al. 1985; Ricks 1985). Because we believe that it is important to assess the parental perspective in studies of attachment beyond infancy, we think that continued research in this area should be given high priority.

3. Research must be conducted to demonstrate the relative contribution of constitutional and relationship factor influences on the development of attachment during the preschool period and beyond.

Although one of the basic tenets of attachment theory always has been that infants' attachment classifications are a result of their particular experiences with their attachment figures (Sroufe 1985), speculations about the determinants of attachment patterns have not been without controversy (Kagan 1982). The findings of a number of prospective longitudinal investigations also have provided support for the notion that innate differences in temperament determine, at least in part, the attachment behaviors of anxious-avoidant, anxious-resistant, and secure relationships (see Goldsmith & Alansky 1987 for a review). According to the most recent constitutionally based theory of attachment, avoidant infants are viewed as representing children who have higher thresholds of arousal, and resistant infants are children who have lower thresholds of arousal. Belsky and Rovine (1987) provide further evidence to support this temperamental theory. However, these investigators also demonstrated that although temperamental differences influence the form of the infant's attachment pattern, they were not predictive of whether children would develop secure or insecure attachments to their caregiver. Together, these results suggest a gene/environment interaction in the development of attachment relationships and call for future research on this topic.

4. Continued investigations that address the relation between attachment

and other stage-salient developmental issues (e.g., the self-system, peer relations, identity, intimacy, etc.), both concurrently and over time, merit investigation with normal and pathological groups as well.

5. Future studies of attachment beyond infancy must integrate relational, family systems theory approaches with other theoretical positions on relationship formation (Hinde and Stevenson-Hinde 1987; Marvin & Stewart, this vol.; Minuchin 1985; Sroufe & Fleeson 1986, 1988).

6. More empirical focus should be placed upon the study of the goal-corrected partnership phase of attachment (Marvin 1977). A promising extension of the goal-corrected partnership to older ages is Selman and Demorest's (1986) description of the development of interpersonal negotiation strategies.

7. Ongoing validation of the "Disorganized/Disoriented" type D attachment category is critical.

We believe that work on this newly discovered attachment pattern holds great promise for the discipline of developmental psychopathology. For example, Spieker and Booth (1988) have documented a high-percentage (28%) of type D attachments in lower-SES disadvantaged mother-child dyads. Likewise, Carlson et al. (1989) have found that approximately 80% of maltreated infants, when reclassified by blind raters unaware either of the infants' diagnostic status or of their prior attachment classification, had type D attachments with their maltreating mothers. Questions such as the temporal stability of the D classification, how to classify D's during the preschool period, and the relation between D attachment status and later adaptation/maladaptation all will provide crucial information to the field. Given their apparent high base-rate of type D attachments (see Crittenden's 1988 A/C pattern), studies of maltreated children should prove promising for understanding the antecedents, correlates, and consequences of disorganized/disoriented attachments.

8. Additional work with high-risk and pathological populations is necessary to enhance our understanding of relationship formation, maintenance, and dissolution across the life span.

9. The vast majority of research in the area of attachment and developmental psychopathology has been conducted with high-risk populations of infants and toddlers. It is essential that this work be extended to a more life-span perspective and include studies of both children and adults with DSM-III-R (American Psychiatric Association 1987) diagnosed mental illnesses. Of course, parallel progress must be made in our understanding of normal attachment relationships across the life span.

10. Developmental knowledge gained from the study of attachment relationships beyond infancy should be used to guide clinical decision making.

11. Further prospective longitudinal studies on the processes underlying the relation between attachment during the preschool years and later developmental outcomes are needed in both normal and clinical populations.

REFERENCES

Ainsworth, M. D. S. (1967). *Infancy in Uganda: Infant care and the growth of love.* Baltimore: Johns Hopkins University Press.

Ainsworth, M. D. S. (1969). Object relations, dependency and attachment: A theoretical review of the infant-mother relationship. *Child Development* 40, 969–1025.

Ainsworth, M. D. S. (1973). The development of infant-mother attachment. In B. M. Caldwell & H. N. Ricciuti (eds.), *Review of child development research* (vol. 3, pp. 1–94). Chicago: University of Chicago Press.

Ainsworth, M. D. S. (1974). The secure base. Unpublished manuscript, Johns Hopkins University.

Ainsworth, M. D. S. (1977). Attachment theory and its utility in cross-cultural research. In P. H. Leiderman, S. R. Tulkin, & R. Rosenfeld (eds.), *Culture and infancy* (pp. 49–67). New York: Academic Press.

Ainsworth, M. D. S. (1985). Attachments across the life span. *Bulletin of the New York Academy of Medicine* 61, 792–812.

Ainsworth, M. D. S. (1989). Attachments beyond Infancy. *American Psychologist* 44, 709–716.

Ainsworth, M. D. S.; Blehar, M. C.; Waters, E.; & Wall, S. (1978). *Patterns of attachment: A psychological study of the strange situation.* Hillsdale, N.J.: Erlbaum.

Ainsworth, M. D. S., & Wittig, B. A. (1969). Attachment and the exploratory behavior of one-year-olds in a strange situation. In B. M. Foss (ed.), *Determinants of infant behavior* (vol. 4, pp. 113–136). London: Methuen.

American Psychiatric Association Committee on Nomenclature (1987). *Diagnostic and statistical manual of mental disorders, III-R.* Washington, D.C.: American Psychiatric Association.

Anderson, J. W. (1972). Attachment behaviour out of doors. In N. Blurton Jones (ed.), *Ethological studies of child behaviour* (pp. 199–215). Cambridge: Cambridge University Press.

Armsden, G., & Greenberg, M. (1987). The inventory of parent and peer attachment: Individual differences and their relationship to psychological well-being in adolescence. *Journal of Youth and Adolescence* 16, 427–454.

Bandura, A. (1978). The self system in reciprocal determinism. *American Psychologist* 33, 344–358.

Bates, E.; Bretherton, I.; Beeghly, M.; & McNew, S. (1982). Social bases of language development: A reassessment. In H. W. Reese & L. P. Lipsitt (eds.), *Advances in child development and behavior* (vol. 16, pp. 7–75). New York: Academic Press.

Bates, J. E.; Maslin, A.; & Frankel, K. A. (1985). Attachment security mother-child interaction, and temperament as predictors of behavior-problem ratings at age three years. In I. Bretherton & E. Waters (eds.), *Growing points of attachment theory and research. Monographs of the Society for Research in Child Development* 50 (1–2, Serial No. 209), 167–193.

Baumrind, D. (1971). Current patterns of parental authority. *Developmental Psychology Monograph* 4(1, pt. 2).

Beeghly, M., & Cicchetti, D. (1987). An organizational approach to symbolic development in children with Down syndrome. *New Directions for Child Development* 36, 5–29.

Belsky, J. (1984). The determinants of parenting: A process model. *Child Development* 55, 83–96.

Belsky, J., & Nezworski, T. (1988). *Clinical implications of attachment.* Hillsdale, N.J.: Erlbaum.

Belsky, J., & Rovine, M. (1987). Temperament and attachment security in the strange situation: An empirical rapprochement. *Child Development* 58, 787–795.

Belsky, J.; Rovine, M.; & Taylor, D. G. (1984). The Pennsylvania Infant and Family Development Project, 3: The origins of individual differences in infant-mother attachment: Maternal and infant contributions. *Child Development* 55, 718–728.

Belsky, J., & Vondra, J. (1989). Lessons from child abuse: The determinants of parenting. In D. Cicchetti & V. Carlson (eds.), *Child maltreatment: Theory and research on the causes and consequences of child abuse and neglect.* New York: Cambridge University Press.

Bemporad, J.; Smith, H.; Hanson, C.; & Cicchetti, D. (1982). Borderline syndromes in childhood: Criteria for diagnosis. *American Journal of Psychiatry* 139, 596–602.

Berndt, T. J., & Perry, T. B. (1986). Children's perceptions of friendships as supportive relationships. *Developmental Psychology* 22, 640–648.

Bertalanffy, L. von (1968). *General systems theory: Foundations, development, applications.* New York: Brazilier.

Bischof, N. A. (1975). A systems approach toward the functional connections of attachment and fear. *Child Development* 46, 801–817.

Bleuler, E. ([1911] 1950). *Dementia praecox or the group of schizophrenias.* New York: International Universities Press.

Bowlby, J. (1944). Forty-four juvenile thieves: Their characters and home life. *International Journal of Psychoanalysis* 25, 19–52 and 107–127.

Bowlby, J. (1958). The nature of the child's tie to his mother. *International Journal of Psychoanalysis* 39, 350–373.

Bowlby, J. ([1969] 1982). *Attachment and loss: Vol. 1. Attachment.* New York: Basic Books.

Bowlby, J. (1973). *Attachment and loss: Vol. 2. Separation.* New York: Basic Books.

Bowlby, J. (1977a). The making and breaking of affectional bonds. *British Journal of Psychiatry* 130, 201–10.

Bowlby, J. (1977b). The making and breaking of affectional bonds. *British Journal of Psychiatry* 130, 421–431.

Bowlby, J. (1980). *Attachment and loss: Vol. 3. Loss, sadness and depression.* New York: Basic Books.

Bowlby, J. (1988a). *A secure base: Parent-child attachment and healthy human development.* New York: Basic Books.

Bowlby, J. (1988b). Developmental psychiatry comes of age. *American Journal of Psychiatry* 145, 1–10.

Bretherton, I. (1980). Young children in stressful situations: The supporting role of attachment figures and unfamiliar caregivers. In G. V. Coelho & P. Ahmed (eds.), *Uprooting and development* (pp. 179–210). New York: Plenum.

Bretherton, I. (ed.), (1984). *Symbolic play: The development of social understanding.* Orlando, Fla.: Academic Press.

Bretherton, I. (1985). Attachment theory: Retrospect and Prospect. In I. Bretherton & E. Waters (eds.), *Growing points of attachment theory and research. Monographs of the Society for Research in Child Development* 50(1–2, Serial No. 209), 3–35.

Bretherton, I. (1987). New perspectives on attachment relations: Security, communication, and internal working models. In J. Osofsky (ed.), *Handbook of infant development* (2d ed.). New York: Wiley.

Bretherton, I., & Ainsworth, M. D. S. (1974). Responses of one-year-olds to a stranger in a strange situation. In M. Lewis & L. A. Rosenblum (eds.), *The origins of fear* (pp. 131–164). New York: Wiley.

Bretherton, I.; Bates, E.; Benigni, L.; Camaioni, L.; & Volterra, V. (1979). Relationships between cognition, communication and quality of attachment. In E. Bates, L. Benigni, I. Bretherton, L. Camaioni, & V. Volterra, *The emergence of symbols cognition and communication in infancy* (pp. 223–269). New York: Academic Press.

Bretherton, I., & Beeghly M. (1982). Talking about internal states: The acquisition of an explicit theory of mind. *Developmental Psychology* 18, 906–921.

Bretherton, I.; McNew, S.; & Beeghly-Smith, M. (1981). Early person knowledge as expressed in verbal and gestural communication: When do infants acquire a "theory of mind"? In M. E. Lamb & L. R. Sherrod (eds.), *Infant social cognition* (pp. 333–373). Hillsdale, N.Y.: Erlbaum.

Bronfenbrenner, U. (1979). *The ecology of human development: Experiments by nature and design.* Cambridge, Mass.: Harvard University Press.

Campbell, D. P., & Fiske, D. W. (1959). Convergent and discriminant validation by the multitrait-multimethod matrix. *Psychological Bulletin* 56, 81–105.

Carlson, V.; Cicchetti, D.; Barnett, D.; & Braunwald, K. (1989). Finding order in disorganization: Lessons from research on maltreated infants' attachments to their caregivers. In D. Cicchetti & V. Carlson (eds.), *Child maltreatment: Theory and research on the causes and consequences of child abuse and neglect.* New York: Cambridge University Press.

Carmichael-Olsen, H. (1986). Developmental process and outcome in preterm chidlren: A transactional study. Unpublished doctoral dissertation, University of Washington.

Cassidy, J. (1988). Child-mother attachment and the self in six-year-olds. *Child Development* 59, 121–134.

Cassidy, J., & Marvin, R. S., in collaboration with the MacArthur Working Group on Attachment (1989). Attachment organization in three- and four-year-olds: Coding guidelines. Unpublished manuscript, University of Virginia and Pennsylvania State University.

Cicchetti, D. (ed.), (1984). *Developmental psychopathology. Child Development* 55 (special issue).

Cicchetti, D. (1989). How research on child maltreatment has informed the study of child development: Perspectives from developmental psychopathology. In D. Cicchetti & V. Carlson (eds.), *Child maltreatment: Theory and research on the causes and consequences of child abuse and neglect* (pp. 377–431). New York: Cambridge University Press.

Cicchetti, D. (1990). An historical perspective on the discipline of developmental psychopathology. In J. Rolf, A. Masten, D. Cicchetti, K. Neuchterlein, & S. Weintraub (eds.), *Risk and protective factors in the development of psychopathology* (pp. 2–28). New York: Cambridge University Press.

Cicchetti, D., & Aber, J. L. (1986). Early precursors to later depression: An organizational perspective. In L. Lipsitt & C. Rovee-Collier (eds.), *Advances in infancy* (vol. 4, pp. 87–137). Norwood, N.J.: Ablex.

Cicchetti, D., and Beeghly, M. (1987). Symbolic development in maltreated youngsters: An organizational perspective. In D. Cicchetti & M. Beeghly (eds.), *Symbolic development in atypical children* (pp. 47–68). San Francisco: Josey-Bass.

Cicchetti, D., & Beeghly, M. (eds.), (in press). *The self in transition: Infancy to childhood.* Chicago: University of Chicago Press.

Cicchetti, D.; Beeghly, M.; Carlson, V.; & Toth, S. (in press). The emergence of the self in atypical populations. In D. Cicchetti & M. Beeghly (eds.), *The self in transition: Infancy to childhood.* Chicago: University of Chicago Press.

Cicchetti, D., & Olsen, K. (1990a). Borderline disorders in childhood. In M. Lewis & S. Miller (eds.), *Handbook of developmental psychopathology.* New York: Plenum.

Cicchetti, D., & Olsen, K. (1990b). The developmental psychopathology of child maltreatment. In M. Lewis & S. Miller (eds.), *Handbook of developmental psychopathology.* New York: Plenum.

Cicchetti, D., & Rizley, R. (1981). Developmental perspectives on the etiology, intergenerational transmission, and sequelae of child maltreatment. *New Directions in Child Development* 11, 31–55.

Cicchetti, D., & Schneider-Rosen, K. (1984). Theoretical and empirical considerations in the investigation of the relationship between affect and cognition. In C. Izard, J. Kagan, & R. Zajonc (eds.), *Emotions, cognitions, and behavior* (pp. 366–406). New York: Cambridge University Press.

Cicchetti, D., & Schneider-Rosen, K. (1986). An organizational approach to childhood depression. In M. Rutter, C. Izard, & P. Read (eds.), *Depression in young people: Clinical and developmental perspectives* (pp. 71–134). New York: Guilford.

Cicchetti, D., & Serafica, F. C. (1981). The interplay among behavioral systems: Illustrations from the study of attachment, affiliation, and wariness in young Down syndrome children. *Developmental Psychology* 17, 36–49.

Cicchetti, D., & Sroufe, L. A. (1978). An organizational view of affect: Illustration from the study of Down's syndrome infants. In M. Lewis & L. Rosenblum (eds.), *The development of affect* (pp. 309–350). New York: Plenum.

Cicchetti, D., & Toth, S. (1987). The application of a transactional risk model to intervention with multi-risk maltreating families. *Zero to Three* 7, 1–8.

Cicchetti, D.; Toth, S.; & Bush, M. A. (1988). Developmental psychopathology and incompetence in childhood: Suggestions for intervention. In B. Lahey & A. Kazdin (eds.), *Advances in child clinical psychology* (vol. 11, pp. 1–73). New York: Plenum.

Cicchetti, D.; Toth, S.; Bush, M. A.; & Gillespie, J. F. (1988). Stage-salient issues: A transactional model of intervention. *New Directions for Child Development* 39, 123–145.

Cleckley, H. (1937). *The mask of sanity.* St. Louis: Mosby.

Connell, J. P. (in press). Context, self, and action: A motivational analysis of self-system processes across the life-span. In D. Cicchetti & M. Beeghly (eds.), *The self in transition: Infancy to childhood*. Chicago: University of Chicago Press.

Coster, W.; Gersten, M.; Beeghly, M.; & Cicchetti, D. (1989). Communicative behavior in maltreated toddlers. *Developmental Psychology* 25, 1020–1029.

Crittenden, P. M. (1981). Abusing, neglecting, problematic, and adequate dyads: Differentiating by patterns of interaction. *Merrill-Palmer Quarterly* 27, 201–208.

Crittenden, P. M. (1985). Maltreated infants: Vulnerability and resilience. *Journal of Child Psychology and Psychiatry and Allied Disciplines* 26, no. 1, 85–96.

Crittenden, P. M. (1988). Relationships at risk. In J. Belsky & T. Nezworski (eds.), *Clinical implications of attachment theory* (pp. 136–174). Hillsdale, N.J.: Erlbaum.

Crockenberg, S. (1981). Infant irritability, mother responsiveness, and social support influences on the security of infant-mother attachment. *Child Development* 52, 857–869.

Cronbach, L. T., & Meehl, P. E. (1955). Construct validity in psychological tests. *Psychological Bulletin* 39, 123–131.

Crowell, J., & Feldman, S. S. (1988). Mothers' internal models of relationships and children's behavioral and developmental status: A study of mother-child interaction. *Child Development* 59, 1273–1285.

Cummings, E. M. (1980). Caregiver stability and day care. *Developmental Psychology* 16, 31–37.

Cummings, E. M. (1987). Coping with background anger in early childhood. *Child Development* 58, 976–984.

Cummings, E. M., & Cummings, J. L. (1988). A process-oriented approach to children's coping with adults' angry behavior. *Developmental Review* 8, 296–321.

Cummings, E. M.; Zahn-Waxler, C.; & Radke-Yarrow, M. (1981). Young children's responses to expressions of anger and affection by others in the family. *Child Development* 52, 1274–1282.

Damon, W. (1977). *The social world of the child*. San Francisco: Jossey-Bass.

Damon, W. (1983). *Social and personality development*. New York: Norton.

Damon, W., & Hart, D. (1982). The development of self-understanding from infancy through adolescence. *Child Development* 53, 841–864.

Dean, A. L.; Malik, M. M.; Richards, W.; & Stringer, S. A. (1986). Effects of parental maltreatment on children's conceptions of interpersonal relationships. *Developmental Psychology* 22, 617–626.

Decarie, T. G. (1929). A study of the mental and emotional development of the thalidomide child. In B. M. Foss (ed.), *Determinants of infant behaviour* (vol. 4). London: Methuen.

Earls, F. (ed.), (1980). *Studies of children*. New York: Neale Watson Academic Publications.

Egeland, B.; Jacobvitz, D.; & Sroufe, L. A. (1988). Breaking the cycle of abuse. *Child Development* 59, 1080–1088.

Egeland, B.; & Sroufe, L. A. (1981). Developmental sequelae of maltreatment in infancy. *New Directions for Child Development* 11, 77–92.

Ekman, P; Friesen, W.; & Ellsworth, P. (1972). *Emotion in the human face*. New York: Pergamon.

Epstein, S. (1983). *The mother-father-peer scale*. Unpublished manuscript, University of Massachusetts, Amherst.

Erickson, M. F.; Sroufe, L. A.; & Egeland, B. (1985). The relationship between quality of attachment and behavior problems in preschool in a high-risk sample. In I. Bretherton & E. Waters (eds.), *Growing points in attachment theory and research. Monographs of the Society for Research in Child Development* 50(1–2, Serial No. 209).

Erikson, E. H. (1950). *Childhood and society*. New York: Norton.

Feldman, S. S., & Ingham, M. (1975). Attachment behavior: A validation study in two age groups. *Child Development* 46, 319–330.

Freud, A. (1946). *The ego and the mechanisms of defense*. New York: International Universities Press.

Freud, A. (1965). *Normality and pathology in childhood: Assessments of development*. New York: International Universities Press.

Garbarino, J., & Gilliam, G. (1980). *Understanding abusive families*. Lexington, Mass.: Lexington Press.

George, C.; Kaplan, N.; & Main, M. (1985). The Berkeley Adult Attachment Interview. Unpublished protocol, Department of Psychology, University of California, Berkeley.

Gersten, M.; Coster, W.; Schneider-Rosen, K.; Carlson, V.; & Cicchetti, D. (1986). The socioemotional bases of communicative functioning: Quality of attachment, language development, and early maltreatment. In M. E. Lamb, A. L. Brown, & B. Rogoff (eds.), *Advances in developmental psychology* (vol. 4, pp. 105–151). Hillsdale, N.J.: Erlbaum.

Gewirtz, J. L. (1972). On the selection and use of attachment and dependence indicators. In J. L. Gewirtz (eds.), *Attachment and dependency*. Washington, D.C.: Winston.

Gilbreath, B., & Cicchetti, D. Psychopathology in maltreating mothers. In preparation.

Goldsmith, H. H., & Alansky, J. (1987). Maternal and Infant temperamental predictors of attachment: A meta-analytic review. *Journal of Consulting and Clinical Psychology* 55, 805–816.

Goodman, G. S., & Rosenberg, M. S. (1987). The child witness to family violence. In D. J. Sonkin (ed.), *Domestic violence on trial: Psychological and legal dimensions of family violence*. New York: Springer-Verlag.

Goslin, D. A. (ed.), (1969). *Handbook of socialization theory and research*. Chicago: Rand McNally.

Graham, P. J. (ed.), (1977). *Epidemiological approaches in child psychiatry*. London: Academic Press.

Greenberg, J., & Mitchell, S. (1983). *Object relations in psychoanalytic theory*. Cambridge, Mass.: Harvard University Press.

Greenberg, M. T., in collaboration with the MacArthur Working Group on Attachment (1984). Working paper on the measurement of attachment during the preschool years. Technical Report No. 1, University of Washington, Seattle.

Greenberg, M. T., & Marvin, R. S. (1979). Attachment patterns in profoundly deaf preschool children. *Merrill-Palmer Quarterly* 25, 265–279.

Greenberg, M. T. & Marvin, R. S. (1982). Reactions of preschool children to an adult stranger: A behavioral system approach. *Child Development* 53, 481–490.

Greenberg, M. T.; Siegel, J. M.; & Leitch, C. J. (1983). The nature and importance of attachment relationships to parents and peers during adolescence. *Journal of Youth and Adolescence* 12, 373–386.

Greenberg, M. T.; Slough, M. N.; Carmichael-Olson, H.; & Crnic, K. (1988). The organization of attachment in five-year-olds. Unpublished manuscript, Department of Psychology, University of Washington.

Greenberg, M. T. & Speltz, M. (1988). Attachment and the ontogeny of conduct problems. In J. Belsky & T. Nezworski (eds.), *Clinical implications of attachment* (pp. 177–218). Hillsdale, N.J.: Erlbaum.

Greenspan, S. I. (1981). *Psychopathology and adaptation in infancy and early childhood*. New York: International Universities Press.

Greenspan, S., & Porges, S. (1984). Psychopathology in infancy and early childhood: Clinical perspectives on the organization of sensory and affective-thematic experience. *Child Development* 55, 49–70.

Greenspan, S. I.; Wieder, S.; Lieberman, A.; Nover, R.; Lourie, R.; & Robinson, M. (eds.), (1987). *Infants in multirisk families*. New York: International Universities Press.

Grossmann, K.; Grossmann, K. E.; Spangler, G.; Suess, G.; & Unzner, L. (1985). Maternal sensitivity and newborns' orientation responses as related to quality of attachment in Northern Germany. In I. Bretherton & E. Waters (eds.) *Growing points of attachment theory and research. Monographs of the Society for Research in Child Development* 50 (1–2, Serial no. 209), 233–256.

Guidano, V. F., & Liotti, G. (1983). *Cognitive processes and emotional disorders: A structural approach to psychotherapy*. New York: Guilford Press.

Hansburg, H. G. (1972). *Adolescent separation anxiety: A method for the study of adolescent separation problems*. Springfield, Ill.: Thomas.

Hartmann, H.; Kris, E.; & Lowenstein, R. ([1949] 1964). Notes on the theory of aggression. In H. Hartmann, *Papers on psychoanalytic psychology*. New York: International Universities Press.

Hartup, W. (1983). Peer relations. In P. Mussen (ed.), *Handbook of child psychology* (pp. 103–196). New York: Wiley.

Hartup, W., & Lempers, J. (1973). A problem in life-span development: The interactional analysis of family attachments. In P. Baltes & K. W. Schaie (eds.), *Life-span developmental psychology: Personality and socialization*. New York: Academic Press.

Henderson, S. (1974). Care-eliciting behavior in man. *Journal of Nervous and Mental Disease* 159, 172–181.

Hesse, P., & Cicchetti, D. (1982). Toward an integrative theory of emotional development. *New Directions for Child Development* 16, 3–48.

Hinde, R. A. (1976) On describing relationships. *Journal of Child Psychology and Psychiatry* 17, 1–19.

Hinde, R. A. (1979). *Towards understanding relationships*. London: Academic Press.

Hinde, R. A. (1982). Attachment: Some conceptual and biological issues. In C. Parkes & J. Stevenson-Hinde (eds.), *The place of attachment in human behavior* (pp. 60–76). New York: Basic Books.

Hinde, R. A., & Stevenson-Hinde, J. (1987). Interpersonal relationships and child development. *Developmental Review* 7, 1–21.

Hunter, R. S., & Kilstrom, N. (1979). Breaking the cycle in abusive families. *American Journal of Psychiatry* 136, 1320–1322.

Kagan, J. (1981). *The second year: The emergence of self-awareness*. Cambridge, Mass.: Harvard University Press.

Kagan, J. (1982). *Psychological research on the human infant: An evaluative summary*. New York: W. T. Grant Foundation.

Kagan, J., & Lamb, S. (eds.), (1988). *Emergence of morality in young children*. Chicago: University of Chicago Press.

Kaplan, B. (1966). The study of language in psychiatry: The comparative developmental approach and its application to symbolization and language in psychopathology. In S. Arieti (ed.), *American handbook of psychiatry*. New York: Basic Books.

Kaplan, N. (1984). Internal representations of separation experiences in six year olds: Related to actual experiences of separation. Unpublished master's thesis, University of California, Berkeley.

Kegan, R. (1982). *The evolving self*. Cambridge, Mass.: Harvard University Press.

Klagsbrun, M., & Bowlby, J. (1976). Responses to separation from parents: A clinical test for young children. British Journal of Projective Psychology 21, 7–21.

Kobak, R., & Sceery, A. (1988). Attachment in later adolescence: Working models, affect regulation, and perceptions of self and others. *Child Development* 59, 135–146.

Kotler, T., & Omodei, M. (1988). Attachment and emotional health: A life span approach. *Human Relations* 41, 619–640.

Kovacs, M.; Feinberg, T.; Crouse-Novak, M.; Paulauskas, S.; & Finkelstein, R. (1984). Depressive disorders in childhood: A longitudinal prospective study of characteristics and recovery. *Archives of General Psychiatry* 41, 229–237.

Kraepelin, E. ([1921] 1987). *Manic depressive insanity and paranoia*. Salem, N.H.: Ayer Company Publishers.

Lamb, M. E. (1981). The development of father-infant relationships. In M. E. Lamb (ed.), *The role of the father in child development* (rev. ed.). New York: Wiley.

Lamb, M. E. (1987). Predictive implications of individual differences in attachment. *Journal of Consulting and Clinical Psychology* 55, 817–824.

Lempers, J.; Flavell, E.; & Flavell, J. H. (1977). The development in very young children of tacit knowledge concerning visual perception. *Genetic Psychology Monographs* 95, 3–53.

Lewis, M., & Brooks-Gunn, J. (1979). *Social cognition and the acquisition of self*. New York: Plenum.

Lewis, M.; Feiring, C.; McGuffog, C.; & Jaskir, J. (1984). Predicting psychopathology in six-year-olds from early social relations. *Child Development* 55, 123–136.

Lieberman, A. F. (1977). Preschoolers' competence with a peer: Influence of attachment and social experience. *Child Development* 48, 1277–1287.

Lyons-Ruth, K.; Connell, D.; Zoll, D.; & Stahl, J. (1987). Infants at social risk: Relationships among infant maltreatment, maternal behavior, and infant attachment behavior. *Developmental Psychology* 23(2), 223–232.

Maccoby, E. E., & Feldman, S. S. (1972). *Mother-attachment and stranger-reactions in the third year of life. Monographs of the Society for Research in Child Development* 37(1, Serial No. 146), 1–85.

Maccoby, E. E., & Masters, J. C. (1970). Attachment and dependency. In P. H. Mussen (ed.), *Carmichael's manual of child psychology* (3d ed., vol. 2, pp. 73–157). New York: Wiley.

MacFarlane, J.; Allen, L.; & Honzik, M. (1954). *A developmental study of the behavior problems of normal children between 21 months and 14 years.* Berkeley: University of California Press.

Mahler, M.; Pine, F.; & Bergman, A. (1975). *The psychological birth of the human infant.* New York: Basic.

Main, M., & Cassidy, J. (1985). Assessments of child-parent attachment at six years of age. Unpublished scoring manual.

Main, M., & Goldwyn, R. (1984). Predicting rejection of her infant from mother's representation of her own experiences: A preliminary report. *International Journal of Child Abuse and Neglect* 8, 203–217.

Main, M.; Kaplan, N.; & Cassidy, J. (1985). Security in infancy, childhood and adulthood: A move to the level of representation. In I. Bretherton & E. Waters (eds.), *Growing points of attachment theory and research. Monographs of the Society for Research in Child Development* 50 (1–2, Serial No. 209), 66–104.

Main, M., & Solomon, J. (1986). Discovery of an insecure disorganized/disoriented attachment pattern: Procedures, findings and implications for the classification of behavior. In M. Yogman & T. B. Brazelton (eds.), *Affective development in infancy.* Norwood, N.J.: Ablex.

Mandler, J. H. (1983). Representation. In J. H. Flavell & E. M. Markman (eds.), P. H. Mussen (series ed.), *Handbook of child psychology: Vol. 3. Cognitive development* (pp. 420–494). New York: Wiley.

Marvin, R. S. (1972). Attachment and cooperative behavior in two-, three-, and four-year-olds. Unpublished doctoral dissertation, University of Chicago.

Marvin, R. S. (1977). An ethological-cognitive model for the attenuation of mother-child attachment behavior. In T. M. Alloway, L. Krames, & P. Piner (eds.), *Advances in the study of communication and affect: Vol. 3. The development of social attachments* (pp. 25–60). New York: Plenum.

Marvin, R. S., & Greenberg, M. T. (1982). Preschooler's changing conception of their mothers: A social-cognitive study of mother-child attachment. In D. Forbes & M. T. Greenberg (eds.), *Children's planning strategies, No. 18: New directions in child development.* San Francisco: Josey-Bass.

Matas, L.; Arend, R. A.; & Sroufe, L. A. (1978). Continuity of adaptation in the second year: The relationship between quality of attachment and later competence. *Child Development* 49, 547–556.

Minuchin, P. (1985). Families and individual development: Provocations from the field of family therapy. *Child Development* 56, 289–302.

Miyake, K.; Chen, S-j; & Campos, J. J. (1985). Infant temperament, mother's mode of interaction, and attachment in Japan: An interim report. In I. Bretherton & E. Waters (eds.), *Growing points of attachment theory and research. Monographs of the Society for Research in Child Development* 50(1–2, Serial No. 209), 276–297.

Morris, M. G., & Gould, R. W. (1963). Role reversal: A necessary concept in dealing with the battered child syndrome. *American Journal of Orthopsychiatry* 33, 298–299.

Pepper, S. (1942). *World hypotheses.* Berkeley: University of California Press.

Provence, S., & Naylor, A. (1983). *Working with disadvantaged parents and their children.* New Haven, Conn.: Yale University Press.

Radke-Yarrow, M.; Cummings, E. M.; Kuczynski, L.; & Chapman, M. (1985). Patterns of attachment in two- and three-year-olds in normal families and families with parental depression. *Child Development* 56, 884–893.

Rheingold, H. L., & Eckerman, C. O. (1970). The infant separates himself from his mother. *Science* 168, 78–83.

Richters, J. E., & Waters, E. (in press). Attachment and socialization: The positive side of social influence. In M. Lewis & S. Feinman (eds.), *Social influences and behavior.* New York: Plenum.

Ricks, M. H. (1985) The social transmission of parental behavior: Attachment across generations. In I. Bretherton & E. Waters (eds.), *Growing points of attachment theory and research. Monographs of the Society for Research in Child Development* 50 (1–2, Serial No. 209), 211–227.

Rosenberg, M. S. (1987). New directions for research on the psychological maltreatment of children. *American Psychologist* 42, 166–171.

Ruppenthal, G. C.; Arling, G. L.; Harlow, H. F.; Sackett, G. P.; & Suomi, S. J. (1976). A 10-year perspective of motherless mother monkey behavior. *Journal of Abnormal Psychology* 85, 341–349.

Rutter, M. (1979). Maternal deprivation, 1972–1978: New findings, new concepts, new approaches. *Child Development* 50, 283–305.

Rutter, M. (1986). Child psychiatry: The interface between clinical and developmental research. *Psychological Medicine* 16, 151–169.

Rutter, M. (1989). Intergenerational continuities and discontinuities in serious parenting difficulties. In D. Cicchetti & V. Carlson (eds.), *Child maltreatment: Theory and research on the causes and consequences of child abuse and neglect.* New York: Cambridge University Press.

Rutter, M., & Garmezy, N. (1983). Developmental psychopathology. In P. Mussen (ed.), *Handbook of child psychology* (vol. 4, pp. 775–911). New York: Wiley.

Rutter, M.; Quinton, D.; & Liddle, C. (1983). Parenting in two generations: Looking backwards and looking forwards. In N. Madge (ed.), *Families at risk* (pp. 60–98). London: Heinemann.

Saarni, C. (1978). Cognitive and communicative features of emotional experience, or Do you show what you think you feel? In M. Lewis & L. A. Rosenblum (eds.), *The development of affect.* New York: Plenum.

Saarni, C. (1979). Children's understanding of display rules for expressive behavior. *Developmental Psychology* 15, 424–429.

Sagi, A.; Lamb, M. E.; Lewkowicz, K. S.; Shoham, R.; Dvir, R.; & Estes, D. (1985). Security of infant-mother, -father, and -metapelet attachments among kibbutz-reared Israeli children. In I. Bretherton & E. Waters (eds.), *Growing points of attachment theory and research. Monographs of the Society for Research in Child Development* 50 (1–2, Serial No. 209), 257–275.

Sameroff, A. J., & Chandler, M. J. (1975). Reproductive risk and the continuum of caretaking casualty. In F. D. Horowitz (ed.), *Review of child development research* (vol. 4, pp. 187–244). Chicago: University of Chicago Press.

Schneider-Rosen, K.; Braunwald, K. G.; Carlson, V.; & Cicchetti, D. (1985). Current perspectives in attachment theory: Illustration from the study of maltreated infants. In I. Bretherton & E. Waters (eds.), *Growing points in attachment theory and research. Monographs of the Society for Research in Child Development,* 50 (1–2, Serial No. 209), 194–210.

Schneider-Rosen, K., & Cicchetti, D. (1984). The relationship between affect and cognition in maltreated infants: Quality of attachment and the development of visual self-recognition. *Child Development* 55, 648–658.

Selman, R. (1980). *The growth of interpersonal understanding.* New York: Academic Press.

Selman, R., & Demorest, A. (1986). Putting thoughts and feelings into perspective: A developmental view on how children deal with interpersonal disequilibrium. In D. Bearison & H. Zimiles (eds.), *Thoughts and emotion* (pp. 93–128). Hillsdale, N.J.: Erlbaum.

Serafica, F. C. (1978). The development of attachment behaviors: An organismic-developmental perspective. *Human Development* 21, 119–140.

Shatz, M., & Gelman, R. (1973). *The development of communication skills: Modifications in the speech of young children as a function of the listener. Monographs of the Society for Research in Child Development* 38(5, Serial No. 152).

Skolnick, A. (1986). Early attachment and personal relationships across the life course. In P. Baltes, D. Featherman, & R. Lerner (eds.), *Lifespan development and behavior* (vol. 7). Hillsdale, N.J.: Erlbaum Associates.

Slough, N. (1988). Assessment of attachment in five-year-olds: Relationships among separation, the internal representation, and mother-child functioning. Unpublished doctoral dissertation, University of Washington.

Slough, N. S., & Greenberg, M. T. (1986). Unpublished manual, University of Washington. Available from the authors.

Slough, N. S., & Greenberg, M. T. (in press). Attachment and mental representations of self and other in five-year-olds. In I. Bretherton & M. Watson (eds.), *New directions in child development*. San Francisco: Jossey-Bass.

Spieker, S. J., & Booth, C. L. (1988). Maternal antecedents of attachment quality. In J. Belsky & T. Nezworski (eds.), *Clinical implications of attachment* (pp. 95–135). Hillsdale, N.J.: Erlbaum.

Sroufe, L. A. (1979a). Socioemotional development. In J. Osofsky (ed.), *Handbook of infant development* (pp. 462–516). New York: Wiley.

Sroufe, L. A. (1979b). The coherence of individual development. *American Psychologist* 34, 834–841.

Sroufe, L. A. (1983). Infant-caregiver attachment and patterns of adaptation in preschool: The roots of maladaptation and competence. In M. Perlmutter (ed.), *Minnesota Symposium in Child Psychology* (vol. 16, pp. 41–81). Hillsdale, N.J.: Erlbaum.

Sroufe, L. A. (1985). Attachment classification from the perspective of infant-caregiver relationships and infant temperament. *Child Development* 56, 1–14.

Sroufe, L. A. (1986). Bowlby's contribution to psychoanalytic theory and developmental psychopathology. *Journal of Child Psychology and Psychiatry* 27, 841–849.

Sroufe, L. A. (1988). The role of infant-caregiver attachment in development. In J. Belsky & T. Nezworski (eds.), *Clinical implications of attachment* (pp. 18–38). Hillsdale, N.J.: Erlbaum.

Sroufe, L. A., & Fleeson, J. (1986). Attachment and the construction of relationships. In W. Hartup & Z. Rubin (eds.), *Relationships and development*. Hillsdale, N.J.: Erlbaum.

Sroufe, L. A., & Fleeson, J. (1988). The coherence of family relationships. In R. Hinde & J. Stevenson-Hinde (eds.), *Relationships within families: Mutual families* (pp. 27–47). Cambridge: Oxford University Press.

Sroufe, L. A.,; Jacobvitz, D.; Mangelsdorf, S.; DeAngelo, E.; & Ward, M. J. (1985). Generational boundary dissolution between mothers and their preschool children: A relationship systems approach. *Child Development* 56, 317–325.

Sroufe, L. A., & Rutter, M. (1984). The domain of developmental psychopathology. *Child Development* 55, 1184–1199.

Sroufe, L. A., & Waters, E. (1976). The ontogenesis of smiling and laughter: A perspective on the organization of development in infancy. *Psychological Review* 83, 173–189.

Sroufe, L. A., & Waters, E. (1977). Attachment as an organizational construct. *Child Development* 48, 1184–1199.

Stern, D. N. (1985). *The interpersonal world of the infant*. New York: Basic Books.

Stevens, S. S. (1951). *Handbook of experimental psychology*. New York: Wiley.

Stewart, R., & Marvin, R. S. (1984). Sibling relations: The role of conceptual perspective-taking in the ontogeny of sibling caregiving. *Child Development* 55, 1322–1332.

Thompson, R. A.; Cicchetti, D.; Lamb, M. E.; & Malkin, C. M. (1985). The emotional responses of Down syndrome and normal infants in the strange situation; The organization of affective behavior in infants. *Developmental Psychology* 21, 828–841.

Trad, P. V. (1986). *Infant depression: Paradigms and paradoxes*. New York: Springer-Verlag.

Trivers, R. L. (1974). Parent-offspring conflict. *American Zoologist* 14, 249–264.

Tronick, E. Z., & Field, T. (eds.), (1986). *Maternal depression and infant disturbance*. San Francisco: Jossey-Bass.

Vaughn, B.; Egeland, B.; Sroufe, L. A.; & Waters, E. (1979). Individual differences in infant-mother attachment at 12 and 18 months: Stability and change in families under stress. *Child Development* 50, 971–975.

Vaughn, C., & Leff, J. (1976). The influence of family and social factors on the course of psychiatric illness: A comparison of schizophrenic and depressed neurotic patients. *British Journal of Psychiatry* 129, 125–137.

Waddington, C. H. (1957). *The strategy of genes*. London: Allen & Unwin.

Waters, E., & Deane, K. E. (1985). Defining and assessing individual differences in attachment relationships: Q-methodology and the organization of behavior in infancy and early childhood. In I. Bretherton & E. Waters (eds.), *Growing points of attachment theory and re-*

search. *Monographs of the Society for Research in Child Development* 50(1–2, Serial No. 209), 41–65.

Watson, M. (in press). Development of self as reflected in children's role playing. In D. Cicchetti & M. Beeghly (eds.), *The self in transition: Infancy to childhood*. Chicago: University of Chicago Press.

Watson, M., & Fischer K. (1980). Development of social roles in elicited and spontaneous behavior during the preschool years. *Developmental Psychology* 16, 483–494.

Weiss, P. (1969). *Principles of development*. New York: Hafner.

Weiss, R. S. (1982). Attachment in adult life. In C. M. Parkes & J. Stevenson-Hinde (eds.), *The place of attachment in human behavior*. London: Tavistock.

Werner, H. (1948). *Comparative psychology of mental development*. New York: International Universities Press.

Werner, H., & Kaplan, B. (1963). *Symbol formation: An organismic-developmental approach to language and the expression of thought*. New York: Wiley.

Winnicott, D. (1965). *The family and individual development*. London: Tavistock.

Zigler, E., & Glick, M. (1986). *A development approach to adult psychopathology*. New York: Wiley.

2 · A Family Systems Framework for the Study of Attachment

Robert S. Marvin and Robert B. Stewart

Consider the following situation. A young mother brought her 3-year-old son to see a clinical psychologist who specializes in attachment. Mother stated that for the past two months her son has become extremely distressed whenever they are not in close physical proximity with one another. He refuses to play outside, follows her from room to room, insists on sleeping in his parents' bed (and then only when they have gone to bed), and is very easily frightened. Things have actually gotten to the point where mother must allow her son to accompany her when she uses the bathroom. If she does not he becomes extremely upset.

On questioning, mother informed the psychologist that two months ago the boy was riding with his father in the family truck when they were sideswiped by another vehicle, forced off the road, and overturned. While no one was injured, both were shaken and scared. In a subsequent session including both parents and the child, it became clear that all three family members had been frightened by the incident. Under these circumstances, it is appropriate that intensive caregiving-attachment interactions very easily be activated for a short period of time. In this case, the continued maintenance of these interactions over such a prolonged period was clearly attributable at least in part to the parents' own fear, to their continuing alarm over their son's intense attachment behavior, and to their own increased levels of caregiving behavior. During this two-month period both parents had remained exclusively focused on their child: they had spent no time together as spouses and no time apart with their own friends and other activities. Both felt these losses and resented them, felt guilty for being resentful while their son was suffering so, and responded by focusing even more caregiving attention on him. This, of course, had the effect of further escalating his attachment behavior and continuing the cycle.

We would like to thank John Bowlby and Sue Molumphy for their helpful comments on an early draft of this chapter. Reprints can be obtained from Robert S. Marvin, Department of Pediatric Psychology, Children's Rehabilitation Center, 2270 Ivy Road, Charlottesville, Virginia 22901.

The intervention consisted of educating these young parents about the appropriateness of a temporary increase in their son's attachment behavior and obtaining an agreement from the parents that they would go out on a "date" twice each week for the next month. While their son initially objected, by the second "date" he accepted the situation, and on one-month follow-up the problem had completely resolved.

The presenting problem was clearly an attachment problem. It is also clear that the existing framework for studying attachment-caregiving interactions does not easily encompass either the problem or the intervention. Contemporary analyses of attachment interactions are based on dyads and do not yet include larger units consisting of simultaneous relations among multiple family members, friends, teachers, etc. Yet the continuing attachment problem experienced by this family stemmed as much from the change in the spouse relationship as it did from any change in the child or in the mother-child relationship. And as family therapists experience regularly, the solution to the "child's problem" consisted of a change in the spouse relationship.

This and other examples, such as the birth of a younger sibling, entrance into day care or school, involvement of grandparents and other extended family members, and the expansion of the range of attachment figures which is so typical of children during the preschool years, all point to the need to think of attachments within a larger context. At this point in the development of this field of research there is a pressing need for a conceptual framework which will allow us to expand our scope beyond the parent-child dyad but will do so in a manner not contradictory to that narrower scope.

INTRODUCTION

IN DEVELOPING his theory of infant-mother attachment, Bowlby ([1969] 1982) utilized advances in modern biological thought which focus on the constructs of information and organization and view living organisms as being open rather than closed systems. Bowlby's later work (e.g., 1973, 1980), and much of the research on attachment which has followed his work, has directly or indirectly been influenced by these themes from "general systems theory," or by logical derivatives of that theory, for example, communication theory, cybernetics, control systems theory, etc. The usefulness of this set of theories for the field of child develoipment more generally is suggested in the recent work of Sameroff (1983) and P. Minuchin (1985).

The purpose of this chapter is to summarize briefly some of the important constructs of general systems theory, to review some of the existing applications of systems thinking to attachment theory and research, and to suggest a general systems framework for expanding the scope of attachment theory and research to the family systems level. We agree with Minuchin (1985) that, of all areas of current research in developmental psychology, the area of attachment behavior is most consistent with a systems framework. In fact, we feel that much of the existing research in attachment has been consistent with a general systems model as applied to families and that some of it has made substantive contributions to such a model. At the same time, many recent attempts to expand attachment research to include family members other than baby and a single caregiver have suffered precisely because they failed to comprehend—or at least to account for—the systemic nature of development within a complex family organization. In this chapter we will present the outlines of a framework which is both consistent with the work of Bowlby and Ainsworth and explicitly accounts for this complex systemic organization.

General Systems Theory

The formal origin of general systems theory is generally attributed to L. von Bertalanffy (e.g., 1968) who, in the 1930s, described an interdisciplinary set of principles and models that apply to systems in general, irrespective of the particular kind of elements and forces involved. He viewed most scientific disciplines of his time as trying to isolate phenomena into simpler units of analysis with the assumption that this *analysis* was the sole and proper approach to understanding. L. von Bertalanffy argued that to understand scientifically any phenomenon, one needs to understand not only the elements of that phenomenon in isolation from one another but, more important, their *interrelations*. This basic change in perspective has evolved into a more contemporary general systems framework, a broad set of approaches to complex phenomena based on the metaphor of the purposive, self-regulating system which naturally grows in complexity (negative entropy). It is, in Berrien's (1968, p. 13) terms, "neither a formula nor a doctrine, but a cluster of strategies of inquiry; not a theory but an organized space within which many theories may be developed and related." In this chapter we will use a general systems framework to argue that attachment theory and family systems theory can be thus related to the advantage of both.

Recent research in family relationships, in attachment and in developmental psychology generally, has begun to reflect some of the basic logic and concerns of systems theory. For example, Belsky (1984) examined the reciprocal effects between the marital relationship and the child's development; Sroufe and his coworkers (Sroufe, Jacobvitz, Mangelsdorf, DeAngelo, & Ward 1985) have begun to study the systemic relationship between the mother's relationship with her son and that with her daughter; and Sameroff (1983) has made significant progress in conceptualizing the manner in which multiple environmental factors regulate the child's development and keep it within certain limits in what approximates a self-regulatory process. Certainly the best example of a general systems theory within developmental psychology is

Bowlby's theory of attachment (Bowlby [1969] 1982, 1973, 1980). It is significant and (we will argue) problematic that to date the development of Bowlby's theory has been restricted to the individual and dyadic levels rather than being expanded to the level of the family.

Perhaps the most highly developed systemic theory of *families* is Salvatore Minuchin's (1974) structuralist theory of families and family therapy. We are convinced that this very powerful theory, and Bowlby's, are essentially consistent with one another and that both can be integrated within a general systems framework. In working toward this integration, our primary focus will be on expanding attachment theory to the level of the family system. We will draw extensively from Minuchin's theory in doing so, and especially from a recent paper by Patricia Minuchin (1985), in which she outlines a number of basic principles of structural family theory and their relationships to developmental psychology. The list of general systems principles discussed below are equally applicable at an individual, dyadic, or family level and should be recognizable to those familiar with Bowlby's first volume (Bowlby [1969] 1982). It should be pointed out that this set of principles itself constitutes an interrelated system within which each principle contains elements of, or implies, each of the others.

Wholeness and Order

This first systems property refers to the notion that the whole is more than the sum of its parts by noting that a whole adds the property of relationships among the parts. The concept of wholeness escapes its metaphysical connotations in a general systems framework by directing attention to issues such as hierarchic structure, stability, differentiation, steady state, and goal-directedness—all terms that are consistent with attachment theory.

The essential thrust of this principle is that no individual can be understood outside the context in which he or she is functioning. Rather than attempting to understand the individual by relying solely on analysis, that is, understanding that individual's component parts, the systems researcher will attempt to describe and understand patterns in the larger organizations that constitute both the individual and/or the system of which that individual is a part. While studying these patterns, the systems researcher can either describe the structure of the individual himself, or can treat the individual as a "black box" without violating conceptual or methodological rules.

An excellent example of the application of this principle at an individual level is the work of Ainsworth and her associates (e.g., Bretherton and Ainsworth 1974; Ainsworth, Blehar, Waters, & Wall 1978) on the interplay among the three behavioral systems of attachment, fear/wariness, and exploration. This interplay yields a complex behavioral pattern—use of the attachment figure as a secure base for exploration—certainly a pattern that is more than the sum of its parts and one that would not have been discovered if Ainsworth had maintained a strictly analytic approach in her research.

At the family systems level of analysis, this principle of wholeness and order suggests that to understand the relationship between infant and mother one must also have sufficient information concerning the infant-father and mother-father relationships. An even more thorough understanding would be obtained by having further information concerning (1) the relationships among all members—the structure of the family as a whole, and (2) the functional outcomes of members' interactions crucial in establishing and maintaining the integrity and coherence of the family. As an illustration of how the marital relationship may affect the ontogeny of the infant-mother relationship, recall that Pedersen, Yarrow, Anderson, and Cain (1978) found that tension and conflict between husband and wife were strongly and negatively associated with maternal feeding competence, while the husband's esteem for his wife as a mother was positively related to feeding skill.

Circular Causal Relationships

The notion of causality has probably done more to hamper progress within the field of developmental psychology than any other single concept. Historically, psychologists have searched for a single cause for a single effect, or at best for multiple causes for that effect. The belief that cause-effect relationships are linear, that is, that they "go" in one direction, has interfered with many aspects of the field. In the search for these simple causal relationships, the field has largely abandoned its descriptive phase and has ignored the fact that "effects" often feed back and become their own "cause." As a result, generations of parents have been given advice that simply does not reflect accurately the complexity of the developing child and the family of which he or she is a part.

Within a general systems framework, on the other hand, "causal" relationships are viewed as complex, often circular feedback loops where it is largely arbitrary at which point the observer begins his causal analysis. Within this framework, a causal analysis amounts to a careful, temporal *description* of the (interactive) pattern under consideration and of the contributions made by each element (e.g., person) within the pattern. Certainly some elements may have more "power," or degrees of freedom, within the pattern than others, but it is difficult to imagine the output of one element constituting the "cause" of the structure or functioning of the other.

Brazelton's (e.g., Brazelton, Koslowski, & Main 1974), Stern's (1974), and Tronick, Als, and Adamson's (1979) work on the reciprocal control of early infant-mother face-to-face interaction are good examples of systemic causal analysis. These studies have culminated in detailed temporal descriptions of the steps involved in this complex, circular interaction and of the contributions to the pattern made by each participant. As to what "caused" this complex pattern—it only makes sense to ascribe the cause to the pattern itself. Almost any other attempt to formulate a causal statement will find itself returning to a temporal description of the pattern.[1]

Throughout this chapter we will argue that a complete understanding of a youngster's attachments (even the dyadic attachment of child to mother) will require this description-based circular causal analysis. Even more important, the causal loops involved will include not only that consisting of the interaction between child and mother but also that between mother and father, and child and father (and other siblings, grandparents, etc., if present). Family therapists have long known that a specific pattern of interaction between mother and child is often "caused" as much by a pattern of interaction between mother and father as by one between mother and child. This will certainly be the case with attachment interactions as well as interactions of other types.

Maintenance of Invariant Relationships

This proposition states that in order to survive there must be order, or constraint, within a system and within its coupling with the environment. In a complex system, it is not necessary that all relationships with the environment be invariant but rather that in certain essential respects—which ones depending on the particular system-environment coupling—variety in that coupling must be maintained within certain limits (Ashby 1952, 1956). This becomes particularly important in the case of complex open systems such as the child, the child-caregiver dyad, or the family, where information received by the system alters its state or organization. If the change resulting from this information extends beyond some necessary invariant limit, the organization of the system will be disturbed or destroyed. Bowlby ([1969] 1982) employs this principle when he speaks of the "predictable outcome" (invariant) of infant-mother proximity as functioning to protect the infant from danger. Family theorists employ the same principle in describing how both normal and mal-adapted families must maintain certain variables within set limits or face disturbance or destruction, and that children are often "chosen by the family" to play a major role in this process.

Ashby develops this concept further with his Law of Requisite Variety (Ashby 1956). The law states that only variety can destroy (or control) variety: if two systems are coupled, for example, child and environment, and if certain variables must be maintained within certain limits, then only the system with the greater variety, that is, greater degrees of freedom, can reduce, limit, or control the amount of variety in the coupling of the two. For ex-

---

1. However, see Hinde's (1970) discussion of the roles that phylogeny, ontogeny, and biological function play in the causation of behavior.

ample, if the child is subject to dangers (greater variety being found in the environment), and if he is unable to protect himself (less variety in himself than in the environment), then in order to maintain his "essential variables" within certain limits he must be coupled with (attached to) a system of more complexity—in this case the caregiver. This coupling must be maintained until either the child possesses the necessary variety (knowledge and skills) within himself and/or can become coupled to another system which can provide the necessary variety (Marvin 1977).

This child-caregiver coupling itself becomes a unit, or system—a system that, because of the mother's high amount of variety, possess enough degrees of freedom to destroy, control, or counteract most variety emanating from the environment. In our own species (as well as in others) this mother-child system tends to be coupled with others (e.g., spouse, other children, extended family) to form a yet larger system with even more variety, thus substantially increasing the entire family system's chances of survival.

Adaptive Self-Regulation

This fourth property refers to a cybernetic stability that self-regulates a system to compensate for changing conditions in the environment by making coordinated changes in the system's internal values (Sameroff 1983). This proposition formally presents the logic by which the system maintains those essential variables discussed above. The basic unit of such self-regulation is the negative feedback loop, through which the organism acts to reduce the effects of deviation from a standard (which may or may not be represented internally).

Attachment researchers are already familiar with this principle in a number of contexts, the most obvious being that of "goal-corrected proximity seeking." The young child compensates for changes in the environment (e.g., mother leaving the room) by activating a self-corrective behavior system, and terminates that system when feedback from his or her activity indicates no deviation from an internal standard (e.g., contact with mother). At a dyadic level, a slightly more complex example occurs when both mother *and* child alter their internal settings (e.g., from visual to rapidly established physical contact) when both notice some startling change in environmental conditions (e.g., a large dog approaching the child).

As Minuchin (1985) states, when this principle is operating at a family level, the self-regulatory mechanisms reside in the *family* rather than in the individual. In most instances these processes are adaptive, as when father feeds the baby in the middle of the night in order to relieve mother. Family therapists, however, are constantly confronted by families in which there is much unresolved conflict between the spouses, and in which the integrity of the family is self-regulated through parental focus on some symptomatic behavior of a child. When a therapeutic change is induced in this family (e.g., parents begin to resolve their conflicts, or the child decreases his symptomatic behavior), it is quite typical that other family members behave in a way that has the "predictable outcome" of returning the family to its former, maladaptive state.

Adaptive Self-Organization

The fifth property refers to a reorganization that alters the parameters within the system when it is subjected to the effect of a new constant in the internal or external environment. That is, a new event acts upon the internal constraints of the system, and the system reorganizes itself, establishing a new homeostatic balance. In a successful self-organizing system, this reorganization takes place in a way that continues to maintain the system's essential variables within limits necessary for its survival. This property differs from adaptive self-regulation in that the latter allows the system to resist temporary disturbances and return to the former steady state without permanent changes being imposed. It should also be noted that while many instances of self-organization refer to developmental or "stage" changes, others are non-developmental (e.g., changes in residence, occupation, financial status, occurrence of a physical disability, etc.).

At an individual level, some of the best-known examples are those of cognitive developmental changes (e.g., Piaget 1970; Flavell 1985). Strong arguments have been made that family systems undergo formally similar, discontinuous developmental changes (e.g., Haley 1986; Carter & McGoldrick, 1980). Although arguably nondevelopmental, the research of Entwisle and Doering (1981) and of Cowan, Cowan, Coie, and Coie (1978) illustrates this principle of self-organization at a family level. Both studies found that families in their samples moved toward traditional role structure and differentiation of household responsibilities soon after the birth of the first child, in spite of previously held egalitarian beliefs and practices. This new division of labor and role structure is established often without regard to whether the mother returns to the work force after a maternity leave. Much the same conclusion can be inferred from studies of families with physically handicapped children (e.g., Kazak & Marvin 1984).

Subsystems and Boundaries

This principle states that any system is itself composed of subsystems and that any system constitutes a subsystem for a yet larger or more inclusive system. Formally, subsystems within a system are distinguished from each other by differences in the rules by which they are governed and self-regulated. The differences in the rules therefore constitute the boundaries separating the subsystems. Communication or interaction across these boundaries are also governed by rules which maintain their integrity. In many biological systems, these boundaries are not always firm, and one member of a system can belong to different subsystems either coincidentally or at different times. However, membership in different subsystems still implies different sets of operational rules for membership in each subsystem.

The subsystems typically attributed to families are the spouse subsystem, the parenting subsystem (which may or may not be occupied by the same members as the spouse subsystem), the parent-child subsystem, the sibling subsystem, and other subsystems composed of specific alliances within the family, grandparental relations, etc. Each of these subsystems is characterized by its own set of operating rules and rules for communication with other subsystems. Individuals are often interchangeable from one subsystem to another, for example, father is also husband, member of a friendly alliance of "boys against girls," etc. This flexibility of subsystem membership is usually adaptive, but it can become maladaptive when individuals are forced into two conflicting/contradictory subsystems simultaneously, when they occupy a developmentally inappropriate subsystem for too long, or when an appropriate member is excluded while an inappropriate member is included. Thus, an older girl, for example, can be a member of a parenting subsystem only as long as she is given the power as well as the responsibility, and as long as she is also given adequate membership in the sibling subsystem. A young boy can enjoy some intimacy with his mother only as long as father is not excluded from the spouse subsystem and clear boundaries are drawn as to when the boy is excluded from that subsystem. When these boundaries or rules are "violated," one or more individual or familial essential variables are at risk.

The rules that constitute the boundaries around subsystems, and individual membership in these subsystems, are established by recurrent patterns of interaction among all family members. These rules undergo changes when a family member, or the family itself, reaches a new developmental transition, and/or when some significant internal or external event impacts the family, such as divorce or significant economic change. Healthy families will realign boundaries and subsystems membership to reflect these new realities. It is when families are too fearful or resistant to these changes that they become truly maladapted, static, symptomatic, and require therapeutic intervention.

In terms of attachment, some of the more important questions here are the following: What effect does the birth of a first or later-born child have on already existing subsystems within the family? How do attachment interactions vary among different family members occupying positions within the parenting subsystem? What repetitive patterns of interaction within the spouse subsystem contribute to the development and maintenance of a secure versus insecure attachment? And reflecting the specific focus of this volume, how do various family subsystems facilitate or hinder the young child's transition away from the very close mother-infant relationship, and what impact does that transition have on those other subsystems? In a later section of this chapter, we present an outline of a framework for the study of attachment within the family system, based on the six principles discussed above. While we propose partial answers to some of these questions, our primary goal is to encourage attachment researchers to think, and conduct research, within a family systems framework.

SYSTEMS THOUGHT IN ATTACHMENT THEORY

As stated earlier, attachment theory as developed by Bowlby and Ainsworth is thoroughly systemic. However, it has been applied almost exclusively at the individual and dyadic (infant-caregiver) levels. On the other hand, and this is one of the most powerful advantages of a general systems approach, the model they have developed is highly consistent with a family-systems model and in fact can easily be seen as a subset of that model. The purpose of this section of the chapter is to review briefly some of the systems aspects of attachment theory, especially as they relate to increasingly inclusive levels of analysis, and thereby to set the stage for the presentation of a family systems model of attachment.

Bowlby's theory of attachment posits that humans develop a number of behavioral systems, each system consisting of a number of structurally different but functionally equivalent behaviors, that is, they all tend to have the same outcome (Bretherton & Ainsworth 1974; Sroufe & Waters 1977; Greenberg & Marvin 1982). The behavior systems which have been used most often in the study of attachment are the attachment behavior system, the exploratory system, the fear/wariness system, and the caregiving system. Each behavior system is described as being "teleonomic" in that it is assumed to result in a predictable outcome when activated in the environment of evolutionary adaptedness. The predictable outcomes (proximity to a caregiver in the case of the attachment system) function, in Ashby's (1956) terms, to maintain the system's essential variables within those limits that increase the likelihood of continued functioning, or survival. As the infant develops, the attachment behavior system comes to function as a purposive, or "goal-corrected," control system using negative feedback and comparison with an internal image, or goal-setting, to gain or maintain this outcome of proximity and contact.

A major thrust of any systemic approach to attachment is that, however important this individual behavior system level of analysis may be, that system cannot fully be understood within this isolated framework. While each behavior system can be studied in isolation, it must be mapped conceptually into a larger system. This is, of course, formally the same point made by family theorists who insist the individual cannot be understood without reference to the family of which he is one subset. An excellent illustration of this point is the "secure base" phenomenon (Ainsworth 1967, Ainsworth & Bell 1970), a concept that involves not only the attachment behavior system but also the exploratory behavior system and (often) the fear/wary behavior system. This construct refers to the way the young child uses access to the mother as a protective base from which to explore and presumably increase his own level of competency. Were the attachment system to be considered in isolation, it would make sense for evolution to have designed the child to maintain *constant* contact. It is only when we consider the attachment system in conjunction with the other behavior systems that constitute the child as a whole that we can see that this behavior system functions within a larger, suprasystem which is learning more about, and operating with ever-increasing variability on, the surrounding environment.

In the same way that individual behavior systems can only be understood fully when viewed in the context of the child-as-system, both mother and child considered as separate systems can only be understood when viewed in the context of the mother-child-dyad-as-system. While the attachment behavior system has commonly been conceptualized as existing to enhance the survival of the individual child, it may also be seen to serve a particular interpersonal relationship, that is, the attachment-caregiving relationship between the child and mother. The attachment and caregiving behavior systems are complementary to one another, and each individual in the dyad is able to incorporate sensitivity to and (eventually) expectations about the other participant (Hinde, 1982). It is interesting and important to note that in the second edition of volume 1 of the *Attachment* volume, Bowlby ([1969] 1982) acknowledged that this work and the research it had generated had examined primarily only half of the dyadic relationship between infant and mother, and that future research in attachment should be focused on the interplay of the attachment and caregiving behaviors of both parties. In doing so, Bowlby may be seen to suggest that (at least) two levels of systems analysis will be necessary to study attachment adequately, that is, the intraorganism analysis of mutually regulatory behavior systems and the interpersonal analysis of mutually regulatory partners.

An intriguing example of how the infant's attachment behavior cannot be understood fully unless placed in the context of infant-mother-as-dyad is Bowlby's description of how the predictable outcome of proximity is nonpurposive on the infant's part for the first 6–8 months of life, and only thereafter is it purposive. Even at birth, however, the infant's behavior may *appear* purposive, or goal-corrected. The resolution of this seeming-contradiction is the idea that the infant-as-system, and the mother-as-system, are each embedded in the infant-mother-dyad-as-system. Specifically, the infant's attachment behavior is automatically elicited by conditions such as fatigue, hunger, pain, and sudden changes in stimulus conditions. At this point, the mother attributes some distress or discomfort to the baby and increases proximity or contact in order to eliminate the source of the baby's distress. The proximity or contact serves as feedback which terminates the baby's attachment behavior. Thus, the young infant's behavior only *appears* purposeful because it is coupled with that of the mother, and the "predictable" result of the patterns of interaction within this dyad is proximity and contact. In other words, from the perspective of infant-as-system we are presented with a paradox: the infant's attachment behavior is activated and terminated in a way that is both highly predictable and serves an important survival function but is itself not goal-corrected. This paradox is resolved only by analyzing the behavior from the level of infant-mother-as-system. For a more detailed explanation, see Bowlby ([1969] 1982).

The work of John Anderson (1972) takes us a step closer to a family systems analysis by illustrating the operation of a dyadic system in which the behavior of *both* individuals is goal-corrected. Anderson observed the naturally occurring organization of proximity between mothers and child in a park setting. He described how babies, in making forays away from mother, tended to oscillate around a set distance from her. In cases where the infant exceeded the distance without soon returning, the mothers themselves tended to follow or retrieve the infant. Anderson's work illustrates the interplay of two coupled, goal-directed systems, both of which are operating to maintain a shared set-goal for proximity. The operation of any one element of the system (i.e., behavior of either infant or mother) is fully understood only when viewed and described in the context of the dyad. It is generally unimportant *who* acts to decrease the distance when the set-goal is exceeded: it is only important that either one or the other element (or both) of the dyadic system do so. It is the dyadic *system* that is engaged here in self-regulating the distance among its elements.

Any complex human relationship beyond infancy, whether between individuals or among family members, will involve communication about and negotiation of shared goals and plans or, more generally, of shared working models. This is illustrated at a dyadic level by the work of Bowlby ([1969] 1982), Marvin (1977), and Marvin and Greenberg (1982) on the goal-corrected partnership. Bowlby introduced the idea by describing the way in which the young child, as he becomes less egocentric, is able to make increasingly accurate inferences concerning his mother's goals and plans for proximity and contact (e.g., Marvin, Greenberg, & Mossler, 1976). Coincidental with this is an improvement in the child's attempts to alter his mother's goals and plans. Marvin (1977) proposed that, as these two skills develop, at least two important changes will occur in the dyad's organization of attachment behavior. First, it will become important to *both* that they share common goals and plans with respect to proximity and contact. Second, in a dyad where mother and child are able to negotiate a shared plan for separation and reunion, the child should experience decreased levels of distress upon separation. Marvin (1977) and Marvin and Greenberg (1982) have demonstrated in a sample of 3- and 4-year-olds that successful negotiation of shared plans for separation and reunion is in fact associated with less distress during separation episodes of the Strange Situation and with less proximity seeking upon mother's return.

In proposing the existence of the goal-corrected partnership, Bowlby ([1969] 1982, p. 355) commented, "When two individuals are each attempting to alter the goals of the other, it may become logically impossible to dissociate the two goal-complexes. The individuals have then acquired a relationship in which their individualities have partly merged (MacKay, 1964)." Again, it is the mother-child *system* or, perhaps more specifically, the operation of their negotiated and shared working models regulating their behavior rather than either one or both individuals considered separately.

Whenever two goal-corrected systems are coupled, there is bound to be occasional conflict of working models. In the case of the goal-corrected partnership, each member of the dyad attempts to change the others' goals/plans to conform with his or her own through persuasive communication. In most mother-child dyads, conflict is reduced by a strategic combination of accommodation of one person's goals/plans to those of the other, mutual accommodation of goals/plans through compromise, and/or turn-taking, where the dyad alternates which of its members' goals/plans will prevail. In any case, a smoothly functioning dyad—or family—will experience these shared working models much of the time.

In summary, nearly all of the research based upon Bowlby's theory of attachment has been limited to the study of intraorganism behavioral control systems and to the dyadic relationship in which these control systems operate. Bowlby, however, has maintained that the family, with its many attachment-caregiving relationships, is the basic social unit for the study of attachment. It is our contention that a family systems model is necessary for a complete understanding of attachment and that attachment theory, as developed to date, is both suggestive of, and completely consistent with, such a model.

A FAMILY SYSTEMS APPROACH TO ATTACHMENT

In this section we present an outline, based on the six general systems principles discussed earlier, of a family systems model of the study of attachment.

Wholeness and Order

Our initial assumption is that all attachment-caregiving relations exist within a *network* of ordered relationships and cannot fully be understood except in that context. Assuming a nuclear family with one child and no extended family, these relationships include child-mother, child-father, mother-father, and mother-child-father. With the addition of more children, grandparents, etc., the network of relationships becomes that much more complex but nonetheless real. The central role extended family members, and particularly maternal grandmothers, play in attachment-caregiving relations is clear from the work of Minuchin (e.g., Minuchin, Montalvo, Guerney, Rosman, & Schumer 1967) and Bowlby (1973).

The significance of the mother-child relationship for the development of attachment is obvious and well documented since it is the basis for most of the research on attachment (e.g., Ainsworth et al. 1978). The importance of the father-child relationship has also received some attention. It is apparent that fathers *do* serve as caregivers, that babies do use their fathers as attachment figures, albeit often as subordinate figures, and that the quality of the baby-mother attachment may or may not differ from that of the baby-father attachment (Lamb, Hwang, Frodi, & Frodi 1982; Main & Weston 1981). While some systems therapists and researchers have insisted that the husband-wife and father-mother subsystems are crucially important to the developing child (S. Minuchin 1974; Belsky 1985; P. Minuchin 1985), there has been very little research on these less direct relationships by researchers on attachment. However, there is already some inferential and direct evidence that the spouse and parental subsystems have important implications for the development of attachment. For example, there is evidence that the satisfaction experienced by the marital partners, and the father's support and approval of mother's caregiving behavior, are associated with a smoother relationship between mother and baby (e.g., Crnic, Greenberg, & Slough 1986). Hart (1985) found that marital satisfaction and fatherly support of the mother's caregiving was directly associated with a secure infant-mother attachment as measured in the Strange Situation. Overall, these studies, combined with others such as Pedersen, Zaslow, Cain, and Anderson (1980), and Weinraub and Wolf (1983), suggest that it is the expressive elements in the husband's relationship with the wife that contribute strongly to her morale and sense of competence as a mother and, by inference, to the security of the baby's attachment to the mother.

In addition to studies similar to those mentioned above, what is needed for a family systems approach to attachment are studies describing attachment-related patterns of interaction among *all* family members, not just separate studies of interactions between child-mother, child-father, and mother-father. An infant or child's attachment behavior is as frequently activated and terminated in the presence of many or all family members, and the attachment-caregiving interactions often affect other subsystems within the family as much as they do the infant-caregiver subsystem. In most homes at least part of the time, the child's attachment behavior will elicit changes in the behavior of many family members. This can take the form of more than one person responding directly to the child (in similar or different ways), mother responding to the attachment behavior of the infant while father "substitutes" for mother in caring for an older child, and other variations of the division of caregiving behavior. These changes can also take the form of interrupting an ongoing interaction within the spouse subsystem, which can often have significant effects and require accommodation on the part of that subsystem. As Dunn and Kendrick (1980), Stewart, Mobley, Van Tuyl, and Salvador (1987), and common experience indicate, the activation of attachment behavior on the part of the infant will often interrupt an interaction between mother and an older sibling, with significant consequences for the mother–older child relationship and the sibling subsystem. How a family adjusts to these situations is a topic of concern in family therapy and should be a concern as well in research on attachment.

The systemic concept of wholeness and order implies the existence of certain patterns of interaction and expectation which serve definable outcomes and maintain the coherence of the family as a system. Family sociologists have focused on outcomes such as provision of food, shelter, and other broadly economic and educational necessities. Attachment theorists (e.g., Heard 1978), on the other hand, have focused on patterns that organize physical proximity and contact among all family members in a way that increases the likelihood of protecting family members from danger. At a purely behavioral level, the shift from applying this concept to the infant-mother relationship to applying it to the family is a relatively obvious shift.

One of the primary means through which family coherence is maintained is that of shared expectations and plans, or "working models" (Bowlby [1969] 1982, 1973) of how the family organizes physical proximity and contact. Families certainly vary in the degree to which they engage in close physical contact, in the conditions that tend to activate and terminate members' attachment and caregiving behavior, and in the impact attachment-caregiving interactions have on other subsystems within the family. Each family member (beyond a certain developmental point) has a working model of his own and other member's contributions to the patterns. Each member's contribution will not be identical: what *will* be shared is a complex working model representing the various attachment-caregiving relations within the family. The use of these shared working models probably accounts for much of the smooth patterning of attachment interactions within the family, in that each individual can anticipate the outcomes of his and others' behavior and select his plans accordingly. This is, of course, equivalent to Bowlby's notion of the "goal-corrected partnership" applied to the level of family-as-system.

At least two important research implications derive from the assumption that shared working models play an important role in family attachments. First, as Bowlby ([1969] 1982) and Marvin (1972) argue with respect to the child-mother partnership, there will be frequent conflict within the family regarding how proximity and contact will be organized at any particular time. The conditions under which this conflict occurs, the means by which it is handled, the degree to which it is resolved, and the effects of the conflicts on other interactions and subsystems within the family will all constitute important research questions.

Second, in studying attachment in children older than the early preschool years, and in families generally, the question arises whether this study should be restricted to those interactions involving concrete, literal physical proximity and contact. As children develop through the preschool years they "imitate," "internalize," or "identify with" their attachment figures' working models for relationships. In systemic information-processing terms, they map internally some model of their relationships with significant others, and of their understanding of observed relationships among dyads not including themselves. For an infant, sharing mother's physical proximity is crucially important: for a school-aged child, sharing her goals, plans, values, and working models for relationships may be equally important. Older children share and resolve intimate emotional conflicts with their attachment figures and use shared emotional states as a "secure base" from which to explore their own emotions and working models. Other family members also use each other in this fashion, and interactions of this type are certainly a major aspect of intimate affectional bonds within families. The question is, To what extent should they be considered to be within the category of attachment interactions per se? While further discussion of this topic would go beyond the scope of this chapter, we believe they *should* be considered attachment interactions.

Other important research questions related to this systems issue of family wholeness and order are as follows: What are the effects of attachment interactions, and quality (e.g., secure, avoidant, etc.) of attachment, on other subsystems within the family (e.g., see the fascinating study by Sroufe et al. 1985)? What are the differential effects of first- and later-born attachment-caregiving relationships on other family subsystems, including the spouse, parenting, sibling, etc., subsystems? How do family attachment patterns change as individual children proceed through development, for example, develop a "goal-corrected partnership," enter adolescence, and leave home as a young adult? The same questions can be applied to developmental changes in the family as a whole. How do attachment interactions affect, and how are they affected by, the breakdown and impending divorce of the spouse subsystem? And how do attachment interactions affect, and how are they affected by, common "crises" experienced by families?

Systemic Causal Relationships

As one part of a focus on recurrent patterns of interaction, attachment researchers adopting a family systems perspective must make a distinction between the immediate *cause* of behavior, and the *effect* or *function* of behavior.[2] Research on attachment at all ages requires detailed descriptions of how

---

2. Because of the widespread use of the term "*function*" in family therapy literature, a distinction is made here between *function* and *biological function* (see related discussions in Bowlby [1969] 1982 and Hinde 1970). In addition, effect and function are used essentially synonymously, with function connoting some degree of (not necessarily conscious) purpose.

various patterns of attachment behaviors and attachment-caregiving interactions affect further interactions within a family, rather than just focusing on what effects family interactions have on subsequent attachment interactions. Moreover, we need not merely look for single, reciprocal causes and effects but should consider multiple systemic causes and effects of interaction. Once these multiple causes and effects are identified, complex recurrent *patterns* of interaction can be described. For example, one of the most consistent findings from studies of triadic family systems is that the amount of interaction between two individuals (i.e., the mother and infant) consistently diminishes when another person (i.e., the father) enters the interactive context (e.g., Hart 1985). This is often accounted for by the increase in spouse interaction resulting from the father's presence. Interactions between mother and infant become synchronized with spouse interactions. Identifying the various "circular" cause-effect relationships and, more important, the overall *patterns* of interaction among the three participants, enables us more fully to grasp the gestalt of the interaction. Perhaps more important, it allows us to recognize and operationalize the cyclic flow of the *focus* of the interaction: from spouse interaction while mother's secondary attention is on the baby to mother-infant interaction while father either observes or is otherwise momentarily occupied. The change of focus can be "caused" by some specific behavior of any of the three participants, and it is more meaningful to attribute the cause of father's momentary return to some other activity to the overall pattern of interaction than to either the baby's cry, mother turning her attention to the crying baby, or father's desire to free mother from spouse interaction so she can attend to caregiving activities.

The adoption of this orientation provides researchers in attachment with at least three major types of research questions regarding causality: those concerning moment-to-moment interaction, those concerning ontogeny, and those focusing on maladaptive behavior. An example of a systemic causal analysis of the first may be found in a description of the bedtime rituals parents and children adopt (e.g., M. T. Greenberg 1989, unpublished data). Such rituals may be seen as analogous to the negotiations commonly observed at points of separation in the Strange Situation procedure. The set-goal of the child may be to remain up, awake, and in proximity to his attachment figures. Requests for one more story to be read, one more glass of water, or one more trip to the bathroom thus appear to be quite purposeful. On the other hand, the parent putting the child to bed, who in all probability is fatigued, may have as his or her primary goal to get the child to bed with the least amount of conflict. Permitting a number of these small diversions is viewed as an attractive alternative to a direct, prolonged confrontation with the child. One might also consider that the parents may have as their goal (shared or not) to leave the parenting subsystem and return to activities of the spouse subsystem. The result is that each participant in the interaction is equally active in shaping or causing the entire pattern. Questions of cause and effect must therefore be framed at the level of the pattern of interaction rather than at the level of one or more of the individuals involved in the interaction. The ritual is *caused* by all family members involved, and perpetuates itself because all members will gain by the predictability of outcome obtained from the pattern.

An ontogenetic example of systemic causal relationships is the changes in the spouse subsystem associated with the birth of a first child. Cowan et al. (1978) and Entwisle and Doering (1981) have reported that couples move toward a traditional role structure and differentiation of household responsibilities soon after the birth of a child in spite of previously held egalitarian beliefs and practices. Attributing this change to one or more individuals in the system is probably too restrictive and linear a view. Certainly the baby, mother, and father are all involved in the change, as are extended family tradition and the need for specialization. The "cause" of this change is probably best attributed to the intricate patterns of expectation and interaction within the entire family system, patterns that are a solution to a disequilibrating input (birth of a child) adopted not only by "normal" families but even more so by families with a handicapped child (Kazak & Marvin 1984).

A second ontogenetic example of systemic causal relationships within the family involves the "cause" of the young child's expanding interests and horizons beyond the close, mother-child relationship. It would be incomplete to attribute this change to variables such as other developmental changes in the child, mother's interest in other activities, the birth of a younger sibling, or father's insistence on more time with his wife. The "real" cause is not a listing of the factor(s) involved, along with statements stating the relative contributions of each factor. A complete analysis of the cause of this change must be based on a description of the specific patterns of interaction within each family which establish and maintain this move toward a wider subsystem membership.

An example of maladaptive behavior most appropriate to this volume on attachment relationships beyond infancy is that of an overly close, "enmeshed" relationship between mother and preschool or school-aged child. This relationship is usually characterized by abnormally high frequency of, and low threshold for, attachment-caregiving interactions. This problem is often associated with tantrums and behavior problems on the part of the child, school refusal, physically handicapping and other chronic medical conditions, and psychosomatic conditions such as diabetes, asthma, and anorexia nervosa (e.g., Minuchin, Rosman, & Baker 1978).

Traditional developmental psychologists are likely to search for the cause of this problem by examining the caregiving behavior of the mother and perhaps mother's relationship with her own attachment figure(s). The family systems researcher or therapist would expand this approach by observing and describing, in addition, the patterns of interaction among *all* family members. In doing so, the systems analyst is likely to discover two things. First, he is likely to discover that interactions among and between other subsystems in the family contribute to the problem in a way that makes it most difficult to attribute the problem solely to maternal caregiving behavior. For example, fathers in these families often are peripheral to both the spouse and parenting subsystems, and enmeshed interactions between mother and child are often initiated by the functional withdrawal of father from one or both of these subsystems. In most of these families there is also a significant amount of unresolved spouse and parental conflict, and mother's only intimate relationship may be the one she has with her child. In many families, father and an older sibling may constitute an alliance "against" mother and younger child, thus providing positive feedback for that enmeshed relationship. The situation can become even more complex with the addition of problematic relations with grandparents and other extended family members.

Second, the systems analyst is likely to discover that one reason for the problem is that this enmeshment serves an "equilibrating" function for the family. For example, in families whose shared working models do not include effective plans for confronting and resolving conflict, "symptomatic" behavior on the part of the child(ren) can function to divert the spouse subsystem from conflict which might be destructive to the integrity of the family system as a whole. Over time the entire family comes to recognize implicitly, although perhaps not consciously, that extreme forms of attachment-caregiving interactions reduce the likelihood of open conflict. The enmeshment between mother and child comes to be an adaptive (for the short term) family strategy and part of its unspoken, shared working model. The important point is that "maladaptive" attachment-caregiving relationships tend to be a function of, and function for, the entire family system and can best be understood within that context. Family therapists best exemplify this belief by viewing the "symptomatic" family member as having been *chosen by the family to exhibit the behaviors.*[3]

Maintenance of Invariant Relationships

Ashby's notion of invariant limits and Law of Requisite Variety have at least two important implications for attachment research within a family perspective. The first concerns Bowlby's ([1969] 1982) proposal that the biological function of attachment behavior is protection of the infant from various sources of danger. This proposal, however, requires an ontogenetic proviso, as illustrated by the facts that, as the child develops, he learns skills which allow him to protect himself, and at some point in development he is likely to be required to relinquish his position in the family to a newborn sibling. Obviously, this is not meant to imply that the primary attachment-caregiving re-

---

3. The term "chosen" is used almost metaphorically in this context and is not meant to connote conscious intention; such roles are often the *unintended* consequences of the actions of family members.

lationship is dissolved, but only that it undergoes change as the youngster develops more "variety" within himself and enters into other relationships, both of which continue to maintain essential variables within necessary invariant limits. Perhaps an ontogenetically "correct" statement of Bowlby's thesis would be that the biological function of attachment behavior is protection of the young child from various sources of danger while he is developing the skills necessary to assume that protective function himself.

At later ages, a systems framework for the study of attachment becomes particularly important because the child is also protected by membership in systems beyond the dyadic relationship with his primary attachment figure. The most important examples of this expanded system-membership are the father-child subsystem (e.g., Kotelchuck 1972; Lamb 1978), the sibling subsystem (Minuchin 1974; Stewart & Marvin 1984), the peer system (Konner 1976), and the teacher-child system. Since membership in these systems, without proximity to the primary attachment figure, begins well before the youngster is able to protect himself, it would certainly increase the youngster's chances of survival if he established a (subordinate) attachment-caregiver relationship with one or more individuals in each system or subsystem. While research in this area has only recently begun, it does in fact appear that even though attachment-caregiving interactions may not predominate, they do occur with predictability when the youngster is frightened, hurt or distressed (e.g., Konner 1976; Stewart & Marvin 1984). How the young child expands his subsystem membership, how this expansion affects and is affected by his attachment to (usually) his mother, and how subordinate attachment-caregiving relationships are structured and protect the youngster within these subsystems will all be important research questions.

The second implication of Ahsby's notions of invariant limits and Requisite Variety involves the "points of equilibria" which families operate to maintain. Certainly some of the most important of these points involve attachment, not only between the youngster and his primary attachment figure but among the larger family system. Examples range from the manner in which most or all family members tend to operate such that proximity is maintained between young child and at least one attachment figure, to stable patterns of proximity and contact between and among all family members. These stable patterns are maintained to a significant degree by the family's shared working models of its own operation. While these shared models aid in the *adaptive* maintenance of invariant limits, they also often interfere with the developmental changes which are as much a part of families as they are of individual. Therapists often experience this as "resistance" to a therapeutic change.

Self-Regulation

In much the same way that attachment theorists have described how the 12-month-old infant is able to use corrective feedback to maintain a set-goal for a certain degree of proximity to mother (Bowlby [1969]; Ainsworth 1969;

Bischof 1975), and Anderson's (1972) results suggest that the mother-infant dyad as a system accomplishes the same, family therapists have described how the *family* as system uses negative feedback from individual members in conforming ongoing interaction to established and familiar patterns (e.g., Jackson 1957; Minuchin 1974). This corrective feedback can be initiated by any individual or subsystem within the family, and *which* part of the family initiates it is often interchangeable. In the same way that infant and mother feel more secure when they are in proximity or contact, family members tend to feel more secure when their shared goals are being maintained, and are being maintained through familiar, well-established patterns of interaction.

Families engage in this corrective feedback process across a wide range of types of interactions and shared set-goals. In terms of attachment-caregiving interactions, the process organizes family patterns in ways that conform to the family's shared working models of: availability of attachment figures to young or infirm members, conditions that activate and terminate attachment and caregiving behavior, specific patterns of attachment-caregiving interactions, how patterns of interaction within other family subsystems affect and are affected by attachment-caregiving interactions, resolution of conflict concerning the recipient or organization of caregiving behavior during a specific interaction, etc.

The study of families' self-regulation of attachment-caregiving interactions will require much research, including an early *descriptive* phase, of the shared working models referred to here. Three examples occur to us as variations in the form these shared working models may take. First, the shared working model can be one in which the roles, and plans to achieve the set-goal, are similar for all family members: an illustration is a large family gathering, for example, a picnic, where the 2-year-old youngster becomes separated from the rest of the family. A typical sequence in this situation would be: the remainder of the family gathers and recognizes that they are in a major family disequilibrium, develops a search plan, and then executes the plan in which all family members fulfill essentially the same role.

In many situations the shared working model will be one in which different family members play differentiated roles in the self-regulatory process. It is important to note that this makes the working model no less shared. A simple example involving the regulation of proximity between a toddler and his primary attachment figure is a rough-and-tumble play interaction between a toddler and father, where there is one tumble too many and the toddler is slightly hurt and cries. In many families the child will run to mother for comfort, and even though father feels guilty and wants to comfort his child, he accommodates to the division of roles understood and shared by all family members and resumes interaction with his child only after the child's attachment behavior is terminated (see Lamb 1977).

A third form of shared working model consists of differentiated but *interchangeable* roles and plans. These allow the family to operate together efficiently in compensating for short-term changes in the environment, enabling the primary attachment figure to participate in other family subsystems, etc. Two examples take what has become the hallmark of attachment research, infant-caregiver separations and reunions in the Strange Situation, and expand this from a dyadic to a family perspective.

In one study, Stewart (1977) observed mothers, fathers, and babies in a modified Strange Situation. He found that fathers tended to interact very little with the babies when mother was present in the room: the fathers tended to engage in solitary activities such as reading a magazine. As mother left the room, however, most fathers ceased solitary activity and engaged the baby in playful activity as if to distract the baby from any distress which might be initiated by mother's leaving the room. The fathers tended to remain engaged with the baby throughout mother's absence, whether a stranger was in the room or not. When mother returned, the fathers tended to return to their solitary activities. The fact that the babies tended to display very brief, almost casual greetings to their mothers and then to return to exploration suggests that the families already possessed a smoothly operating self-regulatory strategy which actually *anticipated* a disturbance and corrected for it before the babies became distressed.

In a second study (Stewart & Marvin 1984), mothers and the sibling subsystem (consisting of older preschooler and 1-year-old sib) were observed in the Strange Situation. The results were similar to those described above, in that the older siblings tended to substitute as attachment figures for the mother during her absence, and the babies tended not to become upset. Interestingly, this occurred only in those families where the older sibling had reached the developmental point where he or she possessed social-cognitive skills (i.e., perspective-taking) which would allow him or her to construct and execute a shared plan with mother in a goal-corrected way. Older siblings who had not yet reached that developmental point tended *not* to function as subordinate attachment figures to their younger siblings. It seems to us that since, in most families, a significant proportion of separations and reunions take place in the company of more than just mother and infant, it will be important for attachment researchers to study them in the context of whole families. Only then will we completely understand how families (and therefore mothers and babies) regulate proximity and contact in a way that minimizes disturbances to the family and each of its members.

Self-Organization

In addition to regulating itself to compensate for temporary changes in the environment, a family must, from time to time, undergo major reorganizational changes to compensate for more lasting changes occurring either in its environment or in itself. With reference to attachment-caregiving relationships, examples are the birth of a first- or later-born child, entrance of children into school or adolescence, loss of a close family member through death, divorce, or leaving home as a young adult, mother (re)turning to a career outside the home, changes in economic conditions which *require* mother to earn wages outside the home, etc. To any of these changing conditions the family as a whole must adjust and establish a new set of stable interaction patterns and self-regulatory processes. All families meet these or similar changing conditions, and most family therapists see them as "normal" family crises. In fact, most "stages" of family development stem from changes in the organization of affectional bonds within the nuclear and extended family (see Haley 1986; Pittman 1987).

For the purposes of this chapter, the best example of these organizational changes may be the birth of a second child when the firstborn is still a preschooler. Research by Dunn and Kendrick (1980, 1982) offers some insight into the changes involved in this situation. They report that the firstborn child tends to become more demanding of the mother's attention and care, and more deliberately naughty, especially at times when mother is occupied with the newborn. Moreover, they report a decrease in maternal attention to the firstborn child during periods when mother is *not* occupied with the baby. This tends to lead to an increase in the number of confrontations between mother and firstborn child. Stewart and his colleagues (1985, unpublished data) replicated the findings of Dunn and Kendrick and extended them to include changes in the relationship between father and firstborn child. Their data indicated that fathers become more active in caregiving and terminating the attachment behavior of the firstborn following the birth of the second child, as if to relieve their wives of the burden of caring for two children simultaneously and to supplement the attention received by the firstborn. As one father put it, "It took only one child to make my wife a mother, but two to make me a father."

The results of these studies are reminiscent of Trivers's (1974) interpretation of parent-offspring conflict over parental investment in the youngster, and they suggest that the birth of the second-born child initiates a process whereby the entire family reorganizes its stable patterns of attachment-caregiving interactions. As the relationship between mother and newborn develops, less time is spent with the firstborn. The firstborn attempts to initiate a return to familiar patterns of interaction (the process of family self-regulation) by becoming more demanding and aggressive toward both mother and infant. The family as a whole must now reorganize its familiar patterns of interaction. There is often a period of instability as the family experiments with and negotiates new patterns for maintaining important variables within certain limits. In many families, one of the newly negotiated patterns involves a closer attachment-caregiving relationship between father and firstborn child, which will in turn imply further changes in the mother-firstborn child relationship. In addition to changes in the parenting and parent-child subsystems, there undoubtedly will be changes in the spouse subsystem as well. As exemplified by the father's statement quoted above, the family's shared working model changes as much as do its patterns of interaction. Finally, if the family systems researchers are correct, this family will again experience a period of stability once these newly negotiated patterns of family interaction (and shared working model) become familiar and more secure. At that point in its development, the family will return to making ongoing self-regulatory adjustments until it must again reorganize when it encounters its next expected or unexpected "crisis."

Systems/Subsystems

Throughout this chapter we have made repeated reference to subsystems within the family and have discussed some of the ways they affect, and are affected by, attachment-caregiving interactions. In this section we would like to focus on one theme—how the youngster, from the security of his relationship with his primary attachment figure(s), gradually expands his membership, during the preschool years, in familial and extrafamilial subsystems. What little research that is available suggests that even during infancy, and especially during the early preschool years, most children become actively involved in relationships other than that with the primary attachment figure. These relationships are characterized by shifting but familiar patterns of interaction: patterns that, in being distinct from patterns in other relationships, define boundaries around that subsystem. The work of Lamb (e.g., 1977), Dunn and Kendrick (e.g., 1982), Stewart (1983), and others coincides with common experience in suggesting that three of these distinct subsystems are the father-child, sibling and peer (often with teacher or daycaregiver) subsystems. The very patterns that establish boundaries around these subsystems enable the young child to develop the play, learning, collaboration, and conflict-resolution skills which will increase his or her own chances of survival and which, because of the nature of the mother-child relationship, are not easily learned within that relationship.

Research suggests that the roles played by both the child and older members of these subsystems vary, with the older member(s) playing the role of playmate, teacher, protagonist, or subordinate attachment figure as the situation warrants, and dependent on the presence/absence of the primary attachment figure. For example, in the presence of mother, the young child may play with father or older sibling, yet seek proximity to *mother* if his or her attachment system is activated (Stewart 1977). If mother is absent, on the other hand, the young child will direct his or her attachment behavior toward the father or older sibling, and the father, older sibling, or teacher will actively take the role of caregiver/attachment figure (Stewart & Marvin 1984). Thus, as Konner (1976) was the first to imply, and as is completely consistent with attachment theory, the young preschooler's membership in subsystems other than the mother-child subsystem probably implies the presence of a member of that subsystem who "doubles" as a subordinate attachment figure. This would certainly increase the child's chances of survival while developing these new skills and learning to operate relatively independently of his primary attachment figure for increasing periods of time.

The question of what factors cause the young child to expand his membership in these subsystems will eventually occupy much time of attachment researchers. Bowlby ([1969] 1982) suggested that one factor is the youngster's curiosity and interest in other relationships, and Ainsworth's notion of the use of mother as a secure base for exploration certainly implies that she may serve this function in her child's expanding subsystem membership. A family systems perspective suggests at least two other factors. The first is the already established attachment-caregiving relationships between the young child and one or more members of each subsystem, making this transition less anxiety producing for the child.

An equally important factor, and one which almost *requires* a family systems perspective, is the tendency within a family to establish and maintain clear, firm but flexible boundaries between various subsystems. One of the functions of these boundaries is to exclude inappropriate members during those times when the subsystem is functioning. In well-functioning families, children often will be excluded from the spouse subsystem when it is actively functioning. This exclusion will tend, in families with more than one child, to "force" the young child to spend time either alone or within the sibling subsystem. For example, most of us have known families confronted with the problem of an infant or young child who insists on sleeping with one or both parents. This problem is resolved usually by an alliance between the members of the spouse subsystem to exclude the child from that subsystem and to restrict his or her involvement with them to times when they are functioning as a *parental* subsystem. A second example of a subsystem boundary which occasionally excludes a child is when mother and another child place temporary boundaries around *their* interaction. The classic instance of this situation is the birth of a younger sibling, which is often the precipitating "cause" of the older child's increased membership in the father-child subsystem (Stewart, Van Tuyl, Mobley, Salvador, & Walls 1985). A third and perhaps less obvious example consists of those times when the sibling subsystem tends, either actively or because of the parents' respect for that boundary, to exclude the parents. It is largely within this latter situation that children learn to resolve conflict among relative equals and to cope with fearful situations without recourse to activating attachment behavior toward a parent.

Thus, family subsystem boundaries probably function in an adaptive manner to "push" the very young child out of a *relatively* exclusive relationship with mother into an expanded subsystem membership. As already mentioned, one important question concerns the necessity for, and role of, subordinate attachment figures within those other subsystems. A related question concerns the relationship between the security of the youngster's attachment to his mother and his interest and success in engaging in this process of expanding horizons.

For example, an insecure, "resistant" child-mother attachment, with relatively restricted involvement by the child in other family and extrafamilial subsystems, is commonly seen by family therapists as part of a *family* pattern. The child's continual presence with mother (maintained through the child's "insecure" behaviors, mother's overly active caregiving system, and father's lack of involvement with both) denies the child the opportunity to develop memberships in other subsystems. At the same time, the tendency of other family subsystems to exclude either child and/or mother functions as positive feedback to increase the degree of their enmeshment. This insecure, overinvolved relationship between young child and mother is actually a family "dance" and serves some stabilizing function for the family as a whole. This is illustrated repeatedly in family therapy, when a change (for the better) in the behavior of any family member is vehemently opposed by other family members. Our understandings of an insecure, "avoidant" attachment can be refined in the same manner.

The successful expansion of the securely attached child's subsystem membership also is caused by other patterns of interaction within the family as a whole. In addition to the child's interest, his use of mother as a secure base, and the presence of subordinate attachment figures in those other subsystems, important factors include the family's tendency to insist on spouse and sibling interaction with clear subsystem boundaries; a change in the conditions that activate attachment behavior toward mother as the child develops more competent coping skills; and a willingness on the part of all family members to struggle with the process of reorganizing the family itself, and its shared working model for attachment-caregiving interactions, as the child develops.

A family systems analysis of the young child's expanding subsystem membership includes not only a description of the process of that change, and of the causal processes involved, but also a description of its *effects* or *functions*. Since cause and effect often overlap, and in fact the effect of an interaction or developmental change often feeds back as a stabilizing cause of that same interaction or change, much of this issue has already been covered in the above discussion. At this point we would like to merely to list some further effects of this change before moving to the topic of maladaptive attachments.

From a family systems perspective, one of the most important functions of the young child's expanded subsystem membership is that it increases the child's degree of autonomy within his relationship with mother, and prevents their relationship from becoming inappropriately enmeshed. In addition, it allows for an increased involvement between the spouses, something that often suffers during the early months/years of an infant's life. In turn, this increased involvement, with the youngster's protection on a moment-to-moment basis being fulfilled significantly by other subsystems, increases both the availability and likelihood for another pregnancy. Finally, the child's expanded subsystem membership allows for more diversified attachment plans between mother and child since those plans can now include interactions with other family members.

INDIVIDUAL DIFFERENCES: MALADAPTIVE ATTACHMENTS FROM A FAMILY SYSTEMS PERSPECTIVE

With the possible exception of construct validation studies, the most popular focus of attachment research to date has been that of individual differences or the study of "normal" versus "maladaptive" attachment-caregiving relationships. Undoubtedly, this will also be the case in research on attachment from a family systems perspective. We would like to highlight a few relevant issues.

One commonalty of both attachment and family systems theory is that both have identified three major organizations of, or individual differences in, the respective system under study (this does not include the "disorganized" group recently identified by Main & Solomon 1986). Even more striking is the similarity across the two research traditions in the structure of these three organizations. Ainsworth (e.g., Ainsworth et al. 1978) and other attachment researchers have classified infants' attachments as either "secure," "insecure-avoidant," or "insecure-ambivalent." Similarly, the best-known classification of family organizations (e.g., Minuchin 1974) describes families—or family subsystems—as either "adaptive" (mutually sensitive, openly communicative, and supportive while respectful of developmentally and situationally appropriate autonomy), "disengaged" (avoidant or underinvolved, angry and insensitive), or "enmeshed" (overinvolved, intrusive, ambivalent, and disrespectful of appropriate autonomy and boundaries).

The similarities between these two classificatory systems are extensive and intriguing, and could provide one important shared base from which to integrate the two paradigms. A major contribution to attachment research from such an integration would be consideration of the relationship between the "quality" of the child's attachment to his primary attachment figure and the quality or organization of the family (or subset of the family) system. A fascinating example of one step in this direction is implicit in the recent work of Sroufe et al. (1985), exploring the implications of an enmeshed, inappropriate mother-son relationship on the mother-daughter relationship. One potentially puzzling result emerging from current attachment research is that a child may not have the same quality of attachment to mother as to father. Presumably (as implied by the work of Sroufe et al.), different children in a given family can also have different qualities of attachment to the same attachment figure. While these differential relationships would present an immediate problem within attachment theory as currently developed, they may be assimilated within, and even predicted by, family systems theory.

A reciprocal contribution, of attachment to family systems theory, would be a significantly missing element of the latter, that is, the element of loving relations. Family systems theory currently focuses primarily on boundaries, roles, subsystems, hierarchical relations, communication and conflict-resolution, and homeostasis and change. What has been significantly lacking is equally detailed coverage of *loving relations:* we are convinced that attachment theory can provide/stimulate this coverage in a matter to expand and strengthen both paradigms.

One important distinction made by family systems researchers that we think will be useful in attachment research is the distinction between a *maladaptive* family structure and the temporary condition or process known as *a crisis of transition* (Pittman 1987). Maladaptive implies a structure or pattern inappropriate to the goals of a family, destructive, and extremely resistant to change, that is, family members act so as to maintain this pattern and persistently counteract any family member's attempts to change it. A crisis of transition implies, on the other hand, a disturbance of family equilibrium accompanying a developmental or situational change to which the family attempts to accommodate through the earlier described process of self-organization. These changes, for example, the birth of a new child or the loss of a family member, tend to be quite disruptive and painful, but they also tend to be resolved through changes in the family's structure and patterns of interaction. This period of change is followed by a different, but once again comfortable and adaptive, organization and set of interaction patterns. The important point is that the period of crisis is characterized by discomfort and unfamiliar (and often less adaptive) patterns of interaction. These periods are seen by family therapists as normal and necessary rather than maladaptive or pathological.

The implication for attachment research is that as the youngster proceeds from one phase of development to another, or as a major change takes place in the family, a normal "crisis of transition" will take place for the entire family as well as for the child himself. It is likely that during these transitions the attachment relationship between child and mother will suffer a loss of equilibrium or homeostasis and be characterized by a coincidental increase in conflict and decrease in security. Almost by definition, in well-functioning families this period will be followed by a return to a secure attachment between child and mother. In fact, this process could serve a critically important learning function for the child in equipping him with basic strategies for resolving crises of transition for the remainder of his life.

The idea that the security of the youngster's attachment may temporarily be disturbed during periods of transition could also account in part for one of the puzzling findings in some longitudinal studies of individual differences in attachment. Specifically, most studies have demonstrated 60%–80% stability in the organization of attachment behavior toward mother across six-month periods during infancy (e.g., Connell 1976; Owen, Easterbrook, Chase-Landsdale, & Goldberg 1984), and from 1 to 6 years of age (Main, Kaplan, & Cassidy 1985). As impressive as this stability is, an important question remains: What accounts for the instability in that 20%–40%? While measurement error, specific risk factors associated with lower SES, etc., may account for some changes in security of attachment (e.g., Vaughn, Egeland, Sroufe, & Waters 1979), a family systems perspective would predict that some of this documented instability could be a result of assessments having been conducted during normal crises of transition. During normal and necessary periods of significant change, the relationship between a child and his mother is likely to be stressed. These periods will usually be temporary, with a return to security and relative homeostasis (albeit with a different set of interaction patterns) defining the end of the crisis of transition. Some of the results obtained by Egeland and Farber (1984) are consistent with this hypothesis.

Turning to attachments which are unquestionably maladaptive, we would like briefly to discuss two related issues: one an example of a family systems perspective on a specific maladaptive organization of attachment, and the other a consideration of the role of attachment behavior and the organization of proximity among family members in the development and maintenance of symptomatic behaviors. With both of these issues, it is understood that cause-effect relationships are primarily systemic rather than linear or dyadic in nature; that the family's interaction patterns select each family member to play a certain role; that a family's shared working models, as described earlier, play a crucial role in the process; and that equally important roles are played by each of the other major "principles" of family systems theory as outlined earlier in this chapter.

One of the most common maladapted family structures encountered by family therapists is one in which mother and (at least one) child are overinvolved, or enmeshed (Minuchin 1974). This enmeshed relationship is usually characterized by a number of the following: reciprocally intrusive, controlling behavior on the part of mother *and* child; much insecurity and distress on the part of both over real or threatened separation, sometimes even to the point where the child refuses to attend school; treatment of the child as if he or she were younger than is actually the case; a strong tendency for one or both to speak for the other and assume knowledge of what the other is thinking and feeling without "checking it out" (a really palpable lack of psychological boundaries); role reversals in attachment and caregiving behaviors; an inability to resolve conflict; and relative isolation from familial and extrafamilial support systems while at the same time maintaining a degree of intimacy with one another inappropriate to their relative ages and positions in the family.

This set of patterns is reminiscent of one of the classificatory groups identified by attachment researchers in their work with infants and young children. Labeled "insecure-resistant" (Ainsworth et al. 1978) or "insecure-controlling" (Marvin 1972, 1977; Main et al. 1985), these groups of children and their mothers display patterns of interaction covering most of the patterns characteristic of enmeshed dyads (Minuchin 1974).

Both research traditions also identify these groups of children as being at risk for emotional and interpersonal maladaptation, and psychopathology. For example, Ainsworth and her colleagues have described these children as being fearful at 12 months of age even in their own homes (Ainsworth et al. 1978), Sroufe (1983) has demonstrated that they are significantly less functional than secure children in kindergarten, and Bowlby (1973) has outlined a number of other "psychological" problems for which they are at risk. Family therapists have noted that these children often become "symptomatic"—for example, phobic behavior in a preschooler or school refusal in an 8-year-old (Haley 1971), intractable psychogenic pain in a 12-year-old (Marvin, in preparation), or anorexia nervosa in a 15-year-old (Minuchin et al. 1978). Further research will be required to determine whether these two traditions are speaking of the "same" child. We strongly suspect they are.

At least three systemic questions arise in thinking about this problem. What family issues or variables—in addition to maternal characteristics such as intrusiveness, insensitivity and unpredictability to signals, etc.—foster this type of insecure attachment? In families where this is an entrenched pattern resistant to change, what homeostatic or self-regulatory outcome is this attachment pattern helping to maintain? And what developmental, self-organizational change is the pattern operating to inhibit? As in any systemic process, these questions, and the answers to them, are very much interrelated.

Family therapists would have a number of hypotheses concerning these questions, with the specifics differing from family to family. The general outline, however, would be something like the following. In this family, it is likely that the spouse dyad lacks an adequate degree of intimacy and/or conflict-resolution strategies. The emotional distance between the spouses leads to resentment between them and makes it difficult as well to work together as parents. Mother begins to experience her intimacy within her relationship with the child rather than with her husband/parenting partner, and father focuses his energy on his job, hobbies, another child, etc.

In a reciprocal fashion, this enmeshed relationship tends further to increase the emotional distance between husband and wife. Because of the closeness of mother and child, father gets little or no opportunity to develop a relationship with the child; mother is caregiving so much of the time that there is little or no opportunity for spouse interactions; the youngster has such a low "threshold" for the activation of attachment behavior that mother's caregiving system is activated too frequently; and husband is too peripheral and preoccupied with other things to entice his wife into spousal interactions. The youngster is then often called upon to serve as caregiver for mother's emotional state, and paradoxically is treated by mother as younger than the child's chronological age would dictate, in order to keep the child in that caregiving role. Finally, the existence of all these inappropriate roles fosters resentment and ambivalence within all the relationships.

At any given time this complex pattern can be initiated by any of the three family members, for example, fearful behavior on the youngster's part, withdrawal of the father or worry/caregiving on the mother's part. If these interaction patterns become repetitive and stable, that is, if no "intervention" originating within or outside the family system manages to change the pattern, then the pattern can take on a stability of its own and constitute a homeostatic outcome maintained in a self-regulatory fashion.

What is the purpose of this self-regulatory pattern, and ultimately of this insecure, enmeshed relationship between child and mother? The answer depends on one's perspective, and can range from the circular argument that the purpose of the pattern is to maintain itself, to arguments based on the individual perspective of a specific family member (e.g., mother's need for *some* intimacy, the only source of which is her child at this time).

Family therapists tend to view the spouse dyad as the "core" of most families, and believe that this is the family subsystem with the most "degrees of freedom" in influencing all other subsystems, including the parenting subsystem. In other families (some with and some without a husband/father), the core, at least with respect to parenting, consists of mother and a member of the extended family (usually the maternal grandmother). While we refer primarily to the spouse subsystem in what follows, much the same can be applied to any variant of the parenting subsystem.

In answering the question as to the purpose of the insecure attachment, family therapists are likely to focus on its effect: its role in distracting attention from spousal resentment and conflict, or at least from spousal interaction, and in maintaining family integrity by stabilizing the system around the mother-child dyad. A family in which the spouses are unable to resolve conflicts and who maintain emotional distance from, or continual conflict with, one another is certainly unstable and at risk for divorce. This systemic pattern of peripheral father and enmeshed mother-child dyad, with its focus on the youngster as helpless and needing constant attention, turns out to be a fairly successful (albeit painful) strategy for keeping the family together as an intact unit. The same applies to the systemic pattern of a controlling grandmother and seemingly incompetent mother, both of whom are enmeshed with the child in an endless cycle of conflict with each other.

The developmental, self-organizational changes this maladapted attachment inhibit can be changes at the level of the child, or of the family as a whole. For the child this relationship, and the corresponding family patterns, will operate to inhibit the youngster's competent entrance into other familial and extrafamilial subsystems as discussed earlier, as well as to inhibit the development of a secure, smoothly operating goal-corrected partnership with the mother (Bowlby [1969] 1982; Marvin 1977). For the family, this systemic pattern will operate to inhibit those changes families usually make as they move from being a family with infants and preschool children to one with school-age children. Among others, these changes include denser boundaries between the parent and child/sibling subsystems, more independence for the child, and closer alliance within the spouse (or mother-grandmother) subsystem, which tends naturally to foster the child's gradual movement out of the family.

The second issue mentioned earlier concerns the role of attachment behavior in the formation and maintenance of those extreme forms of behavior labeled "symptoms" (see the related discussion by Bowlby 1973). Family therapists are constantly confronted with family members (more often than not one of the children) who engage in repetitive patterns of behavior such as those identified with school refusal, stealing, fire-starting, psychogenic pain, anorexia nervosa, etc. Rather than (or in addition to) searching for the intrapersonal reasons for these patterns, the family therapist will usually search for the self-regulatory role the symptom serves for the family system. Fortunately for the therapist attempting to diagnose the family, this role often becomes apparent by observing what *effect* the symptom has on other family members, even in the context of a single family therapy session.

With surprising frequency, this effect turns out to be one of mobilizing the caregiving behavior of other family members toward the "identified patient." This caregiving behavior can be of a gentle, protective, nurturing sort in the case of psychogenic pain or anorexia nervosa; of a firm, even angry, sort in the case of fire-starting, stealing, and other behavior problems; or even oddly reversed in the case of the youngster who refuses to attend school because of fear of what might happen to his parent(s).

With even more regularity, these families are characterized by much unresolved conflict and resentment between mother and her primary parenting partner (usually either father and/or maternal grandmother). The term "unresolved" is important here, because some of these families avoid any open conflict, while others engage in many *unproductive* fights. In either case, the family interaction patterns usually provide some stimulus which diverts the spouses (or mother and grandmother) from successful resolution of their conflict(s). Activation of the spouse subsystem is so uncomfortable that the family as a whole would rather avoid it.

Family therapists find that this diversion is often provided by symptomatic behavior of one or more of the children. This is so common that therapists usually, as Bergman says,

> assume (with a family in which there is a particularly resistant symptom)
> that an intense, often covert marital conflict is present and that there will

be considerable resistance to treatment because of the family's fear (real or imagined) that if treatment were to be successful someone (usually one of the parents) would leave (divorce, become seriously ill, or die). (1985)

Thus the diversion is often an extreme form of attachment behavior (symptom) on the part of the child, with subsequent activation of the parental caregiving system. Usually no one in the family is (consciously) aware of the systemic role played by this intense attachment behavior, and the family is stabilized around, for example, its focus on the child's "medical" problem. The symptom is so resistant to change precisely because these attachment-caregiving interactions stabilize the family and decrease the chances of loss of a family member.

CONCLUSIONS

In this chapter we have argued that attachment theory and family systems theory can be integrated within their shared relationship to general systems theory. General systems theory, while offering a framework that draws one's attention to the organization of a system, needs to be supplemented with some theoretical framework from which observations can be drawn. Bowlby's theory of attachment has been noted for its eclecticism (Hinde 1982), and has served well as a means for integrating ideas from cybernetics, biology, ethology, cognitive development, and evolutionary thought. That it shares a common theoretic space with structural family systems theory should come as no surprise. Attachment researchers can broaden the range of their inquiry by becoming more familiar with the research being conducted in disciplines such as family sociology and family therapy, and thereby provide a means for sustaining Bowlby's claim that "attachment theory is still growing: its potential and its limitations remain unknown" ([1969] 1982, p. 313).

Two alternatives exist for studying attachment from a family perspective: the approach of family therapists and sociologists, who conceptualize the *family* as the basic social system; and the approach of developmental psychologists, who take the *child* as the basic unit of conceptualization but who also hold the conviction that we cannot truly understand the child without understanding the entire system of which he is a part. In the past, there has always been a struggle as to which of these two scientific paradigms is the "correct" one, with the result that members of each discipline often lack a clear understanding of the research accomplishments of the other (see Minuchin 1985). We wish to emphasize that, given the utility of the general systems perspective for *both* disciplines, there is no substantive battle, only a political one. Whether one's ultimate focus is on the child or on the family is a personal decision of the individual scientist and not a reflection of the superiority of one orientation over the other. In fact, it will be absolutely necessary, given the complexity of attachment at a family systems level, that individual scientists from each perspective conduct research from their own points of view. One of the primary advantages of adopting a general systems framework is that this interdisciplinary work may be accomplished and integrated without conflict across disciplines.

REFERENCES

Ainsworth, M. D. S. (1967). *Infancy in Uganda: Infant care and the growth of love.* Baltimore: Johns Hopkins University Press.

Ainsworth, M. D. S. (1969). Object relations, dependency and attachment: A theoretical review of the infant-mother relationship. *Child Development* 40, 969–1025.

Ainsworth, M. D. S., & Bell, S. M. (1970). Attachment, exploration and separation: Illustrated by the behavior of one-year-olds in a strange situation. *Child Development* 41, 49–67.

Ainsworth, M. D. S., Blehar, M. C., Waters, E., & Wall, S. (1978). *Patterns of attachment: A psychological study of the strange situation.* Hillsdale, N.J.: Erlbaum.

Anderson, J. (1972). Attachment behavior out of doors. In N. G. Blurton-Jones (ed.), *Ethological studies of child behavior.* London: Cambridge University Press.

Ashby, W. R. (1952). *Design for a brain.* London: Wiley.

Ashby, W. R. (1956). *An introduction to cybernetics.* London: Chapman & Hall.

Belsky, J. (1984). The determinants of parenting: A process model. *Child Development* 55, 83–96.

Belsky, J. (1985). Experimenting with the family in the newborn period. *Child Development* 56, 407–414.

Bergman, J. S. (1985). *Fishing for barracuda: Pragmatics of brief systemic therapy.* New York: Norton.

Berrien, F. K. (1968). *General and social systems.* New Brunswick, N.J.: Rutgers University Press.

Bertalanffy, L. von. (1968). *General systems theory.* New York: Braziller.

Bischof, N. A. (1975). A systems approach toward the functional connections of attachment and fear. *Child Development* 46, 801–817.

Bowlby, J. ([1969] 1982). *Attachment and loss: Vol. 1. Attachment.* New York: Basic Books.

Bowlby, J. (1973). *Attachment and loss: Vol. 2. Separation.* New York: Basic Books.

Bowlby, J. (1980). *Attachment and loss: Vol. 3. Loss, sadness and depression.* New York: Basic Books.

Brazelton, T.; Koslowski, B.; & Main, M. (1974). The origins of reciprocity: The early mother-infant interaction. In M. Lewis & L. A. Rosenblum (eds.), *The effect of the infant on its caregiver.* New York: Wiley.

Bretherton, I., & Ainsworth, M. D. S. (1974). Responses of one-year-olds to a stranger in a strange situation. In M. Lewis & L. A. Rosenblum (eds.), *The origins of fear.* New York: Wiley.

Carter, B., & McGoldrick, M. (1980). *The family life cycle.* New York: Gardner.

Connell, D. (1976). Classification of individual differences in strange situation behavior. Unpublished doctoral dissertation, Syracuse University.

Cowan, C.; Cowan, P.; Coie, L.; & Coie, J. (1978). Becoming a family: The impact of the first child's birth on the couple's relationship. In W. Miller & L. Newman (eds.), *The first child and family formation* (pp. 296–324). Chapel Hill: Carolina Population Center.

Crnic, K. A.; Greenberg, M. T.; & Slough, N. M. (1986). Early stress and social support influences on mothers' and high risk infants' functioning in late infancy. *Infant Mental Health Journal* 7, 19–33.

Dunn, J., & Kendrick, C. (1980). The arrival of a sibling: Changes in patterns of interaction between mother and first-born child. *Journal of Child Psychology and Psychiatry* 21, 119–132.

Dunn, J., & Kendrick, C. (1982). *Siblings: Love, envy, and understanding.* Cambridge, Mass.: Harvard University Press.

Egeland, B., & Farber, E. (1984). Infant-mother attachment: Factors related to its development and changes over time. *Child Development* 55, 753–771.

Entwisle, D., & Doering, S. (1981). *The first birth: A family turning point.* Baltimore: Johns Hopkins University Press.

Flavell, J. H. (1985). *Cognitive Development* (2d ed.). Englewood Cliffs, N.J.: Prentice-Hall.

Greenberg, M. T., & Marvin, R. S. (1982). Reactions of preschool children to an adult stranger: A behavioral systems approach. *Child Development* 53, 481–490.

Haley, J. (1971). *Changing families.* New York: Grune & Stratton.

Haley, J. (1986). *Uncommon therapy.* New York: Norton.

Hart, N. J. (1985). Family system influences on the quality of infant-mother attachment. Unpublished doctoral dissertation, University of Virginia.

Heard, D. H. (1978). From object relations to attachment theory: A basis for family therapy. *British Journal of Medical Psychology* 51, 67–76.

Hinde, R. A. (1970). *Animal behaviour: A synthesis of ethology and comparative psychology* (2nd ed.). New York: McGraw-Hill.

Hinde, R. A. (1982). Attachment: Some conceptual and biological issues. In C. Parkes & J. Stevenson-Hinde (eds.), *The place of attachment in human behavior.* New York: Basic Books.

Jackson, D. (1957). The question of family homeostasis. *Psychiatric Quarterly Supplement* 31, 79–90.

Kazak, A., & Marvin, R. S. (1984). Differences, difficulties, and adaptation: Stress and social networks in families with a handicapped child. *Family Relations* 33, 67–77.

Konner, M. (1976). Maternal care, infant behavior and development among the !Kung. In R. Lee & I. DeVore (eds.), *Kalahari hunter gatherers: Studies of the !Kung San and their neighbors.* Cambridge, Mass.: Harvard University Press.

Kotelchuck, M. (1972). The nature of the child's tie to his father. Unpublished doctoral dissertation, Harvard University.

Lamb, M. E. (1977). Father-infant and mother-infant interaction in the first year of life. *Child Development* 48, 167–181.

Lamb, M. E. (1978). Interactions between eighteen-month-olds and their preschool siblings. *Child Development* 49, 51–59.

Lamb, M. E.; Hwang, C.; Frodi, A.; & Frodi, M. (1982). Security of mother- and father-infant attachment and its relations to sociability with strangers in traditional and non-traditional Swedish families. *Infant Behavior and Development* 5, 355–367.

MacKay, D. (1964). Communication and meaning: A functional approach. In F. Northrop & H. Livingston (eds.), *Cross-cultural understanding: Epistemology in anthropology.* New York: Harper & Row.

Main, M.; Kaplan, N.; & Cassidy, J. (1985). Security in infancy, childhood and adulthood: A move to the level of representation. In I. Bretherton & E. Waters (eds.), *Growing points in attachment theory and research. Monographs of the Society for Research in Child Development* 50 (1–2, Serial No. 209), 66–104.

Main, M., & Solomon, J. (1986). Discovery of an insecure-disorganized/disoriented attachment pattern. In T. B. Brazelton & M. Yogman (eds.), *Affective development in infancy.* Norwood, N.J.: Ablex.

Main, M., & Weston, D. (1981). The quality of the toddler's relationship to mother and father: Related to conflict behavior and readiness to establish new relationships. *Child Development* 52, 932–940.

Marvin, R. S. (1972). Attachment-, exploratory-, and communicative-behavior in 2, 3 and 4 year-old children. Unpublished doctoral dissertation, University of Chicago.

Marvin, R. S. (1977). An ethological-cognitive model for the attenuation of mother-child attachment behavior. In T. Alloway, L. Krames, & P. Pliner (eds.), *Advances in the study of communication and affect: vol. 3. Attachment behavior* (pp. 25–60). New York: Plenum.

Marvin, R. S. (in preparation). Brief, family-focused treatment of reflex sympathetic dystrophy and related childhood disorders.

Marvin, R. S., & Greenberg, M. T. (1982). Preschooler's changing conceptions of their mothers:

a social-cognitive study of mother-child attachment. In D. Forbes & M. T. Greenberg (eds.), *New directions for child development: Children's planning strategies* (no. 18). San Francisco: Jossey-Bass.

Marvin, R. S.; Greenberg, M. T.; & Mossler, D. G. (1976). The early development of conceptual perspective-taking: Distinguishing among multiple perspectives. *Child Development* 47, 511–514.

Minuchin, P. (1985). Families and individual development: Provocations from the field of family therapy. *Child Development* 56, 289–302.

Minuchin, S. (1974). *Families and family therapy.* Cambridge, Mass.: Harvard University Press.

Minuchin, S.; Montalvo, B.; Guerney, G. B.; Rosman, B. L.; & Schumer, F. (1967). *Families of the slums: An exploration of their structure and treatment.* New York: Basic Books.

Minuchin, S.; Rosman, B. L.; & Baker, L. (1978). *Psychosomatic families: Anorexia nervosa in context.* Cambridge, Mass.: Harvard University Press.

Owen, M. T.; Easterbrook, M. A.; Chase-Lansdale, L.; & Goldberg, S. (1984). The relation between maternal employment status and stability of attachments to mother and father. *Child Development* 55, 1894–1901.

Pedersen, F.; Yarrow, L.; Anderson, B.; & Cain, R. (1978). Conceptualization of father influences in the infancy period. In M. Lewis & L. A. Rosenblum (eds.), *The social network of the developing infant.* New York: Plenum.

Pedersen, F.; Zaslow, M.; Cain, R.; & Anderson, B. (1980). Caesarean birth: The importance of a family perspective. Paper presented at the International Conference on Infant Studies, New Haven.

Piaget, J. (1970). *Structuralism.* New York: Basic Books.

Pittman, F. S. (1987). *Turning points: Treating families in transition and crisis.* New York: Norton.

Sameroff, A. (1983). Developmental systems: Contexts and evolution. In W. Kessen (ed.), *Handbook of child psychology* (vol. 1). New York: Wiley.

Sroufe, A. (1983). Infant-caregiver attachment and patterns of adaptation in preschool: The roots of maladaptation and competence. In M. Perlmutter (ed.), *Minnesota Symposium in Child Psychology* (vol. 16). Hillsdale, N.J.: Erlbaum.

Sroufe, A.; Jacobvitz, D.; Mangelsdorf, S.; DeAngelo, E.; & Ward, M. (1985). Generational boundary dissolution between mothers and their preschool children: A relationship systems approach. *Child Development* 56, 317–325.

Sroufe, A., & Waters, E. (1977). Attachment as an organizational construct. *Child Development* 48, 1184–1199.

Stern, D. (1974). Mother and infant at play: The dyadic interaction involving facial, vocal and gaze behaviors. In M. Lewis and L. A. Rosenblum (eds.), *The effect of the infant on its caregiver.* New York: Wiley.

Stewart, R. (1977). Parent-child interactions in a quasi-naturalistic setting. Unpublished master's thesis, Pennsylvania State University.

Stewart, R. (1983). Sibling attachment relationships: Child-infant interactions in the strange situation. *Developmental Psychology* 19(2), 192–199.

Stewart, R., & Marvin, R. S. (1984). Sibling relations: The role of conceptual perspective-taking in the ontogeny of sibling caregiving. *Child Development* 55, 1322–1332.

Stewart, R.; Mobley, L.; Van Tuyl, S.; & Salvador, M. (1987). The firstborn's adjustment to the birth of a sibling: A longitudinal assessment. *Child Development* 58, 341–355.

Stewart, R.; Van Tuyl, S.; Mobley, L.; Salvador, M.; & Walls, D. (1985). The transition at the birth of a second child: Sources of parental stress and support. Paper presented at the Southeastern Conference on Human Development, Nashville, Tenn.

Trivers, R. (1974). Parent-offspring conflict. *American Zoologist* 14, 249–264.

Tronick, E.; Als, H.; & Adamson, L. (1979). Structure of early face-to-face communicative interactions. In M. Bullowa (ed.), *Before speech: The beginning of interactional communication.* New York: Cambridge University Press.

Vaughn, B.; Egeland, B.; Sroufe, A.; & Waters, E. (1979). Individual differences in infant-mother attachment at twelve and eighteen months: Stability and change in families under stress. *Child Development* 50, 971–975.

Weinraub, M., & Wolf, B. (1983). Effects of stress and social supports on mother-child interactions in single- and two-parent families. *Child Development* 54, 1297–1311.

3 · Theoretical and Methodological Considerations in the Study of Attachment and the Self in Young Children

Jude Cassidy

THE NOTION that the self develops not in a vaccum but rather in relation to social interaction has been widely held by psychologists for nearly a century (Baldwin 1897; Cooley 1902; Mead 1934). Despite convergent theoretical predictions, however, the investigation of connections between the self and any of a number of familial factors has been notoriously difficult. Wylie (discouragingly) stated at the end of her extensive review: "The most impressive thing which emerges from an overview of this book is that null or weak findings have been obtained many times in each of a number of areas in which theory and conventional wisdom very confidently predicted strong trends" (1979, p. 690).

One aspect of social interaction that has been considered particularly relevant to the formation of the self is early interaction with principal caregivers, that is, with attachment figures (Bowlby [1969] 1982, 1973, 1980; Sroufe, in press; Stern 1985; Sullivan 1953). This chapter explores a number of both theoretical and methodological considerations relevant when investigating the connection between attachment and the self in early childhood. The work presented in this chapter reflects previous theoretical and empirical emphasis on the child's relationship with the mother only; the self within the family context is addressed briefly at the end of this chapter.

TERMS RELATED TO THE SELF

For many years, psychologists have examined aspects of the self from a variety of perspectives. This extensive interest in the self stems from the idea that self-related beliefs and feelings play a key role in development. For instance, several theorists have emphasized the notion that the child uses what he already knows and feels (part of which are beliefs and feelings about himself) in constructing his own reality and in contributing to his own experience

The author is grateful to the following people, whose helpful comments on earlier drafts of this paper improved its quality: Mary Ainsworth, Dante Cicchetti, Phil Cowan, Mark Greenberg, and Irving Sigel.

(e.g., Bowlby 1980; Piaget 1955). Other theorists have viewed the self as important to development because of its close tie to affect. For instance, a close intertwining of self-love and love of others has been proposed: unless one loves himself, he will feel a basic hostility toward others (e.g., Horney 1950; Rogers 1951). In addition, there are both theoretical and empirical connections between low self-esteem and depression (Bibring 1953; Harter 1986).

A wide array of terms is connected with research related to the self. These concepts are often used vaguely, inconsistently, and interchangeably. Wylie (1974, 1979) has suggested that this vagueness of vocabulary reflects fragmented theoretical conceptualization, which, in turn, contributes to difficulty in operationalization. Therefore, it may be helpful to review the distinctions among several terms related to the self.

Many of these terms can be divided into one of two major groupings: one related to self-cognition, and the other related to self-affect. Terms related to self-cognition include self-concept, self-image, self-schema, and self-understanding. Terms such as these (referred to here as self-concept) suggest a descriptive reference to the self: a definition of the nature and qualities of the self, without necessarily being evaluative.[1] Aspects of one's self-concept might include the statements that one is female, a biologist, a bridge player, a moviegoer, a hard worker. These are beliefs about the self thought of as undisputable facts.

Terms related to self-affect include self-esteem, self-worth, self-evaluation, and self-feeling. These terms are used to describe the *value* a person places on himself: the extent to which he views himself as valuable, worthwhile, and meaningful. Thus, for example, self-esteem as defined here is a global judgment of the person's overall sense of worth. It is viewed as a relatively stable underlying component of personality, not subject to wide daily fluctuations. Coopersmith (1967) described self-esteem as "a personal judgment of worthiness that is expressed in the attitudes the individual holds toward himself." Harter described feelings of "general self-worth" as including those of "being happy with the way one is, feeling good about the way one acts, and thinking that one is a good person" (1982, p. 88).

"Perceived competence," a term used by Harter (1982) to describe a person's perception of his abilities in specific areas, can be viewed as a self-cognition, but as a self-cognition with close ties to self-esteem. Cooley (1902) first described the connection between competence and self-esteem by saying that self-esteem

appears to be associated chiefly with ideas of the exercise of power, of being a cause . . . The first definite thoughts that a child associates with

---

1. In both common usage (e.g., "He has a poor self-concept") and elsewhere (e.g., The Piers-Harris Children's Self-Concept Scale), the term "self-concept" is used to suggest an evaluative component. Here a distinction is made between self-concept as descriptive of the self, and self-affect as evaluative of the self.

self-feeling are probably those of his earliest endeavors to control visible objects—his limbs, his playthings, his bottle, and the like. Then he attempts to control the actions of the persons about him, and so his circle of power and self-feeling widens without interruption to the most complex of mature ambition. (Pp. 145–146)

In more recent years, the connection between competence and self-esteem has been explored by White (1963) as well as by Seligman (learned helplessness) (1975), Bandura (self-efficacy) (1977), and Harter (1982). Bowlby referred to both competence and self-esteem, and related them to a variety of theoretical viewpoints:

> Typically these [securely attached] children grow up to be secure and self-reliant, and to be trusting, cooperative, and helpful toward others. In the psychoanalytic literature such a person is said to have a strong ego; and he may be described as having "basic trust" (Erickson 1950), "mature dependence" (Fairbairn 1952) or as having "introjected a good object" (Klein 1948). In terms of attachment theory, he is described as having built up a representational model of himself as being both *able* to help himself and as *worthy* of being helped should difficulties arise. (Italics added; 1979, p. 136)

Harter (1982, 1986) has extensively described perceived competence and its connections with self-esteem. She has suggested (*a*) that perceived competence in one area can be independent from that in another area, (*b*) that there is great variation in the extent to which the child's perceived competence matches either actual competence or the perceptions of the child's competence by others, and (*c*) that there is great variation in the extent to which perceived competence in a particular area relates to self-esteem. One factor frequently considered to influence the impact that competence in a particular area has on a person's self-esteem is the importance of that particular area to that particular person (e.g., Harter 1982; James [1890] 1963; Rogers 1959). James gave an eloquent personal illustration of this point:

> I, who for the time have staked my all on being a psychologist, am mortified if others know much more psychology than I. But I am contented to wallow in the grossest ignorance of Greek. My deficiencies there give me no sense of personal humiliation at all. Had I "pretensions" to be a linguist, it would have been just the reverse. (P. 310)

In addition to the importance of an area of performance, a person's aspirations are relevant, a point central to James's ([1890] 1963) definition of self-esteem: "self-esteem=success/pretensions." Both the extent to which an area is important to the person and, more specifically, how much he expects and desires to achieve success in it, play a direct role in his evaluation of himself. Coopersmith (1967) identified both importance and aspiration ("pretensions") along with performance and defenses as important elements:

The process of self-judgment derives from a subjective judgment of success, with that appraisal weighted according to the value placed upon different areas of capacity and performance, measured against a person's personal goals and standards and filtered through his capacity to defend himself against presumed or actual occurrences of failure. (P. 242)

A person can use aspects of his self-concept in forming his self-esteem: "I am a good bridge player and a hard worker, therefore I am a good person"; "I am only a mediocre biologist and therefore a worthless person." Self-esteem can also be independent of specific aspects of the self-concept: that is, "I am a good bridge player, yet nonetheless worthless." Yet, self-esteem is, above all, a subjective perception, a perception that may or may not relate to reality. The extent to which self-esteem reflects reality is subject to great individual variation. James ([1890] 1963) stated that although "self-feeling" is usually "the good or bad actual position one holds in the world," it is not necessarily so:

. . . there is a certain average tone of self-feeling which each one of us carries about with him, and which is independent of the objective reasons we may have for satisfaction or discontent. That is, a very meanly-conditioned man may abound in unfaltering conceit, and one who's success in life is secure and who is esteemed by all may remain diffident of his powers to the end. (P. 306)

James's reference to "self-feeling" emphasizes the affective, "felt" component of self-esteem, an aspect emphasized by a number of other theorists (e.g., Cooley 1902). James discussed the difference between what a person *knows* about himself and what he *feels* about himself. A person may know objectively that he is successful, competent, and important to society but may nonetheless *feel* worthless.

Thus, the relations between cognitions and affects related to the self are complex. Many theorists have suggested a hierarchical structure, with self-concept including all self-descriptive statements, and self-esteem as the evaluative component (Epstein 1973; Harter 1983; Rosenberg 1979). Cicchetti (Cicchetti & Hesse 1983; Cicchetti & Schneider-Rosen 1984; Hesse & Cicchetti 1982) has written extensively about the importance of clear distinctions between cognitions and affects, and about the important implications (both theoretical and methodological) of the nature of their interconnections. Cicchetti proposed an interactionist view of the relation between self-affect and self-cognition. He suggested, for instance, that

it may be expected that certain self-cognitions cause specific feelings of self-esteem to arise and that these feelings will have a positive or negative polarity depending upon the content of the cognition. In a reciprocal manner, an intense or enduring affect of self-esteem may be expected to lead to congruent self-cognitions. (Cicchetti & Schneider-Rosen 1986, p. 98)

Most important, clear distinctions between cognitions and affects permit exploration of many questions which can lead to a richer understanding of the complex processes involved in both aspects of the self: What is the nature of the interaction? What is the developmental progress of this interaction? In what cases does self-cognition lead to or affect self-feeling and vice versa?

Not all concepts fall neatly into the two categories of self-cognition and self-affect; there are terms that cut across the distinction between self-cognition and self-affect. "Self-confidence," for example, is such a term. As defined here, self-confidence describes the extent to which the individual believes in his abilities to succeed, to make the appropriate decisions, and/or to act effectively. Self-confidence is considered subject to large and sudden fluctuations dependent on immediate feedback, and it is thus considered less stable than self-concept or self-esteem.

BOWLBY'S "WORKING MODELS"

A concept that also incorporates components of both self-cognition and self-affect is Bowlby's notion of "working models" ([1969] 1982) (Bowlby later referred to these as "representational models" [1980]). Bretherton (1985, in press) and Main (Main, Kaplan, & Cassidy 1985) have extensively discussed working models; they will not be discussed in detail here. Briefly, Bowlby states that the individual creates mental representations which provide him with models of the workings, properties, characteristics, and behavior of attachment figures, the self, others, the world. These models are similar to cognitive maps that permit successful navigation of an organism's environment. Unlike maps, however, working models are not static images but are flexible and adaptable representations. Thus, the concept of these models is similar to Piaget's object concept, in that both are active constructions rather than static representations.

For Bowlby, the foundations of working models are laid during the infant's first year. Bowlby relates working models to the ability to plan, and asserts that it is within the framework of these working models that the child can assess the situation and plan his behavior. Main has suggested that in addition to influencing behavior, working models can also influence feelings, attention, memory, and cognition (Main et al. 1985).

Working models become so deeply ingrained in the individual that the ways in which they influence feelings and behavior may become automatic. This situation carries with it both advantages and disadvantages. Working models can serve a useful purpose for the child, making unnecessary the construction of a new set of expectations for each new situation. For example, a baby who has a working model of his mother as available when needed may spend less time monitoring her movements than a baby unsure of his mother's availability. This use of existing models to appraise and guide behavior in new situations increases efficiency. When models become inaccurate or outdated, however, their automatic nature may be a disadvantage. Bowlby views working models as remaining to a certain extent open to new input. Nonetheless, he believes that with development working models, particularly working models that are unconscious, become increasingly resistant to change. Thus, when working models are no longer accurate, they may remain to guide an individual's behavior in repetitive and even pathological ways. (See Cicchetti 1988 for further discussion of the role of working models in psychopathology.)

The working models of the self differ from other working models only in that their object is the self. In other ways, they are similar to working models in general: they are active constructions which, because they guide behavior, perception, and feelings, can serve a useful purpose; yet their automatic and unconscious nature renders them resistant to change, and thus potentially pathological when the model becomes outdated or inaccurate.

In connection with his notion of "working models of the self," Bowlby does not make the distinction between self-cognition and self-affect that other theorists have made (e.g., Cicchetti & Schneider-Rosen 1986). For Bowlby, working models have both cognitive and affective components. In fact, Bowlby stated that "the concept of a working model of the self comprehends data at present conceived in terms of self-image, self-esteem, etc." (1979, p. 117), thereby incorporating the terms of both self-cognition (self-image) and self-affect (self-esteem). Bowlby deals with the self *in relation to attachment,* which is, of necessity, the self in an affective context. Bowlby does not deal with neutral concepts such as "I am a piano player" and "a tax-paying citizen," but rather with highly affectively charged cognitions such as "I am lovable," and "I am worthy of being helped in times of trouble." It is logically tenable that, if cognition and affect are separate, it is *possible* that a person could connect the cognition of "I am unworthy of help in times of trouble" with positive self-affect. It is undoubtedly true that some cognitions and affects are independent. However, Bowlby believes that this is not the case for affectively charged cognitions about the lovableness and worthiness of the self. For Bowlby, an apparent discrepancy between self-cognition and self-affect—for example, a person who *thinks* he is lovable but *feels* unlovable with an accompanying negative self-affect—does not reflect a discrepancy at all. Rather, the individual is operating with multiple models: in this example, with one model of being lovable and another of being unlovable. Consequently, it is this latter model of being unlovable that meshes with feelings of negative self-affect. Bowlby's notion of multiple working models will be discussed in greater detail in the final section of this chapter.

The Self and the Role of Social Interaction

The notion that the self arises from the context of social interaction has been common since the last century. Baldwin (1897) was perhaps the first psychologist to describe the importance of social interaction in the formation of the self. He saw the self and the "alter" (the other person) as two poles of one entity. Baldwin's central idea can be summarized as follows: "My sense of self grows by imitation of you, and my sense of yourself grows in terms of my sense of myself. Both ego and alter are thus essentially social; each is a socius, and each is an imitative creation" (1897, p. 7). Cooley (1902) was the next major theorist to deal with the importance of social interaction for the development of self-esteem. For Cooley, sense of self is always intimately connected with a sense of other people. Cooley introduced the concept of the "looking-glass self," which suggested that an individual's sense of self reflects his perception of what others think of him.

Mead (1934) believed that the child is born without a sense of self and that this gradually develops through experiences with parents, siblings, and others. The role of social interaction is central: "The self, as that which can be an object to itself, is essentially a social structure, and it arises in social experience . . . it is impossible to conceive of a self arising outside social experience" (p. 40). Mead introduced the idea that over time the child extends his view of others to form a "generalized other" (i.e., others in general, society at large) and comes to view the self as seen by this "generalized other." He stated, "We are more or less consciously seeing ourselves as others see us" (p. 272). Mead introduced the idea of the "generalized other." Mead believed that although the self acts differently in different settings, there is an underlying unified self. This notion is necessary if we believe in the construct of *global* self-esteem.

Sullivan (1953), although working in a psychoanalytic perspective, had an interpersonal emphasis rather than an intrapsychic one. In the social interactionist tradition of Baldwin, Cooley, and Mead, he believed that the self is learned through "reflected appraisals." Unlike Mead, however, his emphasis was on interaction with significant others rather than the generalized other. He felt that these appraisals are set in motion long before the acquisition of language, and was the first theorist to emphasize the mother-infant relationship in relation to the development of the self.

Like Sullivan, Bowlby (1969, 1973, 1980) emphasized the infant-mother (principal caregiver) relationship as central to the development of the self. For Bowlby, there is an inextricable intertwining of the working model of the attachment figure and the working model of the self. Over time, the child comes to believe that his mother will behave in certain predictable ways. Based on these experiences, the child simultaneously develops a complementary view of himself. For example, if the child is loved and valued, he comes to feel lovable, valuable, and special. If, however, the child is neglected or rejected, he comes to feel worthless and of little value. Bowlby stated that this intertwining exists despite the fact that this may not necessarily be so:

> An unwanted child is likely not only to feel unwanted by his parents but to believe that he is essentially unwantable, namely unwanted by anyone. Conversely, a much-loved child may grow up to be not only confident of

his parents' affection but confident that everyone else will find him lovable too. Though logically indefensible, these crude overgeneralizations are none the less the rule. Once adapted, moreover, and woven into the fabric of working models, they are apt henceforward never to be seriously questioned. (1973, p. 204–205)

For Bowlby, working models are strongly influenced by the child's repeated daily experiences, "in fact far more strongly determined by a child's actual experience throughout childhood than was formerly supposed" (1979, p. 117). Bowlby viewed the ultimate determinant of working models of both the attachment figure and the self as related to the question:

To what extent and in what ways has a [child] had his attachment behavior met, not only during infancy, about which information is uncertain and often entirely speculative, but throughout all the later years of childhood also? (1973, p. 207)

ISSUES IN THE MEASUREMENT OF QUALITY OF ATTACHMENT IN YOUNG CHILDREN

It is proposed here (as it is, in depth, in Main et al. 1985) that the patterns of the child's behavior on reunion with the parent reflect his working model of the relationship with that parent, and that it is for this reason that the study of reunion behavior has yielded important information about relationships. It is important to note here that what is meant by "reunion behavior" is not the specific discrete behaviors but rather the underlying organization of the *patterns* of behavior.

The study of patterns of reunion behavior following brief laboratory separations through the use of Ainsworth's Strange Situation has played a central role in the study of infant social-emotional development. The Strange Situation is a twenty-minute assessment during which the mother and a female "stranger" alternately leave and return to the baby who remains in the toy-filled laboratory room. Patterns of attachment in the Strange Situation in infancy have proven a powerful measure: they have repeatedly been shown to be stable, and have been related both to prior aspects of the infant-mother relationship as well as to a wide variety of later aspects of infant and child functioning (Ainsworth, Blehar, Waters, & Wall 1978; Belsky, Rovine, & Taylor 1984; Cassidy 1986b; Main & Weston 1981; Matas, Arend, & Sroufe 1978; Waters 1978; Waters, Wippman, & Sroufe 1979). (See Bretherton 1985 and Belsky & Isabella 1988 for comprehensive reviews of this literature.)

Of particular relevance to the investigation of self-esteem is the well-replicated finding that the patterning of Strange Situation reunion behavior is related to the qualities of parental sensitive responsiveness which, within attachment theory, theoretically predict self-esteem. This relationship has been found in at least ten different samples (Ainsworth et al. 1978; Belsky et al. 1984; Egeland & Farber 1984; Frodi, Grolnick, & Bridges 1985; Grossman, Grossman, Spangler, Suess, & Unzer 1985; Main, Tomasini, & Tolan 1979; Maslin & Bates 1983; Matas et al. 1978; Smith & Pedersen 1988; and Sroufe & Rosenberg 1982). One would expect, therefore, that reunion behavior within the Strange Situation would be related to the child's later self-esteem. Support for this expectation has, in fact, been provided by Sroufe and Egeland's longitudinal project (Sroufe 1983). Teachers rated the self-esteem of preschool children using three measures, and found that children who had been securely attached to mother in infancy had higher self-esteem than children who had been insecurely attached.

Until recently, examination of the connection between attachment and the self invariably necessitated a longitudinal study. Thus, if a connection between attachment and the self were to exist, it would be evident only if (*a*) there were long-term stability in attachment, or (*b*) there were a sensitive period in infancy whereby early quality of attachment affected later functioning irrespective of changes in attachment. Yet these issues are quite separate from the issue of a connection between attachment and the self. In order to examine the concurrent, rather than the predictive connection between attachment and self-esteem, age-appropriate measures of attachment at later ages are needed.

Few studies have examined child-parent reunion behavior in children after infancy. Marvin (1972, 1977) examined normative trends in the attachment behavior of 2-, 3-, and 4-year-olds in the Strange Situation. He found that 2-year-olds behaved in much the same manner as 1-year-olds: most cried during separation, and those who did were not comforted by the stranger and actively sought mother's proximity on reunion. The 3- and 4-year-olds, however, behaved differently from younger children: those who cried at separation could be comforted by the stranger. Most of the 3-year-olds approached the mother on reunion, whereas the 4-year-olds fell into two groups: one group separated easily and did not seek proximity on reunion; the other group greatly protested separation and engaged in manipulative, controlling behavior on reunion. Marvin used two converging assessments—a delay task, and a series of perspective-taking tasks—as the basis for an ethological-cognitive model for the attenuation of child-mother attachment behavior. Marvin's study has shown that reunion behavior continues to reflect important aspects of the nature of the relationship beyond infancy. This study also revealed that it is with the development of the child's underlying cognitive skills that the organization of attachment behaviors undergoes developmental change as well. Similarly, a study of deaf children indicated that communication skill/competence related to developmental change in the organization of attachment behaviors when measured independently of age and nonverbal IQ (Greenberg & Marvin 1979).

More recently, there is evidence to suggest that reunion behavior of children ages 5–7 reflects the quality of the child-parent attachment. Main and Cassidy (1987) have devised a procedure for scoring the behavior of children this age on reunion with the parent following a laboratory separation. The most striking evidence that patterns of reunion behavior at this age reflect quality of attachment comes from the finding that patterns of attachment in infancy predicted patterns of reunion at age 6 (Cassidy & Main 1984; Main & Cassidy 1988; Main et al. 1985). Although the specific behaviors were naturally different at the two ages, there was stability of the underlying patterns. In Main's longitudinal Berkeley sample of children seen in the Strange Situation at 12 months with mother and at 18 months with father, 84% of the children (twenty-eight of thirty-three) were placed in the same category with mother as they had been in infancy; the corresponding number with father was 60%.[2] Additional evidence comes from the findings that patterns of attachment at age 6 relate to the child's concurrent functioning in a number of theoretically predicted areas: general social-emotional functioning, responses to questions about what a child might do in situations related to separation, responses to presentation of a photograph of the child's family, and responses to a brief period of aloneness in the playroom (Cassidy & Main 1985; Kaplan 1984; Kaplan & Main 1985; Main et al. 1985). As expected, the functioning of children insecurely attached to mother in infancy was substantially below that of children who had been classified securely attached to mother. Similarly, patterns of reunion behavior at age 6 were found *not* to relate to several variables (i.e., family income, maternal and paternal education) not theoretically related to attachment (Cassidy 1986a). Finally, behavior on reunion with mother at age 6 is independent of that on reunion with father (as it is in infancy), suggesting that this behavior reflects a particular dyadic relationship rather than a trait of the child (Cassidy & Main 1984; Main et al. 1985).

The sixth-year reunion procedure is described in detail in Main and Cassidy (1988) and will be described here only briefly. The procedure is such that the child, parent, and experimenter are together in the toy-filled playroom for approximately twenty minutes. The parent then leaves the room while the child remains in the playroom with the experimenter for approximately one hour. During that time, the child may participate in a variety of assessments, but the fifteen-minute period prior to reunion is spent in free play.[3] When the parent returns to the room, reunion is not emphasized, and the parent is given no instructions for reunion. The experimenter is responsive but does not initi-

---

2. The striking stability of attachment from infancy to age 6 found in Main's Berkeley sample (Main & Cassidy 1988) has recently been replicated with the Grossmanns' German sample. Wartner (1986) found that, from infancy to age 6, 78% of the children showed the same pattern of attachment when classified into one of the three basic groups of Ainsworth's original system.

3. The validity of our system for coding reunion behavior when this procedure is altered has not been demonstrated.

ate interaction. The child's behavior during the three–five minutes following reunion is used for two forms of assessment: ratings and classifications. The security versus insecurity of attachment reflected by reunion behavior is rated on a nine-point scale devised by Main and Cassidy (1987). Ratings at the secure end of the scale are given to the child who initiates (or at least participates in) a warm, intimate relationship with the parent. This is manifested by either physical proximity and/or contact of an affectionate nature, or through eager, responsive, continuing conversation. Ratings at the insecure end of the scale are given for a variety of patterns of behavior: (*a*) avoidance of the parent; (*b*) rejecting or punitive treatment of the parent; (*c*) nervousness and expressed feelings of inadequacy; (*d*) excessively bright, subtly disorganized responses to reunion; or (*e*) caregiving and subtly parental responses to the parent.

Each child's behavior on reunion is also rated on a nine-point scale of avoidance devised by Main and Cassidy (1987). This scale, not intended to be independent from the security versus insecurity scale, deals with the intensity and persistence of the child's avoidance of physical or emotional interaction, proximity, or contact. Avoidant behaviors are defined as any behaviors that function to maintain or increase the physical or affective-emotional distance between child and parent, through a shift of attention away from the parent, or through preserving attention to other occupations, conversations, or objects. The tone of avoidance is neutral. Both affection and anger are hidden.

Reunion behavior is also classified as indicating one of four patterns of child-parent attachment: secure, insecure/avoidant, insecure/ambivalent, or insecure/controlling (Main & Cassidy 1987). Children classified as securely attached show some genuine pleasure in the parent and are either initiating or readily responsive to the parent in a relaxed manner. The relationship is personal, warm, and intimate. Children classified as insecurely attached/avoidant avoid the parent in a neutral and nonconfrontational manner. Children classified as insecurely attached/ambivalent show elements of avoidance, sadness, fear, and/or hostility, and are clearly ambivalent about proximity to the parent. Children classified as insecurely attached/controlling have taken control of the child-parent interaction. This role reversal takes one of two forms: (*a*) the child may take confrontational control of the parent and overtly reject the parent; or (*b*) the child may subtly attempt to care for or comfort the parent through overly bright greetings or attempts to helpfully orient and guide the parent. Children given the insecurely attached/controlling classification are also given an alternative classification equivalent to one of the three basic patterns of Ainsworth's original system: secure, insecure/avoidant, or insecure/ambivalent. There is also the option of classifying a child who is judged to be insecure but who does not fit into one of the other existing insecure categories as "insecurely attached/other." One child from the Berkeley sample was given this classification.

A more recent study with a separate Charlottesville sample (Cassidy

1986a, 1988) provided data that suggested stability of attachment across two sessions of the sixth-year procedure itself. Over a one-month period, 84% of the children showed the same pattern of reunion behavior when given a classification equivalent to one of the three basic groups of Ainsworth's original system, and 62% showed the same pattern when the fourth group (insecure/controlling) was included. (It was not uncommon for reunion behavior to vary across sessions in the extent of controllingness, yet to show the same *underlying* organization across sessions; in such cases, the child would be considered not stable when the controlling pattern was included and stable when it was not.) This stability across different sessions in which the immediate context may vary supports the notion that the child carries with him an underlying organization related to attachment.

This underlying organization means that, despite situational variation, a child with an avoidant organization in relation to the parent will find a way to be avoidant of her, a child with a secure organization in relation to the parent will find a way to show this security with her, etc. For example, when the mother ignores the child or talks to the stranger, a mother-avoidant 6-year-old can avoid the mother and remain preoccupied with the toys. But if the mother presses for interaction, the child, knowing the rules of social interaction, cannot remain preoccupied with the toys. In order to maintain neutrality and not call attention to the relationship, he must respond. Responses, however, are minimal, and true interest, warmth, and intimacy are lacking—as indeed they are in the relationship itself. This stability is an example of what Kagan (1971) has referred to as "heterotypic continuity." The particular behavioral manifestation varies (in this case, due to changes in the room, toys, and/or maternal behavior), but an underlying organization in the child remains. Nonetheless, this stability of pattern of behavior on reunion at age 6 across a one-month period does not *in itself* tell us much more than that, following a one-hour separation in an unfamiliar playroom, children behave to their parents in much the same way on different days. This is, however, a necessary step if we are to be able to say that patterns of reunion behavior reflect the quality of the underlying child-parent attachment.

Main and Cassidy (1988) have outlined a number of reasons why the sixth-year reunion procedure is more difficult to code than Ainsworth's strange situation. These reasons relate to both the child (the greater social skills of the 6-year-old; the acquisition of language) and the procedure (the lack of constraints on parental behavior; the use of only one reunion). For these reasons, Main and Cassidy have suggested that classifications based on reunion at age 6 be accompanied with either a second-reunion classification or with a measure tapping the child's representation of attachment (e.g., assessment of the child's family drawing [Kaplan & Main 1985]).

Although the sixth-year reunion procedure has been successful in differentiating children in a number of theoretically predicted ways, there remains much work to be done in relation to this procedure. In infancy, Ainsworth had extensive home observations to support her claim that the pattern of reunion behavior in the Strange Situation reflected the quality of attachment. Similar empirical support from home observations is essential at age 6 to further substantiate the validity of reunion patterns.

This sixth-year procedure may prove useful when examining the connection between child-parent attachment and the self for several reasons. First of all, it avoids many of the problems characteristic of many previous measures. Wylie critically stated that

> the parental or other familial measures variables were most frequently assessed by instruments of unknown reliability and validity. Often children's retrospective reports were used. Or parental interviews, which are notoriously subject to bias and distortion, were often depended upon . . . *No studies used independent observations of parental behaviors and characteristics.* (Italics added; 1979, p. 336)

It is suggested here that the child's behavior on reunion with the parent provides an observational measure of a family variable, that is, child-parent attachment. In addition, it is suggested that attachment may be a more sensitive measure of the components of the child-parent relationship likely to be related to self-esteem than many commonly used measures (e.g., parenting beliefs, punishment practices, family size, birth order, marital status of the parents, parent's reported level of regard for the child, intrafamilial tension, and the parent's own level of self-esteem). Finally, the finding in Main's Berkeley study that specific *patterns* of reunion behavior were related to consistent, coherent, and specific *patterns* of working models suggests that the six-year reunion procedure may prove particularly useful in understanding development.

Although the great majority of research investigating attachment has involved observations of infant/child reunion behavior (see also Cassidy & Marvin's [1988] system for coding reunions of 3- and 4-year-olds), the important work of devising additional attachment measures is well underway, most importantly by Waters and his colleagues (Waters & Deane 1985). These researchers devised a Q-sort set of 100 items containing a variety of behaviors theoretically linked to quality of child-parent attachment. Following naturalistic observations in any of a number of settings, observers (or parents or teachers) sort these items into a fixed distribution ranging from "most characteristic of this child" to "least characteristic of this child." A measure of attachment security is derived by comparing the child's Q-sort with a criterion sort of a securely attached child. Scores consist of Pearson correlations ranging from $+1.0$ to -1.0. This technique permits the researcher to treat normatively the ipsative Q-sort data. Advantages of the Q-sort method include the following: (*a*) a number of constructs can be scored from the same sort, and observers can be kept blind about the constructs of interest; (*b*) detailed knowledge of norms is unnecessary; (c) response biases are reduced; and (d) a distinction can be made between a behavior's significance and its frequency. Item content can be varied to be age appropriate; Waters Q-sort was originally used with a sample of children ages 3–4, and a study with infants age 1 year is currently underway. Work with this method is new, and the extent to which the behaviors described by the items in this Q-sort reflect the prior quality of the infant/child-parent relationship in the home has yet to be demonstrated. This procedure has a number of strengths; its particular advantages and limitations should be examined with reference to particular populations and particular data collection constraints.

DEVELOPMENTAL LEVEL AND MEASUREMENT OF SELF-ESTEEM

A central issue of self-esteem measurement in young children is the question of whether or not children younger than 8 think in terms of global self-esteem. It may be the case that young children can make judgments about specific abilities ("I can run faster than any other kid on the block"; "I make great popcorn") but cannot make integrated judgments of the type comprising global self-esteem (e.g., "I am a worthwhile person"). Several researchers and theorists (e.g., Bannister & Agnew 1976; Harter 1983; Peevers & Secord 1973; Shantz 1983) have suggested that young children think of themselves in concrete, specific ways and that they develop more global integrated views only later. Harter (1983, 1986), for instance, has repeatedly cited Piaget's developmental theory as strong support for the notion that young children do not perform the complex mental operations needed for global judgments of self. For instance, she said,

> It had been our conviction, derived from general developmental theory, that children would not be able to make meaningful judgements about their worth as a person until approximately the age of 8. The very concept of "personness," as a generalization about the self, is not yet firmly established among younger children. As a result, we reasoned, young children cannot make judgements of global self-worth, although they can evaluate their performance in the particular domains of their lives. (1986, p. 143)

Harter has stated that, although chidlren below the age of 8 may *possess* underlying self-esteem, they do not *conceptualize* it in terms similar to older children (Harter 1986, March 28, personal communication). Empirical support for Harter's position came from her findings that young children's responses to the global self-esteem component of her scale did not consistently load on a particular factor as they did with older children. In addition, her studies with mentally retard children whose mental ages were similar to those of young children revealed that "the self-worth subscale did not emerge as a separate factor as it did for the normal sample, nor did the self-worth items systematically or meaningfully load on any factor" (1986, p. 145).

This issue of overall developmental level has been addressed also by Damon and Hart (1982) who have attributed problems in self-esteem measurement with young children to the fact that "there is no measure of self-esteem that includes in its determination of scores a recognition that the conceptual bases of a subject's self-evaluation may be differently construed and differently weighted at different periods in the subject's development" (p. 842). The authors pointed out that it is possible that the preoperational child is unable to examine the self from as many perspectives as is necessary to produce a global sense of self-worth. A continually growing body of literature, however, suggests that the young child does indeed have perspective-taking and other skills said by Piaget not to occur until age 7 or 8 (Abrahams 1979; Flavell 1974; Flavell, Botkin, Fry, Wright, & Javis 1968; Gelman 1978; Marvin, Greenberg, & Mossler 1976; Mossler, Marvin, & Greenberg 1976; Shantz 1983).

In contrast with these theories which suggest a developmental progression in which global self-esteem does not emerge until the age of 8 is Bowlby's attachment theory. Bowlby ([1969] 1982) suggested that a global sense of one's worth develops much earlier, in conjunction with one's relationship with the attachment figure. Bowlby proposed that the infant develops a working model of the attachment figure based on his daily experiences of her availability and responsiveness; the infant then develops a complementary working model of the self as one worthy of the treatment he receives. More recently, attachment theorists have proposed that it is a working model of the attachment *relationship* that first develops:

> Together with Sroufe and Fleeson (in press) we presume instead that even a young infant will have a working model of relationships. Knowledge of self and of other will then be embedded in event-based relationships from the outset (cf. Piaget, 1954). In sum, *because a concept of "the attachment figure" apart from the event-relevant relationship between the attachment figure and the young infant does not exist, different relationships will be represented differently from the beginnings of representation.* (Main et al. 1985, p. 75)

In a similar vein, Main has proposed that from infancy onward there exist "individual differences in the mental representation *of the self in relation to attachment*" (italics added; Main et al. 1985). The model of "the self in relation to attachment" refers to such representations as the extent to which the child feels that he is participating in a relationship in which (when appropriate) he is accepted and valued, the relationship is acknowledged as relevant and important, the child feels safe and protected, and conflict or stressful situations are acknowledged and resolved successfully through the relationship.

Yet even if these representations (of the attachment relationship; of the self in relation to attachment, are present from infancy onward as attachment theorists have proposed, can these be considered equivalent to global self-esteem? What is the nature of the link between the working model of the self *within the relationship with the attachment figure,* and the working model of the self *separate from this relationship?* As Harter pointed out (1983), it is not necessarily the case that, when the relationship with the attachment figure is insecure, the child makes the assumption that there is something wrong with himself. The child's self-esteem may be high, and he may decide that his parent is treating him poorly. Main has found, through use of the Berkeley Adult Attachment Interview, that there are cases in which the adult recalls feelings of this sort: "I was abused, but I knew even then that I did not deserve it" (Main, personal communication, July 1985). Clinical experience, however, has led Bowlby to believe, in general, otherwise:

> Logically these variables are independent. In practice they are likely to be confounded. As a result, the model of the attachment figure and the model of the self are likely to develop so as to be complementary and mutually confirming. (1973, p. 204).

Thus, with young children, it may be important to explore both the model of the self within the relationship with the attachment figure as well as the model of the self separate from this relationship.

Support for the notion that young children do make global judgments comes from recent research on children's memory. Eder, Gerlach, and Perlmutter (1987) postulated that previous *research on the self* (including Harter's) led to an expectation that young children would respond to both specific and global questions about themselves (e.g., "What did you do in school today" and "What do you do at school?") with *specific* responses ("I painted pictures today"). They also postulated that, in contrast, previous *research on children's memory* led to an expectation that young children would respond to both kinds of questions about themselves with *general* responses ("I usually play"). In a study designed to examine the responses of young children to these questions, the authors found that children as young as 3½ years provided general responses to general questions and almost never provided specific responses to general questions. Thus, these children did *not* use specific information about the self to make global summations of themselves. On the other hand, although children usually provided specific responses to specific questions, they also provided general responses to specific questions approximately 25% of the time. The authors interpret the predominance of general statements/memories of the self as indicating that these young children have global, context-free conceptions of themselves.

Clearly, the issue of whether global self-esteem in early childhood exists (as attachment theory suggests), or does not (as Harter suggests), is an important one. Although Harter's data (1986) suggest an important conceptual change at age 8, a recent study with 6-year-olds revealed that the responses to Harter's global self-esteem subscale of children at this somewhat younger age were consistent (Cronbach's alpha=.74) with a theoretically predicted correlate (security of attachment, r=.40, p=.002; Cassidy 1988). It is possible that the developmental pathway follows a course that can best be understood by examination of both theoretical perspectives. The infant's earliest sense of self-worth may be in large part global, a function of his early relationships with attachment figures. During the preschool years, the child's greater cognitive, physical, and peer skills may be paralleled by a capacity to evaluate competence in each of these specific domains. And finally, in the early school years, there may be a shift in conceptualization (perhaps related to connections between domain specific and global judgments) or in articulation skills (the younger child may be unable to articulate his global feelings of self-worth). It is not, however, the intent of this portion of this chapter to integrate these two theoretical perspectives but rather to present them for the consideration of researchers. It is not clear that such an integration is possible. Yet it is also not clear that both positions cannot provide a contribution to understanding the self in young children. Continued empirical exploration and further refinement and precision of models will be necessary to fully understand the contributions of each perspective.

MEASUREMENT OF THE SELF IN YOUNG CHILDREN

The history of self-esteem measurement is filled with problems. Many of these problems are common to all research dealing with internal cognitive and affective structures. Historically, self-esteem measures have fallen into three categories: (a) self-report measures, (b) projective measures, and (c) behavioral observations. Each category of measures, with its own set of advantages and disadvantages, is discussed below.

Self-Report Measures

Self-report self-esteem measures share problems common to all self-report measures. Their usual reliance on verbal skills can be viewed as an important limitation. Because both statements and responses usually involve verbal processes, these measures can be particularly problematic when used with young children. In addition, the responses may require a level of reflectivity of which the young child is not capable. Another characteristic feature of these measures is that they overtly and directly ask about the child himself. There is no need to infer, as there is with projective measures, that when the child speaks of "a boy" he is thinking of himself. Yet there is much debate over whether this overt focus on the self is an advantage or a disadvantage (Harter 1983; Wylie 1974). Combs and Soper (1957) described several additional factors that interfere with the interpretability of self-report measures: the extent to which the individual is consciously aware of his self-perceptions, the individual's level of necessary expressive abilities, the individual's level of motivation and his desire to cooperate, and the level of social desirability in the measurement interaction combined with personal ability of the individual to admit unfavorable attributes. Wells has stated that, "as these factors become salient, the connection between self-conception and self-report becomes vague and indeterminant" (1976, p. 124).

The problem of socially desirable answers is (if possible) even more problematic in self-esteem research than it is in other areas of research. It is reasonable to assume that most people have a natural tendency to want to be seen in a positive, socially desirable light. Yet this tendency may be tied to self-esteem, and when it is self-esteem that is being measured, the difficulties multiply. A child's need to appear perfect may mask low self-esteem. For such a child, the admission of *any* imperfection may be excessively threatening. The ability to openly admit weaknesses, faults, and room for improvement may require a strong self-esteem. Chodorkoff (1954) reported that "relatively well-adjusted people" were less defensive. Thus, the interpretation of very high scores is problematic. Do they reflect truly high self-esteem, or do they reflect a self-esteem so poor and fragile that the individual cannot tolerate discovery of the slightest imperfection? (Specifically in relation to attachment, there is a growing body of literature suggestive of a connection between the avoidant pattern of attachment and a variety of forms of defensiveness. See Cassidy and Kobak 1988 for a review.)

There are three types of self-report self-esteem measures most commonly used: one type uses direct assessment of global self-esteem, one type asks questions about capabilities in a variety of areas and derives a summed score of overall self-esteem, and a third type uses any of a number of rationally derived equations that relate component parts of self-esteem.

Measures that directly assess global self-esteem use global questions such as, "Do you like yourself?" "Do you think you are a worthwhile person?" Rosenberg's (1965) ten-item self-esteem scale for adolescents and adults is a representative measure. Rosenberg described the reasoning behind his choice:

> The subject himself may be as ignorant as the investigator about how this complex synthesis of elements has been achieved, but he is in a unique position to recognize, as a matter of immediate experience, the final results. He alone can experience whether he has a generally favorable or unfavorable, positive or negative, pro or con feeling toward himself as a whole. (1979, p. 21)

Harter's (1982) global self-esteem subscale for children age 8 and older, with questions tapping feelings of being a "good" child and "doing the right thing," is also such a measure.

Another type of self-report measure asks specific questions in a variety of areas ("Do you do well in school?" "Are you good at sports?") and lumps them together to come up with a summed overall score (e.g., Coopersmith's Self-Esteem Inventory [1967]; and the Piers-Harris Children's Self-Concept Scale [1969]). Wylie (1974) has argued that claims that these summed scores represent a true global and content-free measure of self-esteem cannot be considered valid. Similarly, Rosenberg (1979) pointed out that "the assessment of [e.g.,] one's academic ability and the view of one's general self-worth are two separate attitudes whose relationship must be investigated, not assumed" (p. 21).

An additional commonly used type of self-report measure involves attempts to break down self-esteem into component parts, measure each component, and devise an equation describing the relations among the component parts (e.g., Dickstein 1977; Harter 1986). James's equation of "self-esteem = success/pretensions" is such an attempt. Equations of this sort involve complex, juggling, weighing of component parts of the equation, and appropriate identification (and weighing) of the relevant performance domains. Researchers are left with a complex array of elements to be identified, weighed, and integrated, and there is, as a result, considerable room for error. Assessment of the validity of these equations is problematic. Researchers can operationalize a theoretically based equation, but they cannot directly test whether it reflects self-esteem. Rather, researchers generally *assume* that their particular equation equals self-esteem and then use it to relate to other variables.

It is possible that even if the proper components of a self-esteem equation could be identified, and even if the proper weighting could be determined, there would be a significant portion of self-esteem unaccounted for through equations of this sort. In James's discussion ([1890] 1963) of his equation, he assumed a unilateral direction of effect: that it is the individual's perception of his success, albeit related to his desires, that yields self-esteem. According to this thinking, if a child has pretensions of being team captain and isn't, his resulting low self-esteem is attributed to the fact of his failure. It is entirely possible, however, that the reverse process is also in operation, that is, that self-esteem influences pretensions. Thus, if the child becomes captain he may raise his pretensions to being class president and may maintain his low self-esteem. No matter how successful he is, he is never satisfied, it is never enough, and he continually feels of little value. In such a case, self-esteem is not determined by the equation of success divided by pretensions, but rather the low self-esteem leads to a continual reshuffling of what constitutes success divided by pretensions. In the case of the aspiring class president, pretensions keep getting higher so that self-esteem is never high. Thus, a child with low self-esteem might think that whatever he is capable of doing must not be worth very much. Groucho Marx expressed feelings of this sort when he said, "Any club that would have me as a member, I wouldn't want to join."

Self-esteem might also determine the level of pretensions in another way. For example, a child with low self-esteem might set his pretensions at a minimal level; a child with high self-esteem, confident that he has resources to succeed and knowledgeable that he will be supported and accepted if he fails, might set his pretensions at a high level. On the other hand, there are, of course, plenty of people with low self-esteem who set their sights high, at times excessively high. It may be that they think they need to excel in order to compensate for being such a worthless person.

There are thus several reasons why an approach to self-esteem measurement through the use of equations of this sort may be subject to methodological problems: it is difficult to identify the appropriate equation, the equation may change, and there are likely to be significant elements related to self-esteem that fall outside the equation. Harter (1983) described an experience with a 10-year-old subject who had participated in a series of measures designed to tap various components of global self-esteem. In a statement acknowledging the fact that certain components of self-esteem fall outside any possible equation, the child said (helpfully), "Are you trying to find out how I feel about myself *in general?*"

It would, however, certainly be premature to imply that measures involving what Harter (1983) has referred to as "delicate equations" are without merit. Certainly they have several advantages: the component parts and their psychometric properties are relatively easy to obtain; there is no difficulty with interrater reliability; the source of the information comes directly from the subject, and he is overtly describing himself; the relationship between the components can be explicitly and precisely (i.e., mathematically) laid out. These advantages suggest that continued exploration of measures of this type is very much worthwhile. Harter (1986) has reported the widely used formula "self-esteem = ideal-self minus real-self" to be useful. Block (1985) assessed the self-esteem of adolescents by comparing real-self and ideal-self Q-sorts and found correlates with theoretically predicted constructs (see, however, Hoge & McCarthy 1983 and Wylie 1974 for critiques of that particular formula).

Projective Techniques

The advantages and disadvantages of projective measures have been discussed extensively (e.g., Sigel & Hoffman 1955) and are nearly the reverse of those related to self-report measures. Because the child is not the direct focus of the questions he is less likely to give socially desirable answers. Because he is unaware of what the researcher is interested in there is less censorship. The material received may be quite rich in quality because these measures tap unconscious material, permit a multiplicity of responses, and have no rules of right or wrong. However, there is the possibility that the child's answers do not truly refer to himself but rather to his brother, his friend, a storybook hero, etc. It is difficult to tell whether the child is fantasizing about the way he'd like to be or describing himself as he truly believes he is. Other problems may arise because of the fact that interpretations are based on external factors rather than being taken at face value. Thus, interpretation may be subjective, and adequate interrater reliability may be difficult to obtain. In addition, it may be difficult to convert interpretations into quantitative scores. Nonetheless, if these difficulties can be dealt with, these techniques can yield rich data. In any case, these are expensive assessments in terms of time spent training, administering, and scoring.

Direct Observation

A third category of measures, consisting of measures derived from direct observation, involves the notion that particular behaviors reflect particular underlying beliefs about the self. Although this assumption seems highly reasonable, unless observations are made over a considerable period, the role of situation specificity can be large. There are clearly cases in which what is being measured is self-confidence rather than self-esteem (e.g., Coopersmith 1967).

Long-term repeated systematic observations of child behavior in natural settings seem more likely to reflect true self-esteem. Waters and his associates (Waters, Noyes, Vaughn, & Ricks 1985) have developed a measure that uses such long-term observation of children as a basis. Observers watch the child repeatedly in one or more naturalistic settings and then complete the California Child Q-set (Block & Block 1969). A measure of self-esteem is derived by comparing the description of the child with this Q-sort to a Q-sort defined by Waters as indicative of the "most highly self-esteeming preschool child." Scores are Pearson correlations. This measure is helpful when a behavioral assessment is particularly desirable, or when the behavior of particularly young children is of interest. (It has been used with children as young as age 3.) Another important factor is that this measure permits investigation of the extent to which a connection exists between "self-esteeming" behavior and the child's own internal representations of his self-worth.

SPECIFIC MEASURES OF THE SELF IN YOUNG CHILDREN

There are two self-esteem measures most widely used with older children, both self-report measures: Coopersmith's Self-Esteem Inventory (1967) and the Piers-Harris Children's Self-Concept Scale (1969). Both measures are somewhat problematic. Coopersmith's Inventory (developed for adolescents) is a fifty-item self-report paper and pencil test that uses items drawn from an adult scale that fall into the domains of parents, peers, school, and global statements about the self. Coopersmith found no evidence that children differentiate across domains of competence, and scores across all domains are summed to form a single global self-esteem score. This summing is an extremely problematic practice because there is *no* evidence to suggest that an unweighted summing of responses related to specific domains, uniform across individuals, bears any resemblance to global self-esteem (Harter 1986; Rosenberg 1979; Wylie 1974). The Piers-Harris Scale is a similar eighty-item paper and pencil test. The fact that its items were drawn from questions asked to children makes it an improvement over the Coopersmith Inventory, and, in general, it is considered to be less problematic (Wylie 1974, 1979; Robinson & Shaver 1973). Neither scale, however, considers the value the child places on the particular domain considered, and neither guards against responses that excessively reflect social desirability. A third self-esteem measure, Rosenberg's scale (originally designed for use with adolescents and adults) has more recently been used with school-age children, although this use is not widespread (Rosenberg 1979).

Another self-report measure used with increasing frequency (for children age 8 and older) is Harter's Self-Perception Profile for Children (1985). This scale addresses several of the problems found in other measures. The format of the scale, with the presentation of two different types of children, was designed to reduce the possibility of socially desirable answers. In addition, the scale was designed to separately assess the child's feelings of worth in different domains important to children: the domains of scholastic competence, social acceptance, athletic competence, physical appearance, and behavioral conduct. The scale has been used on a number of samples of children, and results support the use of separate domains. Factor analyses reveal high loadings on the four relevant factors across samples, with "no systematic cross-loadings" (Harter 1982). The scale also contains a measure of global self-esteem (as separate from the specific domains). It is this subscale that can be used as a self-esteem measure.

Harter has designed two versions of her scale for younger children called the Pictorial Scales of Perceived Competence and Social Acceptance for Young Children—one for children ages 3–5, and one for children ages 6–7 (Harter & Pike 1984). During scale construction, careful attention was paid to what is particularly relevant to children of particular ages. The pictorial format minimizes the influence of the child's verbal skills. In both versions, the subscale of global self-esteem is replaced with a subscale of maternal acceptance, and a two-factor solution emerges. The first, called "general competence," is defined by the physical and cognitive subscales. The second, called "social acceptance," is defined by the mother and peer acceptance subscales. Although this scale can be used reliably to examine a variety of research questions related to self-esteem (see Harter 1983), it is not in itself a self-esteem measure. And Harter makes it clear that it was not so intended: "[We] have urged that the scale be treated as a measure of what the title indicates, perceived competence and perceived social acceptance, rather than treating it as a singular measure of 'self-concept' or 'self-esteem'" (1986, p. 143). Part of what necessitates this limitation is the fact that there is no way of assessing the relative importance to the child of the various domains, a component of self-esteem assessment Harter clearly agrees is essential. And the self-esteem subscale, useful for assessing self-esteem in older children, is not present.

Thus, at this time, there is no widely used self-esteem measure for children under ages 7–8. Coopersmith's Inventory and the Piers-Harris Scale were both designed for use with somewhat older children, and their usefulness with younger children is not known. Harter designed a version of her scale for younger children, but, as discussed above, it has no component of self-esteem. Construction of new assessments that consider the many methodological pitfalls thus appears necessary.

With our Charlottesville sample, we have developed and are currently refining an assessment measure for 5–7-year-olds of the child's perception of the way an "unspecified other" views him. This measure is an interview of a large hand puppet, a green frog named Bix. The interview questions are about the child. The voice of the puppet belongs to the child. The assumption is that the child answers questions about himself through the puppet as he imagines this "unspecified other" would answer. It is expected that this interview will reveal the way in which the child imagines that others view him. The way the child imagines that others view him is important in itself. And, if one accepts the widely held notion that the child views himself as he imagines others view him, then his answers to the interview can be interpreted as a reflection of his self-esteem. Whether or not this interpretation is valid, however, particularly with children this young, is an empirical question.

In the puppet interview procedure, the experimenter introduces Bix to the child and demonstrates how Bix works. Following a brief familiarization period, the experimenter looks directly at Bix rather than at the child and interviews Bix. Sample questions to Bix include: (3) Do you like (child) the way he is, or do you want to make him better? How? (16) Do you think (child) is important or not important? (17) Do you care what happens to (child)? The interview lasts approximately ten minutes.

The interview is coded in two ways: on a five-point scale, and by placement into one of three classificatory groups—(a) responses perfect in every way, even after repeated pressing; (b) responses globally and excessively negative; and (c) responses generally positive but with the realistic admission of room for improvement.

After pilot testing, the interview was administered to our sample of fifty-two white, middle-class 6-year-olds. Because a high correlation between the responses of different puppets on different days would strengthen the case that the puppet's responses reflect the child's view of how the "unspecified other" perceives him, the interview was administered one month later with a yellow duck puppet, Quax. Interrater reliability in both sessions exceeded .85. The interviews of 71% of the children were placed in the same classification group across sessions. Both interviews related (modestly, but significantly) to attachment as assessed in the sixth-year reunion procedure, and particular patterns of responses were related to particular patterns of attachment. The avoidant pattern was associated with "perfect" responses, the controlling pattern was associated with "negative" responses, the ambivalent pattern was associated with both "perfect" and "negative" responses, and the secure pattern (more than any other pattern) was associated with positive but open responses. Although the perfect response was more characteristic of the insecure/avoidant child than of the securely attached child, there were a substantial number of the latter whose responses were in this category. Like other self-report measures, this measure has difficulty distinguishing children who accurately perceive optimal functioning from those who are defensive. In a replication with a smaller German sample consisting of avoidant, controlling, and secure children only, a priori contrasts between securely attached and avoidant children as well as between securely attached and controlling children revealed significantly more optimal functioning for the securely attached children. *Patterns* of response, however, did not distinguish groups, although there was a trend for more securely attached children than avoidant and controlling children to fall into the open category (35% vs. 18% and 15%, respectively; see Cassidy [1986a, 1988] for additional details).

A second assessment on which we are currently working examines the self *within the relationship with the attachment figure* (in this case, the mother). The child is asked to complete a series of incomplete doll stories using a doll house and family. Each story is designed to last approximately two–three minutes. The stories explore what Main has referred to as "the mental representation of the self in relation to attachment" (Main et al. 1985). They explore the extent to which the child views himself as participating in a secure relationship with mother—one in which (when applicable) the child is accepted and valued, the relationship is acknowledged as relevant and important, the child feels safe and protected, and conflict or stressful situations are acknowledged and resolved successfully through the relationship.

Two stories deal with potentially emotionally charged mother-child interactions. In one, the child gives a present he made to his mother. In the other, the child approaches his mother and says, "I'm sorry, mom." Two stories (taken from Walsh 1956) deal with conflict within the family, principally with the mother. In one story, the child does not like what is served for dinner. In the other, the child has to do the one thing he most hates doing. The final two stories deal with conflict or a threat from outside the family. In one, the child discovers his bicycle has been stolen and sees an unfamiliar child riding it away down the street. In the other, the child is awakened by a loud noise in the middle of the night.

Stories are assessed in two ways. First, each of the six stories is rated from verbatim transcripts separately (i.e., with the rater blind to remaining stories) on a different five-point scale. These scales varied to fit the particulars of the story, but, in general, scores were given at the high end of the scale for stories in which, as described earlier, the child feels accepted and valued, the relationship is acknowledged as relevant and important, the child feels safe and protected, and conflict or stressful situations are acknowledged and resolved successfully through the relationship. Second, stories are placed into one of three classifications: secure/confident, avoidant, or hostile/negative. The doll story procedure was administered to our Charlottesville sample of fifty-two 6-year-olds. Mean interrater agreement for classification group was 86%; stability of story classification across one month for the one story that was repeated was 73%. There were significant connections between responses to the stories and attachment as assessed in the six-year reunion procedure, and particular patterns of some stories related to particular patterns of attachment. When there were connections, there were tendencies for the stories of children securely attached to their mothers to be secure/confident, for stories of children avoidant on reunion to be avoidant, and for stories of children controlling on reunion with mother to be hostile/negative. Stories of children ambivalent on reunion fell evenly across categories (see Cassidy [1986a, 1988] for additional details).

A third assessment consists of a twenty-item question interview in which the child is asked directly to talk about himself. This interview is direct in that the child (rather than a puppet) describes himself (rather than a doll protagonist). Sample questions include: (1) Can you tell me something you like about yourself? (3) What do you think is not so good about yourself? (5) Do you think you're special? (7) Is there any way you could be a better kid? (15) Is there any way you would change yourself so you'd be happier? (19) Can you tell me five words about you? (20) If I was going to tell somebody just one thing about you, what would it be? Responses to the interviews fell into four categories: (*a*) open/flexible—the child described the self in a positive way, yet was able to recognize and admit less than perfect aspects of the self; (*b*) avoidant/perfect—the child described the self as perfect, and relationships were neither acknowledged nor used as relevant descriptors of the self; (*c*) negative—the child made excessive negative and few positive statements about the self; and (*d*) body preoccupied—the child made pervasive references to his body to the extent that references to additional components of the self were excluded. This fourth category was not anticipated prior to review of the transcripts. Interrater reliability for group placement of the interview was 90%. Stability of responses has not yet been established.

Patterns of interview responses were significantly related to patterns of attachment assessed both in the same session and one month later. There was a tendency for responses of children classified securely attached to fall in

the open category, for responses of children classified insecurely attached/
avoidant to fall into the avoidant/perfect category, and for responses of
children classified insecurely attached/controlling to fall into the negative
category. The responses of children classified insecurely attached/ambivalent
fell evenly across categories; all three interviews in which there was an
emphasis on the child's body were interviews of children classified insecurely
attached/ambivalent.

The development of self-esteem assessments for young children must be
continued with great care, given the uncertainty related to the young child's
representational and cognitive capacities. There is some evidence that the doll
stories procedure, the puppet interview, and the interview of the child may be
moderately successful in assessing aspects of the self in young children. Yet
there is clearly much work to be done in relation to these assessments. It may
be helpful here to provide for other researchers a summary of some of the
major problems with existing self-esteem measures that should be carefully
considered when exploring the connection between self-esteem and attachment. These problems include the following:

1. There is confusion over whether children below age 8 can make global
judgements relevant to self-esteem.

2. Developmental level is not always sufficiently considered when designing both form and content.

3. The difficulty that young children may have with verbal expression or
with understanding abstract concepts is not always considered.

4. There is difficulty differentiating between conscious and unconscious
models of the self.

5. Scores in various domains are often combined to yield summary
scores; questions about global self-esteem are often combined with questions
about other domains.

6. The importance the child places on the domain is often overlooked.

7. Problems with social desirability are large, and the interpretation of
very high scores is difficult.

8. Behavioral measures often reflect self-confidence, persistence, and
frustration tolerance rather than the child's underlying sense of self-esteem.

ADDITIONAL ISSUES

Direction of Effects

It is important here to mention the issue the direction of effects. In studies with correlational designs, the issue of causation cannot be addressed.
Although historically many theoreticians have believed that it is the child-
parent relationship that leads to the quality of self-esteem (Bowlby promi-
nently among them), it is possible that the reverse is the case. For instance, a

child with low self-esteem may make it difficult for the parent to establish a good relationship, in which case the poor self-esteem would be causing the poor child-parent relationship. Another possibility is that both the child-parent relationship and the child's self-esteem are both mediated by other variables. For instance, a child's poor performance in sports and/or school may lead both to poor self-esteem and a poor child-parent relationship. None of these simple formulae is likely to be entirely valid. Of course, even if it is the child-parent relationship that primarily influences self-esteem, characteristics of both the child and the parent are likely to play a role in the quality of that relationship. Thus, once there is support for the existence of a connection between self-esteem and the child-parent relationship, examination of precisely what leads to this connection will be important as well.

Further Components of Self-Esteem

Wylie (1974) has proposed, and it has been proposed here, that much of the difficulty in illustrating a connection between social relationships and the self stems from methodological failings. However, Bretherton (1985) has pointed out two important reasons why the issue of the relationship between social interaction and self-esteem is a complex one, and why it may prove difficult to discover a strong relationship between the two. First, there may be two or more models of the self and of the attachment figure. For example, a child may have a large global model of the parent based on what he has been told by his parents and others (Bowlby refers to this as being based on semantic memory). Examples of this type of model might be: "My mother adores me," and "We're one big happy family which comes together on holidays for really nice times." Conflicting with this model may be a model based on concrete, specific instances of behavior and interaction that the individual experiences (Bowlby refers to this as being based on episodic memory). Examples of this type of model might be: "My mother told me to go away when I fought with my best friend and really needed her," and "Everybody fought a lot during preparations for Easter dinner last year, and we were all relieved when the holiday was over." In dysfunctional families, it is common for children to have two (or even more) such competing models. One model is dominant and readily accessible and the other less readily accessible. The less accessible model can influence feelings and behavior more or less outside of awareness. Bowlby described this as follows:

> When multiple models of a single figure are operative they are likely to differ in regard to their origin, their dominance and the extent to which the subject is aware of them. In a person suffering from emotional disturbance it is common to find that the model that has the greatest influence on his perceptions and forecasts, and therefore on his feeling and behavior is one that developed during his early years and is constructed along

fairly primitive lines, but that the person may be relatively, or completely, unaware of; while, simultaneously, there is operating within him a second, and perhaps radically incompatible, model, that developed later, that is much more sophisticated, and that the person is more nearly aware of and that he may mistakenly assume to be dominant. (1973, p. 205)

Thus, when examining connections between the child's working models of the self and of the attachment figure, the existence of multiple conflicting models of the attachment figure complicates the issue.

A second factor discussed by Bretherton (1985) is that there is usually more than one attachment figure. The role of additional attachment figures must be considered. Are they as influential? Do they influence the child in different ways? What happens when one attachment figure suggests that the child is lovable and valuable and another suggests that the child is of little value? Do these conflicted views become integrated into the formation of one representational model of the self? If so, through what process does this occur? Can secure attachment to one parent serve as a buffer (i.e., contribute to positive self-esteem) in light of an insecure attachment to the other parent? Are same-sex linkages (i.e., father-son, mother-daughter) particularly important in relation to self-esteem? Can sibling relationships play a role? Use of a family systems approach to attachment may be helpful (Marvin & Stewart, this vol.) In addition to these factors discussed by Bretherton, other variables that may contribute to self-esteem include quality of the marital relationship, the child's physical attractiveness, and support from the social network of both child and family. The impact of external events impinging upon the family must be considered. What is the role of such factors as race, socioeconomic status, and family composition? What is the role of temperament? What are the roles of the child's basic capacities and limitations (e.g., his cognitive ability, athletic skill, etc.)? Are particular aspects of self-esteem more sensitive to the child-parent relationship than are others? The extent to which these factors relate to self-esteem is an empirical question important for researchers to continue to explore.

Summary

Several theories converge to suggest a connection between social interaction, particularly interaction with principal caregivers, and the child's self-esteem. Despite this convergence, empirical support for this connection has been difficult to find. Part of this difficulty may stem from the inherent complexity of this connection, and part may stem from methodological problems with measures of both social interaction and self-esteem. Bowlby's attachment theory emphasizes the attachment component of the parent-child relationship as being of particular importance, yet there has been little work specifically assessing the connection between attachment and self-esteem.

When attachment is assessed in infancy, investigation of this connection necessitates a longitudinal study, a design that raises a host of additional questions and contingencies. More recently, assessments of attachment beyond infancy permit simultaneous investigation of the connection between attachment and self-esteem.

The developmental level of the child is important in any investigation involving a complex mental representation such as self-esteem. There remains a great deal of uncertainty about the specific representational abilities of young children. Careful attention to definitions and to the specific delineation of precisely what is being assessed (i.e., perceived competence in particular areas vs. the self within the relationship with the attachment figure vs. the self as the child imagines others view him vs. global self-esteem, etc.). These various components of the self in young children may not be integrated in the way theory predicts or as they may be in older children and adults.

This chapter has emphasized a number of theoretical and methodological issues to be considered when investigating the connection between attachment and self-esteem in young children. This connection is complex, and it may never be possible to account for a great deal of the variance. Nonetheless, given the central role of the self throughout the life span, continued attempts to understand its correlates are crucial.

REFERENCES

Abrahams, B. A. (1979). An integrative approach to the study of the development of perspective-taking abilities. Unpublished doctoral dissertation, Stanford University, Palo Alto.

Ainsworth, M. D. S.; Blehar, M. C.; Waters, E.; & Wall, S. (1978) *Patterns of attachment: A psychological study of the strange situation*. Hillsdale, N.J.: Erlbaum.

Baldwin, J. (1897). *Social and ethical interpretations in mental development*. New York: Macmillan.

Bandura, A. (1977). Self-efficacy: Toward a unifying theory of behavioral change. *Psychological Review* 84, 191–215.

Bannister, D., & Agnew, J. (1976). The child's construing of self. In J. Cole (ed.), *Nebraska Symposium on Motivation* (pp. 100–125). Lincoln: University of Nebraska.

Belsky, J., & Isabella, R. (1988). Maternal, infant, and social-contextual determinants of attachment security. In J. Belsky & T. Nezworski (eds.), *Clinical implications of attachment* (pp. 41–94). Hillsdale, N.J.: Erlbaum.

Belsky, J., Rovine, M., & Taylor, D. (1984). The origins of individual differences in infant-mother attachment: maternal and infant contributions. *Child Development* 55, 718–728.

Bibring, E. (1953). The mechanism of depression. In P. Greenacre (ed.), *Affective disorders* (pp. 13–48). New York: International Universities Press.

Block, J. (1985, October). Some relationships regarding the self emanating from the Block and Block longitudinal study. Paper presented at the SSRC Conference on Selfhood, Palo Alto.

Block, J., & Block. J. (1969) *The California Child Q-Set*. Berkeley: Institute of Human Development, University of California.

Bowlby, J. ([1969] 1982). *Attachment and loss: Vol. 1. Attachment*. New York: Basic Books.

Bowlby, J. (1973). *Attachment and loss: Vol. 2. Separation*. New York: Basic Books.

Bowlby, J. (1979). *The making and breaking of affectional bonds*. London: Tavistock.

Bowlby, J. (1980). *Attachment and loss: Vol. 3. Loss, sadness and depression*. New York: Basic Books.

Bretherton, I. (1985). Attachment theory: Retrospect and prospect. In I. Bretherton & E. Waters (eds.), *Growing points of attachment theory and research. Monographs of the Society for Research in Child Development* 50 (1–2, Serial No. 209), 3–35.

Bretherton, I. (1987). New perspectives on attachment relations: Security, communication, and internal working models. In J. Osofsky (ed.), *Handbook of infant psychology* (2 ed., pp. 1061–1100). New York: Wiley.

Cassidy, J. (1986a). Attachment and the self at age six. Unpublished doctoral dissertation, University of Virginia, Charlottesville.

Cassidy, J. (1986b). The ability to negotiate the environment: An aspect of infant competence as related to quality of attachment. *Child Development* 57, 331–337.

Cassidy, J. (1988). Child-mother attachment and the self at age six. *Child Development* 57, 331–337.

Cassidy, J., & Kobak, R. (1988). Avoidance and its relation to other defensive processes. In J. Belsky & T. Nezworski (eds.), *Clinical implications of attachment* (pp. 300–326). Hillsdale, N.J.: Erlbaum.

Cassidy, J., & Main, M. (1984, April). Quality of attachment from infancy to early childhood: Security is stable but behavior changes. Paper presented at the International Conference on Infant Studies, New York.

Cassidy, J., & Main, M. (1985). The relationship between infant-parent attachment and the ability to tolerate brief separation at six years. In R. Tyson & E. Galenson (eds.), *Frontiers of infant psychiatry* (vol. 2, pp. 132–136). New York: Basic Books.

Cassidy, J., & Marvin, R. S., with the Attachment Working Group of the John D. and Catherine T. MacArthur Network on the Transition from Infancy to Early Childhood (1988, April). A system for coding the organization of attachment behavior in 3- and 4-year-old children. Paper presented at the International Conference on Infant Studies, Washington, D.C.

Chodorkoff, B. (1954). Self-perception, perceptual defense, and adjustment. *Journal of Abnormal and Social Psychology* 49, 508–512.

Cicchetti, D. (1988). Attachment and developmental psychopathology. Unpublished manuscript, University of Rochester.

Cicchetti, D., & Hesse, P. (1983). Affect and intellect: Piaget's contributions to the study of infant emotional development. In R. Plutchik & H. Kellerman (eds.), *Emotion: Theory, research, and experience* (vol. 2, pp. 115–169). New York: Academic Press.

Cicchetti, D., & Schneider-Rosen, K. (1984). Theoretical and empirical considerations in the investigation of the relationship between affect and cognition in atypical populations of infants. In C. Izard, J. Kagan, & R. Zajonc (eds.), *Emotions, cognition, and behavior* (pp. 366–408). New York: Cambridge University Press.

Cicchetti, D., & Schneider-Rosen, K. (1986). An organizational approach to childhood depression. In M. Rutter, C. Izard, & P. Read (eds.), *Depression in young people: Developmental and clinical perspectives.* New York: Guilford.

Combs, A., & Soper, D. (1957). The self: Its derivation, terms, and research. *Journal of Individual Psychology* 13, 134–145.

Cooley, C. (1902). *Human nature and the social order.* New York: Scribner's.

Coopersmith, S. (1967). *The antecedents of self-esteem.* San Francisco: Freeman.

Damon, W., & Hart, D. (1982). The development of self-understanding from infancy through adolescence. *Child Development* 53, 841–864.

Dickstein, E. (1977). Self and self-esteem: Theoretical foundations and their implications for research. *Human Development* 20, 129–140.

Eder, R.; Gerlach, S.; & Perlmutter, M. (1987). In search of children's selves: Development of the specific and general components of the self-concept. *Child Development* 58, 1044–1050.

Egeland, B., & Farber, E. (1984). Infant-mother attachment: Factors related to its development and changes over time. *Child Development* 55, 753–771.

Epstein, S. (1973). The self-concept revisited or a theory of a theory. *American Psychologist* 28, 405–416.

Erikson, E. H. (1950). *Childhood and society.* New York: Norton.

Fairbairn, W. R. (1952). *Psychoanalytic studies of the personality.* London: Tavistock.

Flavell, J. (1974). The development of inferences about others. In T. Mischel (ed.), *Understanding other persons*. Oxford: Blackwell.

Flavell, J.; Botkin, P.,; Fry, C.; Wright, J.; & Jarvis, P. (1968). *The development of role-taking and communication skills in children*. New York: Wiley.

Frodi, A.; Grolnick, W.; & Bridges, L. (1985). Correlates of stability and change in infant-mother attachment between 12 and 20 months. *Infant Mental Health Journal* 6, 60–67.

Gelman, R. (1978). Cognitive development. *Annual Review of Psychology* 29, 297–332.

Gersten, M.; Coster, W.; Schneider-Rosen, K.; Carlson, V.; & Cicchetti, D. (1986). In M. E. Lamb, A. Brown, & B. Rogoff (eds.), *Advances in developmental psychology* (vol. 4, pp. 105–151). Hillsdale, N.J.: Erlbaum.

Greenberg, M., & Marvin, R. (1979). Attachment patterns in profoundly deaf preschool children. *Merrill-Palmer Quarterly* 25, 265–280.

Grossmann, K. E.; Grossmann, K.; Spangler, G.; Suess, G.; & Unzer, L. (1985). Maternal sensitivity in Northern Germany. In I. Bretherton & E. Waters (eds.), *Growing points of attachment theory and research. Monographs of the Society for Research in Child Development* 50 (1–2, Serial No. 209), 233–256.

Harter, S. (1982). The perceived competence scale for children. *Child Development* 53, 87–97.

Harter, S. (1983). Developmental perspectives on the self-system. In E. M. Hetherington (ed.), *Handbook of child psychology* (pp. 275–385). New York: Wiley.

Harter, S. (1985). *Manual for the self-perception profile for children*. Denver: University of Denver.

Harter, S. (1986). Processes underlying the construction, maintenance, and enhancement of the self-concept in children. In J. Suis & A. Greenwald (eds.), *Psychological perspectives on the self* (vol. 3, pp. 137–181). Hillsdale, N.J.: Erlbaum.

Harter, S., & Pike, R. (1984). The pictorial scale of perceived competence and social acceptance for young children. *Child Development* 55, 1969–1982.

Hesse, P., & Cicchetti, D. (1982). Perspectives on an integrated theory of emotional development. In D. Cicchetti & P. Hesse (eds.), *New Directions for Child Development, Emotional development* (no. 16, pp. 3–48) San Francisco: Jossey-Bass.

Hoge, D., & McCarthy, J. (1983). Issues of validity and reliability in the use of real-ideal discrepency scores to measure self-regard. *Journal of Personality and Social Psychology* 44, 1048–1055.

Horney, K. (1950). *Neurosis and human growth*. New York: Norton.

James, W. ([1890] 1963). *Psychology*. New York: Fawcett.

Kagan, J. (1971). *Chance and continuity in infancy*. New York: Wiley.

Kaplan, N. (1984). Internal representations of separation experience in six-year-olds: Related to actual experiences of separation. Unpublished master's thesis, University of California, Berkeley.

Kaplan, N., & Main, M. (1985, April) Internal representations of attachment at six years as indicated by family drawings and verbal responses to imagined separations. In M. Main, Attachment: A move to the level of representation. Symposium conducted at the biennial meeting of the Society for Research in Child Development, Toronto.

Klein, M. (1948). *Contributions to psychoanalysis 1921–1945*. London: Hogarth Press.

Lewis, M.; Feiring, C.; McGuffog, C.; & Jaskir, J. (1984). Predicting psychopathology in six-year-olds from early social relations. *Child Development* 55, 123–136.

Main, M., & Cassidy, J. (1987). Reunion-based classifications of child-parent attachment organization at six-years of age. Unpublished scoring manual, University of California, Berkeley.

Main, M., & Cassidy, J. (1988). Categories of response to reunion with the parent at age six: Predictable from infant attachment classifications and stable over a one-month period. *Developmental Psychology* 24, 415–426.

Main, M.; Kaplan, N.; & Cassidy, J. (1985). Security in infancy, childhood and adulthood: A move to the level of representation. In I. Bretherton & E. Waters (eds.), *Growing points in attachment theory and research. Monographs of the Society for Research in Child Development* 50 (1–2, Serial No. 209), 66–104.

Main, M.; Tomasini, L.; & Tolan, W. (1979). Differences among mothers of infants judged to differ in security. *Developmental Psychology* 15, 472–473.

Main, M., & Weston, D. (1981). The quality of the toddler's relationship to mother and to father: Related to conflict behavior and the readiness to establish new relationships. *Child Development* 52, 932–940.

Marvin, R. S. (1972). Attachment, exploratory and communicative behavior of two, three, and four year old children. Unpublished doctoral dissertation, University of Chicago.

Marvin, R. S. (1977). An ethological-cognitive model for the attenuation of mother-child attachment behavior. In T. Alloway, L. Krames, & P. Pliner (eds.), *Advances in the study of communication and affect: Attachment behavior* (vol. 3, pp. 25–60). New York: Plenum.

Marvin, R. S.; Greenberg, M.; & Mossler, D. (1976). The early development of conceptual perspective taking: Distinguishing among multiple perspectives. *Child Development* 47, 511–514.

Maslin, C., & Bates, J. E. (1983, April). Precursors of anxious and secure attachments: A multivariate model at age six months. Paper presented at the biennial meeting of the Society for Research in Child Development, Detroit.

Matas, L.; Arend, R.; & Sroufe, L. A. (1978). Continuity of adaptation in the second year: The relationship between quality of attachment and later competence. *Child Development* 49, 547–556.

Mead, G. (1934). *Mind, self, and society.* Chicago: University of Chicago Press.

Mossler, D.; Marvin, R. S.; & Greenberg, M. (1976). Conceptual perspective taking in 2- to 6-year-old children. *Developmental Psychology* 12, 85–86.

Peevers, B., & Secord, P. (1973). Developmental changes in attribution of descriptive concepts to persons. *Journal of Personality and Social Psychology* 27, 120–128.

Piaget, J. (1955). *The child's construction of reality.* London: Routledge & Kegan Paul.

Piers, E., & Harris, D. (1969). *The Piers-Harris Children's Self-Concept Scale.* Nashville, Tenn.: Counselor Recordings and Tests.

Robinson, J., & Shaver, P. (1973). *Measures of social psychological attitudes.* Ann Arbor, Mich.: Institute for Social Research.

Rogers, C. (1951). *Client-centered therapy.* Boston: Houghton-Mifflin.

Rogers, C. (1959). A theory of therapy, personality, and interpersonal relationships, as developed in the client-centered framework. In S. Koch (ed.), *Psychology: A study of science* (vol. 3, pp. 184–256). New York: McGraw-Hill.

Rosenberg, M. (1965). *Society and the adolescent self-image.* Princeton: Princeton University Press.

Rosenberg, M. (1979). *Conceiving the self.* New York: Basic Books.

Rutter, M., & Garmezy, N. (1983). Developmental psychopathology. In E. M. Hetherington (ed.), *Handbook of child psychology* (vol. 4). New York: Wiley.

Schneider-Rosen, K., & Cicchetti, D. (1984). The relation between affect and cognition in maltreated infants: Quality of attachment and the development of visual self-recognition. *Child Development* 55, 648–658.

Seligman, M. (1975). *Helplessness: On depression, development, and death.* San Francisco: Freeman.

Shantz, C. (1983). Social cognition. In J. Flavell & E. Markman (eds.), *Handbook of child psychology: cognitive development* (vol. 3, pp. 495–555). New York: Wiley.

Sigel, I., & Hoffman, M. (1955). The predictive potential of projective techniques. *Journal of Projective Techniques* 20, 261–264.

Smith, P., & Pederson, D. (1988). Maternal sensitivity and patterns of infant-mother attachment. *Child Development* 59, 1097–1101.

Sroufe, L. A. (1983). Individual patterns of adaptation from infancy to preschool. In M. Perlmutter (ed.), *Minnesota Symposium in Child Psychology* 16, 41–85.

Sroufe, L. A. (in press). An organizational perspective on the self. In D. Cicchetti & M. Beeghly (eds.), *Transitions from infancy to childhood: The self.* Chicago: University of Chicago Press.

Sroufe, L. A., & Rosenberg, D. (1982, April). Coherence of individual adaptation in lower class infants and toddlers. Paper presented at the International Conference on Infant Studies, Austin, Texas.

Stern, D. (1985). *The interpersonal world of the infant.* New York: Basic Books.

Sullivan, H. (1953). *The interpersonal theory of psychiatry.* New York: Norton.

Walsh, A. M. (1956). *Self-concepts of bright boys with learning difficulties.* New York: Teachers College, Columbia University.

Wartner, U. (1986). Attachment in infancy and at age six, and children's self-concept: A follow-up of a German longitudinal sample. Unpublished doctoral dissertation, University of Virginia, Charlottesville.

Waters, E. (1978). The reliability and stability of individual differences in infant-mother attachment. *Child Development* 49, 483–494.

Waters, E., & Deane, K. (1985). Defining and assessing individual differences in attachment relationships: Q-methodology and the organization of behavior in infancy and early childhood. In I. Bretherton & E. Waters (eds.), *Growing points of attachment theory and research. Monographs of the Society for Research in Child Development* 50 (1–2, Serial No. 209), 41–65.

Waters, E.; Noyes, D.; Vaughn, B.; Ricks, M. (1985). Q-sort definitions of social competence and self-esteem: Discriminant validity of related constructs in theory and data. *Developmental Psychology* 21, 508–522.

Waters, E.; Wippman, J.; & Sroufe, L. A. (1979). Attachment, positive affect, and competence in the peer group: Two studies in construct validation. *Child Development* 50, 821–829.

Wells, L. (1976). *Self-esteem: Its conceptualization and measurement.* Beverly Hills, Calif.: Sage Publications.

White, R. (1963). Ego and reality in psychoanalytic theory. *Psychological Issues.* Monograph 3. New York: International Universities Press.

Wylie, R. (1974). *The self-concept: A review of methodological considerations and measuring instruments* (rev. ed., vol. 1). Lincoln: University of Nebraska Press.

Wylie, R. (1979). *The self-concept: Theory and research on selected topics* (vol. 2). Lincoln: University of Nebraska Press.

4 · Procedures for Identifying Infants as Disorganized/Disoriented during the Ainsworth Strange Situation

Mary Main and Judith Solomon

*The ends of scientific classification are best
answered when the objects are formed into groups respecting
which a greater number of general propositions can
be made, and those propositions (being) more important,
than could be made respecting any other groups into
which the same things could be distributed.*
—John Stuart Mill 1874, pp. 466–467.

THE AINSWORTH Strange Situation is a laboratory-based observation of the infant's response to two brief separations from, and reunions with, the parent (Ainsworth, Blehar, Waters, & Wall 1978). Infant responses to this situation are customarily classified as fitting to one of three overall patterns of behavioral organization: *secure* (the infant shows signs of missing the parent upon separation, greets the parent actively upon reunion, then settles and returns to play, identified as category *B*); *insecure-avoidant* (the infant shows little or no distress at separation from the parent, and actively avoids and ignores the par-

Mary Ainsworth provided continuing encouragement and support while we were engaged in developing this expansion of her original system for classifying infant attachment organization. Bryan Cowley, Vicki Carlson, Jude Cassidy, Dante Cicchetti, Pat Crittenden, Bob Harmon, Nancy Kaplan, and Ulrike Wartner were helpful in critiquing earlier editions of this manuscript. We are grateful for the extensive and careful critiques provided by Mary Ainsworth, Carol George, Erik Hesse, and Marinus Van IJzendoorn.

We are grateful to the following researchers for permitting us to view their Strange-Situation videotapes: Leila Beckwith, UCLA School of Medicine; Wanda Bronson, Institute of Human Development, Berkeley; Vicki Carlson, Washington University, and Dante Cicchetti, University of Rochester; Mary J. O'Connor, Marian Sigman, and Nancy Brill, UCLA; Susan Spieker and Kathryn Barnard, Child Development and Mental Retardation Center, University of Washington, Seattle.

Support from the Harris Foundation of Chicago made the preparation of this paper possible. In its earlier phases, the Berkeley Social Development Project was supported by the William T. Grant Foundation, and by Bio-Medical Support grants 1-444036-32024 and 1-444036-32025. Tom Rigney undertook the drawings from videotape utilized in figure 1.

ent upon reunion, category *A*); or *insecure-ambivalent/resistant* (the infant is highly distressed by separation and seeks or signals for contact on reunion, but cannot be settled by the parent and may show strong resistance, category *C*). Infant responses to a particular parent in this situation are considered by Ainsworth and her colleagues to reflect the history of the interaction the infant has experienced with that parent in the home (Ainsworth et al. 1978), and to predict important differences in later functioning. (See Bretherton 1985 for a relatively recent review of studies related to infant Strange-Situation behavior. See the Appendix to this chapter for a more complete description of the Strange-Situation procedure, and of infant behavioral responses to the procedure leading to infant *A*, *B*, or *C* attachment classifications.)

Investigators working with middle-class parent-infant dyads have typically "forced" every infant in a given sample to a best-fitting *A*, *B*, or *C* attachment classification, despite the difficulties presented by the occasional infant whose Strange-Situation behavior does not fit well to the criteria assigned to any given classification as described by Ainsworth (Ainsworth et al. 1978). In a recent paper, however (Main & Solomon 1986), we described the Strange-Situation behavior of fifty-five infants whose response to separation and reunion had failed to meet either group *A*, *B*, or *C* classification criteria. Given that the three original *A*, *B*, *C* attachment categories had been discovered on the basis of the response variation found among only twenty-three infant-mother dyads, we expected that in a sample of unclassified infants this large, a number of different, coherent, and distinct, for example, *D*, *E*, *F*, and *G* Strange-Situation responses might be uncovered.

The central discovery we reported earlier was the absence of clear new categories of infant Strange-Situation behavior (Main & Solomon 1986). Surprisingly, infants who could not be classified within the present *A*, *B*, *C* system did not appear to us to resemble one another in coherent, organized ways. What these infants shared in common was instead bouts or sequences of behavior which seemed to lack a readily observable goal, intention, or explanation. The term we selected to describe these diverse behavior patterns was *disorganized and/or disoriented*. In some infants, behavior could be seen as disorganized only when it was considered at an abstract level, as for example with respect to the observer's expectations regarding the usual temporal patterning of infant behavior. In others, there were episodes of more obviously disorganized or disoriented behavior (e.g., approaching with head averted, stilling or freezing of movement for thirty seconds with a dazed expression). We described the behavior of these *D* infants as including one or more of the following features: *disordering of expected temporal sequences; simultaneous display of contradictory behavior patterns; incomplete or undirected movements and expressions, including stereotypies; direct indices of confusion and apprehension;* and *behavioral stilling.* Different indices of disorganization and disorientation appeared in different infants.

The primary intention of this paper is heuristic. We hope to provide a sufficiently clear description of disorganization and disorientation in infant Strange-Situation behavior that a reader can identify this behavior in other samples. Some behaviors considered as indices of disorganization and disorientation (e.g., stereotypies) are not uncommon among children suffering neurological abnormalities. Therefore, the reader may wish to know whether in medically normal samples we have evidence that such behavior could be a function of neurological or other difficulties experienced by the infant as an individual, having little to do with the relational issues which concern most research in attachment. Relatedly, the reader may wish to know whether this category could be associated with any particular experience the parent or infant may have undergone, and whether, like the traditional Strange-Situation categories, this new category of Strange-Situation behavior has distinct sequelae in later childhood.

In earlier or separate papers investigators have reported the following with respect to the *D* attachment category:

1. D *attachment status is independent across caregivers.* Of the thirty-four Strange Situations judged *D* within our Bay Area sample (Main & Weston 1981), only three involved the same infant, thirty-one of our thirty-four infants being disorganized or disoriented only in the presence of one parent. Comparable evidence for independence of *D* attachment status (previously called "unclassifiable" attachment status) across caregivers was presented in a 1982 doctoral thesis completed by Krentz (reviewed in Main & Solomon 1986).[1]

2. *The parents of* D *infants in low-risk samples have been found to differ from the parents of* A, B, *and* C *infants in that they suffer from still-unresolved attachment-related traumas.* Infant *D* attachment status was found strongly associated with the parent's lack of resolution of mourning of attachment figures lost through death in both our own Bay Area sample and in a recent sample of parents and infants studied in Charlottesville (Main 1983, 1985; Main & Hesse, this vol., and 1989; Ainsworth & Eichberg, in press). In both samples, there was some suggestion that other unresolved attachment-related traumas might also predict infant *D* attachment status.

3. *In two independent high-risk samples studied to date in the Strange Situation, the great majority of infants of maltreating parents have been judged disorganized/disoriented as compared to a minority of control infants.* Main and Hesse (this vol., and 1989) have suggested that unresolved trauma may lead to frightened and/or frightening behavior on the part of the parent.

---

1. Krentz used an "unclassified" rather than a "disorganized/disoriented" title to describe infants who could not be classified using the *A, B, C* attachment classification system. Several infants who showed extreme disorganization with their day-care caregivers in the Strange Situation were judged very secure (*B*3) with their mothers.

They reason further that, since an infant cannot easily approach a frightening or frightened parent, disorganization or disorientation of behavior may appear in the infant in stressful situations. Partial support for the disorganizing effect of frightening behavior on the part of the parent was obtained in two recent studies of maltreated infants, in which the great majority were judged disorganized/disoriented (Lyons-Ruth, Zoll, Connell, & Odom 1987; Carlson, Cicchetti, Barnett, & Braunwald 1989).

It is critical to recognize that the above findings do not indicate, however, that D infants in normal samples have been abused or maltreated in any way. Main and Hesse propose that behavior patterns which are associated with the parent's own anxiety or distress—as, for example, unintended displays of conflicting signals, displays of anxiety, or the assumption of certain bodily postures—will also be found disorganizing or disorienting to infants (Main & Hesse, this vol.).

4. *Children who were categorized* D *with a particular parent in infancy in our Bay Area sample were distinguishable from other children for their behavior five years later.* The majority of these previously disorganized children seemed controlling and parental toward their parents at 6 years of age, being either punitive or caregiving (Main & Cassidy 1988). In addition, when a child had been judged D with a particular parent in infancy, parent-child discourse for *that* dyad was judged dysfluent five years later, while discourse with the second parent reflected the original attachment classification with the second parent and hence was likely to be fluent (associated with group B infancy classifications) or fluent-restricted (associated with group A infancy classifications; Strage & Main 1985). Finally, interview transcripts showed that children who had been categorized as D with mother in infancy were fearful, or even somewhat irrational and still disorganized in discussing children's responses to separation from their parents at 6 (Kaplan 1987). These follow-up studies are, again, based upon study of a single upper-middle-class sample of intact families.

The set of findings considered above points to the probable utility of distinguishing a new, disorganized/disoriented (D) Strange-Situation response pattern. Considered together, these reports also suggest that in medically normal samples, infant D attachment status with respect to a particular parent most likely reflects some aspect of the infant's interaction with that parent rather than reflecting neurological or other difficulties.

To date, we have reviewed the (videotaped) Strange-Situation behavior of at least 200 infants whom we judged to be disorganized/disoriented. Whereas thirty-four of fifty-five D infants in our earlier report came from our stable, upper-middle-class sample, we have now reviewed almost 100 videotapes of D infants from high-risk samples. The D classification criteria that identify "not A, B, or C" infants in normal samples seem to serve equally well to identify "not A, B, or C" infants from maltreatment and high-risk families.

On the basis of this more complete review, we have developed an expanded set of thematic headings for the various typologies of disorganized/disoriented behavior patterns (see table 1, pp. 136–40).

The main purpose of the present paper is to formally present a set of indices of disorganization and disorientation in Strange-Situation behavior that will permit the identification of *D* patterning by other workers. We begin with a review of previous studies reporting difficulties in placing ("forcing") every infant in a given sample into one of the three traditional categories. We then discuss (*a*) the process by which we developed and obtained reliability for the set of classification criteria to be presented, (*b*) the classification criteria themselves, and (*c*) some theoretical issues in the modification of classification systems.

REVIEW OF PREVIOUS STUDIES REPORTING DIFFICULTIES IN STRANGE-SITUATION CLASSIFICATION

Continued use of the Ainsworth Strange Situation has gradually led to a number of reports of difficulties in assigning every infant in a given sample to an *A, B,* or *C* classification. Difficulties have been reported both for normal and for maltreatment and/or high-risk samples, by workers in several independent laboratories (esp. Crittenden 1985, 1987; Gaensbauer & Harmon 1982; Egeland & Sroufe, 1981b; Main & Weston 1981; Radke-Yarrow, Cummings, Kuczynski, & Chapman 1985; Spieker & Booth 1985). Here, we review the difficulties that led these investigators to set aside some infants as unclassifiable.

Readers not yet familiar with the Ainsworth Strange Situation should move briefly to the Appendix to this chapter which contains a review of the procedure and classification instructions. Throughout the remainder of this text we will refer to *A, B,* or *C* classifications assigned to (or "forced" upon) infants whose Strange-Situation behavior does not, in fact, fit to the *A, B, C* classification descriptors. These "forced" classifications will alternately be described as the infant's "*best-fitting*" *A, B,* or *C* classification, with the understanding that the infant's Strange-Situation behavior is actually disorganized and/or unclassifiable with respect to the traditional system.

Informal Notice of Difficult-to-Classify Infants in White, Middle-Class Samples

The first observation of "unclassifiable" infant Strange-Situation behavior was made by Sylvia Bell, who judged one of of thirty-three infants studied in conjunction with her doctoral dissertation unclassifiable with respect to the *A, B, C* classification system: however, a best-fitting *A* classification was ultimately assigned to this infant (Ainsworth 1989, March, personal communication; see also Ainsworth et al. 1978, p. 63; Bell 1970). Similarly, in conjunction with her 1973 doctoral thesis, Main (unpublished data) described the Strange-Situation behavior of five out of forty-nine (10.2%) of the infants in her sample as difficult to classify. These were each ultimately assigned (forced) to a best-fitting *A, B,* or *C* attachment classification, but most were informally termed *A-C* infants within the laboratory. For four out of five of these infants, informal home observations suggested unusual degrees of difficulty in the mother-infant relationship.

The first published reference to classification difficulty was made by Sroufe and Waters (1977), who found that 10% of their white, middle-class Minnesota sample (seven out of seventy infants) could not readily be fitted to one of Ainsworth's three categories. Similarly, in her study of the stability of infant-mother attachment classifications over a two-week period, Ainsworth reported that *A, B, C* classifications were very difficult to make on the basis of the second procedure (Ainsworth et al. 1978). Infants judged to fit to the *A* classification instructions in the first Strange Situation were difficult to classify in the second procedure, but were ultimately assigned to a "forced" or best-fitting *B* classification. The difficulty was partially attributable to intensified distress, which was shown in increased crying and proximity seeking.

Direct Identification of Difficult-to-Classify Infants within White, Middle-Class Samples

It was not until the early 1980s that investigators began to publish the results of studies in which some infants were formally left unclassified. Working with families studied in Bielefeld, West Germany, Grossmann, Grossmann, Huber, and Wartner (1981) used *A, B, C* and a fourth "not to classify (n.t.c.)" category in reporting the results of their Strange Situation analyses—the n.t.c. category having been used by the first author (MM) in her analysis of this sample in 1977. In the same year, Main and Weston (1981) published a study intended in part "to identify characteristics of infants judged unclassifiable within the Ainsworth system." One hundred and fifty-two Strange Situations (infant and mother, or infant and father) were reviewed. Of these, nineteen (12.5%) were judged unclassifiable using the Ainsworth criteria. Justifications for placement in the unclassifiable category included "behaves to parent in reunion as a secure infant but behaves identically to the stranger," and "extreme avoidance is combined with extreme distress throughout the situation." Judges felt strongly that these infants were insecure even on the basis of observation of their Strange-Situation behavior: in addition, in a separate parent-infant-Stranger Situation (the "clown session"; Main & Weston 1981), several exhibited strong *conflict* behavior (quite possibly, behavior which would be termed *disorganized/disoriented*). Nonetheless, thirteen out of nineteen would have been identified as secure (group *B*) with the parent had standardized classification procedures been utilized.

Difficulties in the Classification of Infants in High-Risk and Maltreatment Samples

In the first report of classification difficulties in a high-risk/maltreatment sample, Egeland and Sroufe (1981a) reported a striking dissonance between infant-mother histories and infant Strange-Situation classification. Infants in their large Minnesota poverty sample were seen in the Strange Situation at 12 and again at 18 months with a subsample of mothers identified as neglecting, abusing, or both neglecting and abusing. At 12 months, eight out of twenty-four neglected infants (33%) were classified as secure with mother in the Strange Situation, while at 18 months 47% were classified secure. At 12 months, two of the four abused infants were classified secure with mother in the Strange Situation; at 18 months, all four abused infants were classified secure.

Given the supposition that the "secure" pattern of response to the Strange Situation is dependent upon a history of sensitive, responsive interactions with the parent, findings such as these raised serious questions regarding the traditional classificatory system. If abused and neglected infants respond exactly as do secure infants to the Ainsworth Strange Situation, then the procedure would have to be considered severely limited in its ability to represent an infant's interactional history. On the other hand, it could be that closer examination of the Strange-Situation behavior of these infants would reveal important differences, and, with this reasoning in mind, Egeland and Sroufe reexamined Strange-Situation behavior within their maltreatment sample (Egeland & Sroufe 1981b). Their inquiry resulted in informal recognition of a new, *D* pattern of insecurity. The *D* category was composed of infants "considered anxiously attached but neither avoidant nor resistant (for example, apathetic or disorganized)." Many of the abused and neglected infants were found to fit.

Gaensbauer and Harmon (1982) also studied abused and neglected infants using a separation-and-reunion procedure involving a single separation. They did not attempt to alter the present classification system, but did examine the behavior of some of their abused infants in detail. This examination led to emphasis upon the contrast between behavior seen *immediately* upon reunion, for example, strong proximity seeking, and behavior that followed, for example, "depression and withdrawal." They describe one 12-month-old infant as showing separation and reunion behavior (to a foster mother) "consistent with secure attachment. At the same time, he exhibited clear evidence of depression and withdrawal intermittently throughout the session, most notably in the minutes immediately following the reunion." Other maltreated, "secure" infants were also observed to "demonstrate affective behavior during other portions of the session indicative of possible developmental disturbance."

Like Egeland and Sroufe (1981a, 1981b), Crittenden had found a substantial number of abused and neglected children assigned to the *B* (secure) Ainsworth attachment classification (1987, see also 1985; Crittenden & Ainsworth, in press). Following a particularly thorough reexamination of her videotapes (described below), Crittenden ultimately developed a new *A–C* category for use with her second maltreatment sample.

The maltreated children who had been placed in the *B* (secure) category in Crittenden's first sample showed several distinct characteristics. They often sought proximity obliquely, or accompanied by moderately strong avoidance, or without the expected accompanying positive affect. Their resistance often took the form of whiny petulance accompanied by noncontextual aggression, for example, aggression directed at aspects of the inanimate environment. Many displayed "clinical indicators of stress, such as face covering, head cocking, huddling on the floor and rocking, and wetting."

In order to see as many offspring of abusing and neglecting families as possible in the succeeding study, Crittenden (1987, see also 1985) used the Strange Situation with children from 11 to 48 months of age. The Ainsworth systems were modified so that verbal contact and smiling were included as greetings, while leaning on, holding onto, or touching the mother without actually clambering up were considered indicative of a full approach and maintenance of physical contact. The interactive scoring systems were further modified so that indirect approaches were scored on both the proximity-seeking and proximity-avoiding scoring systems, while crankiness and noncontextual aggression were considered additional indices of contact-resistance. A new classification, *avoidant-ambivalent* (*A-C*), was then identified "as consisting of extremely anxious infants whose scores on Ainsworth's scales combined (1) moderate to high proximity-seeking, (2) moderate to high avoidance, and (3) moderate to high resistance. In addition, these infants often displayed unusual, stress-related maladaptive behaviors." In this second study, Crittenden found that the new *A/C* classification was associated with the older and more severely maltreated children, particularly those who had been both abused and neglected.

In another study of a sample at high risk for maltreatment, Spieker and Booth (1985) identified 18% of infants as unclassifiable within the traditional Ainsworth system. Fourteen percent of the sample were termed *A-C* infants, defined as infants who showed strong avoidance and resistance within the same reunion episode. These infants "were extremely distressed at separation and would be waiting at the door for mother's return. But when mother entered the playroom, these infants would turn and walk away from her and avert their attention, while remaining extremely distressed. If the mothers made contact, the infants would be resistant. They sometimes seemed depressed, fearful or helpless." Another 4% of infants exhibited behavior that disqualified them from inclusion in the *A, B, C,* or *A-C* categories. These infants were termed "unclassifiable" but were judged insecurely attached.

Mothers of *A-C* infants in the Spieker and Booth sample reported more depression, more chronic life difficulties, and more physically uncomfortable symptoms in pregnancy than other mothers. These workers suggested that the *A-C* pattern is distinct from other insecure patterns and may reflect greater insecurity and more inadequate rearing environments.

In a study of attachment patterns in families with depression, *A-C* children were identified largely through their exhibition of moderate to high avoidance and moderate to high resistance during reunion (Radke-Yarrow et al. 1985). In addition, most of the children also displayed one or more of the following: "affectless or sad with signs of depression," "odd or atypical body posture or movement," and "moderate to high proximity seeking." The investigators felt their *A-C* category was "similar, although not identical" to Crittenden's *A-C* classification and Main and Weston's "unclassified" category. Insecure attachments were common among children of mothers with a major depressive disorder. The *A-C* attachments were associated with histories of the most severe depression in the mother.

Summary

A number of investigators have reported difficulties in applying the *A, B, C* classification system to every infant in a given sample. Partitioning out unclassifiable children has proven particularly necessary in maltreatment and high-risk samples, in which application of the *A, B, C* system often leads to describing the Strange-Situation behavior of the maltreated infant as secure. Several investigators have offered descriptions of the Strange-Situation behavior of infants who fail to fit one of the traditional categories, but different criterion behaviors and behavior constellations have been highlighted for different samples, and descriptions have been offered at different levels of formality.

Main and Weston (1981) noted the existence of "unclassifiable" infants in a stable, middle-class sample, but did not provide directions for the identification of new cases by succeeding workers. The term *A-C* was used by several investigators working with high-risk samples to emphasize the occurrence of both avoidance and resistance in combinations that rendered an infant unclassifiable. The *A-C* category has been described differently across investigators, however, and is based upon differing combinations of (sometimes previously adjusted) interactive scores in different laboratories. Finally, Egeland and Sroufe (1981a, 1981b) developed not an *A-C* but rather a *D* unclassifiable category for their own maltreatment sample, precisely in order to describe insecure, unclassifiable infants who did *not* show substantial avoidance and resistance.

The studies reviewed lead to four principal conclusions:

1. Infants who cannot be classified within the traditional *A, B, C* classification system are found in both high-risk and in low-risk samples.

2. Although many of these infants are judged secure (*B*) when forced to the best-fitting traditional classification, observations of their Strange-Situation behavior, their behavior in separate laboratory sessions, or knowledge of their parenting history have led investigators to conclude that they are insecurely attached to the parent with whom they are seen in the Strange Situation.

3. Misidentification of unclassifiable infants as "secure" by continued application of "forced" or best-fitting *A, B, C* classification criteria to every infant in a sample is therefore likely to diminish overall coherency of results even within low-risk populations.

4. We are in need of a unifying set of procedures for the description and designation to one or several new categories of infants who do not fit the present system. These procedures should be based upon a broad selection of infants, that is, a group that includes infants from both middle-class and poverty families, and infants from high-risk and from maltreatment samples.

Steps Taken in the Development of the Disorganized/Disoriented Strange-Situation Category

1. We noted that the Strange-Situation behavior of some infants previously termed unclassifiable could also be described as failing to represent coherent attachment-related "strategies" for dealing with this mildly stressful situation (Main & Hesse, this vol.; Main & Solomon 1986). While to some extent our earlier "unclassifiable" category (Main & Weston 1981) simply reflected a given infant's failure to meet the *A, B, C* classification criteria (Ainsworth et al. 1978), infant "unclassifiable" attachment status can also be conceptualized at a more abstract level—that is, as reflecting inconsistencies in what we have elsewhere termed "attachment strategies" (Main & Hesse, this vol.; Main & Solomon 1986).

In general, the attachment behavioral system is understood as being organized to increase infant-caregiver proximity in situations of threat or alarm, but to permit the activation of exploratory behavior when the situation is not threatening and caregiver proximity is assured (Bowlby [1969] 1982). A relatively smooth alternation between exploratory behavior and attachment behavior is observed in the Strange-Situation response of secure infants, who explore the environment so long as proximity to the parent is assured; turn their attention to attachment when proximity is threatened; and following a display of attachment behavior directly upon reunion with the parent, return once more to exploration.

We have described the *A* and *C* infant attachment organizations as attachment-related "strategies" for obtaining whatever proximity to the caregiver is possible, in the face of a history of limited rejection of attachment behavior (category *A*) or unpredictable caregiver responsiveness (category *C*). The infant of the relatively rejecting mother may then be seen as adopting a strategy of *minimizing* the display of attachment behavior relative to the actual level of activation of the attachment behavioral system (pattern *A*), while a *maximization* strategy may conceivably be adopted instead when the caregiver is insensitive, nonrejecting, and unpredictable (Main, in press; Main & Hesse, this vol.).

Given this understanding of the *A, B,* and *C* attachment patterns, the Ainsworth classification instructions seem to describe the behavior expected for an infant who is using one of these three central strategies in responding to parental leave-taking and return within an unfamiliar environment. With Ainsworth's classification instructions viewed in terms of infant attachment strategies, we can see why Main and Weston (1981) had earlier judged "unclassifiable":

a) otherwise classifiable "group *A*" infants who, though avoidant on reunions, were greatly distressed by each separation from the parent, and thus seemed unable to maintain a "strategy" of minimizing the exhibition of attachment behavior by diverting attention from attachment-related events;

b) otherwise classifiable "group *B*" infants who followed strong, full proximity seeking on reunion by turning sharply away and standing motionless in the center of the room with a dazed expression, thus failing to fulfill the general description of the secure infant as being occupied either with regaining the caregiver or with exploration and play;

c) otherwise classifiable "group *C*" infants[2] who failed to cry upon separation or interrupted strong distress with sudden strong avoidance, thus violating the expectancy of consistently heightened focus upon the attachment figure and consistently heightened displays of attachment behavior.

2. We decided to review the thirty-six "unclassifiable" infants to determine the specifics of their Strange-Situation behavior. What could serve as a behavioral basis for developing new classifications? One possibility was to identify unusual combinations of scores already assigned to the infants, for example, proximity seeking, proximity avoiding, contact maintaining, and contact resisting (Ainsworth et al. 1978). One or several new classifications could then have been developed by setting aside infants whose score profiles were inconsonant with the expected *A, B,* and *C* patterning.

This approach seemed inadequate because most of the behaviors that had led to "unclassifiable" infant attachment status—for example, hand-to-mouth

2. The Strange-Situation behavior of infants in the insecure-ambivalent group seems less well organized to most observers than that of either secure or insecure-avoidant infants. Within the Bay Area sample, however, a high proportion of infants for whom the best-fitting traditional classification was *C* were in fact ultimately judged *D*/unclassifiable (as see Main & Hesse, this volume, and 1989).

gestures at the moment of reunion—were not contributors to any of the preexisting scoring systems established by Ainsworth (Ainsworth et al. 1978). The new system could only be developed, therefore, by renewed study of the Strange-Situation videotapes themselves.

3. *We discovered that almost all (thirty-four of thirty-six) of the "unclassifiable" Bay Area infants showed what we at first could only identify as inexplicable, "odd," or conflicted patterns of behavior during the Strange Situation: the particular behaviors exhibited differed across infants.* As noted earlier, we originally expected that a thorough examination of the Strange-Situation behavior of unclassified infants might yield a set of several new organizations of infant Strange-Situation behavior, for example, *D, E, F,* and *G* attachment classifications. However, while two infants had been set aside as "unclassifiable" because it was not clear that they were attached to the parent with whom they were seen in the Strange Situation (the father), no two of the remaining thirty-four infants behaved similarly enough to warrant the creation of new categories. Rather, these infants showed a diverse set of behavior patterns. The very lack of organization implicit in the diverse behavioral characters observed mitigated against the conclusion that we had discovered new "patterns of organization" (see Ainsworth et al. 1978; Sroufe & Waters 1977). Indeed, the array of behaviors observed seemed to be identified as things of a kind chiefly by using an exclusion criterion: at the moment of the (diverse) behavioral displays we marked as conflicted, odd, or inexplicable, what the unclassified infants shared in common was that they were *without* an obvious strategy for dealing with surrounding circumstances, and/or that they were *not* oriented or *not* organized.

4. *We searched for a single thematic heading which, while adequately describing the behaviors observed, would remain general enough to permit recognition of new instances by other workers.* No term was considered completely satisfactory—however, "disorganized and/or disoriented" was selected with the proviso (*a*) that it describes behavior only and (*b*) that it is not equivalent to the extreme mental states sometimes defined as such in adult psychiatry.

The common theme in the diverse list of "inexplicable, odd, or conflicted" behavior patterns shown by unclassified infants was the lack of a readily observable goal, purpose, or explanation. Selecting a final descriptive heading for the diverse array of behaviors observed was difficult. While many of the behaviors observed could be interpreted as evidencing conflicting behavioral tendencies, in fact a broad range of infant Strange-Situation behaviors—particularly those exhibited by insecure infants—can be seen as the outcomes of conflict. Diverting attention to a toy at the moment of reunion with the parent can, for example, be seen as an example of what ethologists term *displacement* behavior, while repeatedly clinging to the parent and then pushing away may be seen as *alternation* (see Hinde 1970). Therefore, "conflict behavior" seemed too broad a heading to distinguish the Strange-Situation behavior of unclassifiable infants from the behavior of other infants for whom the return of the parent also aroused conflicting tendencies.

The most striking theme running through the list of recorded behaviors was that of *disorganization* or, very briefly, an observed contradiction in movement pattern, corresponding to an inferred contradiction in intention or plan. The term *disorientation* was also needed, because, for example, immobilized behavior accompanied by a dazed expression is not so much disorganized as seemingly signaling a lack of orientation to the immediate environment. While a review of the actual behaviors observed (table 1) shows that our category title is still not fully satisfactory (see esp. the discussion of apprehensive movements, pp. 136–40), "disorganized/disoriented" still seems an acceptable descriptive heading.

Note again that the terms are applied *only to specific aspects of the infant's behavior.* The terms *disorganized* and *disoriented* have been used within the discipline of psychiatry to describe severe adult mental states. Our use of the term is descriptive of infant movement patterns.

5. *We reviewed these thirty-four Strange-Situation videotapes again and constructed a descriptive narrative record of the behavior patterns which had seemed disorganized and/or disoriented.* We described the behavior in detail, together with the context and time of occurrence.

6. *We studied the narrative descriptions of the disorganized/disoriented behaviors seen in these infants with the aim of developing a set of more abstract or thematic headings under which the particular behaviors could be organized.* Necessarily, no exhaustive list of disorganized or disoriented behavior patterns can be provided. Study of the behaviors exhibited, however, permits us to identify higher-order themes under which we can organize examples. The final list of thematically oriented indices of disorganization and disorientation in behavior is presented in table 1.

7. *We used our list of thematic headings and behavior examples in conjunction with a review of sixty* classifiable *(A, B, C) infants from the same Bay Area sample. Our aim was to determine whether these classifiable infants had in fact shown the same array and intensity of D behaviors as unclassifiable infants during the Strange Situation.* Although we had already established that thirty-four of thirty-six infants who had originally been left unclassified showed disorganized/disoriented behavior patterns, the possibility remained open that similar patterns had also been shown by infants earlier determined to be classifiable. Reviewing our videotapes of *A, B,* and *C* infants to determine whether they too showed substantial indices of disorganization and/or disorientation was, therefore, an important step in the development of the category. Our review showed that seven of the sixty infants did come close to *D* attach-

ment status using these identifiers (Main & Solomon 1986), but none matched the unclassifiable infants in intensity or timing. Therefore, these indices appeared to distinguish a special category of infant behavior.

Following our review,[3] we continued to consider only previously "unclassifiable" infants as D (disorganized/disoriented). Of the thirty-four out of 268 dyads who were ultimately judged disorganized/disoriented with a particular parent (12.7% of the sample), the majority (twenty-one, or 62%) were judged "secure" in terms of traditional classifications, eight (23%) were judged "insecure-ambivalent/resistant" in terms of traditional classifications, and five (15%) were alternately "insecure-avoidant." Infants exhibiting strong avoidance and resistance in the same reunion episode (Spieker & Booth's A-C infants, 1985) were virtually nonexistent in the original Bay Area sample (Main & Weston 1981).

8. We established interjudge agreement with new coders working in our laboratory, and with coders in other laboratories working with high-risk/ maltreatment samples. Using videotapes taken from a new middle-class sample, we established interjudge agreement on D/non-D attachment status with new judges in our own laboratory (77%–80% agreement). However, while the D system had been developed on our stable, upper-middle-class sample, it would now need to be applied to a broad range of samples—specifically, to samples of the type in which A-C and depressed/apathetic Strange-Situation responses had previously been reported. The first author (MM) established 83% "D/non-D" agreement with a coder in one high-risk/maltreatment sample (Lyons-Ruth et al. 1987), and 94% agreement with a coder working with another high-risk/maltreatment sample (Carlson et al., 1989). Within-laboratory agreement across all four Strange-Situation (ABCD) categories in Carlson's study was 88% (forty-three cases).

9. In order to broaden our understanding of disorganized/disoriented behavior, and in order to further clarify our classification criteria, we continued to study Strange-Situation videotapes loaned to us by investigators working with poverty, high-risk, and/or maltreatment samples. As noted earlier, this paper is based upon study of 200 Strange-Situation videotapes of D infants. The group now includes approximately 100 infants from high-risk and/or maltreating families.

INDICES OF DISORGANIZATION AND DISORIENTATION

Table 1 represents an attempt to order examples of the various types of disorganization and disorientation in behavior seen in the Strange Situation

---

3. Our review of these sixty classifiable (A, B, C) videotapes took place in 1985, before any efforts toward assigning D-scale values had been devised. While there is no doubt regarding the greater intensity and frequency of D behaviors in the thirty-four unclassifiable tapes, it is pos-

under seven thematic headings: (1) sequential display of contradictory behavior patterns; (2) simultaneous display of contradictory behavior patterns;
(3) undirected, misdirected, incomplete, and interrupted movements and expressions; (4) stereotypies, asymmetrical movements, mistimed movements,
and anomalous postures; (5) freezing, stilling, and slowed movements and expressions; (6) direct indices of apprehension regarding the parent; and (7) direct indices of disorganization or disorientation. The headings are selected for
heuristic purposes and are not mutually exclusive. Some patterns could be
placed equally well under several headings, for example, a fearful smile
directed to the parent at entrance could be described either as an instance of
"simultaneous exhibition of contradictory behavior patterns" or as a "direct
index of apprehension."

Sequential Display of Contradictory Behavior Patterns

One of the most striking types of disorganized/disoriented behavior
occurs in the form of quick displays of contradictory behavior patterns, such
as strong displays of attachment behavior succeeded almost immediately by
avoidance. Avoidance, an "organized shift of attention" away from the parent
(Main & Weston 1982), is a relatively frequent response to separation. With
respect to the Strange Situation, avoidance *followed by* proximity seeking,
either in response to assurance that the parent intends to remain with the infant
in a given reunion or in response to a second separation and reunion, is seen
as a natural sequencing of events and is associated with a mildly avoidant
"secure" subcategory of Strange-Situation behavior (subcategory *B*2; see
Ainsworth et al. 1978). In these contexts, avoidance can be understood as
"reserve." Such reserve may be seen as having "melted" with time over the
course of a single reunion episode, or as "breaking down" across two reunion
episodes in response to a second leave-taking. To most observers, there is
nothing inherently disorganized in this sequencing, despite the shifts which
occur in behavior.

Consider now in contrast the temporal organization of behaviors described as *disorganized* in table 1. In an earlier paper, we described these unexpected shifts as a "disordering of expected temporal sequences" (Main &
Solomon 1986).[4] Rather than avoiding the parent upon reunion for a few seconds, and then gradually initiating interaction or contact, some infants give
the parent a full greeting with raised arms and active bids for contact, then
suddenly succeed this search for contact with avoidance. Others show high

---

sible that a current review of these tapes would now lead to an estimate of a somewhat higher
overall proportion of *D* classifications within our sample.

4. Originally, we described patterns similar to these as exemplifying a "disordering of expected temporal sequences." We are grateful to Bryan Cowley for suggesting "sequential display
of contradictory behavior patterns" as a heading referencing a more inclusive array of examples.

TABLE 1.   INDICES OF DISORGANIZATION AND DISORIENTATION
(For Infants 12–18 Months Observed with Parent Present)

---

1.   Sequential Display of Contradictory Behavior Patterns

Very strong displays of attachment behavior or angry behavior suddenly followed by avoidance, freezing, or dazed behavior. For example:

— In the middle of a display of anger and distress, the infant suddenly becomes markedly devoid of affect and moves away from the parent.

— *Immediately following strong proximity seeking and a bright, full greeting with raised arms, the infant moves to the wall or into the center of room and stills or freezes with a "dazed" expression.*

— *Infant cries and calls for the parent at the door throughout separation: immediately upon reunion, however, the infant turns about and moves sharply away from the parent, showing strong avoidance.*

Calm, contented play suddenly succeeded by distressed, angry behavior. For example:

— *Infant calm and undistressed during both separations from the parent, but becomes extremely focused upon the parent, showing highly distressed and/or angry behavior immediately upon reunion.*

---

2.   Simultaneous Display of Contradictory Behavior Patterns

The infant displays avoidant behavior simultaneously with proximity seeking, contact maintaining, or contact resisting. For example:

— While held by or holding onto parent, infant shows avoidance of parent such as the following: (*a*) infant sits comfortably on parent's lap for extended period but with averted gaze, ignoring parent's repeated overtures; (*b*) infant holds arms and legs away from the parent while held, limbs stiff, tense, and straight; (*c*) infant clings hard to parent for substantial period while *sharply* averting head/gaze. (Note: Disorganized only if infant is clinging hard while sharply arching away. Many infants look away or turn heads away while holding on lightly after a pick-up.)

— Infant approaches while simultaneously creating a pathway which avoids and moves away from parent, and this cannot be explained by a shift of attention to toys or other matters. Thus, from its inception the infant's "approach" seems designed to form a parabolic pathway.

— *Movements of approach are repeatedly accompanied by movements of avoidance such as the following:* (b) *infant approaches with head sharply averted,* (b) *infant approaches by backing toward parent,* (c) *infant reaches arms up for parent with head sharply averted or with head down.*

— *Distress, clinging, or resistance is accompanied by marked avoidance for substantial periods, such as the following:* (a) *infant moves into corner or behind item of furniture while angrily, openly refusing or resisting parent;* (b) *infant cries angrily from distance, while turning in circles and turning away from parent.* (Note: Arching backward with flailing arms, and throwing self backward on floor are part of normal infant tantrum displays and are not necessarily considered disorganized.)

— *Extensive avoidance of parent is accompanied by substantial distress/anger indices, such as: infant silently averts head and body away from parent who is offering or attempting pick-up but makes stiff, angry kicking movements and hits hands on floor.*

Simultaneous display of other opposing behavioral propensities. For example:

— Infant's smile to parent has fear elements (*very strong index* if marked, see no. 6).

— *While in apparent good mood, infant strikes, pushes, or pulls against the parent's face or*

TABLE 1. (*continued*)

eyes. (These usually subtle aggressive movements are sometimes immediately preceded by a somewhat dazed expression, or may be accompanied by an impassive expression.)

3. Undirected, Misdirected, Incomplete, and Interrupted Movements and Expressions

Seemingly undirected or misdirected movements and expressions. For example:

—Upon becoming distressed, infant moves away from rather than to parent. (Note: Do not consider brief moves away from parent disorganized when an infant has been crying and displaying desire for contact for a long period, and parent has failed to satisfy infant. Infant may briefly move away while crying in response to frustration in these circumstances, coming back to parent to try again, without being disorganized.)

—Infant approaches parent at door as though to greet parent, then attempts instead to follow stranger out of the room, perhaps actively pulling away from the parent. (This pattern seems more misdirected or redirected than undirected; see no. 7 for similar behavior.)

—Initiation of extensive crying in parent's presence without any move toward or look toward the parent. (Note: This is not necessarily disorganized if parent is already nearby and attentive. It also is not disorganized if the infant, having already been crying and focused on the parent for an extended period, simply does not look at or move closer to the parent for a few seconds.)

—Any marked failure to move toward the parent when path is not blocked and infant is clearly frightened.

—Similarly, expression of strong fear or distress regarding an object while staring at it, without withdrawing from it or looking toward parent.

—*Extensive or intense expressions of fear or distress accompanied or followed by moves away from rather than to parent, as, infant appears frightened of stranger in parent's presence, moves away and leans forehead on wall.*

—*Infant cries at stranger's leave-taking, attempts to follow her out of room. (This behavior pattern may be more misdirected or redirected than undirected; see also no. 7.)*

Incomplete movements. For example:

—Movements to approach parent are contradicted before they are completed, for example, infant moves hand toward parent and withdraws hand quickly before touching parent, without rationale. Or repeated, hesitant, stop-start approach movements (or reach movements) toward parent.

—Exceptionally slow or limp movements of approach to parent, as though the infant is resisting the movements even while making them ("underwater" approach movements).

—*Exceptionally slow, limp, movements of striking at, pushing at, or pulling at the parent's face, eyes, or neck ("underwater" movements). The subtle but definite aggressive intent is almost indiscernible because of the incomplete, slow nature of the movements. See also 5.*

Interrupted expressions or movements. For example:

—After a long period of contented play, sudden out-of-context crying or displays of distressed anger without rationale.

—*Infant interrupts approach to parent on reunion with a bout of angry behavior, directed away from the parent, then continues approach. As, begins strong approach upon reunion but interrupts approach to look away and strike hand on floor with angry sounds, then completes full approach.*

—*Infant rises or begins approach immediately upon reunion, but falls prone in "depressed" (huddled) posture.*

138

TABLE 1. *(continued)*

---

4. Stereotypies, Asymmetrical Movements, Mistimed Movements, and Anomalous Postures

Asymmetries of expression or movement. For example:

—Asymmetries of movement on approach to parent (asymmetrical creeping, heavy or fast on one side only), with or without sudden, unpredictable changes of direction.

—Asymmetries of facial expression directly upon the appearance of the parent, for example, an extremely swift "tic" which lifts only the left side of the facial musculature.

Stereotypies. For example:

—Extended rocking, ear pulling, hair twisting, and any other rhythmical, repeated movements without visible function. (Note: Do not include "stereotypies" that make sense in the immediate context, as rubbing eyes in a tired infant, or some initial ear pulling or hair pulling in the stranger's presence).

—Marked stereotypies while held by the parent. (Do *not* include rubbing eyes if infant has been crying, or brief continuation of previous stereotypies while in arms in an infant who showed the same stereotypies during separation.)

Assumption of anomalous postures. For example:

—*Repeated assumption of uninterpretable postures, as, head cocking with arms crooked over head.*

—*Assumption of huddled, prone, depressed posture for more than twenty seconds, unless infant is clearly tired.*

—Any posture stereotyped for a particular baby, as, closing eyes and holding hands forward at shoulder height for several seconds in response to each reunion.

Mistimed movements. For example:

—Unpredictable bouts of activity or movement which seem to lack normal preparation time for initiation, and/or which have a jerky, automaton-like (unmonitored) quality. For example, a sudden burst of jerky arm and leg activity in an infant who had been sitting tense and immobilized a second prior.

---

5. Freezing, Stilling, and Slowed Movements and Expressions

Freezing is identified as the holding of movements, gestures, or positions in a posture that involves active resistance to gravity. For example, infant sits or stands with arms held out waist-high and to sides. *Stilling* is distinguished from freezing in that infant is in comfortable, resting posture which requires no active resistance to gravity. Freezing is considered a stronger marker of disorientation than stilling.

Freezing and stilling suggestive of more than momentary interruption of activity. For example:

—*Freezing lasting twenty seconds or more, and stilling lasting thirty seconds or more, accompanied by dazed or trance-like facial expression. For example, freezing accompanied by tense, smooth closing of the lids or by lifeless stare.*

—*Interrupting a bout of resistant or distressed behavior, freezing (ten or more seconds) or stilling (twenty or more seconds) is accompanied by a dazed or trance-like expression.*

—*Freezing lasting twenty-five seconds or more, and stilling lasting thirty-five seconds or more, while held by parent unless infant has recently been engaged in hard crying (below).* (Notes: [1] Context should be considered. [2] Do not consider stilling during the first thirty seconds of reunion if the infant is being held by parent, has been crying hard, and is clearly simply in transition from crying. [3] Infant should not be considered to be freezing or stilling if infant is watching something with lively interest, as, watching stranger demonstrate working of a toy. [4] The C2 infant is passive by definition: general passivity should not be confused with stilling.)

TABLE 1. (*continued*)

Slowed movements and expressions suggesting lack of orientation to the present environment. For example:

—Markedly apathetic or lethargic movements, as though infant is without purpose in moving forward.

—Slack, depressed, dazed, or apathetic facial expression especially when unexpected, as accompanying approach to parent on reunion ending in raised arms. (Note: Consider only expressions specified above. Neutral or impassive expressions are not considered indicative of disorientation with respect to the current environment.)

---

6. *Direct Indices of Apprehension Regarding the Parent*

Expression of strong fear or apprehension directly upon return of parent, or when parent calls or approaches. For example:

—*Immediate responses to noting parent's entrance such as the following:* (a) *jerking back, with fearful expression;* (b) *flinging hands about, over, or in front of face, or over mouth, with fearful expression;* (c) *dashing away from the door/parent upon reunion, with hunched or tucked head and shoulders.*

—Other expressions of fear or apprehension soon following reunion, such as *fearful facial expression on pick-up.*

Other indices of apprehension regarding the parent. For example:

—Moving behind chair or behind furniture without immediate rationale (pursuit of toy, interest in object behind chair, or brief exploration), especially when infant is then out of reach or out of sight of parent.

—Following a hesitant, seemingly cautious approach to the parent with a rapid, tense "away" movement.

—Offering objects to the parent with tense arm and over an unusual distance, as though avoiding parental "reach" space.

—Raising or tensing shoulders when approaching or in contact with parent.

—Highly vigilant posture or appearance when in presence of parent. Movements or posture tense, infant gives impression of being hyperalert to parent even or especially when parent positioned behind her.

---

7. *Direct Indices of Disorganization or Disorientation*

Any clear indices of confusion and disorganization in first moment of reunion with the parent. For example:

—Raising hand or hands to mouth directly upon the return of the parent without accompanying confused, wary, or fearful expression. (Do not include thumb or finger sucking, putting objects in mouth, or removing objects from mouth. Do not include if hands already near face.)

—*"Greeting" stranger brightly at the moment of reunion with parent, that is, approaching stranger with raised arms immediately as parent enters.* (Note: Distinguish from the bright or happy look to stranger made by many infants at the moment of the parent's return, often accompanied by pointing to parent to further mark the event.)

—*Flinging hands over, about, or in front of face directly upon return of the parent and in clear response to return of the parent.*

—*Raising hand or hands to mouth directly upon the return of the parent with a clearly confused or wary expression.*

TABLE 1. (*continued*)

—*Confused or confusing sequences of very rapid changes of affect in first few seconds of reunion with parent, as,* (a) *rapid movement of withdrawal* (b) *accompanied by confused cry-laugh* (c) *succeeded by approach movement.*

Direct indices of confusion or disorientation beyond the first moments of reunion with the parent. For example:

- —Fall while approaching parent when infant is good walker. Similar unexplained falls when parent reaches for infant, or when parent calls from outside of door.
- —Disorganized wandering, especially when accompanied by disoriented expression.
- —Rapidly pursuing parent to door, protesting departure, then smiling at door as though in greeting as door closes.
- —Disoriented facial expression. Sudden "blind" look to eyes, where infant has previously used eyes normally.

NOTE: Italics mark very strong indices, which in themselves are usually sufficient for *D* category placement.

distress upon separation, calling and crying for the parent, then backing away immediately upon reunion, their faces suddenly expressionless. They then exhibit strong avoidance.

One of us was able to identify an infant as disorganized/disoriented immediately upon seeing her first reunion episode. The infant went at once to her mother at the door, arms up for contact in a full, strong, "secure" reunion response. She was identified as disorganized, however, when she turned away from the door with a confused, puzzled expression, advanced a few steps into the room, and stood with a dazed look staring straight ahead. This was an abused infant who, on the basis of her strong, immediate proximity-seeking behavior, had been classified as secure within the traditional system.

Simultaneous Display of Contradictory Behavior Patterns

In our review of the literature concerning difficult-to-classify infants, we have already described several instances of the simultaneous display of contradictory patterns. In a previous study, abused infants were described as creeping or walking toward their caregivers sideways, or with head averted, or backing toward them rather than approaching face-to-face (George & Main 1979). Similar behaviors were observed in some *D* infants: for example, an infant in our Bay Area sample "approached" mother by moving backward toward her on her stomach, face averted. Other infants in our sample reached strongly for the parent immediately upon reunion—but with head held sharply down. The impression in each case was that approach movements were being partially but unsuccessfully inhibited through simultaneous activation of avoidant tendencies (see George & Main 1979). Thus, contradictory patterns were activated but were not sufficiently inhibitory to lead to the complete overriding of approach movements.

An even more striking example of the simultaneous display of contradictory patterns was *avoidance while in contact with the parent*. This appeared in reunion episodes, often after the infant seemed settled from previous distress. Infants who were marked unclassifiable sometimes sat upon the parent's lap—perhaps even comfortably molded to the parent's body—while looking away, either sullen or dazed. One infant seemed comfortable seated on his mother's lap, his body conforming to hers, his arms and hands relaxed. His expression was, however, peculiarly avoidant, and he turned his head away and sullenly, impassively ignored her many overtures. A second baby sat on the floor for several moments with her hand on mother's lap, leaning toward her mother but simultaneously turned slightly away as though intending to approach the toys: silent and trance-like, she failed to turn completely either to the toys or to her mother. A third 12-month-old stood similarly at mother's knee for several seconds looking at the floor, holding onto mother but turned partially away with a dazed expression: face heavy and somber, he seemed unable to play, and unable to seek interaction.

The behavior of these three infants suggests mutual inhibition of the attachment and exploratory behavioral systems. If, comfortably settled on the parent's lap, these infants were not yet ready to return to play, why did they actively refuse the parent's initiations of interaction, or fail to initiate interaction or further contact? And, if the infants were either satisfied with respect to contact with the parent, or preferred to "avoid" the parent by turning attention to exploration of the environment, why were the infants seemingly unable to move away from the parent? Seemingly, these infants could neither respond to the parent, approach the parent, or fully shift attention away.

Undirected, Misdirected, Incomplete, and Interrupted Movements and Expressions

Seemingly undirected, incomplete, and interrupted movements and expressions appeared in many unclassifiable infants. Most examples seemed to involve fear, distress, or aggression, and/or inhibited or interrupted approach movements.

"Undirected" expression of strong fear or distress—that is, strong fear or distress neither accompanied by nor quickly succeeded by physical or communicative orientation to the parent—is one of the strongest markers of the *D* category. One infant appeared frightened of the stranger in the third episode of the Strange Situation, as shown by a high, whimpering cry with mouth corners down and back. Without looking or even slightly orienting toward the parent, she moved away from both the stranger *and* the parent to lean forehead against the wall with a fear-face, her eyes opened widely and cast far to the side. A less extreme example was that of an infant who moved away from his mother to the far side of the room during the first reunion episode. Remaining at this distance, this year-old infant suddenly began a full, continuous cry. While crying, he neither looked at the mother, oriented to her, or undertook an approach movement. Rather, he cried while looking straight ahead of him.

Expressions of anger toward the mother appear in infants in each of the three central Ainsworth categories. In each category, the expression of anger takes a characteristic form. While insecure-avoidant infants do not express anger openly, sometimes they throw a toy at the parent's feet. Strong, direct expressions of anger combined with proximity seeking characterize infants identified as actively insecure-resistant/ambivalent ($C1$). Finally, secure infants can also express anger toward the mother upon reunion, and in our Bay Area samples infants have occasionally been classified as secure even when an openly frustrated, expressive "swipe" has been taken. For these infants, "hitting at" mother seems a brief, communicative expression of frustration— often at being offered a toy when contact with mother is wanted instead.

Review of our tapes of D infants showed an occasional very slow striking at the parent's face, but in incomplete, weak movements which initially appeared undirected and therefore innocuous. Viewing the videotape at normal speed, the movements of the infant's hand might seem, for example, to indicate only an effort to grasp the parent's glasses which had led to accidental jabbing of the parent's face or eyes. That these movements were in fact deliberately directed at the parent's face or eyes—rather than being undirected— could often be inferred from slow motion analysis. In several cases, we observed a change to a dazed, faintly aggressive facial expression just prior to initiation of the slow and apparently undirected aggressive movement.

Proximity seeking was also sometimes interrupted by sudden aggressive movement patterns. The infant of a father who had recently attempted suicide and who was frequently subject to homicidal fantasies provided an especially strong example. During the second reunion, the infant interrupted her strong approach with a simultaneous expression of anger and avoidance. Creeping rapidly forward toward father, she suddenly stopped and turned her head to the side and—while gazing blankly at the wall—slapped a toy and then her empty hand on the floor in a clearly angry gesture, still with head averted and gaze blank. This interruption lasted only three to four seconds. She then continued her strong approach and reached to be picked up. A minute later, while still being held by father, she three times brought her arm down in a gesture that involved apparently accidental striking of father's face with a toy.

This infant's face remained impassive or expressed a good mood on each of these occasions. The child was identified as D solely on the basis of the above patterning and without any knowledge of the father's history. Aside from these brief gestures, she appeared secure.

In another example of subtly interrupted, incomplete approach movements, one infant repeatedly leaned toward the mother while standing at her knee, but in a slow, heavy manner suggesting that he was resisting and pushing away at the same time. Others approached in an abbreviated, start-stop manner, seemingly unable to make smooth forward movements. Two infants quickly approached the parent but then as quickly veered away before arriving beside her, one (below) then sharply rocking on hands and knees.

Stereotypies, Asymmetrical Movements, Mistimed Movements, and Anomalous Postures

Stereotypies and anomalous postures are observed in animals in conflict situations (Hinde 1970) and are also commonly associated with neurological difficulties. The patterns considered here include anomalies of posture such as head cocking; stereotypies such as rocking, ear pulling, hair pulling, and head banging; and asymmetrical or mistimed movements. For example, one infant repeatedly raised both hands to her ears whenever she was hugged by the mother: the mother was later identified as abusive. Another infant approached the mother on reunion, then veered away and rocked violently on hands and knees, facing the wall. These patterns have no obvious orientation with respect to the immediate environment and may have no obvious stimulus. They are often described as "clinical indicators of stress" (Crittenden 1987) and, when seen in medically normal infants, are among those considered most worrisome by observers.

Asymmetrical facial expressions immediately upon hearing or seeing the parent were observed in three infants from maltreating families. The immediate response to reunion observed in one seriously maltreated 12-month-old infant was as follows:

> B hears M's voice and turns and looks to the door. Her look is initially blank, brows somewhat raised. Looks up at M, averts gaze for a moment, facial expression then *divides in two* (left vs. right half of face), uplifting left mouth-corner only. In these microseconds her eyes widen, and as she looks at M, the asymmetry makes her appear puzzled, disgusted or fearful. Her face then breaks into an extremely wide smile.

On the next reunion, this infant showed a fear-smile immediately at mother's entrance.

Mistimed movements appeared in several infants. Three infants crept across the room with highly asymmetrical movements, one hand slapping against the floor belatedly as the other hand made forward progress. Such movements could be interpreted either as the outcome of neurological difficulties, or as the outcome of partial inhibition of approach movement. Whether for reasons of physical or psychological experience, however, mistimed or asymmetric movements occurred largely in infants in maltreatment samples.

Freezing, Stilling, and Slowed Movements and Expressions

Like freezing and stilling, slowed movements and slack, apathetic, or depressed facial expressions seem to indicate more disorientation with respect to the present environment than active disorganization in behavior. Marked periods of "freezing of movement" (defined by us as cessation of movement in a posture requiring resistance to gravity, e.g., ceasing movement for several seconds with arms at shoulder height) and "stilling" (defined by us as cessation of movement in a relatively restful posture, e.g., falling prone and ceasing motion, or leaning back against the parent, unmoving) occurred in many infants who had previously been identified as unclassifiable. The infant usually had a dazed, somewhat disoriented expression during these episodes.

The infant of a clinically depressed mother stilled immediately following reunion. When mother entered the room in the first reunion episode he rose, took two steps toward her, and then fell prone in a depressed, huddled posture for many seconds. At mother's second entrance, he placed his hands over his mouth, bowed his head, and fell prone again, crying. Lifted and held on mother's lap, he again bowed his head and stilled completely for one minute.

Direct Indices of Apprehension Regarding the Parent

Main and Hesse (this vol.) have suggested that a state of fear or apprehension regarding the parent (originating in a parent whose behavior is *either* frightening or frightened) may be involved in the development of the disorganized/disoriented response pattern for many infants. As such, it may play a role in many of the behavior patterns listed earlier in table 1 (e.g., interrupted approach movements and avoiding the parent directly following a greeting). However, in some dyads—particularly those seen in maltreatment or high-risk samples—we have observed more direct indices of apprehension. For example, one maltreated infant approached her mother hesitantly, then moved quickly away with raised shoulders, her neck bent forward in a tense, hunched posture. Others approached the mother with head and chin tucked, leaving quickly.

At a theoretical level, signs of apprehension may seem less disorganized or disoriented than many of the other behavior patterns listed in table 1. Simply increasing one's distance from a feared individual is hardly an indication of behavioral disorganization. *Fear of the attachment figure in an attached infant,* however, usually *results* in disorganization of behavior, because the infant is not in a position to completely withdraw from the attachment figure and in stressful situations may need to approach her. Thus, the attached but fearful infant may greet the parent with a fearful smile or approach in a disorganized manner rather than simply withdrawing (see George & Main 1979).

Direct Indices of Disorganization or Disorientation

Table 1 describes only a few of many direct indices of confusion, disorganization, or disorientation. Turning and "greeting" the stranger rather than the parent was observed in several infants at the moment of the parent's entrance. Two maltreated infants pursued the parent, protesting departure,

Figure 1. Responses of four infants, 12–18-month-olds, to parent's entrance to the room (drawings taken directly from film). All gestures occurred within eight seconds of entrance. For three of these four infants, the best-fitting traditional category was *B* ("secure").

then smiled immediately "at" the closed door. Some infants crept rapidly after the stranger, crying at her departure as though at the departure of the parent.

Directly upon sighting (or even hearing) the approach of the parent, some infants exhibited confusion. We observed one infant hunch her upper body and shoulders at hearing her mother's call, then break into extravagant laugh-like screeches with an excited forward movement. Her braying laughter became a cry and distress-face without a new intake of breath as she hunched further forward. Then, suddenly, her face lost all expression.

One of the most striking expressions of confusion was a hand-to-mouth gesture which occurred immediately upon reunion in several of the disorganized infants (see fig. 1). One child had been crying and calling during separation but immediately on reunion bowed his head, stepped backward away from the parent, and put hand to mouth in a gesture resembling indecision, shame, or apprehension. Two of the infants put both hands to mouth and cheeks immediately upon hearing the mother's call. The impression in one case was of confusion, and in the other confusion mixed with fear. Several of these direct indices of confusion, disorganization, and/or apprehension observed at the parent's entrance are shown in the drawings taken from videotape in figure 1.

DIRECTIONS FOR DETERMINING WHETHER AN INFANT SHOULD BE ASSIGNED TO DISORGANIZED/DISORIENTED ATTACHMENT STATUS

This is a list of steps to be taken in determining, first, whether a given infant's Strange-Situation response is or is not classifiable within the traditional system (A, B, C, U_{ABC}) and, second, whether the infant is to be assigned to disorganized/disoriented attachment status. The directions given in this section are summarized in table 2 (page 148). The system should be applied only under the following conditions:

1. The individual working with the system must be thoroughly familiar with, and reliable in utilizing, the Ainsworth A, B, C infancy classification system (Ainsworth et al. 1978). The worker must be familiar enough with the A, B, C system to recognize an infant who fails to meet the traditional classification criteria. This will also assist the worker in, for example, recognizing expected versus unexpected temporal patterning in infant behavior.

2. The sample being studied should be one in which subjects are presumed neurologically normal. Obviously, an occasional subject will have unexpected neurological or motor difficulties, which may be recognized by the researcher only following interviews with the parent or, indeed, following direct observation.

3. The D system should be applied to the infant's behavior only when the

parent is present. Conflict behaviors such as ear pulling and indices of fear such as inhibition of movement are not unexpected when the infant is alone or is confronted by a stranger in the parent's absence.

4. The D classification system is designed for use with infants between 12 and 18 months old. Children who show disorganization and disorientation in the Strange Situation in infancy may later show considerably less or even no overtly disorganized behavior, and instead exhibit controlling, placating, or other response patterns. The D infants in our Bay Area follow-up study typically exhibited a relatively well-organized controlling-punitive or a controlling-caregiving response toward the parent by 6 years of age (Main & Cassidy 1988). Similarly, Crittenden has noted that well before 6 years some maltreated children develop a compliant, "pseudocooperative" response pattern (Crittenden 1987).

We have applied the D criteria shown in table 1 successfully with children up to 18 months, but at 21 months we have experienced some difficulty since the beginnings of "controlling" and other more sophisticated patterns now make an appearance in some children. Whether this system can be used unaltered following 21 months seems doubtful.

5. The Strange Situation must be structured so that there is nothing inherently confusing to the infant in the arrangement of the room or in the instructions to the parent. If the parent opens the door at one location and then walks to another part of the room before beginning her approach, the infant will naturally appear disoriented at the first moment of reunion or may make a seemingly "disorganized" approach by setting off for the parent in one direction, stopping, and moving away. Similarly, the parent should not have to stop and step over a barrier in the middle of her approach to the infant; call from one door but appear at a second; read throughout the reunion against her own inclination but in accordance with laboratory directions; or be directed in her movements by a loudspeaker in room center. Parental behavior of this type may disorganize or disorient an otherwise well-organized infant.

6. Clear video recording, complete with a record of infant facial expression and small motor movements throughout most of the situation, is required. If a stationary camera placed in one corner of the room has made the sole record of the Strange Situation; if the film is of poor quality; or if the infant's back is to the camera upon reunion, it is unlikely that D scoring will be accurate. In such cases, expressions of confusion or apprehension will not be visible on the film, so that some D behavior is missed, or the infant may be inaccurately judged D on account of prolonged stilling when in fact the infant was watching something closely, with a lively expression.

7. The observation and recording of D behavior can only be made in conjunction with repeated, slow-motion study of the film. Not only must the observer find and describe the behaviors, but lengthy consideration must be

TABLE 2.   DIRECTIONS FOR DETERMINING WHETHER AN
INFANT IS TO BE ASSIGNED TO DISORGANIZED/DISORIENTED
ATTACHMENT STATUS

This system is applied to samples of normal infants 12–18 months of age, and to episodes of the Strange Situation in which the parent is present. It is presumed that the worker is already reliably trained in the traditional, A, B, C system; that a clear video recording sufficient to permit study of infant facial expression and small-motor movements is available; and that nothing within the conduct of the situation itself is likely to produce disorganization.

1. Attempt to assign an "Ainsworth" (A, B, C) classification and subclassification. If the infant is unclassifiable (U_{ABC}), two or more best-fitting A, B, or C attachment classifications will be assigned in order of descending fit (priority).

2. Review table 1: Can the infant's Strange-Situation behavior be described as fitting to one of several of the thematic headings, or to one of the behavior examples?

3. Make a written record of all behaviors seeming to qualify as indices of disorganization or disorientation, specifying social, behavioral, and temporal context.

4. If any of these are "very strong" indicators (shown in italics in table 1) occurring without immediate explanation or rationale, the infant is assigned to D.

5. If there are no italicized indicators, the worker must decide whether the recorded indices are sufficient to warrant placement in the D category on the basis of the following categorical decisions. Thus (pp. 146–47), D attachment status is assigned if Strange-Situation behavior appears *inexplicable with respect to the immediate context in which it is observed;* and/or if the infant appears to the observer to be *without a behavioral "strategy"* for dealing with its immediate situation; and/or if the behavior can be explained only by the assumption that the infant is either *fearful of the attachment figure, or is fearful of approaching the attachment figure.*

6. Assign a rating to the infant for degree of disorganization, utilizing a simple nine-point rating scale.

7. If the infant has been assigned to D attachment status because of only one type of behavioral display, the worker may elect to assign a tentative D subcategory, as, "stilling/freezing of movement," "apprehensive movements and expressions," "depressed/apathetic," or "A/C."

8. Review the final classification assignment. Each tape will ultimately be assigned to one of five major categories (A, B, C, D, or U), in conjunction with other best-fitting categories where necessary. With respect to infants who cannot be directly classified using the traditional A, B, C system, note that some infants will be D while being otherwise classifiable (e.g., $D/A1$); many will be D as well as being unclassifiable (e.g., $D/UA1/B4$); and a few still will be simply unclassifiable ($U/A1/B4$).

given to the context in which the behaviors appear (see table 2). Application of this system (in conjunction with the Ainsworth system) is expected to take between one and two hours.

Presuming that the conditions of observer experience with the A, B, C system, sample selection, and video recording are met, the steps taken in assigning classification are now as follows:

I. Attempt to make an "Ainsworth" classification and subclassification: this will either result in assignment to an A, B, or C subcategory, or in a determination (U_{ABC}) that the infant cannot be satisfactorily classified within the Ainsworth system. Even if the infant is primarily unclassifiable within the A, B, C system, one or several best-fitting Ainsworth subcategories are still assigned.

Although this chapter is concerned chiefly with the identification of

D behavior patterns, in practice the worker should begin study of the video-tape by attempting to assign an *A, B,* or *C* classification and subclassification. In the first search to determine whether the infant can be assigned to an *A, B,* or *C* classification or is in fact U_{ABC} (unclassifiable), it may be helpful to note the following:

a) The infant may be unclassifiable in *A, B, C* terms because he or she qualifies almost equally well for two incompatible attachment classifications, either by mixing behavior patterns in a given reunion (e.g., *A* and *C*), or by qualifying for one classification on the basis of behavior observed in the first reunion, but for a second and unexpected classification in the second reunion, for example, *B*4 followed by *A*1. (Behaving as an *A* infant on the first reunion and a *B* infant on the second reunion represents, of course, an expected sequencing of responses to reunion and usually qualifies the infant for Ainsworth's subgroup *B*2 attachment classification.)

b) The infant may be unclassifiable because of other violations of expectancies regarding the sequencing of behavior for an infant exhibiting a given attachment strategy. Specifically, an infant who avoids the parent strongly on both reunions, but cries and calls for the parent in distress when left with the stranger, cannot be given an *A* classification. Similarly, an infant who is calm and undisturbed during separation, but becomes distraught and resistant only upon reunion, cannot be given a *C* classification.

c) Note that Ainsworth has recently revised the descriptors for the *B*4 subcategory as presented in Ainsworth et al. 1978 (personal communication, January 1985). Stereotypies, and gazing away while held, are no longer to be considered criteria for the *B*4 subcategory. If intense, marked, or frequent, they are more likely to be indicators of *D* attachment status (see table 1). The lines to be omitted from the current classification directions (Ainsworth et al. 1978, p. 62) are: "He may show other signs of disturbance, such as inappropriate, stereotyped, repetitive gestures or motions," and ". . . he may avoid (the mother) by drawing back from her or averting his face when held by her."

II. Review table 1: Can the infant's behavior during those episodes of the Strange Situation in which the parent is present be described in terms of one or more of the seven thematic headings?

The worker should begin by reviewing the thematic headings, using the specific behaviors listed only as examples. The behavior examples are offered as illustrations of the range and type of behavior that to date has been observed to fit under each particular heading. The behavior of many or even most *D* infants will fail to match any particular behavior example listed but will instead serve as a new example of, for example, "apprehensive movement." Note that any particular behavior example may fit to several thematic headings.

III. Make a written record of all behaviors seeming to qualify as indices of disorganization and disorientation, specifying social, behavioral, and temporal context. This written record will be vital to any future development of *D* subcategories.

IV. If the infant shows one of the "very strong" indicators (indicators given in italics in table 1), the infant should be considered for immediate assignment to the *D* category. In many cases, one of the behavior patterns italicized has appeared as virtually the only example of *D* patterning during the Strange Situation for an infant later discovered to be maltreated, or for a dyad in which the parent was later discovered to have had psychotic episodes or very marked, unresolved trauma.

V. If no italicized ("very strong") indicators, but one or several other indicators of disorganization and disorientation are present, the worker must decide whether these are sufficient to warrant placement in the *D* category. The worker will observe disorganized/disoriented behaviors in many infants. What, then, are the cut-off criteria distinguishing organized infants who are simply slightly to somewhat disorganized from infants who should definitely be placed within the *D* category? We suggest that consideration be given to each of the following factors:

a) Whether the infant's behavior seems inexplicable; and/or indicative of momentary absence of a behavioral strategy; and/or can be explained only by presuming that the infant is either fearful of the parent, or is unable to shift its attention away from the parent while simultaneously being fearful of or inhibited in completing approach movements (Main & Hesse, this vol., and 1989). A review of table 1 shows that almost all the behaviors listed are either *inexplicable* considering the immediate Strange-Situation context; and/or suggest the absence of an immediate behavioral goal or strategy; or, otherwise, are explicable only if we presume that:

(1) the infant is fearful of the attachment figure, or

(2) is actively inhibited from approaching the attachment figure without being able to successfully shift its attention away from that figure to the immediate environment.

The less evidence there is of an *immediate* goal, rationale, or explanation for the infant's behavior, the more seriously the infant should be considered for *D* attachment status. If nothing in the immediate situation explains, for example, why the infant suddenly freezes all movement in the middle of a bout of distress, or cries loudly while moving away from the parent to lean against the wall, the infant is a candidate for assignment to *D* attachment status. Note that these particular behaviors also suggest that the infant is experiencing stress but is without an accompanying behavioral strategy, being neither able to engage in an "organized shift of attention" away from the attachment figure (and possibly the stressful experience) in the manner of avoidant infants (Main 1981; Main & Weston 1982), nor to approach the attachment figure in the manner of infants judged secure or insecure-ambivalent (Main & Hesse, this vol., and 1989).

Close attention to the full videotape will often be required to provide a rationale for behaviors that otherwise would be considered disorganized. An infant may push a toy angrily against mother's body in the midst of an apparently good mood without being considered disorganized if this is a toy mother is continuing to attempt to "force" on the infant, despite the infant's having several times already communicated its dislike.

b) *The timing of the appearance of* D *behavior* with respect to the Strange Situation. A given disorganized behavior pattern appearing in the initial moments of reunion is a stronger index of disorganization of relationship than that pattern appearing later within the reunion episode, and reunion episodes are generally treated more seriously with respect to *D* behavior than are the preseparation episodes. Thus, freezing of all movement in immediate response to parent entrance is different from initial freezing at stranger entrance, when a shy infant may be caught in a location that prevents approaching the parent without first drawing closer to the stranger. Sometimes, however, infants show *D* behavior *only* in episode 3, but the behavior is sufficiently marked to lead to *D* categorization in itself—as, very extensive freezing, or crying while moving away to the wall rather than the parent when frightened.

c) *Whether episodes of apparent disorganization* (for example, out-of-context distress or undirected distress) *are immediately succeeded by an approach to the parent, suggesting an organized and appropriate use of the parent as a "solution" for whatever stress the infant may be experiencing.* If the infant approaches the parent following a small episode of disorganized behavior and in obvious immediate response to it, the parent still appears to provide a solution for the infant's experience of stress. A *D* classification is then less likely to be made on the basis of this single incident.

VI. Given that infants differ in the intensity, context and frequency of their display of *D* behaviors, a nine-point scale for disorganized/disoriented behavior can be utilized. The Ainsworth interactive scales for proximity seeking, contact maintaining, and proximity avoidance offer good examples of the complex but readily comprehensible behavior scoring which can be used to order superficially differing behavior patterns in terms of apparent similarity of function (see Sroufe & Waters 1977 as well as Ainsworth et al. 1978 for particularly clear elaborations of this point). In one of these scales, for example, looking away from the parent, moving away, and failure to respond to parental initiation are all seen as indices of avoidance, despite the differences in movement pattern. Each of these behavior patterns seems to be used to maintain or to increase the distance between child and parent.

It is in contrast initially a radical notion that the many, highly diverse indices of disorganization and disorientation listed in table 1 can be placed under one heading. Unlike indices of avoidance, the *D* indices are not similar to one another in any ordinary sense: rocking on all fours does not look like stilling, crying at the stranger's leave-taking is not rocking, and neither of these patterns resembles a hand-to-mouth gesture made immediately upon reunion with the parent.

In point of fact, we recognize the similarity of this diverse set of behaviors partly in terms of what they seem *not* to represent. These are not behaviors that can be grouped in terms of similarity of function, serving to increase or maintain proximity between infant and attachment figure, or to shift attention away from the attachment figure toward the inanimate. They are not exploration or play behaviors, nor attempts at social interaction with the stranger. In other words, these behaviors are recognized in part by an *exclusion* principle: they are not readily seen as serving the set goals of the several behavioral systems typically activated by the Strange Situation (as see Bretherton & Ainsworth 1974; see also Ainsworth et al. 1978). Most of the behaviors listed as *D* indices do not, in other words, have even a superficial similarity, and it is only by defining them through exclusion criteria—as *dis*organized and *dis*oriented—that we can hope to recognize them as things of a kind.

For the above reasons, no exhaustive list of *D* behaviors can be constructed, and because *D* behaviors follow an exclusion principle rather than serving an obvious single function, a satisfactory interactive scoring system comparable to those devised by Ainsworth cannot yet be constructed. Nevertheless, an infant who leans her forehead against the wall and cries in the parent's presence, rises and then falls prone on reunion, and later interrupts her avoidance with tantrum behavior seems more disorganized than an infant who freezes briefly at the stranger's entrance. Note, however, that while avoidance can be scored without knowledge of the full classification system, and without the judge having yet decided upon *A*/not-*A* as a categorical judgment, suggestions for scaling *D* behavior as given below depend upon a complete consideration of the suitability of the tape for *D* classification. We may then recognize a simple ordering which presupposes that the nature of the behavior, the context of the behavior being considered, its potential rationale or explanation, and its sequelae have already been taken into account:

1. No signs of disorganization/disorientation. Any behaviors that initially seemed to be indices of disorganization or disorientation have been explained in other terms.

3. Slight signs of disorganization/disorientation. There are some indices of disorganization or disorientation, but the worker does not even begin to consider placement in a *D* category.

5. Moderate indices of disorganization/disorientation which are not clearly sufficient for a *D* category placement. No very strong (italicized) indicators are present, and the indices that are present are not frequent enough, intense enough, or clearly enough lacking in rationale for the worker to be certain of a *D* category placement. The worker using a 5 will have to "force" a decision regarding whether the infant should be assigned to a *D* category. (Note: ratings below a 5 (e.g., 4.5) mean the infant is not to be assigned to the

D category, and ratings above a 5, for example, 5.5, indicate assignment to the D category.)

7. Definite qualification for D attachment status, but D behavior is not extreme. There is one very strong indicator of disorganization/disorientation, or there are several lesser indicators. There is no question that the infant should be assigned to D status, even though exhibition of D behavior is not strong, frequent, or extreme.

9. Definite qualification for D attachment status: in addition, the indices of disorganization and disorientation are strong, frequent, or extreme. Either several very strong indicators are present, or one very strong indicator and several intense exhibitions of one or several other indices.

VII. If fitting (below), assign the infant to a tentative D subcategory, as, "stilling/freezing," "apprehensive movements," "depressed/apathetic," or "A/C." Many infants show several types of disorganization. In some infants, however, signs of apprehension, freezing, or depressed affect et al. are the *only* indices that have led to assignment to the D category. Another particularly strong candidate for special status is Crittenden's A-C infant Strange-Situation behavior category (Crittenden 1985, 1987; see also use of A-C unclassifiable categories by Spieker & Booth 1985 and Radke-Yarrow et al. 1985, above), which may identify young children subjected to extremes of maltreatment and hence not usually met with in our Bay Area studies.[5]

This tentative assignment to subcategory should not lead to early reification of the concept of D subcategories. For any potential subclassification to meet the criteria for a coherent subcategory, we will need evidence for predictable and distinct sequelae, and for a specific and distinct history. Recording such tentative subgroup distinctions as "A-C," "apprehensive," and "apathetic/depressed" will provide the material necessary to eventual validation of meaningful subcategories, if and where they exist.

VIII. Make the final classification assignment. Each tape will be assigned to one of five major classifications (A, B, C, D, or U_{ABC}), in conjunction with other best-fitting categories. Ultimately, four combinations are possible:

Classifiable as A, B, *or* C *(to subcategory).* The infant is classifiable using the traditional system. In this case the classification is simply recorded as, for example, $A2$, $B4$. This assignment is used for an infant who fits satisfactorily to the Ainsworth categories and scores (at or) below 5 for disorganization.

Disorganized/disoriented but otherwise readily classifiable as A, B, *or* C

---

5. Crittenden (Crittenden & Ainsworth, in press) has suggested that, as opposed to D, A-C may be an organized pattern of response for children meeting with circumstances of extreme abuse and/or neglect. However, many of the Strange-Situation subjects described as A-C by Crittenden (1987) were well beyond 12–18 months, and indeed the A-C pattern was found associated with the older children in her sample. It is possible that, just as a controlling reunion response pattern developed only following infancy for many D dyads in our middle-class sample, A-C patterns of response to the parent may also appear somewhat later.

with subcategories. The infant scores (at or) above 5 for disorganization and disorientation during the Strange Situation, but is otherwise readily classifiable using the traditional *A, B, C* classification system. Thus, the infant may fit almost perfectly to *A*2 but freezes all movement for two minutes during episode 3. In this case the primary *D* classification is recorded together with the best-fitting traditional category, as *D/A*2.

Disorganized and unclassifiable as A, B, *or* C. The infant scores (at or) above a 5 for disorganized/disoriented behavior, and in addition cannot be satisfactorily classified using the traditional *A, B, C* system. The infant is therefore *both* disorganized and unclassifiable. Although the infant is primarily judged disorganized, the final classification record will now be more extensive as, for example, $D/U_{ABC}/A1/B4$. As noted, in our experience to date with both low-risk and high-risk dyads, most disorganized infants are also unclassifiable.

Unclassifiable as A, B, *or* C *but not disorganized.* The infant is unclassifiable within the *A, B, C* classification system, but scores for disorganization/disorientation are *at or below* a 5. Here again, while the primary assignment is U_{ABC} (unclassifiable as *A, B, C*), the classification is recorded as, for example, $U_{ABC}/A1/B4$ (an unclassifiable infant who shows virtually no disorganized/disoriented behavior), or $U_{ABC}/D/A1/B4$ (an unclassifiable infant who scores, for example, 4 for disorganized behavior). Infants who are unclassifiable rather than disorganized/unclassifiable are rare in our experience.

No matter what the primary classification, every Strange Situation will now have a best-fitting "Ainsworth" classification and subclassification assigned, and in many cases several classifications may be assigned, always in the order of descending best-fitting priorities. (An infant assigned to D/U_{ABC} /*B*2/*A*2 is therefore presumed to fit to the *D* descriptors; to be also *U*/unclassifiable within the traditional system; and, if forced into the traditional system to fit slightly better to the *B*2 classification than to *A*2.)

The reader should note again that (1) *D* scores above a 5 always lead to a primary *D* assignment, and (2) that *U* is interpreted as U_{ABC} only. At present we retain our earlier usage of *U* as reflecting an infant's failure to fit to *A, B, C* criteria (Main & Weston 1981). Unclassifiable status would otherwise reflect an infant's failure to fit to *A, B, C, or D* criteria, and an infant classified as *D* would not be given an alternative *U* assignment as well. Our continued usage of U_{ABC} reflects our present uncertainty with respect to the status of *D* as a category comparable in meaning to the relatively well-organized *A, B, C* attachment classifications recognized by Ainsworth, and our continued interest in distinguishing between infants who meet *D* criteria *while being readily classifiable in the* A, B, C *system* from infants who meet *D* criteria and are *unclassifiable* with respect to *A, B, C.*[6]

---

6. An "explicable/inexplicable" cut-off criterion for the *D*/not-*D* distinction was also used in scoring "disordered/disoriented" infant behavior during a mildly stressful infant-parent-

This full an accounting is recommended because of its use in distinguishing infants in terms of history, or in later development. In later studies, researchers may want to distinguish between infants who were assigned to *D* because of strongly disorganized behaviors but were otherwise easily classifiable within the traditional system, and infants who were not only disorganized but also unclassifiable within the *A, B, C* system. These infants may have different interactional histories and differ in later development. Similarly, the *D* infant whose best-fitting traditional classification is *A*1 (*D/A*1) may differ in history or in later development from the *D/B*4 infant. Finally, it is possible that for infants who are *both* disorganized and unclassifiable, the *D* classification will be more predictive of later behavior, or more stable, than for those infants who are disorganized but otherwise readily fit to "forced" *A, B,* or *C* categories.[7] The observer who has kept the most complete record will be the most advantaged in the application of this new system.

SOME THEORETICAL ISSUES IN THE
MODIFICATION OF CLASSIFICATION SYSTEMS

We have now completed the description of our modifications to the traditional Ainsworth system for classifying infant-parent attachment relationships. In describing the process through which these modifications evolved, it may be helpful to draw an analogy with the development of biological classification systems, and particularly upon a series of essays concerning the devel-

---

stranger "clown session" (Main & Weston 1981) in South Germany. In this mildly stressful session, the infant is seated near the parent as she observes an initially masked clown who later attempts to make friends with her. As noted, infant *D* behavior in the Ainsworth Strange Situation predicted controlling or still unclassifiable responses to reunions with the parent at 6 years of age in the Berkeley sample (Main & Cassidy 1988). In the South German study (Wartner 1987), mothers and children returned to the laboratory at 6 years, and the sixth year attachment classification system developed in Berkeley was applied to reunion behavior. Children who had shown "inexplicable" disordered/disoriented behavior in the parent's presence during the clown session (receiving scores of 3.5 or above on the nine-point scale) were most often judged controlling or still unclassifiable in their response to the parent five years later. Wartner's study not only reinforces the explicable/inexplicable *D* cut-off criterion, but also suggests the possibility of recognition of *D* patterning outside of the Strange Situation—that is, whenever the infant is exposed to mildly stressful situations in the parent's presence.

7. As evidence for the independent status of *D* as a category, our original Bay Area reports are flawed in that all *D* infants in our sample *were also unclassifiable* within the *A, B, C* system. While our review of "classifiable" tapes within this same sample stressed differing degrees of disorganization in classifiable versus unclassifiable infants, there is no way to determine with certainty that the predictors and sequelae of *D* attachment status were not simply the predictors and correlates of unclassifiability with respect to the *ABC* system (U_{ABC}). Ainsworth and Eichberg (in press), however, found lack of resolution of trauma highly related to the *D* attachment category in an *A, B, C, D* Strange-Situation analysis which did *not* include an unclassifiable (U_{ABC}) category. Finally, three infants seen with their mothers in a new Bay Area study have been determined to fit to *D* attachment status without also being unclassifiable with respect to the traditional system. These disorganized but classifiable infants (e.g., *D/B*2, *D/A*1) each had mothers experiencing considerable attachment-related traumas, suggesting similarity in meaning between *D* and U_{ABC} attachment status.

opment of biological taxonomy by Ernst Mayr (1976). According to Mayr, a central question in biological systematics during the 1950s and 1960s had been to identify the proper basis for developing new classifications—whether the organism's phylogenetic history exclusively (the positions taken by biologists identified as *cladists*), or its present appearance exclusively (the position of *pheneticists*), or instead some combination of history and appearance should be utilized. To the pheneticists, classifications were ideally to be based upon similarities and dissimilarities of appearance among organisms, and not upon speculations regarding phylogenetic history. At the opposite extreme were those ("cladists") who advocated basing the classification purely upon a monophyletic view of the organism's descent. To these workers, an ideal system would completely reflect a single phylogenetic process.

Mayr argued that a joint consideration of *history and appearance* typically yields a more fruitful classification system than does exclusive attention either to an organism's appearance or to its phylogenetic descent. The appearance of an organism reflects its history, and dissimilar appearances are often cues to dissimilar histories, not artifacts of measurement or perception. To this extent, the "cladist" is correct in searching for a system behind appearances. At the same time, phylogenetic history can never be identified completely, and classification systems are always therefore provisional abstractions intended to assist in the organization of knowledge.

Our position with respect to the dialectic between history and appearance in the development of new classification systems parallels that of Mayr. We are interested jointly in behavioral *appearance* (i.e., the infant's response to the Strange Situation) and in the infant's interactional *history* with the caregiver (e.g., maltreated or not maltreated). It is not behavioral appearance (infant Strange-Situation behavior) in itself that is of interest but rather what behavior can reveal about the outcomes of interactional histories. At the same time, the import of differing interactional histories lies in their consequences both for behavior and for mental organization. Appearance (whether of an individual or of a species) often reflects history (whether phylogenetic or ontogenetic). A "new" appearance, then, whether in species' morphology or in individual behavior, is frequently the result of differences in history. Conversely, if there are substantial differences in history, differences can likely be found within appearances.

We believe that the related discoveries of unclassifiable and of disorganized/disoriented attachment status—discoveries shared among a number of investigators—demonstrate the usefulness of the "dialectical" approach to behavioral classification. As we had discussed earlier, investigators working with high-risk families had originally been concerned with the "appearance"-based classifications of maltreated infants as "secure" within the earlier system (Crittenden 1985, 1987; Egeland & Sroufe 1981a, 1981b; Gaensbauer & Harmon 1982; Spieker & Booth 1985; Radke-Yarrow et al. 1985). Their knowledge of an infant's history led them to inspect the "appearance" of infant Strange-Situation behavior particularly closely, and ultimately to discriminate *D, A-C,* and other response patterns from what had previously been considered secure attachment classifications. In this case, knowledge of the infant's interactional history led to a successful discrimination among the appearances.

In our own laboratory we began with an attention to appearance (behavior form), and moved from this to discoveries regarding a particular experiential history (Main & Weston 1981; Main & Solomon 1986). We had no knowledge of infant attachment history when we set aside infants whose Strange-Situation behavior did not fit any of the existing (*A, B, C*) classificatory criteria (Main & Weston 1981). But exacting attention to a distinction between individuals in terms of "appearance" led us to the later discovery of corresponding differences in "history," that is, to the discovery of second-generation effects of unresolved trauma (Main & Hesse, this vol., and 1989; Ainsworth & Eichberg, in press). Later, it served to discriminate maltreated from control infants in poverty samples (Carlson et al., in press: Lyons-Ruth et al. 1987).

The study of infant attachment organization rests upon the classification of individuals. The attachment classifications recognized to date are taken as meaningful rather than arbitrary, but also as provisional rather than immutable. Revision of any existing system is possible but only insofar as it is informed by a dialectic between history and appearance. In the future, recognition of new distinctions in a dyad's history may lead workers to search for corresponding distinctions in the patterning of infant behavior in mildly stressful situations. At the same time, recognition of as yet unclassified infant behavioral patterns may lead to still further discoveries regarding the history or experiences of the dyad.

APPENDIX:
THE AINSWORTH STRANGE SITUATION
The Strange-Situation Procedure

The Ainsworth Strange Situation is a brief, structured laboratory procedure involving infant and parent in two separations and two reunions within an unfamiliar setting. It was devised with the intention of highlighting the operation of the attachment behavioral system (Bowlby [1969] 1982) as it is organized in normal infants 12 months of age. The situation is designed to elicit exploratory behavior in the early episodes and then, through a series of mildly stressful events, to shift the infant's attention to the maintenance of proximity and contact with the attachment figure.

The Strange Situation is divided into eight episodes, each except the first being three minutes long. In the opening episode, infant and parent are introduced to an unfamiliar, comfortable laboratory room filled with toys. A stranger enters the room; the parent leaves the infant in the company of the stranger; the parent returns; the parent leaves the infant alone; the stranger returns; the parent returns once more for the second and final reunion episode. (In our laboratories, episodes in which the infant is distressed are reduced to thirty seconds.)

During each reunion, the parent is instructed to pause in the doorway and greet the infant, permitting time for the infant to mobilize a response to the parent's arrival. On the second reunion, the parent is instructed to pick the infant up. A more complete description of this procedure (together with the classification and coding procedures described below) can be found in Ainsworth et al. 1978.

The critical systems of analysis devised by Ainsworth for classification of infant attachment focus upon the two reunion episodes of the Strange Situation, when infant and parent are alone together. As would be expected for a system designed to highlight the organization of individual differences in attachment, there is some emphasis upon proximity seeking and efforts to maintain physical contact with the parent. Greatest emphasis is placed, however, upon two types of negative behavior (avoidance and angry resistance) observed in relation to the parent.

Classification Procedures, Reliability, and Stability

As noted earlier, the Ainsworth classification system is designed to permit assignment of infants to one of three categories—secure, insecure-avoidant, or insecure-ambivalent in relation to the parent. Classifications are based upon infant rather than parental behavior during the Strange Situation.

Infants are classified as *secure* (group B) in relation to the parent when they actively seek proximity and contact following separation, and when these behaviors appear unmixed with strong anger or avoidance. In the preparation episodes, securely attached infants may examine the toys and explore the strange environment. They may or may not be distressed upon separation, but if they are, the mother's return provides comfort and enables them to return either to exploration or to interactive play with the parent.

Infants are classified as *insecure-avoidant* (group A) in relation to the parent when they actively avoid and ignore the parent during both reunion episodes. Avoidance of the parent is considered strong when the infant turns away and moves away from the parent upon reunion, indicates a desire to be put down when picked up (often in an affectless manner), and ignores the parent's efforts toward communication. Infants classified as avoidant show no distress specific to the parent's absence and often explore the room and toys actively throughout the Strange Situation. They are most striking for the apparent absence of fear, distress, or anger.

Infants are classified as *insecure-ambivalent/resistant* (group C) in relation to the parent when they both seek proximity and contact upon reunion and resist it (actively or passively), seeming to find little security in the parent's return or presence. Infants classified as insecure-ambivalent may be distressed even before the first separation and fearful of the person playing the part of the stranger. They are often extremely distressed upon separation. Proximity seeking may be weak rather than active.

Interjudge agreement on the three major classifications is high (Ainsworth et al. 1978; Main and Weston 1981; Matas, Arend & Sroufe 1978). The majority of infants are usually classified as secure, one-fifth to one-third as insecure-avoidant, and a small minority as insecure-ambivalent/resistant (Van IJzendoorn & Kroonenberg 1988).

REFERENCES

Ainsworth, M. D. S.; Blehar, M. C.; Waters, E.; & Wall, S. (1978). *Patterns of attachment: A psychological study of the strange situation.* Hillsdale, N.J.: Erlbaum.

Ainsworth, M. D. S., & Eichberg, C. G. (in press). *Effects on infant-mother attachment of mother's unresolved loss of an attachment figure or other traumatic experience.* In P. Marris, J. Stevenson-Hinde, & C. Parkes, *Attachment across the life cycle.* New York: Routledge.

Bell, S. M. (1970). The development of the concept of the object as related to infant-mother attachment. *Child Development* 41, 291–311.

Bowlby, J. [1969] 1982. *Attachment and loss, Vol. 1: Attachment.* New York: Basic Books.

Bretherton, I. (1985). Attachment theory: Retrospect and prospect. In I. Bretherton & E. Waters (eds.), *Growing points of attachment theory and research. Monographs of the Society for Research in Child Development* 50 (1–2, Serial No. 209), 3–35.

Bretherton, I., & Ainsworth, M. D. S. (1974). Responses of one-year-olds to a stranger in a strange situation. In M. Lewis & L. A. Rosenblum (eds.), *The origins of fear* (pp. 131–164). New York: Wiley.

Carlson, V.; Cicchetti, D.; Barnett, D.; & Braunwald, K. (1989). Disorganized/disoriented attachment relationships in maltreated infants. *Developmental Psychology* 25, no. 4, 525–531.

Crittenden, P. M. (1985). Maltreated infants: Vulnerability and resilience. *Journal of Child Psychology and Psychiatry* 26, 85–96.

Crittenden, P. M. (1987). Relationships at risk. J. Belsky & T. Nezworski (eds.), *Clinical implications of attachment.* Hillsdale, N.J.: Erlbaum.

Crittenden, P. M., & Ainsworth, M. D. S. (in press). Child maltreatment and attachment theory. In D. Cicchetti (ed.), *Handbook of child maltreatment theory and research: A life-span developmental perspective.*

Egeland, B., & Sroufe, L. A. (1981a). Attachment and early maltreatment. *Child Development* 52, 44–52.

Egeland, B., & Sroufe, L. A. (1981b). Developmental sequelae of maltreatment in infancy. In R. Rizley & D. Cicchetti (eds.), *Developmental perspectives in child maltreatment* (pp. 77–92). San Francisco: Jossey-Bass.

Gaensbauer, T. J., & Harmon, R. J. (1982). Attachment behavior in abused/neglected and premature infants: Implications for the concept of attachment. In R. N. Emde & R. J. Harmon (eds.), *The attachment and affiliative systems* (pp. 245–299). New York: Plenum.

George, C., & Main, M. (1979). Social interactions of young abused children: Approach, avoidance and aggression. *Child Development* 58, 306–318.

Grossmann, K. E.; Grossmann, K.; Huber, F.; & Wartner, U. (1981). German children's behavior towards their mothers at 12 months and their fathers at 18 months in Ainsworth's strange situation. *International Journal of Behavioral Development* 4, 157–181.

Hinde, R. A. (1970). *Animal behavior: A synthesis of ethology and comparative psychology* (2d ed.). New York: McGraw Hill.

Kaplan, N. (1987). Individual differences in 6-year-old's thoughts about separation: Predicted from attachment to mother at age 1. Unpublished doctoral dissertation, Department of Psychology, University of California, Berkeley.

Krentz, M. S. (1982). Qualitative differences between mother-child and caregiver-child attachments of infants in family day care. Unpublished doctoral dissertation, California School of Professional Psychology, Berkeley.

Lyons-Ruth, K.; Zoll, D.; Connell, D. B.; & Odom, R. (1987, April). Maternal depression as mediator of the effects of home-based intervention services. Paper presented at the biennial meeting of the Society for Research in Child Development, Baltimore.

Main, M. (1973). Exploration, play, and cognitive functioning as related to child-mother attachment. Unpublished doctoral dissertation, Johns Hopkins University.

Main, M. (1981). Avoidance in the service of attachment: a working paper. In K. Immelmann, G. Barlow, L. Petrinovich, & M. Main (eds.), *Behavioral development: The Bielefeld interdisciplinary project* (pp. 651–693). New York: Cambridge University Press.

Main, M. (1983). New prospects in the study of attachment. Paper presented at the annual meeting of the American Academy of Child Psychiatry, San Francisco.

Main, M. (1985). An adult attachment classification system: Its relation to infant-parent attachment. Paper presented at the biennial meeting of the Society for Research in Child Development, Toronto.

Main, M. (in press). Cross-cultural studies of attachment organization: Recent studies changing methodologies, and the concept of conditional strategies. *Human Development.*

Main, M., & Cassidy, J. (1988). Categories of response to reunion with the parent at age six: Predictable from infant attachment classification and stable over a one-month period. *Developmental Psychology* 24, no. 3, 415–426.

Main, M., & Hesse, E. (1989). Adult lack of resolution of attachment-related trauma related to infant disorganized/disoriented behavior in the Ainsworth strange situation: Linking parental states of mind to infant behavior in a stressful situation. Submitted ms.

Main, M., & Solomon, J. (1986). Discovery of a new, insecure-disorganized/disoriented attachment pattern. In M. Yogman & T. B. Brazelton (eds.), *Affective development in infancy* (pp. 95–124). Norwood, N.J.: Ablex.

Main, M., & Weston, D. (1981). The quality of the toddler's realtionship to mother and father. *Child Development* 52, 932–940.

Main, M., & Weston, D. (1982). Avoidance of the attachment figure in infancy: Descriptions and interpretations. In C. M. Parkes & J. Stevenson-Hinde (eds.), *The place of attachment in human behavior* (pp. 31–59). London: Tavistock.

Matas, L.; Arend, R. A.; & Sroufe, L. A. (1978). Continuity of adaptation in the second year: The relationship between quality of attachment and later competence. *Child Development* 49, 547–556.

Mill, J. S. (1874). *A system of logic, ratiocinative and inductive, being a connected view of the principles of evidence and the methods of scientific investigation* (8th ed.). London: Longmans, Green.

Mayr, Ernst. (1976). *Evolution and the diversity of life: Selected essays.* Cambridge, Mass.: Belknap Press.

Radke-Yarrow, M.; Cummings, E. M.; Kuczynski, L.; & Chapman, M. (1985). Patterns of attachment in two- and three-year olds in normal farmilies and families with parental depression. *Child Development* 56, 884–893.

Spieker, S. J., & Booth, C. (1985, April). Family risk typologies and patterns of insecure attachment. In J. O. Osofsky (chair), Intervention with infants at risk: Patterns of attachment. Symposium conducted at the biennial meeting of the Society for Research in Child Development, Toronto.

Sroufe, L. A., & Waters, E. (1977). Attachment as an organizational construct. *Child Development* 48, 1184–1199.

Strage, A., & Main, M. (1985, April). Parent-child discourse patterns at 6 years predicted from the organization of infant attachment relationships. Paper given at the biennial meeting of the Society for Research in Child Development, Toronto.

Van IJzendoorn, M. H., & Kroonenberg, P. M. (1988). Cross-cultural patterns of attachment: A meta-analysis of the strange situation. *Child Development* 59, 1, 147–156.

Wartner, U. (1987). Attachment in infancy and at age six and children's self-concepts: A follow-up of a German longitudinal study. Unpublished doctoral dissertation, University of Virginia.

5 · Parents' Unresolved Traumatic Experiences Are Related to Infant Disorganized Attachment Status:

IS FRIGHTENED AND/OR FRIGHTENING PARENTAL BEHAVIOR THE LINKING MECHANISM?

Mary Main and Erik Hesse

THE STUDY OF human attachment can be encompassed within two major branches of inquiry. The first has been concerned with (*a*) describing the normal development and functioning of an attachment behavioral system, a system presumed to have evolved to take continual account of the whereabouts of caregivers (attachment figures), and to promote proximity to those figures whenever necessary (Bowlby [1969] 1982); and (*b*) with describing the effects of potentially traumatic events, such as loss of attachment figures, upon the further functioning of the individual. Traumatic loss of parents or other attachment figures and abuse by attachment figures are considered likely to overwhelm the developing attachment behavioral system (Bowlby 1973, 1980) and to be contributory factors in depression (Brown, Harris, & Bifulco 1985) and later difficulties in parenting (Quinton & Rutter 1985).

The second branch of inquiry has centered upon individual differences in attachment organization. During infancy, these individual differences are usually identified through an examination of infant behavioral responses to the parent in a separation and reunion observation conducted in the unfamiliar laboratory environment (Ainsworth, Blehar, Waters, & Wall 1978). The three traditional categories of infant response to this situation are: *secure*/B (the infant shows signs of missing the parent, seeks proximity on reunion, and then returns to play); *avoidant*/A (the infant ignores and avoids the parent upon reunion); and *ambivalent*/C (the infant is highly distressed and highly focused on the parent, cannot be settled by the parent, and may seek proximity and display anger in quick succession). In several studies, these response categories have been found associated with parental behavior toward the infant, independent across parents (a given infant may be secure with one parent but avoidant with the other), and predictive of the child's later social-emotional functioning (see Bretherton 1985 for review).

This study would not have been possible without the assistance of Carol George, Ruth Goldwyn, and Nancy Kaplan, who were critical to the design and conduct of the Adult Attachment Interviews, and Anitra DeMoss, who coded them. This paper has been through many drafts and editions, and we gratefully acknowledge the criticisms, queries, and commentaries of Mary Ainsworth, Anne Beuter, John Bowlby, Jude Cassidy, Giovanni Liotti, and Judith Solomon.

161

Recently, we have developed an interview centered upon the adult's description and evaluation of his or her attachment-related history (George, Kaplan, & Main 1985). Study of the verbatim transcripts of this interview permits judges to classify each adult into one of three adult attachment categories: secure-autonomous with respect to attachment, dismissing of attachment, or preoccupied by past attachments. These adult classifications have been found to predict the infant's Strange-Situation response to the parent, such that, for example, secure parents typically have secure infants while dismissing parents have avoidant infants (Main 1985; Main, Kaplan, & Cassidy 1985; Main & Goldwyn, in press; Ainsworth & Eichberg, in press). In addition, the parent's adult attachment classification has been found directly predictive of behavior toward the offspring (Crowell & Feldman 1988; Ward, Carlson & Kessler 1989b; see also Grossmann, Fremmer-Bombik, Rudolph, & Grossmann 1988).

In this chapter, we discuss a significant connecting link between these two central areas of inquiry, that is, an association between *unresolved loss of attachment figures (or other attachment-related trauma)* as experienced by the parent, and the infant's *failure* to fit to one of the traditional, organized Strange-Situation response categories. This is in essence the discovery of a second-generation effect of unresolved loss of attachment figures, with the infants of parents who are judged unresolved with respect to this potentially traumatic experience being found to fit to a new (fourth) infant attachment category now termed "disorganized/disoriented" (Main & Solomon, this vol., and 1986) and previously termed "unclassifiable" (Main & Weston 1981).

The reader should note that (1) the term "trauma" traditionally refers to experiences of intense fear, terror, or helplessness (see DSM-III-R [American Psychiatric Association 1987]), which threaten an individual with psychological or behavioral disorganization, although (2) whether any given experience is actually traumatic ultimately rests with the history the individual brings to the experience, and individual perceptions. Experiences such as physical or sexual abuse by a parent are almost inevitably traumatic, while loss experiences are only potentially traumatic, with the effects dependent upon the individual and upon surrounding conditions.

Recent studies have demonstrated that not only unresolved loss of important figures through death, but also unresolved experiences of physical or sexual abuse, and even more general recent traumas (such as a recent close brush with death on the part of the parent) are associated with infant D attachment status (see below). At this point, only a very few of our original Bay Area subjects have described traumas other than the potential trauma implied in loss of important figures. Hence in this chapter our attention will be chiefly confined to loss experiences.

We begin with a review of disorganized/disoriented behavior patterns and their sequelae in recent studies. We next discuss the association discovered between parental lack of resolution of loss experiences and infant disorganization (Main 1983, 1985; Main & Hesse 1989), which has led to the development of a new, unresolved *adult* attachment category, and studies replicating and extending our findings to include unresolved experiences of physical and sexual abuse as predictors of infant *D* attachment status (Ainsworth & Eichberg, in press; Friedman 1986; Main, Kaplan, & Hesse, unpublished data; Levine, Ward, & Carlson 1989; Ward, Carlson, Altman, Levine, Greenberg, & Kessler 1989a). We then examine the patterning of infant disorganized/disoriented behavior observed in the Ainsworth Strange Situation, which suggests that the infant may at times be experiencing a fear or distress too intense to be deactivated through a shift in attention (the Ainsworth *A* pattern), yet at least momentarily cannot be ameliorated through approach to the attachment figure (the Ainsworth *B* and *C* patterns). This leads to a discussion of the role that fear may sometimes play in the *D* infant's experiences with the parents, and to a discussion of the hypothesis that *the traumatized adult's continuing state of fear together with its interactional/behavioral concomitants (frightened and/or frightening behavior) is the mechanism linking unresolved trauma to the infant's display of disorganized/disoriented behavior.* Such behavior could be particularly puzzling or frightening to the infant because its immediate cause would often lie in the parent's response to memories aroused by ongoing events rather than resulting from those events directly.

Since the attachment figure is normally the "solution" provided to the infant for dealing with stressful or alarming experiences, an infant who is frightened by the attachment figure is presented with a paradoxical problem— namely, *an attachment figure who is at once the source of and the solution to its alarm.* The chapter concludes with a discussion of the *A, B,* and *C* infant attachment classifications as indicative of relatively well-organized behavior patterns and infant *D* response patterns as indicative of a momentarily irresolvable conflict.

Disorganized/Disoriented Infant Attachment Status: Description and Sequelae

In this section, we briefly review the development of the *D* attachment category and describe some of the behavior patterns which are regarded as disorganized and/or disoriented. For a more complete description of the *D* system, see Main and Solomon (this vol.).

"Unclassifiable" Responses to the Ainsworth Strange Situation

The *A, B, C* classificatory system was developed in conjunction with Ainsworth's study of a sample of Baltimore infants and mothers living in relatively stable circumstances, and has repeatedly been successfully applied to the study of infants and parents in similar low-risk, middle-class samples. Within our own upper-middle-class Bay Area sample, we had earlier reported difficulties in classifying the Strange-Situation response of about 13% of infants (Main & Weston 1981). Studies of high-risk/maltreatment samples in which children were observed with maltreating or psychotic parents in contrast yielded reports of frequent classification difficulties. Recognition of these difficulties often began with the observation that, using the traditional system that classifies every infant as *A, B,* or *C,* infants were being classified as *B* (secure) with respect to a parent who was in all likelihood maltreating or frightening (see Main & Solomon, this vol., for a review of these studies).

Disorganized/Disoriented Infant Attachment Status

Recently, Main and Solomon (1986) conducted an analysis of the Strange-Situation behavior of fifty-five infants who were originally considered *unclassifiable* within the traditional system (Main & Weston 1981), and were now found to exhibit a diverse array of *disorganized/disoriented* and sometimes seemingly *undirected* behaviors. The more recent instructions for identifying infant *D* Strange-Situation response were, however, based upon thorough study of 200 infants judged to be disorganized/disoriented, including 100 infants from maltreatment and high-risk samples (Main & Solomon, this vol.).

Infants are judged to fit to the *D* (hereafter, disorganized) category when they show strong or combined indices of disorganization or disorientation in the presence of the parent such as freezing of all movement; approaching the parent with head averted; rocking on hands and knees following an abortive approach; moving away from the parent to the wall when apparently frightened by the stranger; screaming for the parent by the door upon separation, then moving silently away upon reunion; or rising to greet the parent on reunion, and then falling prone to the floor. Most of these behaviors appear to be of a type ethologists term "conflict behaviors," that is, behaviors that result from the simultaneous activation of incompatible behavioral systems (see, e.g., Hinde 1970).

While it is not uncommon for an infant to show some of these behaviors at low levels of intensity in stress situations in which the parent is absent (e.g., freezing briefly as the stranger approaches during a separation episode), when behaviors of this type are seen at higher levels of intensity *in the parent's presence* they appear difficult to explain. For example, upon reunion, an infant is held on mother's lap for a long period, during which time the infant has a dazed expression and repeatedly twists its hair and raises hands to ears. Or, an infant is crying loudly in the first moments of reunion and attempting to gain the parent's lap, then suddenly "freezes" in a given posture for several seconds. In such cases (*a*) the observer cannot determine what, if anything, is causing the distress, or (*b*) why, if the infant wished to gain the parent's lap, it stopped moving in mid-activity.

Some of these behavior patterns (such as stereotypies) are expected in neurologically impaired infants. There is no evidence to date, however, that *D* reflects any stable constitutional deficiency on the part of infants in normal samples. In the larger Bay Area sample (141 infant-mother Strange Situations analyzed to date), only three out of thirty-four infants judged *D* with one parent were also judged *D* with the second parent (Main & Solomon, this vol.). Independence of "unclassifiable" (now, *D*) attachment status was also found between mothers and day-care caregivers (Krentz 1982). A relation between the *D* category and parental behavior patterns was suggested in two independent studies comparing maltreating to well-matched control families. In both studies, the *D* category was found strongly and specifically associated with maltreatment (Carlson, Cicchetti, Barnett, & Braunwald 1989; Lyons-Ruth, Zoll, Connell, & Odom 1987).

We underscore here that the infant's *D* Strange-Situation response in low-risk samples such as ours is not normally an indication of maltreatment. Indeed, we will argue here for a quite different, although related, mechanism.

Follow-up Studies of Unclassifiable or D Infants in Low-Risk Samples

In our upper-middle-class Bay Area sample, children initially judged unclassifiable (and later recoded as "disorganized") with a particular parent in infancy most often showed *controlling* (role-reversing) responses to reunion with that parent at age 6, being generally either punitive toward the parent on reunion or else caregiving. In addition, when a child had been judged *D*/unclassifiable with a particular parent in infancy, parent-child discourse for that dyad was judged dysfluent five years later, while discourse with the second parent reflected the original attachment classification with the second parent being, for example, fluent (associated with group *B* infancy classifications) or fluent-restricted (associated with group *A* infancy classifications; Strage & Main 1985). Finally, *D* attachment status with mother in infancy predicted apparent difficulties with thinking regarding attachment-related events: thus fearful, disorganized, and contradictory or irrational-seeming thought processes regarding parent-child separations appeared in children who had been classified *D* five years previously (Kaplan 1987).

Similarly, in a Charlottesville study, Cassidy found negative self-descriptions, and bizarre or violent descriptions of interactions between a child and mother doll in attachment-related situations where 6-year-olds were judged *controlling* in their (*D*-equivalent) reunion response to the mother (Cassidy 1986, 1988). Still more recently, George and Solomon (1989) found that both a mother's narrative description of herself as helpless with respect to the child, and her perception of the child as out of her control were strongly correlated with her 6-year-old's controlling response to reunion with her in the laboratory.

LACK OF RESOLUTION OF MOURNING FOR ATTACHMENT FIGURES LOST THROUGH DEATH: RELATED TO INFANT DISORGANIZED/DISORIENTED ATTACHMENT STATUS

The association between parental lack of resolution of mourning for lost attachment figures and infant D attachment status was discovered in conjunction with a sixth-year follow-up study of our Bay Area sample (Main 1983, 1985; see Main & Weston 1981, and Main et al. 1985 for a more complete description of the characteristics of this sample). In this study, we compared the transcripts of a mother's discussion of her own attachment history with her child's Strange-Situation classification during infancy (five years earlier). In the larger sample from which the subjects for this study were drawn (189 dyads observed over a four-year period, 141 infant-mother Strange Situations analyzed to this date), a majority of children had been classified as B (secure) with mother, and only 16% had been considered unclassifiable/disorganized-disoriented (Main & Weston 1981). In contrast, this report is based upon a selected subsample of fifty-three mothers and infants (twenty-four girls, twenty-nine boys), selected to include as many D infant-mother dyads as were available during the period of the study (seventeen, or 32%), as close to equal numbers of B and A infant-mother dyads as possible (sixteen dyads, seventeen dyads) and three C dyads. The report includes the forty infant-mother dyads who participated in the follow-up study described in Main et al. 1985, together with thirteen dyads brought in within the succeeding year. A more detailed description of our findings relating lack of resolution of mourning to infant D attachment status can be found in Main and Hesse (1989).

The Adult Attachment Interview: Procedure, Reports of Experiences of Loss, and the Original Three Category Adult Attachment Classification System

While their children were being seen in a series of assessments involving attachment-related issues, the parents in our follow-up study were interviewed regarding their own attachment histories, and were asked to evaluate the effect of their histories upon their personality and functioning. The hour-long Adult Attachment Interview (George et al. 1985) began with a request for a description of the adult's relationship to each parent during childhood, and later moved to request a description of the relationship to any other individual(s) considered the equivalent of a parent. Adults were asked whether they had experienced the death of any parent or parental figure, any close family member, or anyone else who was especially important to them; how they reacted to the loss at the time; how they thought the loss had affected their adult personalities; and how it may have affected their response to their child. For the purposes of the current study, data concerning loss were categorized as follows: loss of a close family member (older than the subject) prior to the completion of high school; later loss of older family members, and loss of any other important persons at any point in time; no important loss experiences.

As noted earlier, Adult Attachment Interviews are transcribed verbatim, and each transcript is assigned to a single overall classification for the adult's "state of mind with respect to attachment" irrespective of particular relationships and experiences. In keeping with the three-part Ainsworth infant attachment classification system, our original adult attachment classification system assigned each adult to one of three categories, each equivalent to and predictive of infant categories: secure/autonomous with respect to attachment (associated with the parents of *B* infants), dismissing of attachment (associated with the parents of *A* infants), or preoccupied by past attachment relationships and experiences (associated with the parents of *C* infants). Earlier studies employing the Adult Attachment Interview also used this original, three-part scoring system (e.g., Kobak & Sceery 1988; Crowell & Feldman 1988; Main & Goldwyn, in press).

Scoring Subjects for Lack of Resolution of Mourning of Important Figures Lost through Death

A fourth, *U* ("unresolved") adult attachment category has now been developed, which is assigned to subjects in conjunction with scores above 5 on a nine-point scale assessing lack of unresolved loss (described below). Like infant *D* attachment status, which is assigned in conjunction with a best-fitting, alternative, or "forced" *A, B,* or *C* classification (so that the infant is actually classified *D/A, D/B,* or *D/C;* see Main & Solomon, this vol.), adult unresolved attachment status is also assigned in conjunction with a best-fitting alternative adult category. Thus, an adult who is judged unresolved with respect to trauma will be classified as, for example, unresolved/secure or unresolved/dismissing of attachment. Insofar as possible, separate scores are assigned to the discussion of each individual lost. The transcript is assigned the highest score given to any loss experience.

Bowlby (1980) uses the term "mourning" to refer to "all the psychological processes, conscious and unconscious, that are set in train by loss." In constructing a scale intended to assess unresolved loss, we focused on the concept of disorganization and disorientation in mental (cognitive and affective) process as it might be made evident in speech transcriptions. We searched specifically for signs of disorganization both because (1) mental processes in an attached individual are normally organized with some continuing reference to attachment figures—hence, loss of an attachment figure through death will inevitably lead to some disorientation—and (2) because of several specific findings from the literature concerning responses to bereavement. Thus, among the disorganizing and disorienting experiences affecting the bereaved in the first months succeeding a loss are (*a*) necessarily incomplete mental and behavioral search processes, (*b*) vulnerability to a disbelief that the loss has occurred or is permanent (as in fleeting illusions that the dead person is present or is approaching), (*c*) experiences of disorientation in places or situations in which the dead figure had commonly been found, and (*d*) unfounded fears of having been causal in the death itself (Bowlby 1980; Parkes 1972, 1980; Raphael 1982).

If, however, the outcome of mourning is favorable, a reorganization of mental processes will ultimately take place, leading to renewed orientation to the present environment. Indeed, healthy mourning is identified by Bowlby (1980) as "the successful effort of an individual to accept both that a change has occurred in his external world and that he is required to make corresponding changes in his internal, representational world and to *reorganize,* and perhaps to *reorient,* his attachment behavior accordingly" (italics ours).

Our present scale for assessing unresolved loss from interview transcripts takes account of statements indicative of continual mental disorganization and disorientation as shown in (1) lapses in metacognitive monitoring of reasoning processes, (2) lapses in metacognitive monitoring of discourse processes, or (3) reports of extremely disorganized or disoriented behavioral responses to a death when such statements are not accompanied by convincing evidence of later successful resolution of mourning (Main, DeMoss, & Hesse 1989). Lapses in metacognitive monitoring of the types to be described appeared in adults who were functioning well in intellectually demanding contexts, and in a recent analysis we have suggested that these lapses may result from unexamined early beliefs regarding a particular loss or loss in general (Bowlby 1980), and/or from experiences of fear and/or anxiety which occur during the discussion of the loss experience (Main & Hesse 1989). Note that we do not consider "dismissing" discussions of a major loss experience ("I just considered it a blessing by the time it happened. The next year, I started high school.") as indicative of disorganization and/or disorientation. Rather, such discussions would seem to indicate "failed mourning"—that is, that the process of mourning has yet to begin.

Examples of apparent lapses in the *metacognitive monitoring of reasoning processes* include (1) indications of disbelief that the person is dead—for example, "It's really better for him that he is dead, because now he can go on being dead and I can take care of things like he wanted." (2) Feelings of being materially causal in a death where no material cause is present—for example, "I still think it might have happened because I was so angry with her that Sunday that I just hoped she would die." (3) Efforts to manipulate the mind so as to ignore the facts or implications of a death—for example, "I haven't had to go back there since he died, so most of the time I sort of pretend he's still there and I can always call him up if I wanted." (Note that indications of religious belief in a metaphysical life after death are not taken as lapses in reasoning processes. Moreover, such beliefs are often stated as hopes, or as matters of speculation, as, "I like to believe that he is still watching me from Heaven.")

Indications of apparent *lapses in the metacognitive monitoring of discourse processes* take the form of altered discourse during the discussion of a death, suggesting that the individual has entered into a special state of mind in which orientation to the usual conversational strictures are absent. These include: (1) Unusual attention to detail—for example, "He died forty-two years ago last month, on November 7, a Monday, and right before his forty-second birthday. He would have been eighty-four, no, eighty-five, on this November 8." (2) Poetic phrasing (rhetorical/eulogistic speech)—for example, in discussing a death and not elsewhere within the interview, the subject uses eulogistic/rhetorical phrasing, as, "She was young, she was lovely, she was dearly beloved by all who knew her and who witnessed her as she was torn from us."

Reports of *extreme disorganization or disorientation in behavior* following a death are also taken as indices of unresolved mourning, unless accompanied by statements convincingly evidencing resolution. These include reports of attempted suicide and reports of redirected grief, for example, extreme responses to the death of a pet or a public figure following absence of response to a lost attachment figure.

As noted earlier, each subject is scored on a nine-point scale for lack of resolution of mourning for each individual lost through death. Scores of 3 or less are assigned when the subject's discussion of the loss indicates some continuing feeling of regret, and continuing or reemerging affection or sorrow, without accompanying disorganization, for example, brief tears in remembering a shared love of music ("My father loved the violin!"), or regrets expressed for not having had a longer time together.

Ratings of 7 are assigned to individuals who indicate excessive fear or guilt surrounding the loss, or extreme bereavement reactions, or whose speech becomes distinctly disoriented during discussions of the loss. Finally, ratings of 9 are assigned to individuals whose thought processes regarding the lost figure are highly disorganized, or are in clear violation of the usual understanding of physical reality and causality. Subjects are assigned a rating of 9 when, for example, they fear having caused the death of an attachment figure through their own thought processes during childhood, or indicate subtly that the dead person is still believed to be alive. Note that scores indicative of definite unresolved mourning in our system would also often be indicative of frightening ideation (having caused the death of a loved person, or believing a person to be both alive and not-alive), or of frightening or overwhelming experiences (e.g., suicide attempts).

Interjudge Reliability, Sex Differences, and Birth Order

Ratings assigned by one judge (Anitra DeMoss) were used for all fifty-three cases. To estimate interjudge reliability, two judges (Hesse and DeMoss) rated thirty cases blind to one another's ratings and to all information regarding the infant. Interrater reliability was high ($r = .87$).

Tests for sex differences and birth order yielded no significant results. Neither infant disorganization nor mother's score for lack of resolution of mourning was related to the sex or birth order of the child.

Direct Relations between Mother's Loss Experiences and Infant Disorganization

Fifteen mothers in this selected sample had lost an older family member with whom they had lived prior to the completion of high school. Nine of these fifteen experiencing early loss (60%) had infants judged disorganized[1] with them in the Strange Situation, while only eight of the thirty-eight remaining mothers (21%) had D infants ($p = .009$). Note that these results do *not* provide an estimate of the relation between early loss and D attachment status in the population from which they are drawn, since we deliberately selected for as many mothers of D infants as possible.

Infant Disorganization Related to Mother's Unresolved Mourning

The relation between mothers' experience of loss and infant D attachment status was found to be mediated by lack of resolution of mourning, which differed significantly according to infant D or non-D attachment status. Among the fifteen mothers experiencing early loss, nine had infants assigned to D attachment status, and six had non-D infants. The mean score for LRM for the mothers of the nondisorganized infants was 3.9 on the nine-point scale, while the mean score for mothers of the D infants was 7.2. Thus, mother's experience of early loss of an older family member did not in itself lead to infant D attachment status, *unless the mother had experienced lack of resolution of mourning as a consequence.*

Six mothers had not experienced loss. None of these had disorganized infants. We divided the remaining forty-seven mothers experiencing loss into three classes: few or no indications of unresolved mourning (scores 1–3), neither definitely resolved nor unresolved mourning (4–6), unresolved mourning (7–9). Only three out of nineteen mothers (16%) showing no indices of unresolved mourning had disorganized infants. In contrast, eleven out of twelve unresolved mothers (91%) had infants who had been judged disorganized with

---

1. For our follow-up studies of both parents and children in our original Bay Area sample, we relate our findings to infants who were *both* unclassifiable (within the traditional *A, B, C* classification system) and disorganized.

them in the Strange Situation five years previously. The twelfth infant had been originally assigned to the extremely avoidant $A1$ category, but was placed in the D-equivalent *controlling* category when observed again at 6 years. It is interesting to note that this mother described herself as having been rethinking her early losses only recently.

More Recent Studies Relating Mother's Traumatic Experiences to Infant D Attachment Status

Ainsworth and Eichberg (in press) studied an unselected Charlottesville sample of forty-five infants and mothers, comparing infant A, B, C, and D Strange-Situation attachment classifications to mother's Adult Attachment Interview responses a few months later. The Adult Attachment Interview transcripts were scored for lack of resolution of mourning by Mary Ainsworth who was blind to infant Strange-Situation attachment status. As in the Bay Area study, individuals assessing infant Strange-Situation attachment status were blind to all other information regarding the dyad. As opposed to the Bay Area study, however, the Charlottesville sample was unselected for infant-mother attachment categories.

1. In our own study, we found mother's lack of resolution of mourning significantly associated with the infant's best-fitting group C (insecure-ambivalent) attachment category (Main & Hesse 1989). Thus, the *mother* was significantly more likely to show unresolved mourning for lost attachment figures when the *infant's* best-fitting attachment category was C than when the best-fitting category was A or B (using a traditional A, B, C infant attachment category analysis). Ainsworth and Eichberg found mother's unresolved mourning significantly associated with her placement in the (infant C-equivalent) preoccupied adult attachment category. This suggests that adults whose state of mind with respect to attachment is preoccupied may be especially vulnerable to loss and other traumatic experiences, and makes sense of the fact that we found a higher proportion of C than A or B infants disorganized.

2. Few Charlottesville mothers had experienced early loss of a parent: none of these (five) had D infants. When loss was more inclusively defined to include loss of important persons at any point, an association with infant D attachment status appeared as a trend but failed to reach statistical significance. Twelve out of thirty mothers experiencing loss had D infants (40%), while three out of fifteen (20%) mothers with no loss experience had D infants ($p = .20$).

3. Fifteen of the forty-five infants in the Charlottesville study were assigned to D attachment status. *All* (eight) mothers judged unresolved with respect to loss of attachment figures (using an earlier version of our scale) had disorganized infants, while post-hoc analyses indicated that two more mothers of D infants would have been assigned to unresolved status using a more completely developed scale (Main et al. 1989). These findings support our Bay

Area study (Main 1983, 1985) in concluding that it is unresolved mourning for loss of an attachment figure that is especially strongly associated with infant D attachment status and not the death as such.

4. Finally, for the mothers of five D infants in the Charlottesville study, there were no definite indications of unresolved mourning. In two of these five cases, however, infant D attachment status was predicted in advance from other traumas which were considered unresolved. In one case, the mother had been abused by her parents. In a second especially instructive case, the mother had almost died of an extremely dangerous disease with sudden onset just prior to the Strange Situation. From the mother's discussion of this close brush with death, the judge (Ainsworth) considered the mother still unresolved and again correctly predicted infant D attachment status.

Recently, comparison between adult and infant attachment status has been extended to two poverty samples of black and Hispanic teenaged mothers living in inner-city New York, some of whom experienced physical or sexual abuse. Both studies used the new infant and adult attachment classification systems, that is, including infant D and adult unresolved categories. In one study, infant attachment status was found highly concordant (87.5% four-category match) with concurrent assessments of the teenage mother's attachment organization (Levine et al. 1989); in another, the Adult Attachment Interview was administered prenatally, and the mother's attachment category was again found predictive of the infant's (69% four-category match; Ward et al. 1989).

In both of these samples, as in the Bay Area and Charlottesville samples, the mother's unresolved status was found specifically predictive of the infant's disorganized/disoriented attachment status. These adolescent mothers were often found unresolved with respect to maltreatment experiences.

A history of physical or sexual abuse in parents of some D infants had also been noted in a small ($n = 15$) study of blind and partially sighted infants (Friedman 1986). Not only unresolved loss of attachment figures, but also unresolved abuse and other recent unresolved traumatic experiences appear to be linked to D attachment status in our in-progress analysis of a new Bay Area sample (Main, Kaplan, & Hesse, unpublished data).

ANALYSIS OF THE DIVERSE ARRAY OF DISORGANIZED/DISORIENTED INFANT BEHAVIORS: IS FEAR AND/OR INHIBITION OF ATTACHMENT BEHAVIOR INVOLVED?

Consideration of the behavior of infants placed in the D category leads naturally to speculation regarding both the immediate cause of the behavior observed within the Strange Situation (e.g., why the infant falls prone at a particular moment) and the more general, ontogenetic cause (e.g., experiences in interaction with the parent which have led the infant to develop this particular pattern of response). As the reader is already aware, we will shortly suggest that frightened and/or frightening parental behavior may provide the link between the parent's experience of unresolved trauma and the infant's disorganized/disoriented behavior as exhibited in the Strange Situation. Here we examine some of the diverse forms of *D* behaviors observed.

One salient theme that runs through the disorganized/disoriented behavior of *D* infants is that of *contradiction or inhibition of action as it is being undertaken*—indeed, an undermining of action which occurs almost as soon as action is initiated. In many cases, this appears to be an inhibition or contradiction of action begun specifically with respect to attachment. Thus, immediately upon the parent's appearance in the doorway, the infant orients, then places hand to mouth; or rises, then falls prone; or cries, calls, and eagerly approaches the parent, then turns about and avoids the parent with a dazed expression. Later, in the same episode, the infant may approach the parent obliquely or with head averted; cling to the parent while averting gaze; cry, while moving away from the parent; make hesitant, stop-start movements on approach to the parent; or undertake movements of approach which have a slow, limp, "underwater" quality as though being simultaneously inhibited or contradicted.

Several of these behavior patterns suggest that the presence of at least a limited fear may act to inhibit or contradict movements of approach or proximity seeking. Fear may also play a role in "freezing," a frequently appearing disorganized/disoriented behavior also exhibited by some animal species when frightened. The infant who stills or freezes in moments of distress impresses the observer as having no alternative solution (neither a person, nor a location, to which flight may be taken). When the parent is present, this seems an anomalous pattern.

There are also more direct markers of fear among the behaviors which we have labeled "disorganized." Apprehensive movements and expressions are markers for the *D* category, as are fearful expressions, extremely tentative approaches, moving swiftly away immediately upon or just following approach to the parent, and tense, vigilant body postures. Our impression is, then, that D *behavior often involves the start, followed by the inhibition of an attachment sequence.* Moreover, we may note that it is often precisely *movements or expressions of apprehension* which replace (inhibit) or accompany (contradict) the initiation of action with respect to attachment.

This analysis of some of the disorganized/disoriented response patterns is speculative only, and may be disconfirmed by later observations or experiments (e.g., in an individual case freezing could occur in imitation of the parent's behavior in similar circumstances, or could have been reinforced by some parental response pattern). Further, some instances of disorganized/disoriented behavior will undoubtedly be the result of neurological impairments, while in other instances the infant's disorganized/disoriented behavior may be more indicative of confusion than of fear, since the infant may be responding either to obviously conflicting signals, or to signals or events it perceives as conflicting or confusing (see Krentz 1982; see also Volkmar & Siegel 1979; and Volkmar, Hoder, & Siegel 1980 for a discussion of conflicting signals from a stranger which appear to lead to disorganized/disoriented behaviors in some toddlers). Nonetheless, at present the above analysis does appear to fit well with many of our observations of *D* infants, and with our informal observations of the behavior of some parents of *D* infants, described below.

SPECULATIONS REGARDING THE ONTOGENY OF *D* ATTACHMENT STATUS: FRIGHTENING OR FRIGHTENED BEHAVIOR ON THE PART OF THE PARENT?

If we are correct in presuming that an experience of fear plays a causal role in at least some types of disorganized/disoriented infant behavior, then we may presume that these behaviors have something to do with the history of infant-parent interactions, and that these interactions may be frightening to the infant. As we have already indicated, investigators working with two different maltreatment samples have found a high proportion of *D* infants (about 80%), and certainly we can expect that experiences of parental maltreatment will be directly frightening to an infant (Carlson et al. 1989; Lyons-Ruth et al. 1987; see also Radke-Yarrow, Cummings, Kuczynski, & Chapman 1985 who found many infants of parents suffering from psychotic episodes were unclassifiable within the traditional *A, B, C* classification system). Here, however, we are concerned with samples in which the observed (potential) trauma lies in the parent's history rather than in the infant's direct experience, and usually consists in the loss of significant attachment figures through death rather than physical or sexual abuse. In this case, we must ask why unresolved loss on the part of the parent would lead to infant behavior patterns which are at all similar to those displayed by maltreated infants.

We suggest that a parent suffering from unresolved mourning may still be frightened by her loss experiences. As a result, she may display an anxiety that could in turn be frightening to her infant. As we have already indicated, loss is not an inevitably frightening or overwhelming (traumatic) experience, but may have been traumatic for those particular individuals who appeared to us to be unresolved. Thus, a particular loss may have been traumatic because of the age at which it occurred, because of the conditions which surrounded it, or because the individual had also suffered a history of abuse.

We are not able to examine this issue in a satisfactory way on the basis of our present sample. In order to begin to determine whether trauma might have contributed to disorganized/disoriented discussions of loss, however, we conducted a post hoc analysis of our interviews. Early trauma was narrowly defined as any of the following experiences occurring prior to the completion of high school: loss of a close family member through accident, loss of both parents, sexual abuse by a parent, physical abuse by a parent. Only nine of our fifty-three mothers reported events of this type, with at least one mother experiencing at least one of these traumas.

These experiences did appear to be associated with unresolved mourning. Five of the twelve mothers (41%) were judged to experience definitely unresolved mourning, but only four among the remaining forty-one women (10%) had experienced traumas of this kind.

Our own informal and nonblind observations of the behaivor of the parents of *D* (disorganized) infants—as opposed to the parents of organized infants—during the Strange Situation tend to provide support for our hypothesis that the parent of the *D* infant may be frightening or frightened. In these informal observations, we have noted the following patterns, each of which seems to us likely to frighten an infant, either by being directly threatening or by indicating fright on the part of the parent. (Most of the more frightening patterns listed here have *not* yet been noted in our studies of low-risk samples and are instead taken from videotapes of maltreatment and high-risk dyads.)

Unusual Vocal Patterns

These include: (1) simultaneous voicing and de-voicing intonation (especially during greeting or when initiating physical contact) leading to an ominous, or "haunted," tone or effect. Thus, the parent may greet the infant with a simultaneously voiced and de-voiced "Hi." This is a breathy, extended, falling intonation which can be recreated by saying "Hi" while pulling in on the diaphragm. (2) Parent's voice has sudden marked drop in intonation to deep or low pitch. When marked, such changes are startling, especially when the speaker is a woman whose pitch and intonation suddenly seem to belong to a male speaker.

Unusual Movement Patterns

These include: (1) parent suddenly moves object or own face very close to infant's face ("looming"). (2) Parent's movements or postures are part of a pursuit sequence. (3) Parent presents conflicting signals by, for example, calling infant while standing with hands on hips and neck and chin jutted forward in a threatening posture. (4) Unpredictable invasions of the infant's personal space, as the parent's hands suddenly sliding from behind or across the infant's face or throat. (5) Parent's handling of the infant suggests extreme timidity. (6) Parent is extremely responsive to any indications of rejection on the part of the infant, as, for example, slumps and folds previously extended hands on lap and waits, focused on infant with a pleading look, when infant makes an impatient gesture.

Unusual Speech Content

These include: (1) parent implies that infant's actions could have harmful consequences—(*a*) "You'll kill that little (stuffed) bear if you do that!" (*b*) "Uuuohh! (Frightened intake of breath as infant moves toy car across bare floor.) Gonna have an accident! Everybody's gonna get killed!" (2) Sudden initiation of games with a frightening speech content, if accompanied by an unusual, frightening pattern of movement and intonation—"I'm gonna get you!" (3) Direct indications of fear of the infant, as, for example, backing away from the infant while directing the infant not to follow in a stammering, apprehensive voice—"Don't follow, d-don't."

It is self-evident that a maltreating parent will behave in ways that are frightening to an infant. Why, on the other hand, a parent who displays only frightened rather than threatening behavior would produce fear in an infant is less obvious and is a topic that demands closer examination. As stated above, it seems likely that such qualities of parental behavior are often related to the parents' own traumatic experiences rather than to some aspect of the ongoing parent-infant interaction. If this is the case, these parental behaviors are no doubt all the less comprehensible to the infant and most likely seem not only unpredictable as patterns of behavior but also inexplicable in origin.

Further Consideration of Dynamics Occurring When the Parent's Frightened Behavior Results from Past Traumas

We presume that the infant is equipped with behavioral systems which continuously monitor the environment as well as the accessibility of the attachment figure. Depending on the circumstances, cues to danger within the environment will then trigger inhibition of action about to be taken, flight, and/or attachment behavior. The parent's observed expressions of fear will provide one such cue, and, in the usual case, these expressions will (*a*) alert the infant to some observable danger in the immediate environment, for example, an approaching animal, or an apparently dangerous edge or surface; (*b*) lead to changes in the infant's behavior which in some way effectively reduces its danger; and (*c*) be rapidly succeeded by protective parental action, thus reducing the infant's state of alarm.

Under these more usual circumstances, the source of the danger to the infant is in fact external to both infant and parent. When, however, the source of the "danger" leading to parental expressions of fear or anxiety is internal to the (still-traumatized) parent, (*a*) the parent may not be oriented to any obviously frightening aspect of the environment, or (*b*) may be oriented to an aspect of the environment which has become associated with her history and internal state but is not intrinsically alarming, and (*c*) is at any rate unlikely to take satisfactory protection action. In this case:

1. The parent's frightened behavior will be *incomprehensible* because,

stemming from internal factors, its source will be either (*a*) indiscernible; or (*b*) if discernible due to the parent's orientation it will be something that the parent has associated with her own thought processes—for example, a photograph with remote associations to her earlier trauma.

2. Owing to the fact that what is producing fear in the parent is attachment-related, the infant may occasionally become confused in the parent's mind either with the parent herself or with those attachment figures whose death or behavior produced the original trauma. In these cases—when, for example, the parent fears having been causal in the death of an attachment figure—the parent may *indicate to the infant that the infant itself is the source of the alarm.*

3. Adding to these potential complications is a natural tendency toward flight in individuals experiencing fear. Hence, the parent (*a*) *may indicate a desire to get away from the immediate environment and/or the infant* (which would greatly intensify the infant's state of fear), or instead (*b*) *may even subtly indicate a propensity to flee to the infant as a haven of safety.*

It appears, therefore, that many of the likely sequelae to a parent being alarmed by an internal source would lead to confusion and fear on the part of the infant, and hence to disorganization and disorientation (below).

DISORGANIZATION, DISORIENTATION AND THE ATTACHMENT BEHAVIORAL SYSTEM

To this point, we have shown that (1) an interview-based method of assessing unresolved trauma has been developed which relies chiefly upon apparent lapses in the metacognitive monitoring of reasoning or discourse during discussions of loss or other attachment-related trauma[2] (2) to predict infant *D* attachment status. High scores for unresolved trauma on the part of the parent have been found predictive of infant *D* attachment status in two white middle-class samples—our original Bay Area sample (Main & Hesse 1989), and the Charlottesville sample studied by Ainsworth and Eichberg (in press). As this chapter goes to press, the relation between infant *D* attachment status and unresolved adult attachment status[3] has been replicated in two ado-

---

2. Until very recently, researchers were advised to use the indices of disorganization and disorientation in thought processes during discussions of a loss in order to identify unresolved trauma of other kinds. We have now completed a draft of a separate scale for assessing unresolved experiences of physical abuse, and we are applying it to a new Bay Area sample of infants and mothers.

3. In both the Bay Area and Charlottesville samples, almost all infants whose mothers were judged unresolved had infants judged disorganized, but the *D* attachment status of a minority of infants in each sample remained unexplained. While some instances could conceivably be accounted for by traumas not described by the parent, we underscore that in all probability other factors are operating in a substantial minority of *D* cases: for example, neurological difficulties,

lescent poverty samples and infant disorganized/disoriented Strange-Situation response has been predicted prior to the birth of the child (Levine et al. 1989; Ward et al. 1989).

Above, we suggested a possible relation between unresolved trauma and frightened and/or frightening behavior on the part of the parent. We conclude with a discussion of how such behaviors may be related to infant D attachment status.

Bowlby ([1969] 1982) has described the attachment behavioral system as (*a*) developing in all ground-living primates raised in any but highly abnormal rearing conditions, (*b*) leading to a focus upon maintaining proximity to one or a few selected caregivers, and (*c*) providing the infant with the chief behavioral means by which it can assure its own survival. The system is presumed to take continual account of these environmental and internal conditions that would normally lead to the activation or termination of displays of attachment behavior—and hence to be continually *context-sensitive*. In general, the system is organized to increase infant-caregiver proximity in situations of threat or alarm, but to permit activation of exploratory behavior when the situation is not threatening and proximity is assured. Among the conditions provoking alarm are (1) unfamiliar environments and (2) threatened or actual separations from the attachment figure.

In considering individual differences in patterns of attachment as observed in the Strange Situation, it is worthwhile to note that the functioning of the attachment behavioral system as described above is most readily observable in infants judged *secure* within the Strange Situation. Thus, a relatively smooth and organized transition between exploratory behavior and attachment behavior is observed in the response of these (and only these) infants, who explore the environment so long as proximity to the parent is assured; turn their attention to attachment when proximity is threatened; and, following a display of attachment behavior directly upon reunion with the parent, return once more to exploration.

The A and C infant Strange-Situation responses also appear relatively well-organized, although more complex and conceivably more vulnerable to disorganization than the secure attachment patterns. At a theoretical level, we understand the avoidant infant to be *minimizing* the display of attachment behavior relative to the level of activation of the attachment behavioral system, by *reducing reactivity to fear-eliciting (attachment-eliciting) cues* (Bowlby 1980; Main, in press, and 1981). Behavioral organization is then maintained through a shift in attention away from the parent which is largely accomplished through exploration—a strategy that may also serve to maintain what-

---

confusion regarding parental signaling or some other aspect of the experimental procedure, and temporary stresses of other kinds.

ever proximity to the parent seems possible (Main 1981; Main & Weston 1982).[4] The insecure-ambivalent infant also appears organized in its persistent focus upon the caregiver. Expressing alarm over even relatively unalarming events—hence, *maximizing* the display of attachment behavior—this seemingly "hypervigilant" infant draws or attempts to draw the attention of an unpredictably responsive caregiver.

The factors leading to the production of the *D* pattern of behavior are inherently complex. A comprehensive discussion would require (1) a more detailed focus upon the role of conflict in infant responses to the Strange Situation, and relatedly (2) consideration of the number and nature of the parameters which serve to control responses for infants assigned to differing attachment classifications. The Strange-Situation behavior of the secure infant may, for example, be under the control of caregiver location only and therefore involve little or no conflict. The behavior of the avoidant and ambivalent infants may be additionally controlled by the past behavior of the attachment figure, so that for these infants likely caregiver response as well as caregiver location must continually be taken into account (Main, in press). In that their caregivers have typically failed to provide negative (terminating) feedback to attachment behavior in the home situation, being either rejecting of attachment behavior (Ainsworth et al. 1978; replicated in two further samples by Main & Stadtman 1981) or unpredictably responsive (Ainsworth et al. 1978), the behavior of these infants in the more stressful Strange Situation may be in part the product of conflict—a conflict that can nonetheless produce relatively organized outcomes (as the avoidant infant's exploration, which may be a form of displacement behavior).[5] Finally, the more dramatically conflicted behaviors appearing in disorganized infants—unpredictable both in timing and form—may seem chaotic precisely because of a history of frightening experiences which (below) provide mixed positive and negative feedback to the attachment behavioral system.

A complete discussion of the origin and significance of pattern *D* behavior would involve simultaneous examination of the behavior of *A, B,* and *C* infants and is beyond the scope of this chapter. Previously, however, we had

4. The avoidant pattern may be vulnerable to breakdown under increased stress, however, at which time the previously avoidant infant may approach the parent in a disorganized manner (as see Ainsworth et al. 1978 description of difficulty-to-classify proximity seeking in pattern *A* infants subjected to a second Strange Situation).

5. To many people accustomed to observing infant Strange-Situation behavior using the three-part category system, the ambivalent pattern seems much the least well organized. This may be in part because a majority of *C* infants are in fact disorganized (Main & Hesse 1989) but may also result from observations of the infant who first seeks, then angrily rejects, the mother—an *alternation* in behavior patterns which is one possible result of conflict.

If, however, we consider the *C* (nondisorganized) infant as *maximizing* of attachment behavior, this alternation may appear less disorganized. Bowlby (1973) suggests that, inside of some relationships, angry behavior is ultimately proximity promoting.

drawn attention to the conflict experienced by the infant who is physically rejected by the attachment figure (Main 1981; Main & Weston 1982). We suggested that this (insecure-avoidant) infant is theoretically captured within a positive feedback loop in which rejection arouses attachment behavior which, rejected again by the attachment figure, leads to still further arousal of the attachment behavioral system. We described this situation as inherently disorganizing, but we suggested that the rejected infant escapes behavioral disorganization through a shift in attention away from the attachment figure and from attachment-eliciting changes in the environment. This shift in attention can probably only be accomplished, however, when (*a*) the experience of parental rejection has been relatively consistent and nonthreatening and (*b*) when the conditions in the surrounding environment are only moderately stressful.

If we are correct regarding the unpredictably frightening behavior patterns shown on occasion by still-traumatized parents, then we can see that their infants are confronted with an inherently perplexing set of circumstances. In contrast to both avoidant and ambivalent infants—who may be frightened by difficulties in obtaining caregiver responsiveness in stressful situations—the fear the *D* infant experiences stems from the parent as its source. Placed in the Strange Situation in the company of a parent whose behavior has been unpredictably frightening, then, the *D* infant may at moments unavoidably experience an alarm sufficiently intense that the activation of attachment behavior cannot be systematically controlled. When the effects of attachment-eliciting cues cannot be minimized (as they apparently can for the avoidant infant), increasing proximity to the attachment figure is the usual solution. For the infant who has been alarmed unpredictably by the attachment figure, however, approach to the parent may be occasionally interrupted by displays of disorganized/disoriented behavior precisely because memories involving fear of the parent have momentarily become aroused.

In conclusion, it seems apparent that frightening behavior on the part of the still-traumatized parent should lead to disorganized/disoriented infant behavior, since the infant is presented with an irresolvable paradox wherein the haven of safety is at once the source of the alarm. Moreover, the conflict between opposing tendencies to approach and to flee from the attachment figure stems from a single external signal (threatening or fearful parental behavior); is internal to the infant; is self-perpetuating; and is exacerbated by placement in a stressful situation.

REFERENCES

Ainsworth, M. D. S.; Blehar, M. C.; Waters, E.; & Wall, S. (1978). *Patterns of attachment: A psychological study of the strange situation.* Hillsdale, N.J.: Erlbaum.
Ainsworth, M. DE. S., & Eichberg, C. G. (in press). Effects on infant-mother attachment of

mother's unresolved loss of an attachment figure or other traumatic experience. In P. Marris, J. Stevenson-Hinde, & C. Parkes, *Attachment across the life cycle*. New York: Routledge.

American Psychiatric Association Committee on Nomenclature (1987). *Diagnostic and statistical manual of mental disorders, III-R*. Washington, D.C.: American Psychiatric Association.

Bowlby, J. ([1969] 1982). *Attachment and loss: Vol. 1. Attachment*. New York: Basic Books.

Bowlby, J. (1973). *Attachment and Loss: Vol. 2. Separation*. New York: Basic Books.

Bowlby, J. (1980). *Attachment and loss: Vol. 3. Loss, sadness and depression*. New York: Basic Books.

Bretherton, I. (1985). Attachment theory: Retrospect and prospect. In I. Bretherton & E. Waters (eds.), *Growing points of attachment theory and research. Monographs of the Society for Research in Child Development* 50(1–2, Serial No. 209), 3–35.

Brown, G.; Harris, T.; & Bifulco, A. (1985). Long-term effects of early loss of parent. In M. Rutter, C. Izard, & P. Read (eds.), *Depression in childhood: Developmental perspectives*. New York: Guildford.

Carlson, V.; Cicchetti, D.; Barnett, D.; & Braunwald, K. (1989). Disorganized/disoriented attachment relationships in maltreated infants. *Developmental Psychology* 25, no. 4, 525–531.

Cassidy, J. (1985, April). Attachment and the self at six. Paper presented at the biennial meeting of the Society for Research in Child Development, Toronto.

Cassidy, J. (1986). Attachment and the self at six. Unpublished doctoral dissertation, University of Virginia.

Cassidy, J. (1988). Child-mother attachment and the self in six-year-olds. *Child Development* 59, 121–134.

Crowell, J., & Feldman, S. (1988). The effects of mothers' internal models of relations and children's developmental and behavioral status on mother-child interactions. *Child Development* 59, 1273–1285.

Friedman, C. T. (1986). Interaction and attachment: Determinants of individual differences in a sample of visually impaired one- and two-year-olds and their mothers. Unpublished doctoral dissertation, Department of Education, University of California, Berkeley.

George, C.; Kaplan, N.; & Main, M. (1985). The Berkeley Adult Attachment Interview. Unpublished protocol, Department of Psychology, University of California, Berkeley.

George, C., & Solomon, J. (1989, April). Internal working models of parenting and security of attachment at age 6. Paper presented at the biennial meeting of the Society for Research in Child Development, Kansas City.

Grossmann, K.; Fremmer-Bombik, E.; Rudolph, J.; & Grossmann, K. E. (1988). Maternal attachment representations as related to patterns of child-mother attachment and maternal sensitivity and acceptance of her infant. In R. A. Hinde & J. Stevenson-Hinde (eds.), *Relations within families*. Oxford: Oxford University Press.

Hinde, R. A. (1970). *Animal behavior: A synthesis of ethology and comparative psychology* (2d ed). New York: McGraw-Hill.

Hinde, R. A. (1982). Attachment: Some conceptual and biological issues. In C. M. Parkes & J. Stevenson-Hinde (eds.), *The place of attachment in human behavior*. New York: Basic Books.

Kaplan, N. (1987). Individual differences in 6-year-old's thoughts about separation: Predicted from attachment to mother at age 1. Unpublished doctoral dissertation, Department of Psychology, University of California, Berkeley.

Kobak, R. R., & Sceery, A. (1988). Attachment in late adolescence: Working models, affect regulation, and representations of self and others. *Child Development* 59, 135–146.

Krentz, M. S. (1982). Qualitative differences between mother-child and caregiver-child attachments of infants in family day care. Unpublished doctoral dissertation, California School of Professional Psychology, Berkeley.

Levine, L.; Ward, M.; & Carlson, B. (1989, September). Attachment across three generations: Grandmother, mother and infants. Paper presented at World Association of Infant Psychiatry and Allied Disciplines, Lugarno, Switzerland.

Lyons-Ruth, K.; Zoll, D.; Connell, D. B.; & Odom, R. (1987, April). Maternal depression as mediator of the effects of home-based intervention service. Paper presented at the biennial meeting of the Society for Research in Child Development, Baltimore.

Main, M. (1981). Avoidance in the service of attachment: A working paper. In K. Immelmann, G. Barlow, L. Petrinovich, & M. Main (eds.), *Behavioral development: The Bielefeld inter-disciplinary project* (pp. 651–693). New York: Cambridge University Press.

Main, M. (1983). New prospects in the study of attachment. Paper presented at the annual meeting of the American Academy of Child Psychiatry, San Francisco.

Main, M. (1985, April). An adult attachment classification system: Its relation to infant-parent attachment. Paper presented at the biennial meeting of the Society for Research in Child Development, Toronto.

Main, M. (in press). Cross-cultural studies of attachment organization: Recent studies, changing methodologies, and the concept of conditional strategies. *Human Development.*

Main, M., & Cassidy, J. (1988). Categories of response to reunion with the parent at age six: Predicted from infant attachment classifications and stable over a one-month period. *Developmental Psychology* 24, no. 3, 415–426.

Main, M.; DeMoss, A.; & Hesse, E. (1989). A system for assessing lack of resolution of mourning from interview transcripts. Unpublished manuscript, Department of Psychology, University of California, Berkeley.

Main, M., & Goldwyn, R. (in press). Interview-based adult attachment classifications: Related to infant-mother and infant-father attachment. *Developmental Psychology.*

Main, M., & Hesse, E. (1989). Interview-based assessments of a parent's unresolved trauma are related to infant "D" attachment status: Linking parental states of mind to infant behavior observed in a stressful situation. Submitted manuscript, working title.

Main, M.; Kaplan, N.; & Cassidy, J. (1985). Security in infancy, childhood and adulthood: A move to the level of representation. In I. Bretherton & E. Waters (eds.), *Growing points of attachment theory and research. Monographs of the Society for Research in Child Development* 50(1–2, Serial No. 209), 66–104.

Main, M., & Solomon, J. (1986). Discovery of a new, insecure-disorganized/disoriented attachment pattern. In T. B. Brazelton & M. Yogman (eds.), *Affective development in infancy* (pp. 95–124). Norwood: Ablex.

Main, M. & Stadtman, J. (1981). Infant response to rejection of physical contact by the mother: Aggression, avoidance and conflict. *Journal of the American Academy of Child Psychiatry* 20, 292–307.

Main, M., & Weston, D. (1981). The quality of the toddler's relationship to mother and father. *Child Development* 52, 932–940.

Main, M., & Weston, D. (1982). Avoidance of the attachment figure in infancy: descriptions and interpretations. In C. M. Parkes & J. Stevenson-Hinde (eds.), *The place of attachment in human behavior* (pp. 31–59). London: Tavistock.

Parkes, C. M. (1972). *Bereavement: Studies of grief in adult life.* London: Tavistock.

Parkes, C. M. (1980). Bereavement counseling: Does it work? *British Medical Journal* 1, 740–743.

Quinton, D., & Rutter, M. (1985). Parenting behavior of mothers raised in care. IN A. R. Nichol (ed.), *Longitudinal studies in child psychology and psychiatry: practical lessons from research experience* (pp. 157–261). Chichester and New York: Wiley.

Radke-Yarrow, M.; Cummings, E. M.; Kuczynski, L.; & Chapman, M. (1985). Patterns of attachment in two- and three-year-olds in normal families and families with parental depression. *Child Development* 56, 884–893.

Raphael, B. (1982). *Tha anatomy of bereavement.* New York: Basic Books.

Strage, A., & Main, M. (1985, April). Parent-child discourse patterns at 6 years predicted from the organization of infant attachment relationships. Paper given at the biennial meeting of the Society for Research in Child Development, Toronto.

Volkmar, F. R.; Hoder, E. L.; & Siegel, A. E. (1980). Discrepant social communications. *Developmental Psychology* 16, no. 5, 495–505.

Volkmar, F. R., & Siegel, A. E. (1979). Young children's responses to discrepant social communications. *Journal of Child Psychology and Psychiatry* 20, 139–149.

Ward, M.; Carlson, B.; Altman, S. C.; Levine, L.; Greenberg, R. H.; & Kessler, D. B. (1989a). Predicting infant-mother attachment from adolescent's working models of relationships. Submitted manuscript.

Ward, M.; Carlson, B.; & Kessler, D. B. (1989b). Adolescent mother-infant attachment: Interactions, relationships and adolescent working models. Submitted manuscript.

PART TWO

Research on the Normal Development of Attachment in Preschool Years

6 · The Developmental Reorganization of Attachment Relationships

GUIDELINES FOR CLASSIFICATION BEYOND INFANCY

Karen Schneider-Rosen

THE ESTABLISHMENT of an attachment relationship is considered to be a critical socioemotional task that must be accomplished during the infancy period, that provides the basis for competence and effective functioning, and that prepares the infant for the successful resolution of subsequent developmental tasks in the socioemotional and cognitive domains (Ainsworth 1972; Bowlby [1969] 1982, 1973, 1980; Sroufe 1979; Sroufe & Waters 1977). Once an attachment relationship has developed during the first year of life, it is characterized by a pattern of behavioral organization that is mediated by affect (Sroufe & Waters 1977) and that operates in transaction with other organized behavioral systems that regulate the infant's interactions with her environment (Bischof 1975; Bretherton 1980; Bretherton & Ainsworth 1974; Waters & Deane 1982, 1985).

Individual differences in the way that attachment relationships become organized during infancy have been evaluated in an effort to better understand the factors associated with the emergence of various attachment patterns and the consequences of these patterns for subsequent development. The study of individual differences has been contingent upon the classification of attachment relationships. Therefore, with methodological advances and the development of laboratory-based procedures for evaluating and operationally defining qualitative differences in attachment relationships (e.g., Ainsworth, Blehar, Waters, & Wall 1978), theoretical conceptualizations about the nature and importance of early attachment relationships have been subjected to empirical testing and verification by attachment researchers.

These efforts have been restricted to the period of infancy, since it is during the first 2 years of life that attachment relationships have been considered to be most important (e.g., Bowlby [1969] 1982; Sroufe 1979). The classification system developed by Ainsworth et al. (1978) was originally intended for use at 12 months of age. While it has been used with children at 18 months (e.g., Main & Weston 1981; Matas, Arend, & Sroufe 1978; Schneider-Rosen & Cicchetti 1984; Waters 1978), Ainsworth maintains that beyond that age, a modified classificatory system is desirable for the valid identification of attachment patterns (Ainsworth 1982). While some theorists have argued that attachment occurs at all ages (e.g., Ainsworth 1969; Bowlby [1969] 1982) and should be studied as a life-span construct (e.g., Antonucci 1976; Stern 1985; Weiss 1982), empirical efforts to evaluate qualitative differences in the organization of attachment behaviors beyond infancy have been limited.

Bowlby ([1969] 1982) contends that, while the course that attachment takes beyond infancy is not well-chronicled or understood, attachment behaviors during childhood, adolescence, and adulthood are in many ways a continuation of early attachment behaviors. He emphasizes the fact that, at least during the second and third years of life, attachment behavior is shown at neither less frequency nor less intensity than it is at the end of the first year (Bowlby [1969] 1982). A major difference, however, occurs in *the nature of the circumstances that elicit attachment behaviors.* Thus, while it may be the case that an attenuation of attachment behaviors is observed when traditional assessment procedures (e.g., the Strange Situation) are employed with children beyond the age for which they were originally intended, new assessment techniques that are designed specifically for use beyond the infancy period may provide important information about individual differences in attachment relationships as the infant enters toddlerhood.

In considering the classification of attachment relationships beyond infancy, several issues need to be addressed. First, it is important to consider some reasons as to why researchers have studied attachment during the infancy period and not beyond the first 2 years of life. Several theoretical and methodological factors that shed light on this issue will be discussed. Second, if one were to study attachment beyond infancy, then it is critical to have a theoretical framework for conceptualizing attachment relationships and for guiding the development of an appropriate classification scheme. The organizational approach to development will be discussed in terms of its implications for the study of attachment beyond the first 2 years of life. Third, several empirical efforts have been made to study attachment relationships beyond infancy. These classification schemes will be reviewed with special reference to the ways in which they integrate the principles of the organizational approach and contribute to our understanding of developing attachment relationships. This chapter will illuminate the ways in which it *is* possible to extend the work of attachment researchers to date so as to be able to describe and classify individual differences in attachment relationships beyond infancy.

REASONS FOR THE CLASSIFICATION OF INDIVIDUAL DIFFERENCES IN ATTACHMENT DURING INFANCY AND NOT BEYOND

There are several important reasons as to why the analysis and classification of qualitative differences in attachment have been reserved for the period of infancy. These include: (1) the theoretical framework out of which attachment theory has emerged, (2) the developmental perspective within which attachment research has evolved, and (3) the underlying assumptions that have been made by current researchers with regard to those situations that activate attachment behaviors and enable the organization of attachment behaviors to be classified.

The study of individual differences in attachment relationships is tied historically to psychoanalytic theory. Freud described the relationship between the infant and the mother, calling it "unique, without parallel, established unalterably for a whole lifetime as the first and strongest love-object and as the prototype of all later love relations—for both sexes" (Freud 1940, p. 188). Thus, the basic insights of psychoanalytic theory, as they relate to attachment theory and research, are not tied to a drive-reduction model of motivation or a mechanistic model yielding a passive view of the individual (Bowlby [1969] 1982). Rather, they are related to Freud's changing metapsychology which shifted from an early position based on trauma and repression of affect to an increasing emphasis on the quality of significant early relationships (Loevinger 1976; Sroufe 1983). According to this position, anxiety is a signal to the individual that there is a threat of a significant interpersonal loss. The vulnerability to disorganization in the face of anxiety, the characteristic ways of dealing with conflict and anxiety, and the occurrence and magnitude of anxiety are seen to be determined by experiential history within the early relationship (Freud 1940).

The evolution of psychoanalytic theory has continued to emphasize the special significance of the earliest relationships since they are seen to represent the prototype for later interpersonal relationships and to provide the context for the emergence of the self (e.g., Breger 1974; Erikson 1950; Klein 1976; Loevinger 1976; Mahler, Pine, & Bergman 1975; Sander 1975; Sullivan 1953). It is generally agreed that the infant's first meaningful relationships develop during the first year of life and have an enduring significance for the child. It is not surprising, therefore, that early attachment theory (e.g., Ainsworth 1969; Bowlby 1958, [1969] 1982), with its roots in psychoanalytic thinking, emphasized the importance of the infancy period.

Much of the recent attachment research, directed toward classifying and understanding individual differences in patterns of attachment, has been influenced by the organizational approach to development. Within the organizational perspective (Cicchetti & Sroufe 1978; Santostefano & Baker 1972; Sroufe 1979; Werner 1948; Werner & Kaplan 1963), development is depicted as a series of behavioral reorganizations around a set of developmental tasks or issues (see Cicchetti & Schneider-Rosen 1986; Erikson 1950; Greenspan 1981; Sander 1962; Sroufe 1979; Sroufe & Rutter 1984). Thus, for example, physiological regulation and the management of tension are issues of the first

6 months of life, establishing an attachment relationship is an important task for the second half of the first year, exploration and mastery are issues for the period from 12 to 18 months, individuation and autonomy and the regulation and control of emotional reactions are the tasks for 18–30 months, and peer relations, the management of impulses, empathy and prosocial behavior, and sex-role identification represent the issues from 30 to 54 months of age. A developmental task is resolved in a manner that is considered to be competent if it (1) allows for an organization of behaviors that reflects a balance between internal, motivational needs and external environmental demands; and (2) promotes effective, flexible functioning in adaptation to specific environmental constraints.

The adoption of this perspective reflects a commitment to characterizing behavior and development in terms of the changing integration and organization of capacities in the social, emotional, and cognitive domains. Empirical investigations on the coherence of the developmental process have employed this organizational view to evaluate the relative competence with which children are meeting developmental challenges (Sroufe 1983; Sroufe & Rutter 1984; Waters & Sroufe 1983). This conception of competence implies that the successful resolution of stage-salient tasks by children in one behavioral domain at one point in time should be associated with the successful resolution of salient tasks in other domains at the same time as well as in subsequent periods of development. Therefore, early adaptation tends to promote concurrent and later adaptation, given continuity in the caregiving environment. Alternatively, problems in the resolution of stage-salient tasks may result in the development of compensatory mechanisms which may provide alternative pathways to achieving competence, or which may leave the child vulnerable to developing psychopathology (see Cicchetti & Schneider-Rosen 1984 for a review).

Researchers adopting this perspective have used it to guide the questions that they have asked about competence and adaptation at different ages and stages of functioning during infancy and childhood. An implicit assumption of the organizational perspective is that the unfolding series of developmental issues or tasks, upon emergence, remain critical to children's continual adaptation, although they decrease in salience relative to other, newly emerging developmental tasks (see Cicchetti & Schneider-Rosen 1986 for an elaboration of this view). Each of these issues represent life-span tasks that require continual organization and coordination (see Erikson 1950; Sroufe 1979). Thus, for example, while the development of an attachment relationship is a salient task of the infancy period, important changes in attachment relationships occur as children move into toddlerhood.

Why, then, have attachment researchers only focused on the period of infancy in their investigation of qualitative differences in attachment? In their efforts to demonstrate the construct and predictive validity of the attachment construct, researchers have evaluated individual differences in attachment and then moved on to demonstrate the way in which the behavioral organization evolved with respect to attachment lays the groundwork for subsequent behavioral organization, such as in exploration or mastery of the environment or in the negotiation of peer relationships (e.g., Arend, Gove, & Sroufe 1979; Matas et al. 1978; Waters, Wippman, & Sroufe 1979). Attachment researchers have perpetuated inadvertently a notion that the development of an attachment relationship is a milestone or hurdle that needs to be negotiated and mastered during infancy and then decreases in importance relative to other emerging issues. It is, therefore, not surprising that researchers have not evaluated developmental changes in attachment relationships that occur beyond infancy.

These theoretical issues that may be seen to have restricted the study of attachment to the infancy period are paralleled by specific methodological issues that have served the same function. In order to accurately capture the organized patterning of attachment behaviors and to account for individual differences in attachment relationships, researchers employing the Strange Situation (Ainsworth et al. 1978) make an implicit assumption that the increased stress that children experience during the prescribed sequence of episodes activates attachment behaviors. The observed organization of these behaviors, considered within and between episodes, provides an index of the overall quality of the relationship. A critical part of the Strange Situation is the separation/reunion sequence that occurs twice during the twenty-one-minute paradigm. The separations, in particular, are presumed to cause anxiety and to elicit attachment behaviors, that is, those behaviors that will have the effect of bringing the infant into closer proximity to the caregiver so as to achieve contact and derive comfort.

The assumption that separations in the Strange Situation are important for eliciting attachment behaviors has implications for the evaluation of individual differences in attachment relationships beyond the first 2 years of life. Two important questions that need to be asked as one considers the use of the Strange Situation beyond infancy are: (1) Do the episodes elicit the same degree of stress for older children? (2) Do children respond to stress through the overt manifestation of the same interactive behaviors after the first 2 years of life as they do before?

By 2 years of age, children tend to protest less than do younger infants when undergoing a separation from the caregiver not of their own initiative (Maccoby & Feldman 1972; Marvin 1977). Their improved coping skills and increased experiences with separations from their caregivers may make them less likely to respond to separations with overt signs of distress or with a heightened need to seek contact and maintain proximity. However, the diminution in the overt manifestation of these attachment behaviors in response to separation does not imply a decreased importance of attachment. Rather, the implication is that developmentally appropriate coding schemes are necessary to capture the organization of more advanced behaviors that serve to regulate contact and proximity in the Strange Situation (e.g., Schneider-Rosen 1984; Schneider-Rosen, Braunwald, Carlson, & Cicchetti 1985).

There is some evidence suggesting that other laboratory-based separation-reunion sequences may be meaningful for assessing attachment in children older than 2 years of age (see Cassidy & Marvin 1987; Greenberg & Marvin 1979; Main & Cassidy 1986, 1988; Main, Kaplan, & Cassidy 1985; Radke-Yarrow, Cummings, Kuczynski, & Chapman 1985). Thus, while it is more difficult to "see" attachment behaviors beyond infancy since they become more subtle and may be visible only in highly stressful situations, there may be other situations or contexts that are more effective for classifying the attachment relationship. Current classification systems may be inadequate for conceptualizing and evaluating qualitative differences in attachment. New systems are needed that do not rely so heavily on a sequence of episodes that may not elicit the same kind of reactions in older children as have been observed in infants.

The attachment relationship is undergoing qualitative change (Sroufe 1983, 1985; Sroufe & Fleeson 1986), influenced by the development of both the child and the parent, new experiences to which the dyad is exposed, and environmental demands. Therefore, while empirical efforts have focused on evaluating the factors that relate to the development of a particular pattern of behavioral organization within the dyad during the first year (i.e., a secure or insecure attachment pattern), it is equally critical to capture the quality of the parent-child attachment relationship beyond the infancy period.

IMPLICATIONS OF A DEVELOPMENTAL PERSPECTIVE FOR RESEARCH ON ATTACHMENT BEYOND INFANCY

The ability to assess attachment beyond the limited age range within which it has been studied to date requires a sound theoretical framework to guide the development of new classificatory schemes. The integration of a developmental perspective (e.g., Santostefano 1978; Sroufe & Rutter 1984) into research on attachment reflects a commitment to acknowledging the progressive reorganization of behavior that occurs as the developing child transacts with the environment. While attachment has been viewed as an organizational *construct* (e.g., Sroufe & Waters 1977), there are some important implications of an *organizational-developmental approach* to the study of attachment relationships beyond the first 2 years of life. In the following section, several propositions of this developmental perspective will be discussed in terms of their specific relevance to the study of attachment beyond infancy.

Differentiation and Reorganization

The qualitative reorganizations that are characteristic of development proceed according to the orthogenetic principle (Werner 1957). The developing organism moves from a globally undifferentiated and relatively diffuse state to a state of greater articulation and organized complexity as a result of differentiation and hierarchical integration. As the individual develops, earlier forms of behavior are hierarchically integrated within more complex forms (Werner 1957). For example, the behavior of the young infant may be conceived of as governed largely by physiological processes; biological and temperamental factors influence their reactions to particular stimulus situations and guide their behavior. With development, cognitive factors play a more important role in determining behavior as children interpret, filter, and actively "construct" their experience. Behavior and thought are no longer distinct. Behavior is not dependent solely upon changes in the external environment but rather reflects an integration of the child's physiological reactions and cognitive responses to the surroundings.

The changes that take place in the relationship between the individual and the environment reflect the process of differentiation as well. Because physiological processes determine so much of the behavior of young infants, they may be seen as relatively psychologically undifferentiated from their environment. With development, the gradual differentiation that occurs may be studied as a social-cognitive phenomenon—the differentiation and integration of bonds between children and their caregivers—and as an affective-cognitive phenomenon—children's developing conceptions of themselves and of their emotions (Cicchetti & Schneider-Rosen 1986). As a result of the differentiation that occurs, the attachment relationship undergoes transformation. Therefore, both processes of differentiation and integration are directly relevant to the study of attachment beyond infancy in several ways.

First, the implication of differentiation and hierarchic integration for the classification of attachment is that developmental changes in attachment behaviors will be functionally related to children's emerging competencies. For example, increasing cognitive sophistication results in a reorganization of attachment behaviors in a manner that allows children to adjust and modify specific plans and intentions according to situational cues and demands and to caregiver signals. With the development of linguistic and locomotor skills and the cognitive capacity for representation and memory, children do not need to rely as much upon physical closeness or proximity to maintain the attachment relationship. Distal modes of interacting, such as looking, talking, or offering toys across a distance, may take the place of proximal behaviors such as touching or physical closeness (Serafica 1978; Waters 1978). Distress upon brief separation from the caregiver decreases with an increase in age and in cognitive sophistication (Kotelchuck, 1972; Maccoby & Feldman, 1972; Weinraub & Lewis 1977), and children are capable of spending a greater amount of time physically away from the caregiver. Following brief separations, children may be content with mere proximity to their caregiver rather than requiring the close bodily contact sought by 1-year-olds; later, they are likely to be content merely with reestablishing interaction from across a distance. Gaze aversion, which may be an index of avoidance in infants too young to walk away, may be an index of distraction or lack of interest in toddlers.

An important question that needs to be addressed, therefore, is whether a given behavior or set of behavior maintains a consistent relationship with the presumed underlying construct (i.e., attachment) over age, or whether there is a more fluid combination of behaviors, open to transformation over time, that is required to allow for the classification of attachment beyond infancy. The developmental perspective recognizes that various alternatives are possible. Thus, according to this perspective, any classification scheme needs to consider and reflect the fact that there will be age changes in the frequency, intensity, and occurrence of certain attachment behaviors, both during separation and at other times of stress. Specifically, the growing capacities for verbal communication, autonomous functioning, independent exploration, affiliation with unfamiliar adults, emotional control, and flexibility in the modification of goals and plans, represent emerging competencies that result in qualitative changes in attachment behaviors, and in their organization, over time.

With increasing age and cognitive sophistication, children construct alternative means of affecting the behaviors of others around them. They also learn to inhibit goal-directed behavior and to communicate their goals and plans through language, thereby providing for further changes in the organization of the relationship between children and their caregivers. They move toward what Bowlby ([1969] 1982) calls the goal-corrected partnership. The relationship is characterized by increasing behavioral integration reflecting cooperation and consideration for each individual's plans, goals, attitudes, and feelings; there is a cooperative balance in perspective-taking abilities, and there is a reciprocal control of behavior (Marvin 1977). This is not to say that physical proximity and contact are no longer important; rather, they decrease in importance relative to the integration and balance of goals, attitudes, feelings, plans, and behaviors.

Second, with the differentiation that occurs between the individual and their environment, children develop greater flexibility in responding to their surroundings. They become capable of conceptualizing alternative means for responding to their social and nonsocial environments and of substituting various means for obtaining a desired goal (Santostefano 1978). This enables the individual to express behavior in more indirect, organized, and stage-appropriate terms, while simultaneously facilitating adaptation to the environment. Increasingly flexible behavioral organization provides a criterion for examining individual differences in attachment relationships.

Specifically, while early attachment behaviors are incorporated into later ones by means of hierarchical integration, the early structures remain accessible and ready to be activated. The individual does not operate solely in terms of behaviors that define a particular stage of development; early modes of functioning may become manifest, for example, during times of stress. When the attachment system is activated, children may display certain behaviors that appear "regressive" or that are less differentiated relative to their current developmental level. Yet, the availability of previous modes of functioning is relevant to the individual's ongoing adaptation.

To consider an example: a 24-month-old girl and her father enter a playroom in which there are many new toys for her to play with. She moves rather quickly over to the box of toys and becomes actively involved in play. When her father gets up to leave the room, she becomes distressed immediately and runs to the door. She remains at the door for a while, crying and calling for her "daddy" but without attempting to leave the room (i.e., by reaching for the doorknob or banging on the door). Her crying gradually diminishes and she starts talking, saying "Daddy come back, Sara see daddy." After listening for her father's return, but not hearing his footsteps or seeing him enter the room, she goes over to the toy box, picks up the toy phone, and has a "conversation" with her "daddy" on the phone. When her father returns, she runs to greet him at the door and then resumes play.

In this example, the flexible use of early structures facilitates the negotiation of the stressful situation. The toddler initially becomes distressed and makes some attempts to retrieve her father. Yet these efforts, which are characteristic of the way in which she might have sought to regain her father's presence when she was younger (i.e., crying, calling his name, and running after him), are then replaced by more developmentally appropriate behaviors (e.g., pretend play that enables her to calm herself and regain an image of her father). The toddler's flexibility and her capacity to substitute relatively immature behaviors with those that are more suitable for her age represents the "mobility of functioning" (Werner 1957) that promotes adaptation to the environment.

On the other hand, the inflexible use of early structures with regard to the current adaptational task may connote a maladaptive behavioral pattern. Had the toddler remained at the door, crying and calling for her "daddy" with an intensification of distress and an inability to calm down and return to play when her father returned to the room, this would have signified a regression to an earlier mode of functioning that prevented adaptation to the current situation. Thus, it is not the presence or even the use of early, less differentiated behaviors that is atypical; rather, it is the inability to negotiate a stressful situation by modulating one's responses and integrating earlier modes of functioning with more recently developed patterns that signifies an atypical pattern of responding. Therefore, any classification system intended for use beyond the infancy period must be able to identify both normal and atypical patterns of adaptation in response to stress, with flexibility and an ability to redifferentiate after regression, a signal for adaptation.

Holism

The significance of behavior can only be understood within the context in which that behavior occurs (Werner & Kaplan 1963). This principle of *holism* derives from the fact that two relatively similar behaviors may have very different meanings and serve different functions, while two dissimilar behaviors may be equivalent in different contexts (Santostefano 1978; Sroufe & Waters 1977; Werner & Kaplan 1963). Interrelationships between behaviors may become meaningful only to the extent that those behaviors play the same or related functions.

This principle has been considered in the study of attachment during infancy (e.g., Sroufe & Waters 1977); it also has several consequences for the study of attachment beyond infancy which need to be emphasized. First, it is clear that one needs to transcend a focus on frequency counts or lists of relevant attachment behaviors. Even if the behaviors that should be considered are developmentally appropriate and selected according to expectations for a particular level of functioning, they do not have very much meaning for the researcher if they are considered in isolation from the context in which they occur. Thus, it is necessary to examine situational variables and antecedent and consequent events before interpreting the meaning of any particular attachment behavior.

For example, the presence of gaze aversion upon reunion with a caregiver in and of itself is not a sufficient index of avoidance in a 24-month-old. The gaze aversion may be accompanied by movement away from the caregiver, in which case it may signify avoidance, or it may enable the child to redirect attention back to an ongoing activity. In the latter instance, the discrete behavior has a very different meaning. Therefore, the consideration of context enables the observer to better understand the significance and meaning of those behaviors that have been integrated into a particular pattern in a specific context.

Second, it is necessary to consider how the behaviors of interest reflect motivational, emotional, and biological needs of the child as well as influence those needs as a result of their occurrence. While these internal needs are not directly observable, they could have a major impact on the individual's behavior, and they therefore need to be inferred from the ongoing situation. The significance that is ascribed to these internal needs will in some sense define the context in which the child is operating and influence the meaning of the child's behavior as well.

Third, the context also implies the basic unit that is being conceptualized, observed, and analyzed, that is, the relationship and various interactions between individuals. Although the individuals are relatively autonomous, they develop an integrated and well-organized pattern of relating to one another. As the infants' social world expands, multiple attachment relationships may be developed and modified. Attachment relationships will be renegotiated as new modes of interaction are established within each dyad and alternations are made in the maintenance of each relationship. Unique patternings of behaviors will be achieved within *each* dyadic relationship. Qualitatively different attachments will be formed between children and each of their parents as well as between children and alternative caregivers. Thus, it is necessary to study attachment behaviors in the context of *each* of these relationships.

The Coherence of Development over Time

A central proposition underlying the developmental perspective is that the course of development follows a lawful pattern. There is a coherence to each individual's development across periods of discontinuous growth and despite fundamental transformations in manifest behavior (Sroufe & Rutter 1984). Thus, one does not expect to observe an isomorphism in behavior across development; rather, the growing organism displays diverse and increasingly more complex behaviors over time.

In accordance with this principle, consistency is expected in the general adaptive or maladaptive pattern of organizing experiences and interacting with the environment (Block & Block 1979; Rutter 1977; Sroufe 1979). Continuity of development is expressed in organized patterns of behavior over time rather than in isolated behaviors. Therefore, according to the organizational-developmental perspective, a particular pattern of behaviors displayed in a particular context at one developmental level is not necessarily predicted to recur in the same form or in similar contexts at a later point in development. Rather, in spite of behavioral change and homotypic discontinuity (Kagan 1971; Kohlberg, LaCrosse, & Ricks 1971; Masters & Wellman 1974; Mischel 1968), there is an underlying organization and continuity of functioning.

The implication of such an organizational-developmental perspective for the classification of attachment beyond infancy is that classification schemes should emphasize the organization of attachment behaviors at various developmental levels rather than simply identifying static traits or behaviors that are constant across development. Some notion of the coherence of the individual, in terms of his or her manner of organizing and integrating experiences, as well as adaptive and pathological patterns of responding to the environment, need to be included in a developmentally appropriate classification system.

Thus, while the adaptive significance and set-goals of attachment may be maintained from one developmental period to the next, the means by which these objectives are achieved will be modified according to age-appropriate advances. The attachment relationship will retain its important biological function presumed to be operating from birth. Physical proximity and contact will continue to be necessary to fulfill the biological function of protecting children from various sources of danger (e.g., from potentially harmful interactions with others, from physical hazards, etc.). It will also continue to provide the child with a sense of "felt security" and a "secure base" that promotes exploration.

Yet, the emergence of new competencies may impact children's ability to interpret and organize their environment, to interact with others, and to experience and express emotions. These maturational changes will result in developmentally different, yet organized, behavioral patterns. Moreover, the role that caregivers need to play in providing protection will decrease as children's roles increase, such that the relationship continues to maintain an organized quality in which caregivers complement the lack of competencies and skills on the part of their children. There may be moments when caregivers need to take greater responsibility for protecting their children when they perceive that their children's resources are not adequate. But there is also an increase in children's responsibility which is not merely the result of physical growth and the capacity for locomotion; it is a consequence of differences in children's physiological, emotional, cognitive, and linguistic capacities at different ages. A classification system that is based on the organization of attachment behaviors, in relation to the caregiver and in the context of environmental demands, at different developmental periods, will facilitate the identification of more meaningful behavioral patterns over time.

Behavioral Systems

Within the organizational-developmental approach, it is presumed that a hierarchical organization exists within and between interacting behavioral systems. The concept of behavioral systems has its roots in neurophysiology, ethology, and computer science (Cicchetti & Schneider-Rosen 1986). The systems are constructs; they are hypothesized to account for the organization of behavior observed in naturalistic surroundings or in experimental laboratories. With development, emerging competencies become hierarchically integrated *within* each behavioral system; moreover, competencies in each system become integrated *between* behavioral systems (Bischof 1975; Bronson 1972; Cicchetti & Serafica 1981).

The application of this behavioral systems perspective to the study of attachment relationships requires that attachment relationships be viewed in terms of the organization of behaviors both *within* the attachment behavioral system and *between* attachment and other behavioral systems. In particular, investigators have examined the affiliative, exploratory, and fear-wariness behavioral systems in relation to attachment (Bretherton & Ainsworth 1974). An interplay among behavioral systems is presumed to occur such that a single behavior may serve two or more systems (e.g., moving toward the mother in the presence of a stranger could be both an attachment and a wary behavior) or, alternatively, many seemingly unrelated behaviors (e.g., crying, moving toward the mother, termination of play, and inhibition of communication) may all serve the same behavioral system (in this case, the attachment system). Furthermore, behavioral systems may be activated sequentially (e.g., retreat to the mother's side following the entrance of a stranger [attachment] followed by approaching and offering the stranger a toy [affiliation]).

When viewed in this way, the set-goal of the attachment behavioral system is not simply maintenance of proximity to the attachment figure (Bowlby [1969] 1982). Rather, the set-goal is a degree of "felt security" for the child (Ainsworth 1973; Sroufe 1979; Waters 1981), one that promotes exploration and affiliation and reduces fear and wariness. The securely attached dyad will develop its capacity to negotiate changes in its degree of proximity such that each member is allowed freedom and independence while simultaneously remaining aware of the availability of the other (Marvin 1977). This reformulation of attachment theory accommodates the motivation of infants to leave their caregivers in an effort to explore the environment.

Therefore, a major function of the attachment behavioral system, both during and beyond the infancy period, is to assist infants in their excursions into their world and to modulate the balance between exploratory behavior and proximity seeking in response to various environmental contingencies. The control system functions using information not only about the discrepancy between exploration and the set-goal of proximity or contact. An evaluative component is included that allows for a determination to be made of the meaning of the discrepancy to the child (Kopp, Vaughn, & Cicchetti 1982). The evaluation on which these decisions are made will be influenced by developmental changes in children's abilities to perceive and cope with stress. Modifications in distance from the attachment figure may be made depending on the context and the threats to children's "felt security" in that context. Thus, the meaning of those behaviors that serve the various behavioral systems can only be understood within the context in which those behaviors occur.

In sum, the developmental perspective has many implications for the study of attachment beyond infancy. Given the developmental changes in children, and in the relationship between children and their caregivers, several methodological considerations become salient in proposing guidelines for the classification of attachment beyond infancy. First, it is necessary to employ age-appropriate assessment techniques in contexts that elicit a range of behavior patterns considered to be relatively adaptive for a particular age. Second, the complexity of attachment relationships beyond infancy necessitates that qualitative differences be evaluated across contexts and levels of analyses. Therefore, various assessment techniques need to be employed for purposes of classification. Third, alternative means for classifying the quality of the relationship need to be developed that do not rely upon exposure to stress. This becomes especially important beyond infancy since exposure to stress may not elicit the same overt manifestations of attachment behaviors with children's improved coping skills and increased capacity to make cognitive appraisals of the relative safety or danger of new situations.

Finally, the classification system must transcend a focus on discrete behaviors and instead focus on the way in which attachment behaviors become organized and represent a regulated pattern of adaptation that satisfies certain functions necessary for children's survival. This consideration is particularly important since category systems based on discrete responses have been found to fail to predict consistent individual differences (see, e.g., Masters & Wellman 1974). Moreover, it implicates the importance of considering the context in which the behavior has occurred and of infering the meaning of behavior from the situational context, since any single behavior may have many different meanings, depending on the situation in which it occurs. A corollary to this point is that it is necessary to evaluate attachment behaviors in relation to those behaviors serving related behavioral systems. It has been suggested that the attachment-exploration balance, for example, is so characteristic of the infant-caregiver relationship that clear evidence of this kind of organization in behavior in diverse situations provides the best criterion for evaluating and classifying the quality of attachment relationships (Stayton, Ainsworth, & Main 1973).

RECENT DEVELOPMENTS IN THE CLASSIFICATION OF ATTACHMENT BEYOND INFANCY

There are several implications of the developmental perspective for classifying qualitative differences in attachment beyond infancy. It is critical to integrate the theoretical and methodological guidelines evolving from this perspective and to illustrate their importance with reference to classification systems that have been or are being developed currently to characterize attachment relationships beyond infancy. Three different general approaches will be examined. While there are additional systems that are being used by other researchers (e.g., Crittenden 1985; Cummings, this vol.; Waters & Deane 1985), the systems to be described were chosen because of their relation both to existing classification systems and to the proposed guidelines that emanate from the developmental perspective.

One direction that recent research has taken integrates the principles of the developmental approach by providing a modified scheme to classify the quality of the attachment relationship using the Strange Situation (Schneider-Rosen et al. 1985). While many researchers have used the Strange Situation (Ainsworth et al. 1978) for children older than the age for which it was originally intended (i.e., 12 months), no formal classification system has been used to characterize the observed attachment behaviors or their relation to qualitative differences in patterns of attachment. The framework proposed by Schneider-Rosen et al. (1985) enables classification of children at 18 and 24 months of age. It assumes that the organization of the child's behavior across the seven three-minute episodes of the Strange Situation will provide significant information about (and will allow for the classification of) the attachment relationship, so long as the meaning of the child's behavior is inferred from the context, developmentally appropriate manifestations of the interactive behaviors are evaluated, and behaviors serving the attachment behavioral system are considered in relation to those serving the exploratory, affiliative, and fear-wariness behavioral systems.

The classification system was developed by first scoring the interactive behaviors across the seven episodes of the Strange Situation and then examining the individual patterns of these behaviors in a sample of twenty 18-month-old and twenty 24-month-old toddlers. Following the procedure used by Ainsworth et al. (1978) in their development of the classification scheme for 12-month-olds, behavioral protocols were used to divide the toddlers into the three patterns of attachment, that is, anxious-avoidant (group *A*), secure (group *B*), and anxious-resistant (group *C*). The groupings were made by identifying those behaviors that paralleled some of the defining features of the three attachment groups. For example, children who were classified as anxious-avoidant showed little or no tendency to seek interaction with or proximity to the parent, avoidance of the parent upon reunion, and a tendency to interact with the stranger. Securely attached children sought interaction with their parent, although not always in close proximity to them. If they were upset by their parent's departure, they were easily calmed upon their parent's return to the room. And anxious-resistant children were less likely to explore the new toys, wary of the stranger, and combined both a strong desire to maintain proximity to the parent following separation with an angry resistance to the parent upon reunion.

The criteria for classifying children into these three attachment groups were then prepared by identifying the behavioral similarities and differences that distinguished each of the three attachment patterns. The resulting descriptions, which are organized in terms of the behavioral systems activated by the Strange Situation, are delineated in table 1. This framework takes into account the developmental reorganization that occurs *within* the attachment behavioral system as well as *between* the attachment, exploration, affiliation, and fear/wariness behavioral system. It follows the work of others who have developed models to account for many aspects of seeking proximity with or avoidance of both familiar and strange individuals and situations (e.g., Bischof 1975; Bretherton & Ainsworth 1974; Greenberg & Marvin 1982; Waters & Deane 1982, 1985). Moreover, it extends the position that, during infancy, the balance between the attachment and exploratory systems represents the best criterion for evaluating the presence and the quality of the attachment relationship (Stayton et al. 1973). The consideration of affiliative and fear/wariness behaviors in response to novel people and situations represents an additional dimension along which the overall quality of the relationship may be assessed.

With development, the specific behaviors that serve these related systems, the contexts that elicit these behaviors, and the nature of the behavioral

TABLE 1. GUIDELINES FOR CLASSIFYING THE QUALITY OF ATTACHMENT RELATIONSHIPS IN 12, 18 AND 24-MONTH-OLD INFANTS IN THE STRANGE SITUATION (ORGANIZATION OF BEHAVIORAL SYSTEMS)

12 Months	18 Months	24 Months
	Group A: Anxious/Avoidant Attachment	

1. Attachment:

12 Months	18 Months	24 Months
	Does not involve mother in play or exploration.	
	May mix some proximity seeking with avoidance.	
	Ignores mother actively by looking or turning away.	
	Lack of distance interaction.	
	Avoidance more apparent on second reunion.	
	Objects to mother's contact when picked up by looking away or signaling to be put down.	
	Ignores mother's entrance by not looking, averting gaze, turning, or moving away from mother.	
	Little or no tendency to seek interaction or contact with mother.	
	May move toward mother by approaching her sideways, backwards, or circuitously.	
	Maintains ongoing activity with toys without requesting help or involving mother in play.	
	Little or no affective sharing with mother.	
		Verbally requests to be put down or left alone.

2. Exploration:

12 Months	18 Months	24 Months
	Active exploration of toys and room.	
	Little proximity seeking to mother.	
	Lack of distance interaction.	
	Ignores mother by not looking at her and maintaining focus on play with toys.	
	Little or no affective sharing with mother.	
	Independent involvement in play.	
	Little or no communication about toys.	

3. Affiliation:

— — — — — — — — — — — — — — — — Affiliative with stranger, whether or not mother is present.
— — — — — — — — — — — — — — — Responds positively to stranger's initiative in play.
— — — — — — — — — — — — — — May maintain proximity to stranger.
— — — — — — — — — — — — — Frequent interaction with stranger across a distance.
— — — — — — — — — — — — Affective sharing with stranger.
— — — — — — — — — — — Offers toys to stranger.
— — — — — — — — — — Shows toys to stranger across a distance.
— — — — — — — — — Engages in give-and-take object exchanges with stranger.
— — — — — — — — Initiates verbal communications with stranger.

4. Fear/Wariness:

— — — — — — — — — — — — — — Shows little wariness toward new room or toward stranger.
— — — — — — — — — — — — — Easily able to become involved in play with stranger.
— — — — — — — — — — — — Shows little or no distress upon mother's departure.
— — — — — — — — — — — Shows little or no search for mother during her absence.
— — — — — — — — — — Rarely cries but, if so, generally when alone.

TABLE 1. *(continued)*

12 Months	18 Months	24 Months
	Group B: Secure Attachment	

1. Attachment:

12 Months	18 Months	24 Months
—	Active in seeking interaction and/or contact with mother.	—
—	Can move away from mother to explore toys or room but may return to her frequently before moving away again.	—
—	Engages in give-and-take object exchange with mother.	—
—	May show toys and engage in distance interaction without seeking proximity.	—
—	May search for mother during her absence by moving toward her chair or going to the door.	—
—	If distressed during mother's absence:	—
—	(a) immediately approaches mother and seeks contact upon reunion	—
—	(b) contact is effective in terminating distress	—
—	(c) infant is capable of returning to play.	—
—	If not distressed during mother's absence:	—
—	(a) greets mother with smile, approach, or offer of toy	—
—	(b) takes strong initiative in interaction with mother.	—
—	Distress upon mother's departure may result in passivity or exploration or inhibition of play rather than crying.	—
—	Shows toys to mother across a distance.	—
—	Involves mother actively in play.	—
—	Affective sharing of play.	—
—	May search for mother by calling her or symbolically "talking" to her on the telephone.	—
—	Engages in symbolic play activity with mother.	—
—	May greet mother with verbalization.	—
—	—	Engages in dialogue with mother.

202

2. Exploration:

Mother is used as a secure base to explore toys and room.

Affective sharing of play.

May seek proximity to mother but is able to move away.

May show toys and look to mother across a distance.

May approach mother periodically to involve in play or seek contact.

Engages in give-and-take object exchanges with mother.

Independent exploration of and involvement with toys.

Verbally discusses and describes play.

3. Affiliation:

Affiliative with stranger in mother's presence.

Affiliative with stranger during mother's absence if not distressed.

May be comforted by stranger if distressed during mother's absence.

Responds positively to stranger's initiative in play.

May seek contact with or proximity to mother when stranger enters room or initiates play, but gradually able to respond to stranger.

May engage in distance interaction with stranger.

Shows toys to stranger across a distance.

Approaches stranger to give and take toys.

Affective sharing with stranger.

Initiates verbal communication with stranger.

4. Fear/Wariness:

May show some wariness upon entrance to room, but gradually able to explore toys and room and become involved in play.

May show some wariness toward stranger, but gradually capable of interacting with her.

Able to become involved in play initiated by stranger.

May show some distress upon mother's departure and exhibit active search behaviors.

May indicate distress upon mother's departure by passivity of exploration or inhibition of play.

203

TABLE 1. (continued)

12 Months	18 Months	24 Months
	Group C: Anxious/Resistant Attachment	

1. Attachment:

12 Months	18 Months	24 Months
	Passive exploration of toys and room.	
	Little effort to interact with mother in close proximity or across a distance.	
	May seek proximity to mother, but approach/avoidance conflict manifested by looking or turning away while seeking to maintain contact or proximity.	
	Immediate and/or intense distress upon separation from mother.	
	Passive or no search for mother upon separation.	
	Resists contact (e.g., squirming, kicking, hitting) upon reunion.	
	Difficult to comfort upon reunion.	
	Crying intensifies on second separation and second reunion.	
	Continues to cry and/or fuss upon reunion.	
	Has difficulty returning to play, or may not be able to resume play.	
	Continues to show striking passivity in play and in interaction with mother.	
	Anger may be displayed toward mother, alternating with desire to be in close contact with mother.	
	Almost no affective sharing or distance interaction.	
	Little involvement in play with mother.	
		Little or no verbal communication with mother.

2. Exploration:

12 Months	18 Months	24 Months
	Difficulty separating from mother to explore.	
	Gradually able to explore toys and room, but frequent movements back to mother.	
	Little involvement in play with mother.	
	Little distance interaction with mother.	
	Exploration characterized by extreme passivity.	
	Unable to explore toys or room following second separation.	

3. Affiliation:

Frequent glances at mother but little affective sharing.

Increase in inhibition of play following first separation.

Little or no verbal communication during exploration.

Little or no affiliation with stranger during mother's presence or absence.

Does not accept or respond to stranger's attempt to involve infant in play.

Little distance interaction with stranger.

Does not show or offer toys to stranger.

Resists stranger's attempts to comfort infant when distressed by mother's absence.

Little or no affective sharing with stranger.

Does not approach stranger.

Does not initiate give-and-take object exchanges with stranger.

Does not initiate verbal communication with stranger.

4. Fear/Wariness:

Unusually wary of stranger and of room.

Not able to become involved in interaction with stranger.

Strong resistance of contact with stranger during separation from mother.

Wariness of stranger intensifies following separation from mother when alone in room.

Passive or no search for mother upon separation.

Manifests distress upon separation by immediate and/or intense crying, inhibition of play, passivity.

205

organization will be altered. Therefore, children's emerging repertoire of more advanced modes of responding to the environment are integrated into this age-appropriate scoring system for use with the Strange Situation. The developing capacities for verbal communication, autonomous functioning, independent exploration, affiliation with unfamiliar adults, emotional control, and flexibility are considered.

In order to classify the quality of the attachment relationship using this new scheme, Ainsworth et al.'s (1978) detailed description of the six interactive behaviors that are rated during the Strange Situation are used. For each of the seven three-minute episodes, ratings of proximity and contact seeking, contact maintenance, avoidance, resistance, search, and distance interaction are made using the seven-point rating scales delineated by Ainsworth et al. (1978). Then, instead of using Ainsworth et al.'s (1978) classification scheme for assigning children into one of the three attachment groups, the organization of the interactive behaviors is considered following the framework delineated in table 1. This enables the quality of the attachment relationship to be classified into one of the three categories originally defined by Ainsworth and her colleagues, that is, securely attached (group B) or insecurely attached and avoidant (group A) or resistant (group C) (when necessary, classifications of attachment relationships are "forced" into the most appropriate of these three categories when minor variations from, or inconsistencies in, the described patterns emerge).

This classification scheme therefore replaces the one originally developed by Ainsworth and her collegues when one is classifying individual differences in attachment at 18 and 24 months of age. It is possible to see the way this new scheme is related to the one proposed by Ainsworth et al. (1978) by comparing the organization of behaviors at 12, 18, and 24 months across the attachment, exploratory, affiliative, and fear-wariness behavioral systems (as has been done in table 1). The patterning of interactive behaviors included in the table at 12 months of age represents that proposed by Ainsworth et al. (1978); the organization of these interactive behaviors in children at 18 and 24 months represents that which emerged from the detailed analysis of behavior protocols of children at these older ages.

This new classification system has been used in several studies where qualitative differences in attachment were evaluated in children at 18 and 24 months of age (Gersten, Coster, Schneider-Rosen, Carlson, & Cicchetti 1986; Schneider-Rosen 1984; Schneider-Rosen et al. 1985). High rates of reliability (89%–92%) have been obtained. This indicates that the Strange Situation may be used for reliably classifying the quality of the attachment relationship in children up to 2 years of age.

It is likely that further modifications of the scoring criteria would enable the Strange Situation to be used for children at older ages, although additional methods would probably be useful as well. There may be other techniques for arousing mild distress in older children that would provide the context for making qualitative ratings about the relationship. For example, responses upon reunion with the parent following brief separations in a laboratory setting are being used to assess the quality of the attachment relationship in 3- and 4-year-old children (Cassidy & Marvin 1987) and in 6-year-old children (Cassidy & Main 1985; Main & Cassidy 1986, 1988). In addition, Main and her colleagues are currently developing a system to classify dyads using a structured Clown Session (Main & Weston 1981) involving an unfamiliar adult in a situation arousing mild apprehension. Parents are classified in terms of their "emotional availability" (Emde 1980; Sorce & Emde 1981) to their child during the structured and mildly stressful situation. While the focus is on classifying parents, the presumption is that qualitative characteristics of the relationship (e.g., its security) may be understood. Moreover, while this work has been focused on the infancy period, it is certainly likely that similar procedures—that is, those that involve children in situations arousing apprehension and conflict and examine parents' emotional availability to their child—would provide important contributions to classifying the security of the relationship beyond infancy.

Another direction taken by recent empirical work relevant to the classification of qualitative differences in parent-child relationships beyond infancy focuses on the analysis of parental behaviors relevant to attachment. This analysis, however, is not restricted to the observation of parents and children in situations arousing apprehension or stress for the child (see Emde 1980, Sorce & Emde 1981). Rather, the Parental Acceptance Scoring System (Rothbaum & Schneider-Rosen 1988), designed for parents of 1½–4-year-old children, allows for an evaluation of individual differences in the extent to which parents are capable of integrating their child's needs with their own and with reality constraints in the context of *any* ongoing interactive situation. It is presumed that, while the focus is on parental behaviors, the analysis will reveal important information about the quality of the relationship.

The relative success with which parents are capable of perceiving and responding to their child's needs during the first year of life has been demonstrated to impact on the quality of the attachment relationship at 1 year of age (e.g., Ainsworth, Bell, & Stayton 1971; Belsky, Rovine, & Taylor 1984; Grossmann, Grossmann, Spangler, Suess, & Unzer 1985; Maslin & Bates 1983). In particular, sensitivity, accessibility, cooperation, and acceptance are parental behaviors that are associated with the development of a secure attachment relationship (Ainsworth et al. 1978). There has been a paucity of work that has examined these characteristics of parental behavior beyond the first year. Therefore, it is not known whether they continue to bear any relation to the quality of attachment beyond the infancy period. Moreover, while associations have been reported between early attachment and later functioning during nursery school and kindergarten (for reviews, see Bretherton 1985; and

Sroufe 1983), it is not clear that these findings are the result of continuities in parental behavior that contribute to the quality of the relationship over the same period of time. No direct assessments of the parent-child relationship beyond infancy have been made to substantiate this presumed continuity. It is important to extend the work that has been done during the first year of life and to evaluate specific parental behaviors that may be relevant to the emergence of particular patterns within the parent-child relationship beyond the infancy period.

An analysis of parental behaviors that takes into account the success with which parents accept and respond to their child's psychological needs in a developmentally appropriate manner provides a means for evaluating and describing qualitative differences in the parent-child relationship beyond infancy. The Parental Acceptance Scoring System (Rothbaum & Schneider-Rosen 1988) provides a means for illuminating these qualitative characteristics of the developing parent-child relationship. The classification of parental acceptance may be seen as a way of characterizing an organization of behaviors that has evolved within the dyad over time. The use of the scoring system is contingent upon an evaluation of behaviors of *both* the parent and the child within the specific context in which they are interacting. Thus, while the parent's behavior is the object of assessment, the child's behavior is important inasmuch as it "sets the stage" for the parent's subsequent behavior. The child's behavior must be evaluated in order to determine the developmental level at which the child is functioning and the specific needs that are being expressed in a particular situation.

Implicit in the system is a recognition that the parent and child are continually renegotiating their relationship as developmental advances in cognitive, social, and emotional functioning during infancy and childhood enable the child to interact with the caregiver in a manner that is increasingly more sophisticated. This is crucial because the child's specific needs are going to change depending upon the child's age and level of functioning. The Parental Acceptance Scoring System relies on a consideration of the parent's ability to modify her behavior and adjust to the continually changing demands placed upon her by her child. Therefore, the assessment of the transaction between the parent and child is an inherent component of the scoring system.

The scoring system defines five levels of parental acceptance that fall along an acceptance-rejection continuum and that represent a consideration of the transactional nature of the parent-child relationship. The three anchoring levels may be briefly summarized as follows: level 1—*opponents contending*—parent fails to meet child's needs; parent assumes that one party will win (i.e., his/her needs will be met), and one party will lose; level 3—*business partners bargaining*—parent partially meets child's needs; there is a sense that both party's needs can be partially met but there is tension along the way; level 5—*companions harmonizing*—parent works with child to meet their mutual needs; the parent's major concern is the strengthening of their relationship.

The levels of acceptance are arranged on a continuum ranging from extreme incompatibility in need for control (hence, enmity) to extreme compatibility (hence, harmony). At level 1, parents behave as if they perceive their children's need for control as incompatible with their own; thus, they seek control by thwarting or ignoring the child's methods and goals. At level 3, parents behave as if they perceive their children's need for control as partially compatible with their own; they thus seek control by bargaining over methods and goals. At level 5, parents behave as if they perceive their own and their child's needs as harmonious. They thus seek control by sharing control with the child. In this case, granting and exercising of control are mutually reinforcing (for a fuller description of the general construct of acceptance, levels of acceptance, and the notion of integration of child's need for control, see *Parental Acceptance Scoring Manual* (Rothbaum & Schneider-Rosen 1988).

There are three control-related needs with which this scoring system is concerned: the need for evaluation, for availability, and for structure (see table 2). These are assumed to be pervasive needs that are usually manifest in even brief episodes of parent-child interaction. Associated with each need are several criteria which are used in scoring parental acceptance. For example, criteria of acceptance associated with the need for evaluation are (*a*) the affective tone of the parent's evaluation; (*b*) the extent to which evaluative messages are tailored to the individual child; (*c*) the extent to which effort is encouraged; and (*d*) the emphasis on the child's acceptable, as opposed to unacceptable, behavior.

The criteria are conceived of as different ways that the parent can integrate the child's need for control. The criteria are defined in terms of parental behavior as well as children's needs (e.g., evaluation criteria are defined in terms of parental evaluations as well as children's needs for evaluation). Minute-by-minute analyses of parent-child interactions provide the basis for making the ratings (see description of scoring procedures and guidelines in *Scoring Manual*). Each minute of interaction is evaluated for those criteria (from each of the three categories, i.e., evaluation, availability, and structure) that are relevant to the child's needs and the parent's response to those needs within that minute. A level score is then assigned to at least one criterion from each of the three categories. The level score reflects how well the parents have integrated the child's needs with their own and with reality constraints (definitions of the criteria and levels of the criteria are contained in the *Manual*). Once the entire interaction has been evaluated, an overall parental acceptance score (the average of the level scores assigned during each minute of analysis) is representative of one of the five levels along the acceptance-rejection continuum.

The definition of parental acceptance implicit in the scoring system is based in part on previous conceptual models and scoring systems (e.g., Ainsworth et al. 1978; Baldwin, Kalhorn, & Breese 1945; Maccoby & Martin

TABLE 2.   CRITERIA OF PARENTAL ACCEPTANCE

I. *Evaluation criteria*. These criteria are scored when the child needs, or parent provides, evaluative verbal or nonverbal feedback regarding the child or the child's behavior. Evaluation ranges from approval of the child (but not necessarily of the child's behavior) to disapproval of the child.

1. Evaluative affect: nonverbal (tone, facial and bodily) reactions to child which convey positive vs. negative evaluation; includes enthusiasm, liking, joy vs. flat affect, anger or annoyance; match vs. mismatch between parent evaluation/affect and child behavior/mood. Recovery of positive mood vs. failure to recover after limit setting.

2. Evaluative content: individualizing and tailoring of evaluative messages to fit the child's positive behavior; information value of message; focus on child's vs. parent's concerns; separation of child and child's behavior; child's feelings are accepted even if behavior is not.

3. Encouragement of effort: amount and consistency of positive behaviors, such as expressing confidence and cheerleading, in response to child's efforts vs. negative behaviors, such as ignoring, expressing pessimism and disappointment about child's efforts; timing and grading of encouragement of effort.

4. Emphasizing child's acceptable behavior: duration and amount of focus on acceptable vs. unacceptable child behavior; proportion of opportunities for positive vs. negative evaluations of which parent takes advantage.

II. *Availability criteria*. These criteria are scored when the child needs, or the parent provides, the parent's physical or verbal presence or involvement. Ranges from providing a secure base to unavailable or intrusive.

5. Physical presence: receptivity and approach to vs. disdain for and withdrawal from initiations of physical contact or proximity by child, communicated physically; considerateness, sensitivity of timing, sustaining and warmth of physical responsiveness; pleasurable vs. unpleasurable initiations of physical interaction.

6. Acknowledgement: comments or actions which convey attention, understanding, caring, or concern; reflecting back child's feelings and needs; includes willingness to assist vs. ignoring or rejecting requests for assistance.

7. Participation: initial willingness vs. unwillingness to engage in joint activity with child; emphasis on togetherness/collaboration with vs. separation/opposition to child when child desires former; when immediate availability is not feasible, conveying desire for availability (e.g., by proposing alternatives) vs. unavailability; mirroring vs. uncooperative behavior.

8. Standing back: space given to allow child to engage in autonomous or solitary activity vs. intruding parent's presence or actions into child's space; separating parent's and child's agendas vs. confusing them.

III. *Structure criteria*. These criteria are scored when the child needs, or the parent provides, guidance in achieving a goal. Guidance includes directives, suggestions, cues, information and behavioral assistance. Ranges from supportive to undermining.

9. Helpfulness of guidance: clarity, grading, and relevance (vis à vis child's interest and goals) of guidance; making clear to child what to do vs. what *not* to do; helpful vs. unhelpful preparations and setting up environment.

10. Explanations: comprehensibility, richness (informativeness), and relevance of explanations intended to provide an understanding of "why" events and expectations occur as opposed to "what" they are.

11. Mood/motivation setting: induces positive vs. negative affect via modeling affect or via method of presenting task (i.e., highlighting positive vs. negative aspects); naturalness and compellingness of incentives vs. grossly inappropriate, something parent should not or cannot follow through on); redirecting child's attention toward positive vs. negative aspects of tasks.

12. Consistency: consistency vs. inconsistency over time, and between actions and words, especially regarding suggestions and directives; abruptness vs. smoothness of transitions; modeling acceptable behavior vs. leading the way toward unacceptable behavior.

13. Regulation of options: giving child a manageable sense of options vs. too few or too many options; providing a sense of choice vs. coercion; limiting vs. not limiting options when child needs limits.

1983; Newberger & Cook 1983; Sroufe, Matas, & Rosenberg 1979). It is also based, in part, on a review of factor analytic findings from numerous studies of parents of older children (see Rothbaum, 1986, for a review) and several studies of parents of infants (e.g., Ainsworth, Bell, & Stayton 1974; Clarke-Stewart 1973; Stayton, Hogan, & Ainsworth 1971; Martin 1981; Martin, Maccoby, Baran, & Jacklin 1981). The factor analytic findings yield an acceptance factor which typically accounts for a large portion of the total variance in the behavior of parents in both laboratory and home settings. Moreover, the findings indicate which behaviors are involved in acceptance. While there are differences between the factor analytic studies in the items loading on the acceptance factor, the latter almost always includes items relevant to evaluation, availability, and structure.

Current research efforts are directed toward establishing the reliability and validity of the scoring system. For example, we are analyzing the relationship between attachment classifications at 18, 24, and 30 months of age (employing the modified scoring criteria for use with the Strange Situation described above) and parental acceptance in free-play, problem-solving, and clean-up situations, as assessed using this scoring system (Schneider-Rosen & Rothbaum 1990). Relationships between children and both their mothers and fathers are being evaluated. It is predicted that parents of securely attached children will be classified at a higher level on the acceptance-rejection continuum as compared to parents of insecurely attached children. This analysis, which is currently in progress, will provide an empirical base for making explicit the association between parental acceptance and patterns of attachment, thus providing an extension of the work that has been done with infants documenting the connection between maternal behavior during the first year and quality of attachment at 1 year (Ainsworth et al. 1978). Moreover, it will allow for an examination of the extent to which the scores derived from the Parental Acceptance Scoring System reflect qualitative differences in the parent-child relationship.

Other efforts are being directed toward demonstrating the concurrent and predictive associations between level of parental acceptance and the child's functioning. This will provide much needed information that will extend the work done by attachment researchers during the infancy period. In one study, we are evaluating 18-, 24-, and 30-month-old children with their mothers and fathers and examining the association between parental acceptance and self-control (Schneider-Rosen, Rothbaum, & Wenz-Gross 1989). In a second study, we are evaluating a 2-year-old sample and assessing the relation between parental acceptance and (a) the child's capacity to display empathy toward the parent, and (b) the child's competence in interacting with same-sexed peers (Schneider-Rosen, Spada, & DeVirgilio 1989). And in a third study, we are examining the predictive validity of acceptance. Fifty children who were seen at 18 or 24 months of age are being studied at 4 years of age, again with both their mothers and fathers. In this longitudinal follow-up, the stability of parental acceptance is being examined and the association between early acceptance and later child functioning (specifically, compliance, perceived competence, and empathy) is being assessed (Schneider-Rosen, Beatty, & Rothbaum 1989). Ultimately, these analyses will provide information regarding the usefulness of the Parental Acceptance Scoring System for evaluating individual differences in the parent-child relationship beyond infancy. Comparisons between father's and mother's acceptance of their children will provide a means for assessing the implications of different patterns of parental acceptance for the child's development.

While these classification schemes have been focused at the level of verbal and nonverbal behavior, another means for classification of qualitative differences in attachment beyond infancy is at the level of representation. The cognitive sciences have influenced the recent emphasis on "internal working models" of attachment (Bowlby [1969] 1982, 1973, 1980; Bretherton 1985; Kobak & Sceery 1988; Main et al. 1985). Through continual transactions with the environment, children are seen to construct increasingly complex models of their world, the significant people in that world, and themselves in relation to others.

During the first months of life, internal working models of specific relationships are developing. By 12 months of age, individual differences in attachment behaviors with a particular caregiver are reflected in the infant's internal working model *of that specific infant-caregiver relationship* (Main et al. 1985; Sroufe & Fleeson 1986). Bowlby (1973) has proposed that working models of attachment figures continue to be formed during early childhood and serve to maintain continuity in the individual's developmental pathway. However, it has not been possible to investigate this prediction without having a means available to specify attachment relationships in a manner that enables investigators to infer invariance at an organizational level despite major developmental change. The concept of internal working models represents a significant advance in providing a means for evaluating attachment organization across developmental periods; the use of representational tasks (e.g., George, Kaplan, & Main 1985) that rely upon thought and language allows for individual differences to be evaluated in the organization of representation and memory relevant to attachment.

Internal working models of attachment are thought to serve a heuristic function. They provide the individual with a rule system for appraising experience and for guiding behavior in new situations (Main et al. 1985). They may facilitate the process of regulating distress in those situations that normally elicit attachment behaviors. Thus, working models are seen to influence the overt manifestation of attachment behaviors as children grow older. Specifically, because children become more capable at evaluating the intentions, motives, and future behaviors of attachment figures, because they learn to appraise the relative safety of new situations, and because they gradually acquire coping skills, their attachment behaviors become more subtle (Bretherton 1985).

This recent line of thinking with regard to the importance of internal working models of attachment relationships illuminates the social-cognitive and affective factors involved in the process of differentiation which results in the construction of complementary models of attachment figures and of the self (Bretherton 1985; Cassidy 1988; Epstein 1980; Marvin & Greenberg 1982; Sroufe & Fleeson 1986). Developmental changes in social cognition are therefore important to consider in the formulation of assessment techniques that focus on internal working models of attachment relationships. Moreover, because the study of internal working models is contingent upon the use of language (Main et al. 1985), developmental changes in linguistic abilities need to be considered.

Main et al. (1985) have provided some valuable contributions to empirical investigations of internal working models by conducting extensive analyses of attachment related behaviors in 6-year-old children and their parents and comparing these to classifications of the quality of the attachment relationship with the mother that had been made when the children were 12 months of age. In particular, the children's emotional openness in discussing imagined parent-child separations or in conversation with their parents was seen to reflect important aspects of the children's mental representations of their relationships with their parents. Children who were secure in their early attachment relationships were found to have free-ranging access to affect, plans, and memories at 6 years of age, while children who had been insecure displayed varying types of restrictions that influenced the organization of information and of attention.

These findings point to the importance of considering the ways in which language is used to communicate and/or censor information regarding relationships and feelings about the self and others in relationships. They demonstrate continuity in attachment organization from 12 months to 6 years in terms of working models that guide both behavior as well as attention and memory. Moreover, the methods used represent a new and developmentally appropriate means for evaluating qualitative differences in internal models of relationships in childhood. The acquisition of new representational capabilities during childhood and adolescence poses additional questions about the ways in which attachment can be assessed at the level of thought and language, with implications for the development of additional means for understanding attachment organization in adolescence and adulthood as well.

More recent work on internal models of attachment in adolescence demonstrates the presence of coherent patterns of affect regulation and representations of self and others associated with particular models of attachment (Kobak & Sceery 1988). This research evolved out of work conducted during infancy and childhood, indicating a close connection between attachment and affect regulation (e.g., Arend et al. 1979; Cassidy & Kobak 1988; Lutkenhaus, Grossmann, & Grossmann 1985; Main & Stadtman 1981; Matas et al. 1978; Sroufe, Schork, Motti, Lawroski, & LaFreniere 1984; Waters et al. 1979). In Kobak and Sceery's (1988) study of first-year college students, it was found that those adolescents judged as "secure" on the Adult Attachment Interview (George et al. 1985) demonstrated a style of affect regulation and information processing that was based on a capacity to tolerate and process distress-related affect. This was evident in the ability to recall distressing events and a low idealization of parents. Adolescents judged "secure" showed a high level of ego-resilience, as rated by peers. On self-report measures, they rated themselves at higher levels of perceived social competence and perceived levels of support from friends and family, and they did not report extensive loneliness or social isolation. These findings contrasted with those judged "insecure" who lacked ego-resilience and differed from each other in the type of negative affect representations of self and others. Those judged "dismissing of attachment" were more hostile and minimized personal difficulties and distress on self-report measures; those judged "preoccupied with attachment" showed a great deal of anxiety on peer measures and were more likely to acknowledge difficulties and distress.

The results indicate that working models of attachment represent an organizational construct associated with other aspects of affective functioning. They have implications for the exploration of related questions about the organization of attachment beyond infancy. For example, if working models of attachment are associated with styles of affect regulation, then how do they influence the quality of affective communication in current attachment relationships? Methods are currently being developed for examining affective communication (Grossmann, Grossmann, & Schwann 1986; Lutkenhaus et al. 1985) and responsiveness to affective signals (e.g., Rothbaum & Schneider-Rosen 1988) associated with patterns of attachment during infancy and early childhood; new methods for evaluating effective communication within attachment relationships over the life-span need to be developed to extend this important work. In addition, it is critical to examine the ways in which working models are modified over time and the extent to which they influence current attachment relationships (cf. Hazan & Shaver, in press; Shaver, Hazan, & Bradshaw 1988). Research that addresses these questions will extend the important empirical contributions that have been made by those who have explored the representation of attachment in working models.

CONCLUDING REMARKS

This review of recent empirical efforts directed toward the classification of attachment relationships beyond infancy represents some new directions that have been taken by attachment researchers. While the underlying experience of attachment may remain constant across the life span, researchers have acknowledged that important changes occur as a result of the developmental process. The theoretical and methodological considerations that evolve from the developmental perspective should provide a framework for additional work that will extend the contributions made to date. Taken together, current research on attachment beyond infancy indicates that it is both theoretically important and empirically meaningful to study individual differences in attachment relationships beyond the first 2 years of life. This work, contingent upon the development of appropriate classification schemes, will allow for increased understanding of the differential developmental experiences associated with various attachment patterns and of the consequences of these patterns for subsequent development.

REFERENCES

Ainsworth, M. D. S. (1969). Object relations, dependency, and attachment: A theoretical review of the infant-mother relationship. *Child Development* 40, 969–1025.

Ainsworth, M. D. S. (1972). Attachment and dependency: A comparison. In J. L. Gewirtz (ed.), *Attachment and dependency* (pp. 97–177). Washington, D.C.: Winston.

Ainsworth, M. D. S. (1973). The development of infant-mother attachment. In B. M. Caldwell & H. N. Ricciutti (eds.), *Review of child development research* (vol. 3, pp. 1–94). Chicago: University of Chicago Press.

Ainsworth, M. D. S. (1982). Attachment: Retrospect and prospect. In C. M. Parkes & J. Stevenson-Hinde (eds.), *The place of attachment in human behavior* (pp. 3–30). New York: Basic Books.

Ainsworth, M. D. S.; Bell, S.; & Stayton, D. (1971). Individual differences in strange situation behavior of one-year-olds. In H. R. Schaffer (ed.), *The origins of human social relations* (pp. 17–57). New York: Academic Press.

Ainsworth, M. D. S.; Bell, S.; & Stayton, D. (1974). Infant-mother attachment and social development: "Socialization" as a product of reciprocal responsiveness to signals. In M. P. M. Richards (ed.), *The integration of a child into a social world* (pp. 99–135). London: Cambridge University Press.

Ainsworth, M. D. S.; Blehar, M.; Waters, E.; & Wall, S. (1978). *Patterns of attachment: A psychological study of the strange situation.* Hillsdale, N.J.: Erlbaum.

Antonucci, T. (1976). Attachment: A life-span concept. *Human Development* 19, 135–142.

Arend, R.; Gove, F.; & Sroufe, L. A. (1979). Continuity of individual adaptation from infancy to kindergarten: A predictive study of ego-resilience and curiosity in preschoolers. *Child Development* 50, 950–959.

Baldwin, A., Kalhorn, J., & Breese, F. H. (1945). Patterns of parent behavior. *Psychological Monographs* 58(3, Whole No. 268).

Belsky, J.; Rovine, M.; & Taylor, D. (1984). The origins of individual differences in infant-mother attachment: Maternal and infant contributions. *Child Development* 55, 718–728.

Bischof, N. A. (1975). A systems approach toward the functional connections of attachment and fear. *Child Development* 46, 801–817.

Block, J. H., & Block, J. (1979). The role of ego-control and ego-resiliency in the organization of behavior. In W. A. Collins (ed.), *Minnesota Symposia on Child Psychology* (vol. 13, pp. 39–101). New York: Erlbaum.

Bowlby, J. (1958). The nature of the child's tie to his mother. *International Journal of Psychoanalysis* 39, 350–373.

Bowlby, J. ([1969] 1982). *Attachment and loss: Vol. 1. Attachment.* New York: Basic Books.

Bowlby, J. (1973). *Attachment and loss: Vol. 2. Separation.* New York: Basic Books.

Bowlby, J. (1980). *Attachment and loss: Vol. 3. Loss, sadness and depression.* New York: Basic Books.

Breger, L. (1974). *From instinct to identity.* Englewood Cliffs, N.J.: Prentice-Hall.

Bretherton, I. (1980). Young children in stressful situations: The supporting role of attachment figures and unfamiliar caregivers. In G. V. Coelho & P. Ahmed (eds.), *Uprooting and development* (pp. 179–210). New York: Plenum.

Bretherton, I. (1985). Attachment theory: Retrospect and prospect. In I. Bretherton & E. Waters (eds.), *Growing points of attachment theory and research. Monographs of the Society for Research in Child Development* 50 (1–2, Serial No. 209), 3–35.

Bretherton, I., & Ainsworth, M. D. S. (1974). Responses of one-year-olds to a stranger in a strange situation. In M. Lewis & L. A. Rosenblum (eds.), *The origins of fear* (pp. 131–164). New York: Wiley.

Bronson, G. W. (1972). *Infants' reactions to unfamiliar persons and novel objects. Monographs of the Society for Research in Child Development* 37(3, Series No. 148), 1–45.

Cairns, R. (1972). Attachment and dependency: A psychobiological and social-learning synthesis. In J. L. Gewirtz (ed.), *Attachment and dependency* (pp. 29–80). Washington, D.C.: Winston.

Cassidy, J. (1988). Child-mother attachment and the self in six-year-olds. *Child Development* 59, 121–134.

Cassidy, J., & Kobak, R. (1988). Avoidance and its relation to other defensive processes. In J. Belsky & T. Nezworski (eds.), *Clinical implications of attachment* (pp. 300–323). Hillsdale, N.J.: Erlbaum.

Cassidy, J., & Main, M. (1985). The relationship between infant-parent attachment and the ability to tolerate brief separation at six years. In J. D. Call, E. Galenson, & R. L. Tyson (eds.), *Frontiers of infant psychiatry* (vol. 2, pp. 132–136). New York: Basic Books.

Cassidy, J., & Marvin, R. S., in collaboration with the MacArthur Working Group on Attachment (1987). Attachment organization in three- and four-year-olds: Coding guidelines. Unpublished manuscript, University of Virginia.

Cicchetti, D., & Schneider-Rosen, K. (1984). Theoretical and empirical considerations in the investigation of the relationship between affect and cognition in atypical populations of infants. In C. Izard, J. Kagan, & R. Zajonc (eds.), *Emotions, cognition, and behavior* (pp. 366–406). New York: Cambridge University Press.

Cicchetti, D., & Schneider-Rosen, K. (1986). An organizational approach to childhood depression. In M. Rutter, C. Izard, & P. Read (eds.), *Depression in children: Developmental perspectives* (pp. 71–134). New York: Guilford.

Cicchetti, D., & Serafica, F. (1981). The interplay among behavioral systems: Illustrations from the study of attachment, affiliation, and wariness in young Down syndrome children. *Developmental Psychology* 17, 36–49.

Cicchetti, D., & Sroufe, L. A. (1978). An organizational view of affect: Illustration from the study of Down's syndrome infants. In M. Lewis & L. A. Rosenblum (eds.), *The development of affect* (pp. 309–350). New York: Plenum.

Clarke-Stewart, K. A. (1973). *Interactions between mothers and their young children: Characteristics and consequences. Monographs of the Society for Research in Child Development* 38 (5–6, Serial No. 153), 1–108.

Crittenden, P. M. (1985). Maltreated infants: Vulnerability and resilience. *Journal of Child Psychology and Psychiatry and Allied Disciplines* 26, 85–96.

Emde, R. N. (1980). Levels of meaning for infant emotions: A biosocial view. In W. A. Collins (ed.), *Minnesota Symposia on Child Psychology* (vol. 13, pp. 1–37). Hillsdale, N.J.: Erlbaum.

Epstein, S. (1980). The self-concept: A review and the proposal of an integrated theory of personality. In E. Staub (ed.), *Personality: Basic aspects and current research* (pp. 81–132). Englewood Cliffs, N.J.: Prentice-Hall.

Erikson, E. (1950). *Childhood and society.* New York: Norton.

Freud, S. (1940). *An outline of psychoanalysis* (Standard Ed., vol. 23). London: Hogarth Press.

George, C.; Kaplan, N.; & Main, M. (1985). The attachment interview for adults. Unpublished manuscript, University of California, Berkeley.

Gersten, M.; Coster, W.; Schneider-Rosen, K.; Carlson, V.; & Cicchetti, D. (1986). Quality of attachment, language development, and early maltreatment. In M. E. Lamb, A. L. Brown, & B. Rogoff (eds.), *Advances in developmental psychology* (vol. 4, pp. 105–151). Hillsdale, N.J.: Erlbaum.

Greenberg, M. T., & Marvin, R. S. (1979). Attachment patterns in profoundly deaf preschool children. *Merrill-Palmer Quarterly* 25, 265–279.

Greenberg, M. T., & Marvin, R. S. (1982). Reactions of preschool children to an adult stranger: A behavioral systems approach. *Child Development* 53, 481–490.

Greenspan, S. I. (1981). *Psychopathology and adaptation in infancy and early childhood*. New York: International Universities Press.

Grossmann, K. E.; Grossmann, K.; & Schwann, A. (1986). Capturing the wider view of attachment: A reanalysis of Ainsworth's strange situation. In C. Izard & P. Read (eds.), *Measuring emotions in infants and children* (vol. 2, pp. 124–171). New York: Cambridge University Press.

Grossmann, K. E.; Grossmann, K.; Spangler, G.; Suess, G.; Unzer, L. (1985). Maternal sensitivity in Northern Germany. In I. Bretherton & E. Waters (eds.), *Growing points of attachment theory and research. Monographs of the Society for Research in Child Development* 50 (1–2, Serial No. 209), 233–256.

Hazan, C., & Shaver, P. (in press). Romantic love conceptualized as an attachment process. *Journal of Personality and Social Psychology*.

Kagan, J. (1971). *Change and continuity in infancy*. New York: Wiley.

Klein, G. S. (1976). *Psychoanalytic theory: An explanation of essentials*. New York: International Universities Press.

Kobak, R. R., & Sceery, A. (1988). Attachment in late adolescence: Working models, affect regulation, and representations of self and others. *Child Development* 59, 135–146.

Kohlberg, L.; LaCrosse, J.; & Ricks, D. (1971). The predictability of adult mental health from childhood behavior. In B. Wolman (ed.), *Manual of child psychopathology* (pp. 1217–1279). New York: McGraw-Hill.

Kopp, C. B.; Vaughn, B. E.; & Cicchetti, D. (1982). In C. B. Kopp & J. B. Krakow (eds.), *The child: Development in a social context* (pp. 92–153). Reading, Maine: Addison-Wesley.

Kotelchuck, M. (1972). The nature of a child's tie to his father. Unpublished doctoral dissertation, Harvard University.

Loevinger, J. (1976). *Ego development*. San Francisco: Jossey-Bass.

Lutkenhaus, P.; Grossmann, K. E.; & Grossmann, K. (1985). Infant-mother attachment at twelve months and style of interaction with a stranger at the age of three years. *Child Development* 56, 1538–1542.

Maccoby, E. E., & Feldman, S. S. (1972). *Mother-attachment and stranger-reactions in the third year of life. Monographs of the Society for Research in Child Development* 37 (1, Serial No. 146), 1–85.

Maccoby, E. E., & Martin, J. A. (1983). Socialization in the context of the family: Parent-child interaction. In P. H. Mussen (ed.), *Handbook of child psychology: Socialization, personality, and social development* (vol. 4, pp. 1–101). New York: Wiley.

Mahler, M.; Pine, F.; & Bergman, A. (1975). *The psychological birth of the human infant*. New York: Basic Books.

Main, M., & Cassidy, J. (1986). Assessment of child-parent attachment at five to seven years of age. Unpublished Manuscript.

Main, M., & Cassidy, J. (1988). Categories of response to reunion with the parent at age six: Predictable from infant attachment classifications and stable over a one-month period. *Developmental Psychology* 24, 415–426.

Main, M.; Kaplan, N.; & Cassidy, J. (1985). Security in infancy, childhood and adulthood: A move to the level of representation. In I. Bretherton & E. Waters (eds.), *Growing points of attachment theory and research. Monographs of the Society for Research in Child Development* 50 (1–2, Serial No. 209), 66–104.

Main, M., & Stadtman, J. (1981). Infant response to rejection of physical contact by the mother: Aggression, avoidance, and conflict. *Journal of the American Academy of Child Psychiatry* 20, 292–307.

Main, M., & Weston, D. (1981). The quality of the toddler's relationship to mother and father. *Child Development* 52, 932–940.

Martin, J. A. (1981). *A longitudinal study of the consequences of early mother-infant interaction: A microanalytic approach. Monographs of the Society for Research in Child Development,* 46 (3, Serial No. 190), 1–58.

Martin, J. A.; Maccoby, E. E.; Baran, K. W.; & Jacklin, C. N. (1981). The sequential analysis of mother-child interaction at 18 months: A comparison of microanalytic methods. *Developmental Psychology* 17, 146–157.

Marvin, R. S. (1977). An ethological-cognitive model for the attenuation of mother-child attachment behavior. In T. Alloway, L. Krames, & P. Pliner (eds.), *Advances in the study of communication and affect:* vol. 3, *Attachment behavior* (pp. 25–60). New York: Plenum.

Marvin, R. S., & Greenberg, M. T. (1982). Preschoolers' changing conceptions of their mothers: A social-cognitive study of mother-child attachment. In D. Forbes & M. T. Greenberg (eds.), *New directions in child development: Vol. 14. Developing plans for behavior.* San Francisco: Jossey-Bass.

Maslin, C., & Bates, E. (1983). Precursors of anxious and secure attachments: A multivariate model at age six months. Paper presented at the biennial meeting of the Society for Research in Child Development, Detroit.

Masters, J., & Wellman, H. (1974). Human infant attachment: A procedural critique. *Psychological Bulletin* 81, 218–237.

Matas, L.; Arend, R.; & Sroufe, L. A. (1978). Continuity of adaptation in the second year: The relationship between quality of attachment and later competence. *Child Development* 49, 547–556.

Mischel, W. (1968). *Personality and assessment.* New York: Wiley.

Newberger, C. N., & Cook, S. J. (1983). Parental awareness and child abuse and neglect: A cognitive-developmental analysis of urban and rural samples. *American Journal of Orthopsychiatry* 57, 512–524.

Radke-Yarrow, M.; Cummings, E. M.; Kuczynski, L.; & Chapman, M. (1985). Patterns of attachment in two- and three-year-olds in normal families and families with parental depression. *Child Development* 56, 884–893.

Rothbaum, F. (1986). Patterns of parental acceptance. *Genetic Social and General Psychology Monographs 112,* 435–458.

Rothbaum, F., & Schneider-Rosen, K. (1988). Parental acceptance scoring manual: A system for assessing interactions between parents and their young children. Unpublished manuscript. Tufts University and Boston College.

Rutter, M. (1977). Individual differences. In M. Rutter & L. Hersov (eds.), *Child psychiatry: Modern approaches* (pp. 3–21). Oxford: Blackwell.

Sander, L. (1962). Issues in early mother-child interaction. *Journal of the American Academy of Child Psychiatry* 1, 141–166.

Sander, L. (1975). Infant and caretaking environment. In E. J. Anthony (ed.), *Explorations in child psychiatry* (pp. 129–166). New York: Plenum.

Santostefano, S. (1978). *A biodevelopmental approach to clinical child psychology.* New York: Wiley.

Santostefano, S., & Baker, A. H. (1972). The contribution of developmental psychology. In B. Wolman (ed.), *Manual of child psychopathology* (pp. 1113–1153). New York: Wiley.

Schneider-Rosen, K. (1984). Quality of attachment and the development of the self system in maltreated children. Unpublished doctoral dissertation, Harvard University.

Schneider-Rosen, K.; Beatty, M.; & Rothbaum, F. (1989). The stability and predictive validity of parental acceptance: A two-year longitudinal analysis. Manuscript in preparation.

Schneider-Rosen, K.; Braunwald, K.; Carlson, V.; & Cicchetti, D. (1985). Current perspectives in attachment theory: Illustration from the study of maltreated infants. In I. Bretherton & E. Waters (eds.), *Growing points of attachment theory and research. Monographs of the Society for Research in Child Development* 50 (1–2, Serial No. 209), 194–210.

Schneider-Rosen, K., & Cicchetti, D. (1984). The relationship between affect and cognition in maltreated infants: Quality of attachment and the development of visual self-recognition. *Child Development* 55, 648–658.

Schneider-Rosen, K., & Rothbaum, F. (1989). Quality of mother-child and father-child relationships beyond infancy. Unpublished manuscript, Boston College.

Schneider-Rosen, K.; Rothbaum, F.; & Wenz-Gross, M. (1989). Parental acceptance and the development of self-control from 18 to 30 months of age. Unpublished manuscript, Boston College.

Schneider-Rosen, K.; Spada, K.; & DeVirgilio, C. (1989). Parental acceptance and its relation to empathy and peer interactions at two years of age. Manuscript in preparation.

Serafica, F. C. (1978). The development of attachment behaviors: An organizational developmental perspective. *Human Development* 21, 119–140.

Shaver, P.; Hazan, C.; & Bradshaw, D. (1988). Love as attachment: The integration of three behavioral systems. In R. Sternberg & M. Barnes (eds.), *Anatomy of love* (pp. 66–99). New Haven: Yale University Press.

Sorce, J. F., & Emde, R. N. (1981). Mother's presence is not enough: The effect of emotional availability on infant exploration. *Developmental Psychology* 17, 737–745.

Sroufe, L. A. (1979). Socioemotional development. In J. Osofsky (ed.), *Handbook of infant development* (pp. 462–516). New York: Wiley.

Sroufe, L. A. (1983). Infant-caregiver attachment and patterns of adaptation in preschool: The roots of maladaptation and competence. In M. Perlmutter (ed.), *Minnesota Symposium in Child Psychology* (vol. 16, pp. 41–83). Hillsdale, N.J.: Erlbaum.

Sroufe, L. A. (1985). Attachment classification from the perspective of infant-caregiver relationships and infant temperament. *Child Development* 56, 1–14.

Sroufe, L. A., & Fleeson, J. (1986). Attachment and the construction of relationships. In W. Hartup & Z. Rubin (eds.), *Relationships and development* (pp. 51–71). New York: Cambridge University Press.

Sroufe, L. A.; Matas, L.; & Rosenberg, D. M. (1979). Manual for scoring mother variables in tool use task applicable for two-year-old children. Unpublished manuscript, University of Minnesota.

Sroufe, L. A., & Rutter, M. (1984). The domain of developmental psychopathology. *Child Development* 55, 17–29.

Sroufe, L. A.; Schork, E.; Motti, E.; Lawroski, N.; & LaFreniere, P. (1984). The role of affect in social competence. In C. Izard, J. Kagan, & R. Zajonc (eds.), *Emotions, cognition, and behavior* (pp. 289–319). New York: Plenum.

Sroufe, L. A., & Waters, E. (1977). Attachment as an organizational construct. *Child Development* 48, 1184–1199.

Stayton, D. J.; Ainsworth, M. D. S.; & Main, M. (1973). The development of separation behavior in the first year of life: Protest, following, and greeting. *Developmental Psychology* 9, 213–225.

Stayton, D. J.; Hogan, R.; & Ainsworth, M. D. S. (1971). Infant obedience and maternal behavior: The origins of socialization reconsidered. *Child Development* 42, 1057–1069.

Stern, D. (1985). *The interpersonal world of the infant: A view from psychoanalysis and developmental psychology.* New York: Basic Books.

Sullivan, H. S. (1953). *The interpersonal theory of psychiatry.* New York: Norton.

Waters, E. (1978). The stability of individual differences in infant-mother attachment. *Child Development* 49, 483–494.

Waters, E. (1981). Traits, behavioral systems, and relationships: Three models of infant-mother attachment. In G. Barlow, K. Immelman, M. Main, & L. Petrinovitch (eds.), *The development of behavior* (pp. 621–650). Cambridge: Cambridge University Press.

Waters, E., & Deane, K. (1982). Infant-mother attachment: Theories, models, recent data, and some tasks for comparative developmental analysis. In L. Hoffman & R. Gandelman (eds.), *Parental behavior: Causes and consequences* (pp. 19–54). Hillsdale, N.J.: Erlbaum.

Waters, E., & Deane, K. (1985). Defining and assessing individual differences in attachment relationships: Q-methodology and the organization of behavior in infancy and early childhood. In I. Bretherton & E. Waters (eds.), *Growing points of attachment theory and research. Monographs of the Society for Research in Child Development* 50 (1–2, Serial No. 209), 41–65.

Waters, E., & Sroufe, L. A. (1983). Competence as a developmental construct. *Child Development* 3, 79–97.

Waters, E.; Wippman, J.; & Sroufe, L. A. (1979). Attachment, positive affect, and competence in the peer group: Two studies in construct validation. *Child Development* 50, 820–829.

Weinraub, M., & Lewis, M. (1977). *The determinants of children's responses to separation. Monographs of the Society for Research in Child Development* 42 (Serial No. 172), 1–77.

Weiss, R. S. (1982). Attachment in adult life. In C. M. Parkes & J. Stevenson-Hinde (eds.), *The place of attachment in human behavior* (pp. 171–184). New York: Basic Books.

Werner, H. (1948). *Comparative psychology of mental development.* New York: International Universities Press.

Werner, H. (1957). The concept of development from a comparative and organismic point of view. In D. Harris (ed.), *The concept of development.* Minneapolis: University of Minnesota Press.

Werner, H., & Kaplan, B. (1963). *Symbol formation: An organismic-developmental approach to language and the expression of thought.* New York: Wiley.

7 · Security of Toddler-Parent Attachment

RELATION TO CHILDREN'S SOCIOPERSONALITY FUNCTIONING DURING KINDERGARTEN

M. Ann Easterbrooks and Wendy A. Goldberg

THE ISSUE OF how a system can change while simultaneously retaining and preserving its individuality and coherence is a critical question which lies at the heart of many theories of development. The notions of stability, of continuity and discontinuity in development, have been the focus of controversy for many years, which heightened when behaviorists began questioning the tenets of psychoanalytic formulations of development.

In this chapter, we examine the relationships between child-parent attachment measured in toddlerhood, and social-personality organization at kindergarten age. Drawing on ethological attachment theory (Bowlby [1969] 1982, 1973; Bretherton 1985), our point of departure is that there is coherence in individual development (Sroufe 1983) such that early experiences are expected to be associated with later social and personality organization. This perspective assumes a large measure of continuity in development. At the same time, our position emphasizes that the extent of stability or instability in the childrearing environment will influence the strength of the continuity in individual development across time and situations. In order to address this question, we have conducted a study that spans the transition from toddlerhood to early school years. Before presenting our longitudinal data on consequences of early attachment patterns for sociopersonality development, we review the major issues in the debate over continuity in development.

THE CONTINUITY-DISCONTINUITY DEBATE

In Western society the intuitive appeal of continuity in social and personality development is strong (Kagan, Kearsley, & Zelazo 1978, Kagan 1980; Mischel 1969). By embracing the notion that a basic core of personality orga-

This study was supported by a grant from the Foundation for Child Development to Easterbrooks and Goldberg. We are grateful to the families and teachers who participated in this study. We appreciate the dedicated research assistance of Dorothy Feeman, Diane Stephens Cardinas, Laurie Patoff, and Milly Day. Our thanks to Jill Vidas for typing the manuscript.

nization predominates across time and place, adults bring coherence into their complex lives. This "basic core" premise assumes that behavior is organized in a meaningful way, making certain patterns of behavior more likely than others (Sroufe & Waters 1977), although the manifestation of certain attributes (e.g., cheerfulness) may be suppressed in certain situations (e.g., during interpersonal struggles, occupational setbacks, attendance at a somber event) or under conditions of stress. Implicit in this discussion is the relevance of early experiences for later development. The theoretical basis for support of the idea of consistency over time emerges within many paradigms. For example, the intelligence testing tradition is characterized by a search for positive, predictive correlations between infant tests and IQ later in childhood (McCall 1979); continuity in this instance has been measured by standardized tests. In the domain of sociopersonality development, the notion that early interpersonal relationships, or "love relationships," set the stage for future development emerged in large measured from psychoanalytic formulations (Erikson 1963; Freud 1948; Mahler, Pine, & Bergman 1975). According to this tradition, oral preoccupations in adulthood are attributed to failure to gratify oral needs during infancy; conflicts over separation and self-identity in adolescence and adulthood stem from failure to resolve separation issues during toddlerhood.

This particular notion of continuity in development emphasizes that consistency in general patterns, rather than discrete behaviors, may be found across time (Rutter 1984). To illustrate, studies of continuity in temperament (e.g., Thomas, Chess, & Birch 1968) suggest that, with development, the underlying core of characteristics may change in their behavioral manifestations. Thus, an individual who was a "difficult" baby—that is, prone to crying, irritability, irregularity—may not continue to evince these same behaviors, but the cluster of early characteristics will be predictive, in a systematic fashion, of another set of behaviors later on. This position of coherence in patterns, rather than discrete behaviors, contrasts with trait notions of temperament.

In reviewing the continuity-discontinuity debate, Rutter (1984) concludes that the longer-term trajectories of early life experiences appear to differ according to domains of development considered as well as the valence of the critical experiences. In the socioemotional domain, some research suggests that early negative experiences may be especially potent, placing the organism at risk for subsequent developmental problems. Studies of the effects of maternal deprivation on young primates point to the lasting detrimental effects in the absence of intervention (Suomi & Harlow 1978). Similar evidence arises from studies of young children reared in institutions (Bowlby [1969] 1982; Rutter, Quinton, & Liddle 1983). As well, an unstable family life during the early years may be associated with the predictable pattern of risk for later behavioral problems (Rutter 1984). Although positive early experiences are likely to set the tone for future positive adaptation, there is also evidence to suggest that these experiences may not be sufficient to buffer the child from later adversity: a secure, social 3-year-old who is placed with a hostile, violent foster family for ten years likely will be a troubled adolescent (Kagan et al. 1978).

The perspective from psychoanalytic and personality trait theorists, that continuity arises from some basic core of personality, is not universally accepted. Mischel (1969) argues from a learning theory tradition that discontinuity is a part of personality: when response contingencies change, behavior changes. Since behavior is seen as situationally determined, the context of development must be emphasized in the assessment of continuity. If behavior remains the same, it does not reflect a "stable core" of dispositional forces; rather, it means that the conditions that once elicited the behavior are maintained. This is a "person by situation" perspective in which individual behavior is dependent on environmental stimuli.

Longitudinal studies of cognitive development usually have failed to find support for continuity. Weak associations between performance on intelligence tests during infancy and childhood supply evidence for discontinuity (McCall, Eichorn, & Hogarty 1977), but this proposition is tempered by measurement problems (Rutter 1984). The potential for early environmental intervention to remediate cognitive deficits (Kagan & Klein 1973) makes the issue more complex. In the socioemotional area, the fact that discrete behaviors (such as crying, proximity seeking, childhood fears) may vary in frequency during infancy and early childhood (Kagan et al. 1978; Masters & Wellman 1974) is further evidence that "homotypic" continuity (i.e., continuity in the same type of behavior) may not be expected. The suggestion that problems of method or measurement may obscure evidence for developmental continuities is compelling. Over time, behaviors that have the same meaning for the individual or environment may be manifested in ways that appear to be different. We are not without testable theories of development which could be investigated longitudinally. The challenge for the researcher is the development of sensitive and reliable tools to measure individual behavior and environmental conditions over time.

Synthesis of Continuity Debate

In recent years, several theorists, guided by the premises of ethological attachment theory, have addressed the notion of developmental continuity (Bowlby [1969], 1973, 1980; Sroufe 1979; Sroufe & Waters 1977). The idea that there are salient developmental issues that challenge the child, and correspondingly the caregiving environment (Erikson 1963; Sander 1975; Sroufe 1979), is a central tenet of this framework. As such, homotypic continuity of discrete behaviors across situation and time is not expected; rather, the coherence of an individual's development is manifest in the organization of patterns of behavior and may be evidenced in the adaptation to each subsequent developmental issue. Sroufe (1983) addresses the issue by stating that coherence in development is expected, since "development is hierarchical" and "shadows of earlier adaptation remain" (p. 74) in the child's current functioning.

Based on ethological attachment theory, a critical developmental issue for infancy is the establishment of a secure attachment relationship with caregiver(s). The security of infant-caregiver attachment, reflecting the quality of their unique interactive history (Ainsworth, Blehar, Waters, & Wall 1978; Bowlby [1969] 1982; Main & Weston 1981), helps build the foundation for the child's later adaptation/maladaptation and approach to subsequent developmental tasks, such as forming relationships with children outside the family. The mechanism by which this continuity or coherence in development is manifest is through the child's construction of a representational model, or internal working model of him/herself and others which influences the child's view of not only specific relationships, but approaches to life (Bowlby [1969] 1982, 1980; Bretherton 1985; Main, Kaplan, & Cassidy 1985). In describing differences in these models of self and other according to security of attachment, Bowlby (1980) acknowledges that the child who enjoys a secure attachment relationship will have developed a set of expectations that the attachment figure will be sensitively responsible to his/her needs, simultaneously developing a "complementary model of himself as at least a potentially lovable and valuable person" (p. 242). These expectations are reflected in the child's worldview and coping strategies for approaching new or challenging developmental tasks.

Thus, security of attachment lays the foundation for later adaptation. The developmental trajectory for the insecurely attached child should demonstrate similar coherence. According to this view, the inability to form a secure attachment that fosters competent exploration and coping strategies during infancy will set the tone for the child's attempts to master successive developmental tasks. Insecure attachment predicts less optimal functioning in subsequent periods. In stating the case for infant-parent attachment so strongly, we do not mean to imply that attachments at later ages are unimportant. We believe that issues of attachment continue to be important throughout the life span, although attachment behaviors will take different forms at later ages.

DEVELOPMENTAL IMPLICATIONS OF ATTACHMENT TO MOTHERS

The results of a number of studies have contributed to an emerging picture of the importance of quality of child-mother attachment in infancy for later development. The strongest evidence comes from studies which address developmentally salient issues, particularly in socioemotional functioning. Predictive validity of the construct of attachment (as assessed in the Strange Situation [Ainsworth & Wittig 1969]) has been demonstrated in studies of the functioning of the child-mother dyad in problem solving at age 2 (Matas,

stage for later competence. The issue of stability in the caregiving environment highlights critical features of this argument. First, there is empirical support for the notion that changes in the caregiving environment (theoretically of a positive or negative valence) will result in reduced continuity in adaptation (Vaughn, Egeland, Sroufe, & Waters 1979). Although Waters (1978) and Owen, Easterbrooks, Chase-Lansdale, and Goldberg (1984) reported very high continuity in quality of attachment to mother across time in stable middle-class samples, Vaughn and colleagues found much less stability in an economically deprived sample characterized by single-parent families, changes in employment, and unstable family relationships. Because quality of attachment is based on interactive quality, when environmental supports for sensitive (or insensitive) interaction are stable, continuity is maximized. In another study, the association between attachment to mother in infancy and preschool behavior problems was explained in part by knowledge of the continuing presence of the same male in the household during the intervening period (Erickson et al. 1985).

It appears from these studies that the circumstances that engendered early secure or insecure attachments usually persist to perpetuate the child's internal working models of self and others and the quality of ongoing attachments. We would be remiss, though, to overlook the fact that the child, caregivers, and family system are faced with changing developmental tasks as development proceeds. The implication of these changes is the chance for a qualitatively different adaptation to different developmental issues, or across different periods or domains of development (see also Marvin & Stewart, this vol.). In fact, qualitative reorganizations in the domains of attachment also occur. Given the appropriate conditions, attachment quality itself may change, contributing to developmental instability. We know of children with insecure attachments in infancy whose relationship with that parent changed dramatically to become secure in toddlerhood as well as the reverse.

Although the push is for continuity, each developmental phase brings with it the opportunity for reorganization. Thus, some children with insecure attachments in infancy might be able to address the tasks of the preschool period adaptively provided they have sensitive environmental supports (from parents or teachers). Conversely, Erickson et al. (1985) reported that some preschoolers who were securely attached in infancy but who now evinced behavior problems had mothers who were "less effective in helping them negotiate subsequent stages of development . . . able to meet the needs of an infant but not . . . the demands of the maturing, individuating child" (p. 164). Although they acknowledge the impact of the quality of caregiving during intervening years, the authors do suggest that the effects of early experience during infancy remain salient; for example, despite improved conditions, children with early insecure attachments might remain more vulnerable than those with a secure foundation for development. Similarly, securely attached children faced with adversity should retain a more resilient core than those who, though encountering similar adverse experiences contemporaneously, began with insecure attachments in infancy. Thus, later experiences may not totally eradicate the foundation laid during the early years.

OVERVIEW OF OUR CURRENT RESEARCH

The preceding review provides the theoretical and empirical background for our current longitudinal study. Our original question centered around the issues of the influence of family characteristics, notably maternal employment, father involvement, and marital quality, on child-mother and child-father relationships, with attachment as one important manifestation of child-parent relationships. We investigated these issues with a sample of 20-month-old toddlers and their parents, believing that toddlerhood was an important period for attachment to both mother and father and for the role of father involvement in family functioning.

We have written several reports (Easterbrooks & Goldberg 1984, 1985; Goldberg & Easterbrooks 1984) which describe our findings from the toddler period. Briefly, our data supported the notion that securely attached toddlers would display more effective problem-solving behavior and positive affect, and that qualitative differences among mothers' and fathers' childrearing attitudes and behaviors would be systematically related to security of attachment. Furthermore, we found no associations between maternal employment status (nonemployed, part-time, full-time) and quality of attachment to either mother or father. We did demonstrate that marital quality was positively associated with secure toddler-parent attachments and marital discord with insecure attachments. The importance of studying these patterns within a longitudinal framework cannot be overestimated. Our follow-up of these children and families at age 5–6 (the kindergarten period) attempts to address these critical issues.

In the rest of the chapter, we present findings from our longitudinal study that pertain to the issue of predictions from security of attachment during toddlerhood to adaptation during the kindergarten period. Aspects of children's sociopersonality functioning and affective expression are highlighted in this report. Because our study design included assessment of attachment to mother and father, we also present data on the consequences of family attachment patterns for later development.

SAMPLE AND PROCEDURE

The original sample consisted of seventy-five firstborn, caucasian toddlers and their parents. Families were middle- to upper-middle class (assessed on Hollingshead's 1978 four-factor index). Mothers were primary caregivers (with one exception), and two-thirds of the mothers were employed outside the home (see Easterbrooks & Goldberg 1984, 1985 and Goldberg & Easterbrooks 1984 for complete sample description). During the toddlerhood phase of the study, children were seen on two occasions in a laboratory playroom (visits separated by approximately four weeks) to assess security of toddler-mother and toddler-father attachment in the strange situation (Ainsworth & Wittig 1969). Order of child-mother and child-father visits was counterbalanced.

Families were contacted for a follow-up study when the children were in kindergarten. We were able to contact sixty-two of the original seventy-five families, obtaining consent from fifty-eight families (94% participation rate). During the kindergarten assessment period, data was gathered from teachers, home visits, and parental questionnaires. Not all families participated in all phases of the follow-up (i.e., home visits and teacher assessments were not conducted with families who moved out of state). Children's ages when the parent's completed the questionnaires were 5.2–6.8 years (mean age = 6.0). The age range was narrowed at the time of the teacher assessments, which spanned only four months.

Distribution of child gender (thirty boys, twenty-eight girls) and maternal employment status (72% employed; 36% employed fulltime) was similar to the initial phase. Eight couples had divorced in the intervening years between assessments. In this report, our longitudinal analyses are based on the fifty-three children for whom we have kindergarten teachers' assessments of social and personality functioning in the school environment. Teacher ratings were obtained in the middle of the school year to allow children time to become acclimated to school and to allow teachers ample opportunity to know the children. We also present data on children's emotional expression, based on the completed questionnaires returned by forty-nine mothers and forty-four fathers.

MEASURES

Toddlerhood

In the toddlerhood phase, security of child-mother and child-father attachment was assessed in the Strange Situation (Ainsworth & Wittig 1969). Qualitative differences in security of attachment were coded according to the standardized classification scheme of secure, insecure avoidant, and insecure resistant patterns designed by Ainsworth and her colleagues (Ainsworth, Blehar, Waters, & Wall 1978). (Note that this research was conducted prior to the designation of a new insecure category, disorganized/disoriented by Main and her colleagues [Main & Solomon, 1986]). Using this classification scheme, 86% of the toddlers were securely attached to their mothers, while 14% were insecurely attached. With their fathers, 66% had secure attachment relationships, while 34% were insecurely attached. The high proportion of secure attachments to mother is congruent with the high mean scores found for these mothers on our toddlerhood measures of parenting quality: childrearing attitudes, maternal perceptions, and maternal behavior in a parent-child problem-solving task (for details see Easterbrooks & Goldberg 1984; Goldberg & Easterbrooks 1984).

Kindergarten

The criteria for the selection of measures for use during the kindergarten follow-up phase were based on constructs thought to be related to earlier security of attachment and problem-solving behavior as well as on measures used in other longitudinal studies of attachment. Out of a larger array of assessments, those discussed in this chapter focus on teacher and parental reports of the child's social and affective functioning at age 5½: the California Child Q-sort of ego-resiliency and ego-control (Block & Block 1980) and the Differential Emotions Scale (Izard 1972). The California Child Q-sort (CCQ) was used to obtain personality descriptions of each child from their kindergarten teachers, yielding a score for two constructs—ego-resiliency and ego-control, fundamental aspects of developmental adaptation. With this Q-sort measure, teachers described the child's personality according to 100 attributes using a forced-choice distribution. Each child's personality description was then correlated with criterion definitions of ego-resiliency and ego-control established by clinical psychologists (Block & Block 1980). The correlation coefficients are used as scores.

Ego-resiliency represents the flexibility or adaptability of the child, essentially the elasticity of "personality boundaries" according to situational demand characteristics. This ability to respond flexibly, persistently, and resourcefully in problem-solving situations has been considered to be an index of competence (Arend et al. 1979). Low ego-resiliency, thus, would imply being rigid or brittle in new situations and becoming disorganized when confronted with new or stressful events. The construct of ego-control encompasses the child's ability to modulate impulses, delay gratification, and express affect in situationally appropriate ways. Ego undercontrollers (indicated by a negative score) tend toward impulsivity and an inability to delay gratification. On the other hand, overly controlling one's impulses and unduly delaying gratification are characteristics of ego overcontrollers (indicated by a positive score). A continuity theory of development would argue for relationships between early attachment and later ego-resiliency and ego-control, which is indeed what Sroufe (1983) reports for the Minnesota sample of children from economically deprived backgrounds. Our study attempted in part to replicate and extend Sroufe's findings in a middle-class sample.

The second measure of child functioning during the kindergarten phase was an index of parent's reports of the child's emotional expression, the Differential Emotions Scale (Izard, 1972; Izard, Dougherty, Bloxom, & Kotsch 1974). Using Likert-type scales, parents described their child's emotional experience during the past week. Mothers and fathers independently reported on ten fundamental emotions—joy, interest, anger, surprise, fear, disgust, contempt, guilt, shyness, and distress. Three examples of each emotion category were rated (total of thirty emotion words) on a five-point scale from never (1) to very often (5). The three scores for each emotion category were averaged to yield the total emotion scores for each of the ten fundamental emotions. Mothers and fathers independently completed the questionnaires. The Differential Emotions Scale was selected in order to examine specifically the emotional organization of the children with early secure versus insecure attachments; we expected that 5–6-year-old children who were insecurely attached in toddlerhood would display more negative emotions than the securely attached group.

FINDINGS

Security of Attachment and Adaptation in Kindergarten

Predictions from Early Security of Attachment to Each Parent. Based on predictions from attachment theory as well as previous empirical research, we expected that secure toddler-mother and toddler-father attachments would provide a foundation for adaptive functioning during early childhood. Conceptually, the terms "adaptive functioning" and "adaptation" are being used here to connote developmental mental health; operationally, we use the constructs of ego-resiliency and ego-control to index the child's social and personality functioning. Adaptation, then, would consist of a 5–6-year-old child's displaying flexibility and persistence in situations (high ego-resiliency) and a capacity to modulate impulses and emotions (moderate ego-control), as described by the kindergarten teacher. Secure early attachments were expected to predict a profile of high ego-resiliency and moderate ego-control. Insecure attachments would predict less ego-resiliency (i.e., ego-brittleness: inability to respond appropriately to changing situational demands) and either over- or undercontrol (i.e., constrained or impulsive styles).

Attachment to mothers and fathers during toddlerhood was related to later adaptation in the realm of ego-control (see table 1), but not ego-resiliency. Insecurely attached toddlers were perceived as being more overcontrolled kindergartners than were toddlers who had been securely attached to their mothers [trend] or fathers. Thus, these findings were in the expected direction and in accord with the perspective of coherence in individual development.

Inspection of the means for ego-control for the two types of insecure attachments indicated that the source of the overcontrol effect appeared to be the

TABLE 1.   SECURITY OF ATTACHMENT IN TODDLERHOOD
AND ADAPTATION DURING KINDERGARTEN

Security of Toddler-Parent Attachment	Adaptation during Kindergarten	
	Ego-Resiliency	Ego-Control
Attachment to mother:		
Secure $(n = 45)$	.55	−.01[a]
Insecure $(n = 8)$	.50	.10[a]
Attachment to father:		
Secure $(n = 30)$	.52	−.04[b]
Insecure $(n = 21)$	.56	.09[b]

NOTE: A negative score on ego-control signifies undercontrol.
[a] $t(51) = 1.77, p < .10.$
[b] $t(49) = 2.02, p < .05.$

children who were insecure/avoidant during toddlerhood. Means for the A (avoidant), and C (resistant) groups for toddler-mother attachment were .18, −.02, respectively; and for toddler-father attachment were .13, −.06. These data for the insecure avoidant children are in accord with the hypothesis put forth by Arend and colleagues (1979) that avoidance of the attachment figure early in life is associated with overcontrol of impulses and emotions later in childhood.

Predictions from Family Attachment Patterns. One of the major advantages of collecting data on attachment to mothers and fathers is that one can begin to study the complex web of joint and compensatory relationships within the family. In the area of family attachment relationships, two avenues seem particularly promising. One entails investigation of joint influences: effects of having secure attachments to both parents as opposed to insecure attachments to one or both parents. Data are presented below regarding the effects of joint secure attachments on ego-resiliency and ego-control. The second area, that of compensatory attachment relationships, could not be addressed adequately with our sample. We had hoped to explore whether it would be most crucial for a child's later development to have an early secure relationship with mother or with father. Based on the assumptions of ethological attachment theory and the fact that all mothers in our sample were the primary caregivers regardless of employment status, we expected secure attachments to mother during toddlerhood to be more critical to later functioning than secure attachments to father. Unfortunately, we had such a small number of families with both an insecure attachment to mother and a secure attachment to father ($n = 3$) that we could not test this hypothesis.

Returning to the question of the influence of joint secure attachments versus at least one insecure attachment, we again found significant effects for ego-control but not ego-resiliency. In the twenty-eight families with two secure attachments, the childrens' mean ego-control score was −.04. In the twenty-three families with one or both insecure attachments, the mean ego-control score was .08, [$t(49) = -2.10$, $p < .04$]. Thus, we found further support for the contention that insecurely attached children would exhibit the less adaptive pattern of overcontrol of impulses and emotions. This finding also suggests that two secure attachments provide a more favorable environment than one.

The question of the buffering effects of one secure attachment relationship is of great importance. Theoretically, one can ask whether children with one insecure attachment and one secure attachment (in two-parent families) function better than children with no secure attachments. A further critical issue is the difference in adaptation if the single secure attachment is with mother or with father. Our small sample of children with two insecure attachments ($n = 6$) or with an insecure attachment to one parent but secure attachment to the other ($n = 16$) precludes a definitive test of these questions. Nevertheless, examination of the means of the groups with two insecure attachments, a single secure attachment (to either mother or father), and two secure attachments, revealed a theoretically meaningful pattern (but not a statistically significant difference) for ego-control [$F(2,48) = 2.31$, $p = .11$] but not for ego-resiliency [$F(2,48) = 1.02$, n.s.]. Children with two insecure attachments were more overcontrolled ($M = .12$) than their counterparts with only one insecure attachment ($M = .07$) or two secure attachments ($M = -.04$).

Stability in Caregiving Environment and Predictions from Toddlerhood Attachments. During the four years that elapsed between our toddlerhood assessment and follow-up study, a number of the families in our sample experienced major life changes. For example, parents, particularly mothers, changed employment status; some parents divorced during this period, and a few remarried; many families experienced the birth of one or more children, and several families changed their place of residence. Previous empirical work in the attachment field, and theoretical work on continuity in development, led us to expect that the relative stability or instability of family life circumstances would affect the extent of continuity between early attachment and children's functioning during kindergarten. Changes in family life that affect the caregiving environment—the quality and quantity of interaction between child and mother and child and father—were considered to be most salient for the predictions from early attachment to later functioning.

We have just begun to examine our data on stability or change in the caregiving environment. In this chapter, we present data on two aspects of family life that affected the caregiving environment during the intervening years: marital change and maternal employment change. Eight children had experienced parental separation and divorce, entailing changes in household composition. Of the eight children in the marital change group, seven had been securely attached to their mothers during toddlerhood, and four had been securely attached to their fathers. When joint attachment classification was considered, four children had been securely attached to both parents, three had been securely attached to mother and insecurely attached to father, and one child had been insecurely attached to both parents.

Maternal employment changes involved major increases or decreases in maternal work hours between the toddlerhood and kindergarten assessments. Slightly more than half ($n = 28$) of the families in the longitudinal sample of fifty-three (families with Q-sort data) experienced changes in mothers' work patterns. Employment changes encompassed increasing hours ($n = 10$), as in the move from nonemployed to employed, part-time to full-time; changes also included the move to fewer employment hours as in the switch from full-time to part-time ($n = 7$). Many mothers experienced multiple changes in their work over the course of the four intervening years, first decreasing and then increasing hours ($n = 9$), or vice versa ($n = 2$). The net effect of change for the majority of the mothers (nineteen out of twenty-eight; 68%) was an increase in hours of employment. These types of employment changes are conceptualized best as changes in family life. Characteristically, changes in mothers' work hours entailed alterations in the child's caregiving environment: for example, beginning nonmaternal care, changing the number and frequency of contacts with alternate caregivers.

In our analysis, we first examined whether there were main effects of marital change and maternal employment change on ego-resiliency and ego-control. No significant effects for marital change were found, perhaps due to the small sample size in the "change" group [$t(51) = -.34$, n.s., ego resiliency; $t(51) = .85$, n.s., ego-control]. In six of the eight instances of marital change, maternal employment changes also were evident. Discussed below are the effects on children of changes in mothers' work situations.

Interactive effects were investigated between security of attachment and stability in the caregiving environment (indexed by maternal employment) as these two factors related to child functioning during kindergarten. Two-way analyses of variance were conducted which examined the effects of toddler-parent security of attachment (separately for mothers and fathers) and changes in maternal employment status from toddlerhood to kindergarten on kindergarten children's ego-control and ego-resiliency scores (2 [secure, insecure] × 2 [change, no change] ANOVAs). Changes in mothers' work status was related to the extent of ego-resiliency during kindergarten but not to ego-control [$F(2,40) = .50$, n.s.]. A nonsignificant trend was noted for the main effect of maternal work change on ego resiliency [$F(1,40) = 3.15$, $p < .08$], indicating that children who experienced changes in mothers' work patterns displayed less flexibility and persistence than children whose mothers did not change employment involvement (M change $= .49$, M no change $= .61$). Thus, stability in the caregiving environment seems to facilitate the child's adaptive functioning during kindergarten.

TABLE 2.   EFFECTS OF CHANGES IN MATERNAL EMPLOYMENT
AND TODDLERHOOD SECURITY OF ATTACHMENT ON
KINDERGARTEN-AGED CHILDREN'S EGO-RESILIENCY

	Maternal Employment Status	
Security of Toddler- Parent Attachment	Change since Toddlerhood	No Change since Toddlerhood
Attachment to mother[a]	Ego-Resiliency Scores	
Secure (n = 35)	.46 (24)	.70 (12)
Insecure (n = 8)	.65 (4)	.35 (4)
Attachment to father[b]		
Secure (n = 25)	.48 (18)	.66 (7)
Insecure (n = 18)	.50 (9)	.57 (9)

[a]NOTE: Values represent ego-resiliency scores. A two-way (2 × 2) ANOVA was conducted. A significant interaction was found between change in maternal employment and security of attachment: $F (1,40) = 8.75$, $p < .01$.
[b]A two-way ANOVA was conducted; $F (2,39) = 1.26$, n.s.

The two-way ANOVA also revealed a significant interaction between attachment to mother and maternal employment changes (see table 2). (Means for analyses with child-father attachment also are presented in table 2, although the findings were nonsignificant.) Optimal levels of ego-resiliency were yielded when children who had been securely attached to their mothers experienced stability at home; high ego-resiliency also was apparent when children who had been insecurely attached to their mothers experienced changes in the caregiving environment. The least adaptive ego-resiliency was displayed by children who had been insecurely attached and experienced no changes at home. With the caveat of noting the small number of insecure child-mother attachments, these findings suggest that adaptation is enhanced by stability in a good caregiving environment as well as by change from a poorer caregiving environment.

The significant interaction between attachment and family life changes for ego resiliency was consistent with the expected pattern. In three out of the four analyses of the impact of environmental stability and attachment to mother on ego-resiliency and ego-control, the secure group without family life change demonstrated the most optimal functioning, while the insecure group without change had the least optimal scores. Analyses using security of attachment to father in toddlerhood were not significant; but inspection of the means supported the finding of higher ego-resiliency when there was no change in maternal employment (see table 2). There were no differences among the patterns for boys versus girls.

Security of Attachment and Emotional Expression
in the Kindergarten-aged Child

Although based on exploratory data analyses, there was some suggestion in the literature that securely attached children are more emotionally expressive than insecurely attached children (Sroufe 1983). This direction was expected particularly of the insecure avoidant attachment pattern, indicative of overcontrol of emotions. Our analyses failed to provide strong support for the idea that securely attached children would demonstrate different patterns of emotional expressiveness, as reported by their parents, than would insecurely attached children. One might have expected children who were securely attached in toddlerhood to express more of the positive emotions (joy and interest) and less of certain negative emotions (anger, distress, contempt, e.g.) than the insecurely attached group. Of the ten discrete emotions examined by security of attachment to mother and father, none reached conventional levels of significance [F's(1,47) (1,40) < 3.58, n.s.]. However, many of the means for the emotions (eight of ten) displayed the predicted ordering. There were no significant interactions between gender of child and security of attachment.

More informative were the associations between emotional expression and patterns of family attachment. When examining the ten major emotions (using mothers' ratings) in the context of the child having either joint secure attachments or some insecurity, we found that early secure attachments with both parents favored less expression of negative emotions at 5–6 years of age. Compared to children with one or both insecure attachments, children with joint secure attachments were rated as showing less fear [$M_{SS} = 1.71$, $M_I = 2.23$, $t(47) = -2.20$, $p < .03$], less guilt [$M_{SS} = 1.64$, $M_I = 2.08$, $t(47) = -2.92$, $p < .005$], and less surprise[$M_{SS} = 2.21$, $M_I = 2.74$, $t(47) = -2.14$, $p < .04$]. The remaining t-tests for the negative emotions, although nonsignificant, displayed the expected order of secure children showing less expression of negative emotions than insecurely attached children.

When we tried to differentiate among children with one insecure attachment, two insecure attachments, and two secure attachments, we found significant differences for only one of the ten emotions [guilt, $F(2,45) = 4.26$, $p < .02$]. Bearing in mind that the sample size of the group with insecure attachments to both mother and father was very small ($n = 6$), it appears as though a secure attachment relationship with one parent does not protect or buffer the quality of children's emotional experience (as characterized by their mothers).

It is important to recall that these data represent parents' reports of their children's emotions and not actual behavioral observations of the children themselves. Parents may be differentially sensitive to their children's expression of emotions, which could mask the predicted associations. Mothers' and fathers' reports for their child were significantly correlated for only three emotions (anger, fear, and distress: $n = 44$; $.32 \leq r \leq .44$, $p < .05 -.001$); additionally, the emotions of interest, guilt, and contempt demonstrated trends ($.20 \leq r \leq .24$, $p < .10$). The low correlations seem noteworthy. Furthermore, it is surprising that an emotion such as joy, which would appear to be a salient emotion for young children, would demonstrate such low agreement between parents.

Child Gender Differences

In general, few child gender differences emerged from our data, a finding consistent with our results from the toddlerhood period. A nonsignificant trend for child gender emerged on the teacher reports of ego-resiliency, with boys reported as more ego-resilient than girls [M boys $= .60$, M girls $= .47$, $t(49) = 1.67$, $p < .07$]. It is interesting that there were very few differences in parents' reports of boys' and girls' emotions. The only significant difference was mothers' perceptions of boys as displaying more guilt than girls [M boys $= 2.00$, M girls $= 1.68$, $t(47) = 2.38$, $p < .05$]. There were no significant child gender differences with fathers' reports of emotions.

SUMMARY

Results from this study provide evidence for the predictive utility of the quality of early child-parent attachment. Toddlers who distinguished themselves in the Strange Situation by their active seeking of interaction or contact upon reunion with their mothers or fathers were more likely to become kindergartners who, as described by their teachers, had the capacity to modulate impulses and emotions in situationally appropriate ways. On the other hand, toddlers who tended to avoid their parents upon reunion (the majority of our insecurely attached sample was of this type), or toddlers who resisted parental contact, were more likely to display overcontrol of impulses and emotions as kindergartners.

The study's findings underscore the influence of the context of development on developmental processes. The importance of the family context—the caregiving environment—was manifested in three ways: (1) the influence of joint configurations of attachment to mother and to father on later adaptation, (2) the direct influence of stability or change in family life on subsequent adaptation, and (3) the influence of the interactive relationship between stability in family life and early quality of attachment in later adaptation.

Children who enjoyed two secure attachments as toddlers did seem to have an advantage over children with one or both insecure attachments. Again, this difference emerged in the area of ego-control: overcontrol of impulses and emotions in the kindergarten environment typified the children who had one or both early insecure attachments. Joint secure attachments also had implications for later emotional expression. Mothers reported less display of negative emotions, particularly fear, guilt, and surprise, among children who had been securely attached to both parents as compared to children who earlier had one or both insecure attachments. However, these differences, although significant, were small in absolute size.

Our preliminary investigation of the data concerning the effects of having secure attachments to one or both parents in contrast to having insecure attachments to both parents indicated some potential for the buffering ability of a single secure attachment in the area of kindergarten-aged children's ego-control (the manner in which they regulate impulses and emotional expressiveness). We did not find differences in areas of ego-resiliency in kindergarten or emotional expressions (as reported by mothers). We must underscore that these data are based on a very small number of cases of children with joint insecure attachments ($n = 6$), and we do not draw strong conclusions from these analyses.

Two areas of contextual stability and change were examined in this chapter: maternal employment and marriage. The high incidence of change in maternal employment in our sample (52%) offered a good opportunity to study the impact of disruption in the caregiving environment on predictions of continuity. Change in maternal work patterns, which involved changes in the amount of interaction with mother and alternate caregivers, had a modest direct association with less ego-resiliency during kindergarten. Most interesting was the significant interaction between maternal employment changes and quality of child-mother attachment. Stability in the caregiving environment promoted ego-resiliency among those kindergartners who had enjoyed secure attachments to their mothers during toddlerhood. In contrast, change in the caregiving environment had a negative effect on children who had been securely attached, but had a positive effect on children who had been insecurely attached to their mothers. The least adaptive behavior was found when the caregiving environment for insecurely attached children did not change. For the majority of our sample, employment changes involved an increase in maternal work hours, which likely involved changes in the number and type of schedules and settings for alternate care. No main effect was found for marital change, but most families who experienced separation or divorce also experienced changes in maternal employment.

Discussion

The child-parent attachment relationship has been called a hallmark of infant socioemotional development, not only for its immediate significance during infancy but because of the emerging evidence that the quality of this relationship bears directly on adaptation during early childhood. Theoretically and empirically, secure attachments foster favorable self-images, satisfying relationships outside the family, and a stable basis for exploring the environment and mastering new developmental tasks.

This report provides a partial replication of previous studies linking infant-mother attachment to later adaptation, and it extends these findings to the child-father relationship. In so doing, the results lend some measure of support to the notion of developmental continuity. Our findings also lend credence to the idea that continuity in adaptation is most strong under conditions of stability in the caregiving environments. Regulation of affect and impulses in situationally appropriate ways was predicted directly by child-mother and child-father attachments, whereas ego-resiliency was more susceptible to the extent of stability in the caregiving environment. Since ego-resiliency is an index of the child's adaptability to new situations and stresses, it seems reasonable that this construct would be most sensitive to change and stress in the home environment. In future analyses, it may be that stronger, direct associations are found between the toddlers' behavior in a problem-solving situation and kindergarten ego-resiliency, which essentially measures flexibility, persistence, and resourcefulness in problem-solving situations. As part of the toddler assessment, we observed the toddlers with their mothers and with their fathers in a challenging problem-solving task. We found that securely attached toddlers exhibited more positive affect and persistence in problem-solving and that their parents provided a more sensitive environment for this behavior. In our further longitudinal analyses we will examine how early problem-solving behavior, in combination with attachment quality, is associated with kindergarten behavior.

In previous work, exploratory data reported by Arend et al. (1979) pointed to differential associations between the two patterns of insecure attachments in infancy and ego-control at preschool age. Infants who were insecure/avoidant (*A*'s) displayed more overcontrol as preschoolers, and infants who were insecure/resistant (*C*'s) were more undercontrolled. Our study extends the findings for insecure/avoidant attachments to the kindergarten period. That our insecure/resistant children were not undercontrolled may reflect the tentative nature of findings based on the very small number of children in the *C* category in our follow-up sample, or it may reflect a "self-righting" capability, or some other factors promoting change from earlier maladaptive patterns. Differentiation of the developmental effects of the various types of insecure attachments is an important area for future research with larger samples of the different types of insecure attachments.

In general, our data did not demonstrate as strong associations between toddler attachment and kindergarten functioning as those reported by Sroufe (1983). Sampling and other methodological differences between the studies may be contributing factors. The data reported by Sroufe were based on a special preschool program in Minnesota specifically created for study subjects who were living in multiple-stressed lower-class environments. All of our children were living in middle- to upper-middle-class homes which were relatively stable compared with the Minnesota sample. Further, in the Minnesota study, a handful of teachers provided the *Q*-sort descriptions of ego-resiliency and ego-control for all the children, whereas in our study there were nearly as many different teachers as there were children. Thus, Sroufe's study may have eliminated important "noise" from their data, allowing clearer, stronger associations to emerge. Considering the different number of teachers involved in our study, the fact that we were able to detect group differences in itself was confirming.

When we moved from teachers' perceptions of children to parents' perceptions of the childrens' emotional experience, we expected to find that children who were securely attached as toddlers would experience more joy, and less of several of the negative emotions (e.g., anger, distress, contempt), expectations based on attachment theory, and previous empirical work. Although there was some indication of differences according to toddlerhood attachment classification, the data were not as strong as expected. Several factors could serve as potential explanations. The discrete emotion scale may not be the most revealing, due to differences in adults' definitions of the various emotions, the problem of social desirability, and parents' differential sensitivity to the emotions expressed by their children. Certainly, the weak correlations between mothers' and fathers' reports of their children could attest to variation in parental sensitivity; as well, they could indicate differences in parents' contact with the child during the week or in the criteria used to judge the range and frequency of the child's emotional expressions. In further work with these data we plan to look at composite scores of positive and negative emotions reported by the parents. In addition, we will investigate whether there are family styles or patterns of emotional experience by examining parents' reports of their own emotions as well as that of their child. It may be that there are overriding influences related to the socialization of emotional expression within families.

This study is one of a few reports (e.g., Main et al. 1985; Main & Weston 1981) that examine the developmental implications of attachment to father as well as mother. In theory, such study may reveal important information about the relative salience of attachments, and the potential for one secure attachment to protect or buffer the child against an insecure attachment. Further, it could address the question of whether it matters if there is security with the mother or with the father if the child enjoys only one secure attachment. Answers to these questions are elusive for several reasons, one of which is the need for large longitudinal sample sizes in order to compare all possible configurations. In this study, we could address the importance of none or one versus two secure attachments. Our data on the consequences of joint attachment configurations to mother and father suggest that two secure attachments facilitate optimal adaptation later on. If we consider excessive emotional control to be less adaptive for 5–6-year-olds, then children were better off when they enjoyed secure attachments to both of their parents. This finding is consistent with the results reported by Main and Weston (1981) for prediction from joint attachment to later empathic expression.

Understanding the mechanisms that link the organization of early attachment behavior with later behavioral patterns within and outside the family will be advanced by considering both factors in the environment and qualities within the individual (see also Marvin & Stewart, this vol.). Environmental factors such as stability in family life and continuity in the quality of parental care help explain why early secure attachments would foster later adaptation and why early insecure attachments would predispose maladaptation. Not every individual child, however, exhibits this pattern. As others (Erickson et al. 1985; Sroufe 1983) have noted, children are not invulnerable simply because they had secure attachment relationships as toddlers. The quality of parenting may change with different developmental periods or with life changes experienced by families (e.g., marital discord or divorce, loss of employment). Thus, it is important to examine issues of continuity in child adaptation in light of continuity in their environmental supports. In our data, a systems perspective that highlights the transactional experiences between the child and the environment contributes to an explanation of the differential impact of family life change on children who were secure and insecurely attached. Within the individual, the concept of an "internal working model," a mental representation of self and others that guides approaches to experiences (Bowlby [1969] 1982, 1980; Bretherton 1985; Main et al. 1985), provides a mechanism for development being a coherent process. The hypothesis that security of attachment lays the foundation for later adaptation is congruent with each of these perspectives.

Considering the notions of environmental change and the "working" component of internal working models further our understanding of those children who did not follow the predicted developmental trajectory. These children are the securely attached toddlers who were seen by teachers and/or parents to be doing less well than their counterparts, and those insecurely attached toddlers who were functioning very well at ages 5–6. The basis of the working model is that this model, or schema, of self, others, and the world is available for reorganization and change. Thus, a securely attached toddler who experiences dramatic and negative changes in parental sensitivity (which could be encountered in the process of marital disruption and divorce, e.g.) may revise his/her working model of self and others. Commenting on this idea, Bowlby (October 10, 1985) suggested that maximum opportunity for malleability of internal working models occurs during the first few years of life. At the same time, in his theoretical formulation of the self, Epstein (1980) cites the strong resistance to change of "major postulates" of these models (such as "I am loveworthy"), which guides the selection and interpretation of new experiences. Change does occur, but in the context of strong or repeated emotionally salient experiences. In regard to those children who deviated from the predicted pattern, it is especially important to assess their adaptation in multiple contexts. We may discover particular patterns of vulnerability or strength as we continue to analyze and integrate our other data for these families. Speaking to these issues, Erickson and her colleagues (Erickson et al. 1985) commented that individual cases of discontinuity need not necessarily lead to the conclusion that early experiences have no effect on development. Rather, they "expect that children with early maladaptation whose lives have improved remain differentially vulnerable . . . [and that] secure infants who are later showing maladaptation would rebound quickly should life supports again improve." (p. 166). As part of our longitudinal follow-up, we used the Separation Anxiety Test (Hansburg 1980; Main et al. 1985) to assess children's emotional organization and strategies around hypothetical parent-child separations. We hope that this will be a rich base for understanding these children's views of attachment relationships as school-aged children.

Earlier, in our synthesis of the continuity debate, we noted that continuity in the caregiving environment was an important condition for continuity in patterns of behavior across time and situations. Support for this position was found in our data on the consequences of change in maternal availability and alternate care arrangements due to changes in maternal employment. Somewhat more continuity between early secure or insecure attachment patterns and later functioning was found when the caregiving environment was stable. Change in the caregiving environment promoted more discontinuity. It is interesting that the change was toward better functioning for children who had prior insecure attachments to mother. A family systems perspective would suggest that changes in family life serve as an impetus for reorganization in the system. Our data may indicate, then, that children's subsequent adaptation depends on interaction as well as transactions between early experiences and the ways that disequilibrium and the challenge of change are handled. We believe that these preliminary data from our longitudinal study support the idea of developmental continuities but highlight also the need for investigating the continuity of environmental support for children's development provided by the family system.

REFERENCES

Ainsworth, M. D. S.; Blehar, M.; Waters, E.; & Wall, S. (1978). *Patterns of attachment.* Hillsdale, N.J.: Erlbaum.
Ainsworth, M. D. S., & Wittig, B. A. (1969). Attachment and the exploratory behavior of one-year-olds in a Strange Situation. In B. M. Foss (ed.), *Determinants of infant behavior* vol. 4, 113–136. London: Methuen.
Arend, R.; Gove, F.; & Sroufe, L. A. (1979). Continuity of individual adaptation from infancy to kindergarten: A predictive study of ego-resiliency and curiosity in preschoolers. *Child Development* 50, 950–959.
Block, J. H., & Block, J. (1980). The role of ego-control and ego-resiliency in the organization of behavior. In A. Collins (ed.), *Minnesota Symposium of Child Psychology* 13, 39–101. Hillsdale, N.J.: Erlbaum.
Bowlby, J. ([1969] 1982). *Attachment and loss: Vol. 1. Attachment.* NY: Basic Books.
Bowlby, J. (1973). *Attachment and loss: Vol. 2. Separation.* New York: Basic Books.
Bowlby, J. (1980). *Attachment and loss: Vol. 3. Loss, sadness and depression.* New York: Basic Books.

Bretherton, I. (1985). Attachment theory: Retrospect and Prospect. In I. Bretherton & E. Waters (eds.), *Growing points of attachment theory and research, Monographs of the Society for Research in Child Development* 50(1–2, Serial No. 209), 3–35.

Easterbrooks, M. A., & Goldberg, W. A. (1984). Toddler development in the family. Impact of father involvement and parenting characteristics. *Developmental Psychology* 55, 740–752.

Easterbrooks, M. A., & Goldberg, W.A. (1985). Effects of early maternal employment on toddlers, mothers, and fathers. *Developmental Psychology* 21, 774–783.

Easterbrooks, M. A., & Lamb, M. E. (1979). The relationship between quality of infant-mother attachment and infant competence in initial encounters with peers. *Child Development* 50, 380–387.

Epstein, S. (1980). The self-concept: A review and the proposal of an integrated theory of personality. In E. Staub (ed.), *Personality: Basic aspects and current research* (pp. 82–131). Englewood Cliffs, N.J.: Prentice-Hall.

Erikson, E. H. (1963). *Childhood and society* (2d ed.). New York: Norton.

Erickson, M. F.; Sroufe, L. A.; & Egeland, B. (1985). The relationship between quality of attachment and behavior problems in preschool in a high-risk sample. In I. Bretherton & E. Waters (eds.), *Growing points of attachment theory and research: Monographs of the Society for Research in Child Development* 50 (1–2, Serial No. 209), 147–166.

Freud, S. (1948). *The outline of psychoanalysis.* New York: Norton.

Freud, S. (1950). Some psychological consequences of the anatomical distinction between the sexes. In *Collected papers* (vol. 5). London: Hogarth.

Goldberg, W. A., & Easterbrooks, M. A. (1984). Role of marital quality in toddler development. *Developmental Psychology* 20, 504–514.

Grossmann, K. E.; Grossmann, K.; Huber, F.; & Wartner, U. (1981). German children's behavior toward their mothers at 12 months and their fathers at 18 months in Ainsworth's strange situation. *International Journal of Behavioral Development* 4, 157–181.

Hansburg, H. G. (1980). *Adolescent separation anxiety: A method for the study of adolescent separation problems.* New York: Krieger.

Hollingshead, A. B. (1978). *Four-factor index of social status.* Unpublished manuscript, Yale University.

Izard, C. (1972). *Patterns of emotion.* New York: Academic Press.

Izard, C.; Dougherty, F.; Bloxom, B.; & Kotsch, W. E. (1974). The differential emotions scale: A method of measuring the subjective experience of discrete emotions. Unpublished manuscript, Department of Psychology, Vanderbilt University.

Kagan, J. (1980). Perspectives in continuity. In O. G. Brim & J. Kagan (eds.), *Constancy and change in human development* (pp. 26–74). Cambridge, Mass.: Harvard University Press.

Kagan, J.; Kearsley, R.; & Zelazo, P. (1978). *Infancy: Its place in human development.* Cambridge, Mass.: Harvard University Press.

Kagan, J., & Klein, R. E. (1973). Cross-cultural perspective on early development. *American Psychologist* 28, 947–961.

Lamb, M. E. (1978). Qualitative aspects of mother-infant and father-infant attachments. *Infant Behavior and Development* 1, 265–275.

Lewis, M.; Feiring, C.; McGuffog, C.; & Jaskir, J. (1984). Predicting psychopathology in six-year-olds from early social relations. *Child Development* 55, 123–136.

McCall, R. (1979). The development of intellectual functioning in infancy and the prediction of later IQ. In J. Osofsky (ed.), *Handbook of infant development* (pp. 707–741). New York: Wiley.

McCall, R.; Eichorn, D.; & Hogarty, P. (1977). *Transitions in early mental development. Monographs of the Society for Research in Child Development* 42 (Serial No. 171).

Mahler, M.; Pine, F.; & Bergman, A. (1975). *The psychological birth of the human infant.* New York: Basic.

Main, M.; Kaplan, N.; & Cassidy, J. (1985). Security in infancy, childhood and adulthood: A move to the level of representation. In I. Bretherton & E. Waters (eds.), *Growing points of attachment theory and research. Monographs of the Society for Research in Child Development,* 50(1–2, Serial No. 209), 66–104.

Main, M., & Solomon, J. (1986). Discovery of an insecure disorganized/disoriented attachment pattern: Procedures, findings and implications for the classification of behavior. In M. Yogman & T. B. Brazelton (eds.), *Affective development in infancy* (pp. 95–124). Norwood, N.J.: Ablex.

Main, M., & Weston, D. R. (1981). The quality of the toddler's relationship to mother and to father: Related to conflict behavior and the readiness to establish new relationships. *Child Development* 52, 932–940.

Masters, J., & Wellman, H. (1974). Human infant attachment: A procedural critique. *Psychological Bulletin,* 81, 218–237.

Matas, L.; Arend, R. A.; & Sroufe, L. A. (1978). Continuity of adaptation in the second year: The relationship between quality of attachment and later competence. *Child Development* 49, 547–556.

Mischel, W. (1969). Continuity and change in personality. *American Psychologist* 24, 1012–18.

Owen, M. T. (1981). Similarity of infant-mother and infant-father attachments. Unpublished doctoral dissertation, University of Michigan, 1981. *Dissertation: Abstracts International* 42, 2568–B.

Owen, M. T.; Easterbrooks, M. A.; Chase-Lansdale, P. L.; & Goldberg, W. A. (1984). The relation between maternal employment status and the stability of attachments to mother and to father. *Child Development* 55, 1894–1901.

Pastor, D. L. (1981). The quality of mother-infant attachment and its relationship to toddler's initial sociability with peers. *Developmental Psychology* 17, 323–335.

Rutter, M. (1984). Continuities and discontinuities in socio-emotional development. In R. N. Ende & R. J. Harmon (eds.), *Continuities and discontinuities in development* (pp. 41–68). New York: Plenum.

Rutter, M.; Quinton, D.; & Liddle, C. (1983). Parenting in two generations: Looking backwards and looking forwards. In N. Madge (ed.), *Families at risk* (pp. 60–98). London: Heinemann.

Sander, L. (1975). Infant and caretaking environment. In E. J. Anthony (ed.), *Explorations in child psychiatry* (pp. 129–166). New York: Plenum.

Sroufe, L. A. (1979). The coherence of individual development. *American Psychologist* 34, 834–841.

Sroufe, L. A. (1983). Infant-caregiver attachment and patterns of adaptation in preschool: The roots of maladaptation and competence. In M. Perlmutter (ed.), *Minnesota Symposium in Child Psychology* 16 (pp. 41–81). Hillsdale, N.J.: Erlbaum.

Sroufe, L. A.; Fox, N. E.; & Pancake, V. R. (1983). Attachment and dependency in developmental perspective. *Child Development* 54, 1615–1627.

Sroufe, L. A., & Waters, E. (1977). Attachment as an organizational construct. *Child Development* 48, 1184–1199.

Suomi, S., & Harlow, H. (1978). Early experience and social development in rhesus monkeys. In M. E. Lamb (ed.), *Social and personality development* (pp. 252–271). New York: Holt, Rinehart & Winston.

Thomas, A.; Chess, S.; & Birch, H. G. (1968). *Temperament and behavior disorders in children.* New York: New York University Press.

Vaughn, B.; Egeland, B.; Sroufe, L. A.; & Waters, E. (1979). Individual differences in infant-mother attachment at twelve and eighteen months: Stability and change in families under stress. *Child Development* 50, 971–975.

Waters, E. (1978). The reliability and stability of individual differences in infant-mother attachment. *Child Development* 49, 483–494.

Waters, E.; Wippman, J.; & Sroufe, L. A. (1979). Attachment, positive affect, and competence in the peer group: Two studies in construct validation. *Child Development* 50, 821–829.

8 · Attachment as a Basis for Independent Motivation

A VIEW FROM RISK AND NONRISK SAMPLES

Christine Maslin-Cole and Susan J. Spieker

THE QUESTION underlying this chapter, and much of our recent research, is the extent to which a secure attachment during infancy and toddlerhood underlies the development of motivational behavior. In this chapter, we refer specifically to effectance motivation, or mastery motivation. Specifically, we asked, Are the attachment and motivational systems interconnected, and if so, how? What processes, if any, within the attachment system influence the development of motivation? If no relationship between attachment and motivation exists, what implications does this have for our understanding of the role of the attachment relationship in early development?

This chapter discusses four ways in which attachment security and motivational behavior may be linked. A fifth possibility, that attachment security and motivation develop independently, is also discussed. Several sets of data, which address relationships between attachment and motivation, are presented. The data are taken from two longitudinal studies with complementary measures but different sample characteristics; one study used a nonrisk sample, the other a high-social-risk sample. The data from these two studies provide diverse views of how the attachment and motivational systems are interrelated.

CURRENT VIEWS OF ATTACHMENT AND MOTIVATION

Attachment Theory

The ethological-organizational view of attachment (e.g., Bowlby [1969] 1982; Ainsworth, Blehar, Waters, & Wall 1978; Sroufe & Waters 1977a) has provided a useful framework for our work on relationships between attachment and motivation. In this view, attachment behaviors are thought to be or-

The research reported here was supported by grants from the John D. and Catherine T. MacArthur Foundation Research Network on the Transition from Infancy to Early Childhood to Inge Bretherton, George Morgan, and Christine Maslin, co-investigators, and to Kathryn E. Barnard, principal investigator; and the National Institute of Mental Health, grant no. 5 R01 MH 36894, Kathryn E. Barnard, principal investigator. The authors wish to thank the MacArthur Foundation

ganized by an underlying control system. The system operates with various attachment figures, yet is sensitive to expectations about each attachment figure based on past interaction (Hinde 1982). The attachment figure serves as a secure base for the infant's exploration, and activation of attachment behaviors is dependent upon the infant's ongoing evaluation of sense of security (Sroufe & Waters 1977a). If, during separation and exploration, the infant perceives that the attachment figure's availability is threatened, then the infant's attachment system would be expected to be activated.

More recently, the organizational view has been expanded to include developmental changes in the functioning of the attachment system, especially the development of internal working models (e.g., Bretherton, 1985; Main, Kaplan, & Cassidy 1985) and of shared plans which include expectations about the attachment figure's behavior (Marvin 1977; Greenberg & Speltz 1988). How the idea of internal working models is useful for thinking about attachment and motivational behaviors will be discussed in a subsequent section.

Motivational Theory

Traditional views of motivation in young children (e.g., White 1959) refer to an intrinsic motive within the human organism that spurs the organism to interact with the environment in effective ways. White (1959) proposed that, through an "autonomous capacity to be interested in the environment" (p. 13), the organism satisfies an intrinsic need and achieves effective, competent interaction with the environment. White labeled this motive "effectance motivation" and credited it with insuring the organism's progress toward competence.

Current views of childhood motivation emphasize the influence of socializing agents, extrinsic rewards, and internalized views of one's own competence on motivational behavior (e.g., Harter 1978, 1981; Bandura 1982). For example, Harter stresses the importance of adult approval in maintaining a child's mastery motivation and hypothesizes that regular reinforcement given early in a child's development (for both attempts at goals and success) is critical to developing motivation. While Harter's (1978) model incorporates the role of perceived competence in motivational behavior, to date, empirical support is limited to samples of school-age children. Our data, which are drawn from samples of toddler and preschool-age children, help complete the picture of early motivational development.

Working Group on Attachment for the inspiration to further explore the constructs of attachment and motivation and for the opportunity to prepare this chapter.

Correspondence should be directed to the first author at the Department of Human Development and Family Studies, Gifford Building, Colorado State University, Fort Collins, Colo. 80523.

Distinctions in Terminology

Central to understanding a relationship between the attachment and motivational systems is an understanding of the terms used to describe the behaviors associated with each system. The point of greatest confusion (and, perhaps, overlap) concerns use of the terms "exploration" and "goal-directed behavior." In attachment theory, exploration refers to the infant's ability to separate from the attachment figure and turn his/her interest and attention to objects, people, and events in the environment. In the context of motivation research, however, exploration and goal-directed behavior are viewed as conceptually distinct, although some inconsistency in definitions exists. For example, Morgan and Harmon (1984) ascribe motivational qualities to exploration in infancy, but they view it as developmentally less mature than task-directed behavior. They argue that task-directed behaviors require more refined, coordinated, or cognitively complex behaviors (e.g., the performance of steps toward solution in the proper sequence) than exploration. Nevertheless, Morgan and Harmon (1984) also indicate convergence of the two concepts. They equate exploration with curiosity and state that it is measurable at any age and may be indicative of goal-directed behavior throughout the life span. Recently, exploration and goal-directed behavior have been differentiated in methods for assessing independent motivation. Morgan, Maslin, and Harmon (1984) assign the term exploration to those interactions with objects that involve active manipulation of task pieces but are not directed toward an end-goal.

The term "goal-directed" is based on White's (1959) concept of "effectance motivation," which White characterized as being directed, selective, and persistent. Taking White's lead, the accepted behavioral indication of effectance motivation has become a persistent effort to reach an end-goal. Nevertheless, the use of the term "goal-directed" as a synonym for motivated behavior limits the construct of effectance motivation by implying that an end-goal (identifiable by an observer) is necessary in order for a behavior to be considered motivational. As an alternative, we suggest that an organism's behavior can be considered motivational without it leading to an identifiable end-goal. For example, learning about the properties of an object by trying out different ways to use of manipulate the object (what might be called "exploration") can be a goal in itself. Other views of motivation (e.g., Dweck 1986) present a broad view of goal-oriented activity which includes understanding something new.

Motivational behavior can be viewed along a continuum represented by four elements: (1) the purposefulness of behavior, (2) the duration of behavior, (3) the amount of affective engrossment or engagement the individual shows while performing a behavior, and (4) a perception by the individual that either direct positive feedback from the object or insight into the workings of the object is available.[1] In this sense, inherent in highly motivated behavior is a feedback cycle that includes either the availability of direct positive feedback from the object/activity or the belief that a rewarding outcome is pending. The individual's perception that there is something to be gained by continuing to pursue the activity (e.g., knowledge, insight, production of interesting effects) contributes to sustained motivation. Indeed, Harter's (1978) model of effectance motivation emphasizes positive feedback and reward in maintaining motivational level. We hypothesize that it is this interest in outcome that underlies the affective engrossment which accompanies high levels of motivation, and it is the positive feedback (or the promise of it) that contributes to the sustained duration.[2]

Therefore, highly motivated behavior would be purposeful in intent, of substantial duration, accompanied by an affective state of high engagement and/or engrossment, and would occur when the individual perceived the possibility of gaining insight into the object or of producing an interesting outcome or effect. Adjectives used to describe this type of behavior would include determined, persistent, and engrossed as well as goal-directed. Behaviors that reflect only moderate levels of these four characteristics or qualities would also be considered motivational; however, the *level* of motivation would be less.[3] Note that both intrapsychic factors (e.g., fatigue) and external factors, including the degree of challenge or novelty offered by the activity or problem, may influence level of motivation. (See the subsequent discussion in this chapter as well as Morgan & Maslin 1986.)

Much of what has been considered exploratory behavior in the past could be included in the definition of motivational behavior offered here. Rather than using the term "non–goal-directed" to refer to exploratory behavior, it seems more useful to label non–goal-directed those behaviors that lack purpose or intent, are of very brief duration, and are not accompanied by a state of affective engagement. Such behavior is frequently seen in toddlers—for example, tentatively poking at Play Doh without further manipulation (perhaps while casually looking about the room), or hesitantly picking up a puzzle

---

1. Although some may argue that the degree of novelty or challenge afforded by the object and/or activity should play a central role in a definition of motivational behavior, we prefer to view this as a factor external to the individual which contributes to variations in level of motivation. This question has been examined empirically in two recent studies (as described in Morgan & Maslin 1986).

2. The positive feedback we refer to need not take the form of a solution or reward. For some individuals in some settings, simply gaining more information about the properties of an object or a problem (or even the promise thereof) is sufficient reward to maintain engrossment and motivation.

3. In some situations involving exceedingly difficult or impossible tasks, the adaptive response would be to give up and turn attention to other, more productive ends. The term "perseveration" might be used to describe continued persistence toward an end goal when neither indications of progress nor insight into the problem are being gained.

piece and moving it in the direction of the puzzle before dropping it and then looking at something else. These same behaviors (poking at Play Doh and moving a puzzle piece toward a puzzle) would reflect motivation if they were done with determined effort and interest. Therefore, it is not the content of the behavior that determines how motivational it is, rather it is the behavior's purposefulness, duration, and accompanying affect.

Possible Influences of Attachment on Motivation

The ethological-organizational view of attachment generates several interrelated hypotheses concerning the influence of attachment on motivation. The most basic of these is that the attachment relationship serves as a secure base for separation and exploration (Bretherton, Bates, Benigni, Camaioni, & Volterra 1979). Additional advantages which accompany a secure attachment may enhance the effect of secure base behavior on motivation. These possible influences include emotional regulation and positive emotional exchanges with the attachment figure in the context of play, the use of positive feelings and feedback experienced in interaction with the attachment figure in the construction of internal working models of self and others, and active teaching and motivating of the infant by the attachment figure. Each of these possible influences is discussed below.

The Secure Base as a Source of Motivation

Attachment theory points clearly to the role of a secure base in facilitating infant separation and exploration. The feeling of security associated with a secure attachment allows the infant to separate from the caregiver and explore the environment. If the infant's sense of "felt security" is threatened, then the infant ceases exploration and returns to the attachment figure (the secure base), maintaining a balance between exploration and attachment. Whether a secure attachment could also be expected to promote increased levels of motivation and sustained persistence in the face of challenge is less clear. Securely attached infants (group *B*) might be expected to show moderate to high levels of purposeful interaction with objects, since secure infants are able to easily separate from their caregivers and explore when not threatened. Secure infants, however, would not be expected to pursue goals with objects to the extent of ignoring the attachment figure. A securely attached infant may temporarily interrupt object interaction and pursuit of a goal in order to check the attachment figure's proximity and availability, to show the attachment figure some of the "discoveries" uncovered during the course of exploration, or to share pleasure in partially reaching a goal. In the securely attached infant, object-directed and mother-directed behaviors would be expected to be kept in balance. The secure infant would neither be preoccupied with the attachment figure's availability, which would diminish exploration, nor purposely avoidant of interaction with the attachment figure during bouts of exploration.

In contrast, a lack of balance in object-directed and mother-directed behaviors would be expected for groups of anxiously attached infants, and the
exploratory and motivational behavior of infants from these groups could be
expected to be adversely affected. Anxious-avoidant infants (group *A*) tend to
avoid interaction and contact with their attachment figures, even in the face of
stress and a presumed need/desire for comfort. These infants separate easily
from their attachment figure and often show high levels of object interaction
during the Strange Situation. Nevertheless, whether the quality of object interaction shown by avoidant infants is consistent with that of secure infants
and whether it meets the criteria for motivational behavior are not known. For
example, avoidant infants may use many toys quickly and simply without sustained persistence in the face of challenge. Avoidant infants' interactions with
objects may lack affective engrossment, perhaps including tentative or cursory
interactions or repetition which might suggest perseveration.

There has been little research directed at this question. Tracy, Farish, and
Bretherton (1980) found no differences in exploratory behavior between securely attached and avoidant infants. However, Harmon, Suwalsky, and Klein
(1979) found that avoidant infants were more *active* in free play in a modified
Strange Situation, but secure infants sustained a higher *quality* of play. Although avoidant infants engage in active bouts of hitting, banging, and exploration (George & Main 1980), and their high involvement with toys makes
them look motivated and competent (Matas, Arend, & Sroufe 1978), in fact
their behavior may be less mature and focused.

Main (1981; Main & Weston 1982) theorizes that the avoidant infant's
focused attention on objects, at a time when the stress of separation would
normally arouse proximity- and contact-seeking behaviors, serves the purpose
for the infant of maintaining self-organization. This organization is maintained in a situation of theoretically irresolvable conflict: the infant wants to
seek proximity but knows by past experiences of rejection that the mother for-
bids it.

Psychophysiological studies of infants in the Strange Situation provide
some empirical support that avoidant infants turn to objects to maintain organization. Sroufe and Waters (1977b) report that during separations both secure
and avoidant infants showed heart-rate acceleration, but avoidant infants
showed this pattern much longer into the reunion episodes when they were
apparently engrossed in objects and not seeking comfort from their attachment
figure. Thus, while avoidant infants may *appear* to be attentive to objects,
they may actually demonstrate a level of physiological arousal that is incompatible with sustained attention or orientation.

Anxious-resistant infants (group *C*), in comparison, show ambivalent behavior toward their attachment figure. Resistant infants seek contact and comfort from their attachment figure, yet also show resistance and protest behaviors
when contact or comfort is offered (Ainsworth et al. 1978). Some resistant

infants tend to show high levels of attachment behaviors—clinging, fussing, and/or whining—even in the absence of apparent stress or threat of separation. In interactions with objects, they would not be expected to show as much sustained, goal-directed behavior as secure infants and could be expected to show more frustration or distress in the face of a challenging task than secure infants. Preliminary support for this hypothesis is provided by the findings of Tracy et al. (1980), who found that resistant infants were the least competent in exploratory play.

For a third category of infants with insecure attachments, labeled "insecure-disorganized/disoriented" (group *D*) by Main and Solomon (1986, this vol.), no published observations of their exploratory or motivational behavior exist. Indeed, it is unlikely that the motivational behavior of such a heterogeneous group can be comprehensively summarized. Some group *D* infants appear to be simply disorganized. Others, however, display some disorganization or disorientation within a pattern of response that resembles secure, avoidant, or resistant behaviors. Other infants show behavior that is lethargic, affectless, sad, and possibly depressed. We might predict that the greater the infant's overall disorganization in the form of dazed, aimless behavior, high distress, and ambivalence, the lower the infant's motivation is likely to be. Some group *D* infants, however, seem extremely competent. At older ages, they may show evidence of role reversal with the attachment figure and act in a caregiving or punitive manner toward the adult (Main et al. 1985). It is important that we develop the means to determine when excessive competence masks insecurity in some children. Otherwise, we risk assuming that all competent children have feelings of self-efficacy, and this may not be the case.

Emotional Regulation and Positive Emotional Exchanges as Influences on Motivation

The study of emotional development suggests two other possible links between attachment security and motivational behavior. These include the infant's ability to attain and maintain a state of physiological homeostasis (alluded to above) and pleasurable arousal associated with infant-caregiver interaction.

Recent views of the relationship between caregiver and infant have emphasized the regulatory role that primary caregivers play in infant emotional development (e.g., Greenspan & Greenspan 1985). Caregivers serve as regulators of the infant's emotional state, for example, providing experiences of calm alertness for the infant through voice modulation and soothing interactions. Infants whose caregivers regularly assist them in experiencing a state of quiet alertness learn the feeling of emotional homeostasis and, the Greenspans argue, are better able to attain and maintain this state independently. A recent study by Gaensbauer, Connell, and Schultz (1983) points to the organizing function of affective states for attachment behaviors. In this normative study of the relationships between emotional expression and attachment, strong correlations were found between ratings of the infants emotional expression and the strength of concurrent attachment behaviors. The relationship between attachment and emotional functioning seems to be an intimate one. The attachment system seems to both reflect emotional state as well as regulate it.

If the attachment system, when functioning optimally, serves to maintain physiological homeostasis and felt security, then how is it related to information- and sensation-seeking systems such as exploration and motivation? Bowlby ([1969] 1982) considers the attachment and exploratory systems to be competitive in purpose and maintains that the attachment system takes precedence over exploratory systems. The set-goal of the attachment system, maintaining a sense of felt security (Sroufe & Waters 1977a), would need to be met before the exploratory system could be activated. Therefore, infants need to feel assured of their source of security (i.e., access to the attachment figure) before separation and exploration take place.

The notion that optimal exploration takes place only when the organism's more basic needs are met and a state of physiological homeostasis has been achieved is echoed in the work of White (1959), Maslow (1954), and others (e.g., Schachtel 1954; Woodward 1958). White (1959) states that the absence of homeostatic crisis underlies a young child's play and goal-directed behavior. Moreover, like Bowlby, White indicates that systems that service basic biological needs or are associated with high levels of arousal (such as the attachment system) take precedence over systems that are best employed during times of nonarousal and physiological and psychological homeostasis (such as exploration).

If differences in motivational behavior indeed are found between secure and anxious attachment groups, then levels of physiological arousal and ability to maintain homeostasis may underlie the difference. If a secure infant is able to easily attain and maintain a state of physiological homeostasis (i.e., feeling secure), then novel opportunities for activation of the exploratory system would be expected to be more readily exploited than for an anxiously attached infant, who may have difficulty attaining and maintaining homeostasis. By accessing the attachment figure for emotional "refueling," the secure infant would be expected to show greater ease of separation and an absence of unresolved attachment issues which might interfere with exploration. One way that anxiously attached infants might control their physiological arousal is to explore the familiar or the unchallenging.

It is important to consider the affective state that underlies motivational behavior. Young children who are highly task-directed are typically very engrossed and purposeful. To what extent does degree of engrossment reflect a common underlying emotional state or dimension of physiological arousal? Differences in motivational behavior may be ties to differences in ability to regulate affective state and attain (and maintain) a physiological state that supports focused attention and directed effort, although this is yet to be established.

It appears that any influence the attachment bond may have on emotion regulation changes with development, apparently subsiding at some point during childhood. Some adults who have failed to resolve attachment issues or are avoidant of intimacy have, nevertheless, compensated emotionally in order to master the physical and mental aspects of their lives. An understanding of how and when this type of compensation occurs would enhance our understanding of the saliency of childhood attachment-related experiences and self-concept for subsequent behavior.

A second way in which the emotional qualities of a secure attachment might influence motivation is through affective sharing and pleasurable arousal. For example, several recent studies have shown a relationship between the dyad's attachment security and measures of affective sharing and positivity during face-to-face interaction during the infant's first year (e.g., Tronick, Ricks, & Cohn 1982; Kiser, Bates, Maslin, & Bayles 1986).

A young child who is accustomed to experiencing states of pleasurable arousal during joint object-play and challenging activities with the attachment figure may associate feelings of pleasure with goal-directed play. It may not be important to the child's motivational level that the attachment figure have an explicit goal of motivating the child (as is the case with scaffolding, discussed below). Instead, it may be the simple association of shared pleasure during object interaction with the caregiver that contributes to the child's independent efforts with objects. It is likely, however, that an important element of the pleasurable experience is the parent's contingent responsiveness.

Internalized Sense of Effectance as a Source of Motivation

Recent work in attachment has pointed to the importance of the child's internal representation of the attachment relationship for organizing behavior (Bowlby [1969] 1982; Bretherton 1985; Main et al. 1985). As the child interacts with the attachment figure, the child receives feedback that allows an evaluation of his or her ability to effectively elicit desired levels of care and comfort from the attachment figure. As Main et al. (1985) indicate, several theoretical perspectives assert that internal working models develop out of events experienced (e.g., Fairbain 1946; Freud 1952; Spitz 1966). Previous interactions with the attachment figure are basic in the infant's construction of an internal representation of the attachment relationship and of the self (Bowlby 1980; Bretherton 1985).

Bretherton (1985) points out that it is not clear how children integrate feedback about themselves from interactions with several different attachment figures. This question is especially critical in cases in which the child's attachment relationship with one figure is secure while the relationship with another is insecure. Likewise, how children construct an internal representation of themselves when qualitatively different messages about the self and effectiveness are received from social and nonsocial sources has not been established.

Several alternative views of the formation of internal working models are possible. The first might be called a hierarchial view in which messages from diverse sources become subsumed under an overall statement about self-worth, in the type of hierarchial organization of personal reality that Epstein (e.g. 1973, 1976) and Kelley (1955) have proposed. Epstein argues that one of the most basic postulates in an individual's self-theory concerns self-esteem and that concepts about self-esteem are strongly tied to childhood relationships with parents (Epstein 1973; 1987; see Ricks 1985 for a summary).

This approach supports Bowlby's view of the development of internal working models. Children with secure attachment histories would be expected to form more positive self-concepts than children with anxious attachment histories, perhaps regardless of the quality and success of experiences in other domains. If attachment experiences are predominant (i.e., most salient) in the formation of a major postulate about the self, then they may function like a statistical main effect, suppressing the influence of other experiences. Furthermore, a major postulate could be expected to generalize to views of the self in other realms of behavior (e.g., interaction with objects) or in relationships with other individuals.

A second view involves domain-specific differentiation of self-esteem and sense of effectance and might be termed a primacy-differentiation approach. In this view, the types of interaction that are most positive and most rewarding become central to the child's model of self. For a child whose experiences are most positive in social interactions (e.g., attachment relationships), rather than interactions with the nonsocial environment, social experiences may be most salient to early concepts about self-effectance. However, if the reverse is true, then a child's major postulates about the self would be expected to be linked to competency with objects and interaction with the physical environment.

Several questions concerning how a differentiation approach would handle inconsistent evaluations about the self remain to be addressed. For example, would inconsistent evaluations about competency and self-worth in two different situations (e.g., social interactions and interactions with objects) be dismissed, or overridden in favor of a generalized positive view of the self? Perhaps both processes of differentiation and generalization operate, giving rise to an initially context-specific sense of effectance which may be generalized to other areas. Early differentiation in one's model of self-effectance may begin to occur in late infancy and toddlerhood, leading, perhaps, to the type of model proposed by Harter (e.g., 1978, 1981, 1985). As Harter suggests, a child's major postulates about self may be situation-specific and independent across situations.

Finally, the process of forming concepts about the self may be an additive one in which children who have had rewarding experiences in both social and nonsocial contexts would have the most robust sense of their own effectance (a "double plus" experience), while children who have no source of consistent, rewarding interaction (neither social nor nonsocial) would have the most consistently poor sense of their own effectance (a "double minus" experience). Positive feedback or rewarding interaction from at least one source would be expected to temper a poor sense of effectance.

Effective Parental Encouragement as a Source of Motivation

The roles of reinforcement, teaching, and active motivating by a caregiver (scaffolding) need to be considered in a model of effectance motivation. Traditional learning theorists (e.g., Skinner 1953) explain motivation in simple reinforcement terms, and more recent views include positive feedback as a central element in maintaining motivation (e.g., Bandura 1986; Maslow 1955; Harter 1978). Even need-based perspectives (e.g., McClelland 1965) discuss the importance of positive feedback and a sense of progress to maintaining a high level of motivation.

The importance of contingent or controllable stimulation in infancy has been observed by numerous investigators (e.g., Lamb 1981b; Lewis & Goldberg 1969; Suomi 1981; Watson 1979). The perception of contingency is rewarding and motivating to the infant. The opposite condition, "learned helplessness," results from even brief experiences with uncontrollable negative stimulation. In laboratory experiments, animals showing learned helplessness cease trying to control or even avoid aversive, noncontingent stimulation (Seligman, Maier, & Solomon 1971). We may assume that aversive, noncontingent stimulation, over time, would also negatively affect the motivation of human infants. For obvious reasons, however, research in this area has been directed toward successfully *enhancing* learning and self-efficacy, using response-contingent stimulation provided by inanimate objects (Watson 1979) and responsive parents (Riksen-Walraven 1978).

Both frequency of reward and the age at which rewards are first given influence motivational behavior (Harter 1978). Rewards serve as incentives (Harter 1978) and as a source of evaluative feedback to the child concerning the success or failure of performance (Bandura 1986; Harter 1978). More important, positive feedback about performance, in the form of either interesting results from inanimate objects or approval from significant others, seems to be a salient influence on the child's developing sense of his or her own effectance (Bandura 1986; Harter 1978). Other, qualitative aspects of rewards may also be important influences on a child's developing sense of effectance. These may include the timing and pacing of the reward, the appropriateness of the reward to the child's emotional state, and the genuineness of the positive feedback. The potential contributions of various kinds of parental support to young children's mastery attempts needs further investigation.

Jerome Bruner and colleagues (Bruner 1966; Wood, Bruner, & Ross 1976) have elaborated the ways in which an adult supports and assists a child's attempts at a challenging goal. Termed "scaffolding," this process involves adult support and assistance that allows a child to attain a level of performance that exceeds the level the child could attain independently. In Vygotsky's (1978) view, the adult helps the child bridge his or her zone of proximal development.

A key aspect of effective scaffolding is keeping the child motivated and working toward an end-goal. Sensitive, contingent reinforcement is one scaffolding tool that helps maintain enthusiasm for a task. Other aspects of effective scaffolding include appropriate technical support (such as demonstrations of the task and marking of critical features in the solution process) and emotional sensitivity such that child frustration is effectively reduced, the child experiences a sense of accomplishment, and the dyad shares the emotional ups and downs of partial success and temporary setbacks. (See Maslin 1986 for a system for assessing the effectiveness of maternal scaffolding.)

Both Vygotsky (1978) and Wood et al. (1976) propose that effective adult support can raise a child's level of performance beyond what the child can do independently and allow the child to experience success on tasks that would otherwise be too challenging. Harter's (1978) model predicts that success at challenging tasks contributes to intrinsic pleasure and a self-perception of competence and control. These in turn are thought to lead to increases in the child's effectance motivation. In addition, the dyad's emotional exchange (discussed above) or informative feedback to the child about which actions best lead to success may further contribute to child's sense of effectance and may increase motivational behavior.

Scaffolding effectiveness could be expected to be mediated by the dyad's attachment security. Effective scaffolding reflects, in part, the scaffolder's sensitivity to the child's emotional state and ability to effectively modulate it if necessary (as in the case of frustration). Likewise, a certain degree of child receptiveness to the scaffolder's suggestions is necessary for the scaffolding to be effective. Maternal sensitivity to the child and child cooperativeness are considered hallmarks of a smoothly functioning attachment relationship. These qualities also appear to underlie effective scaffolding.

Attachment and Motivation as Independent Processes

The possibility that independent motivation develops separately from (or even in spite of) experiences in attachment relationships must be considered. Motivational behavior may arise primarily from intrinsic or constitutional sources, as White (1959) proposes. Alternately, level of motivation may be situation-specific—for example, as a response to the level of challenge afforded by the activity or task, or as a response to other task characteristics. Robert White's view of motivation includes the notion that the human organism seeks and prefers an optimal degree of challenge, although reinforcement and socialization history could be expected to have an influence (see Harter 1978).

Level of motivation may be a direct function of experience with objects, that is, the amount of time spent away from the caregiver and in interaction with objects and/or the physical environment. Although time spent interacting with objects may be related to ability to separate from the attachment figure and explore, the two are not necessarily equivalent. Nor would a simple linear relationship with security necessarily be expected, since both insecure-avoidant and secure infants would be expected to readily explore and interact with the physical environment. The possibility that simple time away from the attachment figure underlies high levels of object-directed motivation needs further study.

As a final possibility, developmental shifts in motivational behavior may overshadow the influence of early social experiences, pointing perhaps to only temporary influences of attachment-related experiences on motivation. Perceptions of self-efficacy gleaned from other experiences or arenas of functioning may override any early self-doubt in all but the most severe cases.

EMPIRICAL SUPPORT FOR THE INFLUENCE OF ATTACHMENT ON MOTIVATION

In the latter part of this chapter, we will present data from two longitudinal studies of attachment and motivation, each drawing subjects from a different population. The first sample, studied at Colorado State University (CSU), represented a normal, nonrisk population. The second sample, studied at the University of Washington (UW), consisted of mothers, and their young children, judged to be at high social risk. The two studies overlap on several key measures, allowing for comparisons between risk and nonrisk samples. Only selected results from these studies are reported here since more complete reports of findings are available in Maslin, Bretherton, and Morgan (1986) and Spieker and Morisset (1986, 1987).

Overview of the Colorado State University Study

The CSU sample consisted of forty toddlers and their mothers, with equal numbers of male and female children and a balance of firstborns and laterborns. Subjects were primarily white, all families were intact when recruited, and all children were screened for prematurity and major health problems. The dyads are being followed up to 4½ years of age, although this report includes data assessments from 18 months and 25 months only.

Attachment security was assessed at 18 months using the Strange Situation (see Ainsworth et al. 1978), and dyads were assigned to one of four classification groups: secure (group B), anxious-avoidant (group A), anxious-resistant (group C), disorganized-disoriented (group D). The proportions of securely attached and anxiously attached dyads were consistent with other nonrisk samples (see Ainsworth et al. 1978). A five-point security score was computed: score 5 (most secure) = B3; score 4 = B1, B2, B4; score 3 = A2, C1; score 2 = A1, C2; score 1 (least secure) = D, A/C mix.

Motivation was assessed at both 18 and 25 months of age during free play and structured mastery tasks. Toddler free play was scored for the number of seconds of high-level engrossment with two different toy sets (combinatorial and symbolic, ten minutes per set). Structured mastery tasks (Morgan, Maslin, & Harmon 1984) were scored for toddler *persistence* (number of fifteen-second intervals of task-directed behavior) and *mastery pleasure* (number of fifteen-second intervals in which the child smiled while working on the task or immediately after completing part of the task). Each mastery task could be presented at one of three levels of difficulty; however, only scores on that level of each task judged to be moderately challenging for the child were used for analyses (six tasks at 18 months, three tasks at 25 months). In addition, the examiner completed two nine-point ratings of the child following the mastery tasks: goal-directedness and attention span. Maternal ratings of toddler persistence and attention span were obtained on separate days using a temperament questionnaire (compiled from well-known instruments) and the Dimensions of Mastery Questionnaire (Morgan, Maslin, Harmon, Jennings, & Busch-Rossnagel 1988).

Child competence was assessed at both ages using the Bayley MDI (Bayley 1969) and a competence score from the structured mastery tasks, based on the proportion of correct solutions the child attained and weighted for task difficulty. Following the Bayley test, the examiner again completed the two rating scales listed above.

Maternal scaffolding effectiveness was assessed at both 18 and 25 months during a five-minute session of mother-toddler joint play. Each mother was asked to choose a toy or activity that she thought would be a little bit beyond what her child could do independently, to show her child how to do it, and to encourage her child to keep working on it. Each mother was free to vary the difficulty of the chosen task as she saw fit.

Effectiveness ratings were made for three aspects of scaffolding support: motivational, technical, and emotional. The motivation rating reflected the mother's ability to recruit the child's attention, communicate the nature of the end-goal, and maintain direction toward the goal; the technical rating reflected the effectiveness of maternal demonstrations, simplification, marking critical features of the task, and organization; the emotional rating reflected maternal sensitivity to child emotional state, ability to reduce frustration, and contribution to the child's sense of accomplishment. A highly effective scaffolder was able to accurately perceive her child's needs for support and vary the amount and type of assistance accordingly. Results reported below pertain primarily to scaffolding with combinatorial toys, since these toys have clear end goals and require directed effort to successfully complete.

Four indicators of emotional regulation and exchange, from scaffolding with symbolic toys, were included in the present analyses: (1) the frequency of effective reduction of child frustration, as a reflection of maternal ability to help regulate child emotional state; (2) ratings of maternal sensitivity to child emotional state; (3) behavioral counts of maternal physical and critical verbal interruption, rejection, or negation of child attempts at symbolic play, as a second indicator of maternal sensitivity; and (4) ratings of the dyad's affective sharing, as an indicator of mutual pleasure and enjoyment during mother-toddler play. (See Maslin 1986 for a complete description of the scaffolding scoring system.)

Overview of the University of Washington Study

The UW sample consisted of eighty-five mothers and their toddlers. The mothers had been enrolled in an intervention (Mitchell, Magyary, Barnard, Sumner, & Booth 1988) designed to help high-social-risk women improve the quality of their lives and prevent social and developmental problems for their children. High social risk was defined as low social support, low social skills, low education, mental illness, and/or a history of abusing other children. The sample was primarily white, young, and unmarried, with a mean level of education of about eleven years. The intervention began in pregnancy and ended when the children were 12 months. They are being followed in a variety of assessments until the children are 54 months old. This report includes results from assessments at 13 ($n=85$), 20 ($n=75$) and 24 ($n=67$) months.

At 13 months, dyads were videotaped in a ten-minute feeding and a five-minute teaching interaction, and in the Strange Situation. As in the CSU study, dyads were assigned to one of four attachment classifications, and an attachment security score was assigned using the five-point security scale. For the security score, stability from 13 to 20 months was moderate. Of the seventy-two infants with attachment assessments at both ages, 31% were secure at both time points, and 42% were insecure at both time points. The proportions of securely attached infants was less than for nonrisk samples at both ages (44% secure at 13 months, 53% secure at 20 months), and the percentage of disorganized-disoriented attachments was elevated (29% at 13 months, 33% at 20 months).

The mother's interactive behavior in the feeding and teaching episodes was scored using the Nursing Child Assessment Feeding Scale (NCAFS) and the Nursing Child Assessment Teaching Scale (NCATS) (Barnard & Eyers, 1979). The NCAFS and NCATS consist of seventy-six and seventy-three binary items, respectively. Each scale has two infant subscales, clarity of cues and responsiveness to parent, and four parent subscales, cognitive growth fostering, socioemotional growth fostering, sensitivity to cues, and response to distress. Examples of items from the parent subscales of the NCAFS include: "Parent praises child or some quality of the child's behavior during feeding" and "Parent encourages and/or allows the child to explore the breast, bottle, food, cup, bowl or parent during the feeding." Examples of the parent items from the NCATS include: "Parent makes constructive or encouraging statements to the child during teaching" and "Parent describes perceptual qualities of the task materials to the child." The mother subscales from the two scales were independently summed to obtain two total scores, each with excellent internal consistency. For the present analyses, a maternal scaffolding score was computed by adding the NCAFS and NCATS maternal scores.

At 20 months, the dyads were again videotaped in the Strange Situation. In addition, three structured mastery motivation tasks were administered (according to Morgan, Maslin, & Harmon 1984). As in the CSU study, only scores from that level of each task judged to be optimally challenging for the child were used in analyses. Persistence, mastery pleasure, and competence were scored just as they were for the CSU sample. A second competence measure was computed by summing the levels of challenge (low, medium, or high) judged to be appropriate for each child.

At 24 months, the Bayley Scales of Infant Development (Bayley 1969) were administered. The scales provided a measure of developmental competence (MDI) and a measure of motivation. For the motivation measure, the examiner's ratings of the child on four nine-point scales were summed: goal-directedness, attention span, endurance, and responsiveness to objects. This score showed good internal consistency (alpha = .88).

Empirical Questions

Four empirical questions addressing possible influences of attachment on motivation are posed below. We used data from the nonrisk and risk samples to evaluate support for each question. For a fifth question concerning the possible influence of internalized sense of effectance on motivation, a discussion is included in the final section of this chapter, since data were not available from either study to address this question directly.

1. Is there evidence that a secure attachment promotes greater levels of motivational behavior than anxious attachments?

Results from the Nonrisk Sample. Results from the nonrisk sample provide only limited evidence that differences in motivation are related to attachment security. Avoidant infants showed the highest levels of engrossment during play with symbolic toys (at age 25 months), although both the avoidant and secure groups were significantly higher than the resistant and disorganized groups. This finding was not replicated at 18 months nor with combinatorial toys at either age. Results were no more consistent for motivation measures during structured tasks. For example, the avoidant group (at 18 months) showed significantly *more* object interaction (goal-directed behavior plus exploration) during structured tasks than other attachment groups, and the resistant group showed significantly *less* object interaction at the same age. Results at 18 months, however, also indicated that a secure attachment was modestly, but significantly, correlated with goal-directed behavior alone. This same correlation was not significant at 25 months, nor was this finding supported by a test of differences between attachment group means.

Observer ratings of toddler *attention span* during both structured tasks and the Bayley (at 18 months) were positively correlated with the attachment security score. In addition, maternal ratings of toddler attention span (at 18 months) showed a significant difference between attachment groups, and secure toddlers were rated the highest. In contrast, ratings of toddler *persistence* following the structured tasks and Bayley test showed no significant correlations with attachment security nor any significant differences between attachment groups at either age.

Although analyses of motivation and attachment measures showed an inconsistent pattern of statistically significant results, a simple review of attachment group means across motivation measures revealed an interesting pattern: the anxious-resistant group (group *C*) scored the lowest on 88% of motivation measures and next lowest on the other 12% of motivation measures during both free play and structured tasks. The pattern for the highest score was not as consistent. Although the secure group mean was highest on 38% of motivation measures, the avoidant group mean was highest more often (44% of measures). Attachment security seems to be a better predictor of low levels of motivation, especially in the case of resistant attachments, than high levels.

When attachment groups were compared on measures of actual child competence, no significant differences between attachment groups emerged, although a striking pattern did. Results showed that the avoidant group competence level was highest for 86% of competence measures during structured tasks at both ages and for the Bayley MDI at both ages. These results suggest a tendency toward both high motivation and high competence in avoidantly attached toddlers, and they do not support our previous hypothesis that avoidant infants may prefer easy or unchallenging tasks. It is important to note that the mean competence scores for the secure group, which were typically the next highest, ranged from 1% to 10% below the avoidant group mean (for structured tasks) and 5% to 13% below (for Bayley MDI). The resistant group scored lowest most often on competence measures (both structured tasks and Bayley MDI), indicating both low motivation and low competence in this group.

Results from the Social-Risk Sample. The results from the social-risk sample show patterns of relationships similar to those found for the nonrisk sample. For both the 13-month and the 20-month attachment security scores, significant *negative* correlations were found with 20-month persistence during structured tasks. Results of one-way analyses of variance revealed significant difference among both 13- and 20-month attachment groups for 20-month persistence. The post hoc test at 13 months indicated that *A* and *D* toddlers were significantly more persistent than *B* and *C* toddlers. At 20 months the means were in the same order, but the post hoc test indicated only that *A* toddlers were more persistent than *B* and *C* toddlers.

Analyses with competence measures showed that both the 13-month and 20-month attachment security scores were *positively* correlated with one measure of competence during structured tasks (level of difficulty), and the 13-month attachment score approached a significant correlation with the 24-month Bayley MDI. A one-way analysis-of-variance test for differences between attachment group means (at 13 months) indicated a significant difference for competence during structured tasks (level of difficulty). A post hoc test revealed that group *D* infants operated at a significantly lower level of challenge compared to the *A* and *B* groups.

These various analyses describe a rather unexpected finding—that insecure infants from a high-social-risk sample, specifically those categorized as avoidant (*A*) and disorganized (*D*), are more persistent in structured mastery tasks than are secure (*B*) infants. High-risk avoidant infants seem to be persistent *and* competent, while high-risk disorganized infants seem to be persistent and relatively *less* competent. More research is needed to replicate these findings with another high-risk sample, although the results from the risk and nonrisk samples both found that avoidant infants show the highest levels of persistence during structured tasks.

2. *Is there evidence that variations in dyadic emotional regulation or exchange contribute to differences in motivational behavior? If so, does attachment security mediate this relationship?*

Results from the Nonrisk Sample. Our results showed that there was no consistent relationship between maternal reduction of frustration and motivation measures, at either age or during either free play or structured tasks. For measures reflecting maternal sensitivity to the child's emotional state, some interesting findings emerged. High levels of toddler persistence and goal-directed behavior at 25 months were related to *lower* ratings of same-age maternal sensitivity and *higher* frequencies of maternal physical interruption or rejection of child play (both same-age and previously). These correlations held for moderately difficult tasks only. Perhaps the toddler who is highly motivated for tasks that present moderate challenge becomes so absorbed in activity that physical (rather than verbal) interruption or correction is necessary to modify the child's behavior. As an alternative, perhaps toddlers whose mothers are insensitive or who physically interrupt become absorbed in object play as a means of avoidance. Since additional videotape analyses revealed that physical interruptions were not necessarily intrusive in tone (e.g., turning the teacup right-side up before allowing the child to "pour" tea, or temporarily blocking the child's action while filling in missing action in the scenario), the second explanation seems unsupported. Some mothers seemed to prefer physical interruption to verbal feedback and were able to use this tool without compromising effectiveness.

No evidence was found that higher levels of affective sharing predicted higher levels of independent motivation. This was the case for both free play and structured tasks and for both same-age and across-age correlations. There were two *negative* correlations, however, that suggested that higher levels of both persistence at task and overall goal-directed behavior during structured tasks (both 18 months) led to *lower* levels of affective sharing at 25 months. Perhaps the toddler who is highly goal-directed at 18 months loses interest in fun interactions with mother by 25 months. If so, avoidant attachments may mediate this relationship.

Further analyses provided partial support for attachment security as a mediating link between maternal emotional regulation and sensitivity and toddler motivation. The security score was moderately to strongly positively related to same-age ratings of sensitivity to child's emotional state, frequency of reducing frustration, and affective sharing. However, none of these measures at 25 months (seven months after the attachment assessment) were related to attachment security nor was frequency of physical interruptions at either age. The security score was also moderately positively related to same-age expressions of mastery pleasure during structured tasks, although no cross-age correlations were significant. These results suggest that the influence of attachment security on affect exchange may be limited to same-age measures.

Results from the Social-Risk Sample. There were no results addressing this question from the social-risk sample.

3. *Is there evidence that effective maternal scaffolding promotes motivational behavior? If so, does attachment security moderate scaffolding effectiveness?*

Results from the Nonrisk Sample. Our findings suggest a relationship between scaffolding effectiveness and motivation, although the strength and direction of the relationship varies across different aspects of scaffolding, toddler age, and specific motivation measures. Significant correlations were found between both maternal motivational and technical support and child engrossment during free play, although the direction of the relationship varied with age. The effectiveness of technical support at 18 months was positively correlated with later engrossment with combinatorial toys at 25 months. Motivation and technical support at 25 months, however, were each *negatively* related to engrossment with symbolic toys (at both ages). Hence, our "technical" rating (which was made during scaffolding with combinatorial toys) predicted *higher* levels of engrossment with the same toy type (combinatorial) and predicted *lower* levels of engrossment with a dissimilar toy type (symbolic). No significant correlations were found between effectiveness of maternal emotional support and child free-play engrossment at either age or with either toy type.

Concerning motivation during structured tasks, results indicate that the effectiveness of maternal motivational and technical support were, again, related to motivation measures, but emotional support was not. At 18 months, motivational and technical support were both positively related to persistence during structured tasks seven months later (25 months of age). At 25 months, motivational and technical support were both positively related to same-age persistence during cause-and-effect toys only. The effectiveness of maternal emotional support was not significantly related to any measure of motivation during structured tasks at either age.

None of our measures of maternal scaffolding effectiveness showed a relationship with the attachment security score, nor were there any significant differences between attachment group means. However, several aspects of scaffolding effectiveness with symbolic toys showed consistent positive relationships with attachment measures (described in part above and more fully in Maslin 1987). Apparently, the kind of help that effectively supports goal-directed activity with combinatorial toys (most of which involve sequential steps leading to an end-goal) is not influenced by the security of the dyad's attachment relationship.

Results from the Social-Risk Sample. In the social-risk sample, the maternal scaffolding score was not related to any of the motivational or competence measures at 20 and 24 months. It was, however, somewhat correlated with both the 13-month and 20-month rating of attachment security. To more fully investigate whether maternal scaffolding was differentially effective in secure versus insecure dyads, a comparison was made of two subgroups of children with complete data at all age points: those who, at both 13 and 20 months, were securely attached ($n=16$) or insecurely attached ($n=27$). The goal of this approach was to compare the relationships between maternal scaffolding behavior (measured at the beginning of the second year) and both competence and motivational outcomes (assessed at 20 and 24 months, the end of that year), for groups that were stable-secure and stable-insecure. For the stable-secure group, the maternal scaffolding score was highly related only to the Bayley motivation score at 2 years. For the stable-insecure group, there were no significant relationships between maternal scaffolding and motivation or competence measures.

These results suggest that for high-social-risk dyads, attachment has a moderating effect. A secure attachment permits maternal scaffolding behavior to have an impact on the quality of the child's motivational behavior; when the relationship is one of insecurity, the quality of maternal scaffolding does not have much influence. More research to investigate the interrelationships of attachment security, maternal scaffolding, and child motivational behavior is needed to answer this finding fully.

4. *Is there evidence that factors other than the security of the mother-toddler attachment relationship influence motivation? If so, what?*

Results from the Nonrisk Sample. In two studies conducted at CSU of motivation in children from ages 1½ to 3 years (the one described in this report and a second study of similar sample composition), we have observed that children's level of motivation varies by type of task and from session to session. (See Morgan & Maslin 1986 for a complete report.) Early preferences for types of tasks vary from child to child and are not always linked to effect production or variability of feedback. For example, some children clearly prefer cause-and-effect type of tasks, while others show a preference for puzzles, which produce only minor forms of feedback. Our investigation of variations in motivation as a function of task difficulty provides some evidence that persistence varies across different difficulty levels of similar tasks, although this effect was strongest when persistence at moderately challenging and difficult tasks were compared (Morgan & Maslin 1986). Many toddlers persisted equally on moderately challenging and easy tasks. Nevertheless, it appears that the impact of toy type, difficulty level, and within-child characteristics cannot be overlooked as contributors to motivational behavior.

Results from the Social-Risk Sample. No relevant results are available from the social-risk sample.

SUMMARY AND DISCUSSION

The results from these two studies suggest several conclusions about the influence of attachment security on early motivation. The first is that quality of attachment appears to play some role in determining a young child's level of motivation, although our data did not indicate that the influence was highly consistent across various types of motivation measures or ages of assessment. Nevertheless, both studies indicated that avoidant attachments were associated with the highest levels of motivation. Securely attached toddlers, as a group, also showed relatively high levels of motivation, while anxious-resistant toddlers (especially in the nonrisk sample) showed consistently low levels of motivation.

Several issues have influenced the interpretation of these findings. The first concerns the adequacy of the motivation measures used in these studies, and typically in similar studies. The use of persistence during structured tasks may not provide an adequate (or at least complete) measure of motivation, since persistence does not directly tap affective aspects of motivation such as engrossment. Moreover, persistence may have a different meaning for high-social-risk samples than for nonrisk samples. We find it curious that in both samples secure and avoidant infants were equally competent but not equally persistent. We need to look more closely at what the competent, but less persistent, secure infants are doing when not attending to task (a tester-defined end-goal). Are they creatively changing it? Are they attempting to engage the mother or the examiner? Both of these, and probably others, are motivational behaviors which would not be captured by measuring persistence at tester-defined goals alone.

A second issue concerns the stability of patterns of motivation later in childhood and into adulthood. Will the avoidant group continue to show high motivation and competence throughout childhood? And if so, will their motivation become specialized, that is, directed toward a relatively narrow range of goals that primarily involve nonsocial behavior? Will securely attached toddlers, later in childhood and as adults, show motivation for a broad range of activities and tasks, perhaps indicating generalized motivation?

Third, the meaning of low persistence at and low engrossment in object-related activities needs clarification, since low interest in objects does not preclude high interest in social interaction and/or high initiative to be socially competent. The term "social mastery motivation" has been applied to social behaviors that have a motivational component and serve the purpose of attaining an end-goal in a social context (Macturk, McCarthy, Messer, & Klein 1985). Although MacTurk et al. do not interpret social motivation behaviors in an organizational-ethological context, it seems likely that behaviors subsumed under social mastery motivation reflect, at least in part, the way in which a child has organized behaviors relevant to social partners (e.g., the attachment figure). Clearly, studies of early motivation in a variety of contexts, including social ones, are needed in order to fully understand the developmental course of motivational behavior.

A second conclusion suggested by our findings is that certain aspects of emotional regulation and affect communication seem to influence motivation measures. Perhaps the most telling result concerning emotion measures was that high levels of toddler persistence were most often associated with indicator indicators of low maternal sensitivity to emotional state or poor dyadic affective communication. While these results seem to futher support Main's (1981) assertion that avoidant attachments are linked to rejecting and insensitive interactions with the caregiver during infancy, what is not clear is the direction of this effect. Do rejecting mothers create infants and toddlers who turn to objects as a form of compensation for poor social interactions? Or do infants with a high interest in the physical world essentially screen out adult attempts at social communication, perhaps leaving the caregiver feeling disconnected and unneeded? The highest levels of object-directed behavior may occur in those cases in which some inborn preference for the physical world combines with a relatively insensitive, nonsocial caregiver.

Results from both studies point to a link between maternal scaffolding and toddler motivation. In the nonrisk sample, active scaffolding support (especially technical information about the task) emerged as a predictor of toddler motivation. However, this effect seemed to be restricted to combinatorial-type toys which require goal-directed behavior to successfully complete. The influence of effective scaffolding on motivation appears to be relatively short-lived, since cross-age correlations between scaffolding effectiveness and motivation were low despite high cross-age stability in effectiveness.

In the social-risk sample, the findings also suggest that active maternal teaching and scaffolding have a direct effect on toddler motivation and competence—but the effect was restricted to cases with a secure attachment. One possible explanation is that maternal behavior in the laboratory, as scored by the NCATS and NCAFS, provides a more accurate sample of behavior for mothers of secure infants than for mothers of anxious infants. A second possibility is that in social-risk dyads, maternal scaffolding effectiveness is moderated by attachment security. Since maternal scaffolding ability had less of an effect on motivation in anxiously attached dyads than in secure dyads, it appears that an anxious attachment in some way "blocks" the attachment figure's effectiveness as a scaffolder. Perhaps anxiously attached infants have shut out some of their mothers' communications and attempts to assist.

In the nonrisk sample, there was no evidence that attachment security moderated scaffolding effectiveness. Nevertheless, our anecdotal records shed some additional light. Several children showed active avoidance to their mother's attempts to recruit their attention and were difficult to keep engaged for more than brief periods of time. Of the three dyads who clearly fit this pattern, two were anxiously attached; the third was judged "secure" but not especially secure (not $B3$). In addition, we found that all mothers who were judged to be especially effective at scaffolding had secure attachment relationships, while some mothers who received low-scaffolding effectiveness ratings had secure attachments as well. It appears that in a nonrisk sample, a secure attachment helps some mothers be good scaffolders but does not insure against ineffective scaffolding ability.

Neither study addressed the role that an internalized sense of effectance may play in determining level and direction of motivation. We suspect that this will prove to be an especially fruitful area of research for understanding motivation. Further research may show how, if at all, information about self-effectance is integrated from diverse sources and the ways in which an individual's conceptions about the self translate into observable motivational behaviors.

Finally, what implications do the results from these two longitudinal studies have for our understanding of attachment as a predictive construct? Previous work suggests that the attachment relationship serves as a predictor of later development, and the principle of continuity of adaptation across developmental transformations (Sroufe 1979, 1983) has been used to explain these findings. Matas et al. (1978) hypothesize that the toddler who shows competence as an infant (i.e., achieves a secure attachment relationship) would be expected to show continuing competence in toddlerhood through resourcefulness and eager involvement with challenging tasks, and they interpret their results as supporting this claim. A closer look at the Matas et al. study shows that their measure of persistence was an indirect one (the inverse of "time away from task"), and the difference between attachment groups on this measure approached significance but was not actually powerful enough to reach significance. The results from the two studies reported here do not support the Matas et al. claim. In both studies, the highest levels of motivation were most often associated with avoidant (group A) toddlers.

There is closer agreement between the present findings and those previously reported for indicators of engrossment during free play. The results of the nonrisk sample partly agree with Main's (1981) finding of more spontaneous pleasure and more intense involvement during play for the secure group than for the anxious groups. Nevertheless, the results from neither the risk nor the nonrisk study are powerful or consistent enough to suggest that, over time, securely attached infants are at an advantage for developing a longer attention span, "staying power" in the face of challenge, or greater independent motivation. Our results do not preclude, however, the possibility that securely attached toddlers take more pleasure and enjoyment from their interactions with objects, and this finding may be meaningful in itself. Spontaneous expressions of pleasure at this young age may have a stronger influence on a child's developing sense of effectance and may better predict subsequent motivation than measures like persistence and attention span.

Future research in this area should address several points. First, we need greater understanding of the role of early indicators of motivation in the child's developing sense of self, and the degree to which the child's internal working model of self and self-effectance underlies observable motivation. Second, the relationship between attachment security and scaffolding and their interactive effect on motivation need further study. Attachment security may have an influence on scaffolding effectiveness, although the relationship may be subtle, task-dependent, or age-specific. Finally, multivariate models of motivation would identify the relative predictive power of several possible contributors from infancy and toddlerhood to later motivational levels and styles.

REFERENCES

Ainsworth, M. D. S.; Blehar, M. D.; Waters, E.; & Wall, S. (1978). *Patterns of attachment: A psychological study of the strange situation*. Hillsdale, N.J.: Erlbaum.

Bandura, A. (1982). Self-referrent thought: A developmental analysis of self-efficacy. In J. Flavell & L. Ross (eds.), *Social cognitive development*. Cambridge: Cambridge University Press.

Bandura, A. (1986). *Social foundations of thought and action: A social-cognitive theory*. N.J.: Prentice-Hall.

Barnard, K. E., & Eyres, S. J. (eds.), (1979). *Child health assessment: Part 2. The first year of life*. Publication No. DHEW No. HRA 79-25. Washington, D.C.: Government Printing Office.

Barnard, K. E.; Hammond, M. A.; Booth, C. L.; Mitchell, S. K.; & Spieker, S. J. (in press). Measurement and meaning of parent-child interaction. In F. J. Morrisson, C. E. Lord, & D. P. Keating (eds.), *Applied developmental psychology* (vol. 3). New York: Academic Press.

Bayley, N. (1969). *Bayley Scales of Infant Development*. New York: Psychological Corporation.

Bowlby, J. ([1969] 1982). *Attachment and loss: Vol. 1. Attachment*. New York: Basic Books.

Bowlby, J. (1980). *Attachment and loss: Vol. 3. Loss, sadness and depression*. New York: Basic Books.

Bretherton, I. (1985). Attachment theory: Retrospect and prospect. In I. Bretherton & E. Waters (eds.), *Growing points of attachment theory and reseach. Monographs of the Society for Research in Child Development* 50(1–2, Serial No. 209), 3–35.

Bretherton, I.; Bates, E.; Benigni, L.; Camaioni, L.; & Volterra, V. (1979). Relationships between cognition, communication and quality of attachment. In E. Bates (ed.), *The emergence of symbols: Cognition and communication in infancy*. New York: Academic Press.

Bruner, J. S. (1966). *Toward a theory of instruction*. New York: Norton.

Dweck, C. S. (1986). Motivational processes affecting learning. *American Psychologist* 41, 1040–1048.

Epstein, S. (1973). The self-concept revisited or a theory of a theory. *American Psychologist* 28, 404–416.

Epstein, S. (1976). Anxiety, arousal and the self-concept. In I. G. Saranson & C. D. Spielberger (eds.), *Stress and anxiety* (pp. 185–229). Washington, D.C.: Hemisphere.

Epstein, S. (1987). Implications of cognitive self-theory for psychopathology and psychotherapy. In N. Cheshire & H. Thoma (eds.), *Self, symptoms, and psychotherapy*. New York: Wiley.

Fairbain, W. R. D. (1946). Object-relationships and dynamic structure. *International Journal of Psychoanalysis* 27, 30–37.

Freud, A. (1952). The mutual influences in the development of ego and id. *Psychoanalytic study of the child* 7, 42–50.

Gaensbauer, T. J.; Connell, J. P.; & Schultz, L. A. (1983). Emotion and attachment: Interrelationships in a structured laboratory paradigm. *Developmental Psychology* 19, 815–831.

George, C., & Main, M. (1980). Abused children: Their rejection of peers and caregivers. In T. Field (ed.), *High risk infants and children*. New York: Academic Press.

Greenspan, S., & Greenspan, N. T. (1985). *First feelings: Milestones in the emotional development of your baby and child*. New York: Viking.

Greenberg, M. T., & Speltz, M. L. (1988). Contributions of attachment theory to the understanding of conduct problems during the preschool years. In J. Belsky & T. Nezworski (eds.), *Clinical implications of attachment*. Hillsdale, N.J.: Erlbaum.

Harmon, R. J.; Suwalsky, J. D.; & Klein, R. P. (1979). Infants' preferential response for mother versus an unfamiliar adult. *Journal of the American Academy of Child Psychiatry* 18, 437–449.

Harter, S. (1978). Effectance motivation reconsidered: Toward a developmental model. *Human Development* 21, 34–64.

Harter, S. (1981). A model of mastery motivation in children: Individual differences and developmental change. *Minnesota Symposium on Child Psychiatry* 14. Hillsdale, N.J.: Erlbaum.

Harter, S. (1985). Competence as a dimension of self-evaluation: Toward a comprehensive model of self-worth. In R. L. Leahy (ed.), *The development of the self* (pp. 55–121). New York: Academic Press.

Hinde, R. A. (1982). Attachment: Some conceptual and biological issues. In C. M. Parkes & J. Stevenson-Hinde (eds.), *The place of attachment in human behavior*. New York: Basic Books.

Kelley, G. A. (1955). *The psychology of personal constructs* (vols. 1–2). New York: Norton.

Kiser, L.; Bates, J. E.; Maslin, C. A.; & Bayles, K. (1986). Mother-infant play at six months as a predictor of attachment security at thirteen months. *Journal of the American Academy of Child Psychiatry* 25, 68–75.

Lamb, M. E. (1981a). Developing trust and perceived effectance in infancy. *Advances in Infancy* 1, 101–127.

Lamb, M. E. (1981b). The development of social expectations in the first year of life. In M. E. Lamb & L. R. Sherrod (eds.), *Infant social cognition: Empirical and theoretical considerations.* Hillsdale, N.J.: Erlbaum.

Lewis, M., & Goldberg, S. (1969). Perceptual-cognitive development in infancy: A generalized expectancy model as a function of the mother-infant interaction. *Merrill-Palmer Quarterly* 15, 81–100.

McClelland, D. C. (1965). Toward a theory of motive acquisition. *American Psychologist* 20, 321–333.

MacTurk, R. H.; McCarthy, M. E.; Messer, D. J.; & Klein, R. P. (1985, April). The stability and change in social motivation during infancy and early childhood. Paper presented at the biennial meeting of the Society for Research in Child Development, Toronto.

Main, M. (1981). Avoidance in the service of attachment: A working paper. In K. Immelmann, G. Barlow, L. Petrinovich, & M. Main (eds.), *Behavioral development: The Bielefeld interdisciplinary project* (pp. 651–693). New York: Cambridge University Press.

Main, M.; Kaplan, N.; & Cassidy, J. (1985). Security in infancy, childhood and adulthood: A move to the level of representation. In I. Bretherton & E. Waters (eds.), *Growing points of attachment theory and research. Monographs of the Society for Research in Child Development* 50(1–2, Serial No. 209), 66–104.

Main, M., & Solomon, J. (1986). Discovery of an insecure-disorganized/disoriented attachment pattern. In T. B. Brazelton & M. W. Yogman (eds.), *Affective development in infancy* (pp. 95–124). Norwood, N.J.: Ablex.

Main, M., & Weston, D. R. (1982). Avoidance of the attachment figure in infancy: Descriptions and interpretations. In C. M. Parkes & J. Stevenson-Hinde (eds.), *The place of attachment in human behavior* (pp. 31–59). New York: Basic Books.

Marvin, R. S. (1977). An ethological-cognitive model for the attenuation of mother-child attachment behavior. In T. M. Alloway, L. Kramer, & P. Pliner (eds.), *Advances in the study of communication and affect: Vol. 3. The development of social attachments.* New York: Plenum.

Maslin, C. A. (1986). Scales for assessing maternal scaffolding effectiveness. Unpublished manuscript, Department of Human Development and Family Studies, Colorado State University, Fort Collins, Colo.

Maslin, C. A. (1987). Maternal scaffolding effectiveness: How mothers support their toddlers' attempts at challenging tasks. Paper presented at the biennial meeting of the Society for Research in Child Development, Baltimore.

Maslin, C. A.; Bretherton, I.; & Morgan, G. A. (1986, April). The influence of attachment security and maternal scaffolding on toddler mastery motivation. Paper presented at the International Conference on Infant Studies, Beverly Hills, Calif.

Maslow, A. H. (1954). *Motivation and personality.* New York: Harper.

Maslow, A. H. (1955). Deficiency motivation and growth motivation. In M. R. Jones (ed.), *Nebraska Symposium on Motivation* (pp. 1–30). Lincoln: University of Nebraska Press.

Matas, L.; Arend, R.; & Sroufe, L. A. (1978). Continuity of adaptation in the second year: The relationship between quality of attachment and later competence. *Child Development* 49, 547–556.

Mitchell, S. K.; Magyary, D. L.; Barnard, K. E.; Sumner, G. A.; & Booth, C. L. (1988). A comparison of home-based prevention programs for families of newborns. In L. A. Bond (ed.), *Families in transition: Prevention programs* (pp. 73–98). Beverly Hills, Calif.: Sage.

Morgan, G. A., & Harmon, R. J. (1984). Developmental transformations in mastery motivation. In R. N. Emde & R. J. Harmon (eds.), *Continuities and discontinuities in development.* New York: Plenum.

Morgan, G. A., & Maslin, C. A. (1986, April). The influence of task difficulty on toddler mastery motivation. In R. H. MacTurk (chair), Mastery motivation and optimally challenging tasks: Issues in conceptualization and measurement. Symposium presented at the International Conference on Infant Studies, Los Angeles.

Morgan, G. A.; Maslin, C. A.; & Harmon, R. J. (1984). Mastery Motivation Tasks: Manual for 15- to 24-month old children. Unpublished manuscript, Department of Human Development and Family Studies, Colorado State University, Fort Collins, Colo.

Morgan, G. A.; Maslin, C. A.; Harmon, R. J.; Jennings, K. D.; Busch-Rossnagel, N. A. (1988). Assessing mothers' perceptions of mastery motivation: The development and utility of the Dimensions of Mastery Questionnaire. Unpublished manuscript, Department of Human Development and Family Studies, Colorado State University.

Ricks, M. (1985). The social transmission of parental behavior: Attachment across generations. In I. Bretherton & E. Waters (eds.), Growing points of attachment theory and research. Monographs of the Society for Research in Child Development 50(1-2, Serial No. 209).

Riksen-Walraven, M. J. (1978). Effects of caregiver behavior on habituation rate and self-efficacy in infants. International Journal of Behavioral Development 1, 105-130.

Schachtel, E. G. (1954). The development of focal attention and the emergence of reality. Psychiatry 17, 309-324.

Seligman, M. E. P., Maier, S., & Solomon, R. (1971). Unpredictable and uncontrollable aversive events. In F. R. Brush (ed.), Aversive conditioning and learning. New York: Academic Press.

Skinner, B. F. (1953). Science and human behavior. New York: Macmillan.

Spieker, S. J. & Booth, C. L. (in press). Maternal antecedents of attachment quality: What makes social risk risky? In J. Belsky & T. Nezworski (eds.), Clinical implications of attachment. Hillsdale, N.J.: Erlbaum.

Spieker, S. J., & Morisset, C. (1986, April). Competence, persistence and motivation: Relationships in structured and unstructured assessments of high-social-risk 13-month olds. In R. H. MacTurk (chair), Mastery motivation and optimally challenging tasks: Issues conceptualization and measurement. Symposium conducted at the International Conference on Infant Studies, Los Angeles.

Spieker, S. J., & Morisset, C. (1987, April). Persistance, competence, and affect: Profiles of adaptation related to attachment security. Presented at the biennial meeting of the Society for Research in Child Development, Baltimore.

Spitz, R. (1966). Metapsychology and direct infant observation. In R. M. Loewenstein, L. M. Newman, M. Shure, & A. J. Solnit (eds.), Psychoanalytic study of the child 2, 313-342.

Sroufe, L. A. (1979). The coherence of individual development. American Psychologist 34, 834-841.

Sroufe, L. A. (1983). Infant-caregiver attachment and patterns of adaptation in preschool: The roots of maladaptation and competence. In M. Perlmutter (ed.), Minnesota Symposium in Child Psychology (vol. 16, pp. 41-81). Hillsdale, N.J.: Erlbaum.

Sroufe, L. A., & Waters, E. (1977a). Attachment as an organizational construct. Child Development 48, 1184-1199.

Sroufe, L. A., & Waters, E. (1977b). Heart rate as a convergent measure in clinical and developmental research. Merrill-Palmer Quarterly 23, 3-27.

Suomi, S. J. (1981). Contingency, perception and social development. In M. E. Lamb and L. R. Sherrod (eds.), Infant social cognition: Empirical and theoretical considerations. Hillsdale, N.J.: Erlbaum.

Sutton-Smith, B. (1986). Toys as culture. New York: Gardner Press.

Tracy, R. L.; Farish, G. D.; & Bretherton, I. (1980, April). Exploration as related to infant-mother attachment in one-year-olds. Paper presented to the International Conference on Infant Studies, New Haven.

Tronick, E. Z.; Ricks, M.; & Cohn, J. F. (1982). Maternal and infant affective exchange: Patterns of adaptation. In T. Field & A. Fogel (eds.), Emotion and early interactions (pp. 83-100). Hillsdale, N.J.: Erlbaum.

Vygotsky, L. S. (1978). Mind in society: The development of higher psychological processes. Cambridge, Mass.: Harvard University Press.

Waters, E., & Deane, K. E. (1985). Defining and assessing individual differences in attachment relationships: Q-methodology and the organization of behavior in infancy and early childhood. In I. Bretherton & E. Waters (eds.), Growing points of attachment theory and research. Monographs of the Society for Research in Child Development 50 (1-2, Serial No. 209), 41-65.

Watson, J. S. (1979). Perception of contingency as a determinant of social responsiveness. In

E. B. Thoman (ed.), *Origins of the infant's social responsiveness*. Hillsdale, N.J.: Erlbaum.

White, R. W. (1959). Motivation reconsidered: The concept of competence. *Psychological Review* 66, 297–333.

Wood, D.; Bruner, J. S.; & Ross, G. (1976). The role of tutoring in problem solving. *Journal of Child Psychology and Psychiatry* 17, 89–100.

Woodward, R. S. (1958). *Dynamics of behavior.* New York: Holt.

9 · Assessing Internal Working Models of the Attachment Relationship

AN ATTACHMENT STORY COMPLETION TASK FOR 3-YEAR-OLDS

Inge Bretherton, Doreen Ridgeway,

and Jude Cassidy

IN A GROUND-BREAKING paper, Bowlby (1958) reconceptualized psychoanalytic views of the infant-mother relationship in terms of new insights from the ethological literature (Hinde 1961; Lorenz 1957; Tinbergen 1951). He proposed that the infant's attachment to the mother has the basic survival function of protection and that it is regulated by a motivational-behavioral system (the attachment system) which is neither subordinate to nor derivative from motivational systems that subserve feeding or sex. For this reason, attachment theory is often categorized as an evolutionary-ethological theory.

Bowlby's reworking of Freud's instinct theory should not be allowed to obscure the fact, however, that attachment theory still shares many basic assumptions with several psychoanalytic theories of interpersonal relatedness (see Greenberg & Mitchell 1983 for a review). Such theories, usually known as (love) object relations theories, are concerned with the crucial role played by self and object representations in the conduct of close human relationships. Bowlby not only elaborated on the ideas of the object relations theorists but also made them more amenable to empirical investigation. He used a new metaphor, *internal working model* of self and attachment figure, to underscore the dynamic and functional aspect of representations. In addition, he built on current advances in the academic study of information processing and cognition to carry attachment theory beyond the older psychoanalytic formulations.

In this paper, we will first review Bowlby's initial postulates regarding the significance, function, and development of internal working models and consider subsequent developments of these ideas. We will then link these theoretical formulations to a number of recent empirical studies that attempted to investigate internal working models of attachment relations in 6-year-olds and

This study was funded by the Colorado Node of the MacArthur Foundation Research Network for the Transition from Infancy to Early Childhood. Portions of the material presented in this chapter were presented at the biennial meeting of the Society for Research in Child Development, Baltimore, April 1987. We would like to thank the mothers and children who participated in this study, and Linda Wilcox, Bryan Ockert, and Jackie Street who helped with data transcription.

adults. After outlining these findings, we will present results of an exploratory study in which we tried to examine 3-year-olds' internal working models of the attachment relationship.

The Construct of Internal Working Models

Like other psychoanalysts, Bowlby (1973) was greatly concerned with the relationship between outer reality and an individual's inner world. He was drawn to the term "internal working model" (Craik 1943) because it had the functional and dynamic connotations that other related terms like "representation" or "image" lacked. This is how Craik, a psychologist interested in devising intelligent cybernetic systems, describes his conception of working models:

> By a model we thus mean any . . . system which has a similar relation-structure to that of the process it imitates. By "relation-structure" I do not mean some obscure nonphysical entity which attends the model, but the fact that it . . . works in the same way as the process it parallels . . . My hypothesis then is that thought models, or parallels reality . . . If the organism carries a "small-scale model" of external reality and of its own possible actions within its head, it is able to try out various alternatives, conclude which is the best of them, react to future situations before they arise, utilize the knowledge of past events in dealing with the present and future, and in every way to react in a much fuller, safer and more competent manner to the emergencies which face it. (P. 61)

Bowlby was not the only theoretician who noted the usefulness of Craik's metaphor of representation as internal working models. In his recent book on *Mental Models,* Johnson-Laird (1983), building on Craik, placed the concept in an evolutionary perspective very compatible with attachment theory. Working models, Johnson-Laird suggested, owe their origin to the survival advantage that they afford an organism by permitting insightful and foresightful behavior. Because the essential feature of a mental model is its functional role in guiding adaptive behavior, structural correspondence between the representation and what is represented (similarity in "relation-structure," in Craik's terms) is crucial. The more adequately internal working models can simulate relevant aspects of the world, the better the potential planning and responding capacity of an organism.

Bowlby (1973) suggested that, *within* an individual's working model or representation of the world, working models of the self and of principal caregiving figures are of special significance. It is these models that allow an individual to interpret and predict the attachment partner's behavior and to plan immediate and future responses. Because working models of self and other in the attachment relationship have their origin in actual interpersonal transactions, they complement each other—or, as Sroufe and Fleeson (1986) have recently expressed it, taken together they represent both sides of the relationship. For example, a child who experiences—and hence represents—attachment figures as primarily rejecting, is likely to form a complementary internal working model of the self as unworthy or unacceptable. Similarly, a child who experiences a parental figure as emotionally available and supportive, is likely to construct a complementary working model of the self as competent and lovable.

At this point, it is important to note how these ideas relate to other psychoanalytic theories of interpersonal (object) relations (see Greenberg & Mitchell 1983, for a review). The technical terms are different. Object relations theories do not make reference to internal working models but use terms like "introject," "projective identification," "internal objects," "self," and other representations. Nevertheless, the basic notion that representations of self and parent developed in childhood are imposed on future close relationships are held in common with attachment theory. Several crucial differences, however, should not be overlooked. Bowlby's theory ([1969] 1982, 1973, 1980) is both narrower and more general than those psychoanalytic theories of object relations that it most closely resembles (Sullivan 1953; Fairbairn 1952). Attachment theory is narrower, because it is concerned with relationships in which one person serves as secure base and secure haven to another, not with all types of social relationships. It is more general than other object relations theories, becuase the construct of internal working model is used to explain the development of healthy as well as pathological relationships. Sullivan and Fairbairn, in contrast to Bowlby, focused primarily on the internalization of unsatisfying relationships, because they wanted to explain the puzzling distortions in adult relationships that seemed to be derived from representation and subsequent repression of early experiences with parents (see Bretherton 1987 for an overview; see also Cummings & Cicchetti, this vol.).

Inspired by Craik's (1943) as well as by Piaget's (1951, 1954) writings, Bowlby suggested that the construction of internal working models of self and attachment figure is a natural consequence of the human ability to construct representations of the world. Internal working models ordinarily have the adaptive function of providing an adequate representation of self, attachment figures, and the environment. The development of healthy attachment relationships is based, therefore, on continued updating and fine tuning of internal working models. It is only when *defensive* information processing subverts the normally adaptive function of *selective* information processing that development is diverted into nonoptimal pathways. We will return to this issue in a later section.

Theories of Event Representation as Related to the Construct of Internal Working Models

When Bowlby incorporated the term "internal working model" into attachment theory, it was little more than a metaphor with useful connotations that allowed us to think about representation in a new way. However, recent developments in the study of event representation have provided a useful basis for fleshing out the notion of working models. These theories are very compatible with Bowlby's theorizing because they share the configurational and dynamic approach to memory processes that is implied in the term "working model." Representational processes are viewed as governed by event schemata or scripts (Mandler 1979; Nelson & Gruendel 1981; Schank & Abelson 1977) that summarize skeletal information about repeated similar events in a person's life. The structure of event schemata or scripts is said to simulate the spatiotemporal-causal structure of the original experience in connected form, or, as Craik (1943) would have said, event schemata or scripts imitate the "relation-structure" of the event they represent.

Schank and Abelson's original version of script theory (1977) had several disadvantages as far as attachment theory and the concept of internal working models was concerned. The definition of the term "script" was too vague. In addition, there was little discussion on how scripts or generalized event schemata were related to autobiographical memory, whether they were organized into larger structures, how new scripts might be generated, and what role affect might play in event representation. The revised formulation of the theory (Schank 1982) provides, we suggest, a more adequate basis for thinking about the acquisition, use, and change of internal working models.

Schank now argues that information derived from episodic or autobiographical memories (including affect) is reprocessed, partitioned, cross-indexed, and summarized in a variety of ways. All of the diverse resulting schemata preserve a spatiotemporal and causal relation structure that simulates real-world event structures. Some of these structures link mini-event representations into coordinated longer-event sequences (the former scripts), others generalize across mini-events (e.g., feeding situations regardless of context), and yet others generalize across event categories (e.g., all caregiving routines). Schank's conceptualization deliberately blurs the distinction between episodic and semantic memory proposed by Tulving (1972, 1983), and substitutes for Tulving's two-level memory system multiple interconnected hierarchies of schemata that are graded from very experience-near to very general-abstract. These hierarchies are constructed, continually reconstructed, and revised on the basis of new input. Existing schemata determine how new experiences are decoded or processed, although new event schemata will be generated if an initially unexpected event is reencountered several times. Moreover, new schematic memories will be parsed and information fed into many other structures that represent generalized event information about agents, actions, intentions, goals, and emotions. These parsing and ordering processes can therefore explain how events experienced with attachment figures can influence more general normative working models of the caregiving role, or, more generally, how autobiographical memories become incorporated into a variety of general knowledge structures.

Stability, Change, and Distortion
in Internal Working Models

Theories of event representation are helpful tools in thinking about representational stability and change. Once a schema is in place, it guides the processing of incoming information. The resulting stability and efficiency in processing events is, however, bought at the cost of oversimplification. Individuals will feel compelled to accommodate internal working models to a changed reality only when the lack of fit between the working model and actual circumstances becomes very obvious. Some distortion of incoming information in the service of adaptive simplification is therefore normal and unavoidable.

Although attachment theory posits some constraints on the updating of working models, they must adapt as the attachment relationship develops. A more competent child will need the caregiver's support in different ways than an infant. If such changing needs are not reflected in revisions of the child's and the parents' working models, the models will become seriously outdated and, therefore, inadequate. External factors impinging on the relationship (chronic illness, parental job loss, and so forth) are also likely to make the restructuring of internal working models necessary. Finally, cognitive development itself must be presumed to lead to change in the complexity and elaboration, and hence in the adequacy, of internal working models (see Bretherton, 1990, for further discussion of this point).

Clinical case studies cited by Bowlby (1980) suggest that defensive processes may interfere with the adequate development of internal working models of self and caregiver. This is most likely to occur in response to intolerable mental pain or conflict—for example, when an attachment figure habitually ridicules a child's security-seeking behaviors, reinterprets rejection as motivated by parental love, or otherwise disavows or denies the child's anxious, angry, or loving feelings toward attachment figures (Bowlby 1973, 1980). Under such circumstances, it is common for a child to defensively exclude from awareness the working model of the "bad" unloving parent and retain conscious access only to the loving model ("the good parent"). Since the internal working model of an unconditionally loving and supportive parent cannot possibly correspond to reality, a working model of an idealized parent is ultimately maladaptive. Defensive processes bring relief because they keep the individual from experiencing unbearable mental pain, confusion, or conflict in the present. Unfortunately, they are also likely to make the adequate accommodation of internal working models to reality problematic. Inadequate working models, in turn, will interfere with effective coping and with optimal development.

In his discussion of defensive processes, Bowlby (1980) makes use of the distinction between episodic and semantic memory proposed by Tulving

(1972; see also Tulving 1983). Episodic memory is said to store autobiographical memories of specific events in a person's life history, whereas semantic memory stores generic propositions (general knowledge as opposed to specific memories). Tulving believes that the two memory systems are based on different storage mechanisms. Building on this hypothetical distinction, Bowlby (1980) emphasizes that autobiographical memories can only be derived from actual experience, whereas generic knowledge (semantic memory) may also be based on information supplied by others. When the two sources of stored information (memories of actual experience and knowledge based on communications from others) are highly contradictory, severe psychic conflict is likely to arise. Under these circumstances, defensive processes may be brought to bear on episodically stored memories derived from actual experience as a means of eliminating the conflict.

Although Schank (1982) did not specifically discuss defensive processing, we suggest that his revised version of script theory sheds further light on this topic. If portions of autobiographical memories enter into cross-referenced schemata at many hierarchical levels, it is possible to see how material that has been defensively excluded from autobiographical memory can nevertheless be included in schemata at these other levels and thus influence a person's thinking and behavior.

The Intergenerational Transmission
of Working Models

Bowlby suggests that internal working models of self and parents developed in childhood play a major part in the intergenerational transmission of attachment patterns (Bowlby 1973, p. 322). Individuals who grow up to become relatively stable and self-reliant, he postulates, normally have parents who are supportive when called upon but who also permit and encourage autonomy. Such parents tend not only to engage in fairly frank communication of their own working models of self, of their child, and of others but also indicate to the child that working models are open to questioning and revision. To quote Bowlby:

> Because in all these respects children tend unwittingly to identify with parents and therefore to adopt, when they become parents, the same patterns of behaviour towards children that they themselves have experienced during their own childhood, patterns of interaction are transmitted, more or less faithfully, from one generation to another. Thus the inheritance of mental health and of mental ill health through the medium of family microculture is certainly no less important, and may well be far more important, than is their inheritance through the medium of genes. (P. 323)

Bowlby cites longitudinal studies by Peck and Havighurst (1960), Offer (1969), and Murphey, Silber, Coelho, Hamburg, and Greenberg (1963) in support of these claims. More recent studies supporting the intergenerational hypothesis in an attachment-theoretical are reviewed by Ricks (1985).

The Development of Internal Working Models

How relevant are these new insights about representational processes to infancy and childhood? Stern's (1985) recent writings about generalized inter-action schemata, also based on Schank's (1982) writings, provide some con-ceptual tools for studying emergent (presymbolic) working models even during the first year of life. Moreover, from the end of the first-year onward, there is some empirical evidence suggesting that infants can invoke working models in order to think about and forecast an attachment figure's probable behavior in the *future,* not only to adjust their behavior to a partner who is present (Izard 1978; Sroufe 1979). In the second and third years, toddlers' pretend play and language about emotions demonstrates that information about every-day events with the caregiver is available to them in schematic form (Brether-ton 1984; Bretherton, Fritz, Zahn-Waxler, & Ridgeway 1986). In addition, a number of studies inspired by script theory (Nelson & Gruendel 1981: Nelson & Ross 1982) report that 3-year-olds have a good grasp of the order in which action sequences within routine everyday events occur, especially when event sequences are causally related to each other. Research has also shown that children do not have to experience a large number of exposures to an event in order to construct an event schema (Price & Goodman 1985). With respect to the construction of internal working models, it is especially interesting that when 3-year-olds were asked to produce specific memories of a routine event (such as eating dinner last night), they tended to recall event schemata or scripts, not autobiographical memories of specific episodes. Only extraordi-nary events were recalled as episodic memories (Nelson & Gruendel 1981).

Studies of event representation in infancy and toddlerhood have focused on children's knowledge of routine events (having dinner, going to a birthday party), not qualitative differences in attachment experience. They may, there-fore, seem to have little to offer to attachment theory. However, anecdotal evi-dence suggests that event schemata enacted by toddlers *do* represent qualitative aspects of relationships. For example, the 2-year-old who reenacts separations and reunions with dolls may be activating his or her working model of actual experience with parents; or the toddler who is upset about mother's repeated absences and who reassures herself solemnly that "mommy always coming home" may have formed an event schema about her mother's behavior, based on many leave-takings and returns. The same can be said of the child who categorizes long and short maternal absences by whether the hairdryer did or did not remain behind, although the degree to which mention of the hairdryer replaces direct mention of mother's absence may indicate the onset of defen-sive processing.

Such anecdotal information suggests play and language could be useful vehicles for accessing even a toddler's internal working models of self and other in the attachment relationship, though we must be cautious. As Bowlby (1980), Stern (1985), and Sullivan (1953) point out, language has a rather curious relationship to internal working models. A verbal child can be given verbal guidance on how to construe specific interpersonal events and thus acquire internal working models vicariously. This secondhand information may clarify the child's nonverbal experience, but it may also be at odds with it. In other words, language may serve to communicate or miscommunicate, to create concordances or discordances within internal working models. The adaptive function of language with respect to attachment, namely, to better align intentions and goals in an attachment partnership (Greenberg & Marvin 1979), can become subverted. We must, therefore, validate our inferences about children's and adult's internal working models of attachment derived from play and conversation against observational assessments of the actual attachment relationship.

Empirical Studies of Internal Working Models of Attachment and Their Correlates

The theories of event representation briefly reviewed in the last section, suggest that internal working models of self and attachment figure could be studied through representational activities from late infancy onward. Until quite recently, however, empirical work specifically concerned with internal working models has been limited to 6-year-olds and adults. Since this work bears importantly on our own study of 3-year-olds (to be reported in a later section of this chapter), it will be reviewed here in some detail.

The findings summarized in this section constitute pioneering attempts to examine qualitative differences in working models of the self and caregiver, and to relate them to qualitative differences in the attachment relationship assessed behaviorally in the Strange Situation or other separation-reunion procedures. Our review will concentrate on three major studies and on some attempts at replication.

Berkeley Longitudinal Study. The most extensive study of attachment from the representational perspective was undertaken by Main and her colleagues (for an overview, see Main, Kaplan, & Cassidy 1985). The study began in infancy, with Strange Situation procedures at 12 and 18 months, but many of the participating families were seen again when the children were 6 years of age. During the 6-year phase of this longitudinal study, the following representational measures of attachment were obtained from a subsample of forty families that included approximately equal proportions of subjects classified as secure, avoidant, and disorganized in infancy (see Main and Solomon, this vol., for an account of the disorganized or *D* classification): (*a*) child responses to a picture set involving separation scenes, (*b*) child responses to a family photo, (*c*) child drawings of the family, (*d*) parent-child conversations upon reunion after a one-hour separation, and (e) the parents' mental representation of attachment relationships obtained during a one-hour interview. This interview was given to a larger sample of parents, including some whose children who were classified as insecure-ambivalent. The following results were obtained:

(a) Those 6-year-olds classified as secure with mother in infancy gave coherent, elaborated, and open responses to a series of separation pictures adapted from the Klagsbrun-Bowlby (1976) version of the Hansburg (1972) Separation Anxiety Test. Secure subjects also sometimes volunteered information regarding their own separation experiences. By contrast, subjects earlier judged as insecure-avoidant with mother described the children in the more severe separation pictures as sad, but claimed they did not know what the pictured child could have done in response to separation. Subjects classified as disorganized/disoriented were either completely silent or gave irrational or bizarre responses (Kaplan 1984).

(b) 6-year-olds judged secure with mother at 12 months responded to a family photograph presented during separation from the parents by looking at it, smiling at it, and commenting on it. Subjects judged insecure-avoidant with mother in infancy turned away from the photograph, dropped it, or handed it to the examiner. Subjects who were insecure-disorganized with mother at 12 months showed depressed affect or became disorganized in response to the photograph (Main 1985).

(c) In response to a request to draw a picture of their family, 6-year-olds classified as secure with mother in infancy depicted family members as close but not overly so. Figures were well individuated, and not all of them were smiling. Arms tended to be held out in an embracing position. By contrast, drawings by subjects earlier classified as avoidant with their mother had an aura of falseness, with all family members bearing similar smiles, and with greater distance among family members. Figures tended to be armless. Drawings by subjects judged to have disorganized/disoriented attachments to mother in infancy showed a mixture of elements observed in the drawings of secure and avoidant children, but were bizarre in a number of ways. Strange marks were added, unfinished objects or figures were present. Parts of the work were sometimes scratched out. In addition, overbright and cheery elements such as hearts and rainbows were added to the setting without being integrated into the overall design (see Kaplan & Main 1985).

(d) Discourse patterns during mother-child reunions at 6 years of age were systematically related to earlier Strange-Situation classifications with the same parent. Dyads classified as secure in infancy were fluent and discussed a wide range of topics. Dyads classified as avoidant in infancy were restricted in discourse, emphasizing impersonal topics (focusing on activities or objects), showed little topic elaboration, and asked questions that were rhetorical or had yes/no answers. Dyads classified as disorganized/disoriented in infancy were dysfluent, with much stumbling and false starts. The focus of the conversation was on relationship topics (not activities or objects), with the child steering the conversation (Strage & Main 1985).

(e) Infant-parent attachment patterns were strongly related to parental patterns of responding during the Adult Attachment Interview (Main 1985). This interview probed for parental recollections (general and specific) of childhood attachment figures. Main (1985) found that the parents of subjects classified as secure with them in infancy valued both attachment and autonomy, and were at ease when discussing the influence of attachment-related issues upon their own development (whether or not they recalled a secure childhood). Parents of children earlier classified as insecure-avoidant dismissed and devalued attachment, or felt that early attachment experiences had little effect on their own development. They frequently claimed not to remember any incidents from childhood. Specific memories that emerged despite this denial were likely not to support the generalized (usually highly idealized) descriptions of parents. Parents of children earlier classified as insecure-resistant seemed preoccupied with earlier family attachments. They were able to recollect many specific, often conflict-ridden, incidents about childhood attachments but could not integrate them into an overall picture. In sum, both the dismissing and preoccupied groups had difficulty in discussing attachment relationships in a coherent way. Finally, parents of children classified as insecure-disorganized in infancy seemed to be struggling with unresolved issues concerning loss of a parent before maturity (Main & Hesse, this vol.). These results have been replicated in two other samples (Eichberg, 1987; Grossmann, Fremmer-Bombik, Rudolph, & Grossmann, in press).

Charlottesville Study I (6-Year-Olds). The second set of results comes from a study by Cassidy (1988). Fifty-two 6-year-old children were seen twice, one month apart. During each of the two sessions a separation-reunion procedure developed and validated for the Berkeley study was used to assess the quality of child-mother attachment. A puppet interview and story completion task concerning the child's view of self in the attachment relationship were administered to the child in the mother's absence. Data from both sessions were aggregated and considered jointly.

In the puppet interview, subjects judged to be secure on the basis of reunion behavior with mother tended to represent the self in a positive way, but most were also able to acknowledge less than perfect aspects of the self. Insecure-avoidant children tended to depict the self as completely perfect, but without mentioning interpersonal relationships, while insecure-ambivalent subjects showed no clear pattern of responses and insecure-controlling subjects (found to be linked to the disorganized classification in infancy in the Berkeley sample; see Main et al. 1985) tended to make excessively negative statements about themselves.

In the story procedure, children were asked to use a doll family to complete six story beginnings in which self-esteem, familial conflict, and outside threat were enacted in the context of the mother-child attachment relationship. Secure subjects tended to present the doll protagonist as someone worthy, with a warm, supportive relationship to mother. Insecure-avoidant subjects depicted the doll protagonist as isolated or rejected; insecure-ambivalent subjects showed a variety of different responses, and insecure-controlling subjects tended to involve the doll protagonist in violent, hostile, negative, or bizarre behavior enacting a disorganized relationship to mother.

Charlottesville Study II (Young Adults). In a third empirical study of internal working models, Kobak and Sceery (1988) administered the Berkeley Attachment Interview (Main 1985) to fifty-three first-year college students.

When the interview classifications were compared with other assessments, it was found that peers rated secure young adults as significantly higher on social adjustment and positive affect than those classified as preoccupied (ambivalent) or dismissing (avoidant). Young adults classified as secure were also judged by peers to have more ego-resilience (flexibility and coping ability). Insecure young adults were rated as lower on social relatedness, insight, and achievement motivation than their secure peers. When these findings were compared with self-report measures, somewhat different patterns emerged. Surprisingly, the secure and dismissing groups resembled each other in terms of self-esteem, and only the preoccupied group had significantly lower scores than the secure group. These seemingly contradictory results are explained in terms of defensive processes that may have led the dismissing (avoidant) group to deny personal imperfections. It is interesting that, when asked to rate supportiveness by family and friends, the dismissing group differed from the preoccupied and secure groups by reporting much less support.

The findings from these three empirical studies point in the same direction. Secure children, parents, and young adults see attachment figures and the self as primarily good but not perfect. In addition, secure children and adults are able to communicate with ease, tend to be flexible in interpersonal conduct (to have ego-resilience), to express empathy for others, and to discuss attachment relationships coherently without idealizing them. By contrast, avoidant children and adults (those dismissing of attachment) tend to defend themselves against close relatedness by processes that interfere with the construction of adequate working models of relationships. They tend to be non-empathic and somewhat aloof, but at the same time to idealize relationships with parents when speaking of them in general terms. Ambivalent children are less easy to characterize. Their reunion behavior at 6 years of age shows elements of avoidance, sadness, fear, and/or hostility. The corresponding adult pattern is defined by preoccupation with difficult attachment relationships but without an accompanying ability to resolve these difficulties. A fourth pathway begins with disorganized/disoriented reunion behavior in infancy. In childhood, this pattern seems to be characterized by controlling behavior toward the parent during reunions and with negative and somewhat bizarre responses to representational assessments of the attachment relationship. Moreover, it tends frequently to be associated with unresolved mourning for the loss of an important childhood attachment figure in parents.

The suggested link between the ability to coherently discuss (and presumably think about) attachment relations and secure attachment at the behavioral level is interesting and provocative. We propose that this link exists because a security-providing parent is operating with fairly well integrated internal working models of self and other in attachment relations. This enables such a parent to acknowledge the child's bids for emotional support rather than to consistently disavow and disown them. In this context, the child not only receives affirmation and acknowledgement but is free to elaborate, fine tune, and update working models of self and attachment figure so that they adequately reflect the attachment relationship. Let us illustrate this with an analogy. Patterned visual input is necessary for normal development of the visual processing system to occur (Riesen 1966). Similarly, we suggest, support and confirmation from an attachment figure are needed for stabilizing the child's interpretations of the interpersonal world. The quality of the emotional feedback from the parental figures (Ainsworth, Bell, & Stayton 1974 would say "sensitivity to signals"; Emde & Sorce 1983 would say emotional availability) appears to have far-reaching effects on how the social environment comes to be mentally represented and hence ultimately on parental *behavior* in the next generation (see Bretherton 1987, and 1990, for further elaborations of this point).

AN ATTACHMENT STORY COMPLETION TASK FOR 3-YEAR-OLDS

The empirical findings reviewed in the previous section show that the study of internal working models of attachment in children and adults can shed considerable light on our understanding of attachment relationships. Until now, however, similar studies have not been conducted with children under 6 years of age.

In what follows we will report on a study in which we attempted to access the internal working models of attachment of 3-year-olds through a story-completion task, acted out with small family figures. The stories were designed to elicit individual differences in the children's enactment of a variety of attachment-related issues. Building on studies reviewed in the previous section, a system for classifying story completions as indicative of secure or insecure attachment was then developed and compared to a variety of other concurrent and prior assessments. These included attachment, family functioning, temperament, and cognitive development.

Method

Subjects. The children and parents in this study had already participated in a longitudinal study of hypothesized links between mastery motivation and the mother-child relationship at 18 and 25 months (Maslin, Bretherton, & Morgan 1986). Their families were originally identified through newspaper birth announcements. A few days after sending a letter explaining the study, the families were called on the telephone to invite their participation. Eighty percent of parents thus contacted were recruited to the study. Altogether, thirty-six families took part in the first two phases of the study. Of these, twenty-nine families were able to take part in the thirty-seven month phase (the remainder had either moved away and in two cases were unable to participate for personal reasons).

Some attachment-related information was available from earlier phases of the project: Strange Situation classifications at 18 months and attachment Q-sorts (Waters & Deane 1985) performed by the mother at 25 months. In addition, the mother had filled out the Spanier Dyadic Adjustment Scale at 18 and 25 months (Spanier 1976), the Family Adaptability and Cohesion Evaluation Scale (FACES II) at 25 months (Olson, Bell, & Portner 1983), and the Colorado Child Temperament Inventory at 18 months (Rowe & Plomin 1977). The mother had also completed a vocabulary checklist at 25 months (Bretherton, McNew, Snyder, & Bates 1983). A Bayley Test of Infant Development was administered at 18 and 25 months.

Procedure

The thirty-seven-month phase of this study included a laboratory and a home visit. During the laboratory visit we administered the attachment story completion task which is the focus of this chapter. In addition, we included a mother-child separation and reunion procedure as well as a mother-child affect communication task devised by Ridgeway (1987). During the home visit we administered the Waters and Deane Attachment Q-sort to the mother.

Attachment Story Procedure (Laboratory Visit). This procedure took place in a carpeted playroom furnished with a table, small chairs, and a beanbag seat. The entire session was videotaped.

After an initial brief encounter with the tester, mother and child spent about ten minutes engaged in free play with toys. The tester then returned, joining mother and child in additional free play. When the child seemed comfortable (after five–ten minutes), the mother was asked to sit in a corner of the room to fill out a questionnaire while the experimenter cleared away the toys and arranged the small table and chairs for the child and herself.

The administration of the story task began with a warm-up story about a birthday party to ensure that the child understood the procedure. Five attachment-related story beginnings were then narrated and acted out for the children by the tester, using small family figures and props. A mother, father, and two child figures were used for the first three stories, a grandmother was added for the last two stories (three additional stories were concerned with other issues and are not discussed here). The two child figures—one older, one younger—were always of the same sex as the subject (for further details see the Appendix).

The story beginnings introduced the following themes:

1. *Spilled juice.* While the family is seated at the dinner table, the younger child accidentally spills juice on the floor, and the mother exclaims about it (issue: an attachment figure in authority relation to the child).

2. *Hurt knee.* While the family is taking a walk in the park, the younger child climbs a rock, falls off, hurts a knee, and cries (issue: pain as an elicitor of attachment and protective behavior).

3. *Monster in the bedroom.* After the child is sent upstairs to go to bed, the child cries out about a monster in the bedroom (issue: fear as an elicitor of attachment and protective behavior).

4. *Departure.* The parents leave for an overnight trip, with grandmother remaining behind to look after the two children (issue: separation anxiety and coping ability).

5. *Reunion.* Grandmother looks out of the window the next morning and tells the children the parents are coming back (issue: welcoming vs. avoidant, resistant, or disorganized reunion behavior).

After presenting each of these stories according to a standard protocol, the experimenter asked the subject to "show me and tell me what happens next." In addition, three types of prompts were used. The first type focused on the story issue and was used only if the subject failed to do so ("What did they do about the juice, hurt knee, monster, when mommy and daddy were gone, after mommy and daddy came back?"). Second, clarifying prompts were used if the subject talked about unspecified agents ("Who put on the Band-Aid?") or moved the figures without describing their action ("What is she doing?"); a third kind of prompt was designed to elicit more elaboration ("Anything else?"), unless the child indicated by speech or action that the story was finished. These prompts were worded so as not to suggest specific responses to the child. Instructions for the story completion task (Bretherton & Ridgeway) can be found in the Appendix.

Separation-Reunion (Laboratory Visit). This procedure was also videotaped. Upon completion of the story task, the tester asked the mother to go to the room next door in order to discuss her completed questionnaire with the research assistant. The mother had previously been told that she could say whatever she wished prior to her departure.

Experimenter and child remained in the observation room, with all family figures and props left out on the table for free play. The experimenter busied herself with paperwork and only interacted with the child if requested to do so. At the end of three minutes, the experimenter said, "I'm going to get your mommy now," leaving the child alone in the room for an additional three minutes. The mother then returned, and mother and child were free to talk or play with the family figures for three minutes.

After the separation-reunion procedure, mother and child participated in an affect communication task. Results from this part of the session will be reported elsewhere (Ridgeway 1987).

Data Analysis

Detailed verbal and behavioral transcriptions were made of the videotaped story completions. Verbatim records were made of the subject's verbal narratives and the tester's prompts. In addition we described as precisely as possible (sometimes with the aid of diagrams) how the family figures were moved and placed in relation to each other, especially noting emotional components of the subjects' enactments (e.g., aggressive, angry, gentle placement of the figures; sad or happy facial expression, tone of voice, or posture). Emotional responses during the story enactment (smiling, pouting, frowning) were also recorded. Three research assistants worked on each transcript. The first recorded only verbal utterances, the second transcribed behavior (including emotion) and checked/queried the accuracy of the verbal record, while the third checked the accuracy of the behavioral record, indicating disagreements and filling in omissions. Where there were disagreements, the judgements of the last coder were accepted. Only for one transcript out of the twenty-nine were the disagreements such as to affect classification of the child as secure or insecure.

The transcripts were subsequently analyzed in two ways. First, a content analysis was undertaken to examine the children's ability to understand the story issues and to create a story resolution. Second, each child's protocol was examined as a whole in order to classify the children's story presentations as reflective of secure or insecure attachment patterns. These classifications were based on structure *and* content of the stories. We looked for fluent presentation and coherent, benign story resolutions indicative of a secure attachment relationship. Note that the classifications took into account the child's total performance (language and enactment with figures) and were not primarily based on verbal fluency. One factor which facilitated the interpretation of enactments was the subject's willingness to respond to queries ("What are they doing?") when the nature of the behavior was unclear. A satisfactory response could be a one-word reply such as "Hug."

Criteria for Security. The classification system was developed by the first author and applied to the written protocols without knowledge of the 18-month
Strange-Situation classifications (except in two cases). Separate criteria for
security were established for each story. In the "spilled juice" story, responses were classified as secure if the juice was cleaned up, and parental discipline or anger (if mentioned) were not violent or extreme. In the "hurt
knee" story, responses were classified as secure if one of the parents or the
older sibling responded to the hurt child's pain by hugging or administering a
Band-Aid. A positive ending to the story (children or parents climb the rock
and jump off without falling) was classified as secure only if the story protagonist's initial pain was also acknowledged. In the "monster" story responses were categorized as secure if the parents dealt with the child's fear of
the monster or the child approached the parents for comfort, allowing the
child eventually to go to sleep. In the "departure" story, responses were regarded as secure if the children displayed coping behavior in response to the
parents' absence (looking for the parents, playing with grandma, going to
sleep). Finally, in the "reunion" story, responses were judged secure if the
family figures faced each other, sometimes hugged each other, engaged in reunion conversations, and/or undertook a joint family activity. Furthermore, to
be scored as secure, responses had to be given without more than one prompt
for the story issue.

Criteria for Insecurity. On the basis of prior findings, especially those of Cassidy (1988) and Kaplan (1984), two types of criteria for scoring insecure responses were used: (1) avoidance of the story issue, and (2) incoherent or odd
responses. Story responses were coded as avoidant if the subject responded
only after several "don't know"s and prompts, or gave no response other than
"I don't know" or "I want another story." Some subjects avoided the story
issue despite responding (e.g., one subject reenacted the hurt knee story beginning but then merely labeled all the figures instead of completing the
story). We regarded this as indicative of avoidant insecurity, because we attributed such behavior to defensiveness with respect to attachment issues.
Where a subject requested another story after giving a minimal though appropriate response, this was coded as a very mild form of avoidance only if it
occurred repeatedly across several stories.

　　Odd and disorganized responses (e.g., violently throwing the child figure
on the floor; a car wreck after father rejoined mother and children who left on
a second trip; giving answers that did not make sense within the story, such as
"I bumped my head" when asked "What did they do about the monster?"
were regarded as indicative of a different type of insecurity.

　　Subjects who resolved the story issues fluently (without many prompts)
and appropriately (i.e., in line with the criteria described above) were classi-

fied as very secure if this occurred for all five stories (akin to the $B3$ classification in the Strange Situation). If the children showed slight avoidant or odd responses on one or two stories they were classified as fairly secure (akin to the $B1$ and $B2$ classifications in the Strange Situation). Subjects who displayed strong defensive responses ("don't know," or responded but with complete avoidance of the issue) over three or more stories were classified as avoidant-insecure even if they also showed some disorganized responses, while subjects with odd or disorganized responses over three or more stories were classified as insecure-disorganized even if they also displayed some avoidant responses. That is, classification was determined by the predominant type of response. In difficult-to-classify cases (mild avoidance on one or two of the first two stories, strong avoidance on the departure and reunion stories), responses to the departure and reunion stories were especially heavily weighted. Cassidy's (1988) story completion data for 6-year-olds did not suggest any consistent pattern for ambivalent children, and none was detected in this study. With further use of the procedure, we expect that considerable refinements in the method of analysis will be worked out and that an ambivalent category of responding will be identified.

Separation-Reunion Procedure. Videotapes of the children's behaviors during the separation/reunion procedure were classified by Cassidy without any prior information about the children, including their Strange-Situation attachment classifications at 18 months and the story classifications at 37 months. The 3-year reunion classifications were based on a coding scheme developed by Cassidy, Marvin, and the MacArthur Attachment Group (1987) for separation/reunion situations with children of this age range.

Children were classified as secure in the 37-month separation-reunion procedure if their behavior suggested a warm and intimate relationship with the mother, and if they showed positive interest in the mother's presence, either verbally (conversing freely and smoothly with the mother, asking the mother to join in play) or physically (orienting toward the mother, approaching the mother, or remaining close to her). Children were classified as insecure-avoidant if their behavior conveyed distance and coolness in the relationship. Insecure-avoidant children responded minimally to the mother when spoken to and did not initiate or expand conversation. They also moved or turned away from the mother. Children classified as insecure-ambivalent showed dependent, resistant, and/or immature behavior. The latter consisted of wriggling or whining. Finally, children classified as insecure-controlling tended to take charge of the interaction with the mother, either in a hostile-punitive or in a caregiving fashion. Such responses had previously been noted by Main and Cassidy (1989) in the reunions of 6-year-olds who had been classified as disorganized in infancy.

RESULTS

The findings are presented in two parts. Without evidence that 37-month-old children were able to respond meaningfully to the attachment story completion task, individual differences would be meaningless. We therefore first describe normative responses to the story beginnings. The second section is devoted to individual differences in the story task as related to other assessments of attachment quality, to measures of family and child social functioning, and to cognitive variables.

NORMATIVE FINDINGS

The content analysis performed on the transcripts of the story completion task showed that, as a group, the children understood the major issue presented in each story and that they were able to enact appropriate and differentiated story resolutions.

The Spilled Juice Story

Detailed responses are listed in table 1. The most common response was for the subject to have one of the family members (most often the mother) clean up the mess. In some cases the cup was put back on the table, and the child received more juice. Punitive parental behavior was enacted only by a minority of children, and in very few cases was this behavior violent (vehement hitting of the figures against each other or throwing them on the floor). A number of subjects reenacted the juice-spilling episode with the younger child; others made mother, father or the older child also spill juice. A few subjects seemed uncomfortable with the situation and reenacted or renarrated the story without coming up with a solution.

The Hurt Knee Story

As may be seen in table 2, a large majority of the subjects enacted sympathetic responses of some sort (putting on a Band-Aid, being picked up, going to the doctor, hugging or holding). Mother and father were about equally involved in these caregiving episodes. Many subjects replayed the story with a positive ending, using the target child or other family members (the person climbing the rock did not fall but jumped off). A few subjects made one of the figures give admonitions about being careful. On the other hand, some subjects avoided the issue of pain altogether, either by making the child get up without commenting on the pain, by denying the pain, or by reenacting the story beginning without acknowledging the pain. Four subjects gave nonempathic responses (e.g., the parents abandoned the child in the park or spanked

TABLE 1.   RESPONSES TO THE SPILLED JUICE STORY

Dealing with the mess:			22
Wiping or cleaning juice off floor		20	
Mother	11		
Father	2		
Younger child	5		
Subject	1		
Unspecified	3		
Picking up the cup		5	
Mother	1		
Father	1		
Older child	2		
Younger child	1		
Subject	1		
Discipline:			12
Get no more juice		1	
Reproach		5	
Mother	3		
Father	4		
Children cry at reproach	1		
Mother is angry		3	
Child or children sent to room		5	
Mother	3		
Father	2		
Child or children are spanked		4	
Mother	3		
Father	1		
Get more juice:			5
Mother	2		
Child	1		
Unspecified	2		
Reenactments:			9
With spilling		8	
Mother	2		
Father	1		
Older child	1		
Younger child	3		
Without spilling (younger child)		1	
No resolution attempted			3

NOTE: Totals in the subordinate categories may add up to more than the total in the superordinate category because subjects could show more than one response.

the child). A number of subjects also smiled at the story protagonist's pain when the tester enacted the story beginning.

The Monster Story

Findings are displayed in table 3. The most common response was for the parents (father somewhat more often than mother) to get rid of the monster by a variety of means (shooting, throwing in the water, etc.). In a few cases one of the children coped with the monster without the parents' aid. Only in one case did the parents come to the child's bedroom to say that they did not see

TABLE 2.   RESPONSES TO THE HURT KNEE STORY

Empathetic responses:			21
Someone helps hurt child with Band-Aid		11	
Mother	4		
Father	5		
Subject	1		
Unspecified	1		
Hurt child is taken to hospital or doctor (in one case whole family who all hurt themselves)		3	
Hurt child is taken home, to bed		2	
Hurt child or other hurt person is picked up, hugged, kissed		9	
By mother	6		
By father	3		
Concerns about carefulness:			6
Parents issue warnings to be careful		4	
Subject claims family will not do it again, will walk on grass		1	
Subject reprimands mother for rock climbing		1	
Nonempathic responses			4
Parents leave child in park (then return)		1	
Parent spanks child		1	
Subject smiles at hurt		2	
Ignoring of hurt:			7
Child gets up after initial hurt and fall, gets better by self		7	
Reenactments:			14
Subject reenacts fall and hurt		9	
With mother	1		
With father	2		
With mother and father	1		
With older child	3		
With younger child	1		
With older and younger child	1		
Subject reenacts rock climbing without fall		9	
With father	1		
With mother and father	3		
With older child	4		
With younger child	2		
With older and younger child	2		
No resolution attempted at all			5

NOTE: Totals in the subordinate categories may add up to more than the total in the superordinate category because subjects could show more than one response.

the monster. Many subjects brought this story to a resolution by having the child or children go to bed, and sometimes to sleep, after the monster had been vanquished. Only three subjects enacted no resolution to the monster story.

The Departure Story

In response to the departure story (see table 4), about half the subjects were able to put the parental figures in the car and drive them off without hesi-

TABLE 3.   RESPONSES TO THE MONSTER STORY

Disposal of the monster:			27
Parents or child hits, beats, bangs down, gets out, gets rid of, steps on, fights, or kills monster		23	
Mother	7		
Father	11		
Older child	1		
Younger child	2		
Subject	2		
Unspecified	1		
States explicitly that monster is "out of action"		12	
Monster is gone	9		
Monster is all dead	3		
Parents tell children they don't see any monster (in one case after chasing it)		2	
Children leave room to go to parent		2	
Parents then lock room		1	
Father then saves family		2	
Activities after disposal of monster:			13
Asserts that family can stay in room now		1	
Child or children go to sleep		11	
Older child	7		
Younger child	1		
Both children	3		
Parents go to sleep too		2	
Mother tells father she got rid of monster		1	
No resolution of monster problem:			3
Initial resolution but monster comes back		1	
No resolution		2	

NOTE: Totals in the subordinate categories may add up to more than the totals in the superordinate category because subjects could show more than one response.

tation. In a few cases, special leave-taking behavior was also enacted (e.g., parents told grandma to look after the children, family members hugged each other). The other half of the subjects showed mild anxiety about completing the departure story. Some found it difficult to drive the car away after having placed the parents in it, others took the parents out of the car again without making them leave. Yet others tried to make the children accompany the parents on their trip. Once the car had left (had been put under the table by the tester), a sizable number of subjects commented that the children would look or cry for the parents. Some also anticipated the reunion by either talking about it or by reaching for the car under the table. A few subjects were unable to say what the children would do while the parents were gone.

The Reunion Story

Most of the subjects pulled the car back "home" once the tester brought it back out onto the table, and the majority took the parents out of the car and placed them near the children. At this point some children enacted reunion conversations (e.g., making the parents ask the children, "Did you have a

TABLE 4. RESPONSES TO THE DEPARTURE STORY

Departure:		
Subject puts parents in car, makes them leave without problem		14
Subject reluctant in allowing parents to leave		15
Tries to include children in trip	9	
Takes parents out of car, after initiating departure or puts them in without driving off	9	
Family enacts special leave-taking behavior		3
During separation:		
Subject enacts or talks about child or parental activities (not related to separation anxiety)		22
Children sleep while parents are gone	9	
Children stay with grandma	6	
Children play	3	
Children walk	2	
Children have got to clean house	1	
Parents have dinner in park	1	
Subject enacts or talks about separation anxiety or reunion		17
Children search, call or cry for parents	12	
Subject talks about or tries to make parents come back	5	
Subject does not know what children might do in parents' absence		3

NOTE: Totals in the subordinate categories often add up to more than the total in the superordinate category because children could show more than one response.

TABLE 5. RESPONSES TO THE REUNION STORY

During reunion:		
Drives parents home (after experimenter brings car back on table)		17
Takes parents out of car and places near children (or reunion takes place in car)		27
Enacts greetings or welcome		11
Denies parental return		1
Removes grandmother from scene immediately		2
After reunion:		
Reports or acts out family activities		15
Children or family go to sleep	2	
Family goes on joint trip or engages in joint activity (going out to eat, going to church)	8	
Children stay home with mother (father leaves in 2 cases)	4	
Children pack to go home with parents	1	
Reenacts separations		6
Parents leave again (without children)	2	
Grandmother leaves with child or children	3	
Child leaves alone	1	
Don't know what happens after reunion		2

good time?"). In many cases the figures were placed facing each other, and sometimes affection was also enacted. Other children enacted avoidant reunions (the figures were placed so that they did not face each other; the parents came back, but as they did so the children left), or disorganized reunions (e.g., parents returned and the children promptly left with mother; father rejoined them, and there was a car crash).

Not all subjects elaborated the story beyond the immediate reunion scene, but those who did often made the family engage in a joint activity which varied from going to eat pizza, to having a party, going to church, or driving home to eat supper (some children seemed to think that the children were actually staying at the grandmother's house). In a few cases father was made to leave again while mother remained at home with the children (see table 5).

INDIVIDUAL DIFFERENCES

Story-Completion Classifications

On the basis of criteria described earlier, the story completions of ten children were categorized as demonstrating very secure relationships (equivalent of $B3$ in the Strange Situation), and nine children were considered as representing fairly secure relationships (equivalent to $B1/B2$ in the Strange Situation). Of the remaining ten subjects, four were classified as highly avoidant (equivalent to $A1$), two as fairly avoidant (equivalent to $A2$ in the Strange Situation), and four as disorganized (D). For all but one of the subjects classified as insecure (A or D), the avoidant or disorganized behavior was to some degree present in four of the five stories. In addition to using the $ABCD$ system, the classification scores were converted into security scores, using a four-point scale previously employed by Maslin et al. (1986), where $B3 = 4$; $B1$, $B2$, and $B4 = 3$; $A2$ and $C1 = 2$; and $A1$, $C2$, and $D = 1$.

Concordance of Story Completion and Separation-Reunion Procedure Classifications

The classifications and security scores for the story completion task (performed by Bretherton) were then compared with attachment classifications of the thirty-seven months separation-reunion procedure (independently scored by Cassidy). The concordance of secure versus insecure classifications for both procedures was significant at the $p = <.01$ level, using the Kappa statistic (twenty-one concordant, seven nonconcordant, with one separation-reunion missing because of technical problems). However, the classification of the type of insecurity was not consistent across procedures. Whereas children classified as A, C, or D by Cassidy in the separation-reunion procedure tended also to be categorized as insecure in the story completions, the type of secu-

TABLE 6.   CORRELATIONS OF ATTACHMENT: STORY COMPLETION
SECURITY RATINGS WITH OTHER VARIABLES

Variables	Pearson Product-Moment Correlations
37-month separation-reunion procedure	.49***
18-month Strange Situation	.33**
25-month attachment Q-sort (mother)	.61****
37-month attachment Q-sort (mother)	.26**
18-month marital satisfaction (mother) (Spanier 1976)[a]	.39**
25-month marital satisfaction (mother) (Spanier 1976)[a]	.44***
25-month family cohesion (mother) (FACES II)[b]	.53***
25-month family adaptability (mother) (FACES II)[b]	.57****
18-month sociability (mother) (CCTI)[c]	.38**
18-month shyness (mother) (CCTI)[c]	−.35**
18-month Bayley MDI	.38**
25-month Bayley MDI	.49***
25-month vocabulary checklist (mother report)	.60****

[a] Spanier Dyadic Adjustment Scale filled out by mother
[b] Family Adaptability and Cohesion Evaluation Scale II, filled out by mother
[c] Colorado Child Temperament Inventory filled out by mother
*$p < .10$.
**$p < .05$.
***$p < .01$.
****$p < .001$.

rity was not predictable across procedures (children were not systematically classified into the same insecure category in both). Not surprisingly, the correlation between story security scores and thirty-seven-month separation-reunions was also highly significant (see table 6).

Correlations of Story-Completions with Other Attachment Measures

In addition, we were interested in ascertaining whether there were relationships between the story security scores and other measures of attachment security, family climate, temperament, and cognitive development (see table 6), most of them collected during earlier phases of the study. The story security scores were significantly related to the 18-month Strange-Situation classifications, converted into security scores as described above ($B3 = 4$; $B1$, $B2$, $B4 = 3$; $A2$, $C1 = 2$; $A1$, $C2$, $D = 1$), but the correlations were not as strong as the association between story scores and concurrent separation-reunion security. The story security scores were also highly correlated with the attachment Q-sort performed by mother at 25 months, but only marginally with the security scores from the concurrent attachment Q-sort at 37 months. Moreover, the longitudinal consistency of the 25- and 37-month attachment Q-sort security scores—though significant—was not especially high [$r (29) = .39$, $p < .05$] even though the mother performed both sorts.

Correlations of Story-Completion Scores
with Assessments of
Family Functioning and Temperament

Several nonattachment variables of family and child social functioning were also meaningfully related to the attachment story security scores (see table 6). Paper-and-pencil assessments of marital satisfaction (Spanier 1976), filled out by the mother during the 18- and 25-month phase of the study showed highly significant correlations with the story security scores. This was also the case for family adaptability and cohesion assessed at the 25-month visit through the Family Adaptation and Cohesiveness Scales (FACES II, Olson et al. 1983). In addition, there were significant correlations with the sociability and shyness scales of the Colorado Child Temperament Inventory (Rowe & Plomin 1977) filled out by the mother at the 18-month visit, with sociability relating positively and shyness relating negatively to the story scores.

Correlations with Cognitive
and Language Development

Finally, the attachment story security scores were related to the child's level of cognitive and language development during earlier phases of the study. The Bayley MDI at 18 and 25 months, and productive vocabulary assessed through a checklist filled out by the mother (Bretherton, McNew, Snyder, & Bates 1983) were significantly related to the story security scores, despite the fact that story classifications were based on enactments as well as verbal description.

CONCLUDING REMARKS

On the basis of our findings with 37-month-olds, we can claim that, given a structured framework (attachment related story beginnings), props, and non-leading prompts, most children in the early preschool period can produce resolutions to attachment related stories in which their parents are depicted as protective, empathetic, and remarkably nonpunitive and in which separation anxiety and reunion pleasure are activated. This is an interesting finding in terms of 3-year-olds' social -cognitive understanding of parent and child roles, and suggests that story-completion procedures with family figures and props have much to contribute in this area. But what can we say about the significance of individual differences?

Cross-classification of the children as secure or insecure in the story procedure and the concurrent separation-reunion procedure showed statistically significant concordance, but the results of the present study only partially parallel findings obtained by Cassidy (1988) and Kaplan (1984). Remember that both authors were able to predict *subcategories* of insecurity (*A, C, D*) across observational and representational procedures whereas our study did not. We hope that further refinements in the story classification system and replications of the present study will shed light on this issue. In the meantime, however, we have shown that coherent and emotionally open responding to attachment story beginnings *were* successful in predicting 3-year-olds' security versus insecurity in a separation-reunion procedure at the same age.

With respect to cross-age comparisons among the various attachment measures, the expected correlations of attachment story ratings with 18-month Strange-Situation classifications, though significant, were not as strong as findings obtained by Main (1985) had led us to anticipate. She had found very high correlations between Strange-Situation classifications at 1 year of age and several representational measures of attachment at 6. One possible explanation for these divergent findings is that the quality of the mother-child relationship may have changed between 18 and 37 months. The fact that the attachment *Q*-sort security scores were much more highly related to the 37-month story completion scores than the Strange-Situation scores would support this contention. That the 37-month attachment *Q*-sorts, also performed by the mother, were only marginally related to the story completion scores unfortunately undermines this interpretation. It is also noteworthy that security scores from attachment *Q*-sorts at 25 months and at 37 months were not highly stable.

We draw two conclusions from this group of findings: first, that some real change may have occurred in the attachment security of some children during the period from 18 to 37 months; and, second, that the several attachment measures cannot be taken as equivalents of one another although they seem to share some commonality. A further factor, but one only affecting correlations of the story scores with the observational attachment measures, was that the story assessment procedure included father and mother as attachment figure. Main et al. (1985) found that, for 6-year-olds, representational measures of attachment using both father and mother were related only to earlier Strange-Situation classifications with the mother. Whether a better fit between attachment story classifications and the separation-reunion procedure at 3 years of age could be obtained by using only one attachment figure (father or mother) cannot be clarified without further study.

We do find it interesting that maternal reports of marital satisfaction and of family cohesion and adaptability were correlated with the story-based security ratings, supporting earlier studies reporting correlations between family climate and secure attachment (e.g., Belsky & Isabella, 1988; Goldberg & Easterbrooks 1984; for a review see Belsky, Rovine, & Fish, 1990). Such correlations make sense, since the mother's perception of marital and family functioning can plausibly be seen as a factor in her ability to provide a secure base for her child. The correlations of the story-related security scores with the temperament measures are also intriguing, but cannot in and of themselves help to resolve the lively debate between attachment and temperament researchers (see Sroufe 1985 for an overview), because we do not have temperament assessments from earlier periods of the child's life. At 18 months, maternal reports of child temperament are often difficult to distinguish from maternal report of the child-parent relationship (Stevenson-Hinde 1985).

Finally, the correlations between story attachment scores and earlier assessments of the Bayley MDI as well as productive vocabulary may be interpreted in several ways. According to theory (Bowlby [1969] 1982), secure attachment should foster the ability to explore and therefore to learn. In support of this hypothesis, several researchers have reported correlations between secure attachment and cognitive tests (e.g., Ainsworth & Bell 1974; Main 1973), while others have found correlations between secure attachment and language production at 3 years of age (e.g. Beeghly & Cicchetti 1987). The fact that, in this study, the children's Strange Situation scores at 18 months were related to the 18-month Bayley MDI, but not to the 25-month MDI or to word production at 25 months, also corroborates the first hypothesis, but only partially. On the other hand, we cannot rule out the possibility that attachment story classifications were inadvertently influenced by impressions about the children's cognitive and verbal level (in other words that the relationship is spurious), even though every attempt was made to assess appropriate and open responses to the issues presented by the stories irrespective of story complexity.

In conclusion, while this study has answered some important questions regarding the validity of using representational measures of attachment with 3-year-olds, it has also raised several new ones. To resolve these new questions, it will be necessary to do more than apply a refined version of the attachment story procedure and separation-reunion classification to new samples. Although we have been able to show that there is significant statistical association between an observational and a representational assessment of attachment at 37 months, we have not yet established that the 37-month attachment story completions or the 37-month separation-reunion procedure are reflective of the actual attachment relationship as it is played out in the home. It is only when we have validated our laboratory assessments against fairly lengthy observations of parent-child attachment relationships in their natural setting, as Ainsworth and her colleagues did for the Strange-Situation classifications (Ainsworth, Blehar, Waters, & Wall 1978), that we will be on firmer ground in using the attachment story-completion classifications as alternative measures of attachment. Our findings suggest to us that this will be a fruitful goal to pursue.

APPENDIX:
STORY COMPLETION TASKS TO ASSESS
YOUNG CHILDREN'S INTERNAL WORKING MODELS OF CHILD AND
PARENTS IN THE ATTACHMENT RELATIONSHIP

Inge Bretherton and Doreen Ridgeway

This assessment consists of five story beginnings that are to be acted out with small family figures and other simple props. Each story is designed to elicit responses regarding a particular attachment issue. The idea for these stories came from a prior study, designed in collaboration with Marjorie Beeghly, in which we assessed children's understanding of emotions and roles. The issues addressed in the story beginnings are (1) the attachment figure in an authority role (the spilled juice story), (2) pain as an elicitor of attachment and protective behavior (the hurt knee story), (3) fear as an elicitor of attachment and protective behavior (the monster in the bedroom story), (4) separation anxiety and coping (the departure story), and (5) responses to parental return (the reunion story).

ATTACHMENT STORY COMPLETION PROTOCOL

Materials

Family Figures. Two "realistic, bendable" (catalog description) doll families each comprising a father, mother, girl, and boy. The two families can be combined so as to yield a father (F), mother (M), grandmother (GM), and two children (2 Cs), a smaller and larger boy, or smaller and larger girl. To create the grandmother, the hair of one of the mother dolls is painted grayish-white. The dolls can be obtained from several national school supply firms. To prevent the dolls from falling over, they are mounted on plastic stands (those used for Barbie dolls are suitable if you can obtain them).

Other Props. A small wooden box to represent a table; a birthday cake (about the size of a piece of tinkertoy; a set of very small dishes and silverware in suitcase or box; a table cloth (optional); a piece of green felt to represent grass (9×9 inches); a piece of gray or beige artificial sponge, cut to look like a rock; a bed and small felt blanket; a wooden box (4×6 inches) painted like a car.

Administration

The task is administered at a child's table, with the child and tester sitting opposite one another. Bring out the props as needed, naming each one (except for the dolls that are identified at the beginning). After each story, ask the subject to put the figures over to one side, saying, "Can you get them ready for the next story?" To lead into the next story, the tester may say something like, "Now I have an idea for a different story," or "Are you ready for something different now?"

The stories contained in this protocol are part of a larger set developed in collaboration with Helen Buchsbaum and Robert Emde. The remaining stories can be obtained from them. The monster in the bedroom story was developed by Helen Buchsbaum; the remainder were developed by Inge Bretherton and Doreen Ridgeway.

Before beginning presentation of the stories that are part of the assessment, it is a good idea for the tester (T) to present a warm-up story to get the subject to feel comfortable with handling the figures. We have chosen a birthday-party story for this purpose. It is not important to stick precisely to the script for the warm-up story, but it is important to follow standard procedure for the stories that form part of the assessment: "spilled juice," "hurt knee," "monster in the bedroom," "departure," "reunion." The latter is true whether the stories are used as written or whether they are somewhat altered. For example, they could be administered with one parent only, or with a babysitter instead of the grandmother. One change that we are considering for further studies is to present the five stories as events of one day in the family's life (a suggestion we owe to Ned Mueller).

STORIES

Introduction of Figures

T: "Look who we have here." (Bring out family.) "Here's our family. Look. This is the grandma, this is the daddy, this is the mommy, and these are the girls, Jane and Susan (and these are the boys, Bob and George)." (Show them to the subject as you name them.)

T: "Who've we got?" (Point to family figures.) "You know what? I've got an idea. Let's pretend to make up some stories about them. Tell you what, how about if I start a story about our family and you finish it."

Warm-up: Birthday Story. (M, F, GM, 2Cs, table dishes, cake.)

Put out the figures like this:

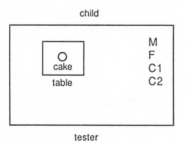

T: "Here's their table and what's this?" (Show cake to subject and wait for subject to name it.) . . . "What kind of cake?" . . . "Yes, it's a birthday cake. You listen carefully to the story. The mommy has baked this beautiful birthday cake and she calls out":

M: "Come on grandma, come on Dad, come on boys (girls), let's have a birthday party."

T: "Show me what happens now." (Inviting tone of voice; let the subject play with the figures or tell a story yourself if the subject does not.)

Spilled Juice Story. (2Cs, M, F, table, dishes.)

T: "O.K., I think I have an idea for a new story." (Put away the grandmother and set out the figures as below, away from the table.)

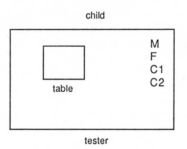

child

table

M
F
C1
C2

tester

T: (Shake the box with the silverware.) "Can you help me set the table for dinner." (Give box to subject, wait till subject has set the table, help if necessary.)

T: "Now put the family around the dinner table so they're ready to eat" (Wait till subject has placed the figures.)

T resumes: "Here is our family eating dinner and Bob (Jane) gets up and reaches and spills his juice" (Make child figure knock cup off toy table so cup is visible to subject.)

M: "Bob (Jane) you spilled your juice!" (Reproachful tone of voice, but don't overdo; turn M toward Bob or Jane, and move her up and down while she is talking.)

T: "Show me what happens now."

Prompting Procedure

T prompt (if subject does not spontaneously mention: "What do they do about the spilled juice?" T prompt if subject gives only one response: "Anything else?" "What else?" or "Then what?" If subject performs ambiguous actions with figures, ask "What are they doing?" and if the subject uses an ambiguous pronoun when talking about the figures, ask "Who was doing it?" T can also repeat the subject's statement in question form, to verify what the subject said ("The mommy wiped the juice? And then what?"). If the subject asks for the GM, say "She's not in the story, we'll get her out again later."

Note that these prompts are designed not to suggest precise ideas to the subject. The only exception is the prompt that focuses the subject's attention on the issue (spilled juice) if it has not been addressed.

Hurt Knee Story. (2 Cs, M, F, felt for grass, sponge for rock.)

T: "O.K. I have an idea for another story. You put our family there and get them ready for the next one while I put these away." (T points to the side of the table; see below. It is important that the rest of the family be about 30 cm away from the rock the story child will climb.)

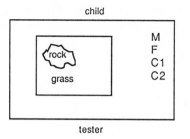

"O.K. Look what I've got." (Set out piece of green felt and sponge rock.) "This is the park. Do you sometimes go to the park with your mom and dad?" "Here is our family and they're out walking in the park, and at this park there is this high, high rock."

C: "Look, mommy and daddy. Watch me climb this high, high rock." (Make child figure climb rock, then fall off.) "Boo-hoo (or ouch), I've hurt my knee (crying voice)."

T: "Show me what happens now."

T prompt (if subject does not spontaneously mention): "What do they do about the hurt knee?") For other prompts, see "spilled juice" story, i.e., ask what the figures are doing if it's not accompanied by speech, ask the subjects to show you what they say the figures are doing, and prompt for elaboration by saying things like "Anything else?" "And then what?" etc.

If the subject seems to have finished, or becomes repetitive, say:

T: "All done? Shall we try another? Let's put these away."

Monster in the Bedroom Story. (2 Cs, M, F, bed with felt blanket.)

T: "Can you get the family ready for the next one?" (Set out the props as below, if subject does not do it. Again, it is important to have the rest of the family at least 30 cm from the bed in the "bedroom.")

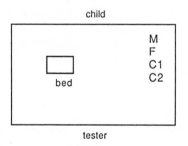

T: "Look what happens now. Listen carefully."

M: (Face M toward story child and move her slightly as she speaks.) "It's bedtime. Go up to your room and go to bed."

F: "Go up to bed now." (Same action as with M, deep voice.)

C: "O.K., mommy and daddy, I'm going." (Make child figure walk to bed.)

T comment: "Bob goes upstairs to his room, and he goes":

C: "Mommy! Daddy! There's a monster in my room! There's a monster in my room!" (Alarmed tone of voice.)

T: "Show me what happens now."

T prompt if subject does not mention spontaneously, "What do they do about the monster in the room?" If necessary, use other prompts given in "spilled juice" story, i.e., ask for clarification of ambiguous action, ask subjects to show you actions they simply described, and for elaboration by saying "Now what?" "Anything else?" etc. If the subject stops playing, or becomes overly repetitive, move on by saying:

T: "Are you ready for the next one?"

Departure Story. (2Cs, M, F, GM, felt grass, box as car.)

T: "Let's use the grandmother this time." (Set out family and grandmother at side of table, with green felt and car as below; it is important to have the car in front of the subject, and the two parents facing the grandmother and two children.)

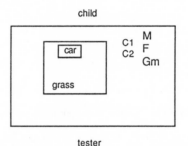

T: "Here we have their front lawn, and here we have their car, this is the family car." (Make mom and dad face the children and grandma, with car in front of subject.)

T: "You know what it looks like to me, (subject's name). It looks like the mommy and the daddy are going on a trip."

M: "O.K. boys (girls). Your dad and I are going on a trip. We are leaving on our trip now." (Move M slightly as she speaks to the children.)

F: "See you tomorrow. Grandma will stay with you." (Move F slightly like M.)

T: "Show me what happens now."

Important: T should let the subject put the figures in the car and make the car drive off. Only intervene if the subject seems unable to make the car drive off. If the subject puts the children in the car say, "No, only the mom and dad are going." After the subject (or if necessary, the tester) makes the car drive off, T puts the car under the table, out of sight. If the subject wants to retrieve the car, T replies, "No, they're not coming back yet."

T: "And away they go." (As the car is moved under the table.)

T prompt if subject does not spontaneously mention, "What do the children do while the mom and dad are gone?" and use other prompts to clarify actions, or actors, and to ask subject to act out what is being described.

Reunion Story. (Same Props as departure story.)

Bring the car with the two parents back out from under the table and set it on table at a distance from the family (i.e., keep it near T, so the subject has to reach for it and can make it drive "home"). If the subject has put the child and grandmother figures in the middle of the table during the previous story, put them back close to the subject to create distance between the returning car and the child figures).

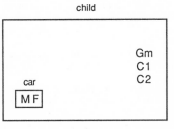

T: "O.K. And you know what? It's the next day and the grandma looks out of the window (make grandma look toward car, move her as she speaks) and she goes":

GM: "Look boys (girls), here come your mommy and daddy. They're home from their trip."

T: "Show me what happens now." (Let subject drive car toward "home," intervene only if the subject does not do so.)

Prompt if subject does not spontaneously take the figures out of the car. "What do we do now that the mom and dad are home?" Also use other prompts given in "spilled juice" story where appropriate.

If the subject asks for other props, like a bed, etc., bring it out. However, do not bring out the grandmother during the earlier stories. Just say, "She'll come back later" or "We'll use her in another story later." It is very important to adhere to the spatial arrangements suggested in each story, especially the distance between parent and child figures in the hurt knee, monster, and reunion stories.

REFERENCES

Ainsworth, M. D. S., & Bell, S. M. (1974). Mother-infant interaction and the development of competence. In K. J. Connolly & J. Bruner (eds.), *The growth of competence*. New York: Academic Press.

Ainsworth, M. D. S.; Bell, S. M.; & Stayton, D. (1974). Infant-mother attachment and social development: "Socialization" as a product of reciprocal responsiveness to signals. In M. P. M. Richards (ed.), *The integration of the child into a social world*. London: Cambridge University Press.

Ainsworth, M. D. S.; Blehar, M. C.; Waters, E.; & Wall, S. (1978). *Patterns of attachment: A psychological study of the strange situation.* Hillsdale, N.J.: Erlbaum.

Beeghly, M., & Cicchetti, D. (1987, April). Child maltreatment, attachment, and the self: The emergence of internal state language. Paper presented at the biennial meetings of the Society for Research in Child Development. Baltimore.

Belsky, J., & Isabella, R. (1988). Maternal, infant, & social-contextual determinants of attachment security. In J. Belsky & T. Nezworski (eds.), *Clinical implications of attachment.* Hillsdale, N.J.: Erlbaum.

Belsky, J.; Rovine, M.; & Fish, M. (1990). The developing family system. In M. Gunnar (ed.), *Systems and development: Minnesota Symposium on Child Psychology* (vol. 22). Hillsdale, N.J.: Erlbaum.

Bowlby, J. (1958). The nature of the child's tie to his mother. *International Journal of Psycho-Analysis* 39, 350–373.

Bowlby, J. ([1969] 1982). *Attachment and loss: Vol. 1. Attachment.* New York: Basic Books.

Bowlby, J. (1973). *Attachment and loss: Vol. 2. Separation.* New York: Basic Books.

Bowlby, J. (1980). *Attachment and loss: Vol. 3. Loss, sadness and depression.* New York: Basic Books.

Bretherton, I. (1984). Representing the social world in symbolic play: Reality and fantasy. In I. Bretherton (ed.), *Symbolic play: The development of social understanding* (pp. 3–41). New York: Academic Press.

Bretherton, I. (1987). New perspectives on attachment relations: Security, communication and internal working models. In J. Osofsky (ed.), *Handbook of infant development* (2d ed.). New York: Wiley.

Bretherton, I. (1990). Open communication and internal working models: Their role in attachment relationships. In R. Thompson (ed.), *Nebraska Symposium on Motivation: Vol. 36. Socio-emotional development.* Lincoln: University of Nebraska Press.

Bretherton, I.; Fritz, J.; Zahn-Waxler, C.; & Ridgeway, D. (1986). Learning to talk about emotion: A functionalist perspective. *Child Development* 57, 529–548.

Bretherton, I.; McNew, S.; Snyder, L.; & Bates, E. (1983). Individual differences at 20 months: Analytic and holistic strategies in language acquisition. *Journal of Child Language,* 293–320.

Cassidy, J. (1988). The self as related to child-mother attachment at six. *Child Development* 59, 121–134.

Cassidy, J., & Marvin, R. S., in collaboration with the MacArthur Working Group on Attachment (1987). Attachment organization in three- and four-year-olds: Coding guidelines. Unpublished manuscript, University of Virginia.

Craik, K. (1943). *The nature of explanation.* Cambridge: Cambridge University Press.

Eichberg, D. (1987). Quality of infant-parent attachment: Related to mother's representation of her own relationship history. In M. Main (chair), Working models of attachment in adolescence and adulthood. Symposium conducted at the biennial meetings of the Society for Research in Child Development, Baltimore.

Emde, R. N., & Sorce, J. E. (1983). The rewards of infancy: Emotional availability and maternal referencing. In J. D. Call, E. Galenson, & R. Tyson (eds.), *Frontiers of infant psychiatry* (vol. 2). New York: Basic Books.

Fairbairn, W. R. D. (1952). *Psychoanalytic studies of the personality.* London: Tavistock.

Goldberg, W. A., & Easterbrooks, M. A. (1984). The role of marital quality in toddler development. *Developmental Psychology* 20, 504–514.

Greenberg, J. R., & Mitchell, S. A. (1983). *Object relations in psychoanalytic theory.* Cambridge, Mass.: Harvard University Press.

Greenberg, M. T., & Marvin, R. S. (1979). Attachment patterns in profoundly deaf preschool children. *Merrill-Palmer Quarterly* 25, 265–79.

Grossmann, K.; Fremmer-Bombik, E.; Rudolph, J.; & Grossmann, K. E. (in press). Maternal attachment representations as related to patterns of infant-mother attachment and maternal care during the first year. In R. A. Hinde & J. Stevenson-Hinde (eds.), *Relationships within families.* Oxford: Oxford University Press.

Hansburg, H. G. (1972). *Adolescent separation anxiety: A method for the study of adolescent separation problems.* Springfield, Ill.: Thomas.

Hinde, R. A. (1961). The establishment of the parent-offspring relation in birds with some mammalian analogies. In W. H. Thorpe & O. L. Zangwill (eds.), *Current problems in animal behaviour.* London: Cambridge University Press.

Isabella, R., & Belsky, J. (1985). Marital consensus during the transition to parenthood and security of infant-parent attachment. *Journal of Family Issues* 6, 505–522.

Izard, C. E. (1978). Emotions as motivations: An evolutionary-developmental perspective. In R. A. Dienstbier (ed.), *Nebraska Symposium on Motivation* (pp. 163–200). Lincoln: University of Nebraska Press.

Johnson-Laird, P. N. (1983). *Mental models.* Cambridge, Mass.: Harvard University Press.

Kaplan, N. (1984). Internal representations of separation experiences in six-year-olds: Related to actual experiences of separation. Unpublished master's thesis, University of California, Berkeley.

Kaplan, N., & Main, M. (1985, April). Internal representations of attachment at six years as indicated by family drawings and verbal responses to imagined separations. In M. Main (chair), Attachment a move to the level of representation. Symposium conducted at the biennial meetings of the Society for Research in Child Development, Toronto.

Klagsbrun, M., & Bowlby, J. (1976). Responses to separation from the parents: A clinical test for young children. *British Journal for Projective Psychology and Personality Study* 21, 7–27.

Kobak, R. R., & Sceery, A. (1988). Attachment in late adolescence: Working models, affect regulation, and perceptions of self and others. *Child Development* 59, 135–146.

Lorenz, K. (1957). *Instinctive behavior,* ed. C. H. Schiller (pp. 83–128). New York: International Universities Press. English trans. of Der Kumpan in der Umwelt des Vogels, *Journal of Ornithology* 83 (1935), 137–213.

Main, M. (1973). Play, exploration and competence as related to child-adult attachment. Unpublished doctoral dissertation, Johns Hopkins University, Baltimore.

Main, M. (1985, April). Adult mental organization with respect to attachment: Related to infant strange situation attachment status. In M. Main (chair), Attachment: A move to the level of representation. Symposium conducted at the biennial meetings of the Society for Research in Child Development, Toronto.

Main, M., & Cassidy, J. (1989). Categories of responses to reunion with the parent at age 6: Predictable from infancy and stable over a one-month period. *Developmental Psychology.*

Main, M.; Kaplan, N.; & Cassidy, J. (1985). Security in infancy, childhood and adulthood: A move to the level of representation. In I. Bretherton & E. Waters (eds.), *Growing points of attachment theory and research. Monographs of the Society for Research in Child Development* 50 (1–2, Serial No. 209), 66–104.

Mandler, J. H. (1979). Categorical and schematic organization in memory. In C. R. Puff (ed.), *Memory organization and structure* (pp. 259–299). New York: Academic Press.

Maslin, C.; Bretherton, I.; & Morgan, G. A. (1986, April). Influence of attachment security and maternal scaffolding on mastery motivation. Paper presented at the International Conference on Infant Studies, Los Angeles.

Murphey, E. B.; Silber, E.; Coelho, G. V.; Hamburg, D. A.; & Greenberg, I. (1963). The development of autonomy and parent-child interaction in late adolescence. *American Journal of Orthopsychiatry* 33, 643–652.

Nelson, K., & Gruendel, J. (1981). Generalized event representations: Basic building blocks of cognitive development. In M. E. Lamb and A. Brown (eds.), *Advances in developmental psychology* (vol. 1, pp. 131–158). Hillsdale, N.J.: Erlbaum.

Nelson, K., & Ross, G. (1982). The general and specifics of long-term memory in infants and young children. In M. Perlmutter (ed.), *Naturalistic approaches to memory* (pp. 87–101). San Francisco: Jossey-Bass.

Offer, D. (1969). *The psychological world of the teenager: A study of normal adolescent boys.* New York: Basic Books.

Olson, D. H.; Bell, R.; & Portner, J. (1983). FACES II (Family Adaptability and Cohesion Evaluation Scales). Unpublished manuscript, Department of Family Social Science, University of Minnesota, St. Paul.

Peck, R. F., & Havighurst, R. J. (1960). *The psychology of character development.* New York: Wiley.

Piaget, J. (1951). *The origin of intelligence in children.* New York: International Universities Press.

Piaget, J. (1954). *The construction of reality in the child.* New York: Basic Books.

Price, D., & Goodman, G. S. (1985, April). Preschool children's comprehension of a recurring episode. Paper presented at the biennial meeting of the Society for Research in Child Development, Toronto.

Ricks, M. H. (1985). The social transmission of parenting: Attachment across generations. In I. Bretherton & E. Waters (eds.), *Growing points of attachment theory and research. Monographs of the Society for Research in Child Development* 50 (1–2, Serial No. 209), 211–227.

Ridgeway, D. (1987, April). The relation between affect communication and attachment security. Paper presented at the biennial meetings of the Society for Research in Child Development, Baltimore.

Riesen, A. H. (1966). Sensory deprivation. In E. Stellar & J. Stellar (eds.), *Progress in physiological psychology* (vol. 1). New York: Academic Press.

Rowe, D. C., & Plomin, R. (1977). Temperament in early childhood. *Journal of Personality Assessment* 41, 151–156.

Schank, R. C. (1982). *Dynamic memory: A theory of reminding and learning in computers and people.* Cambridge: Cambridge University Press.

Schank, R. C., & Abelson, R. P. (1977). *Scripts, plans, goals and understanding.* Hillsdale, N.J.: Erlbaum.

Spanier, G. B. (1976). Measuring dyadic adjustment: New Scales for assessing the quality of marriage and similar dyads. *Journal of Marriage and the Family* 38, 15–28.

Sroufe, L. A. (1979). Socioemotional development in infancy. In J. Osofsky (ed.), *Handbook of infant development* (pp. 462–515). New York: Wiley.

Sroufe, L. A. (1985). Attachment classification from the perspective of infant-caregiver relationships and infant temperament. *Child Development* 56, 1–14.

Sroufe, L. A., & Fleeson, J. (1986). Attachment and the construction of relationships. In W. Hartup & Z. Rubin (eds.), *The nature and development of relationships.* Hillsdale, N.J.: Erlbaum.

Stern, D. N. (1985). *The interpersonal world of the infant.* New York: Basic Books.

Stevenson-Hinde, J. (1985, April). Q-sort attachment data and temperament. Paper presented at the biennial meetings of the Society for Research in Child Development, Toronto.

Strage, A., & Main, M. (1985). Attachment and parent-child discourse patterns. In M. Main (chair), Attachment: A move to the level of representation. Symposium conducted at the biennial meeting of the Society for Research in Child Development, Toronto.

Sullivan, H. S. (1953). *The interpersonal theory of psychiatry.* New York: Norton.

Tinbergen, N. (1951). *The study of instinct.* London: Oxford University Press.

Tulving, E. (1972). Episodic and semantic memory. In E. Tulving & W. Donaldson (eds.), *Organization of memory* (pp. 382–403). New York: Academic Press.

Tulving, E. (1983). *Elements of episodic memory.* New York: Oxford University Press.

Waters, E., & Deane, K. E. (1985). Defining and assessing individual differences in attachment relationships: Q-methodology and the organization of behavior in infancy and early childhood. In I. Bretherton & E. Waters (eds.), *Growing points of attachment theory and research. Monographs of the Society for Research in Child Development* 50 (1–2, Serial No. 209), 41–65.

PART THREE

Developmental Psychopathology of Attachment

10 · Classification of Attachment on a Continuum of Felt Security

ILLUSTRATIONS FROM THE STUDY OF CHILDREN OF DEPRESSED PARENTS

E. Mark Cummings

IT HAS LONG been argued that the emotional bonds that form in early childhood between children and parents influence socioemotional development. Proposals regarding the importance of these early relationships have emerged in many theoretical and research traditions, including psychoanalytic theory (S. Freud 1938), ego psychology (A. Freud 1952; Mahler 1965), social learning theory (Dollard & Miller 1950), operant theory (Bijou & Baer 1965; Gewirtz 1961), object relations theory (Klein, Heimann, Isaacs, & Riviere 1952; Winnicott 1948), and ethology (Blurton-Jones & Leach 1972; Harlow 1958; Lorenz 1935) (for integrative reviews see Bowlby 1958; Bowlby [1969] 1982; Ainsworth 1969). The notion that early emotional bonds have important effects on development has also received impetus from studies of the impact of separation (Bowlby 1973) and loss (Bowlby 1980) on young children and studies of parent-offspring relationships in other species (Bowlby [1969] 1982). Bowlby (1958, [1969] 1982) characterized early emotional bonds as attachments and argued that attachments had biological bases, motivational properties independent of the satisfaction of physiological needs such as hunger or thirst, and served a critical function in providing a secure base for children. The relative security of early attachments was seen as having potentially lasting effects on development. In emphasizing the independence of attachment from other biological systems, and in stressing the positive security provisions function of attachment rather than the more pejorative dependency connotations, Bowlby's notions have enhanced the significance and changed the perceived role of early love relationships.

However, until the relatively recent development of the Strange Situation (Ainsworth & Wittig 1969; Ainsworth, Blehar, Waters, & Wall 1978), there was no reliable and valid measure for assessing qualitative differences in attachment. The development of the Strange-Situation procedure has been critical in providing a means for major empirical advances in an area heretofore dominated by theory. According to attachment theory, a primary function of attachment relationships is to serve as a source of security for the infant in situations that induce fear or anxiety in the child. Consistent with this,

311

Ainsworth's scheme for classifying infant-parent attachments reflects differences between children to the extent they are able to effectively derive security from the parent when faced with stress in the Strange Situation. The patterning or organization of children's use of the parent for security (Sroufe & Waters 1977) serves as the basis for classification, and children's behavior toward parents during reunions following two brief separations is heavily emphasized. Children are classified as securely attached to parents if they actively seek contact with the parent during reunion, and this contact is effective in returning the child to preseparation levels of functioning (pattern B). Children are classified as insecure if they don't effectively use the parent as a source of security during reunion, but avoid the parent (insecure-avoidant, pattern A), or alternate contact seeking and resisting (insecure-ambivalent, group C).

There is ample evidence to suggest that these classifications reflect differences in child-parent relationships that have an impact on development. This evidence takes several forms. First, classifications of attachments in the Strange Situation are related to differences between children in functioning in the home, with securely attached children showing less pervasive anxiety and distress, particularly in stress situations, than insecurely attached children (Ainsworth et al. 1978; Grossmann, Grossmann, Spangler, Suess, & Unzner 1985). Second, classification at 12 or 18 months predicts differences between children in concurrent functioning and functioning at 2–5 years of age (Arend, Grove, & Sroufe 1979; Erickson, Sroufe, & Egeland 1985; Matas, Arend, & Sroufe 1978; Pastor 1981; Schneider-Rosen & Cicchetti 1984; Sroufe, Fox, & Pancake 1983), with securely attached children generally faring better than insecurely attached children. Finally, there are systematic relations between attachment patterns and styles of child-parent interaction (Ainsworth et al. 1978; Belsky, Rovine, & Taylor 1984; Crockenberg 1981; Egeland & Farber 1984; Londerville & Main 1981; Tracy & Ainsworth 1981; Waters, Vaughn, & Egeland 1980), with secure patterns associated with more sensitive and responsive parenting.

While Ainsworth's system has demonstrated validity, however, it is unlikely to describe fully patterns of attachment for the following reasons. First, the criterion sample for Ainsworth's system was small ($n = 23$); thus, some patterns may not have been observed or so infrequently represented as to be difficult to distinguish. Second, the probability of missed patterns is increased by the "normality" of the sample, that is, families were middle class and intact, referred by private pediatricians, and mothers were homemakers. Thus, it might be expected that more diverse and deviant attachment patterns would be found in nonnormal groups, for example, children with abusing or neglecting parents (Schneider-Rosen, Braunwald, Carlson, & Cicchetti 1985), children with parents with psychopathology (Cicchetti & Schneider-Rosen 1986), children with biological deficiencies (Cicchetti & Serafica 1981). Consistent with this notion, there have been a number of recent reports of attachment patterns that do not easily fit Ainsworth's patterns and that have often been found in nonnormal groups (e.g., Crittenden 1983; Main & Hesse, this vol., Main & Weston 1981; Radke-Yarrow, Cummings, Kuczynski, & Chapman 1985; Spieker & Booth 1985).

The goals of this chapter are to examine the conceptual and research bases for rating attachments on a security continuum, and to propose a model system for classifying attachments on a continuum that may have general applicability. Research evidence regarding the existence of multiple behavioral indicators of insecurity is considered, followed by an examination of the conceptual bases for scoring attachments on a continuum of felt security. A model continuum for rating attachments is then proposed and illustrated by scoring attachments of classifiable and difficult-to-classify children of depressed parents. Finally, the use of security continua to score attachment across the life span is discussed.

UNCLASSIFIABLE ATTACHMENTS IN EARLY CHILDHOOD

There has been evidence since the first applications of Ainsworth's system that it did not take into account all information relevant to felt security or describe all possible patterns of attachment. Main (1973, reported in Main & Solomon, this vol.) "force classified" all attachments into A, B, or C groups, but she reported that informally she considered three infants to show an A *and* C pattern, that is, enough avoidance and ambivalence to justify classification in either or both groups. Sroufe and Waters (1977) found that 10% of their infants were not easily classifiable, but they did not specify the characteristics of unclassifiable patterns. Difficulty in classification was also found by Ainsworth in a second sample when 12-month-old infants and their mothers returned to participate in a second Strange Situation two weeks after the first (Ainsworth et al. 1978). Many of the infants scored as insecure in their first Strange Situation were force classified as secure on the basis of their second Strange Situation, but there were reservations about these classifications.

The first systematic report on unclassifiable patterns was by Main and Weston (1981). They assigned infants to an "unclassifiable" (U) category based upon the occurrence of any one of the following patterns: "behaves to the parent in reunion as a secure infant, but behaves identically to the stranger," "extreme avoidance is combined with extreme distress throughout the session," "behaves in one reunion as a secure infant but in the other as an insecure infant," "physical behavior is that of a secure infant—approach, clinging—but infant is affectless with signs of depression." While many U infants were force classified as secure, they behaved more like insecure than secure infants in terms of conflict behavior, defined as behaviors that had a "disordered, purposeless, or odd appearance," and in terms of lack of relatedness to an adult stranger.

Crittenden (1983) explored alternative classifications among children of abusing and neglecting mothers. The unpredictable and/or unresponsive rearing environments in these homes might be expected to lead to the development of atypical, very insecure attachment relationships (Crittenden 1985; Schneider-Rosen et al. 1985). Crittenden (1983) was prompted to reexamine classification according to the *A, B, C* system when children of abusing/neglecting mothers who had behaved "very unusually" in the Strange Situation were force classified as secure. This resulted in the development of an avoidance *and* ambivalent (*A/C*) category characterized by (*a*) moderate to high avoidance, (*b*) moderate to high resistance, and (*c*) moderate to high proximity seeking. *A/C* infants were also significantly more likely than children in other classifications to show unusual or odd behaviors in the Strange Situation such as "face covering, head cocking, huddling on the floor and rocking, and wetting." A link between abusing, neglecting home environments, and the *A/C* pattern was suggested by the fact that this pattern was only observed among children of abusing and neglecting mothers and never found among children of adequate mothers. In a second study, the *A/C* pattern was related to the severity of maternal maltreatment, with the highest incidence found when there was both abuse *and* neglect.

Radke-Yarrow et al. (1985) studied patterns of attachment in another at-risk group, children of bipolar and unipolar depressed mothers. Depressed mothers are more likely to be emotionally unavailable to children for extended periods during depressive episodes. Since maternal unresponsiveness is associated with the development of insecure attachments (e.g., Ainsworth et al. 1978), insecure and very insecure attachments might be expected in this sample (Cummings & Cicchetti, this vol.). Radke-Yarrow et al. classified children according to *A, B, C* criteria, but a sizable proportion of dyads children received high scores on *both* avoidance and ambivalence. Instead of being force classified as *A* or *C*, these children were treated as a separate *A/C* group. Other unclassifiable behaviors also typified children in this group to varying degrees, including sadness, depressed affect, and odd vocalizations, body postures, and movements. Consistent with the hypothesis that depressed parenting is associated with the development of very insecure attachments, the *A/C* pattern was only found in children of unipolar or bipolar depressed mothers; it was never found when mothers were normal or when mothers had minor depression. Further, the incidence of the *A/C* pattern was linked with severity of maternal depression. This is shown in table 1.

Spieker and Booth (1985) examined patterns of attachment in a sample characterized by high socioeconomic, environmental, and birth risk, and reported further evidence for an *A/C* pattern and for its origin in nonnormal

TABLE 1.   MOTHERS' AFFECTIVE FUNCTIONING IN THE
CHILD'S LIFETIME AND QUALITY OF ATTACHMENT RELATIONSHIP

	Attachment		
	Secure	Insecure	
Index	B	A or C	A/C
% child's lifetime mother is ill	26.5	25.9	79.7
Severity of mother's illness[a]	58.3	58.2	44.5
Treatment history[b]	.65	.73	1.60

SOURCE: Adapted from Radke-Yarrow et al. 1985.
[a] GAS scores varied from 0 (needing continuous care and supervision) to 100 (superior functioning); normal mothers are not given ratings.
[b] n forms of treatment received: hospitalization, drug therapy, psychotherapy; maximum score equals three.

rearing environments. The A/C classification was made only when high avoidance and high resistance occurred in the *same* reunion. As in the Radke-Yarrow et al. study, A/C patterns were associated not only with high avoidance and resistance but with the occurrence of other behaviors indicative of insecurity in attachment relations, including depressed affect, fearfulness, or helplessness. Aspects of the adequacy of rearing environments predicted A/C patterns, including more difficult life circumstances, more physically uncomfortable symptoms reported by the mother during pregnancy, and greater maternal report of depression. Instances of children who did not fit prototypical patterns (A, B, C, or A/C) but who showed insecurity by depressed affect or behavioral disorganization were also reported. These results suggest that unclassifiable attachments may be a function of high-risk rearing environments in general and not only the occurrence of specific maternal syndromes (abuse/neglect, or depression).

Main (Main & Hesse, this vol.; Main & Solomon, this vol.) has proposed an insecure-disorganized/disoriented (D) classification based upon further classifications of dyads from the Berkeley Social Development Study (Main & Weston 1981). Multiple classes of behaviors served as bases for D classification: (a) disordering of expected temporal sequences, (b) simultaneous display of contradictory patterns, (c) incomplete or undirected movements or expressions or stereotypes, (d) direct indices of confusion or apprehension, or (e) behavioral stilling. However, D classification was not seen as forming a distinct behavioral pattern but as representing disorganizations of A, B, or C patterns. Ainsworth's patterns were seen as constituting the fundamental organizing principles for attachment. Consistent with this, infants classified as D were also "force classified" in terms of what were viewed as underlying A, B, C patterns. Children classified in terms of the three fundamental patterns also could be alternatively classified as D when there was "marked" evidence of disorganization/disorientation. Multiple behavioral criteria for D as an al-

TABLE 2.   STUDIES FINDING PATTERNS OF ATTACHMENT OTHER THAN A, B, C

Name	n	Family Characteristics	Pattern	%
Crittenden (1983) (two studies)	152	Abuse and/or neglect	A/C	27% of abusing/ neglecting; 0% of adequate
Main and Solomon (this vol.)	270[a]	None specified	D	13%
Main and Weston (1981)	152[a]	None specified	U	12%
Spieker and Booth (1985)	51	Depression, chronic life difficulties, difficult pregnancy	A/C	18%
Sroufe and Waters (1977)	70	None specified	No system developed	10%
Radke-Yarrow, Cummings, Kuczynski, and Chapman (1985)	99	Major unipolar and bipolar depression	A/C	20% of depressed; 0% of normal

[a]Strange Situations with mothers and fathers.

ternative classification are described. While some criteria for the disorganized/ disoriented classification were based upon deviations from "expected" responses (responses expected according to Ainsworth's scheme), others (e.g., A/C patterns, sad or depressed affect, odd body postures, vocalizations, or movements) overlapped with those described by other investigators of unclassifiable patterns and reflected problems in general functioning.

Prediction of 6-year functioning was improved by treating D infants as a separate group. Infants classified as D were more likely to have insecure-controlling attachments, that is, organizations of relationships with parents that were controlling parental (role reversing) or controlling and punitive, at 6 years of age (Main, Kaplan, & Cassidy 1985). There were also differences in terms of parents' experiences. Parents of D infants were more likely to have themselves suffered a loss of a parent prior to maturity.

There is thus accumulating evidence that there are behavioral indices of insecurity in addition to those described by Ainsworth. These studies are summarized in table 2. There is no consensus, however, on how to include these new behaviors in classification decisions. The A/C pattern is not inclusive enough, since other often associated problem behaviors, for example, depressed affect, are not reflected in making the classification. The D pattern may be too inclusive and broad, indexing behaviors widely varying in implications for felt security. A third approach to including unclassifiable behaviors in classification decisions is to classify attachments on a continuum of felt security.

BASES FOR A SECURITY CONTINUUM

Patterns and Continua

The notion that attachments can be represented on a security continuum is not new. Ainsworth has pointed out (1984, personal communication) that when the subcategories of the A, B, C system are considered (Ainsworth et al. 1978), it is possible to order patterns along a continuum of felt security (see fig. 1), with the A_1 and C_2 patterns as extremes of insecurity, and the A/C pattern as the most extreme deviation.

Others have suggested security continua as schemes for attachment classification (Crittenden 1983, 1985; Main et al. 1985). However, conceptual bases for classifying attachment relationships on a security continuum have been little developed.

Classification on a security continuum can both extend and refine the measurement of attachment. With regard to the former, not all attachments may fit "prototypes"; regardless of the behavioral patterning of the attachment relationship, the security that the child derives from the attachment figure can be assessed. Second, even when attachments are classifiable in terms of a prototype, there may be significant differences in felt security among relationships receiving the same classification. Thus, all children classified as A may not derive the same level of security from the relationship. In such cases,

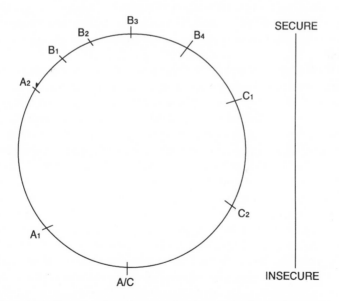

Figure 10.1. Patterns of attachment ordered on a security continuum.

the addition of security ratings can increase the specificity of measurement. Third, when classification decisions require judgments on the borderline between categories, the use of a security continuum can reduce the potential error of measurement (Stevens 1951). For example, when a child is on the borderline between an *A* and *B* classification, a category-based decision makes the difference between a judgment of secure and insecure, but a decision for the same child based upon a security continuum only involves the difference between two close points on a continuum. Thus, the forced-choice format of a pattern system leads to a major loss of power in concurrent and predictive validity that can be avoided with a continuum. From a measurement theory point of view, the use of a continuum system can strengthen the support for the predictive validity of attachment and therefore beneficially affect the progress of research.

Classification on the basis of security provision is always conceptually justified because the security that the child derives from the attachment figure is fundamental to the role and function of attachment. A security continuum, since it is not based upon specific behaviors but on the "message" of any pattern of behaviors regarding security provision, provides a method for assessing attachments that permits the comparison of quality of attachment across a wide range of contexts. Specific patterns of behavior are likely to be age-specific or setting-specific and may not be comparable. However, classification on a security continuum provides a universal basis for assessment that may allow for comparisons across experimental contexts (e.g., Greenberg 1984), across ages (e.g., among adolescents, adults, and the elderly), and across classes of relationships (e.g., day-care caregivers, friends, spouses, parents).

Rather than being an alternative, however, classification in terms of a security continuum should be viewed as a *compliment* to pattern classification; prediction should be best when both systems are used. Pattern classification, since it describes behavioral dispositions, may be particularly useful in predicting styles of affectional relationships and the *form* taken by developmental difficulties (e.g., behavior problems vs. anxiety disorder), whereas security ratings, since they describe level of disturbance, may best predict risk for developmental difficulty and the *extent* of later problems.

This approach to the measurement of difficult-to-classify attachments differs in its assumptions from the approach espoused by Main and Solomon and Main and Hesse (this vol.) in several respects. First, all patterns of attachment, including atypical or very deviant attachments, are seen as organized. Each reflects the history and pattern of relationships between the child and the parent and is a systematic expression of the quality of that relationship (Bowlby 1973). By contrast, Main and her colleagues argue that *D* relationships should be viewed as disorganizations of *A*, *B*, or *C* patterns. While the need to preserve the essentials of the *A, B, C* system, which are of proven value, is recognized and incorporated into the present system, it is not seen as necessary to impart a sort of primacy to these elements of behavior in classifying attachment patterns. Second, we postulate that attachments can be classified unequivocally with regard to felt security, and that a single point on a security continuum can be found to reflect felt security for any attachment relationship. This contrasts with the notion that attachments can be disrupted secure and insecure, for example, *D* (insecure)/forced *B*(secure) or *B d*/forced *B* (secure with some disorganization). Third, unless protypical patterns are present, or can be classified by consistent criteria, it is seen as best not to assign a pattern classification rather than to assign a multiple-defined category. We feel it is more precise simply to note the behaviors indicative of security/insecurity that occur and provide a security rating. Finally, deviations from expected sequences do not constitute a sufficient criterion for classification. Unless behaviors are relevant to judgments of the security provision function of attachment, they should not be included in a rating.

However, there is no doubt that *many D*'s (and certainly the *A/C* subgroup) are at the extremes of insecure attachment. Because of multiple criteria, however, *D* patterns are likely to vary greatly in level of insecurity. This issue is addressed to some extent by scoring level of disorganization on a continuum (Main & Solomon, this vol.). Another promising direction for classification of 3- and 4-year-old attachments are current attempts to identify *well-defined* subtypes within the *D* category.

General Principles of Rating

General principles from attachment theory for classifying attachments on a continuum of felt security are considered next.

One critical issue is to determine which behaviors are properly viewed as relevant to the construct of attachment itself. Some confusion is created by the fact that attachment classification predicts many other aspects of children's functioning. Relationships with other behaviors are not unexpected, since the child's sense of felt security, which originates in part from attachment relationships, underlies and provides a foundation for general functioning. However, this should not be interpreted to mean that all associated behaviors are properly viewed as indices of attachment (Bretherton 1985). Similarly, the fact that problematic or atypical behaviors occur in the Strange Situation does not necessarily mean that they index attachment.

In considering whether behaviors should influence rating, one must decide whether behaviors inform one about the security derived from the attachment relationship. Two fundamental principles should guide classification: (*a*) behaviors considered in classification should reflect the security that the child derives from the relationship, since that is the function specifically served by the attachment bond; and (*b*) judgments should take into account the overall organization and patterning of behavior around issues of the child's felt security rather than treating individual behaviors as discrete entities with diagnostic value in isolation. On the other hand, behaviors do not have to directly serve the attachment behavioral system for them to have import for classification. Behaviors that index a *failure* of this system around issues of derived security may also be relevant to classification.

Felt Security as a Criterion for Classification

The notion that the attachment system revolves around the security that the child derives from the attachment figure is a core concept of attachment theory. The critical role of felt security in the function and operation of the attachment system was made explicit by Sroufe and Waters (1977) but is implicit in virtually all discussions of the role and function of attachment relationships. Bowlby emphasized felt-security issues in many places, particularly in his treatment of the role of attachment figures in allaying children's fears or responses to stress, and in his discussions of anxiety as a response to loss or unavailability of adequate attachment figures (Bowlby 1973, 1980). Ainsworth's classification scheme is based upon the parent's relative effectiveness as a source of derived security in the face of the stresses induced by the Strange Situation.

The role of attachment in security provision can be seen from a biological perspective, from the perspective of current functioning, and in terms of the implications of attachment for later development. Bowlby ([1969] 1982) emphasized the biological function of attachment in protecting the individual from physical harm. However, Bowlby also recognized the secure base function of attachments: ". . . when an individual is confident that an attachment figure will be available to him whenever he desires it, that person will be much less prone to either intense or chronic fear than an individual who for any reason has no such confidence" (Bowlby 1973, p. 202). In this regard, Sroufe and Waters argued that "the concept of the attachment figure as a secure base for exploration . . . is of parallel importance to protection and again makes the concept more valuable as a developmental construct" (Sroufe & Waters 1977, p. 1186). With regard to relationships between the security of early attachments and later development, Bowlby contended, "It is postulated that confidence in the availability of attachment figures, or lack of it, is built up slowly during the years of immaturity—infancy, childhood, and adolescence—and that whatever expectations are developed during those years tend to persist relatively unchanged throughout the rest of life" (Bowlby 1973, p. 202). The impact of early attachments on development has been conceptualized in terms of their influence on the child's developing internal working models of the world (Bretherton 1985; Bowlby 1973; Cassidy, this vol.; Main et al. 1985).

The adequacy of the attachment figures as a source of derived security will not be equally apparent in every situation. The attachment figure's effectiveness as a secure base is most visible in situations that induce stress. Consistent with this, the Strange Situation presents infants with a series of stresses (an unfamiliar setting, an adult stranger, a separation when left with a stranger, and a separation when left alone). Other behavioral systems, for example, exploration, are more likely to be ascendant in nonstress situations. However, even a low-stress situation should activate the attachment behavioral system, and observing security provision in a matrix of low-, moderate-, and high-stress situations may be most informative (Greenberg 1984).

Organizational Schemes and the Rating of Attachment

Another core concept of attachment theory is that attachment relationships should be interpreted from an organizational perspective rather than on the basis of discrete behaviors, for example, separation distress (Bischof 1975; Bowlby [1969] 1982; Bretherton 1985; Sroufe & Waters 1977; Waters & Deane 1982). A focal notion is that attachment relationships are organized as complex, flexible behavioral systems in which behaviors may serve equivalent or interchangeable functions. Thus, in classification, attachment relationships are evaluated in terms of the higher-order goal or purpose of attachment and not in terms of whether specific responses are present or absent. The concept of attachment has demonstrated construct validity, that is, stability (e.g., Waters 1978) and predictive utility (e.g., Main et al. 1985), when treated as an organizational scheme, whereas there is little evidence for the construct validity of attachment when attachment behaviors are treated as discrete units, consistent with trait theories (Sroufe & Waters 1977).

In Bowlby's ([1969] 1982) classic, formulation of a control systems model of attachment behaviors were organized around a set-goal of proximity. However, Sroufe and Waters (1977) have cogently argued that this conceptualization requires elaboration to do justice to the affective and motivational components of attachment brilliantly observed elsewhere in Bowlby's writings, and "to yield a truly developmental construct" (p. 1185). Their position is that the set-goal of attachment should be seen as felt security, that is, attachment relationships should be interpreted in terms of their effectiveness in meeting the individual's security provision needs, with affect serving as a mediator of adaptive behavior.

> Proximity is not automatically elicited but depends on the infant's evaluation of a variety of internal and external parameters, in terms of subjective experience of security-insecurity (Bischof, 1975). Setting, familiarization, preceding events, and other aspects of context, as well as the infant's mood and developmental level, influence the initiation of bids for contact or proximity. And the behaviors which serve to recover an internally represented goal are selected in terms of their efficacy in the

present environment. With development there are increasingly varied means of maintaining contact, and there is decreasing proximity to the caregiver in the absence of stress. (Sroufe & Waters 1977, p. 1186)

Regarding felt security as the higher-order or set-goal of attachment integrates notions of the security-provision function of attachment within an explicitly organizational and control systems perspective. Extending this to classification or ratings of attachments, judgments of the quality of attachment thus should reflect an organizational interpretation of the comparison between the child's security needs and the provision of security by the attachment figure. Within secure attachment relationships there should thus be a match between security needs and security provision, whereas within insecure and very insecure attachment relationships there should be mismatches in this regard. An organizational approach, because of its focus on the attachment relationship rather than attachment behaviors, has a built-in flexibility that allows for the consideration of a multiplicity of behaviors in assessing security.

With regard to the issue of "unclassifiable" attachments, this suggests that when new behaviors are added to those already considered in classification of attachment, they should be chosen because they provide further evidence of the child's ability, or inability, to derive security from the attachment figure. The entire matrix of information with relevance to issues of the child's derived security from the attachment figure should be considered, with allowance for the possibility that interchangeable functions may be served by different behaviors.

Felt Security versus Security

There are several advantages for using an explicit notion of felt security, rather than security, as a criteria for rating attachment. As noted above, felt security provides an anchor for scoring attachments in an organizational/control systems perspective on attachment. Security as a concept is vague, is not clearly grounded in a control systems model, and does not provide a testable, consistent basis for classification. Felt security must be interpreted interactionally, that is, in terms of child-parent interaction, and contextually, that is, in terms of the effectiveness of the parent in providing security to the child when the child needs it, for example, in stressful situations. Of course, all children are insecure at times, and all children use the parents as a secure base from which to explore. However, some are more effective in deriving security from parents when they need it than others, and it is the quality of this give-and-take flow when the individual is stressed that specifies quality of attachment.

The role of affect in this issue presents a difficult challenge for theory. *Overt* displays of distress do not necessarily reflect covert levels of security/insecurity and are not necessarily decisive in classifying attachment relationships. All children, and individuals, can be stressed in some situations.

The issue for classification is whether the attachment figure effectively ame-liorates this distress. For the Strange Situation, the critical issue is what hap-pens in reunion, that is, when the parent is available to provide security, and not what happens in separation, when the child may be distressed but the mother is not available to ameliorate distress. Further, crying when the parent is absent in the Strange Situation can be easily seen as reflecting the child's "secure" expectancy that the parent can be expected to respond to the child's signals. The child's failure to cry in a situation that is naturally threatening is not necessarily a secure response (whether the situation should be seen as "naturally threatening" is undoubtedly age-related).

Defensive processes such as avoidance are attempts to control anxiety, and it may be hasty to conclude that the child that looks okay actually feels that way. Many A-babies don't search or cry during separation, but this may reflect the expectation that the mother won't help or might do something defi-nitely not helpful rather than that the baby doesn't feel anxious. The fact that A-babies avoid interaction or eye contact with the mother when *she becomes available to provide security* completes the picture. As Main (1981) has ar-gued, unresponsiveness and avoidance is not motivated by feeling okay but rather reflects strong covert feelings of anger. Home observations add sup-port: in the home A babies have an interactional history of rejection and are *more easily* distressed by everyday challenges (Ainsworth et al. 1978).

For classification or rating purposes, felt security should be defined from the perspective of the observer's organizational analysis of the message of the individual's entire pattern of overt and covert responses to attachment figures. Insecure individuals should *feel* more insecure but may not appear that way if only single responses are examined; insecure adults may even *report* an ideal-ized picture of high security (e.g., Main et al. 1985). Unfortunately, there is little data that bears on the *covert* responses of children who *appear* okay in stressful contexts. Sroufe and Waters (1977) found that heart rates of A-babies took longer than others to return to baseline levels following reunion in the Strange Situation. One possible interpretation of this finding is that these chil-dren were aroused longer after the mother returned and therefore *felt* more insecure. Other research on children's responses to stressful situations also suggest that overt affective responses may not reflect children's covert re-sponses: 4–5-year-olds who *show* no emotional response to others' anger are most likely to report in an interview that they *felt* angry (Cummings 1987).

CLASSIFYING ATTACHMENTS ON A CONTINUUM OF FELT SECURITY

Characteristics of the Scale

This scheme is meant primarily to serve as an example; the intent is to demonstrate the mechanisms through which multiple sources of information on felt security are integrated in scoring attachments on a continuum of felt security. The presentation of a specific scoring system is only a secondary interest. A large set of behaviors might potentially influence judgments of felt security, and these may change as a function of the context, the sample studied, children's age, or the nature of the affiliative relationship between individuals. The classes of behavior described here represent a selective compilation of schemes proposed by Ainsworth (Ainsworth et al. 1978) and described in recent studies of unclassifiable patterns (see above).

Conceptually, continua for rating security should order attachments on a dimension from very secure at one extreme, representing optimal functioning of the attachment system in the provision of security, to not attached at the other extreme, reflecting the absence of derived security. "Not attached" or "detached" patterns between young children and parents are likely to be rare in normal rearing environments and are probably most often associated with long-term separation (Bowlby 1973), conditions of maternal deprivation (Ainsworth 1962; Bowlby 1951), or instances of extreme neglect (Cicchetti & Schneider-Rosen 1986). In scoring attachments on a security continuum, the choice of the number of scale points is arbitrary, but there are likely to be consistent conceptually meaningful divisions within the scale: very secure, secure, insecure, very insecure, and not attached. In the present instance, the end points are defined as very secure (1.0) and not attached (4.0), with regions in between designated as secure (1.1–1.9), insecure (2.0–2.9), and very insecure (3.0–3.9).

Consistent with the discussion above, general principles guiding classification decisions are (a) to consider only security-relevant behaviors and disregard behaviors irrelevant to security judgments, (b) to consider the overall patterning or organization of behavior and not just one or several "diagnostic" behaviors, and (c) to make judgments based upon the contrast between the child's needs for security and the attachment figures' provision of security. The focal issue is thus the effectiveness of the attachment figure in ameliorating the child's security needs.

Behaviors Included in Judgments of Felt Security

Security ratings are based upon (a) the relative occurrence versus absence of behaviors indicative of successful versus unsuccessful immediate efforts on the child's part to derive security from the parent, and (b) the relative felt-security of the child evident in general functioning which is assumed to indirectly reflect the security derived from the attachment relationship. The behaviors selected as indexing felt security are listed and described in table 3.

Ameliorative behaviors, avoidant and resistant behaviors, and difficulty comforting reflect the immediate effectiveness of the parent in providing security. Ameliorative behaviors index the positive and effective functioning of the attachment relationship. These behaviors include behaviors referred to by

TABLE 3. BEHAVIORAL INDICES OF FELT SECURITY

---

1. Ameliorative. Behaviors include reciprocated contact seeking, proximity seeking, or distance interaction.
2. Avoidance.[a] Behaviors include turning the head away, averting the gaze, avoidance of meeting the parents' eyes, hiding the face, or simply ignoring the parents. Ignoring the parents is most marked when they are trying to gain the attention of the child or get a response from the child.
3. Resistance.[a] Behaviors include pushing away, throwing away, batting away, squirming to be put down, jerking away, stepping angrily, resistance to being picked up or moved or restrained. This also includes more diffuse manifestations of resistance such as angry screaming, throwing self down, kicking the floor, pouting, cranky fussing, and petulance.
4. Difficulty comforting. This is indexed by the time it takes for the child to regain normal emotional and social functioning after the child has been upset or disturbed, and the parent has an opportunity to comfort the child. The most relevant occasion for observing this is in the reunion period. How long does it take the child to recover normal play and affect after the mother returns? However, the entrance of the stranger in episode 3 or simply the beginning of the Strange Situation (exposure for the first time to a strange room) are also occasions for assessing this. Relevant behaviors are (a) an absence of play (fumbling with a toy absently is not play) or exploration, (b) extended crying or whining that may stop and start but never quite goes away, or (c) depressed affect or posture, either in the mother's arms or away from the mother.
5. Depressed affect. Depressed affect can be shown by sadness or depressed body posture. This is likely to be accompanied by persistent flatness of affect, low activity level, and lack of responsiveness to others (the stranger or mother).
6. Conflicted behavior. Behaviors include odd sounds or cries, out of place emotional expressions, body postures or movements, or strange or sudden movements, or incomplete movements.
7. Disconnected. Behaviors include lost, aimless, dazed, or confused responses.
8. Inappropriate caregiving and controlling.[b] The child adapts the role of taking care of the mother. Behaviors include anxious and "overbright" responses with clear behavioral evidence of a role reversal.
9. Inappropriate punitive and controlling.[b] The child attempts to control the mother through directly punitive behavior.

---

[a]Adapted from Ainsworth et al. (1978).
[b]Adapted from Main et al. (1985).

Ainsworth as proximity seeking, contact maintaining, and distance interaction, but the emphasis is placed upon whether these behaviors are reciprocated or otherwise result in the provision of security. The form of expression of ameliorative behavior is likely to change with age (Marvin 1972; Radke-Yarrow et al. 1985). For a 2-year-old, proximity seeking and contact maintaining are likely to be the major forms of expression, whereas a 4-year-old may tend to rely much more on distance interaction.

The conceptual bases for viewing avoidance and resistance as insecure behaviors are thoroughly developed by Main (e.g., Main 1981) and Ainsworth (e.g., Ainsworth et al. 1978). In brief, avoidance reflects an inability of the child to trust the parent as a source of security when the child is vulnerable. Resistance reflects anger and an inability to effectively use the parent as a secure base. Difficulty comforting represents an insufficiency of the attachment relationship in providing security. While it has been linked with insecure patterns of attachment (Ainsworth et al. 1978), it has not, in itself, been used as a criteria for classification. It is viewed here as having face validity as an index of felt security, independent of other responses.

The notion that problems in general functioning are related to attachment relationships is suggested by studies finding links between these behaviors and unclassifiable patterns of attachment. Because of the possibility (which cannot be entirely dismissed) that these behaviors reflect difficulties that are independent of the attachment relationship, it is important that such indices clearly measure insecurity (broadly defined) and that parents have at least a possible role in ameliorating these problems in the Strange Situation. On the other hand, if attachment figures are incorporated into children's internal working models (Bowlby 1973; Bretherton 1985), problems in general functioning may reflect an influence of attachment on general functioning even when such a connection is not visibly apparent.

Conservatively, at least three classes of general functioning problems may reflect felt security in the Strange Situation and are selected for inclusion here: these are termed conflicted behaviors, depressed affect, and disconnectedness. Conflicted behaviors are seen as reflecting general behavioral disorganizations resulting from the intrusion of anxiety or fear. Depressed affect obviously reflects low felt security. These two classes of behaviors have been reported by Crittenden (1983), Main and Weston (1981), Main and Solomon (this vol.), Radke-Yarrow et al. (1985), and Spieker and Booth (1985) in association with unclassifiable patterns of attachment. Disconnectedness suggests the child is lost, confused, aimless, dazed, in short, functioning as if he or she has no internal sense of felt security and no secure base. It may be the most compelling evidence for "not attached." This behavior was observed in both the present sample of children of depressed parents (Radke-Yarrow et al. 1985) and in another sample of children of bipolar parents (Zahn-Waxler, Chapman, & Cummings 1984), but was not formally scored. Main and Solomon (this vol.) report this behavior as a criteria for the D classification.

These behaviors may weigh differently in classification because of their different implications regarding children's felt security. General rules are (a) responses reflecting the pervasive impact of low felt security, for example, depression, reflect greater insecurity than problems in the immediate use of the parent as a secure base, for example, resistance; (b) functional problems (e.g., avoidance of the mother in play) are less worrisome than an absence of functioning (e.g., a failure to play at all); and (c) problematic functioning throughout the Strange Situation is more worrisome than problems localized in one or several periods. Likely links between classes of behavior relevant to felt security and security ratings are shown in figure 2.

Main (Main et al. 1985) has identified two other behaviors in 6-year-olds—controlling and punitive behavior and controlling and parental behavior—that may be relevant to ratings of felt security. From the perspective of felt security, controlling behavior suggests insecurity regarding the parent's

BEHAVIORAL INDICES OF FELT-SECURITY

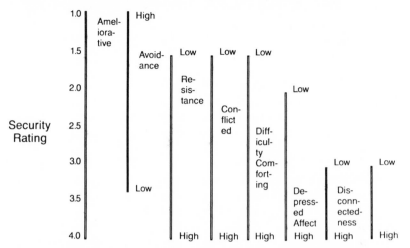

Figure 10.2. Behavioral indices of felt security and security ratings.

availability as a secure base. Punitive behavior may be a developmentally advanced equivalent of resistance. Caregiving behavior reflects an inappropriate role reversal regarding the provision of security: the child is in the role of providing security for the parent rather than the other way around. Bowlby (1973, 1980) has identified the inappropriate adoption of the parental role in childhood as a predictor of later disturbance. However, it is uncertain at what point in development these behaviors first appear within attachment relationships. Moreover, they should be scored as insecure with caution. In moderation and appropriately expressed, independence and assertiveness, and caregiving and prosocial behavior, reflect the effective use of the parent as a secure base and a mature partnership within the attachment relationship.

Scoring Felt Security on a Continuum

It is inconsistent with an organizational perspective to specifically assign individual behaviors ratings on a security continuum, but certain key issues may serve as guidelines for classification, and there may be general correspondences between these guidelines and prototypical pattern classifications. These possible correspondences are given below in parentheses.

Secure (1.0–1.4). Judgments are made about the extent of positive characteristics of attachments: the extent of the parent's reciprocity toward children's bids, the child's emotional and physical access to the attachment figure, and the emotional quality of interactions (B_3).

Secure (1.5–1.9). The issue is to make distinctions among relationships when there is *slight* evidence of insecurity. For example, there may be slight avoidance or resistance (the avoidance and resistance scales in Ainsworth et al.'s 1978 appendix 3 may be useful here), or slight evidence of conflicted behavior (B_1, B_2, B_4).

Insecure (2.0–2.4). The issue is to make distinctions among relationships when there are moderate, but delimited, signs of insecurity. For example, there may be moderate avoidance on reunion with the parent, but in moderate and low stress contexts the child may appear secure (A_2, C_1).

Insecure (2.5–2.9). The issue is to make distinctions among relationships when there are strong, but delimited, signs of insecurity. Thus, evidence of insecurity is still largely confined to high-stress contexts and to the parent's immediate effectiveness in providing security (A_1, C_2).

Very Insecure (3.0–3.4). The issue is to make distinctions among relationships when there are strong, and general, signs of insecurity. For example, there may be multiple signs of insecurity evident in direct interactions with parents, and these may be evident both in reunion and in nonreunion situations. Salient, but delimited, expressions of depressed affect or disconnected behavior may be evident, and there may be significant disharmony (A/C).

Very Insecure (3.5–4.0). The issue is to make distinctions among relationships when there are very strong, and general, signs of insecurity. For example, pervasive depressed affect may be present. High levels of disconnected behavior are particularly significant in indicating the absence or near-absence of a secure base. Main and Solomon (this vol.) describe two instances of detachment in child-father relationships (A/C, not attached).

CLASSIFYING ATTACHMENTS OF CHILDREN OF DEPRESSED PARENTS

A sample of children of depressed parents are given security ratings to illustrate this system (Cummings, Daniel, & El-Sheikh 1986). Attachment relationships in depressed families are of interest because of the provocative issue of whether disturbances in attachment relationships provide an environmental basis in early childhood for the intergenerational transmission of depression (Akisal & McKinney 1975; Cicchetti & Schneider-Rosen 1986; Rutter & Garmezy 1983). Low-felt security resulting from insecure attachment relationships is a potential basis for the development of working models of self and others that are depressionogenic, for example, "I'm not worth loving," "Others won't love me." Consistent with this possible link, the thinking patterns of individuals with insecure attachments and depression (e.g., Beck 1976; Petersen & Seligman 1984) bear marked similarities. Children of depressed parents are more likely to be insecurely attached (Radke-Yarrow et al. 1985; Spieker & Booth 1985). For the present purposes, they provide a sample that is likely to test the full range of an attachment continuum, from very secure to very insecure. The possible role of insecure attachment patterns in the transmission of depression is treated at greater length in Cummings and Cicchetti (this vol.).

Procedure and Sample

A modified version of the Strange Situation (Ainsworth et al. 1978) was employed. The deviations from the traditional procedure were: (*a*) episode 1 was extended in length, increasing its importance for assessing attachment-exploration balance; (*b*) mothers were given no instruction in episode 2 rather than being asked not to interact with the child except in response to the child's initiations; (*c*) more toys were present than in the traditional procedure, and some were defined as forbidden; (*d*) episode 3 was allowed to continue for seven minutes instead of the usual three, and the mother and also the stranger were asked to approach the child in a series of graded steps; and (*e*) when the mother returned in episode 8, she brought with her a small case of toys rather than returning empty-handed.

Families were participants in a longitudinal study of the development of offspring of depressed parents conducted at the Laboratory of Developmental Psychology of the National Institute of Mental Health, and primarily consisted of families recently tested and thus not included in the Radke-Yarrow et al. (1985) report. The present sample consisted of seventeen offspring of bipolar depressive mothers and eight children of mothers with major unipolar depression. Thirteen children of normal mothers were also scored. Children were typically 2 or 3 years old at the time of testing in the Strange Situation.

Families were recruited by advertising for participants in a study of child rearing and development in healthy families and families in which the mother is depressed. All volunteers were given a standard psychiatric interview, the Schedule for Affective Disorders and Schizophrenia (SADS) (Spitzer & Endicott 1977). Father's psychiatric status varied. Fathers could be with or without a diagnosis of depression; however, schizophrenic, alcoholic, and antisocial personalities were excluded.

Coders were trained against criteria tapes and from a coding manual. The author and coders negotiated instances of disagreement, with the author serving as the ultimate judge. Coders usually worked in pairs.

Security Ratings

The expectation that ratings would vary from very secure to very insecure in children of depressed mothers was confirmed. Thus, while having a depressed parent may increase the likelihood of insecure and very insecure attachment, it does not make insecure relationships inevitable. Table 4 shows children's ages, the relative occurrence of each of the target security-related

TABLE 4. SECURITY-RELEVANT BEHAVIORS, FORCED CLASSIFICATIONS
OF ATTACHMENT PATTERNS, AND SECURITY RATINGS
IN CHILDREN OF DEPRESSED PARENTS

| Case | Age (Means) | Security-Relevant Behaviors[a] | | | | | | | Forced Classification (A, B, or C) | Ratings of Felt Security |
		1^b	2	3	4	5	6	7		
1	39	H	L	L	L	L	L	L	B	1.0
2	40	H	L	L	L	L	L	L	B	1.0
3	51	H	L	L	L	L	L	L	B	1.1
4	26	H	L	L	L	L	L	L	B	1.4
5	35	M	L	L	L	L	L	L	B	1.4
6	25	H	M	L	L	L	L	L	B	1.5[c]
7	34	M	M	L	L	L	L	L	B	1.5
8	46	M	M	L	L	L	L	L	B	1.5
9	16	H	L	L	L	L	L	L	B	1.6
10	31	H	M	L	L	L	L	L	B	1.6
11	30	L	H	L	L	L	L	L	A	2.0
12	24	L	H	L	L	L	L	L	A	2.2
13	40	L	H	L	L	L	L	L	A	2.3
14	34	M	M	L	L	M	L	L	A	2.3
15	30	M	M	L	L	L	L	L	A	2.5[c]
16	35	M	H	L	L	L	L	L	A	2.5
17	35	L	H	M	L	L	L	L	A	2.5
18	33	M	H	M	H	L	M	L	A	3.0
19	27	L	M	L	L	L	M	L	A	3.0
20	42	M	M	H	H	M	L	L	C	3.0
21	23	M	L	H	M	L	M	L	C	3.2[c]
22	35	L	H	H	H	L	L	L	A	3.3[c]
23	34	L	H	L	H	L	H	L	A	3.5
24	25	L	H	L	H	M	H	M	A	3.5
25	27	M	M	M	H	M	H	L	A	3.7

[a] 1 = ameliorative; 2 = avoidance; 3 = resistance; 4 = difficulty comforting; 5 = conflicted behavior;
6 = depressed affect; 7 = disconnectedness.
[b] H = high; M = medium; L = low
[c] Includes controlling and punitive or controlling and caregiving behavior.

behaviors, classifications in terms of *A, B, C* patterns (some fit these patterns whereas others were "forced"), and ratings of felt security for children of depressed parents.

These results demonstrate the process of integrating multiple and new sources of information in making classification decisions, and shows how such a process might be carried out throughout a wide range of ages in early childhood. Avoidance was the most commonly observed index of insecurity in children of depressed mothers, followed in prevalence by difficulty comforting, resistance, and depressed affect (the latter two behaviors were equally prevalent). Insecure-controlling behavior was observed in several children and was seen in children as young as 23 months of age.

For the entire sample, pattern *B* children received ratings between 1.0 and 3.1 ($X = 1.51$) and pattern *A* and *C* children received ratings between 2.0 and

3.7 ($X = 2.75$). One child in the normal group that was force classified as *B* received a very insecure rating (3.1) because the child showed problems in multiple domains of functioning, including difficulty comforting, disharmony, and depressed affect. Thus, pattern *B* children are not necessarily always secure. Classification on a security continuum thus (*a*) allowed for the classification of "unclassifiable" patterns, (*b*) allowed for classification across a wide range of ages in early childhood, (*c*) detected insecurity shown by behaviors not included in Ainsworth's system, (*d*) increased discrimination within pattern classification categories, and (*e*) reduced the potential error of measurement at the border between categories.

While attachments are force classified as *A*, *B*, or *C* in table 4, they could also have been scored as *A/C* (Radke-Yarrow et al. 1985; Spieker & Booth 1985). Five children (nos. 17, 18, 20, 22, and 25) clearly fit the *A/C* pattern, receiving a mean security rating of 3.10. *A/C* children were thus among those receiving the lowest security ratings (including the lowest score of 3.7) as expected.

Judgments of felt security on a continuum could be made reliably. Nineteen Strange-Situation sessions were coded by independent observers. Interrater reliability between coders for ratings was $r = .86$. The percentage of agreement for forced classifications of this difficult-to-classify sample was 89%.

Case Studies

Two case studies of attachments classified as *A* are presented to illustrate the wide variation of security possible with traditional pattern classification categories.

A with 2.3 Rating. In episode 2 the child interacted well with the mother and showed average levels of exploration and activity. The child played well with the stranger in episode 3 and comfortably accepted physical contact and play overtures from the mother. During the first separation (episode 4) the child showed a minor drop in activity initially after the mother left but evidenced no distress. The child averted gaze from the mother and maintained distance from her when she returned in episode 5, but then initiated dialogue and play with her. The child alone episode (6) was protested slightly, but the child comforted herself and kept up a moderate level of activity. The child increased activity when the stranger returned (7) and interacted with the stranger. The child did not approach or interact with the mother when she returned (8) and averted gaze when lifted up by the mother. Summary: except for avoidance on reunions, the child generally functioned well throughout the Strange Situation.

A with a 3.5 Rating. In episode 2 the child was whiny toward the mother and hyperactive. The approach of the stranger in episode 3 upset the child, and the child had difficulty being comforted. The child cried loudly when the mother left in episode 4 and could not be comforted by the stranger. The child was extremely difficult (5) to comfort in reunion for the mother, and her cries had an odd quality. The child assumed a huddled, depressed posture and showed sad affect, not looking at the mother in response to her overtures, but eventually functioning improved. The child was affectless and disconnected in appearance throughout episode 6; she didn't greet the mother, averted gaze, and was unresponsive to the mother's overtures in episode 8. Summary: the child didn't function well throughout the Strange Situation, often appearing depressed and sad, and the mother was ineffective in comforting the child.

SECURITY CONTINUA AS A SCORING SYSTEM FOR
RATING ATTACHMENTS ACROSS THE LIFE SPAN

According to attachment theory, attachments are formed throughout the life span and can characterize affectional relations other than the child's bond to the parent (Ainsworth 1985). Bowlby ([1969] 1982) has argued that attachments beyond infancy are organized as goal-corrected partnerships, that is, relationships in which each individual has the capacity to understand and anticipate the others' perspective. Marvin (Marvin 1972, 1977; Marvin & Greenberg 1982) has demonstrated the onset of partnerships in early development. However, while the partnership notion describes the organization of attachment, it does not provide a rubric for classifying qualitative differences in security provision within attachment relationships. Ainsworth (1985) has noted that affiliative relationships other than child-parent relationships, for example, sexual-pair relationships or relationships between friends, companions, and intimates may or may not include attachment bonds. *The* critical issue is whether other relationships serve a security provision function.

"There is a third criterion of attachment that is clearly characteristic of some bonds, notably those of children to parents, which some consider to be essential and to distinguish attachment from other affectional bonds. This is the experience of comfort and security in relationship to the other and yet the ability to move off from this secure base with confidence to engage in other activities—but since not all attachments are secure this should be modified to imply *seeking* to find comfort and security in the other" (Ainsworth 1985, p. 800).

Ainsworth argues that attachments, in common with other affectional bonds, are characterized by being "never wholly interchangeable with or replaceable by another, even though there may be another to whom one is also attached," and "a desire to maintain closeness to the partner as well as a need to keep proximity to him or her." It is important to bear in mind that attachments, in addition to their security-provision function, are fundamentally affectional bonds. Thus, the local policeman or mafioso may provide a person with a sense of felt security and help them to explore (not be scared going outside their house at night), but this does not qualify these individuals as attachment figures.

In this section, the feasibility of using both a security continuum and a pattern classification scheme *in concert* to characterize quality of attachments across the life span is considered.

Classifying Attachments on a Security Continuum

Few attempts have been made to assess the *quality* of child-parent attachments beyond infancy, but the research that has been done suggests the validity of rating attachments on a continuum. Main et al. (1985) rated the quality of attachments of 6-year-olds to the mother on a nine-point security continuum, and found that these ratings correlated significantly with security of attachment to the mother at age 1 and with concurrent measures of functioning, including current overall functioning. Ratings attachments of 6-year-olds to the father also predicted security of attachment to the father at age 1 and current overall functioning. Main also rated the security of the parents' representational model of attachment based upon an Adult Attachment Inventory (Main 1985) and found that this was significantly correlated with the security of the child's attachments to parents.

Ratings of security of attachment are currently being used to assess quality of attachments in middle-age adults and the elderly. Valaik and Cummings (1986) have developed an interview to assess the attachments of the elderly and their middle-age adult children across the life span. Different portions of the interview are designed to assess quality of attachment at different points in development: child-parent attachments, adolescent-parent attachments, adult-parent attachments, and middle-age adult-parent attachments. Questions are also asked about affectional relationships with significant individuals other than the parent. Lists of security-relevant domains are developed for each age period, with specific questions designed to explore different domains of relationships. The quality of attachments to parents and others are rated on the basis of an organizational integration of security-relevant information.

To permit more complete characterization and comparison of attachments when attachments other than child-parent attachments were considered, an attempt is made to construct an attachment hierarchy as well. The place of attachment relationships in the hierarchy corresponds to the individual's preferences between others when faced with significant stress, and is also reflected by reactions to potential separation or loss. Relevant to this issue, Cummings (1980) found that toddlers strongly preferred the mother over day-care caregivers in terms of proximity-seeking measures in an unfamiliar laboratory context (high stress), but easily tolerated day-care caregivers substituting for the mother in a day-care setting (low stress), suggesting that attachments to mothers are stronger than those to day-care caregivers, but that this is only apparent in high-stress contexts. Conceivably, quality and the place of an attachment in a hierarchy of relationships can vary independently, so that, for example, an individual might have insecure bonds with parents, and secure bonds with friends, but prefer parents in times of greatest stress.

Classifying Patterns of Attachment

While the emphasis here has been on unclassifiable patterns and the advantages of a security continuum, it is important not to lose sight of the fact that about 90% of infant-parent attachments fit Ainsworth's A, B, C prototypes in normal samples, and that 80% may fit these prototypes even in samples with parental psychopathology (e.g., Radke-Yarrow et al. 1985). Further, developmental variants of these patterns have been observed in 6-year-olds (Cassidy, this vol.), young adults (Kobak, cited in Ainsworth 1985), and adults (Main & Hesse, this vol.). For example, Main found that adults evidenced three main patterns of attachment: autonomous (corresponding to pattern B), detached (corresponding to pattern A), and enmeshed (corresponding to pattern C). The prevalence and demonstrated predictive power of pattern classification suggests that pattern classification and classification on a continuum are ideally used in concert in order to optimally characterize attachments throughout the life span.

Pattern classification schemes may correspond with significant differences in children's general styles of coping with stress. Internal working models of coping developed in attachment relationships may serve as general guides for coping. For example, Cummings (1987) identified three styles of coping with background anger (anger between others) in 5-year-olds. Pattern A children ignored others' anger but later said they were, in fact, angry about the fight. Pattern B children showed concern and sometimes sought support from the mother or peer and later said they had wanted to intervene and felt empathic (sad) during the fight. Pattern C children were emotionally ambivalent, sought high levels of social support from others, verbalized that they felt impulses to disregulate and subsequently showed heightened levels of aggressiveness to peers. While children's attachments to the mother were not assessed in this sample, and correspondences between attachment and coping with background anger thus could not be directly examined, these results suggest the possible generality of A, B, C styles for describing children's coping patterns.

A Model Classification Scheme

This discussion suggests that the following should be included in assessing attachments across the life span: (a) lists of age-appropriate security-relevant behaviors, (b) ratings on a continuum of security of attachment (corresponding to quality of attachment), (c) ratings on a hierarchy of attachment, and (d) classifications of attachment patterns (if they fit prototypical rubrics). At each age, these dimensions could be assessed separately for different attachment figures, for example, parents, spouses, friends.

CONCLUDING REMARKS

The concept of attachment has become ascendent largely because of its sound conceptual and empirical bases. The challenge for future researchers is to maintain this essential core while expanding the utility of the construct to new domains. While the challenge is exciting, it is also formidable and requires a difficult mix of creativity and consistency with the past, risk-taking, and scientific rigor. The eventual test of any system is not whether it is reliable but whether it predicts functioning and development; that is, whether it succeeds in organizing behavior in a useful manner. Optimally, the present work is consistent with these constraints and successfully takes a step toward progress.

REFERENCES

Ainsworth, M. D. S. (1962). The effects of maternal deprivation: A review of findings and controversy in the context of research strategy. In *Deprivation of maternal care: A reassessment of its effect*. Public Health Paper No. 14. Geneva: WHO.

Ainsworth, M. D. S. (1969). Object relations, dependency and attachment: A theoretical review of the infant-mother relationship. *Child Development* 40, 965–1025.

Ainsworth, M. D. S. (1985). *Attachments across the life span*. Bulletin of the New York Academy of Medicine 61, 792–812.

Ainsworth, M. D. S.; Blehar, M. C.; Waters, E.; & Wall, S. (1978). *Patterns of attachment: A psychological study of the strange situation*. Hillside, N.J.: Erlbaum.

Ainsworth, M. D. S., & Wittig, B. A. (1969). Attachment and the exploratory behavior of one-year-olds in a strange situation. In B. M. Foss (ed.), *Determinants of infant behavior* (vol. 4). London: Methuen.

Akisal, H., & McKinney, W. (1975). Overview of recent research in depression: Integration of ten conceptual models into a comprehensive clinical frame. *Archives of General Psychiatry* 32, 285–305.

Arend, R.; Gove, F.; & Sroufe, L. A. (1979). Continuity of individual adaptation from infancy to kindergarten. A predictive study of ego-resiliency and curiosity in preschoolers. *Child Development* 50, 950–959.

Beck, A. T. (1976). *Cognitive therapy and the emotional disorders*. New York: International Universities Press.

Belsky, J.; Rovine, M.; & Taylor, D. (1984). The Pennsylvania Infant and Family Development Project: III. The origins of individual differences in infant-mother attachment: Maternal and infant contributions. *Child Development* 55, 718–728.

Bijou, S. W., & Baer, D. M. (1965). *Child development* (vol. 2). New York: Appleton-Century-Crofts.

Bischof, N. A. (1975). A systems approach toward the functional connections of attachment and fear. *Child Development* 46, 801–817.

Blurton-Jones, N. G., & Leach, G. M. (1972). Behavior of children and their mothers at separation and greeting. In N. G. Blurton-Jones (ed.), *Ethological studies of child behavior*. London: Cambridge University Press.

Bowlby, J. (1951). *Maternal care and mental health*. Monograph No. 2. Geneva: WHO.

Bowlby, J. (1958). The nature of the child's tie to his mother. *International Journal of Psychoanalysis* 39, 350–373.

Bowlby, J. ([1969] 1982). *Attachment and loss: Vol. 1. Attachment.* New York: Basic Books.

Bowlby, J. (1973). *Attachment and loss: Vol. 2. Separation: Anxiety and Anger.* New York: Basic Books.

Bowlby, J. (1980). *Attachment and loss: Vol. 3. Loss, sadness and depression.* New York: Basic Books.

Bretherton, I. (1985). Attachment theory: Retrospect and prospect. In I. Bretherton & E. Waters (eds.), *Growing points in attachment theory and research. Monographs of the Society for Research in Child Development* 50 (1–2, Serial No. 209), 3–35.

Cicchetti, D., & Schneider-Rosen, K. (1986). An organizational approach to childhood depression. In M. Rutter, C. E. Izard, & P. B. Read (eds.), *Depression in young people.* New York: Guilford.

Cicchetti, D., & Serafica, F. (1981). The interplay among behavioral systems: Illustrations from the study of attachment, affiliation, and wariness in young Down's syndrome children. In M. Lewis & L. A. Rosenblum (eds.), *The development of affect.* New York: Plenum.

Crittenden, P. M. (1983). Maltreated infants: Vulnerability and resilience. Paper presented at the biennial meeting of the Society for Research in Child Development, Detroit.

Crittenden, P. (1985). Maltreated infants: Vulnerability and Resilience. *Journal of Child Psychology and Psychiatry* 26, 85–96.

Crockenberg, S. B. (1981). Infant irritability, mother responsiveness, and social support influences on the security of mother-infant attachment. *Child Development* 52, 857–865.

Cummings, E. M. (1980). Caregiver stability and day care. *Developmental Psychology* 16, 31–37.

Cummings, E. M. (1987). Coping with background anger in early childhood. *Child Development* 58, 976–984.

Cummings, E. M.; Daniel, D. B.; & El-Sheikh, M. (1986). An organizational scheme for the classification of attachment on a secure/insecure/detached continuum. Paper presented at the Fifth Biennial International Conference on Infant Studies.

Dollard, J., & Miller, N. E. (1950). *Personality and psychotherapy.* New York: McGraw-Hill.

Egeland, B., & Farber, E. (1984). Infant-mother attachment: Factors related to its development and change over time. *Child Development* 55, 753–771.

Erickson, M. F.; Sroufe, L.; & Egeland, B. (1985). The relationship between quality of attachment and behavior problems in preschool in a high-risk sample. In I. Bretherton & E. Waters (eds.), *Growing points in attachment theory and research. Monographs of the Society for Research in Child Development* 50 (1–2, Serial No. 209), 147–166.

Freud, A. (1952). The mutual influence in the development of ego. *Psychoanalytic study of the child* 7, 42–50.

Freud, S. (1938). *An outline of psycho-analysis.* London: Hogarth.

Gewirtz, J. L. (1961). A learning analysis of the effects of normal stimulation, privation and deprivation on the acquisition of social motivation and attachment. In B. M. Foss (ed.), *Determinants of infant behaviour* (pp. 213–290). London: Methuen; New York: Wiley.

Greenberg, M. (1984). Working paper on the measurement of attachment during the preschool years: Report of the workshop on attachment in the transition period. Unpublished manuscript, University of Washington, Seattle.

Grossmann, K.; Grossmann, K. E.; Spangler, G.; Suess, G.; & Unzner, L. (1985). Maternal sensitivity and newborns' orientation responses as related to quality of attachment in Northern Germany. In I. Bretherton & E. Waters (eds.). *Growing points in attachment theory and research. Monographs of the Society for Research in Child Development* 50 (1–2, Serial No. 209), 233–256.

Harlow, H. F. (1958). The nature of love. *American Psychologist* 13, 673–685.

Klein, M., Heimann, P., Isaacs, S., & Riviere, J. (1952). *Developments in psycho-analysis.* London: Hogarth; Toronto: Clarke, Irwin.

Londerville, S., & Main, M. (1981). Security of attachment, compliance and maternal training methods in the second year of life. *Developmental Psychology* 17, 289–299.

Lorenz, K. ([1935] 1957). In Claire H. Schiller (ed.), *Instinctive behavior* (pp. 83–116). New York: International Universities Press.

Mahler, M. S. (1965). On early infantile psychosis. *Journal American Academy of Child Psychiatry* 4, 554–68.

Main, M. (1981). Avoidance in the service of attachment: A working paper. In K. Immelmann, G. Barlow, L. Petrinovich, & M. Main (eds.), *Behavioral development: The Bielefeld interdisciplinary project*. New York: Cambridge University Press.

Main, M. (1985). An adult attachment classification system. Paper presented at the biennial meeting of the Society for Research in Child Development, Toronto.

Main, M.; Kaplan, N.; & Cassidy, J. (1985). Security in infancy, childhood and adulthood: A move to the level of representation. In I. Bretherton & E. Waters (eds.). *Growing points in attachment theory and research. Monographs of the Society for Research in Child Development* 50 (1–2, Serial No. 209), 66–104.

Main, M., & Weston, D. (1981). The quality of the toddlers' relationship to mother and to father: Related to contact behavior and the readiness to establish new relationships. *Child Development* 52, 932–940.

Marvin, R. S. (1972). Attachment and cooperative behavior in two-, three-, and four-year-olds. Unpublished doctoral dissertation, University of Chicago.

Marvin, R. S. (1977). An ethological-cognitive model for the attenuation of mother-child attachment behavior. In T. M. Alloway, L. Krames, & P. Pliner (eds.), *Advances in the study of communication and affect: Vol. 3. The development of social attachments*. New York: Plenum.

Marvin, R. S., & Greenberg, M. T. (1982). Preschoolers' changing conceptions of their mothers: A social-cognitive study of mother-child attachment. In D. Forbes & M. T. Greenberg (eds.), *New directions in child development: Vol. 14. Developing plans for behavior* (pp. 47–60). San Francisco: Jossey-Bass.

Matas, L.; Arend, R. A.; & Sroufe, L. A. (1978). Continuity and adaptation in the second year: The relationship between quality of attachment and later competence. *Child Development* 49, 547–556.

Pastor, D. (1981). The quality of mother-infant attachment and its relationship to toddlers initial sociability with peers. *Developmental Psychology* 17, 326–335.

Petersen, C., & Seligman, E. (1984). Causal explanations as a risk factor for depression: Theory and evidence. *Psychological Review* 91, 347–374.

Radke-Yarrow, M.; Cummings, E. M.; Kuczynski, L.; & Chapman, M. (1985). Patterns of attachment in two- and three-year olds in normal families and families with parental depression. *Child Development* 56, 884–893.

Rutter, M., & Garmezy, N. (1983). Developmental psychopathology. In E. M. Hetherington (ed.), P. H. Mussen (series ed.), *Handbook of child psychology: Vol. 4. Socialization, personality, and social development* (pp. 775–911). New York: Wiley.

Schneider-Rosen, K.; Braunwald, K.; Carlson, V.; & Cicchetti, D. (1985). Current perspectives in attachment theory: Illustration from the study of maltreated infants. In I. Bretherton & E. Waters (eds.), *Growing points in attachment theory and research. Monographs of the Society for Research in Child Development* 50 (1–2, Serial No. 209), 194–210.

Schneider-Rosen, K., & Cicchetti, D. (1984). The relationships between affect and cognition in maltreated infants: Quality of attachment and the development of self recognition. *Child Development* 55, 648–658.

Spieker, S. J., & Booth, C. L. (1985). Family risk typologies and patterns of insecure attachment. In J. O. Osofsky (chair), *Intervention with infants at risk: Patterns of attachment*. Symposium conducted at the biennial meeting of the Society for Research on Child Development, Toronto.

Spitzer, R. L., & Endicott, J. (1977). *The schedule for affective disorders and schizophrenia: Lifetime version*. New York: Biometrics Research, New York State Psychiatric Institute.

Sroufe, L. A.; Fox, N. E.; & Pancake, V. R. (1983). Attachment and dependency in developmental perspective. *Child Development* 54, 1615–1627.

Sroufe, L. A., & Waters, E. (1977). Attachment as an organizational construct. *Child Development* 48, 1184–1199.

Sroufe, L. A., & Waters, E. (1977). Heart rate as a convergent measure in clinical and developmental research. *Merrill-Palmer Quarterly* 23, 3–27.

Stevens, S. S. (1951). *Handbook of experimental psychology*. New York: Wiley.

Tracy, R., & Ainsworth, M. D. S. (1981). Material affectionate behavior and infant mother-attachment patterns. *Child Development* 52, 1341–1343.

Valaik, M., & Cummings, E. M. (1986). A lifespan attachment interview. Unpublished manuscript, West Virginia University, Morgantown.

Waters, E. (1978). The reliability and stability of individual differences in infant-mother attachment. *Child Development* 49, 483–494.

Waters, E., & Deane, K. E. (1982). Infant-mother attachment: Theories, models, recent data, and some tasks for comparative developmental analysis. In L. W. Hoffman, R. Gandelman, & R. H. Schiffman (eds.), *Parenting: Its causes and consequences*. Hillsdale, N.J.: Erlbaum.

Waters, E.; Vaughn, B.; & Egeland, B. (1980). Individual differences in mother-infant relationships at age one: Antecedents in neonatal behavior in an urban, economically disadvantaged sample. *Child Development* 51, 208–216.

Winnicott, D. W. ([1948] 1958). Pediatrics and psychology. *British Journal of Medical Psychology* 21, 229–40. Reprinted in D. W. Winnicott, *Collected Papers*. London: Tavistock.

Zahn-Waxler, C.; Chapman, M.; & Cummings, E. M. (1984). Altruism, aggression, and social interactions in young children of manic-depressive parents. *Child Development* 55, 112–122.

11 · Toward a Transactional Model of Relations between Attachment and Depression

E. Mark Cummings and Dante Cicchetti

INTRODUCTION

ATTACHMENT THEORY has its origins in the study of clinical issues and the development of psychopathology (Bowlby 1944, 1958, 1977a, 1977b). After a period characterized by a focus upon the etiology, course, and sequelae of secure and insecure attachments in normal samples (Ainsworth, Blehar, Waters, & Wall 1978; Main, Kaplan, & Cassidy 1985; Sroufe, 1979a, 1979b, 1983), there is now a renewed research interest in the development of attachment relationships in "high-risk" youngsters (Bowlby, 1988; Crittenden, 1988; Schneider-Rosen, Braunwald, Carlson, & Cicchetti 1985; Sroufe & Fleeson 1986). In addition, a number of theoreticians and researchers have begun to apply the principles of attachment theory to clinical work with disturbed and "high-risk" mother-child dyads. The clinical implications of research on the basic processes involved in attachment have been recognized across the life span (Belsky & Nezworski 1988; Cicchetti & Toth 1987; Greenberg & Speltz 1988; Greenspan, Wieder, Lieberman, Nover, Lourie, & Robinson 1987; Guidano & Liotti 1983, Valaik & Cummings 1988).

This resurgent interest in the clinical implications of attachment theory interfaces with an exciting new approach to the study of the developmental origins and pathways of clinical disorder that has been termed developmental psychopathology (Cicchetti 1984; Sroufe & Rutter 1984). The core goals of this approach are to investigate the developmental trajectories of disorder in the context of the study of normal development and to examine and understand the dynamic processes underlying individual adaptation and maladaptation rather than to focus exclusively on between-group differences (Cicchetti, 1990; Cicchetti & Schneider-Rosen 1984; Sroufe & Rutter 1984). The promise of this work is a deeper, richer understanding of the etiology, develop-

Our collaborative work on this chapter was supported, in part, by a grant from the John D. and Catherine T. MacArthur Foundation. Both authors contributed equally to the writing of this chapter. We are grateful to Sheree Toth for her helpful comments and suggestions. Moreover, we profited immeasurably from our discussions with Jill Gentile. Finally, we also would like to thank Victoria Gill for typing this chapter.

mental progression and treatment of mental disorder than has been possible with traditional models for clinical study (Bowlby 1988; Cicchetti, Toth, & Bush 1988; Cicchetti, Toth, Bush, & Gillespie 1988; Cowan 1988; Nannis & Cowan 1988; Rutter 1986).

Developmental Considerations in the Epidemiology and Diagnosis of Depression

The identification of the processes through which depression develops is a compelling problem for theoreticians, researchers, and clinicians alike (Rutter, Izard, & Read 1986). Major depressive disorder is, according to some estimates, the most common serious mental health problem (see Eaton & Kessler 1985). For example, depressive symptoms have an approximate 15%–20% prevalence rate in the adult population (Boyd & Weissman 1982). Moreover, epidemiological estimates of the current and past prevalence rates of the major depressive disorders range from 5% to 15% for adults (Weissman & Boyd 1984). In addition, the incidence of unipolar depression is approximately 3% in the adult male population, with estimates in adult females ranging from 4% to 9% (Weissman & Boyd 1984). The major risk factors for unipolar illness include: (1) having a positive family history for depression or alcoholism; (2) having a generally hostile, disruptive, and negative home environment during childhood; (3) being a female between the ages of 35 and 45; (4) having experienced recent negative life events; (5) the absence of an intimate trusting relationship; and (6) having conceived a child within the preceding six months (Brown & Harris 1978; Nurnberger & Gershon 1984; Orvaschel, Weissman, & Kidd 1980; Paykel 1982; Radloff 1975; Weissman & Boyd 1984; Weissman & Klerman 1977; Winokur 1979). Finally, the risk morbidity estimates for bipolar disorder (i.e., manic depression) across sexes range from 0.6% to 0.88% in industrialized societies (Weissman & Boyd 1984).

Furthermore, estimated prevalence rates of 1%–9% for childhood major depressive disorders have been reported (Kashani, McGee, Clarkson, Anderson, Walton, Williams, Silva, Robins, Cytryn, & McKnew 1983). Weissman, Gammon, John, Merikangas, Warner, Prusoff, and Sholomskas (1987) have found that children of clinically depressed parents had an increased prevalence of major depressive disorder and substance abuse compared with children of normal parents. Children of depressed parents experienced poorer social functioning, increased psychiatric treatment, and more school problems than children of normal parents (Weissman et al. 1987). Moreover, the mean age of onset of major depression occurred significantly earlier in the children of depressed parents (mean age of onset, 12–13 years) than in the children of normal parents (mean age of onset, 16–17 years).

Finally, in recent years, researchers and clinicians alike have become increasingly interested in depression as a disorder that can be present during childhood. While consensus has begun to emerge regarding the presence of depression in childhood, skepticism remains as to the age of onset. Because strict adherence to DSM-III-R (American Psychiatric Association 1987) criteria may underestimate the incidence and prevalence rates of childhood affective disorders (Cicchetti & Schneider-Rosen 1986), some investigators have employed other nosological systems and have argued for the existence of depression during infancy and the preschool period.

Trad (1987), building on the early work of Spitz (1946) and Bowlby (1961), argues that infants can experience depression. While *symptoms* associated with depression can be manifested during infancy, the presence of a depressive disorder in infancy is difficult for most investigators to conceptualize. Although also controversial, the existence of depression in a preschool population has been explored. Kashani, Holcomb, and Orvaschel (1986) reported that preschool children can experience depression and that a sizable number of preschoolers, while not evidencing a diagnoseable depressive disorder, exhibit a significant number of depressive symptoms. According to teacher reports, preschoolers who had symptoms associated with depression also exhibited behavioral problems, including social withdrawal. Moreover, preschoolers evidencing depressive symptomatology had experienced more life stress than children not exhibiting depressive symptoms.

Most scholars in the field agree that childhood depression can be diagnosed as early as 5 or 6 years using DSM-III-R (American Psychiatric Association 1987) criteria (see Rutter et al. 1986). In fact, in an especially important study, Kovacs, Feinberg, Crouse-Novak, Paulauskas, Pollock, and Finkelstein (1984) have found that early age of onset of childhood depression predicted a more protracted depressive illness. If a link ultimately could be demonstrated to exist between potential early precursors of depression and later affective disorder, then there may loom great significance for prophylaxis in later generations.

Thus, on grounds of developmental issues and epidemiological risk, not to mention the cyclicity and the deleterious sequelae which often accompany mood disorders, a research focus on the depressive disorders and a broadening of the current theoretical approaches to their investigation is clearly warranted. Over the course of the past twenty-five years, researchers have examined the potential etiological role of a variety of biochemical, genetic, neuroendocrine, psychological, and psychosocial factors in the development of depression (Post & Ballenger 1984).

In contrast, very little methodologically sound and theoretically informed work exists on the role of parent-child attachment in the etiology of depressive disease. We believe that the use of attachment theory can provide a framework for conceptualizing the specific processes whereby poor quality parent-child relationships can place a child at high risk either for developing a depressive episode and/or for maintaining such episodes throughout various periods of the developmental life course.

GOALS OF THIS CHAPTER

In this chapter, we have two focal concerns, namely, (1) How might depressive symptomatology or depression in the mother contribute to the development of disturbed attachment relationships? (2) How might disturbed attachment relationships, in transaction with other factors, contribute to increased risk for depression, both in the offspring of depressed mothers and in non–high-risk samples of children?

Due to the state of the science, we marshal several forms of evidence and theory toward the goal of mapping a framework for conceptualizing the relationship between attachment and depression. Disturbances in attachment may play a role in the development, maintenance, and intergenerational transmission of depression. Several lines of evidence suggest these relationships. For example, negative self-concepts are associated with insecure parent-child attachments (Armsden & Greenberg 1987; Bretherton 1985) and depression (Beck 1976). In particular, a sense of loss and rejection is likely to characterize both insecure attachment and depression (Bowlby 1980). Conceivably, the negative internal working model of the self that develops in the context of an insecure parent-child attachment relationship could be a major contributor to the development of depressive cognitions and symptomatology. Furthermore, the quality of past and current attachments may figure significantly in the relation between social support and depression. The perceived quality and availability of social exchange, rather than the actual amount given, appears to be most important to the impact of social support on socioemotional functioning (Cohen & Willis 1985; Ingersoll-Dayton & Antonucci 1983). In addition, attachment, like depression, appears to be transmitted intergenerationally (Ricks 1985). An intriguing issue is whether insecure attachment and depression are associated with each other in families in which affective disorders are transmitted.

HISTORICAL PERSPECTIVE

Both theoretical and empirical work support the relevance of a consideration of attachment in the development of depression. The traditions of psychoanalytic and object relations theories have long argued for links between early disturbed parent-child relations and the development of depression (Abraham 1911; Arieti & Bemporad 1978; Bibring 1953; Bowlby 1980, 1988; Freud 1917; Jacobson 1971; Klein 1934, 1940; Mahler 1966; Mendelson 1974; Rado 1928, 1951; Sandler & Joffe 1965). Despite the lack of empirical evidence that has been generated by this work (see Bowlby 1988), one must be impressed by the repeated proposition of relations between problematic attachments and depression by astute clinicians who had considerable experience conducting analyses of depressed patients.

Many traditional psychoanalytic theorists have argued that depression occurs in individuals who cannot complete the "normal" grieving process following loss. Freud (1917) was perhaps the first theorist to underscore that mourning, regardless of whether it was adaptively or maladaptively handled, was a difficult process. Subsequently, several authors have extended Freud's views and have described the mourning process and its accompanying state of grief in detail (Bowlby 1961, 1980). Drawing from his clinical observations of childrens' and adults' responses to separation and loss, Bowlby (1961) delineated three phases of grief he believed characterized the process of mourning.

While others, most notably Parkes (1970), have elaborated upon Bowlby's viewpoint, all agree that not all persons successfully resolve the "normal" grieving process. Instead, as Freud (1917) originally pointed out, some individuals experience melancholia or pathological mourning. This state of melancholia possesses the same behavioral and psychodynamic features as mourning. However, in melancholia there is an accompanying decrease in self-esteem. In a compelling description of the distinction between mourning and melancholia, Freud (1917) stated that "in mourning it is the world which has become poor and empty; in melancholia, it is the ego itself" (p. 246).

An important question to address is, What accounts for the observed individual differences in negotiating and resolving the mourning process? Freud (1917) stated that a loss of self-regard was characteristic of melancholia but not of mourning. Following Freud, psychodynamically oriented theorists interested in the relation between loss and depression have likewise underscored the concomitant loss of a feeling of well-being in the clinically depressed state (Bibring 1953; Joffe & Sandler 1965; Rado 1928).

The theoretical position of Joffe and Sandler (1965) is most germane for our purposes. They proposed that what was really lost in depression was not the loved person per se but the sense of well-being implicit in the attachment or self-object relationship. Consequently, with object loss in melancholia, "attention is focused almost exclusively on the object because it is the key to the retainment of the lost sense of self" (p. 399). By contrast, in "normal" mourning, a sense of well-being is retained despite object loss. Stated differently and from an object relations perspective, in the course of normal mourning, the sense of well-being, implicit in the attachment relationship, has been internalized.

Attachment and object-relations theorists stress that the internalization of the positive attributes of significant people is integral to the development of positive self-esteem. Although the process of internalization continues throughout the life span, it is the quality of internal representations of self and other which develop during the early years of life that are most critical. These early attachment relationships set the stage for the development of healthy as opposed to fragile self-esteem and are subsequently associated with adaptation in the face of loss. Overall, then, the developmental approach utilized by attachment and object-relations theorists is helpful in conveying an understanding of resilience versus fragility following object loss. Because the contributions made by object-relations and attachment theorists are integral to establishing a framework for understanding the links between attachment and depression, their respective contributions will be considered below.

CONTRIBUTIONS FROM OBJECT RELATIONS THEORIES

While internal working models have reached ascendancy within attachment theory only recently, their psychoanalytic roots of self and object representations have been integral to object-relations theory since its inception (Fairbairn 1952; Guntrip 1961; Klein 1932). Broadly defined, object-relations theorists focus on the relationship between external people, the internal representations of these people, and their relevance for psychic functioning (Greenberg & Mitchell 1983). As with attachment theory (see Sroufe 1985), object-relations theories propose a relationship model to explain the impact that early interpersonal relations have on personality development (see Bretherton 1985, 1987).

The concept of internalization is central to object-relations theory (Meissner 1981; Schafer 1968). As with internal working models, the structural derivatives of internalization in the form of self and object representations are theorized to have cognitive and affective components and to be relatively enduring mental representations. Moreover, self and object representations are considered to be an extension of an attachment relationship (Giovacchini 1975). The modification of self and object representations as a function of experience is referred to as separation-individuation (Mahler, Pine, & Bergman 1975). In accord with this model, self and object representations are seen as evolving from a state of symbiosis in which the self and other are merged into a state of empathic relatedness in which the self is able to view the other as separate without fearing for its own integrity.

The process of separation-individuation culminates at approximately 3 years of age and coincides with the child's attainment of object constancy. At this time and if negotiated adequately, the "good enough mother" (Winnicott 1953) has been internalized, thereby enabling the child to function competently, even when the attachment figure is not physically present (Mahler et al. 1975). Accordingly, the losses associated with separation-individuation are minimized by the assimilation of caregiver functions into the self (Giovacchini 1975). The failure to incorporate positive caregiver functions into the self-representation results in vulnerability to future separation and loss experiences (Adler 1985; Horner 1984; Mahler et al. 1975).

CONTRIBUTIONS FROM ATTACHMENT THEORY

Bowlby ([1969] 1982) introduced and subsequently expanded upon the concept of internal working models of attachment figures and of the self and their role in personality development and psychological functioning (Bowlby 1973, 1980). Internal working models are mental representations constructed during childhood and based primarily upon early experiences with significant caregivers. These working models can be modified or "re-worked" during the course of ongoing interpersonal transactions. In addition to representational models of relationships, parallel but interactive models of the self are formed. Thus, with the experience of a caretaker as being reliably available and emotionally responsive, the child's construction of an accessible, responsive internal working model of the attachment figure, as well as a reciprocal representational model of the self as acceptable in the eyes of the attachment figure, is promoted. Such cognitive and emotional representations enable the child to experience the absence of this attachment figure relatively free of insecurity, anxiety, or distress (Bowlby 1973). It follows, then, that an individual's vulnerability or resilience to stress will vary as a function of the "felt security" afforded by his or her working models.

Relevant to the development of insecure internal working models, Bretherton (1985) contends that "if an attachment figure frequently rejects or ridicules the child's bids for comfort in stressful situations, the child may come to develop not only an internal working model of the parent as rejecting but also one of himself or herself as not worthy of comfort or help . . . similar ideas, but clothed in somewhat different terminology, have been proposed by a number of other investigators" (Bretherton 1985, p. 12).

Throughout Bowlby's writings, he focuses on separation and loss experiences (Bowlby [1969] 1982, 1973, 1980). According to Bowlby's formulations, children experience anxiety when separated from their primary attachment figure. In cases of prolonged or sustained loss, an intense mourning process ensues. When this mourning process continues beyond an expected period of time, Bowlby views it as a reflection of an unresolved loss. Without the presence of a reliable internal working model, any loss will be experienced as paramount. Conversely, positive early experiences result in good quality internal working models, and loss may not be a devastating experience. Accordingly, it is postulated that pathological mourning reflects a failure to internalize a positive attachment relationship (Bowlby 1980).

In terms of the development of internal working models, the psychological unavailability of parents for long periods can be seen as a powerful influence in shaping expectations that attachment figures are unavailable and that the self is unlovable. The implicit communication to the child is that the child is unworthy of love, that is, worthless and rejected, and that the parent is "lost" to the child. The recurrent loss of the parent as a function of major depressive episodes that some children experience may be equivalent in impact on the child's self-concept to the effects of recurrent major separations. This "loss" can also be seen as parallel to the perceptions of loss that precipitate depressive patterns (Beck 1976). Early experiences of "loss" may be particularly powerful because they mold fundamental cognitive/emotional/social response patterns. The psychological unavailability of parents, insecure attachment relationships between parent and child, and the child's development of depression or precursors of depression thus may be seen as interrelated processes.

CONSEQUENCES OF SEPARATION AND LOSS FOR ATTACHMENT RELATIONSHIPS

Because loss, whether actual or perceived, is integral to formulations of depression and attachment, this unifying concept merits attention. Children's separation from and loss of their parents have been linked repeatedly in research on the development of the affective disorders (Bowlby 1973, 1980). Both physical and psychological aspects of loss have been studied.

In the case of physical separation, the length of separation is associated with risk for later disturbance. Longer or more frequent separations predict greater risk. Moreover, the availability of adequate alternative attachment figures in the separation or loss setting appears to be associated with a decreased risk for later disturbances in children.

Studies of the effects of physical separation have more often focused on its role in inducing anxiety and anger in children than on its role in inducing depressive affect. Depressed affect, however, is frequently identified as a response to separation. For example, children typically follow a predictable sequence in response to brief separations (Bowlby, Robertson, & Rosenbluth 1952; Heinicke 1956). In the first stage children *protest* the departure of the parent by crying, active efforts at search, and other displays of anxiety. The second stage is marked by *despair*. In this phase of response to separation, children appear to be mourning the loss of the parent, appearing despondent, and often showing depressed affect. In the final *detachment* stage of response to separation, children appear to no longer mourn the absence of the parent. Indicative of the continuing strong impact of the experience on children, however, they will show anger and ambivalence toward the parent when reunification occurs. Depressed affect thus is a frequently observed response to separation from parents in young children.

In contrast to studies of physical separation, the focus of empirical work on parental loss through death has been on grief, mourning, and depression

(Crook & Eliot 1980). Depressed affect is a frequent concomitant of the mourning process. In addition, early loss of parents has been linked with greater risk for depression and suicide in adolescents and adults (Bowlby 1980). Loss through the death of a parent is more often associated with the development of depression than is loss through divorce or separation from parents (Bowlby 1980).

These findings thus make a case for relationships between disrupted early attachments and the later development of depression in some individuals. Persistent insecurity and overdependence are commonly observed outcomes of separation and loss. Bowlby has argued that the effects of these events on child development can be understood through their impact on the development of internal working models of the self and other. Three propositions are made regarding the role of experience in the development of internal working models of the world and the individual in the world: (1) ". . . when an individual is confident that an attachment figure will be available to him whenever he desires it, that person will be much less prone to either intense or chronic fear than will the individual that for any reason has no such confidence"; (2) ". . . confidence in the availability of attachment figures, or lack of it, is built . . . through the years . . .—infancy, childhood, and adolescence— and . . . whatever expectations are developed during those years tend to persist relatively unchanged throughout the rest of life"; (3) ". . . the varied expectations of the accessibility and responsiveness of attachment figures that different individuals develop during the years of immaturity are intolerably accurate reflections of the experiences those individuals have actually had" (Bowlby 1973, p. 202).

The impact of separation and loss on children can thus be understood, in part, in terms of the effects these experiences have on the children's expectations regarding the availability of attachment figures. Separation or loss violates these expectancies. When these experiences occur early in life, the notion that attachment figures will *not* be available when needed is likely to become a fundamental aspect of children's organization of personality, and to result in feelings and perceptions of insecurity that are resistant to change.

This research documents the effects of the physical unavailability of attachment figures on the development of children. From the perspective of attachment theory, however, the fact of physical absence may be less important than the psychological unavailability of the attachment figure to the child during periods of separation or loss. Thus, conditions that result in high levels of psychological unavailability, even when physical absence is not a factor, may produce similar outcomes in terms of increasing children's felt insecurity. One instance where this might occur is when parents have major and extended episodes of unipolar or bipolar depression. Relationships between psychological unavailability in child rearing and parental depression have not been directly and systematically examined; however, there is evidence concerning percentages of insecure and very insecure attachment in children of depressed parents which may bear indirectly on this issue.

Psychological Unavailability, Attachment, and Depression

Psychological unavailability has been linked with insecure attachment in prospective studies of parent-child attachment relationships and is a factor in physical separation and loss (Bowlby 1980; Egeland & Sroufe 1981). Depression in parents is likely to increase their psychological unavailability, at least during depressive episodes. There are thus compelling bases for considering psychological unavailability of the parent to be a risk factor for the development of insecure attachment in children of depressed parents.

Children of depressed parents are particularly likely to be faced with the psychological unavailability of parents for long periods, particularly during depressive episodes. Children of depressed parents are exposed to maternal sad affect, hopelessness and helplessness, irritability, confusions, and, in bipolar depression, to these episodes alternating with periods of euphoria and grandiosity. Although we do not know the effects on children of each of these patterns of behavior, to some degree a common theme during depressive episodes is likely to be that the mother is emotionally unresponsive as well as potentially physically unavailable.

A demonstration of the existence of higher rates of insecure attachment in children of depressed parents is critical if the argument that disturbed early attachments are a factor in the development of depression in children of depressed parents is to be supported. Several recent studies suggest that this is, in fact, the case. Radke-Yarrow, Cummings, Kuczynski, and Chapman (1985) compared patterns of attachment in children of unipolar and bipolar depressed parents with attachments in children of parents with minor depression or with no affective disorder. A higher proportion of insecure attachments was found in children of parents with major affective disorders (i.e., unipolar and bipolar depressive disease) than in children from the other groups. These findings suggest that the severity and extent of parental depression was a significant factor in outcomes. In addition, children of bipolar depressed parents were most likely to develop insecure attachments. In contrast, children of parents diagnosed with minor depression were no more likely than children in the control group to develop insecure attachment relationships. Specific measures of the mother's illness also predicted security of attachment. Insecure attachment was positively associated with how long the mother had been ill in the child's lifetime, the severity of her illness, and the extensiveness of her treatment history.

Children of parents with a major affective disorder are more likely than children from homes without parental affective disorder to be confronted with a highly deviant child-rearing environment. Thus, it might be presumed that, in addition to being at a greater risk for insecure attachment, children in this group would be likely to form *very* insecure attachments. In support of this hypothesis, Radke-Yarrow et al. (1985) observed A/C attachments in their study, but *only* in children of parents diagnosed for major unipolar or bipolar illness. These A/C attachments are marked by combinations of high avoidance and high resistance (see Crittenden 1988). This suggests that severity of depression is associated with greater risk for insecure and *very* insecure attachment.

Zahn-Waxler, Chapman, and Cummings (1984) also found evidence for relationships between bipolar depression in parents and the development of insecure attachments. In this study, the reunion responses of a sample of seven children of parents diagnosed for bipolar depression and a matched group of children from a nondisordered group of parents were compared following a brief separation. Children of parents with bipolar depression were more likely to show responses characteristic of insecurity, with six of seven doing so upon reunion.

Spieker and Booth (1988) report findings from a longitudinal study of children from families at high risk due to socioeconomic, environmental, and reproductive factors. These data provide further support for a link between depression in parents and the development of A/C or very insecure attachments. Spieker and Booth found that the A/C classification was associated with several indices of less than optimal rearing environments, including greater maternal reports of depression.

Evidence from research on maltreating families also is relevant to this issue. Egeland and Sroufe (1981) compared the effects of (*a*) psychological unavailability and depression, (*b*) physical abuse and hostility, and (*c*) neglect. One focus of their study addressed changes in attachment patterns between 12 and 18 months. The greatest increase in insecure attachment between 12 and 18 months was in the group characterized by maternal depression and psychological unavailability. At 18 months, 100% of the children of psychologically unavailable mothers were insecurely attached, with over three-fourths of these children classified as avoidant and the rest classified as resistant.

Carlson, Cicchetti, Barnett, and Braunwald (1989) found that over 80% of maltreated infants had disorganized/disoriented attachments with their primary caregivers. Of particular interest for our purposes, the mothers in the Carlson et al. protective service sample exhibited elevated levels of clinical depression (Gilbreath & Cicchetti, in preparation). Depression may have independently contributed to the development of disorganized attachment in at least some of the maltreated infants in this sample. Furthermore, the suggestion of possible links between depression and child maltreatment is not without support. In their sample, Poznanski and Zrull (1970) found that parents of depressed children were prone to abuse and neglect their children and were angry, punitive, detached, and belittling toward them. In addition, Puig-Antich and his colleagues (Puig-Antich, Blau, Marx, Greenhill, & Chambers 1978) found that nearly all of the families they investigated in which there was a depressed child were characterized by maladaptive parent-child relations. Several of the parents were cruel and physically abusive and/or violent toward their children. Finally, Kazdin, Moser, Colbus, and Bell (1985) reported an association between depression and physical abuse in a group of psychiatrically hospitalized children.

In summary, these findings suggest that parental histories of depression are associated with greater risk for insecure *and* very insecure attachments. Nonetheless, several issues should be considered in interpreting these data. Depression in parents does not always predict insecure attachment. Some children of parents with major affective disorders, including some children of parents with bipolar depression, have been reported to form secure attachments (Radke-Yarrow et al. 1985). In addition, the fact that children of depressed parents develop insecure attachments to parents does not mean that they will necessarily develop depression. Insecure attachment has been linked with aspects of concurrent and later functioning that are considered less than optimal (Crowell & Feldman 1988; Lewis, Feiring, McGuffog, & Jaskir 1984; Main et al. 1985; Sroufe 1983). Of relevance for our purposes, Zahn-Waxler, Mayfield, Radke-Yarrow, McKnew, Cytryn, and Davenport (1988) have reported on a four-year follow-up of the seven toddlers of the bipolar parents they had originally studied (Zahn-Waxler et al. 1984). These children, who as toddlers displayed insecure attachment responses to their caregivers upon reunion, were administered a child psychiatric interview and found to manifest internalizing problems, particularly depressive symptoms, that were corroborated by independent maternal report. In addition, their mothers described these children as showing antisocial behavior patterns.

Despite the compelling results from research conducted with "high risk" and normal youngsters, there is as yet no direct evidence of a relationship between insecure attachment and later depression. Insecure attachment can only be regarded as a risk factor for deviant outcomes, including depression, within the context of a complex developmental model (see our discussion below). It is critical to remember that there are a variety of familial mechanisms through which depression might be linked with insecure attachment and risk for depression. These include maternal attributions toward the child, child-rearing practices associated with the socialization of affect, and facial expression and body posture as aspects of the caregiver's emotion language (Cicchetti & Schneider-Rosen 1986; Cicchetti & White 1988; Cohn, Matias, Tronick, Connell, & Lyons-Ruth 1986; Cohn & Tronick 1983; Tronick & Field 1986). Identification of the connections between parental depression and insecure attachment is only a first step toward specifying the bases for such relations. If depression in parents is linked with insecure attachment, it may be because it shapes important elements of parent-child interaction or broader aspects of the child-rearing environment. An important aspect of this broader environment is likely to be the psychological unavailability of the parent during periods of depression.

COGNITIVE PROCESSES OF DEPRESSION AND
INTERNAL WORKING MODELS OF ATTACHMENT

The case for relationships between attachment and depression is increased if process links between the two domains can be demonstrated. That is, can it be shown that the cognitive and emotional sequelae of early insecure attachment relationships contribute to the later development of depression? The focal question is whether the internal working models of self and others and the generalized sense of felt security that are associated with insecure attachment relationships in infancy and early childhood (Bowlby [1969] 1982; Bretherton 1985, 1987) might be expected to be a developmental precursor of the pattern of expectations and cognitions that have been associated with depression.

According to Bowlby (1973), confidence in the availability of attachment figures rests upon two factors: (*a*) whether the attachment figure is evaluated to be the type of person that can be relied upon to respond when the child is in need; and (*b*) whether the child judges himself or herself to be the type of person the attachment figure, in particular, and others, in general, are likely to respond to in a supportive fashion. While these two factors are logically distinct, they often become confused in the individual's thinking. Thus, the representational model of the attachment figure and self develop in relation to each other and tend to confirm and complement each other. Consequently, in the case of insecure attachment, the rejection by the attachment figure may contribute to the development of low self-esteem and low self-image (see Bifulco, Brown, & Harris 1987; Schneider-Rosen & Cicchetti 1984).

Main et al. (1985) have contributed toward furthering conceptualizations of internal working models of attachment. One of their propositions is that some types of internal working models form in the first year of life. These are characterized as generalized event representations (Nelson & Gruendel 1981), reflecting the history of actions and action outcomes within the attachment relationship. Both events that occur in interaction with caregivers and events that occur in the caregiver's absence are seen as shaping these models. Major separations constitute one sort of event that may influence attachments even in the partner's absence. Main and her colleagues draw explicit parallels between the processes that influence attachment organizations and reorganizations in the partner's presence and absence. A unifying construct is the implication of events for the "emotional availability" of the attachment figure.

Main and her collaborators were the first to use multiple measures to characterize internal working models of attachment in early childhood (see Main & Solomon, this vol.). The results of their study provide strong evidence for the stability of organizations of internal working models across early childhood. Security of attachment to the mother at 1 year in the Strange Situation predicted security at 6 years as reflected in responses to parent-child reunion. Furthermore, 1-year ratings of security predicted fluency of discourse in the mother-child dyad, the child's overall functioning and emotional openness, the sophistication of the child's level of response given to the question concerning parent-child separations, and the child's responses to a family photograph. In addition, security of attachment to the father at 1 year was related to security of father-child attachment at 6 years.

In their follow-up study, Main et al. (1985) included twelve children who had been rated as disorganized/disoriented (type D) in their attachment to their mothers at 12 months of age. At the follow-up assessment, these children's reunion behavior with their mothers was characterized as controlling, either through punitiveness or through overly bright caregiving and role reversal. On other measures of mental representation of attachment, the children rated as disorganized/disoriented in infancy appeared "depressed, disorganized and intermittently irrational in thought processes" (Main et al. 1985, p. 99).

Also relevant to the contents of internal working models, Cassidy (1988) reported relationships between the security of attachment in 6-year-olds and individual differences in self-concept (see also Cassidy this vol.). Likewise, Kobak and Sceery (1988) found relationships between young adults' working models of attachment assessed with the Adult Attachment Interview (George, Kaplan, & Main 1985) and peer assessment of ego-resiliency, ego-undercontrol, hostility, and anxiety, as measured by the California Q-Sort method for assessing adult personality (Block & Block 1980). To provide one example of Kobak and Sceery's findings, adults classified as securely attached were rated as more ego-resilient, less anxious, and less hostile by their peers as compared to groups of insecurely attached adults.

Furthermore, insecurely attached maltreated children have been found to show parallel impairments in the development of their "self-system." Most notably, these youngsters talk less about themselves, their ongoing activities, and their own and others' internal states (Cicchetti & Beeghly 1987; Coster, Gersten, Beeghly, & Cicchetti 1989), as well as show less advanced communicative functioning (Coster et al. 1989).

In summary, while relatively little is known about the specific contents of internal working models of insecure attachments, there are bases for contending that they reflect low self-esteem and uncertain expectations regarding the individual's status and worth to others. In addition, these concepts of self and other would appear to develop early and to be resistant to change.

Exploration of the contents of internal working models is too rudimentary at present to allow systematic comparisons with adult cognitive patterns of depression. However, the evidence to date points in the direction of functional similarities between these domains. For example, Beck (1976) has identified a sense of *loss* as the focal element in depressive patterns: ". . . the sense of loss pervades the person's view of himself, his world, his future, and leads to other phenomenon of depression" (p. 128). Closely related to this sense of loss is low self-esteem and self-image. "The depressed person shows specific distortions. He has a negative view of his world, a negative concept of himself, and a negative appraisal of his future" (pp. 105–106). Certainly, in broad outline, this characterization of depression bears similarities to issues and processes associated with insecure attachment.

An impressive literature has developed around the specification of the particular contents of depressive cognitions. While the attachment literature has only begun to explore the contents of internal working models of attachment, this work provides potentially fruitful bases for further research on internal working models of attachment and their possible links with depressive thought patterns and processes. A variety of distorted thought processes have been found to characterize depression, including negative causal explanatory styles, feelings of worthlessness, self-reproach, and excessive or inappropriate guilt (Peterson & Seligman 1984; Seligman, Castellon, Cacciola, Schulman, Luborsky, Ollove, & Downing 1988). Research aimed at identifying these specific thought processes in insecurely attached children would further advance our understanding of the relationship between insecure attachment and depression.

The functional similarities of these processes, at a global level, make a logical case for insecure attachments as a precursor of depression. However, it is important to emphasize that insecure internal working models not only have cognitive contents, but also have affective and motivational-behavioral components (Cassidy, this vol.). Similarly, depression also clearly has emotional, motivational, and behavioral implications for the individual. A full investigation of this issue thus requires consideration of each of these domains of functioning (see Cicchetti & Schneider-Rosen 1986 for an elaboration of these issues).

A rearing environment that contains these elements, that is, a home in which one or both parents are depressed, is an obvious context for transmitting these processes. In other words, the characteristics of these environments may simultaneously foster both negative working models of the world associated with insecure attachment and depressive affective/cognitive/behavioral tendencies. In fact, one model of the developmental psychopathology of depression might be that insecure attachment and depression are not separate developments, but are related occurrences that first become evident at different stages in the child's life. Thus, insecure attachment might be observed initially in infancy and may be related to an increased risk of becoming depressed in the future.

Multiple mechanisms may be implicated in the transmission of depression from parent to child. One mode may relate to the interactional history between child and parent pertaining to issues of felt security. As we have noted, during depressive episodes, the affected parent, and conceivably both parents (Coyne 1976; Tronick & Field 1986), may be unavailable to the child for long periods of time. However, other factors also may be important. These may be correlated or operate independently of security-relevant issues. For example, parents' cognitive/affective styles may be communicated directly to children within the childrearing environment (Hesse & Cicchetti 1982). One method of transmission might be the parent's patterns of attribution in interaction with the child.

For example, the parent may frequently cause the child to experience inadequacy as a result of the attributions conveyed toward the child. Recently, Radke-Yarrow, Belmont, Nottelman, and Bottomly (in press) selected affectively disordered mothers (thirteen unipolar, four bipolar) and control group mothers (no psychiatric disorder) in order to explore mother-child discourse. Although this study revealed that depressed mothers were similar to nondepressed mothers in the quantity and content of attributions, depressed mothers conveyed significantly more negatively toned affect in their attributions. This occurred most often with respect to negative attributions about their children's emotions. In addition, depressed mother-child dyads evidenced a higher correspondence of affective tone of attributions and of self-reference than did control group dyads. Radke-Yarrow and her colleagues interpreted these results as suggestive of a heightened vulnerability to maternal attributions in the offspring of depressed parents. The potential for increases in negative self-attributions for these children and the impact of this for the development of a depressive disorder is noteworthy.

To provide a final example, another possible mechanism for transmission of cognitive/affective contents is modeling. Parents' depressive verbalizations, emotions, or behaviors may directly teach the children to engage in these patterns (Cicchetti & White 1988). Children thus may learn to adopt insecure working models of the world and depressive affects and cognitions through a complex matrix of related and independent mechanisms.

A Framework: The Transactional Model

In order to better conceptualize the complex relationships that exist between attachment and depression, we advocate the utilization of a transactional developmental perspective. As we have described, factors other than genetics, biochemistry, and neurobiology are involved in the etiology of depression. Parent-child attachment relationships are but one of a variety of nonbiological factors involved in the etiology, maintenance, and/or expression of depressive disease. There are many pathways to the development and perpetuation of a depressive disorder (the principle of *equifinality;* see Wilden 1980). Furthermore, the particular vulnerability factors and challengers may vary in significance over time, as well as in relative importance with regard to the operation of alternative permissive or efficient causes of depression (Cicchetti & Schneider-Rosen 1986). In order to examine these multiple pathways to depressive disease, it is useful to employ a transactional model.

Prior to the 1970s, developmental models were primarily "linear/main-effects" or "early experience" conceptualizations (Reese & Overton 1970). According to early experience models, later developmental outcomes are determined almost exclusively by a childhood experience that lies dormant before manifesting itself through maladaptation and/or psychopathology. Although the main-effects model does not limit the emergence of psychopathology or maladaptation to childhood experiences, it is similar in that it posits psychopathology as the direct and inevitable result of a pathogenic process or experience that exerts an effect on the course of development. For the majority of current research, these models are far too simplistic.

Both of these models are deficient for several reasons. First, they posit a cause-and-effect determinism that is not supported by either clinical experience or research to date. Second, they disregard the individual's initiative in responding to a supposedly pathology-inducing agent. Third, these models are insufficient to explain variations in the duration of determinants preceding the occurrence of psychopathology or the role of subsequent factors in determining type, severity, and course of psychopathology. Finally, a focus on the identification of the role of early experience in determining psychopathology minimizes the importance of intervening experiences that occur throughout the life span. These developmental experiences may either mediate against potentially negative influences, or may result in new vulnerabilities which increase the probability of the emergence of a psychopathological condition.

In the past two decades, researchers, theoreticians, and clinicians have begun to conceive of children's developmental outcomes as having multiple causal determinants rather than positing single-factor etiologies (see Engel 1977). The outgrowth of this thinking is conceptualized in the transactional model, which was described by Sameroff and Chandler (1975) in the mid-seventies. The transactional model viewed the multiple transactions among environmental forces, caregiver characteristics, and child characteristics as dynamic reciprocal contributions to the course of child development.

According to the transactional model, the parent, child, and environment exert reciprocal influences among components. Moreover, if deviant development is manifested over time, it is assumed that the child has been involved in an ongoing maladaptive process. Whether or not the maladaptation continues depends upon the status of the environment, in conjunction with the child characteristics, which reciprocally determine and are determined by the nature of the environment. In contrast, when discontinuities between early and later adaptation are present, reorganizations in the parent-child-environment system are thought to have occurred.

The application of a transactional model of development to the relationship of attachment processes and depression across the life span requires that one consider the specific potentiating and compensatory factors associated with their cooccurrence.

CONSIDERATION OF TRANSACTIONAL MODELS FOR DEPRESSION: THE PLACE OF ATTACHMENT

A critical element for future research on the relations between attachment and depression is the formulation of an adequate model or framework for conceptualizing research issues. As Brown and Harris (1978) and Cicchetti and Schneider-Rosen (1986) have argued, much confusion and lack of progress in the depression literature can be attributed to reliance on inadequate models.

Several models of the relation between attachment and depression can be rejected on grounds of strong empirical evidence. For example, because insecure attachment, in and of itself, does not cause depression, a main-effects model can be refuted. Similarly, early experience models provide insufficient causal explanations because early attachment experiences, no matter how severe (e.g., loss of parents), do not, in themselves, predict depression (Bowlby 1988; Brown & Harris 1978; Brown, Harris, & Bifulco 1986).

We think that the most useful model is one that places attachment in the context of a large array of biological and experiential factors that affect risk for depression. The application of a transactional model of development to the etiology of depression requires attention to the specific risk factors associated with the disorder (see Cicchetti & Aber 1986). A scheme for characterizing the processes whereby an insecure attachment may eventuate in depression must integrate the multiple factors that have been implicated in the etiology of depression (see table 1). Of course, while we are focusing specifically on those risk factors associated with depression, this model could be modified to address factors associated with the links between attachment and other disorders (Cicchetti, in press).

In the current model, factors may be seen to comprise a vulnerability to depression as opposed to resilience to depressive disorder in those infants, children, and adults who possess the risk factors for depression. Following Cicchetti and Aber's (1986) formulation, each outcome may be understood in relation to those enduring or transient influences that either increase or decrease the likelihood of the occurrence of a depressive episode. Cicchetti and Rizley's (1981) transactional model of child maltreatment can be extended to explain the relationship between attachment and depression. The factors associated with depression or resilience to depressive disorder can be broadly classified into two categories: potentiating factors increase the probability of an insecure attachment leading to depression, while compensatory factors decrease the likelihood of the emergence of a depressive episode. Transient factors refer to those influences that lack stability and are of a relatively brief duration, whereas enduring factors represent more permanent attributes or conditions. Both potentiating and compensatory factors may exert either an enduring or transient influence on the likelihood of a depressive disturbance emerging. Within this transactional model of risk factors, vulnerability factors include those relatively enduring characteristics of the child, caregiver, and social environment. Challengers represent more transient factors that could precipitate a depressive episode.

Both the enduring influence of protective factors and the transient effect of buffers comprise compensatory factors that increase resilience, even when risk factors for a depressive disorder are present. Protective factors represent conditions that may be biological, psychological, or sociological/cultural. Buffers, while relatively transient, may serve a protective function during periods of unanticipated stress (see Cohen & Willis 1985). Examples of vulnerability factors, challengers, protective factors, and buffers are presented in table 1. Because for every potentiating factor, there may be a corresponding compensatory factor, those opposites considered to be of particular importance also are included in table 1.

The relevance of development to this transactional model must be kept in mind. For enduring factors, whether vulnerability or protective, specific developmental changes may be necessary before they are activated. For example, the ability to conceptualize multiple emotions, a protective factor, is possible only with cognitive growth. Likewise, transient factors are age-specific in that what constitutes a challenger or buffer will vary with development. A coordination among compensatory and protective factors also is likely. For example, with the emergence of concrete operational thought, the child can make causal attributions to and about the self (vulnerability factor) but at this time also can conceptualize multiple emotions (compensatory factor).

In addition to recognizing the role of development, the action of these factors also can differ. Some are mechanism-specific, while others operate in a general fashion. A factor is mechanism-specific if it potentiates or compensates by playing a role in a proposed mechanism of childhood or adult depression, whereas its action is general if it can potentiate or compensate in a variety of ways in a variety of circumstances. For example, the loss of an ambivalently loved object is mechanism-specific, since it is a challenger according to the psychoanalytic theory of depression, whereas low socioeconomic status and nutritional deficiency would operate in a general manner.

When attempting to understand the utility of this model for the occurrence of depression, it is important to examine all categories of risk factors and their transactions over time. Although there are multiple precipitants of child and adult depression, a vulnerable parent, a vulnerable child, environ-

TABLE 1.   A TRANSACTIONAL MODEL OF EARLY RISK FACTORS
ASSOCIATED WITH LATER DEPRESSION POTENTIATORS

Potentiators	*Compensators*
Enduring	

Potentiators	Compensators

Vulnerability factors:
1. Individual
  Unsuccessful resolution of stage-salient developmental tasks (e.g., insecure attachment)
  Psychologically unavailable caregivers
  Structuralized negative schemata of self
  Nutritional deficiency
  Excessive seriousness, whiney, clingy
  Failure to individuate
  Repeated experiences of noncontingency between action and outcome that result in learned helplessness
  Diminished number of biogenic amines
  Depressive genotype
  Offspring of parent(s) with an affective disorder
  Hypersensitivity to frustration
  Moodiness
  Poor self-control
  Dependency (excessive)
  Absence of affectionate care
  Negative "internal working models" of attachment figures and of the self
  Presence of additional psychiatric disorder(s) (e.g., co-morbid personality disorder)
	Protective factors:
	1. Individual
	  Resiliency to stress
	  Prior experience with stressful events
	  Ability to utilize aggression adaptively
	  Successful resolution of stage-salient developmental tasks (e.g., secure attachment)
	  Emotionally available caregivers
	  Good physical health/resistance to illness
	  Normal biochemistry
	  High hedonic capacity
	  Good temperament
	  High threshold for frustration
	  History of affectionate care
	  Positive "internal working models" of attachment figures and of the self
	  High-derived felt-security
	  Absence of other psychiatric disorder(s)

2. Familial
  Early separation
  Early loss
  Pathological, gloomy, depressed parents
  Manipulative syndrome in parents
  Early spoiling followed by later rejection
  Rejection and depreciation by parents
  Ambivalent, avoidant, or disorganized/disoriented attachment
  Presence of several young children in the home, lack of full-time or part-time employment, absence of a confidant or partner, and loss of mother by separation or death before the age of 11
  Parental alcoholism
  Parental psychopathology
	2. Familial
	  Secure attachment bonds to parents
	  History of good parenting and socialization
	  Sibling attachments
	  Absence of parental psychopathology

3. Social
  Self-esteem based upon others' evaluation
  Poor social support networks
  Poor peer relations.
	3. Social
	  Good peer relations
	  Availability of social support network
	  Good quality care outside the home

4. Environmental
  No extended family
  Unhappiness with neighborhood
	4. Environmental
	  Availability of community resources
	  Availability of economic resources

TABLE 1 (*continued*)

Potentiators	Compensators
Enduring	

Vulnerability factors:
  Early deprivation
  Noncontingent negative reinforcement
  Marital discord
	Protective factors:
	  Good marriage
	  Help from extended family
	  Satisfaction with neighborhood

Transient	

Challengers
1. Individual
  Stress induced changes in
    neurochemistry
  Ineffective coping style
  Physical illness
2. Familial
  Acute mental or physical health prob-
    lems or addictions in parents
  Loss of ambivalently loved object
  Bereavement
  Separations associated with father's or
    mother's job; pregnancy of mother
3. Social
  Stress specific to negative schemata
  Situation specific to earlier noncon-
    tingent reinforcement
  Lack of social supports
 	
4. Environmental
  Situation specific to earlier noncon-
    tingent reinforcement
  Home or day-care changing
	Buffers
	1. Individual
	  Effective coping style
	  Responsive to others (interactive style
	    effective with others)
	
	2. Familial
	  Parents responsive to other and child
	  Parents available
	  Sibling or extended family available and
	    responsive
	
	3. Social
	  Relations with peers and others
	    supportive
	  Presence of social supports within and
	    outside the family
	  Day care caregivers provide security
	4. Environmental
	  Pleasurable activities
	  Absence of discord in home
	  Predictable daily routine

mental challenge, and a relative absence of compensatory protective factors and buffers may occur in any combination. Cicchetti and Aber (1986) argue that depression is expressed only when potentiating factors override compensatory ones and some theoretical threshold is crossed. Anything that reduces vulnerability or stress, or increases buffers or protective factors, should decrease the probability of a depressive episode.

This model represents a framework within which to conceptualize the probability of developing a depressive episode as manifested at any specific point in time. Implicit in the model is the assumption that the presence or absence of a depressive episode represents a multiplicity of factors that need to be considered in combination with one another in order to account for and adequately *explain* the processes whereby a specific depressive outcome has been achieved.

These principles logically lead to predictions regarding the role of attachment and internal working models in the development of depression. As we have argued, linear "main effects" models cannot account for the complexity involved in the development of a depressive disorder. Within this conceptualization, then, attachments are best conceived as important contributors to risk or protection from depression across the life span because of their role in the individual's feelings of security, self-esteem, and perception of social support (Cohen & Wills 1985; Parker & Barnett 1988). In this regard, attachment relations have both a historical and an ongoing significance. Historically, the quality of the child's attachments to parents in early childhood is likely to have had a fundamental impact on the formation of secure versus insecure internal representations of the world. On the other hand, subsequent secure attachments, including the individual's current network of attachments, may alter or modify these models and, in addition, play an important role in buffering the individual from stress that might otherwise precipitate depression (Armsden & Greenberg 1987; Antonucci 1985; Cohen & Willis 1985).

Insecure early attachment relationships may render children more vulnerable to depression by leaving them with very low internalized feelings of felt security. When faced with stress, such children are likely to have few resources for coping and may easily be susceptible to diminished self-esteem, heightened feelings of insecurity, and depressed affect. Second, the content of the cognitions that the insecurely attached individual develops in the context of attachment relationships may facilitate the development of depressive cognitions and affect. As we have stated, these cognitions, which center around loss and the unacceptability of the self, are likely to resemble patterns of cognitive processes that have been linked with depression in adults (Beck 1976).

Even though an early secure attachment relationship with the primary attachment figure increases the probability of maintaining a positive working model of the self and of attachment relations, an insecure attachment can manifest itself at any point across the life span. Accordingly, adherence to a life-span model necessitates that the specifics of the relationship between attachment and depression may change greatly with age. For example, an insecure attachment at one period of development may have very different consequences for depression from that at another developmental period. The resulting causal network will be very complex. Early insecure attachment will have a variety of effects, some of which will tend to perpetuate insecure attachment, while others may potentiate later secure attachment. A depressive episode, when it occurs, may lead to insecure attachment, and this in turn may result in a variety of effects, some perhaps maintaining the depression, others predisposing for future maladaptation, and still others leading to adaptation which may buffer against the experience of subsequent depressive episodes. A sketch of these causal interdependencies is presented in figure 1. This illustrates the complex feedback relationships that we might expect to obtain. Of course, it should be mentioned that insecure attachment and depression will have sequelae dependent upon the ontogenesis of those neurophysiological and biochemical systems that serve as the biological bases of depression.

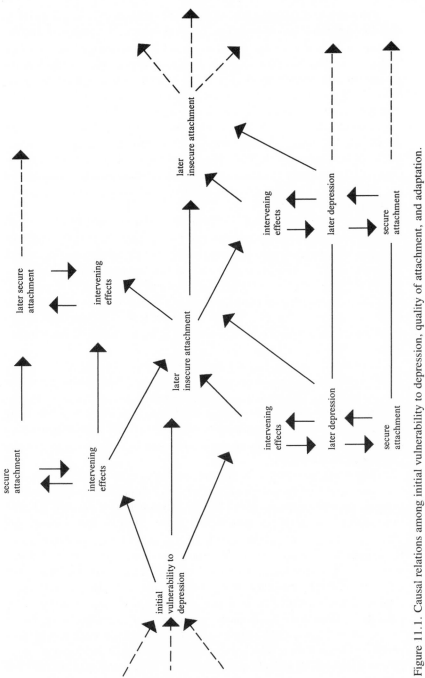

Figure 11.1. Causal relations among initial vulnerability to depression, quality of attachment, and adaptation.

The work of Brown and his colleagues provides an excellent illustration of a life-span transactional model of the relation between attachment and depression in these women. In 1978, Brown and Harris reported that childhood loss of the mother had no association with adult depression in women in the absence of a provoking agent. The risk for depression increased threefold, however, if the childhood loss was combined with threatening life events, long-term problems, or problematic current personal relationships.

According to Brown, Harris, and Bifulco (1986), a serious lack of affectionate care was the key variable which caused maternal loss to create a vulnerability to depression. In fact, this conspicuous lack of affectionate care predicted later depression even in the absence of maternal loss. Important for our purposes, loss per se showed no relation with depression in the presence of affectionate care.

Harris, Brown, and Bifulco (1987) reported that when family circumstances were problematic before maternal loss and there was inadequate care after the loss, women were far more vulnerable to developing depression. These investigators also found that women who had experienced inadequate care were twice as likely to develop a negative self-image as were women who had received adequate care (Bifulco et al. 1987). This evidence is compatible with the hypothesis that the vulnerability factor lack of parental care brings about a cognitive set of helplessness and low self-esteem (see Abramson, Seligman, & Teasdale 1978).

In summary, the data of Brown and his collaborators suggest that attachment-related experience is most relevant to the class of vulnerability-protective factors; however, these experiences may operate at any level of the transactional model. For example, loss of an attachment figure may be a provoking agent, and individual coping strategies may evolve based upon experience in attachment relationships. Past or present attachments could serve as vulnerability or protective factors.

Corroborating evidence for the link between childhood attachment relations and vulnerability to depression is provided through research examining the retrospective recollections that depressed adults have about their relationships with their parents. In the tradition of both object relations theory and attachment theory, these researchers have underscored the importance parental representations might play in the etiology of depression. Though differing with respect to methodology and to the nature of the depressed samples studied, there is much unanimity among these results. For example, Parker has conducted a series of studies employing a wide range of subjects ranging from psychiatric outpatients to adoptees in the general population (see Parker 1979a, 1979b, 1981, 1983). The results of this important work provide supportive evidence for a relationship between low-maternal and parental-caring behavior (e.g., "Did not help me as much as I needed"), high-maternal overprotection (e.g., "Did not want me to grow up"), and depression in adults.

Raskin, Boothe, Reatig, Schulterbrandt, and Odel (1971), in a study of psychiatric inpatients, likewise found that depressed patients recalled their parents as being less positively involved and more likely to employ negative/punitive child-rearing strategies than did normal adults. However, depressed inpatients perceived their mothers to be overpermissive and not overprotective as Parker reported in his work with samples of outpatient and nonpatient populations.

To provide a final example, Crook, Raskin, and Eliot (1981) discovered themes of maternal and paternal rejection in the recollections of early parent-child relationships in a group of depressed outpatients. Most notably here, these depressed adults recalled that they had received more negative evaluations from their parents and had experienced more withdrawal of parental affection than had normal adults.

An additional thread of evidence linking caregiving with the development of depression is provided through research on expressed emotion. Attachment researchers and theoreticians have emphasized that the key concept of attachment is the emotional commitment made to another important person (or persons). We believe that the limits of a purely cognitive control systems model of attachment (see Engel 1971) are highlighted even more in the study of psychopathology (Cicchetti & White 1988). Recent research in experimental psychopathology on the relationship between intrafamilial expressed emotion in schizophrenic and affectively disordered patients and later functioning provides suggestive confirmation of the predictive power of affective constructs in relationship consolidation and dissolution.

Investigations in the area of expressed emotion were pioneered in England by Brown, Monck, Carstairs, and Wing (1962). These researchers rated the levels of criticism, hostility, and dominance of relatives of schizophrenic patients based on an interview administered to family members. The schizophrenic patients with a relative who received a high rating of expressed emotion were found to have a higher relapse rate over a one-year follow-up period than schizophrenic patients whose relatives received a low rating of expressed emotion.

Current research utilizes the Camberwell Family Interview (CFI) (Brown & Rutter 1966; Rutter & Brown 1966) in which the patient's primary relative (generally a spouse or parent) is asked about the patient's illness and its impact upon the household. While the ostensible reason for the interview is to obtain information about the patient, in actuality the primary purpose is to assess the feelings expressed by the relative toward the patient. Recent research has applied the expressed emotion paradigm to the study of depressive and manic-depressive disease. Hooley, Orley, and Teasdale (1986) found that unipolar depressed patients, who lived with a spouse who employed critical expressed emotion comments about them, had a 59% relapse rate for depression within a year. In contrast, depressives living with an emotionally supportive, noncritical spouse evinced a 0% relapse rate.

Miklowitz, Goldstein, Neuchterlein, Snyder, and Mintz (1988) collected measures of expressed emotion and affective style of interactional behaviors from key relatives of twenty-three hospitalized recently manic bipolar patients. The manic-depressive patients subsequently were followed up for a period of nine months after being discharged from the hospital. As has been found to be the case for schizophrenia (Vaughn & Leff 1976), conjoint levels of intrafamilial expressed emotions and interactional affective style predicted the likelihood of patient relapse at follow-up. In fact, bipolar patients from families characterized as low on both expressed emotion and affective style of interaction had a very low relapse rate (17%). Conversely, patients from families rated high on either factor had an extremely high recurrence of their illness (94%). In addition, levels of affective style of interaction predicted degree of social adjustment at follow-up. It is most interesting that the relationships obtained were independent of patient lithium carbonate compliance, baseline symptoms, treatment regimen, demographics, and illness history. These results suggest that the emotional climate of the family during the post-discharge period may be an extremely significant predictor of the clinical course of bipolar disease.

The findings of Miklowitz and colleagues concerning the relationship between intrafamilial affective style of interaction and social adjustment are congruent with those of another group of investigators. Merikangas, Bromet, and Spiker (1983) found that hospitalized patients with an affective disorder who were married to individuals who were themselves psychiatrically disordered were significantly less likely to function well at longitudinal follow-up than were in-patients who were married to spouses without psychiatric illnesses.

A final line of evidence relating parent-child relations and depression is discussed by Puig-Antich, Lukens, Davies, Goetz, Brennon-Quattrock, and Todak (1985a). They discovered that clinically depressed children and their mothers had less affectionate relationships and poorer communication than did groups of normal and nondepressed psychiatric controls and their mothers. In a subsequent paper, the same group of authors (Puig-Antich et al. 1985b) provided data on a follow-up study of those children who had maintained a depression-free state for four months. The investigators found that relations with both parents were significantly associated with the child's recovery. Specifically, the quantity and the quality of mother-child relations improved, and there was less apparent maternal hostility than was the case during the childrens' depressed periods. Unfortunately, Puig-Antich and colleagues (1985b) did not provide information about the parent-child relationships of the depressed children who had not recovered, nor about any possible changes that may have occurred in the parent-child relationships of the control groups. However, despite these limitations, the results of this study suggest that the quality of the parent-child relationship in clinically depressed children can be changed. In other words, it is possible that, regardless of the direction of effects (i.e., Does an improvement in clinical state bring about improved parent-child relations, or does improving the quality of the parent-child relationship result in an improvement in clinical condition, or, as we suspect, is it a transactional process?), the representational models of attachment relations may have been changed in both the parents and children.

CONCLUSION

In this chapter, we have sketched out pathways whereby insecure and secure attachment relationships could either contribute to, maintain, and/or protect against the emergence of a clinical depression. Guided by the contributions and tenets of object relations and attachment theory, we have demonstrated how the quality of parent-child attachment can either eventuate in depression or act as a buffer promoting resilience to the disorder. We have conceptualized our discussion of this process within a transactional model of potentiating and compensatory factors.

To date, the empirical work conducted on the relationship between attachment and depression has stemmed primarily from studies of the young offspring of depressive and manic-depressive parents. Although not all of the offspring of such mood-disordered parents develop insecure attachment relationships, nonetheless they are an especially "high-risk" group. The actual percentage of these children who develop depressive disorders has yet to be demonstrated. Furthermore, a major area awaiting empirical confirmation is the hypothesized links between quality of attachment and the development of depression in normal and non "high-risk" populations.

Our present knowledge base provides several reasons to believe this work will result in promising yields. Retrospective research on the internal working models of depressed parents and on recollections of the quality of care depressed women received in their childhood both provide suggestive transactional links between problematic parent-child relations and the development of depression. Moreover, studies of depressed children interacting with their mothers and follow-up investigations of the affectional style of the relatives and spouses of mood disordered patients likewise implicate the role quality of parent-child and spouse-spouse interaction may have on the emergence of an affective disorder.

Conversely, the presence of childhood and adult mood disorders may clearly contribute to the maintenance of the disorder and/or exacerbate its duration and/or intensity. For example, depression in a child or in an adult could exert a negative impact on the parent-child and spouse-spouse relationship (Cicchetti & Schneider-Rosen 1986; Coyne 1976; Coyne, Burchill, & Stiles, in press; Lewinsohn 1974).

Given the multiplicity of pathways whereby depression can occur, we believe that future research should focus on uncovering the processes and mechanisms linking insecure and secure attachment relationships to depression across the life span. We believe that the model of relations between attachment and depression that we have described can serve as a valuable base for future research. Now that investigators are developing procedures for assessing attachment relationships beyond infancy (George et al. 1985; Greenberg, Cicchetti, & Cummings, this vol.; Valaik & Cummings 1988), prospective studies of the interrelations among attachment, "the self-system," and the psychobiological and biochemical factors associated with depression can be conducted.

REFERENCES

Abraham, K. (1911). Notes on the psychoanalytical investigation and treatment of manic-depressive insanity and allied conditions. Reprinted in K. Abraham (ed.), *Selected papers* (pp. 137–156). London: Hogarth.

Abramson, L. Y.; Seligman, M.; & Teasdale, J. (1978). Learned helplessness in humans: Critique and reformulation. *Journal of Abnormal Psychology* 87, 32–48.

Adler, G. (1985). *Borderline psychopathology and its treatment*. New York: Jason Aronson.

Ainsworth, M. D. S.; Blehar, M. C.; Waters, E.; & Wall, S. (1978). *Patterns of attachment: A psychological study of the strange situation*. Hillsdale, N.J.: Erlbaum.

American Psychiatric Association Committee on Nomenclature (1987). *Diagnostic and statistical manual of mental disorders, III-R*. Washington, D.C.: American Psychiatric Association.

Antonucci, T. (1985). Social support: Theoretical advances, recent findings and pressing issues. In I. Sarason & B. Sarason (eds.), *Social support: Theory, research, and application* (pp. 21–37). The Hague: Martinns Nijhof.

Arieti, S., & Bemporad, J. (1978). *Severe and mild depression*. New York: Basic Books.

Armsden, G., & Greenberg, M. (1987). The inventory of parent and peer attachment: Individual differences and their relationship to psychological well-being in adolescence. *Journal of Youth and Adolescence* 16, 427–454.

Beck, A. (1976). *Cognitive therapy and the emotional disorders*. New York: International Universities Press.

Belsky, J., & Nezworski, T. (eds.), (1988). *Clinical implications of attachment*. Hillsdale, N.J.: Erlbaum.

Bibring, E. (1953). The mechanism of depression. In P. Greenacre (ed.), *Affective disorders: Psychoanalytic contributions to their study*. New York: International Universities Press.

Bifulco, A.; Brown, G.; & Harris, T. (1987). Childhood loss of parent, lack of adequate parental care and adult depression: A replication. *Journal of Affective Disorders* 12, 115–128.

Block, J. H., & Block, J. (1980). The role of ego-control and ego-resiliency in the organization of behavior. In W. A. Collins (ed.), *Minnesota Symposium on Child Psychology* (vol. 13). Hillsdale, N.J.: Erlbaum.

Bowlby, J. (1944). Forty-four juvenile thieves: Their characters and home life. *International Journal of Psychoanalysis* 25, 19–52, and 107–127.

Bowlby, J. (1958). The nature of the child's tie to his mother. *International Journal of Psychoanalysis* 39, 350–73.

Bowlby, J. (1961). Childhood mourning and its implications for psychiatry. *American Journal of Psychiatry* 118, 481–498.

Bowlby, J. ([1969] 1982). *Attachment and loss: Vol. 1. Attachment*. New York: Basic Books.

Bowlby, J. (1973). *Attachment and loss: Vol. 2. Separation*. New York: Basic Books.

Bowlby, J. (1977a). The making and breaking of affectional bonds. *British Journal of Psychiatry* 130, 201–10.

Bowlby, J. (1977b). The making and breaking of affectional bonds. *British Journal of Psychiatry* 130, 421–31.

Bowlby, J. (1980). *Attachment and loss: Vol. 3. Loss, sadness and depression.* New York: Basic Books.

Bowlby, J. (1988). Developmental psychiatry comes of age. *American Journal of Psychiatry* 145, 1–10.

Bowlby, J.; Robertson, J.; & Rosenbluth, D. (1952). A two-year-old goes to hospital. *Psychoanalytic Study of the Child* 7, 82–94.

Boyd, J., & Weissman, M. (1982). Epidemiology. In E. S. Paykel (ed.), *Handbook of affective disorders* (pp. 109–125). New York: Guilford.

Bretherton, I. (1985). Attachment theory: Retrospect and prospect. In I. Bretherton & E. Waters (eds.), *Growing points of attachment theory and research. Monographs of the Society for Research in Child Development* 50(1–2, Serial No. 209), 3–35.

Bretherton, I. (1987). New perspectives on attachment relations. In J. Osofsky (ed.), *Handbook of infancy* (2d ed., pp. 1061–1100). New York: Wiley.

Brown, G., & Harris, T. (1978). *Social origins of depression.* London: Tavistock.

Brown, G.; Harris, T.; & Bifulco, A. (1986). Long-term effects of early loss of parent. In M. Rutter, C. Izard, & P. Read (eds.), *Depression in young people: Developmental and clinical perspectives.* New York: Guilford.

Brown, G.; Monck, E.; Carstairs, G.; & Wing, J. (1962). The influence of family life on the course of schizophrenic illness. *British Journal of Preventative Social Medicine* 16, 55–68.

Brown, G., & Rutter, M. (1966). The measurement of family activities and relationships. *Human Relations* 19, 241–263.

Carlson, V.; Cicchetti, D.; Barnett, D.; & Braunwald, K. (1989). Finding order in disorganization: Lessons from research in maltreated infants' attachments to their caregivers. In D. Cicchetti & V. Carlson (eds.), *Child maltreatment: Theory and research on the causes and consequences of child abuse and neglect.* New York: Cambridge University Press.

Cassidy, J. (1988). Child-mother attachment and the self in six-year-olds. *Child Development* 59, 121–134.

Cicchetti, D. (1984). The emergence of developmental psychopathology. *Child Development* 55, 1–7.

Cicchetti, D. (1990). A historical perspective on the discipline of developmental psychopathology. In J. Rolf, A. Masten, D. Cicchetti, K. Neuchterlein, & S. Weintraub (eds.), *Risk and protective factors in the development of psychopathology* (pp. 2–28). New York: Cambridge University Press.

Cicchetti, D. (in press). Attachment and developmental psychopathology. In D. Cicchetti & S. Toth (eds.), *Rochester Symposium on Developmental Psychopathology* (vol. 2). Hillsdale, N.J.: Erlbaum.

Cicchetti, D., & Aber, J. L. (1986). Early precursors to later depression: An organizational perspective. In L. Lipsitt & C. Rovee-Collier (eds.), *Advances in infancy* (vol. 4, pp. 87–137). Norwood, N.J.: Ablex.

Cicchetti, D., & Beeghly, M. (1987). Symbolic development in maltreated youngsters: An organizational perspective. In D. Cicchetti & M. Beeghly (eds.), *Symbolic development in atypical children* (pp. 47–68). San Francisco: Jossey-Bass.

Cicchetti, D., & Rizley, R. (1981). Developmental perspectives on the etiology, intergenerational transmission, and sequelae of child maltreatment. *New Directions for Child Development* 11, 31–55.

Cicchetti, D., & Schneider-Rosen, L. (1984). Theoretical and empirical considerations in the investigation of the relationship between affect and cognition in atypical populations of infants: Contributions to the formulation of an integrative theory of development. In C. Izard, J. Kagan, & R. Zajonc (eds.), *Emotions, cognition and behavior* (pp. 366–406). New York: Cambridge University Press.

Cicchetti, D., & Schneider-Rosen, K. (1986). An organizational approach to childhood depression. In M. Rutter, C. Izard, & P. Read (eds.), *Depression in young people: Clinical and developmental perspectives* (pp. 71–134). New York: Guilford.

Cicchetti, D., & Toth, S. (1987). The application of a transactional risk model to intervention with multi-task maltreating families. *Zero to Three* 7, 1–8.

Cicchetti, D.; Toth, S.; & Bush, M. (1988). Developmental psychopathology and incompetence: Suggestions for intervention. In B. Lahey & A. Kazdin (eds.), *Advances in child clinical psychology* (vol. 11). (pp. 1–73) New York: Plenum.

Cicchetti, D.; Toth, S.; Bush, M.; & Gillespie, J. (1988). Stage-salient issues: A transactional model of intervention. *New Directions for Child Development* 39, 123–145.

Cicchetti, D., & White, J. (1988). Emotional development and the affective disorders. In W. Damon (ed.), *Child development today and tomorrow* (pp. 177–198). San Francisco: Jossey-Bass.

Cohen, S., & Wills, T. (1985). Stress, social support, and the buffering hypothesis. *Psychological Bulletin* 98, 310–357.

Cohn, J.; Matias, R.; Tronick, E.; Connell, D.; & Lyons-Ruth, K. (1986). Face-to-face interactions of depressed mothers and their infants. In E. Tronick & T. Field (eds.), *Maternal depression and infant disturbance* (pp. 31–45). San Francisco: Jossey-Bass.

Cohn, J., & Tronick, E. (1983). Three-month-old infants' reaction to simulated maternal depression. *Child Development* 54, 185–193.

Coster, W. J.; Gersten, M. S.; Beeghly, M.; & Cicchetti, D. (1989). Communicative functioning in maltreated toddlers. *Developmental Psychology* 25, 1020–1029.

Cowan, P. (1988). Developmental psychopathology: A nine-cell map of the territory. *New Directions for Child Development* 39, 5–29.

Coyne, J. C. (1976). Toward an interactional description of depression. *Psychiatry* 39, 28–40.

Coyne, J. C.; Burchill, S.; & Stiles, W. (in press). An interactional perspective on depression. In C. R. Snyder & D. O. Forsyth (eds.), *Handbook of social and clinical psychology: The health perspective*. New York: Pergamon.

Crittenden, P. M. (1988). Relationships at risk. In J. Belsky & T. Nezworski (eds.), *Clinical implications of attachment theory* (pp. 136–174). Hillsdale, N.J.: Erlbaum.

Crook, T., & Eliot, J. (1980). Parental death during childhood and adult depression: A critical review of the literature. *Psychological Bulletin* 87, 252–259.

Crook, T.; Raskin, A.; & Eliot, J. (1981). Parent-child relationships and adult depression. *Child Development* 52, 950–957.

Crowell, J., & Feldman, S. S. (1988). Mothers' internal models of relationships and children's behavioral and developmental status: A study of mother-child interaction. *Child Development* 59, 1273–1285.

Eaton, W., & Kessler, L. (eds.), (1985). *Epidemiologic field methods in psychiatry.* Orlando, Fla.: Academic Press.

Egeland, B., & Sroufe, L. A. (1981). Developmental sequelae of maltreatment in infancy. *New Directions for Child Development* 11, 77–92.

Engel, G. L. (1971). Attachment behavior, object relations and the dynamic-economic points of view. *International Journal of Psychoanalysis* 52, 183–196.

Engel, G. L. (1977). The need for a new medical model: A challenge for bio-medicine. *Science* 196, 129–135.

Fairbairn, W. (1952). *An object relations theory of the personality.* New York: Basic Books.

Freud, S. ([1917] 1957). *Mourning and melancholia.* (Standard Ed., vol. 14). London: Hogarth.

George, C.; Kaplan, N.; & Main, M. (1985). Attachment interview for adults. Unpublished manuscript, University of California, Berkeley.

Gilbreath, B., & Cicchetti, D. Psychopathology in maltreating mothers. In preparation.

Giovacchini, D. (1975). *Psychoanalysis of character disorders.* New York: Jason Aronson.

Greenberg, J. T., & Mitchell, S. (1983). *Object relations in psychoanalytic theory.* Cambridge, Mass.: Harvard University Press.

Greenberg, M. T., & Speltz, M. (1988). Attachment and the ontogeny of conduct problems. In J. Belsky & T. Nezworski (eds.), *Clinical implications of attachment* (pp. 177–218). Hillsdale, N.J.: Erlbaum.

Greenspan, S.; Wieder, S.; Lieberman, A.; Nover, R.; Lourie, R.; & Robinson, M. (eds.), (1987), *Infants in multirisk families: Case studies in preventive intervention.* New York: International Universities Press.

Guidano, V. F., & Liotti, G. (1983). *Cognitive processes and emotional disorders: A structural approach to psychotherapy.* New York: Guilford.

Guntrip, H. (1961). *Personality structure and human interaction: The developing synthesis of psychodynamic theory.* New York: International Universities Press.

Harris, T.; Brown, G.; & Bifulco, A. (1987). Loss of parent in childhood and adult psychiatric disorder: The role of social class position and premarital pregnancy. *Psychological Medicine* 17, 163–183.

Heinicke, C. (1956). Some effects of separating two-year-old children from their parents: A comparative study. *Human Relations* 9, 105–176.

Hesse, P., & Cicchetti, D. (1982). Perspectives on an integrated theory of emotional development. In D. Cicchetti & P. Hesse (eds.), *Emotional development* (pp. 3–48). San Francisco: Jossey-Bass.

Hooley, J.; Orley, J.; & Teasdale, J. (1986). Levels of expressed emotion and relapse in depressed patients. *British Journal of Psychiatry* 148, 642–647.

Horner, A. (1984). *Object relations and the developing ego in therapy*. New York: Jason Aronson.

Ingersoll-Dayton, B., & Antonucci, T. (1983). Reciprocal and nonreciprocal social support: Contrasting sides of intimate relationships. Paper presented at the annual meeting of the American Psychological Association, Anaheim, Calif.

Jacobson, E. (1971). *Depression: Comparative studies of normal, neurotic and psychotic conditions*. New York: International Universities Press.

Joffe, W., & Sandler, J. (1965). Notes on pain, depression, and individuation. *Psychoanalytic Study of the Child* 20, 394–424.

Kashani, J. H.; Holcomb, W. R.; & Orvaschel, H. (1986). Depression and depressive symptoms in preschool children from the general population. *American Journal of Psychiatry* 143, 1138–1143.

Kashani, J.; McGee, R.; Clarkson, S.; Anderson, J.; Walton, L.; Williams, S.; Silva, P.; Robins, A.; Cytryn, L.; & McKnew, D. (1983). The nature and prevalence of major and minor depression in a sample of nine-year-old children. *Archives of General Psychiatry* 138, 143–153.

Kazdin, A. E.; Moser, J.; Colbus, D.; & Bell, R. (1985). Depressive symptoms among physically abused and psychiatrically disturbed children. *Journal of Abnormal Psychology* 94, 298–307.

Klein, M. (1932). *The psychoanalysis of children*. London: Hogarth.

Klein, M. (1934). A contribution to the psychogenesis of manic-depressive states. In *Contributions of psycho-analysis, 1921–1945* (pp. 282–310). London: Hogarth.

Klein, M. (1940). Mourning and its relation to manic-depressive states. In *Contributions to psycho-analysis, 1921–1945* (pp. 311–338). London: Hogarth.

Kobak, R. R., & Sceery, A. (1988). Attachment in late adolescence: Working models, affect regulation, and representations of self and others. *Child Development* 59, 135–146.

Kovacs, M.; Feinberg, T.; Crouse-Novak, M.; Paulauskas, S.; Pollock, M.; & Finkelstein, R. (1984). Depressive disorders in childhood: II. A longitudinal study of the risk for a subsequent major depression. *Archives of General Psychiatry* 41, 643–649.

Lewinsohn, P. (1974). A behavioral approach to depression. In R. Friedman & M. Katz (eds.), *The psychology of depression: Contemporary theory and research*. Washington, D.C.: Winston.

Lewis, M.; Feiring, C.; McGuffog, C.; & Jaskir, J. (1984). Predicting psychopathology in six-year olds from early social relations. *Child Development* 55, 123–136.

Mahler, M. (1966). Notes on the development of basic moods: The depressive affect. In R. Loewenstein, L. Newman, M. Schur, & A. Solnit (eds.), *Psychoanalysis: A general psychology* (pp. 152–158). New York: International Universities Press.

Mahler, M.; Pine, F.; & Bergman, A. (1975). *The psychological birth of the human infant*. New York: Basic Books.

Main, M.; Kaplan, N.; & Cassidy, J. C. (1985). Security in infancy, childhood and adulthood: A move to the level of representation. In I. Bretherton & E. Waters (eds.), *Growing points of attachment theory and research. Monographs of the Society for Research in Child Development* 50 (1–2, Serial No. 209), 66–104.

Meissner, W. (1981). *Internalization in psychoanalysis*. New York: International Universities Press.

Mendelson, M. (1974). *Psychoanalytic concepts of depression*. New York: Spectrum.

Merikangas, K.; Bromet, E.; & Spiker, D. (1983). Assortive mating, social adjustment, and course of illness in primary affective disorder. *Archives of General Psychiatry* 40, 795–800.

Miklowitz, D.; Goldstein, M.; Nuechterlein, K.; Snyder, K.; & Mintz, J. (1988). Family factors and the course of bipolar affective disorder. *Archives of General Psychiatry* 45, 225–231.

Nannis, E., & Cowan, P. (eds.), (1988). *Developmental psychopathology and its treatment*. San Francisco: Jossey-Bass.

Nelson, K., & Gruendel, J. (1981). Generalized event representation: Basic building blocks of cognitive development. In M. E. Lamb & A. Brown (eds.), *Advances in developmental psychology* (vol. 1). Hillsdale, N.J.: Erlbaum.

Nurnberger, J., & Gershon, E. (1984). Genetics of affective disorders. In R. Post & J. Ballenger (eds.), *Neurobiology of mood disorders* (pp. 76–101). Baltimore: Williams & Wilkins.

Orvaschel, H.; Weissman, M.; & Kidd, K. (1980). Children and depression: The children of depressed parents; the childhood of depressed parents; depression in children. *Journal of Affective Disorders* 2, 1–16.

Parker, G. (1979a). Parental characteristics in relation to depressive disorder. *British Journal of Psychiatry* 134, 138–147.

Parker, G. (1979b). Reported parental characteristics in relation to trait depression and anxiety levels in a non-clinical group. *Australian and New Zealand Journal of Psychiatry* 13, 260–264.

Parker, G. (1981). Parental reports of depressives: An investigation of several explanations. *Journal of Affective Disorders* 3, 131–140.

Parker, G. (1983). *Parental overprotection: A risk factor in psychosocial development.* New York: Grune & Stratton.

Parker, G., & Barnett, B. (1988). Perceptions of parenting in childhood and social support in adulthood. *American Journal of Psychiatry* 145, 479–482.

Parkes, C. M. (1970). "Seeking" and "finding" a lost object: Evidence from recent studies of the reaction to bereavement. *Social Science and Medicine* 4, 187–201.

Paykel, E. (1982). Life events and early environment. In E. Paykel (ed.) *Handbook of affective disorders* (pp. 146–161). New York: Guilford.

Peterson, C., & Seligman, M. (1984). Causal explanations as a risk factor for depression: Theory and evidence. *Psychological Review* 91, 347–374.

Post, R., & Ballenger, J. (eds.), (1984). *Neurobiology of mood disorders.* Baltimore: Williams & Wilkins.

Poznanski, O., & Zrull, J. (1970). Childhood depression: A longitudinal perspective. *Journal of the American Academy of Child Psychiatry* 15, 491–501.

Puig-Antich, J.; Blau, S.; Marx, N.; Greenhill, L.; & Chambers, W. (1978). Prepubertal major depressive disorder: A pilot study. *Journal of the American Academy of Child Psychiatry* 17, 695–707.

Puig-Antich, J.; Lukens, E.; Davies, M.; Goetz, D.; Brennon-Quattrock, J.; & Todak, G. (1985a). Psychosocial functioning in preburtal major depressive disorders: I. Interpersonal relationships during the depressive episode. *Archives of General Psychiatry* 42, 500–507.

Puig-Antich, J.; Lukens, E.; Davies, M.; Goetz, D.; Brennon-Quattrock, J.; & Todak, G. (1985b). Psychosocial functioning in prepubertal major depressive disorders: II. Interpersonal relationships after sustained recovery from affective episode. *Archives of General Psychiatry* 42, 511–517.

Radke-Yarrow, M.; Belmont, B.: Nottelman, E.; & Bottomly, L. (in press). Young children's self-conceptions: Origins in the natural discourse of depressed and normal mothers and their children. In D. Cicchetti & M. Beeghly (eds.), *The self in transition.* Chicago: University of Chicago Press.

Radke-Yarrow, M.; Cummings, E. M.; Kuczynski, L.; & Chapman, M. (1985). Patterns of attachment in two-and-three-year-olds in normal families and families with parental depression. *Child Development* 56, 884–893.

Radloff, L. (1975). Sex differences in depression: The effects of occupational and marital status. *Sex Roles* 1, 249–265.

Rado, S. (1928). The problem of melancholia. *International Journal of Psychoanalysis* 9, 420–438.

Rado, S. (1951). Psychodynamics of depression from the etiologic point of view. *Psychosomatic Medicine* 13, 51–55.

Raskin, A.; Boothe, H.; Reatig, N.; Schulterbrandt, J.; & Odel, D. (1971). Factor analyses of normal and depressed patients' memories of parental behavior. *Psychological Reports* 29, 871–879.

Reese, H., & Overton, W. (1970). Models of development and theories of development. In L. R. Goulet & P. Baltes (eds.), *Life span developmental psychology: Research and theory.* New York: Academic Press.

Ricks, M. H. (1985). The social transmission of parental behavior: Attachment across generations. In I. Bretherton & E. Waters (eds.), *Growing points of attachment theory and research. Monographs of the Society for Research in Child Development* 50 (1–2, Serial No. 209), 211–230.

Rutter, M. (1986). Child psychiatry: The interface between clinical and developmental research. *Psychological Medicine* 16, 151–169.

Rutter, M., & Brown, G. (1966). The reliability and validity of measures of family life and relationships in families maintaining a psychiatric patient. *Social Psychiatry* 1, 38–53.

Rutter, M.; Izard, C.; & Read, P. (eds.) (1986). *Depression in young people: Developmental and clinical perspectives.* New York: Guilford.

Sameroff, A., & Chandler, M. (1975). Reproductive risk and the continuum of caretaking casualty. In F. Horowitz (ed.), *Review of child development research* (vol. 4). Chicago: University of Chicago Press.

Sandler, J., & Joffe, W. (1965). Notes on childhood depression. *International journal of psychoanalysis* 46, 88–96.

Schafer, R. (1968). *Aspects of internalization.* New York: International Universities Press.

Schneider-Rosen, K.; Braunwald, K.; Carlson, V.; & Cicchetti, D. (1985). Current perspectives in attachment theory: Illustration from the study of maltreated infants. In I. Bretherton & E. Waters (eds.), *Growing points in attachment theory and research. Monographs of the Society for Research in Child Development* 50 (1–2, Serial No. 209), 194–210.

Schneider-Rosen, K., & Cicchetti, D. (1984). The relationship between affect and cognition in maltreated infants: Quality of attachment and the development of visual self-recognition. *Child Development* 55, 648–658.

Seligman, M.; Castellon, C.; Cacciola, J.; Schulman, P.; Luborsky, L.; Ollove, M.; & Downing, R. (1988). Explanatory style change during cognitive therapy for unipolar depression. *Journal of Abnormal Psychology* 97, 13–18.

Spieker, S. J., & Booth, C. (1988). Family risk typologies and patterns of insecure attachment. In J. Belsky & T. Nezworski (eds.), *Clinical implications of attachment* (pp. 95–135). Hillsdale, N.J.: Erlbaum.

Spitz, R. (1946). Anaclitic depression. *Psychoanalytic Study of the Child* 2, 313–342.

Sroufe, L. A. (1979a). The coherence of individual development. *American Psychologist* 34, 834–841.

Sroufe, L. A. (1979b). Socioemotional development. In J. Osofsky (ed.), *Handbook of infant development* (1st ed.) (pp. 462–516). New York: Wiley.

Sroufe, L. A. (1983). Infant-caregiver attachment and patterns of adaptation in preschool: The roots of maladaptation and competence. In M. Perlmutter (ed.), *Minnesota Symposium in Child Psychology* (vol. 16, pp. 41–81). Hillsdale, N.J.: Erlbaum.

Sroufe, L. A. (1985). Attachment classification from the perspective of infant-caregiver relationships and infant temperament. *Child Development* 56, 1–14.

Sroufe, L. A., & Fleeson, J. (1986). Attachment and the construction of relationships. In W. Hartup & Z. Rubin (eds.), *Relationships and development.* Hillsdale, N.J.: Erlbaum.

Sroufe, L. A., & Rutter, M. (1984). The domain of developmental psychopathology. *Child Development* 55, 1184–1199.

Trad, P. (1987). *Infant and childhood depression.* New York: Wiley.

Tronick, E. Z., & Field, T. (eds.), (1986). *Maternal depression and infant disturbance.* San Francisco: Jossey-Bass.

Valaik, M., & Cummings, E. M. (1988). Parent-child attachment: Coping and well-being in the elderly. Unpublished manuscript, Department of Psychology, West Virginia University.

Vaughn, C., & Leff, J. (1976). The influence of family and social factors on the course of psychiatric illness: A Comparison of schizophrenic and depressed neurotic patients. *British Journal of Psychiatry* 129, 125–137.

Weissman, M., & Boyd, J. (1984). The epidemiology of affective disorders. In R. Post & J. Ballenger (eds.), *Neurobiology of mood disorders* (pp. 60–75). Baltimore: Williams & Wilkins.

Weissman, M.; Gammon, G.; John, K.; Merikangas, K.; Warner, V.; Prusoff, B.; & Sholomskas, D. (1987). Children of depressed parents. *Archives of General Psychiatry* 44, 847–853.

Weissman, M., & Klerman, G. (1977). Sex differences in the epidemiology of depression. *Archives of General Psychiatry* 34, 98–111.

Wilden, A. (1980). *System and structure*. London: Tavistock.

Winnicott, D. ([1953] 1971). Transitional objects and transitional phenomenon. In D. Winnicott, *Playing and reality*. Middlesex, England: Penguin.

Winokur, G. (1979). Unipolar depression: Is it divisible into autonomous subtypes? *Archives of General Psychiatry* 36, 47–52.

Zahn-Waxler, C.; Chapman, M.; & Cummings, E. M. (1984). Cognitive and social development in infants and toddlers with a bipolar parent. *Child Psychiatry and Human Development* 15, 75–85.

Zahn-Waxler, C.; Mayfield, A.; Radke-Yarrow, M.; McKnew, D.; Cytryn, L.; & Davenport, Y. (1988). A follow-up investigation of offspring of parents with bipolar disorder. *American Journal of Psychiatry* 145, 506–509.

PART FOUR

Clinical Intervention from an Attachment Perspective

12 · Disorders of Attachment and Secure Base Behavior in the Second Year of Life

CONCEPTUAL ISSUES AND CLINICAL INTERVENTION

Alicia F. Lieberman and Jeree H. Pawl

THE GOAL OF this chapter is to present a framework for understanding the etiology of maladaptive behavioral patterns in the second year of life within the context of attachment theory (Bowlby [1969] 1982, 1973, 1980). More specifically, the concept of "secure base" (Ainsworth 1973; Ainsworth, Blehar, Waters, & Wall 1978) will be used as a point of departure for studying some behavioral patterns repeatedly identified in a clinical population of toddlers and their mothers. These mother-toddler dyads were referred for abuse, neglect, and problems of socioemotional development, and received extensive assessment and treatment at the Infant-Parent Program, the infant mental health program of the University of California, San Francisco. A detailed description of the theoretical orientation, structure, and functions of the program is provided elsewhere (Lieberman 1985).

Secure base behavior refers to the contextually determined balance between attachment and exploratory behaviors that allows the baby to use the mother as a safe and reliable anchor from which to explore, returning to her periodically for social exchanges and reassurance (Ainsworth 1973). Detailed observations of our clinical population suggest that persistent deviations from the dynamic balance between attachment and exploratory behaviors represent distortions in the organization of the secure base phenomenon. These distortions are defensive adaptations within the relationship which protect the child against anxiety about the mother's unavailability as a secure base from which to explore. We postulate that such defensive adaptations become a part of the attachment relationship built by the child in the course of repeated transactions with the mother (Bowlby [1969] 1982, 1973). Recurrent experiences of feeling unprotected have a profound influence on the process of internalizing the role of the attachment figure as protector. When the working model of attachment incorporates salient features of unprotectiveness (including abuse and neglect), the child's ability to develop reliable mechanisms for self-protection is in turn jeopardized. Distortions in self-protecting mechanisms may then be observed in many areas of the child's behavior, particularly those that involve the need to negotiate a balance between the attachment system and the child's involvement in exploration and learning.

In offering treatment for these disturbances, it is of crucial importance that symptoms in the child that express distortions in the mother-child relationship be understood as exactly that—"symptoms." In a very real sense, they represent the child's adaptive solution, however aberrant, to problems in that relationship. These problems encompass the impediments within the mother which prevent appropriate responsiveness to the child, in interaction with the child's particular temperament and affective style as these have evolved from the ongoing transactions between constitutional characteristics and the caregiving environment. Given the complexity of the mutual regulation between mother and child, neither partner may be treated either separately or directly regarding these symptoms. The infant and toddler are still so embedded in the matrix of the relationship that making the child aware of the defensive aspects of his behavior does not by itself result in meaningful change. On the other hand, the mother's response to the symptoms may range from bland indifference to irritation with the child. She may not acknowledge or experience these symptoms as problems, or she may perceive them solely as an expression of willfulness, uncooperativeness, or "badness" on the child's part. It is the anxious quality of the attachment that is at issue, and it is the complex origins of this quality that must be understood.

We have developed an approach to therapeutic intervention in which dealing directly or even focusing on the symptoms plays a relatively minor role (Fraiberg 1980; Pawl & Pekarsky 1983; Lieberman 1985). The therapist attempts to appreciate with the mother her more global experience of her child in the context of her own history and present circumstances. As the therapist supports and understands the parent, weaving connections between her individual experience and her perceptions of and feelings toward the child, shifts in the mother's own working models of attachment begin to take place, and these are in turn manifested in changes in her interaction with her child. As the mother's caregiving improves, concomitant improvements are observed in the quality of the relationship.

The child's physical presence during this process is extremely potentiating. The interactions between parent and child can be observed and addressed as they occur in all their variety, immediacy, and emotional intensity, instead of being recollected and selectively reported by the parents. Therapeutic clarifications and interpretations can then focus fully on the affect experienced by both parties. The contribution of a toddler to the relationship is so potent and often so complex that it is easy for parents to believe that all the difficulties are due to the child's behavior and to resist an examination of how their own conflicts are expressed in relating to the child. The joint presence of the parent and the child helps the therapist to understand and address each of the partner's contribution to the interactional difficulties.

In this chapter, we will describe our approach to conceptualizing and treating disturbances of attachment in the second year of life as pathological deviations from the developmental tasks of this period. We will use clinical case vignettes to illustrate our clinical assessment and treatment methods, seeking to highlight the integration of classic psychoanalytic theory and attachment theory in the process.

THE DEVELOPMENTAL TASKS OF THE SECOND YEAR

The concept of development as a normative sequence of salient issues negotiated by the child in transaction with the environment has been described by many influential thinkers using highly personal but largely compatible vocabularies (e.g., Erikson 1963; Piaget 1954; Sander 1962; Mahler, Pine, & Bergman 1975; Sroufe 1979; Greenspan 1981). For the purposes of the present chapter, the concept of attachment as an organizational construct that lays the foundation for later development is particularly useful (Sroufe 1979). In this view, the child entering the second year faces a developmental transition from the salient issue of establishing an affective attachment relationship (6–12 months) to be the salient issue of engaging in exploration and mastery of the environment (12–18 months). In the second half of the second year, these issues coalesce with the gradual consolidation of the child's individuation and autonomy (Sroufe 1979; Waters & Sroufe 1983).

The evolving developmental issues encountered by the infant call for complementary changes in the mother's role. The infant's ability to form a secure attachment relationship is predicated on the mother's responsive availability to a variety of signals (Ainsworth et al. 1978). Once this relationship is reliably established and the infant begins to explore beyond the orbit of the dyad, the mother's role comes to incorporate an increasing emphasis on the encouragement of appropriate exploration, but always in the context of ongoing availability for security and protection. This function of the mother as an external support and reliable extension of the child becomes gradually internalized in the second and third years, a process that enables the child to find increasingly within himself or herself the resources to cope with the challenges of interaction with the environment. The mother's role in facilitating this healthy internalization includes firm support for the child's autonomy and self-control and the provision of clear, predictable, and self-affirming roles and values (Sroufe 1979).

The complex developmental processes involve a multiplicity of transactions between the child and the parent, transactions that may be classified under many different categories to reflect the variety of affective and instrumental functions served by the parent-child relationship both simultaneously and in the course of development. As Bretherton (1980, 1985) points out, the term "attachment," in its technical sense, covers one specific aspect of this multifaceted relationship: that concerning the child's felt security and protection from danger. The behaviors comprising the attachment system have the set goal of promoting and maintaining proximity and contact with the attachment figure, increasing the likelihood of physical safety by maximizing accessibility to the attachment figure as a protector from danger (Bowlby [1969] 1982). The attachment system is continuously active in the sense that there is an ongoing process of monitoring information regarding clues to danger and the availability of the attachment figure (Bretherton 1980, 1985). Attachment behaviors tend to be mobilized in situations that arouse wariness and fear, and the attainment of the set goal of proximity and contact brings about a decline in fear and a psychological experience of security (Bischof 1975). When fear subsides and a feeling of security prevails, the attachment behaviors are attenuated (although the system continues to operate), and exploration at a flexible distance from the attachment figure can take place.

The attachment system operates in such a way that feelings of security tend to coincide with actual safety conditions, although this correspondence is not always exact (Bretherton 1985). From a developmental perspective, however, it is likely that feelings of security are based on repeated experiences in which fear or anxiety had been reliably assuaged by timely interventions from the attachment figure. Such feelings of security develop through the reciprocal quality of the parent-infant interaction throughout the first year, when the parent's functioning with the infant in a mutually regulating manner protects the infant from excessive internal and external stimulation. As a result of reported experiences of caregiving, the child develops expectancies about the parent's availability and responsiveness in a variety of situations, especially those that may elicit anxiety and fear. These expectations, in turn, become building blocks for the child's evolving working model of attachment.

As the infant develops, the actual circumstances experienced as dangerous (fear arousing) differ in degree and kind at different developmental stages in keeping with evolving perceptual and motor skills and with the child's cognitive and affective capacity to appraise and seek protection from danger. Concurrently, the actions of the attachment figure which provide protection from danger (both relief from fear and felt security) should optimally change in consonance with the changing needs and demands of the child, and they gradually come to be perceived by the child as providing protection. In this process, the child's appraisal of danger involves the perception of "natural clues to danger" (Bowlby 1973) as well as learned responses stemming from both active prohibition and literal protection by the parent and from the child's use of the parent for social referencing. From the parent's behavior, the children learn what they should experience as dangerous, and simultaneously what is experienced as dangerous changes with development.

The emphasis of attachment theory on the dynamic balance between the fear, exploratory, and attachment systems around the goal of protection from danger makes an important contribution to the understanding of maladaptive emotional functioning in the second year of life. The issue of protection and its psychological correlate of felt security are lifelong concerns that color in fundamental ways the psychological well-being of the individual. Recent contributions to attachment theory and research have emphasized the importance of recognizing the changing developmental manifestations of this basic underlying theme (Greenberg & Marvin 1979; Marvin & Greenberg 1982; Marvin 1977).

The beginning of the ascendancy of internalization in the second year of life provides a unique opportunity to study how the reliable protection provided by the mother enables the child to become self-protective. Here, as in other developmental issues, deviations from normative patterns of adaptation increase our understanding by altering the relations between the different components of the system and highlighting their specific roles. When a mother is unable to provide reliable protection from danger through contingent responsiveness to the child's signals of fear or distress, the child fails to attain a reliable state of felt security. In the absence of this feeling of security, the child's ability to engage in a confident exploration of the environment is disrupted, and alterations in the balance between exploration and attachment behaviors (secure-base behavior) are observed. The individual manifestations of these alterations differ from child to child depending on a variety of factors—among them, the particular ways in which the mother fails to be available or protective and the specific adaptations made by the child to manage and express fear and anxiety. Children's subjective experiences of their interactions with the mother around the issue of protection will be a major part of the evolving working model of the attachment relationship (Bowlby [1969] 1982, 1973). Since children internalize all the components of a relationship (Sroufe & Fleeson 1986), this working model will also incorporate important components of the mother's performance as perceived by the child. The child's evolving self-concept as deserving and capable of securing protection, or, alternatively, as undeserving or incapable, will be influenced by these early experiences in enduring ways.

DISTORTIONS IN NORMATIVE PATTERNS OF SECURE-BASE BEHAVIOR

In the clinical population of toddlers assessed and treated at the Infant-Parent Program, three major patterns of distortion in secure-base behavior have been identified. These patterns represent qualitatively different adaptations which aid the child in coping with the issue of protection from danger when the mother does not reliably provide such protection. In these situations, the child must find strategies to manage both with the fear of external danger and with the anxiety stemming from the mother's unavailability as a protector. One pattern, recklessness and accident proneness, is seen as a counterphobic defense against perceived danger. A second pattern, inhibition of exploration, is interpreted as a phobic flight from danger. Finally, a third pattern of excessive self-reliance is described as precocious competence in self-protection. In our view, each of these patterns involve efforts to solve the problem of self-protection in the absence of appropriate maternal support for negotiating this developmental task.

In the sections that follow, we will describe our observations of the behavioral and affective features of these patterns as well as their etiology in the mother-child relationship. No systematic effort will be made to link each of these clinical syndromes to existing research-derived classifications of attachment based on behavior in the Strange Situation (Ainsworth et al. 1978). The Strange-Situation classification was based on normative samples, and there are strong caveats to its clinical application (Ainsworth & Lieberman 1985; Main 1985, December, personal communication; Greenspan & Lieberman, in press). Moreover, our clinical population was observed both at home and in our office playroom but not in a Strange-Situation procedure. Thus, elucubrations about the links between the laboratory and the clinical situation, although conceptually intriguing, would be speculative at best.

A Counterphobic Defense against Danger: Recklessness and Accident Proneness

Recklessness in the second year of life may take a variety of forms, but the underlying pattern is the same: the child enters situations that place him at risk for physical harm or actually lead to bodily injury. One manifestation of this phenomenon is the child's tendency to leave ostensibly safe surroundings and wander away from the psychological perimeter encompassed by the mother's presence (Anderson 1972) without either checking back with her or returning to her for reassurance. This departure may occur either at home or in unfamiliar settings. In the home, the child may open the front door and wander down the street or climb over the fence while playing in the yard. In unfamiliar situations, such as stores or other public places, the child may disappear from the mother's sight without showing distress or seeking to restore proximity or contact with her. The child's disappearance is often not noticed until much later, and it is customarily the mother who, in a panic, finds that her child is gone and engages in a frantic search to restore proximity.

A second manifestation of recklessness is the child's tendency to get hurt in the course of exploring the environment. The child may climb on furniture and fall down, or rock on a chair so forcefully that it tips over, or collide into furniture in the process of going somewhere, or bang his head while attempting to retrieve an object from under a chair.

These manifestations of recklessness and accident-prone behaviors may be understood from an attachment theory perspective as a distortion of the secure-base phenomenon. In the adaptive course of development, the mother's roles as a protective regulator and as a secure base from which to explore enable the child to expand his social and cognitive skills without jeopardizing the protection derived from easy accessibility to the attachment figure. In reckless and accident-prone children, the usual dynamic, contextually determined balance between attachment and exploratory behaviors, is altered toward a predominance of the latter at the expense of the former. When exploratory behavior is not balanced by the protection typically afforded by the complementary pull of attachment behaviors, the child's safety is potentially or actually endangered.

Accidents are, of course, notoriously common in the second year of life, and isolated incidents do not in themselves indicate a tendency to recklessness or accident proneness. However, a recurrence of such mishaps suggests a deficiency not only in parental protection but also in the self-protective mechanisms derived from the child's working model of the relationship with the attachment figure. When the mother either does not protect the child from danger or actually exposes the child to it, the child may internalize these behaviors as components of the evolving working model of attachment and of the self. The existence of a deficiency in self-protection is highlighted by the frequent co-occurrence, in reckless and accident-prone children, of behaviors indicative of a turning of aggression against the self (Fraiberg 1982), such as prolonged head banging, self-biting and pinching, and pulling one's own hair. Although the dynamics are different, the co-occurrence is frequent. A possible explanation for this pattern is advanced below.

The balance between attachment and exploratory behaviors postulated in attachment theory resembles, within a different conceptual framework, the balance postulated by psychoanalysis between libidinal and aggressive drives; when the libidinal drives fail to bind the aggressive ones, the result is a personality where destructive impulses are not redirected in order to preserve the integrity of the self and that of others (A. Freud & Burlingham 1944; Fraiberg 1977). This compatibility between the insights derived from the attachment version of psychoanalysis and the explanatory mechanisms suggested by traditional psychoanalytic theory is particularly useful to explore the question of why secure-base behavior should be so disrupted in some children as to place them in severe physical danger. Here again, clinical observation proves useful in searching for understanding. Infants referred for infant-parent psychotherapy because of impulsive, reckless, or self-destructive behavior also tend to engage in behaviors that denote a high level of anxiety. These ambitendent behaviors can be seen as extreme versions of age-appropriate attachment and exploratory behaviors. For example, children who run away from home or dart off from their mother's side in unfamiliar situations may also cling to her frantically and show other signs of distress upon separation when it is the mother who tries to move away. Serious sleep disturbances are also common, signaling a breaking through of anxiety over the child's real or perceived failure to master age-appropriate developmental tasks (Fraiberg 1950).

The seemingly paradoxical coexistence of anxious (fearful) and reckless (danger-seeking) behaviors suggests that recklessness may be a counterphobic defense against danger. Both traditional psychoanalytic theory (S. Freud 1926) and the attachment version (Bowlby 1973) understand anxiety as the reaction to the danger of losing the attachment figure (object), and interpret defense as a mode of dealing with this anxiety. Clinically, the problem is to elucidate the behavioral manifestations and ramifications of this anxiety and how it originates in the first place. In reckless toddlers, the anxiety is triggered by the generalized maternal unavailability, which is experienced by the child as felt insecurity. The additional specific maternal failure to anticipate danger and modulate the child's exposure to it creates a situation in which the child may defend against that anxiety by reckless behavior. When the mother discounts or ridicules the child's fears, ignores situations of danger, entices the child to explore dangerous situations, or minimizes the experience of pain when the child is hurt, the child's fear and attachment behaviors may be strongly aroused but are not responded to and terminated, thus causing severe distress (Bowlby [1969] 1982, 1973).

A repetition of these painful experiences may trigger in the child a defensive exclusion of the information that ordinarily mobilizes attachment behavior (Bowlby 1980). As the attachment behavioral system is deactivated by this defensive exclusion, the exploratory behavioral system has full sway because the child continues to process information about the exploratory potential of the environment without the complementary input from the attachment system. Recklessness and accident proneness can then be seen as expressions of the disruption of secure-base behavior. Phenomenologically, one consequence of this disruption may be to prompt children to seek increasingly dangerous situations as if attempting to discover how much risk they have to endure before mother intervenes. Hence, the counterphobic character of the defense. In effect, the child seems to be asking, "How far do I need to go before my mother will bring me back? How much danger is too much so that my mother will protect me? How much fear do I need to experience before I'm helped to feel safe?" Often, this behavior is labeled as "negative attention seeking" by people who are unaware of the etiology of this pattern and of its psychological function for the child. In attempting to delineate the boundaries of what they will be allowed to endure, the children are simultaneously exploring the limits of their own fear, struggling to defy and ultimately master the sources of danger and anxiety.

While a process of "testing the limits" of what is permissible occurs normally in the second year of life, in the case of reckless children such behavior occurs in the context of a deactivation of the attachment behavior system which ordinarily keeps it in safe balance. Such a deactivation, of course, is seldom complete. Bowlby (1980) indicates that "fragments of the information defensively excluded seep through so that fragments of the behavior defensively deactivated become visible" (p. 65). This explains the simultaneous occurrence in reckless children of behaviors indicative of anxiety over the availability of the attachment figure, such as separation distress and sleeping disturbances. These behaviors represent the breakthrough of affects defended against when the child is engaging in reckless behavior.

There is evidence that a similar but less extreme pattern of deviations in patterns of exploration is present in a nonclinical population observed in the Strange Situation. Cassidy (1986) reports that 18-month-olds classified as anxiously attached/ambivalent (*C* babies) have more difficulty in negotiating the environment than either securely attached (*B*) or anxiously attached/ avoidant (*A*) babies. Cassidy defines negotiation of the environment as the "ability to move safely through space, to be relatively comfortable in the understanding of the physical properties and boundaries of objects, to be aware of weight and balance, to be careful when testing the limits of one's physical skills, and to begin to foresee the consequences of one's physical actions." This definition is congruent with our own conceptualization of the ability of children to protect themselves in the course of exploration. Cassidy's findings, superimposed on our clinical observations, suggest that there may be a continuum along this dimension. Toddlers whose attachment relationship is ambivalent but not clinically so may show moderate disturbances of exploration, whereas toddlers clinically diagnosed as having disturbances of attachment may show more severe self-endangering behaviors. Such a continuum along the dimension of safe negotiation of the environment is consistent with the view that pathological patterns are distortions and exaggerations of adaptive coping mechanisms normally observed in the course of development (Bowlby 1980; Lampl-de Groot 1957).

Clinical Vignette: Joshua, 15 Months. Joshua was referred to our program by his pediatrician after neurological examinations revealed no organic basis for an initially suspected diagnosis of hyperactivity. The behaviors prompting the referral were the child's severe and protracted sleeping difficulties and his disorganized activity during the day. Describing Joshua during the first assessment session, the mother said with exasperation, "Joshua does not know what 'no' means. He puts his fingers in the electrical outlets. He eats dirt from the living room plants. He climbs on the stereo. He fell down and cut his forehead three times. He broke a bowl and cut himself playing with the glass. He pulls things that fall on him and hurt him." The parents interpreted these behaviors as a sign of hyperactivity, whether confirmed by the neurological examinations or not.

As the assessment proceeded for a span of five weekly sessions, more information emerged about Joshua's behavior, and the parents' reports could be corroborated by direct observation. The mother, Estelle, described an episode in which Joshua disappeared from her sight in a crowded store, and she had to search for him for fifteen minutes before finding him under a table, eating the dirt from a nearby plant. This was part of a pattern of darting off from the mother's side—whether while crossing the street, playing in the park, or going shopping.

At the same time, there was much reported distress upon separation. At home, Joshua followed his mother from room to room and cried bitterly outside the door when she went to the bathroom. When left with babysitters, Joshua clung to his mother and cried for a long time after she left. These behaviors were not manifested in Joshua's interactions with his father.

Direct observations of the mother-child interaction confirmed the impression of an intensely anxious attachment on Joshua's part. He rarely looked or smiled at his mother and seldom approached her in the course of play. He also rebuffed his mother's attempts to hug, kiss, or play with him. This behavior contrasted with Joshua's friendliness toward the therapist and his warmth toward his father. An episode that occurred during the third assessment session illustrates this contrast. Joshua spontaneously approached the therapist in the course of his play and kissed her on the nose. When the mother asked him to kiss her, too, he started walking toward her but stopped midway without looking at her and started playing with a toy. Estelle grabbed Joshua and kissed him noisily, but he first averted his gaze and then turned his entire face away from her. Estelle said in a bitterly sarcastic voice, "You would rather kiss a stranger than your mother."

Estelle, in turn, was alternatively intrusive and unavailable to her child. On one occasion, for example, she interrupted Joshua's quiet play with a truck by abruptly throwing a beach ball on his head and inviting him to play with it. Later, when he signaled that he wanted a toy placed on a high shelf, she encouraged him to get it, then abruptly pulled him down when he started climbing the shelves toward it. On other occasions, Estelle rejected Joshua's approaches. When the child tried to stay close to his mother upon first meeting the clinician, Estelle walked away from him. When he tried to hold her hand for reassurance during his first visit to our office playroom, she pushed him on to the toys while calling him a "faker" and went on to express her belief that Joshua only pretended to want to be with her.

Estelle also teased Joshua about separations. She often pretended to leave the playroom without Joshua and laughed at his obvious distress at her departure. Conversely, she encouraged him to leave by opening the door of the playroom and saying, "You can go out, Joshua," or "Bye-bye, Joshua." If Joshua looked at her with hesitation, Estelle continued to encourage him to leave. When he finally complied, the mother turned to the clinician with a resigned expression, as if saying, "Now you yourself see what he does."

These observations indicated a profound disturbance in the mother's ability to respond to Joshua's affective signals. This was most marked in the failure to protect Joshua from danger and to empathize with his fears, and was paralleled by a concomitant inability on the child's part to protect himself. Joshua's behavior mirrored in many ways his mother's interactions with him: she encouraged him to leave, and he independently darted off from her side; she rebuffed his efforts at establishing proximity and contact, and he in turn rejected her overtures; she encouraged dangerous forays, and he engaged in accident-prone behaviors. The anxiety generated in this child by the absence of protective maternal availability was clearly manifested in his night wakings and his acute distress upon separation, which contrasted with the recklessness that was the main focus of the parents' concern.

Treatment in this case consisted of exploring Estelle's own childhood in order to understand the emotional links between her past history and her current difficulties with her child. This technique, known as infant-parent psychotherapy, is used with parents and infants in the first 3 years who are experiencing disorders of attachment (Fraiberg, Adelson, & Shapiro 1975; Fraiberg 1980; Fraiberg, Lieberman, Pekarsky, & Pawl 1981). A basic premise is that the baby represents a powerful transference object for the parents and that problems in the parents' relationship to the infant may be understood as reenactments of their own childhood experiences. The thrust of the intervention is to link negative feelings experienced in the present toward the baby with emerging feelings and experiences from the past. As the parents acquire insight into the sources of their ambivalence toward the child, their positive emotional investment becomes freer from conflict, and the baby can become less engulfed in the parents' intrapsychic difficulties.

In the course of treatment, it became apparent that Estelle's childhood had been as bereft of protection as her own child's was in the present. In session after session, the mother recalled with much pain and anger the physical and psychological abuse she had endured from her older sister, who was diagnosed as psychotic many years later. Estelle remembered being locked in a dark room, thrown downstairs, encouraged to stick her fingers in the electric outlets, and dared into attempting dangerous feats. When she sought refuge in her own mother, the standard reply was, "You girls should work it out between yourselves." Her father, Estelle said, was always working too hard to be of any help.

As the treatment progressed, it emerged that Estelle perceived Joshua as sharing many of her sister's characteristics, and responded to him as if he were a powerful and abusive older sibling rather than an anxious little boy in search of maternal love and protection. Estelle was helped by the therapist to gradually remember and reexperience her own wish for protection in the past and her fear and anger when this was not forthcoming. These early feelings were connected in the course of treatment with Estelle's present feelings toward Joshua, and the transferential character (from sister to son) of the relationship to her child could then be examined and understood. As the childhood anger became redirected to its original targets—the abusive sister and the unavailable, unprotecting parents—and as Estelle could allow herself to remember the pain and fear that once threatened to overwhelm her, she also became better able to empathize with Joshua's fears, to make herself more available to him, and to protect him more reliably from both external and self-inflicted dangers. Estelle's characterological disturbances were much too pervasive to be completely resolved through infant-parent psychotherapy, but her conflicts around nurturance and protection were substantially alleviated, and she began to experience increasing pleasure in being a mother. After one year of weekly treatment, this improvement was clearly reflected in a marked decline in Joshua's recklessness, separation distress, and sleeping disturbances.

A Phobic Defense against Danger: Inhibition of Exploration

Generalized inhibition of exploration in the second year of life is manifested in reluctance to approach, touch, and manipulate objects in the inanimate environment and in avoidance and withdrawal from social interaction with unfamiliar persons, whether adults or peers. There is a restriction of the affective range. The predominant mood is often sober or neutral, and there may be a marked delay in the differentiation of affect. Most noteworthy is the relative scarcity of intense emotional reactions, ranging from delight to negativism, that are so characteristic of this age. In unfamiliar settings, the child engages in a sober scrutiny which, depending on the accompanying affect, may denote either interest and alertness with a concomitant suppression of active exploration, or, alternatively, hypervigilance and fear. When offered a toy, the child's fingers may move almost imperceptibly, or there may be an uncompleted attempt to reach.

The child may or may not seek to maintain close proximity or contact with the mother. When the child does remain close to the mother, the observer's initial impression is one of shyness and slowness to warm up, although as observations accumulate it becomes increasingly apparent that the child's inhibition of action is not merely a temporary situational reaction but a pervasive mode of responding to the environment. When not seeking proximity to the mother, the child often remains immobile or barely moving for a relatively long period.

Murphy and Moriarty (1976) interpreted inhibition as an effort to fend off loss of coordination as a disintegrative response to stress (or, in the vocabularies of psychoanalysis and attachment theory, to anxiety and fear). In this view, inhibition represents an effort to preserve integration. Fraiberg (1982) described an extreme form of inhibition involving "complete immobilization, a freezing of posture, of motility, of articulation" (p. 622) that she called "freezing." The defensive character of this behavior becomes apparent when the inhibition of movement suddenly gives way to disorganized motility. This may happen, for example, when the infant's faint attempt at exploration is followed by a seemingly inexplicable cry that escalates into prolonged screaming and flailing. This motor collapse is seen as the other side of freezing—a complete disintegration of the child's regulatory mechanisms in the face of anxiety or fear.

Inhibition may be interpreted as a distortion in the organization of secure-base behavior due primarily to the exaggerated suppression of exploration. Deviations in the incidence and quality of attachment behaviors, however, are also an integral part of the pattern. As described earlier, some children cling to the mother and refuse to separate from her even after being familiarized with a setting; others tend to avoid proximity to the mother as well as exploration. The choice of pattern is likely to reflect the child's working model of the attachment relationship.

In our clinical population, severe inhibition is often seen in two major groups. One group is the children of psychotic or schizophrenic mothers who are gratified by their baby's total dependence and discourage their unfolding autonomy by responding to it with emotional withdrawal or direct punishment. We speculate that these children perceive and incorporate the mother's intense wish for closeness, and equate physical distance with the withdrawal of maternal emotional availability and, hence, with lack of protection. These children cling to the mother and refuse to separate from her. The second group comprises children who live in extremely chaotic environments where verbal abuse and physical punishment for even minor transgressions are frequent and severe but often unpredictable. These children are likely to perceive the mother as herself a source of danger, and keep their distance from both the physical environment and the mother in an effort to avoid the perils from either source.

Bowlby (1973) elucidated some of the conditions leading to anxious attachment in childhood and established a clear link between anxious attachment and the phobias of childhood. The etiology of school refusal, in particular, is attributed to family patterns where the child is made anxious either by threats (overt or covert) of abandonment by the parent, or by the parents' own difficulties in allowing for age-appropriate separations from the child. Refusal to attend school is interpreted as the child's effort at self-protection from the anxiety engendered by these conditions.

There are interesting parallels between Bowlby's etiological formulations for school refusal in older children and those we propose for inhibition of exploration in the second year: in both conditions, the antecedents include either an inordinate wish for closeness on the part of the parent or undue harshness in the parents' treatment of the child. Attending school is, for older children, the developmental equivalent of exploration of the environment in toddlers; hence, school refusal may be seen as equivalent to inhibition of exploration as a developmental deviation in the balance between attachment and exploration. Both conditions suggest an underlying mechanism of phobic defense against the danger stemming from the attachment figure's behavior. These children avoid situations that highlight the failure of the attachment figure to act as a protector. The avoidance serves as a defense against the helplessness, anxiety, and anger engendered by the attachment figure, and has the function of protecting both the child and the attachment relationship from the overt expression of negative feelings which brings increased fears of abandonment and loss. Main, Kaplan, & Cassidy (1985) described the defensive role of avoidance of the attachment figure following separation. Our observations suggest that a defensive mechanism also may be at work when the child avoids developmentally appropriate situations such as exploration and play.

As a defensive mode, inhibition of exploration has pervasive negative effects on the child's cognitive functioning, most likely due to the constriction of access to opportunities for learning. Expressive language is widely affected, probably because its development is strongly influenced by motivational factors such as the wish to communicate and the expectation of being listened and responded to. In more severe cases of inhibition, gross and fine motor development may be broadly age-appropriate but show inconsistencies that indicate the interference of anxiety, as when a child suddenly stops building a tower made of blocks or walks with a very stiff gait when encountering an unfamiliar situation.

Clinical Vignette: Aleta, 20 Months Old. Aleta and her mother, Natasha, 14 years old, were referred to our program by the Department of Social Services because of their concern about the child's almost complete absence of vocalizations and their questions about the teenage mother's ability to take care of her child. Mother and daughter were living together in a foster home after being expelled from home by the maternal grandmother, who suspected that Aleta was the result of incestuous relations between her daughter and her husband. The husband died soon after being confronted with this accusation, and the grandmother took this as confirmation of her charges in spite of Natasha's vehement denials of them.

The assessment period involved evaluations of Aleta's interactions with her mother and with the foster mother, appraisals of the child's cognitive and socioemotional functioning, an exploration of Natasha's capacity to make use of developmental guidance on behalf of her daughter, and an evaluation of the foster home as a nurturing environment for both mother and child. This process lasted for eight weeks and involved one or two weekly sessions.

The observations and cognitive testing of Aleta revealed an overly controlled and affectively muted child in her interactions both with her mother and with her foster mother. Her range of affect was extremely limited; she never evidenced anger, discontent, upset, or frustration, and seldom showed spontaneous joy or excitement. She frequently displayed a pleasing smile that stayed on her face for long periods at a time, as if it were forced. She seemed to have an extreme desire to please both her mother and her foster mother. During the testing situation, which was conducted in the presence of the foster mother, there were many occasions when Aleta could not look at what she was doing with her hands but instead turned toward the foster mother to watch her reaction. At times, her anxiety during the testing seemed so overpowering as to essentially paralyze her thinking and problem-solving abilities. The same response was observed in free-play situations, where she displayed little curiosity or initiative in exploration. During the initial sessions, Aleta remained frozen in either her mother's or foster mother's lap. She often did not speak or make any sound during the entire visit but gazed about her in an apprehensive way. The therapist's efforts to interest Aleta in toys or to engage her in a conversation were met by frozen watchfulness and at times a hollow smile. Aleta's demeanor was basically the same with both her mother and her foster mother. She showed some preference for them over the therapist in maintaining contact and proximity, but she seemed to derive little security from their presence as evidenced by her inability to use either of them as a base from which to explore.

Visits to the foster mother's home showed that both Natasha and Aleta were treated in demanding, critical, and unsympathetic ways by the foster mother. This woman, herself very talkative and outgoing, felt irritated by Aleta's unresponsiveness, which she interpreted as a personal rejection. She was clearly disappointed by Aleta's performance during the testing and openly berated the child for not speaking more and not performing better. Aleta responded to these remonstrations by lowering her gaze and becoming immobile. When the foster mother commanded her to say her name as a demonstration that she could understand verbal requests, Aleta complied but stuttered in the process of doing so. Aleta had a limited number of toys she was allowed to play with, and the foster mother yelled and slapped her hand when she tried to touch something other than these objects. It was quite apparent from these and similar interactions that Aleta was expected to perform in very exacting ways, that she consistently failed to please the foster mother, that she was punished for this failure, and that she responded by withdrawal and constriction of affect and of motor response.

Aleta's interactions with her mother were equally worrisome. Natasha was a deeply depressed and confused adolescent. Although she wanted to keep her daughter, she did not have the interpersonal resources to establish a reciprocal relationship with her. Natasha often sat sullenly with the child on her lap, herself a frozen and terrified child. These periods of stupor were often interrupted by sharp yelling at Aleta when the child dared to initiate some activity that was not consonant with the mother's image of what child play should be. On one occasion, for example, Aleta moved from her mother's lap to pick up a rubber band from the floor. Natasha yelled "no" and slapped the child's hand. Aleta dropped the rubber band and leaned back in silence against the mother.

Although our preference would have been to place Aleta for adoption because of the dismal quality of the relationship with both her mother and her foster mother, there were insurmountable legal and practical obstacles to this alternative. We were then faced with the need to search for the least detrimental course of action (Goldstein, Freud, & Solnit 1973, 1979) to alleviate the child's predicament. The most immediate course of action was to recommend to the Department of Social Services that Natasha and Aleta be moved to a new foster home, one that would be chosen with an eye to the foster parents' ability to be tolerant and emotionally available to an adolescent and her toddler. Fortunately, such a home could be found, and Natasha was clearly relieved by the change. Once this move was implemented, the therapist offered supportive psychotherapy and developmental guidance to Natasha, and served as a consultant to the foster parents about the day-to-day management of developmental issues both with Natasha and with Aleta. Treatment continued for two years. During this time, the therapist helped to find solutions to such practical problems as education and income, was instrumental in finding and securing financial coverage for good-quality day care for Aleta, served as a mediator between mother and the legal system, supported and encouraged the mother in her struggles to cope with the often conflicting developmental tasks of adolescence and motherhood, served as a secondary attachment figure to support Aleta's development, and helped the foster parents in their struggles to remain patient and responsive to a difficult adolescent and to a very withdrawn toddler.

By the end of treatment, Natasha was doing well in school, working part-time, and getting along well with her foster parents. She had also grown as a mother, showing more awareness of her child's needs, more permissiveness for exploration, and more receptiveness to the child's expression of wish for proximity and contact. Aleta was developing well. She continued to respond to stress through withdrawal, but her affective range was now rich and full, and she showed initiative and pleasure in exploration as well as freedom in initiating interactions with her mother. Her day-care teacher described her as a rewarding child who responded warmly to expressions of affection and who played well with other children, although she still tended to withdraw from conflict situations and had some difficulty claiming her rights to a disputed toy.

Precocious Competence in Self-Protection

Precocious competence in self-protection is characterized by an apparent reversal of roles between mother and child, so that the child engages in protective behaviors ordinarily expected from the mother and is unusually solicitous of the mother's welfare. The self-protection is manifested most strikingly in the child's unilateral initiative in maintaining proximity to the mother in unfamiliar settings. This behavior takes place without concomitant signals of anxiety: the children seem to take for granted that it behooves them to keep track of the mother's whereabouts and do so successfully and with no apparent effort or distress. The solicitousness to the mother's welfare is shown primarily in an unusual awareness of the mother's moods and in behaviors designed to take care of the mother, such as offering her a cookie or consistently centering the symbolic play on nurturing themes such as feeding the mother. This pattern has long been recognized as an indication of developmental disturbance by psychoanalysts (Harley 1975, October, personal communication; Settlage 1986, January, personal communication), and some aspects of it are receiving systematic attention within the attachment theory paradigm (e.g., the "compulsive caregiving" pattern in Bowlby 1980; and the role-reversal patterns described by Main, Kaplan, & Cassidy 1985).

The pattern of precocious competence is often seen in children whose mothers are emotionally invested in their children but too depressed or self-absorbed to remain emotionally available in a consistent fashion. Such mothers may show exquisite empathy for their children's experience and respond sensitively to their needs, but their attuneness is largely dependent on their own affective state. When the mother's own needs take emotional precedence, the child may experience her as unresponsive or unpredictably available. In some cases, the mother's fragile emotional availability breaks down under the pressure of the child's demands, and then she may strike out and become physically abusive.

The children of these mothers seem to internalize sooner than developmentally expected the protective maternal availability that they experience in sporadic fashion. They may also perceive the mother as a loving and beloved figure that is herself in need of protection and take upon themselves the role of being the stronger member of the dyad. This precocious competence is a form of identification with the benign, nurturing aspects of the mother and serves as a defense against the anxiety triggered when the mother's self-absorption interferes with her responsiveness to the child's needs. By internalizing the protective function, the child gains an illusion of safety through premature self-reliance. When the mother becomes occasionally physically abusive, the child's ability for self-care has the additional function of protection from the mother's rage when she cannot tolerate the child's demands.

Precocious competence is not quite readily interpretable as a distortion of secure-base organization because its most striking manifestation is not an alteration of the balance between attachment and exploratory behaviors. A secure-base distortion may nevertheless be inferred because the child does not rely on the mother as the primary source of protection but incorporates into his or her own behavior substantial portions of the mother's normative role as a secure base from which to explore. In this sense, these children show in magnified detail the pattern of internalizing all the components of a relationship described by Sroufe and Fleeson (1986).

The costs to the child's personality development of this defensive process are less immediately apparent than the costs of the two defenses discussed in earlier sections—recklessness and inhibition. Social values stressing independence and self-reliance are so pervasive that it is easy to extoll these children as resilient and to overlook the manifestations of anxiety that coexist with the positively adaptive coping strategies. The most worrisome long-term feature of precocious competence in self-protection is that its core is an effort to compensate for a profound insecurity in the availability of attachment figures. This compensatory effort is by its very nature built on a fragile foundation, a basic personality matrix where mistrust outweighs trust (Erikson 1963). The outward appearance of competence hides painful inner doubts about one's own worth and lovability and becomes the foundation of what has been called the "false self" (Winnicott 1955). In the second year of life, the other side of the self-reliance is manifested in the whole repertoire of behaviors indicative of anxiety at this age, such as night wakings, eating disturbances, frequent and prolonged temper tantrums, and a pervasive soberness of affect.

Clinical Vignette: Tanya, 22 Months. The case of Tanya and her mother, Jody, was published elsewhere as an illustration of a therapeutic intervention aimed at protecting the best interests of the child (Lieberman & Pawl 1984). The following description of the mother-child dyad focuses on the features relevant to Tanya's precociousness in self-protection and her solicitude toward her mother.

Jody and Tanya were referred by the courts as a preventive therapeutic measure after Jody's older son was removed from the home for physical abuse. Tanya had not been abused, and Jody denied feeling toward her daughter the same mixture of love and intense rage that she experienced toward her son. The observations made during the assessment period revealed that Jody was often sensitively attuned to Tanya's moods and signals. During the first sessions, for example, Jody showed great patience and resourcefulness in helping her daughter remove a winter jacket without parting from a cookie the child was holding on to with great determination. In subsequent sessions, Jody was often able to turn her attention to Tanya when necessary even while in the midst of intense emotion, such as grief or anger. On other occasions, however, Jody's need to speak about her experiences was so overpowering that she seemed completely lost in her own memories and barely noticed her daughter's efforts to gain her attention. This self-absorption alternated with occasional outbursts of impatient yelling in which she told Tanya that she could either wait or take care of herself.

Tanya, for her part, seemed intensely attuned to her mother. It was primarily the child who initiated social exchanges with Jody and tended to maintain physical proximity with her, as when she laboriously trotted down the long hall toward the playroom behind her mother. Jody, in contrast, often marched heedlessly on without so much as a backward glance toward her daughter.

Tanya had clearly learned that her mother could respond to her in sensitive and playful ways but that she needed to take the initiative in eliciting these responses by both remaining physically close and being an engaging companion. She also showed a precocious awareness of her mother's moods and a disturbing sense of responsibility for making her mother feel better. For example, on several occasions Tanya stopped her play when Jody cried and gently dried her mother's tears. When Jody left the child at the babysitter's home, Tanya's response was to tell her, "Don't be sad, mommy. Don't cry." These behaviors contrasted strikingly with Tanya's overall developmental delays in language and representational play. This picture indicated that Tanya relied a great deal on a precocious ability to care for herself and her mother and that the roles of mother and daughter were readily reversed. The cost to Tanya's personality development was apparent not only in her developmental delays but also in her predominant affect, which was a mixture of soberness and cheerful resignation, as if she knew that life was difficult but was trying to face it bravely. The effort it took to maintain this stance was also manifested in her response to physical pain: she often winced and began to whimper when she hurt herself, but quickly suppressed these responses and never cried. Equally worrisome was an isolated instance of anxious behavior: Tanya sucked her thumb until it was practically raw, as if to reassure herself in ways that her mother could not.

Treatment in this case involved a multifaceted approach involving practical assistance to stabilize the mother's living circumstances, developmental guidance around Tanya's physical and emotional needs, and infant-parent psychotherapy to explore the ways in which the mother's pain and rage about the abuse she had endured as a child were now interfering with her consistent emotional availability as a mother. In the course of treatment, Jody revealed that she was a heroin addict and that her everyday activities were largely centered on supporting this habit. She confessed that her addiction had become progressively worse and that she could not take care of Tanya when she was worried about where her next "fix" would come from. In response to this information, and with the mother's cooperation, the therapist revised the intervention plan to include a drug rehabilitation program and regular monitoring of the situation by the Child Protective Services. The ongoing criterion for determining the success of the plan was Tanya's socioemotional functioning as assessed in weekly sessions.

Unfortunately, Jody was unable to use the drug rehabilitation services to free herself from her addiction, and she became increasingly defensive and angry when the therapist expressed concerns about her growing inability to take care of her daughter. The situation came to a crisis when a pediatric checkup revealed that Tanya had lost eleven ounces in one week. The child was removed from the home and placed with carefully selected foster parents who were willing to adopt her should the mother's parental rights be legally terminated.

Given these events, the therapist's role changed in keeping with the changing needs of the child. Treatment now involved three main components: (1) weekly individual psychotherapy with Tanya to explain the realities of her life in ways that the child could understand, and to offer a setting for the expression and exploration of the child's feelings around the separation from her mother; (2) developmental guidance with the foster parents to sensitize them to the emotional impact of Tanya's experiences, and to suggest ways of alleviating the child's grief and anger over the loss of her mother; and (3) ongoing consultation to the Department of Social Services and the court system to highlight the importance of making decisions consistent with the best emotional interests of the child, and to work through the often conflicting demands between the legal rights of the mother and the long-term welfare of the child. The therapist also made efforts to maintain contact with Jody, but the mother soon became a fugitive and a warrant was issued for her arrest on a parole violation.

As work with Tanya and the foster parents continued during the ensuing year, the child made a successful adjustment to her new circumstances. She learned to trust and rely on her foster parents, and her development proceeded remarkably well. In a court hearing conducted eighteen months after Jody's disappearance, the therapist acted as an expert witness on behalf of the Department of Social Services and recommended termination of Jody's parental rights and adoption by the foster parents. The judge ruled in accordance with this recommendation, and Tanya is in the process of being legally adopted.

Now 5 years old, Tanya continues to develop well. She remembers Jody and talks about her in ways that show an integration of her original love for her mother and an awareness that Jody could not take care of her. She refers to her adoptive parents as "mommy" and "daddy," a development that was spontaneous, gradual, and consistent with the child's own psychological process in transferring her emotional investment from her biological mother to her adoptive parents. She is joyful, friendly, and unusually articulate in the verbal expression of feelings, a situation that is in marked contrast to her early language delay. After a period of regression in function shortly after being placed with her foster parents, Tanya began a slow but steady recovery. Her cognitive functioning is now well above average.

There is little trace of the precocious competence in self-protection that was one of Tanya's chief characteristics when she was living with Jody. When fearful of separation or loss, she tends to respond by "taking charge," trying to dominate the situation by telling others what to do or expressing anger forcefully. Under ordinary circumstances, however, she is able to express pain when she is hurt and to turn to the consistently nurturing adults in her environment for help and protection. A poignant remnant of the early role reversal occurs occasionally in Tanya's symbolic play: she often likes to play that she is taking care of a baby whose role is assigned to an adult playmate. This theme, however, is nicely balanced by the complementary theme of being a baby who is well taken care of by a benign mother. Tanya is still working at the integration of positive and negative feelings toward attachment figures and at reconciling what she perceives as the polarities of taking care of and being taken care of. However, she is well on her way to an age-appropriate resolution of this developmental task.

CONCLUSION

The framework described above represents an effort to understand some behavioral patterns observed during the second year of life in terms of variations in the development of secure-base behavior. There are multiple factors underlying the specific forms of these variations. Temperament is likely to play a contributory role through the specific reactive patterns that are most readily available to a particular child (Chess & Thomas 1984). These individual differences, in dynamic transaction with the characteristic patterns of maternal caregiving during the first year (Ainsworth et al. 1978), influence the nature and quality of the working model of the attachment relationship gradually internalized by the child. The internalized working model in turn exerts a powerful influence on the child's behavior, generating a process of reciprocal influences that leads both to an increasing elaboration of the mother-child interactive patterns and to a growing consolidation of the internalization by the child of specific aspects of this interaction.

The mutual adaptations between mother and child involved in this process occur normatively in a context of reciprocal regulation. The mother's role demands greater accommodation to the need signals of the child than vice versa, but the child also needs to accommodate gradually and adapt to the characteristic patterns of the mother's caregiving. The "goodness-of-fit" model adopted by Chess and Thomas (1984) summarizes the multifactorial nature of this process. In the transactions between the child and the mother, there exists a continuum of costs and benefits that are gradually established through the mutual adaptations of both members of the dyad. We believe that the greater the demands for the child to accommodate to the mother rather than vice versa, the greater the costs to the child in terms of distortions in the expression of temperamental characteristics and age-appropriate developmental needs that are not met within the mother's caregiving repertoire.

In this context, defenses may be interpreted as costly adaptations made by the child to a caregiver that cannot accommodate to the child's individual style and developmental needs for care and protection. Lampl-de Groot (1957) has written, "Can we speak of normal defense, or does every defensive process belong to the realm of pathology?" (p. 114). She goes on to suggest that "we view the neurotic defense mechanisms as pathologically exaggerated or distorted regulation and adaptive mechanisms, which in themselves belong to normal development" (p. 117). This view is consistent with the position taken

in this chapter. The clinical patterns described are interpreted as costly adaptations to anxiety-arousing caregiving conditions, which in turn create distortions in the dynamic balance between attachment and exploratory behaviors
observed under the normative conditions of a secure attachment relationship.

REFERENCES

Ainsworth, M. D. S. (1973). The development of infant-mother attachment. In B. M. Caldwell &
    H. N. Ricciuti (eds.), *Review of child development research* (vol. 3, pp. 1–94). Chicago:
    University of Chicago Press.
Ainsworth, M. D. S.; Blehar, M. C.; Waters, E.; & Wall, S. (1978). *Patterns of attachment*.
    Hillsdale, N.J.: Erlbaum.
Ainsworth, M. D. S., & Lieberman, A. F. (1985, December). The strange situation: procedure
    and uses of an experimental assessment of attachment. Paper presented at the Training Insti-
    tute of the National Center for Clinical Infant Programs, Washington, D.C.
Anderson, J. W. (1972). Attachment behaviour out of doors. In N. Blurton-Jones (ed.), *Ethologi-
    cal studies of child behaviour*. Cambridge: Cambridge University Press.
Bischof, N. A. (1975). A systems approach towards the functional connections of fear and attach-
    ment. *Child Development* 46, 801–817.
Bowlby, J. ([1969] 1982). *Attachment and loss: Vol. 1. Attachment*. New York: Basic Books.
Bowlby, J. (1973). *Attachment and loss: Vol. 2. Separation*. New York: Basic Books.
Bowlby, J. (1980). *Attachment and loss: Vol. 3. Loss, sadness and depression*. New York: Basic
    Books.
Bretherton, I. (1980). Young children in stressful situations: The supporting role of attachment
    figures and unfamiliar caregivers. In G. V. Coelho & P. Ahmed (eds.), *Uprooting and at-
    tachment*. New York: Plenum.
Bretherton, I. (1985). Attachment theory: Retrospect and prospect. In I. Bretherton & E. Waters
    (eds.), *Growing points in attachment theory and research. Monographs of the Society for
    Research in Child Development* 50 (1–2, Serial No. 209), 3–35.
Cassidy, J. (1986). The ability to negotiate the environment: An aspect of infant competence as
    related to quality of attachment. *Child Development* 57, 331–337.
Chess, S., & Thomas, A. (1984). *Origins and evolution of behavior disorders*. New York:
    Bruner/Mazel.
Erikson, E. (1963). *Childhood and society*. New York: Norton.
Fraiberg, S. (1950). On the sleep disturbances of early childhood. *Psychoanalytic study of the
    child* 5, 285–309.
Fraiberg, S. (1977). *Every child's birthright: In defense of mothering*. New York: Basic Books.
Fraiberg, S. (1980). *Clinical studies in infant mental health: The first year of life*. New York:
    Basic Books.
Fraiberg, S. (1982). Pathological defenses in infancy. *Psychoanalytic Quarterly* 51, 612–634.
Fraiberg, S.; Adelson, E.; & Shapiro, V. (1975). Ghosts in the nursery. *Journal of the American
    Academy of Child Psychiatry* 14(3), 387–422.
Fraiberg, S.; Lieberman, A. F.; Pekarsky, J.; Pawl, J. H. (1981). Treatment and outcome in an
    infant psychiatry program. *Journal of Preventive Psychiatry* 1–2, pts. 1–2.
Freud, A., & Burlingham, D. (1944). *Infants without families*. New York: International Univer-
    sities Press.
Freud, S. (1926). *Inhibitions, symptoms and anxiety*. (Standard Ed., vol. 20, pp. 87–172). Lon-
    don: Hogarth.
Goldstein, J.; Freud, A.; & Solnit, A. J. (1973). *Beyond the best interest of the child*. New York:
    Free Press.
Goldstein, J.; Freud, A.; & Solnit, A. J. (1979). *Before the best interests of the child*. New York:
    Free Press.

Greenberg, M. T., & Marvin, R. S. (1979). Attachment patterns in profoundly deaf preschool children. *Merrill-Palmer Quarterly* 25(4), 265–279.

Greenspan, S. I. (1981). Psychopathology and adaptation: Principles of clinical diagnosis and preventive intervention. *Clinical Infant Reports, No. 1, National Center for Clinical Infant Programs.* New York: International Universities Press.

Greenspan, S., & Lieberman, A. F. (in press). A clinical developmental approach to adaptive and maladaptive attachment. In J. Belsky & T. Nezworski (eds.), *Clinical implications of attachment.* Hillsdale, N.J.: Erlbaum.

Lampl-de Groot, J. (1957). On defense and development: Normal and pathological. *Psychoanalytic Study of the Child* 12, 114–126.

Lieberman, A. F. (1985). Infant mental health: A model for service delivery. *Journal of Clinical Child Psychology* 14, 196–201.

Lieberman, A. F., & Pawl, J. H. (1984). Searching for the best interests of the child: Intervention with an abusive mother and her toddler. *Psychoanalytic Study of the Child* 39, 527–548.

Mahler, M.; Pine, F.; & Bergman, A. (1975). *The psychological birth of the human infant: Symbiosis and individuation.* New York: Basic Books.

Main, M.; Kaplan, N.; & Cassidy, J. (1985). Security in infancy, childhood and adulthood: A move to the level of representation. In I. Bretherton & E. Waters (eds.), *Growing points in attachment theory and research. Monographs for the Society for Research in Child Development* 50 (1–2, Serial No. 209), 66–104.

Marvin, R. S. (1977). An ethological-cognitive model for the attenuation of mother-child attachment behavior. In T. M. Alloway, L. Krames, & P. Pliner (eds.), *Advances in the study of communications and affect: Vol. 2. The development of social attachment.* New York: Plenum.

Marvin, R. S., & Greenberg, M. T. (1982). Preschoolers' changing conceptions of their mother: A social-cognitive study of mother-child attachment. In M. T. Greenberg & D. Forbes (eds.), *Intertonality and the planning of social behavior.* New York: Jossey-Bass.

Murphy, L. B., & Moriarty, A. (1976). *Vulnerability, coping and growth: From infancy to adolescence.* New Haven: Yale University Press.

Pawl, J. H., & Pekarsky, J. H. (1983). Infant-parent psychotherapy: A family in crisis. In S. Provence (ed.), *Infants and parents: Clinical case reports.* New York: International Universities Press.

Piaget, J. (1954). *The construction of reality in the child.* New York: Basic Books.

Sander, L. (1962). Issues in early mother-child interaction. *Journal of the American Academy of Child Psychiatry* 1, 141–166.

Sroufe, L. A. (1979). The coherence of individual development: Early care, attachment, and subsequent development issues. *American Psychologist* 34, 834–841.

Sroufe, L. A., & Fleeson, J. (1986). Attachment and the construction of relationships. In W. Hartup & Z. Rubin (eds.), *Relationships and development* (pp. 51–71). Hillsdale, N.J.: Erlbaum.

Waters, A., & Sroufe, L. A. (1983). Social competence as a developmental construct. *Developmental Review* 3, 79–97.

Winnicott, D. W. (1955). Metapsychological and clinical aspects of regression within the psychoanalytic set-up. Reprinted in *Through pediatrics to psychoanalysis* (pp. 278–294). New York: Basic Books.

13 · The Treatment of Preschool Conduct Problems

An Integration of Behavioral and Attachment Concepts

Matthew L. Speltz

THIS CHAPTER will describe several clinical modifications of a standard behavioral parent-training model for preschool conduct problems (Forehand & McMahon 1981). These modifications have been drawn in large part from the study of mother-infant attachment during infancy and the preschool years (e.g., Ainsworth 1982; Bowlby 1979; Main, Kaplan, & Cassidy 1985; Marvin 1977), including research suggesting a predictive relationship between early attachment classification and the subsequent behavioral competencies of preschoolers (e.g., Bates, Maslin, & Frankel 1985; Erickson & Farber 1983; Lewis, Feiring, McGuffog, & Jaskir 1984; Sroufe 1983). Although the integration of behavioral and attachment constructs is complicated by the very different epistemological models from which these two areas have developed (Reese & Overton 1970), we believe that there is great potential for the development of new parent-training techniques on the basis of conceptual models typically associated with dynamic or analytic styles of treatment intervention (Mahler, Pine, & Bergman 1975).[1]

First some background will be provided regarding the behavioral training of parents with young conduct-problem children, including our clinical impressions about the effects of these treatment procedures on child development. Next, some hypotheses about the relationship between early attachment and subsequent social competency during the preschool years will be discussed as well as the clinical implications of this theorizing for current interventions with young disruptive children. Finally, our modified behavioral

---

This paper is the second in a series of papers on this topic. The first (Greenberg & Speltz 1988) provides a detailed review of the parent-training and attachment literature and proposes an attachment conceptualization for conduct problems. This one will focus more on training procedures and clinical examples, utilizing a conceptualization that integrates attachment concepts and behavioral techniques.

1. The first-person plural will refer in this paper to the author, colleagues, and several interns and graduate students who have contributed to the development of these ideas through their various activities in the Child Psychiatry Outpatient Clinic at Children's Hospital and Medical Center in Seattle.

parent-training model will be described in some detail, followed by a case example of its application.

BACKGROUND

The term "conduct problem" will be used to describe a well-known constellation of preschool problem behaviors including chronic noncompliance, aggressiveness, and frequent dyscontrol. These behaviors generate a high level of parent-child conflict, hinder greatly the child's capacity to function effectively in preschool, and very often lead to a referral for professional help during the preschool years. Longitudinal research (e.g., Loeber 1982) suggests that for many youngsters such difficulties will persist and intensify, although the exact manifestation of these early problems in later years is not altogether clear (Sroufe & Rutter 1984).

During the past decade, operant learning models have strongly dominated the clinical study of conduct disorders both in terms of their conceptualization (Patterson 1976; Atkeson & Forehand 1981) and resulting treatment strategies (Forehand & McMahon 1981). Treatment within this model is almost always a caregiver-focused intervention in which the child's parent or teacher is trained in methods of behavioral control that follow directly from operant principles of reinforcement, punishment, and extinction (see Greenberg & Speltz 1986). Outcome research suggests that, at least under conditions of optimal performance (i.e., experimenter-observed play sessions), parents of conduct-problem preschoolers can successfully demonstrate the operant skills in which they are trained and, when doing so, child compliance and general deportment improves in relation to pretraining measures (e.g., Forehand & King 1974).

We used this model of parent training for several years in our work with conduct-disordered preschoolers. In our early work with these children, we were impressed with the power of operant techniques to reduce intense parent-child conflict in a relatively brief period of time, an effect we initially interpreted as "successful" treatment. As our experience with these young children broadened, however, we began to find that reductions in conflict-producing behaviors with a trained caregiver were often short-lived and seemed not to generalize to the child's social relationships with others (with teachers, peers). Nor did such changes in observable conflict behavior seem to generalize to areas of the child's psychological functioning which are believed to have long-term significance (e.g., self-esteem, self-control, problem-solving skills).

Our clinical impressions of limited generalization are supported in the behavioral literature. When cross-setting measures of parent-training outcome have been taken (e.g., looking at child posttraining behavior with parent *and* with an "untreated" teacher in a classroom), children have been found to either show no change (Forehand, Sturgis, McMahon, Auger, Green, Wells, & Breiner 1979; Bruner & Forehand 1981), or a deterioration in behavioral functioning (Johnson, Bolstad, & Lobitz 1976). Thus, it would appear that, while conflict reduction through contingency management is an important and perhaps necessary step in the treatment process, it may not be sufficient to promote the young child's long-term adjustment or to enhance the quality of the child's relationships.

ATTACHMENT AT THE LEVEL OF OVERT BEHAVIOR

In our attempts to supplement the operant model with other conceptualizations that might foster more generalized change, we became interested in attachment because many of the child behavior problems brought to our attention seemed to reflect the child's attempts—vis à vis "problem" behavior—to control the physical and psychological proximity of caregivers. When we would ask ourselves—initially from a strictly operant perspective—what observable events were "reinforcing" the child's problem behavior, the answer often had to do with achieving greater regulation over the availability of the caregiver. Presenting problems such as hitting a sibling, having a tantrum, frequent accidents or injuries, refusing to eat (or eating too much!), destroying something belonging to the caregiver, running away, taking a toy from a peer, and so on, have obvious capacity to generate rapid and intense caretaker intervention. Further, a common situational antecedent for many of these problem behaviors is one that portends or results in some interruption or termination of the caregiver's proximity to the child (e.g., getting dressed before school, putting toys away, going to bed, parent departures, home or classroom transitions leading to reduced parent/teacher proximity or attention).

Such extreme measures for gaining access to care may result from the child's history of unresponsive parental care in which the parent's behavior has lacked both *contingency* (i.e., lacking immediate, consistent responding; see Skinner 1985) and *sensitivity* (i.e., the content of the parent's response is developmentally inappropriate with respect to the caregiver's interpretation of child signals; see Ainsworth 1967). Although the child's "use" of provocative behavior might successfully improve the contingency of the parent's behavior, it would probably do little to alter the sensitivity of the parent's care. Thus, misbehavior as a strategy for regulating care would do little for the child's further social and emotional development.

This conceptualization at the level of observable interaction could be viewed simply as a less parsimonious way of describing the operant effects of what behavior therapists call "attention." Parental attention is viewed as a powerful social "reward" for child misconduct and serves as the conceptual basis for recommending the use of ignoring as a technique to extinguish problem behavior (Patterson 1976). However, the concept of "attention" as used by most behavior therapists does not explain clearly *why* parent attention is so powerful a reinforcer at particular ages; why some children seem "driven" to elicit potentially harmful parental attention (physical discipline); and why the same or similar behavior problems can occur in relationships with dramatically different patterns or *amounts* of parental attention to the child (neglect vs. overprotection).

ATTACHMENT AT THE LEVEL OF AFFECT AND COGNITION

The proceeding conceptualization represents a relatively simple integration of operant and attachment concepts in that the concept of reinforcement is merely extended in terms of a key developmental task during infancy and beyond—the child's regulation of adult care. The focus, however, is still on the observable interactions between the child and caregiver and, like the more traditional operant formulations of behavior disorders (e.g., Atkeson & Forehand 1981), the cognitive and affectual correlates of this process are not considered. What attachment theory can primarily contribute to the understanding of behavior problems is how the young child's observable relationship with the caregiver (in terms of proximity regulation) serves as the basis for developing cognitive and emotional responses that "represent" the early relationship and potentially exert strong effects on behavior long after physical proximity functions as a salient developmental challenge for the child (Main et al. 1985). This is not to say that the thinking and feeling "products" of early attachment exert enduring, unchangeable effects on behavioral development. Rather, the effects of early responses "transact" with the child's changing social environment (Sameroff & Chandler 1975), altering the probability of future disorder.

There are several ways in which the cognitive and affectual consequences of early unresponsive care can substantially increase a child's risk for preschool conduct problems. The probability of problem behavior may be enhanced by the disregulating effects of chronic anxiety or fear associated with the continued uncertainty of the caregiver's availability. Feelings of anxiousness and fear may also affect social behavior by curtailing the child's exploration of the inanimate and social environment and the child's "experimentation" with new ways of relating to others (what Main et al. 1985 have called "attempts and outcomes"). Such anxiety may foster excessive monitoring of the caregiver's activity (in an effort to assure one's self of parental availability) at the expense of attending to other aspects of the environment which promote social learning (see Cassidy 1986 for a discussion of this possibility with respect to the child's ability to negotiate the physical environment). Chronic uncertainty about the responsiveness of one's caregiver may also directly give rise to feelings of anger and frustration which may become manifested in part as tantrum behavior or aggressiveness toward the parent. Resentment of the caregiver's level of responsiveness may eventually affect the child's willingness to cooperate and please the parent.

When the child cannot regulate or influence the behavior of adults reliably, generalized expectations of incompetence may come to govern the child's willingness to engage in new tasks and solve problems (Lewis & Brooks 1978; Hazen & Durrett 1982; Skinner 1985). Bowlby's concept (Bowlby 1973) of the child's internal "working model," as elaborated by Bretherton (1985), Main et al. (1985), and Sroufe and Fleesen (1986), suggests how the young child's early experiences of coping with caretaker unavailability may later come to foster generalized cognitive rules or expectations about the availability and emotional supportiveness of others, including peers, teachers, and so on. The child's developing self-concept thus may be affected in that the child begins to view himself or herself primarily in terms of the caregiver's responsiveness, or lack thereof. As Bretherton (1985) states:

> . . . if an attachment figure frequently rejects or ridicules the child's bids for comfort in stressful situations, the child may come to develop not only an internal working model of the parent as rejecting but also one of himself or herself as not worthy of help or comfort. Conversely, if the attachment figure gives help and comfort when needed, the child will tend to develop a working model of the parent as loving and of himself or herself as a person worthy of such support.

In a similar fashion, the child who must resort to provocative and/or oppositional behavior as a reliable means of regulating care may develop a self-concept in which such behavior becomes a central part of the internalized self; that is, the child sees himself or herself generally as someone who does or must behave in this manner in order to have influence over the responsiveness of others. This type of self-image may engender "a self-fulfilling prophecy" in that the child may continue to act out in line with self-perception even when the social environment changes and no longer directly supports such behavior (e.g., noncompliance continues at school even when compliance is rewarded in that setting).

Thus, the link between early attachment and later behavioral competence (Sroufe 1983) may be understood at multiple, interdependent levels of functioning including observable patterns of parent-child interaction with respect to proximity regulation (both past and present) and the child's emotional responses and cognitive expectations related to self and other. In this analysis, frequent tantrum behavior (a common ingredient of the conduct-problem presentation during the preschool years) not only results from its overt effect on caretaker proximity but also the child's feelings about the parent and his or her perceptions of self and others.

An important question is raised by this analysis. If an insecurely attached child develops provocative behavior as a primary means of regulating caregiver behavior (which we would presume the clinic-referred child has accomplished "successfully"), are not the child's needs for predictable caregiver behavior now met? Are these behaviors then *adaptive* within the context of the child's attachment relationship? Such behavior, of course, cannot be considered "adaptive" even with reference to the relationship in which such behavior developed. Although, at the level of overt interaction, the *proximity* and *contingency* of parent is enhanced, only in very rare cases would the parent's *sensitivity* to the child's emotional needs be enhanced as well by such behavior. In fact, continued problem behavior over time probably leads to further decline in the parent's sensitivity to the child's affectual needs, creating a "vicious cycle" in which the child's provocative behavior may regulate parent proximity contingently but at the expense of further impairment to the emotional bond between the two.

Within this perspective, the difficulty noted earlier in obtaining generalized change with current parent-training methods may result from the nearly exclusive focus in these procedures on overt parent-child interaction, with relatively little attention to the emotional and communicative aspects of the relationship (Greenberg & Speltz 1988). Naturally, in attempting to change only specific overt behaviors, only overt misbehavior is changed, with little generalization to the emotions and cognitions that come to have increasingly more direct influence on overt behavior as the child develops. Perhaps, if there were an attempt to alter the emotional bond between parent and child, generalized child improvements would occur. In the following sections, our efforts to extend the behavioral parent-training model along these lines is described in close relation to procedural details.

The Role of Parent and Child Working Models

With respect to the search for specific areas in which the conflict reduction methods of operant training might require extension and supplementation, two areas took priority: (1) interventions aimed at the child's cognitive/affectual representations of the attachment relationship (the working model), and (2) interventions that consider the *parent's* working model of relationships as it pertains to their caretaking behavior.

Child's Working Model

The concept of the "working model" follows from Bowlby's (1973) hypotheses about the transition of the attachment system from infancy to the preschool years, a transition in which the child's reliance on mother's physical presence changes to a self-reliance on cognitive/affectual representations of mother in her physical absence. As the child's cognitive capabilities expand to include the understanding of others' perspectives, the potential for mutual negotiations of mother's departures and reunion arises. Marvin (1977) proposed that, as the importance of physical proximity attentuates during the preschool years, the attainment of verbally derived and mutually agreed upon goals and plans regarding parent-child separations and reunions now becomes one of the child's "set-goals" in the relationship, just as physical proximity functioned in this manner during infancy. In this way, *verbal transactions* between child and parent regarding separation contribute importantly to the child's growing accumulation of expectations and "rules" about social relationships and, in particular, expectations regarding the availability and supportiveness of others in the context of such relationships. This relationship between parent-child transactions and the child's working model provides an important clinical opportunity for treatment; that is, the child's working model can be nurtured potentially by exploring in therapy the construction of joint plans for separation and reunion and other situations of potential conflict between parent and child—a strategy that should facilitate generalized behavioral adjustment.

Operant models of parent training for preschoolers have not emphasized the verbal negotiating skills of the parent-child dyad. Indeed, a child's attempt to negotiate a parental limit is often regarded as "noncompliance," and parents are warned about the potential reinforcement of "misbehavior" that would result if they responded verbally in a spirit of negotiation. Parents, thus, are taught to ignore verbal protesting when giving their child a direction and to use a punishment "time out" if such protesting persists without compliance. Since the child seldom participates at a verbal level in the training process, the parents may very likely begin to use these procedures without explanation to the child. The problems with this recommendation from a developmental perspective are: (1) neither the parent nor child learns how to communicate about and/or problem solve issues regarding separation and limit setting (skills associated with smooth child adjustments to separation/reunions; Marvin 1977); (2) the child may internalize an expectation about relationships that caregivers (or others) become unresponsive and possibly punishing when anger or disagreement is expressed; and (3) opportunities for the child to learn and rehearse the verbal labeling of one's own emotional states (a process critical for the development of self-control) are lost. It may be that one characteristic distinguishing the families of conduct-problem preschoolers from nonproblem children is the extent to which the dyad is able to develop joint plans for separations/reunions or other situations stressful for the dyad—a possibility Greenberg and Speltz (1988) have termed a "deficiency of planning" hypothesis.

Parent's Working Model

The responsiveness of the caregiver may be influenced strongly by his or her own working model of relationships, that is, social expectations that have resulted from the parent's attachment relationships with caregivers during infancy and childhood (Main et al. 1985), as modulated by the experiences of subsequent relationships with peers, teachers, spouses, and so on. Implicit "rules" about the general availability and probable responses of others (based on multiple relationships and experiences) mediate the caregiver's *interpretation* of their child's behavior and subsequent interactions with the child.

In a brief training intervention, it is probably not possible to change substantially the working model of an adult; indeed, some believe that working models in large part are beyond conscious awareness and quite resistant to change (Bowlby 1980), thus requiring long-term intervention in a therapeutic relationship that challenges long-held expectations of others. It may be possible, however, to enable parents to recognize that their responses to their child are based on far more than the child's specific behaviors. Rather, the parent can come to understand that in many situations their response to child behavior may be driven by a collection of thoughts and feelings representative of past relationships of which their child's provocation is but a reminder. Thus, for example, when the preschooler "talks back" and the mother becomes angry, this anger may be directed not only at the child but also at others in past relationships (husband, father, boss) who have treated the mother in a similar fashion, recreating a familiar relationship pattern consistent with the parent's cognitive expectations (Sroufe & Fleeson 1986). Although it is unlikely that the working model of the parent with respect to self and others can be changed in a parent-training program, the parent may be able to learn how their parenting behavior is affected by their own attachment history as manifested by current beliefs, attitudes, and expectations about relationships in general. Perhaps the parent can learn to (*a*) recognize when such expectations affect their perception of child behavior, and (*b*) consciously make their child an "exception" to these beliefs.

DESCRIPTION OF TRAINING PROCEDURES

Overview

In developing an integrated model of intervention for conduct problem preschoolers, we wanted to retain those portions of the operant model that have been shown to reduce overt conflict effectively and also to retain this model's overall mode of presentation; that is, a skills-training format which at the point of direct service to the client translates conceptual analyses of unobservable processes into specific caregiver/child behaviors that can be taught and rehearsed in a variety of established methods including didactic teaching, modeling, role playing, videotape feedback, and so on. This is in contrast procedurally with most treatments that follow directly from analytic descriptions of attachment which tend to focus on long-term verbal strategies with adults (psychotherapy) or verbal interpretations of play with children within a supportive therapist-child relationship. These procedures, although important, have limited general applicability, particularly with clients with average or below verbal abilities and the lack of motivation or resources to remain in treatment for long periods. This is not to say, however, that the therapist-client relationship is not an important or necessary treatment ingredient within the proposed model, but only that an overall treatment structure with an emphasis on specific behavioral goals and activities presented in a determined sequence was a primary consideration.

Another consideration of importance at the outset was how to strike a balance between short-term conflict reduction and attention to variables hypothesized as having long-term effects on child development and the parent-child relationship (e.g., partnership skills, child's working model). Just as behavior therapists have tended to overlook developmental variables of long-term significance in their efforts to quell immediate conflict, clinicians of an analytic/attachment persuasion have tended to focus immediately in treatment on long-term variables without adequately addressing factors that have come to exert strong control over day-to-day variations in behavior (interpersonal contingencies). We believe that these clinicians have underestimated the power of simple contingencies to influence interpersonal behavior. For example, many child therapists recommend as a treatment for frequent or prolonged tantrums that the parent hold, comfort, and reassure the child when such behavior occurs. Although this recommendation assumes (correctly) that the child's tantrums reflect in large part a need for greater intimacy with parent, an initial treatment strategy based on this line of reasoning would very likely lead to an even higher rate of tantrums that would continue as long as the parent responded in this manner. Although treatment in the long term should clearly address the child's need for intimacy (and eventually move the dyad to a point where the parent *can* reassure the child during tantrums without ill effects), a more effective short-term (but temporary) solution would minimize the parent's emotional responses to tantrums (both negative and positive) and seek to increase parent-child intimacy in situations that are *independent* of tantrum behavior. Thus, the "ultimate" cause of a behavior problem may not be the one on which to develop an initial treatment strategy; rather, the therapist may need to focus initially on very proximal antecedents (and/or consequences) of conflict, moving "backward" along some hypothesized dimension of temporal causality as treatment progresses.

The model of treatment proposed here attempts to handle this very difficult balancing of short- versus long-term treatment strategies by initially addressing a relatively proximal characteristic of the parent-child relationship: the child's regulation of caregiver behavior during play interactions. Next, short-term conflict reduction using standard operant techniques for limit setting is emphasized. In the final phase of training, cognitive/affectual variables are addressed more directly by focusing on patterns of parent-child communication which manifest the goal-corrected partnership and allow the dyad to move to a level of mutual regulation. These treatment phases follow an assessment phase and a brief orientation/education phase which alerts the parent to key developmental issues relevant to conflict (e.g., attentuation of the child's need for physical proximity). Each of these five phases of training (assessment, education, child-directed play, limit setting, and parent-child communication training) are described below.

Assessment

The first two or three sessions with the family focus on the assessment of the child's presenting problems, the situational features of presenting problems (interactional antecedents and consequences), child developmental status, the attachment history of the parent-child relationship, the parent's own attachment history, and how the parent-child dyad play together and resolve conflict. The attachment histories of the mother-child dyad and each parent are obtained through interview. The interactional properties of the relationship are assessed through direct observation of play interaction and separation/reunion. Two trials of separation/reunion are used (see Speltz, Greenberg, & DeKlyen in press for details), followed by child-directed versus parent-directed play instructions developed by Eyberg and Robinson (1982). Our assessment of separation/reunion is directed equally at both members of the dyad. The reunion behavior of the child is observed with respect to multiple possible forms of affectual expression, including *verbal* manifestations of avoidance and resistance (e.g., child giving the parent commands or asking controlling questions, raising a topic of obvious distress to the parent). We are also interested in the mother's departure style, the parent's immediate and delayed responses to whatever reunion behavior is shown by the child, and the verbal interchange between parent and child prior to the mother's departure. (Is some agreement reached? Does mother suggest to child what can be done in her absence? Is the reunion situation anticipated by the mother?)

This assessment information is collected in order to provide at least tentative answers to the following specific questions which follow from the conceptualization presented in this paper: (1) How developmentally capable is the child of communicating caretaking needs (in terms of cognitive, language, motor development)? (2) How emotionally and psychologically capable is the parent to respond to child communications of need for caretaking (i.e., in terms of parent self-concept, social support, financial/living circumstances)? (3) What are the child's primary observable strategies for regulating caregiver behavior (i.e., "misbehavior" versus "prosocial behavior")? (4) What is the best estimate (based on parent report) of the quality of attachment during the child's first and second years of life? That is, was the child securely attached early in the relationship with problems emerging primarily during the more recent separation/individuation phase? Or was "secure" attachment never evident? (5) To what extent are the parents' relationship conflicts with the child indicative of the parents' relationship with others (with spouse, peers, parents, siblings)? (6) To what extent does the dyad manifest a verbal process for mutual coregulation of attachment versus exploration, child versus parent control of decisions in the relationship? (7) What interactional contingencies are prominent in situations in which presenting problems frequently occur? That is, in what specific ways does the child's problem behavior regulate or control caretaker behavior? (8) To what extent does the family system (including the marital relationship, sibling-child relationships) contribute to dyadic conflict?

Tentative answers to these questions are used to recommend an overall intervention plan that may include (but is certainly not limited to) our parent/child training program or used to make recommendations about a particular sequence about different interventions (e.g., parent/child training followed by family therapy, parent/child training concurrent with individual psychotherapy for the caregiver and/or play therapy for the child). Although no certain rules apply, parent/child training *alone* is usually recommended under the following circumstances: (1) there is some evidence of relatively early secure attachment to a caregiver, (2) current behavioral conflict seems to be attributable to recent difficulties in the dyad's ability to negotiate the separation/individuation phase than to a significantly disruptive attachment early in the relationship, (3) the parents' difficulties in responding to the child seem attributable more to situational factors and/or an inability of the parent to shift from an early to later mode of parenting (e.g., transition from sensitivity and nurturance to "relaxed firmness"; see Greenberg & Speltz 1988) than a personality disorder which significantly limits the caregiver's generalized ability to provide care.

When the decision for a treatment recommendation is made, a feedback session is held with the family in which the results of the assessment phase are presented with an explanation of why we believe the child is displaying the behavioral symptoms brought to us for treatment. We also discuss in what specific ways these causal events are related to the recommended treatment. This session is very often the most important of any for it gives the parents a rationale for treatment which in turn affects motivation for follow-through.

Our causal explanations to parents focus on the role of child temperament (i.e., that some children from quite early on are much more difficult to take care of than others) and the match between the child's temperament and the parent's personality (Thomas & Chess 1977). Some matches engender relatively smooth relationships; other matches are difficult and result in frequent conflict that is not the "fault" of either party but rather a result of this dyadic matching process. Temperamentally, we describe the oppositional child to parents as one who has a very strong "need" for control and self-determination, children who tend to be quite stubborn and strong-willed. Although these characteristics can be channeled into potentially desirable qualities (assertiveness, leadership), they present problems during the preschool years because all children (even those with easy-going temperaments) are striving for self-determination during these years.

These general explanations, as well as specific information pertaining to each child (developmental status, unique historical factors which may have played a causal role in current difficulties), are given to the parents alone. Whenever possible, some part of the feedback session is devoted to providing a simple presentation to the *child* of "what is going on" in terms of why the family is visiting that day, what is generally being discussed, and what the plan is for future meetings. The children are given an opportunity to ask anyone present a question about "what is going on" and assured that they are not "bad" or to blame for anything and that the entire family has been asked to come together to talk about how to "get along better." Although only some preschoolers will participate actively in this part of the session, we believe that this is still an important process for the child to experience because (1) it is in keeping with our general philosophy that the child must be involved in all levels of treatment so as to facilitate self-attribution of change, and (2) it creates a model for the parents that the preschooler, although having limited cognitive capabilities, is a person "worthy" of being regarded in this manner, someone who deserves to be informed of matters greatly affecting his or her life.

PHASE I (1–2) SESSIONS): PARENT EDUCATION IN DEVELOPMENTAL ISSUES

The primary objective of this first phase of treatment is to acquaint the parent with developmental information that bears on the child's social and emotional development. Included are issues pertaining to language and cognitive and motor development, emphasizing what the parent can generally expect of a child at a given age. Usually in this session we are attempting to counter what seems to be a strong tendency for our parents to overestimate their child's capabilities, particularly in areas having to do with their response to parent verbal reasoning during disciplinary transactions. The tremendous degree of individual variation in developmental areas is also emphasized.

These are areas commonly addressed in parent-training programs, but what appears to be less common is our inclusion of developmental information pertaining to the attachment relationship and changes in attachment during the preschool years; that is, the child's transition from physical proximity to verbal/symbolic interaction as the primary mode of maintaining a close relationship with parents. In this regard, we emphasize the preschooler's attempts to become more independent and autonomous than during toddlerhood and the "growth ambivalence" that is characteristic of this stage. Important, too, is the idea of "dual ambivalence" (i.e., it is sometimes the case that the parent can also have ambivalent feelings about the child's growing individuation and that this is "normal").

We also cover the dramatic changes in caregiving behavior that seem to be required during this transition period (e.g., the need to "remain close" during infancy/toddlerhood vs. the need to provide both support for autonomous behavior and limit setting during the preschool years). The obvious difficulty of trying to set limits concurrently and support autonomy is acknowledged as something that is problematic for all parents and quite obviously made even more challenging when the child is also generally difficult to manage. The child's development of behavior problems is described within the context of all of these issues, with the intent of convincing parents that behavior problems at this age are not the symptoms of a "bad" child (which many of our parents truly believe) but rather in part an outgrowth of a normal developmental tendency to assert control.

PHASE II (3–5 SESSIONS): CHILD-DIRECTED INTERACTION

The primary goal of Phase II is to increase the child's actual and perceived level of control in the parent-child relationship, primarily through the use of child-directed play sessions with parents. We attempt to increase not only the *amount* of parent-child play interaction but also the extent to which the parent allows the child to control that interaction. In this way, both the "neglected" child (who has little interaction time with parent) and the "enmeshed" child (who has frequent but excessively controlled interaction with parent) theoretically benefit from child-directed play. Within the conceptual model here, frequent child-directed play will provide the child with a means of caregiver regulation that does not depend for its elicitation on problem behavior. An assumption implicit in this emphasis on play is that the dynamics of play interaction between parent and child are relatively well representative of the entire parent-child relationship.

Another important goal of Phase II is to explicate the parents' subjective *interpretations* of child behavior during play which mediate the parents' capacity and comfort in giving the child control (reflecting presumably, the parents' working model of relationships). Here, we help the parent to (1) recognize and articulate the specific nature of such cognitive interpretations and their emotional impact on the parent; (2) explore the possible relationship between such cognitive/affective processes as applied to "child" versus "others"; and (3) regard the child as an *exception* to the parents' commonly held rules/expectations, that is, getting the parent to "reframe" the child's behavior in a way that facilitates the parents' ability during play to give control.

The idea of teaching parents how to do child-directed play comes from several sources including both those of a behavioral orientation (e.g., Hanf 1969; Eyberg & Robinson 1982) and nonbehavioral orientation (Stover & Guerney 1967). Usually, the parent is taught in such procedures to allow the child to lead whatever play activity develops by occasionally describing to the child what they are doing ("You're stacking the blocks"; "You're driving the car"; etc.), praising the child's efforts, and eliminating commands, questions, and critical comments.

One type of child-directed interaction, called "Child's Game," is the focus of Rex Forehand's first phase of operant parent training for preschoolers (Forehand & McMahon 1981). Our version of child-directed play, although procedurally similar to Child's Game, is different in several ways. First, Child's Game functions primarily in the operant model as an opportunity for parents to rehearse (with therapist coaching) a set of skills with considerable *control-taking* potential (contingent giving/withholding of attention, praising of behaviors that the *parent* desires). Although Child's Game also emphasizes parent verbal behaviors that facilitate child control (describing), the overall goal of the play seems to be the development of the parents' ability to use their attention contingently in order to gain better control of the child's misbehavior. In contrast, the child-directed play in the current model is designed to exaggerate the child's sense of control by looking at very detailed aspects of parents' verbal and nonverbal behavior (including gestures, sitting position) which might conceivably communicate intrusiveness or a sense of expectation or performance. Thus, watching, imitation, and describing are emphasized; praising is *not* introduced initially; and commands, questions, question-like descriptions ("You're building a bridge, aren't you?") and interpretations ("You're getting tired") are all discouraged.

A second difference between the use of play in the operant model versus the current model is the strong emphasis that we place on the parents' cognitive/affective processing of child-play behavior and the effects of these private events on the parents' emotional state and subsequent interactions with the child. Procedurally, this is done by having the therapist identify specific child behaviors that appear to upset or irritate the parent and/or are followed by a parental effort to take control of the interaction (e.g., child gives parent a command; parent looks angry, complies, but then gives the child an idea for a "better" way to play). The play is videotaped, viewed with the parent, and when a selected child behavior occurs (child giving mom a command), the tape is stopped and the parent is asked questions like, What is your first thought about that? How do you feel about what he just said (or did)? What does it remind you of? Have you known anyone else who does (or says) that? The answers to such questions will hopefully allow us to piece together the parents' working model that most strongly mediates their perception of the child during play.

A third difference between the Child's Game procedure and the play in this model is related to the nature of the child's participation. In the operant model, instructions about the play and how to play are directed almost exclusively at the parent, and the child's presence seems to serve primarily the need for having a child to "practice with." Within the present model, the child is included deliberately in the preplay instructions, given a role to play ("It's your job to take the lead, to think of things to do"), and sometimes the child is asked to "watch for things" that the parent might do or say and to let the therapist know what that was like. In this way, we hope to instill in the child a sense of full participation and the potential to attribute whatever positive changes in parent-child play occur to his or her own effort.

Sequence of Procedures

To begin Phase II, the parent is given some instructions and didactic materials pertaining to the "dos and don'ts" of child-directed play and then watches with the therapist a videotape of a mother and son who demonstrate both a parent-directed and child-directed form of interaction. Then, the parent is asked to play with the child for ten to fifteen minutes at the beginning of each session, and this interaction is videotaped. The subsequent videotape review is divided about equally between (1) giving the parent feedback and coaching about their *control-giving* skills, and (2) explicating the parents' subjective cognitive/affectual reactions to child behaviors. This latter process will often lead to discussions of the parents' own experiences of being parented and how this affects their interpretations of child behavior, a process we encourage as long as its relevance to parent-child play interaction is evident. Also at this time, the therapist will attempt to have the parent engage in perspective-taking dialogue in which the parents are asked to "place themselves" in the child's situation, focusing on how the child feels, is thinking about, and so on during stressful interchanges. Between-session assignments focus on doing child-directed play everyday at home and reframing exercises (i.e., planned self-statements) the parents can use to alter their prevailing views of the child during play.

PHASE III (2–3 SESSIONS): LIMIT SETTING

Our approach to limit setting is guided by the principle of "least restraint," that is, using the minimal amount of force needed to insure the child's safety and to meet the needs of the parent to maintain order in the relationship. Of course, parental need to maintain order as well as perceived child safety are both quite subjective—again depending in large part on the parents' working model—and this cognitive process becomes an important part of Phase III.

As child-directed play is clearly a command-free "zone" of interactional territory, Phase III deals exclusively with transactions *outside* of play. Four steps are involved in analyzing and teaching limit setting in these nonplay areas:

1. *Helping the parent identify child behaviors which potentially require limit setting and sorting these into two broad categories:* annoying, but potentially ignorable behaviors (i.e., behavior not likely to lead to harm or destruction, e.g., whining, talking loudly, swearing) and nonignorable, potentially

harmful behaviors (hitting, leaving house, breaking toys). This step almost always leads to a discussion of the subjectiveness involved here as affected by the parent's personality, values, tolerance levels, the marital relationship, and so on. In two-parent families, reaching consensus between partners in these areas is strongly emphasized.

2. *Reducing limit setting in relation to behaviors in the ignorable category.* This step is based on the assumption that the potential effectiveness of any single limit (command) decreases in proportion to the overall frequency of commands given in the relationship. Thus, parents are given assignments in which they are asked to choose a behavior in this category and not respond (ignore) unless it escalates to a level that would place it in the nonignorable category. In this step, the ideas of "letting some things go" and developing greater tolerance for the annoying things that *all* preschoolers do are emphasized.

3. *Using indirect methods for limit setting.* In this step, the intent is to provide the parent with strategies for either (*a*) responding to child behaviors in the ignorable category, or (*b*) gaining child compliance with ordinary requests that still allow the child to have some degree of choice and responsibility in this process. Three deceptively simple techniques are introduced here: (*a*) giving choices or options that are within the parents' desires for the child (e.g., "You can choose the green or red dress. Which do you want?"); (*b*) when/then contingencies that simply state what the child needs to do before a routine, pleasant event in the child's schedule is allowed to occur (e.g., "When you pick up your clothes, then you can go outside"; "When you talk in a quiet voice, then I'll listen"); (*c*) specific labeled praise for acts of compliance (Forehand & McMahon 1981). We have found that the when/then contingency is an important organizing behavior for parents who learn to use it appropriately (i.e., a positive behavior is stated, the parent can afford in this situation to give the child a choice and can tolerate possible noncompliance, a routine reward is used vs. a bribe).

4. *Using direct methods for limit-setting.* Here the procedures of Forehand and McMahon (1981) are used in situations in which a nonignorable behavior occurs or the parent makes a request of the child which is considered important and nonnegotiable. Briefly, this procedure consists of a very structured one command–one warning–punishment sequence the parent is encouraged to carry out in a brisk, assertive, business-like manner which will hopefully override the prolonged and highly volatile interactions that typically characterize the parent's efforts to gain control over an oppositional child (Patterson 1976). This strategy is presented within our model as a procedure for use only in those situations in which the preceding techniques are not appropriate. An important extension of the Forehand and McMahon (1986) program is the gradual, stepwise reduction of the one command–one warning procedure, replaced by the selective use of the parent/child negotiating that becomes the focus of Phase IV.

PHASE IV (4–6 SESSIONS): PARENT-CHILD COMMUNICATION TRAINING

This phase is the most recent addition to our training efforts and certainly the least developed, a component still undergoing continuing modification and fine tuning. Phase IV techniques and skills are drawn from three sources: (1) the concept of "emerging partnership" (Marvin 1977) which describes a pre goal-corrected stage of the parent-child relationship in which the parent lays the basis for later coregulation by modeling and scaffolding verbal negotiation strategies, (2) the cognitive problem-solving approach to parenting (Spivack & Shure 1973) which encourages parents to "hold back" and assist the child in developing their own solutions to problems, (3) the communication training/problem-solving approach of behavior marital therapists who focus on techniques for reciprocity and coregulation in adult relationships (Gottman, Notarius, Gonso, & Markman 1976; Jacobson & Margolin 1979). From a communications standpoint, we conceptualize the ideal goal-corrected partnership as being not unlike a smoothly functioning marriage with two exceptions: (1) the parent must be able to "fill in" the child's part of the negotiating process *temporarily* (until the child can verbally "hold their own"), and (2) one side of the dyad (parent) is responsible for the overall structure within which negotiation takes place.

Table 1 presents a list of specific parent and child behaviors which increase the likelihood of the dyad-reaching agreement for a mutual plan regarding separation or a mutual decision pertaining to other issues in the relationship. It is expected, of course, that agreement or compromise will not always take place, in fact, many occur only some of the time with the parent having to withdraw eventually from the interaction and separating and/or making a unilateral decision. The primary goal, however, is not agreement per se but the *process* of trying to reach agreement in a manner that maximizes the preschoolers' perceived input into the parents' decision-making behavior.

The presentation and rehearsal of the skills in table 1 proceed in three steps. First, the instruction of communication skills for the parent is accomplished during a didactic session in which both the rationale for this approach to communication and the specific behaviors in table 1 are presented, followed by a roleplaying exercise in which the therapist takes the role of the child in a leave-taking situation and then in a decision-making situation in which the "child" and parent initially disagree. Like the earlier videotape review of child-directed play, the therapist's coaching during/after this role-playing covers both the parents' demonstration of skills as well as their cognitive/ affectual processing of "child" behaviors. The child is also taught the three skills presented in table 1 by the therapist using a combination of direct instruction techniques developed for preschool social skills training (Odom et al. 1985; Combs & Slaby 1977) and puppet play. The parent sometimes watches this session from behind an observation window. The primary intent of this instructional session with the child is not to bring the child to a level of

TABLE 1.   PARENT-CHILD COMMUNICATION SKILLS

Parent	Child
1. General communication skills: making feeling statements, nonverbal listening skills; verbal listening skills including paraphrasing and validating of what child says; labeling feelings in self and child.	1. Making a feeling statement ("I feel angry, sad, happy") in relation to the separation/reunion decision.
2. Verbalizing the extent to which the child's plans and intentions vs. the parents plans and intentions are the same or different (e.g., "I need to do this, but it sounds like you want me to do that").	2. Stating own intentions: "I want you to stay here."
3. Verbalizing a possible sequence for separation/reunion: (a) asking children what they can do during parents' absence; (b) suggesting choices of things children could do in parents' absence; (c) giving information about length, destination, reason for separation; (d) giving information about what the dyad can do when parent returns.	3. Helping parents to "brainstorm" about things to do during parents' absence and what the dyad can do upon parents' return.
4. Scaffolding: "filling in" child's part of the transaction.	
5. Detecting when children are ready to do their part on their own: gradually withdrawing the "filling in," allowing children to do their own part.	
6. Using labeled praise to provide children with feedback about their part of the transaction.	

actual performance of these skills but rather to introduce these behaviors to the child, solicit the child's participation, and indirectly model for the parent this type of transaction. It is expected that the child's "real" learning of these skills will take place over the repeated course of these interactions with parent.

The second step in this process consists of in vivo rehearsal. Here, the many brief separations that naturally occur in a therapy session (e.g., a parent leaves the playroom to talk individually with the therapist) are utilized as opportunities for the parent to try out the new skills; or, child behavior problems that emerge during the course of therapy sessions are used as conflict situations in which parent-child negotiating can be rehearsed. These situations are videotaped and then reviewed with the parent as was done in the child-directed play phase.

Homework assignments to continue the rehearsal of negotiation are given with respect to selected situations at home. Initially, these focus on relatively minor separations and/or decisions (e.g., one parent leaves child with another) and gradually move on to potentially more stressful situations (leaving child with the baby-sitter; being dropped off at day-care or preschool). As with all the homework assignments given within this parent-training model, both parent and child are included in the discussion of and instructions regarding the week's forthcoming assignment.

CASE APPLICATION

One recent application of the training procedures described above involved a 4-year-old girl (to be called Lisa) who was brought to our clinic by her parents (to be called Robert and Judy) for a variety of conduct problems (e.g., frequent and intense tantrums, noncompliance, "power struggles," and aggressiveness usually directed at parents but sometimes at peers). The precipitating event for the family's first clinic visit was Lisa's being asked to leave a day-care because of frequent tantrum behavior as well as being "too bossy" with peers and generally "not minding." In her new preschool, similar problems were occurring, primarily during structured group times when Lisa would strongly resist teacher efforts to have her remain with the group, stay seated, answer questions, and so on.

Both parents and teachers reported that Lisa was otherwise "within normal limits" with respect to other major areas of development such as language, gross and fine motor functions, and toilet training. Lisa was somewhat overweight (98 percentile for age and height), and many of the power struggles with her parents centered on interactions related to food consumption (refusing to eat what she was given at mealtimes, eating prohibited foods between meals). Lisa's parents were both somewhat overweight themselves, particularly Judy, who expressed very strong feelings about Lisa not "turning out like me."

The family group consisted of Lisa and her two parents who were both quite involved in the parenting and general care of Lisa. Judy was unemployed, reported having few friends, and it seemed to us that an inordinate amount of this mother's life was devoted to Lisa and the current situation regarding Lisa's "problems."

Assessment Phase

The interviews and observational assessment of this family produced several findings of significance. Observations of parent-child play revealed a maternal style of interaction that was highly controlling and somewhat nonresponsive. This was manifested primarily by a very high rate of verbal behavior, dominated by a teaching or tutorial style of play (quizzing Lisa, asking her questions, having her draw pictures in a certain way). Robert was considerably more child-directed in his play, appearing quite comfortable in following Lisa's directions and ideas. Judy told us that whenever she asked Lisa a teaching question during play, she felt "reassured" that Lisa was developing normally despite her behavior problems. These types of parental play interaction seemed to represent well the general nature of the parent-child relationships in this family, as reported by the parents during interviews. For example, Judy's overall amount of interaction with Lisa seemed to be considerable but largely consisting of parent-directed interaction.

At the beginning of the separation/reunion segment of the observational assessment, Judy announced her departure without warning, simply saying that "the doctor wants me to go." Lisa immediately began to protest in a whining, pleading manner which Judy ignored completely. Lisa then began to cry as her mother left the room. Soon after the door was closed, however, Lisa stopped crying and settled down easily to solitary play with toys.

When Judy returned to the playroom, Lisa initially ignored her completely, including not answering several questions directed at her from Judy. Instead, Lisa played with her back to Judy for several minutes. When Judy's questions went unanswered, she attempted to redirect Lisa's play ("Let's draw some more pictures"). Lisa then began to play aggressively with the blocks. Judy set a limit, and the interaction quickly escalated to an enormous power struggle with Lisa eventually having a tantrum in the playroom. This tantrum lasted for about three minutes with Lisa eventually de-escalating to a level of barely audible crying and asking to sit on Judy's lap. Judy obliged, and Lisa eventually stopped crying and the dyad proceeded to draw pictures together. Robert, who had been observing this interaction from behind the observation window with us, reported that this sequence of events frequently occurred at home (i.e., Lisa acting "standoffish," Judy responding by trying to redirect whatever Lisa was doing, Lisa having tantrums and eventually sitting on mother's lap for reassurance).

Finally, our interview with the family turned up several important historical facts. First, the early attachment relationship between Lisa and Judy had been complicated by a half-year period, beginning when Lisa was about 10 months old, in which Judy experienced what sounded like mild to moderate depression, although professional diagnosis and treatment had not occurred. Judy described this in her own words as a "late postpartum depression" related to feelings of lost independence, uncertainty about the future of her work career, her inability to lose weight, and so on. When asked if this despondency had affected her care of Lisa, Judy replied, "No, I slept a lot on the couch during those days, but I always kept Lisa with me; I always held her next to me." Judy believed that her depression ended when she found a job, leaving Lisa in a full-time day-care situation at about age 16 months.

A second important finding was in relation to Judy's relationship with her own mother, which Judy described as being extremely conflicted. According to Judy, this conflict was the result of her mother having been an exceptionally "bad" parent who always "ran my life." More recently, however, Judy stated that she had become aware of her mother's incompetence and could now "face up to this" and confront her mother, thus producing the conflict noted. Although Judy's mother lived in a different part of the country, telephone contact occurred several times weekly and often consisted of heated arguments regarding the parenting of Lisa. Much of the information that was gathered about this relationship was uncovered during our review of the pretreatment assessment videotapes with the family. In this situation, Judy would very often provide a rationale for a particular parenting behavior by saying that she was deliberately doing something that was the opposite of what *her* mother would have done.

Our interpretation of the most prominent causal factors in the development of Lisa's behavior problems centered on Judy's difficulty in providing care that was sensitive to *Lisa's* needs versus care given primarily in relation to *Judy's* needs and affectual states. Thus, this mother-child relationship could be characterized as one in which the amount (i.e., frequency/duration) of interaction between parent and child was not a problem but rather that this mother's care was lacking both contingency and sensitivity. In many ways, Judy's parenting of Lisa seemed to be a way of "working through" unresolved issues and feelings regarding Judy's own mother. As a result, much of Judy's parenting was organized in relation to the way in which she was parented rather than parenting in relation to Lisa's current expressions of need.

We believe that Lisa was, under these circumstances, developing rather well, due in part to the compensating effects of a father who seemed to be more nurturing and responsive than the majority of fathers that we have seen in our clinic. Despite the fact that many of the reasons for Judy's lack of responsive care seem related to relatively enduring personality characteristics, we elected to go ahead with our parent-training procedures for two reasons: (1) family stability was high, and (2) both parents were highly motivated to try this form of treatment and expressed an exceptional openness to suggestions regarding change.

Responses to Treatment

Phase I

Both parents responded easily to this educational phase of the program, especially Judy who expressed a desire to learn more about "how kids develop." Judy's comments during this phase reflected some change in her perception of Lisa as a "bad" child for having tantrums versus a child expressing a need for normal autonomy seeking. Judy also made frequent remarks during this phase about the incompetence of her mother's parenting in relation to the developmental information presented. That is, she would often use the information we presented as a way to validate her impressions of her mother's incompetence.

Phase II

Training in child-directed play (CDP) with Robert proceeded very smoothly, as this father's usual style of interaction with Lisa was quite compatible with this approach. Lisa in turn played easily with her father, and there was very little conflict between the two of them in this situation. Judy had a very difficult time initially with CDP, made no easier by Lisa's early reaction to CDP with her mother. This consisted of a mixture of aggressive play with toys and an extreme "bossiness" with Judy in which Lisa would give her mother many directions in a disrespectful manner. Judy also expressed considerable discomfort with the idea of Lisa not "accomplishing" anything during CDP; she wondered if this type of play might affect Lisa's school performance adversely.

In a typical early session of CDP between Lisa and Judy, there would be some initial conflict over what to play, followed by a few minutes of problem-free interaction. Then, Lisa would soon begin to give her mother commands, Judy would respond with a direction of her own, and a power struggle would rapidly build. At first, it seemed impossible for this dyad to play for more than a couple of minutes without conflict.

These problems were resolved in several ways. First, during videotape reviews of mother-child play, we isolated Judy's reaction to Lisa's bossiness and explored with her some of the cognitive and emotional elements of this response. Judy was first able to identify "anger" as a prevailing response. With continued discussion and exploration, Judy began to label her response to Lisa's bossiness more as "scariness" because it reminded her of Lisa's school problems (i.e., noncompliance) and of her own perceived responsibility for these problems ("I'm a bad parent to have a child like this"). The "bad parent" idea eventually led, of course, to Judy's use of her own mother as a reference point for establishing one's competence (or incompetence) as a parent. In this way, the mother-grandmother relationship became a treatment issue, but in relation to a very specific and concrete aspect of the current mother-daughter relationship (i.e., responding to Lisa's bossiness during CDP).

This conflict was handled by identifying Judy's "first thought" about Lisa's bossiness ("This is what gets her into trouble at school") and replacing this thought with a self-statement that "reframed" the behavior in terms of a common developmental process ("Preschoolers often act this way when trying to be autonomous"). This procedure worked quite well, not only with specific reference to Judy's reaction to bossy behavior but also with respect to her more general ease in giving Lisa control through the standard CDP procedures (reflecting, describing, and imitation). Further, all of this seemed to heighten greatly Judy's awareness of just how much her preoccupation with her mother's parenting affected in very specific ways her perception of her daughter's behavior. At one point in this discussion, Judy stated, "You know, I'm letting *my* mother parent Lisa through me!"), a statement Lisa overheard and asked her mother to explain. Judy's answer to Lisa's question revealed clearly to us a developing sense of appropriate "boundaries" between these relationships extending across two generations.

By the end of Phase II, both parents began to report modest but discernable improvements in Lisa's behavior outside of play in addition to improved behavior during play itself. This included, for example, a reduction in the frequency of Lisa's tantrums and somewhat more compliant behavior at mealtime.

Phase III

Although Phase II had focused very much on Judy, both parents were involved equally in Phase III. Whereas Robert had problems setting limits because of a general lack of assertiveness and admitted distaste for "confronting people," Judy's difficulty in this area had more to do with giving Lisa inefficient commands (e.g., question commands) with very little follow-up other than simply repeating the same command. Several marital issues emerged in this phase, including different expectations about basic rules for behavior and Robert's tendency to "set up" Judy as the disciplinarian for conflicts initially involving only Robert and Lisa. Robert's reluctance to set limits with Lisa was explored in the same way as Judy's response to bossiness, with the finding that dad feared that Lisa might treat him as she did Judy (with resistance and noncompliance) if he were to follow-up firmly on Lisa's noncompliance. Much of the work in Phase III was devoted to establishing, with Lisa's input, a simple set of rules and expectations about mealtime behavior and snacking between meals, an area in which primary responsibility was given to Robert, with Judy assigned more of a supporting role in this effort.

By the end of Phase III, these parents were reporting a number of clear improvements in Lisa's behavior. The frequency of the tantrums had diminished further to one or two brief episodes per week, and mealtime behavior was no longer considered to be a major problem. Judy was happy about Robert's new involvement in matters of limit setting and discipline. We observed that Judy's references to her mother's parenting had gradually diminished over sessions, and this issue seemed not to play such a prominent role in her parenting of Lisa. School behavior had not changed, however, and problems of compliance with teachers and bossiness with peers were still reported by Lisa's teachers. We also noted that, other than during brief segments of CDP, Judy's level of emotional responsiveness to Lisa had not changed dramatically. There was very little talking about feelings generally in this family or attempts to offer support and reassurance to Lisa when she experienced strong emotions. If anything, as the overall frequency of the tantrums had diminished—with the corresponding decrease in the physical comforting that had often followed them—Judy's opportunities for giving emotional comfort to Lisa had also declined precipitously. This then became a central issue for us in Phase IV.

Phase IV

This phase was made easier for the therapists by the fact that Lisa continued to show relatively strong reactions (for a 4-year-old) to transitions in the clinic involving even brief separations from her parents. Further, there were still occasional conflict situations during treatment sessions in which Lisa would, for example, turn off the lights in the treatment room or persistently nag her parents for something unobtainable at the time (an ice-cream cone). Thus, these situations could be potentially used for the in vivo rehearsal of the communication skills presented earlier in table 1. Before this happened, however, each of the two cotherapists worked separately with the parents and Lisa. The steps in table 1 were first presented to the parents in a didactic fashion followed by role playing in which the therapist usually played the child in separate encounters with each parent.

With Lisa, the therapist used a combination of direct instruction and role playing in which hypothetical conflicts involving separation/reunion and parent limit setting were presented (e.g., You want to eat a cookie. Your mom says "no"). Specific presentation and rehearsal methods were drawn from the Integrated Preschool Social Skills curriculum (Odom et al. 1985). Materials from a preschool curriculum for teaching feelings and talking about feelings were also used (Simon 1986).

After two sessions of this type of training with parents and Lisa separately, each parent took turns, during a subsequent session, leaving Lisa alone in the playroom preceded by a negotiation/planning interaction which was videotaped for later review. During this session, we also were fortunate to "catch" on videotape an unplanned situation in which Lisa wanted to leave the treatment room to join another group of children at play in an adjoining room; instead of simply saying "no" and giving a warning for time out, Judy made an attempt to adapt some of the communication skills presented in the context of leave-taking to this situation.

As has been typical with the majority of families that have participated thus far in Phase IV, the early attempts of this family to plan, negotiate, and problem solve were quite awkward and seemed to promote more conflict than if the parents had just simply ignored the child and carried out their own plan in a unilateral fashion. For example, during the planning phase preceding Judy's departure from Lisa, Judy tended to use frequent controlling interpretations of Lisa's feelings (e.g., "You're looking mad now") instead of helping Lisa to identify—in whatever words she chose—her own feelings. In these early attempts, such interpreting seemed to heighten Lisa's anxiety, and Judy began to question our rationale for teaching these techniques rather than simply continuing to use the ignoring and punishment procedures presented in Phase III.

We dealt with these problems by first emphasizing to these parents our view of the short- and long-term effects of unilateral parent control versus strategies allowing for gradual and increasing levels of child input (see Greenberg & Speltz 1986 for extended discussion of this topic). We then had the parents talk about their personal tolerance levels for verbal conflict in these situations and define as clearly as possible the point at which each parent would feel the need to shift from a negotiating orientation to one in which the parent would ignore Lisa's further protesting and simply carry on with the parent's own plan. Again, videotaped review was very helpful in this regard. We also emphasized repeatedly that neither agreement or any other particular immediate outcome was the primary goal here but, rather, the *process* of providing Lisa with the opportunity to have input.

Eventually, with repeated rehearsals during four additional clinic sessions, these transactions slowly began to take on a smoother and more predictable form with noticeable reductions in Lisa's level of anger and anxiousness, although, as expected, she rarely *verbally* agreed with or totally accepted her parent's plan. At this point, we then helped the parents to formulate a list of what they regarded as "negotiable" and "nonnegotiable" conflict areas (e.g., going outside without permission was not negotiable but bedtime was), and homework assignments to use negotiating in appropriate situations were given.

IMMEDIATE TREATMENT EFFECTS AND FOLLOW-UP

This family participated in a total of eighteen treatment sessions (including two assessment sessions and five sessions during Phase IV). By the end of treatment, all major presenting problems in the home setting had changed substantially and to the parents' satisfaction. We observed a very noticeable increase in Judy's general level of social responsiveness and sensitivity, particularly with respect to her listening behavior when interacting with Lisa and Robert. These parents reported that they sometimes used their new negotiating skills with each other during marital conflict situations. Lisa's teachers reported a sharp decrease in tantrums and aggressiveness toward peers at school over the course of treatment, although we had not formally intervened in this setting in any way. However, Lisa's compliance and attentiveness during structured group situations were still reported as problems. We thus conducted a school visit and helped the teachers to develop a simple behavioral program to reward on-task behavior, which worked exceptionally well (a result we felt would not have occurred prior to treatment).

A six-month, posttreatment follow-up (phone calls to parents and teachers) indicated that Lisa was continuing to do well both at home and at school. Her teachers still regarded her as among the four or five most "time-consuming" children in their classroom group, but Lisa's continuation in this program was assured, and the teachers described her as becoming one of the primary "play organizers" in her peer group.

CONCLUSION

This case example has been presented for the purpose of demonstrating the clinical application of our procedures and some of the problems that can arise in the course of this type of treatment. It does not, of course, confirm the efficacy of these procedures, and, at present, there is little empirical evidence that this approach promotes the type of generalized change that we believe it does. Although there is preliminary evidence that preschoolers referred for treatment are more likely than well-behaved children to show insecure attachment behavior in a clinic observation (Speltz, Greenberg & DeKlyen in press), is not known whether treatment procedures organized in relation to this difference are more effective than current parent training models. Thus, comparative outcome research is needed, especially because our procedures call for considerably more time and therapist involvement than standard parenting programs which usually require only eight to ten weeks of participation and can be provided on a group basis. It is important that research of this nature includes the types of overt interactional measures now used in behavioral parent-training research (e.g., observations of parent-child interaction) as well as direct measures of the cognitive and affectual areas of individual child functioning that are typically overlooked in this area of study (e.g., self-concept, problem-solving skills, ability to talk about feelings, negotiating skills with adults, impulse control).

The objective of such research should not be to determine which approach is better for groups of children but rather (1) to determine what effects current parent training programs have on areas of child development not commonly assessed in previous research, and (2) to determine what child and family variables predict success in one type of treatment approach versus the other. Surely, some types of conduct problems in certain family situations are well-treated by currently available parent-training programs, while other situations will require the more elaborate and costly procedures advocated here. Until data confirming the validity of our impressions and procedures are available, we hope that this paper has provided a convincing argument for the continued exploration of behavioral change techniques within the context of the young child's attachment relationships.

REFERENCES

Ainsworth, M. D. S. (1967). *Infancy in Uganda: Infant care and the growth of love*. Baltimore: John Hopkins University Press.

Ainsworth, M. D. S. (1982). Attachment: Retrospect and prospect. In C. M. Parkes & J. Stevenson-Hinde (eds.), *The placement of attachment in human behavior* (pp. 3–30). New York: Basic Books.

Atkeson, B. M., & Forehand, R. (1981). Conduct disorders. In E. J. Mash & L. G. Terdal (eds.), *Behavioral assessment of childhood disorders*. New York: Guilford.

Bates, J. E.; Maslin, C. A.; & Frankel, K. A. (1985). Attachment security, mother-child interaction, and temperament as predictors of behavior-problem ratings at age three years. In I. Bretherton & E. Waters (eds.), *Growing points in attachment theory and research*.

Monographs of the Society for Research in Child Development 50 (1–2, Serial No. 209), 167–193.

Bowlby, J. (1973). *Attachment and loss: Vol. 2. Separation.* New York: Basic Books.

Bowlby, J. (1979). *The making and breaking of affectional bonds.* London: Tavistock.

Bowlby, J. (1980). *Attachment and loss: Vol. 3. Loss, sadness and depression.* New York: Basic Books.

Bretherton, I. (1985). Attachment theory: Retrospect and prospect. In I. Bretherton & E. Waters (eds.), *Growing point in attachment theory and research. Monographs of the Society for Research in Child Development* 50 (1–2, Serial No. 209), 3–35.

Breiner, J., & Forehand, R. (1981). An assessment of the effects of parent training on clinic-referred children's school behavior. *Behavioral Assessment* 3, 31–42.

Cassidy, J. (1986). The ability to negotiate the environment: An aspect of infant competence as related to quality of attachment. *Child Development* 57, 331–337.

Combs, M., & Slaby, D. (1977). Social skills training in children. In B. Lahey & A. Kazdin (eds.), *Advances in clinical child psychology.* New York: Plenum.

Erikson, M. F., & Farber, E. A. (1983). Infancy to preschool: Continuity of adaptation in high-risk children. Paper presented at the biennial meeting of the Society for Research in Child Development, Detroit.

Eyberg, S. M., & Robinson, E. A. (1982). Parent-child interaction training: Effects on family functioning. *Journal of Clinical Child Psychology* 11, 130–137.

Forehand, R., & King, E. H. (1974). Pre-school children's non-compliance: Effects of short term behavior therapy. *Journal of Community Psychology* 2, 42–44.

Forehand, R. L., & McMahon, R. (1981). *Helping the noncompliant child: A clinician's guide to parent training.* New York: Guilford.

Forehand, R.; Sturgis, E. T.; McMahon, R.; Auger, D.; Green, K.; Wells, K.; & Breiner, J. (1979). Parent behavioral training to modify child noncompliance: Treatment generalization across time and from home to school. *Behavior Modification* 5, 3–25.

Gottman, J.; Notarius, C.; Gonso, J.; & Markman, H. (1976). *A couple's guide to communication.* Champaign: Research Press.

Greenberg, M. T., & Speltz, M. L. (1988). Contributions of attachment theory to the understanding of conduct problems during the preschool years. In J. Belsky & T. Nezworski (eds.), *Clinical implications of attachment.* Hillsdale, N.J.: Erlbaum.

Hanf, C. (1969). *A two-stage program for modifying maternal controlling during mother-child interaction.* Paper presented at the meeting of the Western Psychological Association, Vancouver, B.C.

Hazen, N., & Durrett, M. (1982). Relationship of security of attachment to exploration and cognitive mapping ability in two-year-olds. *Developmental Psychology* 18, 751–759.

Jacobson, N. S., & Margolin, G. (1979). *Marital therapy: Strategies based on social learning and behavior exchange principles.* New York: Brunner/Mazel.

Johnson, S. M.; Bolstad, D. D.; & Lobitz, G. K. (1976). Generalization and contrast phenomena in behavior modification with children. In L. A. Hamerlynck, L. C. Handy, & E. J. Mash (eds.), *Behavior modification and families: Theory and research* (vol. 1). New York: Brunner/Mazel.

Lewis, M., & Brooks, J. (1978). Self-knowledge and emotional development. In M. Lewis & L. Rosenblum (eds.), *The development of affect* (pp. 205–226). New York: Plenum.

Lewis, M.; Feiring, C.; McGuffog, C.; & Jaskir, J. (1984). Predicting psychopathology in six-year-olds from early social relations. *Child Development* 55, 123–136.

Loeber, R. (1982). The stability of anti-social and delinquent child behavior: A review. *Child Development* 53, 1431–1446.

Mahler, M. S.; Pine, F.; & Bergman, A. (1975). *The psychological birth of the child.* New York: Basic Books.

Main, M.; Kaplan, N.; & Cassidy, J. (1985). Security in infancy, childhood and adulthood: A move to the level of representation. In I. Bretherton & E. Waters (eds.), Growing points of attachment theory and research. *Monographs of the Society for Research in Child Development* 50 (1–2, Serial No. 209), 66–104.

Marvin, R. S. (1977). An ethological-cognitive model for the attenuation of mother-child attachment behavior. In T. M. Alloway, L. Krames, & P. Pliner (eds.), *Advances in the study of communication and affect: Vol. 3. The development of social attachments.* New York: Plenum.

Marvin, R. S., & Greenberg, M. T. (1982). Reactions of preschool children to an adult stranger: A behavioral systems approach. *Child Development* 53, 481–490.

Odom, S.; Bender, M.; Stein, M.; McInnes, M.; Doran, L.; Deklyen, M.; Gilbert, M.; Speltz, M.; & Jenkins, J. (1988). *Integrated preschool curriculum.* Seattle: University of Washington Press.

Patterson, G. R. (1976). The aggressive child: Victim and architect of a coercive system. In L. A. Hamerlynck, L. C. Handy, & E. J. Mash (eds.), *Behavioral modification and families: Theory and research* (vol. 1). New York: Brunner/Mazel.

Reese, H. W., & Overton, W. F. (1970). Models of development and theories of development. In L. R. Goulet & P. B. Baltes (eds.), *Life-span developmental psychology: Research and theory.* New York: Academic Press.

Sameroff, A. J., & Chandler, M. J. (1975). Reproductive risk and the continuum of caretaking casualty. In F. D. Horowitz, M. Hetherington, S. Scarr-Salapatek, & G. Siegel (eds.), *Review of child development research* (vol. 4). Chicago: University of Chicago Press.

Simon, L. (1986). Development of a self-esteem and social skills curriculum. Unpublished curriculum, Seattle Public Schools Special Education Department (Preschool Incentive Grant 34118), Seattle.

Skinner, E. (1985). Determinants of mother sensitive and contingent-responsive behavior: The role of childrearing beliefs and socioeconomic status. In I. Sigel (ed.), *Parents belief systems.* Hillsdale, N.J.: Erlbaum.

Speltz, M. L.; Greenberg, M. T.; & DeKlyen, M. (in press). Attachment in preschoolers with disruptive behavior: A comparison of clinic-referred and nonproblem children. *Development and Psychopathology.*

Spivack, G., & Shure, M. B. (1973). *Social adjustment of young children: A cognitive approach to solving real-life problems.* San Francisco: Jossey-Bass.

Sroufe, L. A. (1983). Infant-caregiver attachment and patterns of adaptation in preschool: The roots of maladaptation and competence. In M. Perlmutter (ed.), *Minnesota Symposia on Child Psychology* (vol. 16). Hillsdale, N.J.: Erlbaum.

Sroufe, L. A., & Fleeson, J. (1986). Attachment and the construction of relationships. In W. Hartup & Z. Rubin (eds.), *Relationships and development.* Hillsdale, N.J.: Erlbaum.

Sroufe, L. A., & Rutter, M. (1984). The domain of developmental psychopathology. *Child Development* 55, 17–29.

Stover, L., & Guerney, B. (1967). The efficacy of training procedures for mothers in filial therapy. *Psychotherapy* 4, 110–115.

Thomas, A., & Chess, S. (1977). *Temperament and development.* New York: Brunner/Mazel.

14 · Security of Attachment in Toddlerhood

Modifying Assessment Procedures for Joint Clinical and Research Purposes

J. Lawrence Aber and Amy J. L. Baker

Introduction

ATTACHMENT THEORY and research have emerged in part from considerations of clinical phenomena (Bowlby [1969] 1982, 1973, 1980) and have been used as contexts for current discussions of a variety of clinical and child-care issues (e.g., Barglow, Vaughn, & Molitor 1987; Belsky 1986; Cicchetti & Toth 1987). Nonetheless, they have had surprisingly little direct impact on both the design and evaluation of services for young children. Undoubtedly, there are many reasons for the negligible impact of attachment theory and research on the provision of services to date. For instance, attachment theory is a relatively new perspective compared to the more clinically influential grand theories in psychology like psychoanalytic and social-learning theories. Thus, most senior clinicians and service providers have not been trained in attachment theory (Aber & Slade 1987).

We believe that the relative separation of basic research scientists from clinical and child-care providers has also limited and delayed the influence of attachment theory and research on services. Mistrust between researchers and service providers has contributed to this separation. Some service providers see researchers as investigating narrow, artificial phenomena with little direct clinical and practical value; some researchers see service providers as superstitious believers in programs and/or forms of treatment that cannot pass scientific scrutiny.

The research reported in this chapter was funded by grants from the Barnard College Faculty Grants Program, the Spencer Foundation, and an anonymous donor. Release time to write the chapter was provided to the first author by a Faculty Scholar's Award from the William T. Grant Foundation and by a Spencer Fellowship from the National Academy of Education. The authors wish to thank the children and parents who participated in these studies; Dante Cicchetti for critical advice at several points in the project; Patricia Shimm, Annelie Hartmann, Brenda Berger, Kay Bender, and the rest of the staff, students, and volunteers at the Center for Toddler Development for assistance in data collection and coding; Christina Mitchell, Arietta Slade, Mary Jo Ward, and Mark Greenberg for their comments on an earlier version of this paper; Mary Ainsworth, Inge Bretherton, and Vicki Carlson for their contributions to creating the criterion Q-sort; and Betsy Arnold for help in preparing the manuscript. Send correspondence or requests for reprints to J. Lawrence Aber, Director, Center for Toddler Development, Barnard College, Columbia University, 3009 Broadway, New York, New York 10027.

This separation did not characterize earlier theories (psychoanalysis, social learning) which influenced clinical practice and service provision, or even the earliest work on attachment (Bowlby is a dedicated clinician). Indeed, there appeared to be much more fluid two-way relationships between scholarship (both theory and research) and practice in earlier days. Fortunately, this gap between scientific knowledge development about attachment relationships and the use of such knowledge in service may be starting to close. One way this is being done is for service and research to take place in the same setting and to be designed to contribute to each other. In fact, a number of researchers now are simultaneously investigating basic processes of attachment in normal and clinical populations and providing services to young children and their families (Belsky & Nezworski 1988; Cicchetti & Toth 1987; Lieberman & Pawl, this vol.; Lyons-Ruth, Connell, Zoll, & Stahl 1987; Lyons-Ruth, Zoll, & Connell 1987). A well developed example of such an integration of science and service is presented by Sroufe (1983), who created a preschool service program for his research sample in order to study their development in a school setting.

We join these clinically oriented research scientists in the belief that joint scholarly and service activities will lead to further cross-fertilization between attachment theory and research on the one hand, and practice on the other. But we suspect that productive cross-fertilization will still require some changes in the prevailing cultures of the worlds of both research and practice. While this poses a number of problems, it holds a number of exciting possibilities as well.

It was with both a faith in the potential value of the cross-fertilization of research and service cultures and a foreknowledge of the difficulties that we introduced a program of attachment research to the ongoing service operation at the Center for Toddler Development at Barnard College, Columbia University, five years ago.

This chapter represents our first attempt to take stock of this joint enterprise and to describe some of the strengths and weaknesses of our emerging "service and research" model. First, we will briefly describe the history, goals, and operations of the Center for Toddler Development. Second, we will describe two attachment assessment procedures adapted from existing research to simultaneously serve the Center's service, research, and educational goals. In order to address the theme of this book, we will describe our paradigms, procedures, and initial findings for the older children in our sample: toddlers who were 19–24 months old on intake and 30–36 months old at the end of the program. In the fourth section of this chapter, we will present preliminary data supporting the scientific validity of our adapted assessment procedures. We will then discuss the findings as they relate to conceptualizing and measuring security of attachment in toddlerhood.

For our Center, joint activities are the key to crossing the cultural divide between research and service, or knowledge development and action. It is our belief that our activities should be judged by dual standards: scientific standards and practice standards. Hence, in the last section, we will discuss some potential implications and advantages/disadvantages of our research for both basic knowledge of attachment processes and for the provision of services for young children and their parents.

CENTER FOR TODDLER DEVELOPMENT: THE SERVICE AND RESEARCH MODEL

The Toddler Center at Barnard College, Columbia University, was begun in 1973 to serve three purposes: service, research, and education.

Service

The first goal involves the provision of services to toddlers and their families. This is accomplished by offering a low-key developmental play group. Two groups of twelve children attend the program each year from September through May.[1] The Center is staffed by two teachers and three or four student teachers.

The Toddler Center's "curriculum" is based on the premise that toddlers have their own agenda of exploration and play and that teachers best served toddlers by helping them pursue their own agenda of social and exploratory play. Consequently, children are free to focus their energies and attention on what they pleased.

The program is designed to serve as a toddler play group, and thus parents eventually are expected to leave their child for the morning and return midday. Although parents come to the Toddler Center with an expressed desire to have their child separate from them for the play group, most parents also experience a certain amount of anxiety and doubt about this separation process. Thus, the first month of the play group is designed to slowly facilitate the parent-child separation. This was accomplished by helping the children feel safe and comfortable in the center, and by helping the parents experience their pride and joy in their children's development and growth as well as their sadness that their children are no longer babies. During the first few weeks, the children slowly acclimate themselves to the new environment by increasing their attendance from one to two-and-one-half hours per morning. In parallel, "caretakers" (still usually mothers, sometimes babysitters, and occasionally fathers) slowly increased their time spent out of the classroom away from their children. Usually this procedure met most children's needs for a manageable warm-up to a new, potentially anxiety-provoking setting. How-

---

1. As mentioned earlier, we also ran a small "developmental support program" for toddlers of parents with major affective disorders which we describe briefly in the last section of this chapter.

ever, this process is individualized to accommodate dyads for whom four weeks (eight sessions) is not sufficient to help the child feel reasonably secure when separated from mother.

In addition to the twice-weekly toddler play group, the Center offers a variety of other support services and experiences including parent/teacher conferences, a parenting group, start and end of the year parties for the parents, baby-sitting services, educational planning conferences, and referrals to other helping services as needed.

Research

The second set of goals of the Center is to conduct developmental research. Since 1982, the focus of research has been primarily on early social emotional and personality development from an attachment theory perspective. To that end, children who attend the Toddler Center are involved in a variety of research assessments. Over the course of the year, each child participates in four such out-of-classroom videotaped "research visits," accompanied by his or her primary caretaker, the first and fourth of which are the focus of this chapter. The first research visit, named the Intake Interview, and the fourth visit, named the Spring Assessment, are described in more detail below and are adaptations of the Ainsworth Strange Situation (Ainsworth, Blehar, Waters, & Wall 1978) and the Matas, Arend, and Sroufe (1978) procedure for assessing indices of toddler autonomy. The intake assessment occurs during the spring before children start the Center, and the spring assessment is conducted one year later, near the end of the children's attendance at the Center.

Research visits which are not discussed in this chapter include a peer-peer interaction paradigm which investigates early forms of competence with peers, and a 2-year birthday visit which investigates the ontogeny of the affects of pride and shame. In addition to these videotaped visits of mother-child interaction, parents are also interviewed twice over the course of the year, once receiving the Berkeley Adult Attachment Interview (Main & Goldwyn 1984; Main, Kaplan, & Cassidy 1985) and once receiving the Parent Development Interview, an interview concerned with parents' representations of their relationship with their children (Aber, Slade, Berger, Bresgi, & Kaplan 1985; Slade & Aber 1986).

Finally, data on the children's functioning in the Center are systematically collected via teacher Q-sorts of toddler security of attachment during the fall, in this chapter referred to as Time 2 (adapted from Waters & Deane 1985) and of preschooler ego-strength in the spring (Schacter, Cooper, & Gordet 1968).

Our overall research agenda is guided by the theoretical notion of the coherence of individual development (Sroufe 1979). Thus, we have designed a series of research visits and data collection strategies to assess children's quality of adaptation to stage-salient developmental challenges. For example, attachment is assessed when the children are between 12 and 24 months of age, and indices of autonomy are assessed when the children are between 24 and 36 months of age. Additionally, our research agenda was developed with service goals in mind. For example, our interest in facilitating the mother-child separation process in September contributed to our interest in having a videotaped sample of the mother and child separating before then, that is, the attachment assessment six to eight months prior to the beginning of the school year. And our goal of training teachers to make theoretically guided observations of the children was one impetus for creating a teacher Q-sort of the toddlers for use at the end of the first month of the toddler play group. Thus, the research agenda represents an attempt to combine both science issues and service concerns.

Education

In addition to service provision and ongoing research activities, the Toddler Center also provides a setting for the direct observation of early development (for students in undergraduate psychology courses) and serves as a training program for advanced undergraduates learning to facilitate the development of normal toddlers and for doctoral students in clinical and developmental psychology who care for toddlers at-risk due to parent's major affective disorder. The Center conducts a variety of teaching and training activities each year, including observations of the toddlers by psychology and education classes and visiting students and professionals; year-long seminars (for the undergraduates) and externships (for graduate students) in advanced theory, clinical work, and research with toddlers; sponsorship of senior theses, masters' theses, and doctoral theses; and training in the development of new assessment tools and methods.

Adaption of Attachment Research Paradigms for Joint Scientific and Clinical Use in a Service Setting

One unfortunate byproduct of the apparent separation of attachment research and service programs has been a lack of impetus to create additional or modified assessment procedures which could be tailored for the needs and interests of both researchers and clinicians. To date, the majority of attachment research has focused on 12–18-month-olds and has employed the standard laboratory procedure for such assessments, for example, the Strange Situation (Ainsworth et al. 1978).

Theoretical formulations have also contributed to this focus on assessing security of attachment in infancy. The organizational perspective of Sroufe and his colleagues (Sroufe 1979; Sroufe & Waters 1977) stresses the importance of viewing development as a series of stage-salient issues. Sroufe describes infants as facing one set of challenges—forming a secure attachment relationship with the primary caregiver—and toddlers as facing a different set of challenges—achieving increasing individuation and autonomous functioning vis-à-vis the caregiver. One hallmark of this theoretical perspective has been the assessment of the individual's behavioral organization and quality of adaptation with respect to stage-salient tasks. Thus, the majority of attachment research has been based on the belief that the quality of the infant-parent attachment relationship is systematically related to later, albeit different, stage-salient tasks after 18 months (Lieberman 1977; Matas et al. 1978; Pastor 1981; Waters, Wippman, & Sroufe 1979).

Sroufe's concept that the toddler faces a different set of issues than a younger child is based in part on recognition of the important developmental advances taking place around the second birthday. Gains in language development, acquisitions of symbolic capacities, advances in motor skills, and increased complexity of behavioral and social repertoires all take place over the second year of life (Kagan 1981; Sroufe 1979). Historically, this toddler phase has been differentiated from infancy in a similar manner by theorists from a variety of perspectives (Erikson 1950; Freud 1905; Greenspan 1981; Mahler, Pine, & Bergman 1975; Piaget 1936).

There are, however, a growing number of exceptions to the existing general rule of focusing primarily on 12–18-month-olds in the standard assessment procedure. For instance, some researchers have employed the standard procedure to assess security of attachment in children over 18 months (Greenberg & Marvin 1979; Maccoby & Feldman 1972; Radke-Yarrow, Cummings, Kuczynski, & Chapman 1985; Schneider-Rosen, Braunwald, Carlson, & Cicchetti 1985). Other researchers have made modifications in the standard procedure or used substantially different procedures in order to create stage- and age-appropriate measuring strategies of security of attachment (Bretherton 1985; Kobak & Shaver 1987; Lieberman 1977; Main et al. 1985; Schneider-Rosen, this vol.; Schneider-Rosen et al. 1985). Main et al. (1985) and Marvin (1977) in particular have focused on expanding the assessment procedures to be appropriate for children (ages 2–6) and adults. This work has been based on the belief that the issue of security of attachment remains important at every stage of development, while the specific form it takes and the most appropriate way to measure it depends upon the individual's level of development and the stage-salient contexts in which individual differences in security of attachment will be revealed.

Thus, our research program is consistent with the goals of attachment researchers to broaden the age and contexts within which security of attachment can be assessed (Cicchetti, Cummings, Greenberg, & Marvin, this vol.; Greenberg 1984). In addition, our research agenda was designed to integrate the attachment assessment procedures and resulting data into our ongoing service program. To accomplish this, we devised two different attachment assessment procedures which were both sufficiently standardized to evaluate the children reliably and validly and also flexible enough to be sensitive to the individual needs of the parents and children. The first procedure is a modified Strange Situation for 19–24-month-olds, which also functions as an intake interview into our service program, and the second is a center-based attachment *Q*-sort, which also functions as a teacher-training and staff-development tool. The theoretical rationale for each assessment procedure is described in the next two sections.

Attachment Paradigm/Intake Interview

Ainsworth designed the Strange Situation to place stress on the infant-parent dyad by activating the attachment system through a series of brief separations and reunions. Once the attachment system had been strongly activated by the second separation, the infant's style of interacting with the parent could then be coded and classified as either secure or insecure.

In designing our modified attachment procedure, our intention was to create a situation that would be stressful enough to activate the child's attachment system but could also be used as an intake interview into a service program at the Toddler Center. We started with the basic framework of the associate director's intake interview into the Toddler Center. In collaboration with her, we created an expanded version of her original interview which satisfied both (her) service goals and (our) research goals. The final procedure still allowed her to interview the parents casually, to observe the parents and children interact, and to describe the Toddler Center to the parents. Thus, the final protocol maintained the tone and style of her original interview and was consistent with the philosophy of the toddler program itself.

At the same time, we wanted the intake interview to function as a standardized paradigm to assess security of attachment in both infants and toddlers. With this goal in mind, modifications were made in the standard Strange Situation procedure. Because toddlers have increased motor, language, and social repertoires, assessments were conducted in a large, toddler playroom designed to provide the child with numerous opportunities to play both near and far from the mother. This design allowed individual differences to emerge in older toddlers' abilities to use their mothers as a secure base from which to explore the room, to monitor mother from a distance, and to use distance interaction to communicate with her while engaged in play.

In keeping with the notion that individual differences in socioemotional competence emerge most clearly under moderate-to-high levels of stress (Sroufe 1979), our paradigm was designed to stress the child by activating both the attachment and the exploration systems. The child's attachment system is activated not only by the separation from the mother but also by the presence of two strangers, the unfamiliarity of the room, and the fact that the mother is preoccupied by the intake interview. The child's exploration system is activated by the array and choice of the toys.

One original concern by the program staff was that a two-separation paradigm (with the child left entirely alone during the second separation) could not be justified as part of an intake procedure into a toddler play group. On the contrary, it was felt that such a procedure would give parents the wrong message about our research versus service priorities and might reduce the membership or change the types of families who apply to the Center. In order to make the procedure more naturalistic (i.e., less obviously stressful) and more sensitive to the needs of the parents and children during a program intake interview, the separation/reunion phase was reduced to a single two-minute separation in which the child was left with the stranger. We believed that a series of stressors perceived by the parent to be less intrusive and more ecologically valid would be more in keeping with our service goals than what was allowed by the standard procedure. The preseparation phase of our paradigm was expanded in order to measure a number of preseparation indices of security of attachment (Waters et al. 1979) and to observe in older children emergent features of the fourth phase of attachment, the goal-corrected partnership (Bowlby [1969] 1982; Marvin 1977).

Center-based Q-Sort/Teacher Observations

For a number of reasons, laboratory-based assessments of security of attachment may not be the method of choice for many service providers who might find attachment information clinically useful. For example, one potential problem with laboratory-based assessments is their reactivity; children may respond differently to a second administration of the Strange Situation unless a critical (and unspecified) amount of time has elapsed. Consequently, laboratory assessments involving forced separations may be problematical for studies using repeated measures designs of children's reactions to events such as separations from parent, onset of parental illness, or entry into substitute care arrangements. Second, the technical (video equipment, one-way mirrors) and analytical (subsequent coding) demands of laboratory-based assessments also reduce the practicality and acceptability of the Strange Situation to many service providers. Together with the overtly stressful nature of the Strange Situation, these limits make lab-based attachment procedures less likely to be employed by a wide range of child and family service organizations for research and evaluation purposes.

An attachment procedure based on observations of naturally occurring mother-child interactions in a common and frequented "setting" (home, daycare center, school) may be more ecologically valid, less susceptible to problems of reactivity of the measure, and more likely to be adopted for research and evaluation purposes. One example of such a methodology to assess security of attachment is presented by Waters and Deane (1985). Our modification of their procedure was based on the conviction that entry to a child-care program/toddler play group and the naturally occurring separations/reunions was another valuable natural "setting" for the study of attachment. In addition, it was our belief that student teachers could be trained to observe and to describe reliably toddlers' attachment behaviors (and attachment-relevant exploratory and social behaviors) in a manner that would simultaneously yield scientifically valuable data and improve their training as child-care/early education professionals. To these ends, the Waters and Deane Q-sort deck was modified to eliminate items referencing behaviors only observable in the home (not a center), to include items referencing behaviors only observable at a developmental play group or child-care center (not at home), and to be usable with brief training by novices to both attachment theory and child-care work.

Like Waters and Deane, we followed the advice of Loevinger (1957) to include in the Q-sort references to cognition and affect as well as behavior, and to assess children's behaviors across a variety of domains (attachment, exploration), with a variety of partners (parents, teachers, peers), in a variety of situations (freeplay, structured play), and to do so in an ethological/attachment framework.

In summary, a major aim of this research was to design two modified attachment procedures which could be both consistent with our service goals as well contribute to our basic understanding of how the attachment system is organized in different contexts and at older ages. It was also our aim to begin to validate these assessment procedures. We did this in two ways. First, we examined the relationship between components of the attachment system assessed in the Intake Interview and toddler security of attachment on entry to a play group assessed via the Q-sort six months later. We hypothesized that children who were more secure (exhibited more secure communication with the mother, a more flexible attention-deployment strategy, less separation insecurity, and less reunion rejection) would be rated by teachers via a Q-sort as more secure on entry to the play group. Second, we examined the relationship between attachment assessed in the intake interview and two indices of child autonomy in the problem-solving paradigm assessed twelve months later. We did not want to assume that this pattern of relationships between attachment on intake and autonomy one year later would be the same for boys and girls; therefore, we examined these relationships for all children and then separately by gender.

Initial Validity Studies

Methods

Sample Selection. The children and parents who participated were part of a larger sample of families enrolled in an ongoing study of early social-emotional development at the Toddler Center. The families became involved in this study through their interest in a toddler play group serving children between 18 and 30 months of age in September. Each year, approximately

twice as many families apply as can be accommodated, and priority for acceptance is given to families whose older children had been in the play group or
who were members of the staff or faculty at the university (about 30% of the
children every year). The remaining slots were filled with children whose age
and gender would ensure equal numbers of boys and girls and children of different ages in the play group. Although the Center would not be appropriate
for children with severe emotional or physical problems (e.g., autism, spina
bifida), we make a point not to select out of our longitudinal sample children
or parents on the basis of any less severe problem or personality characteristic.
Such a selection bias would not only be inconsistent with our service goals but
would also decrease the generalizability of our findings.

Because these data represent the first wave of an ongoing research project, to date not every child has been coded for all three assessments. Therefore, the sample of this study was a subset of fifty-eight toddlers who were
between 19 and 24 months old at the time of the intake and who comprise the
first wave of toddlers coded on attachment at Time 1. Because the Time 2
assessment procedure was recently introduced into the ongoing research, only
twenty-four of the fifty-eight toddlers so far have Time 2 data from when they
were between 24 and 30 months of age. Forty-two of the original fifty-eight so
far have completed Time 3 data, when they were between 30 and 36 months of
age. Of the 58, there were 24 males, 34 females, 36 firstborns, and 22 later
borns. The sample came from a primarily middle- to upper-middle class,
well-educated, urban population.

Assessment Procedures. If accepted, the family returned six to eight months
after the initial interview (Time 1) for the play group. The first month of the
play group comprised the time period for the Time 2 assessment. Over the
course of the year, the parents and children participated in a number of additional research visits, one of which occurred in the spring of that year (Time 3).

Time 1: Attachment paradigm/intake interview. The Time 1 assessment
was the modified attachment paradigm/intake interview. The child's primary
caretaker[2] participated in the interview, was encouraged to attend the first
month of the play group, and was expected to participate in all subsequent
research visits.

The assessment was held in a 23 × 15-foot section of a large, sunny,
playroom with a one-way mirror. In the center of the room was a small table
around which the parent, a female stranger, and the interviewer (associate director) sat equidistant from each other. The mother sat facing the mirror. Be-

2. Some parents reject on ideological grounds the notion of a primary caretaker; yet most
families were easily able to specify the parent most involved in raising the child. We consider this
a compromise in light of the parents' busy lives, because for scientific as well as ideological reasons it would be preferable to study both parents (Main & Weston 1981; Goldberg & Easterbrooks 1984; Easterbrooks & Goldberg 1984).

TABLE 1. EPISODES OF MODIFIED ATTACHMENT PARADIGM

Activity	Participants	Duration (in Minutes)
1. Interview begins	(Mother, child, interviewer, and stranger)	5
Stranger initiation		
2. Interview continues	(Mother, child, interviewer, and stranger)	3
Stranger initiation		
3. Interview continues	(Mother, child, interviewer, and stranger)	4
Stranger initiation		
4. Interview continues	(Mother, child, interviewer, and stranger)	3
5. Free play	(Mother, child)	5
6. Free play	(Mother, child, stranger)	3
7. Separation	(Stranger, child)	2
8. Reunion with mandatory pickup	(Mother, child)	3
9. Clean-up	(Mother, child)	2

hind her were shelves with an assortment of small-motor and symbolic toys. A rocking rowboat and a slide were also in the room for large-motor activity. The episodes of the paradigm are outlined in table 1 and described briefly below.

During the first fifteen minutes of the procedure, the mother, interviewer, and stranger were seated at the table. The child was free to explore the room and play with the toys or stay nearby while the mother was interviewed. The interview was standardized and concerned the nature of the parents' work, a medical and social history of the first year of the child's life, and a discussion about what the parent expected from the play group. While the interview was taking place, the stranger watched the child from her seat at the table. At the end of the standardized interview, the interviewer and stranger left the room for five minutes, and the mother and child were free to play "as if they were at home." The stranger then reentered the room for three minutes, after which time the parent left the room for two minutes. While the mother was out of the room, the interviewer instructed her to pick the child up when she returned to the room. Upon the mother's return, the stranger left the room and the mother and child had a three-minute free-play and a subsequent two-minute clean-up period.

Thus, during the first fifteen minutes of this procedure the mother had to balance being interviewed and attending to her child. The child also had the dual tasks of exploring the environment while attempting to gain a feeling of security from the mother who was preoccupied. We believed that the competing demands on both the parent and the child would create a low-level, protracted stress on the dyad which would reveal the nature of their attachment relationship, while still being clinically sensitive.

Time 2: Center-based Q-*sort/teacher observations. Classroom context for teacher observation.* Because the context of the teacher's observations is critical to the quality of the Q-sort data, it will be briefly described below. Six to eight months after the Time 1 attachment assessment, the twenty-four families accepted into the program each year began to attend the play group. For each group of twelve children, there were two full-time teachers (who worked every day) and eight part-time assistant teachers (who each worked one day a week), a total of six teachers per day. The play group was held in the same room as the Time 1 assessment: a long, narrow room (15 × 40 feet) with various play "stations," such as a painting corner, a small-motor activity corner, and a storytelling corner. During the day, the six teachers were stationed around the room at various play areas while the children were free to play wherever they chose. The general schedule of the play group followed the same routine of activities every day, starting with a free playtime, then a snack time, a storytelling time, and a large-motor activity time.

During the first month of the play group, the children began by attending a one-hour session in the first week, and then the length of the sessions increased one-half hour weekly, so that by the fourth week the children stayed for the entire two-and-a-half hours. In addition, during the first month the mothers stayed in or near the playroom with their children and, for the most part, remained seated at one end of the playroom or in an adjacent room. The first week the mothers stayed in the playroom the entire session. In the second week, the mothers went into the adjacent room for fifteen minutes. During the third and fourth weeks, the mothers stayed in the adjacent room the entire time. While they were in the adjacent room, the mothers were out of sight of the children in the playroom but were still available to their children because the door connecting the playroom and their room was always open and the children were free to pass back and forth.

Student teachers were encouraged to observe the children from behind a one-way mirror on the days when they were not working in the classroom, and they also attended a weekly seminar on attachment theory and research.

Q-sort procedure. Student teachers were trained in the Q-sort technique during the first month of the seminar. During the first class, the students were introduced to the ninety-two items in the Q-sort deck. Each of the sixteen teachers was then randomly assigned four children to observe and on whom to write diaries, and eventually to describe with the Q-sort. Because the children's interactions with their parents were of particular interest, only children whose parents were accompanying them for the first month were observed. Consequently, each year approximately twenty of the twenty-four children have Time 2 data. Each child was assigned to be rated by three different teachers.

In the second class, the teachers were encouraged to ask questions about specific items in the Q-sort deck. Most of the third and fourth classes focused on group discussions of the children's behavior. At all times, the teachers were encouraged to decribe the children's actual behaviors rather than make interpretations. It was also stressed that they should refer only to what they actually observed, even if it was discrepant with other teacher's observations or comments. A practice Q-sort was assigned in the fifth class, which entailed the teachers using the deck to describe a child in the classroom who was not originally assigned to any teacher. The purpose of this was to give the teachers an opportunity to learn about doing a Q-sort without jeopardizing the quality of the data on the children in the longitudinal study. Finally, after having spent seven to fourteen hours working with and/or observing the children, and having no other information about the children other than their direct observations, discussions, and completed diaries, each teacher independently completed the Q-sorts for their four assigned children.

Time 3: Problem-solving paradigm. Approximately one year after the Time 1 attachment assessment, the parents and children participated in a problem-solving paradigm designed by Matas et al. (1978) and modified for use with older children by Cicchetti and colleagues (D. Cicchetti 1982, personal communication). The parent and child came to a lab room (10 × 18 feet) on a day in which the Toddler Center play group was not in session. One wall of the lab room was a one-way mirror behind which video equipment was set up. In the center of the room was a small round table at which the mother sat. Against the mirror was a second table on which there was a doll, a truck, and two hand puppets. Against the back wall were two toy cars for large-motor activity. This paradigm consisted of four six-minute episodes: (1) mother was mildly preoccupied filling out a questionnaire while the child could play with the toys, (2) mother was instructed to engage child in play "as if they were at home," (3) problem-solving task predetermined to be below child's developmental capabilities (easy task), and (4) problem-solving task predetermined to be beyond child's developmental capabilities (hard task). Each child worked on two or three of six possible tasks.[3] Prior to the start of the procedure, the mother was shown how the problem-solving tasks worked and instructed to let the child work alone but to give the child whatever help she thought her child needed.

Measures

Time 1. The modifications of the attachment paradigm and the extension of the age group studied recommended the construction of a new code. In Ainsworth's classification system, individual differences in the quality of the infant-parent attachment relationship are identified by examining age- and context-specific behavioral and affective manifestations of the child's expecta-

---

3. A complete description of the problem-solving tasks is available from the authors upon request. An example of an easy task for a 30-month-old is putting together six snap-together beads in the same color sequence of a model. An example of a hard task for a 36-month-old is building a tower of sixteen blocks in the same color and shape sequence as a model.

tions of maternal availability and responsiveness. Specifically, the child's greeting response to the mother after a series of brief separations is considered a reflection of the child's internal working model of the attachment relationship (Main et al. 1985).

In creating a code that would be appropriate for our paradigm and older sample of toddlers (as well as infants), we also decided to measure age- and context-specific manifestations of the child's expectations of maternal responsiveness and availability during the reunion. We also followed Bretherton's lead in conceptualizing the attachment system as always active; for example, the child continuously monitors the mother's location and assesses her availability (Bretherton 1987). To that end, a coding procedure was designed to measure relevant external manifestations of the child's internal working model both over the course of the entire paradigm as well as specifically during the reunion.

Two sets of variables were selected for inclusion into the code. Consistent with the notion that the attachment system is continuously active, the first set focused primarily on the child's behavior and communication with the mother: (1) use of the mother as a secure base from which to explore the room, (2) positive affect expressed toward the mother, and (3) communication with the mother across a distance.

Each of these three variables was coded during five episodes: one (first four minutes of interview), two (fifth through eighth minute of the interview), five (five-minute mother-child free play), six (three-minute mother-child-stranger free play), and eight (three-minute reunion), and was scored on a three-point scale. A score of zero indicated that the child did not exhibit the behavior at all. A score of one indicated that the child exhibited the behavior but in a qualified or somewhat ambiguous manner, and a score of two indicated that the child exhibited the behavior in a definite, clear-cut manner.

The second set of variables consisted of six behaviors during either the separation or reunion episodes (episodes 7 and 8, respectively): (1) visual avoidance of the mother during her departure, (2) not overtly symbolically representing the mother in her absence (i.e., not saying the mother's name or not pretending to talk to the mother on a toy telephone), (3) lack of disruption in ongoing play activity during the separation, (4) negative reunion behavior, (5) rejecting the mother as she approaches in the reunion, and (6) rejecting the mother as she physically picked the child up during the reunion.

These variables were also coded on a three-point scale, with a score of zero indicating an absence of the behavior, a score of one indicating that the child exhibited the behavior in a qualified manner, and a score of two indicating that the child exhibited the behavior in a definite, clear-cut manner.

In addition to the three-point quantitative scale, qualitative aspects of the child's behavior were also coded for all nine variables. For example, there is more than one way to fail to use the mother as a secure base (score of zero on the secure-base variable). A child could be entirely involved with the mother

TABLE 2. CODE FOR VARIABLE: USING MOTHER AS A SECURE BASE

0 = Not at All

0.1.	Child is involved with mother the whole time and never becomes involved in play
0.2.	Child is involved in play the whole time and never becomes involved with mother[a]
0.3.	Child wanders aimlessly or scattered around the room, with fleeting or momentary involvement with mother and/or toys[b]

1 = Somewhat

1.1.	Child is involved with mother the whole time and has brief or casual involvement with toys
1.2.	Child is involved with play the whole time and has brief or casual involvement with mother[a]
1.3.	Child alternates between brief involvement with mother and brief involvement with play without ever really setting into focused play or interaction[b]
1.4.	Child increases level of exploration and play over the course of the episode but is still not fully engaged in play by the end

2 = Definitely

2.1.	Child is involved with both play and interaction with mother, in mother's proximity
2.2.	Child is involved with both play and interaction with mother at a distance[a]
2.3.	Child is involved with both play and interaction with mother both near and far from mother[b]

[a] Indicates an attention deployment style associated with focusing attention on the environment.
[b] Indicates an attention deployment style associated with balancing attention between the environment and mother.

and show no interest or involvement with the environment (a style resembling resistant children, a 0.1 on the secure-base variable). Or a child could be entirely involved with the environment and show no interest in or involvement with the mother (a style resembling avoidant children and a 0.2 on the secure-base variable). An example of the code used for the secure-base variable (which also includes the qualitative style code used to score flexibility of attention deployment) is presented in table 2. (The entire code is available from the authors upon request.)

Four composite variables representing different components of the attachment system in toddlerhood were derived from the nine variables coded: secure communication, flexible attention-deployment strategy, separation insecurity, and reunion rejection (see table 3).[4]

Secure communication. The first set of variables was designed to measure aspects of the child's ability to communicate with the mother while using her as a secure base from which to explore the room. Children's scores on each of

4. The code is designed to capture secure, avoidant, and resistant styles of the child's interaction with the mother. Because the primary focus of the data analysis was on comparing security with avoidance, only the avoidant style is described. The full code is available from the authors upon request.

TABLE 3.   CONSTRUCTION OF THE FOUR COMPOSITE ATTACHMENT MEASURES

	Secure Communication
Component variables	Secure base, positive affect, distance communication
Scored	Zero, one, two
Episodes coded	One, two, five, six, eight
How computed	Each variable is summed across five episodes (range from 0 to 1)
	Summary scores converted to Z-scores
	Z-scores summed
	New summary score is converted to a Z-score
Range	−3 to +3
Alpha	.75

	Flexible Attention-Deployment Strategy
Component variables	Style score for secure-base variable.
Scored	0.1, 0.2, 0.3
Episodes coded	One, two, five, six, eight
How computed	Frequency of avoidant (0.2) style (max = 5) is subtracted from the frequency of the secure or balanced (0.3) style (max = 5)
Range	−5 to +5
Alpha	.63

	Separation Insecurity
Component variables	Avoidance of departure, lack of symbolization, lack of play, disruption
Scored	0, 1, 2
Episodes coded	Seven
How computed	The three variables are averaged with unit weighting
Range	0 to 2
Alpha	.63

	Reunion Rejection
Component variables	Negative greeting, rejection of approach, rejection of pickup
Scored	0, 1, 2
Episodes coded	Eight
How computed	The three variables are averaged with unit weighting
Range	0 to 2
Alpha	.60

these three variables were summed across the five different episodes from which they were coded. Thus, each child received one score for secure base, one score for positive affect, and one score for distance communication. These summary scores ranged from zero to ten. A child would receive a score of zero if he or she never exhibited the behavior (scored zero) across each of the five episodes, and a child would receive a score of ten if he or she exhibited the behavior in a clear-cut manner (scored two) across each of the five episodes.

Children's scores on each of these three summary scores were converted to Z-scores and summed to create a single score which ranged from -6 to $+6$. This score was then converted to a Z-score. Thus, a single continuous variable of the child's secure communication with the mother was created, ranging from -3 (very insecure) to $+3$ (very secure). (See Cummings, this vol., for a discussion of continuous measures of security of attachment.) For this measure, the overall alpha was .75, and each of the three variables correlated at least .70 with the whole.

Flexible attention-deployment strategy. The composite score of the child's attention-deployment strategy was created from the qualitative code of the secure-base variable. The number of episodes during which the child was rated as focusing more attention on the environment than on the mother (0.2, 1.2, or 2.2 on the secure-base code, see table 2 for the code) was subtracted from the number of episodes during which the child was rated as balancing attention between the mother and the environment (0.3, 1.3, or 2.3 on the secure-base code). This variable ranges from -5 to $+5$. A score of -5 indicates that the child focused attention primarily on the environment throughout the paradigm; and a score of $+5$ indicates that the child balanced his or her attention between the mother and the environment throughout the paradigm. For this measure, the alpha was .63 with each episode correlating at or above .61.

Separation insecurity. This third summary variable was constructed from the child's scores on the three separation variables: visual avoidance of the mother's departure, lack of symbolic representation of the mother during her absence, and lack of disruption in ongoing play activity during the separation. Using equal weightings, children's scores on these three variables were averaged to create the summary score. The three variables comprising this measure all correlated at or above .65 with an alpha of .61.

Reunion rejection. The fourth summary variable was constructed from the three reunion variables: negative greeting upon reunion, rejection of the mother as she approached, and rejection of the mother's reunion pick-up. The children's scores on these three variables were also averaged, with each score being unit weighted. If a mother did not pick up the child, the data was considered missing for the rejection of the pick-up variable. The three variables comprising this measure all correlated with the whole at or above .58 with an overall alpha of .60.

Time 2. The center-based toddler attachment Q-sort consisted of ninety-two items and was adapted from the Waters and Deane home-based Q-sort (Waters & Deane 1985) for use in our Toddler Center. Each item described the child's behavior in reference to one of five domains: attachment, exploration, peer interaction, interactions with the teachers, and the child's mood and temperament. Thirty-one of the items were drawn directly from Waters and Deane's original Q-sort. Twenty-four items from the original deck were modified to form the basis for thirty-seven items only observable in the first weeks of a toddler playgroup; and thirty-four items were newly created to replace items from the deck which were not relevant to play-group content.

TABLE 4.   EXAMPLES OF Q-SORT ITEMS AND THEIR RANKINGS
ON THE CRITERION SORT

Characteristic of Security with Rank	
Child smiles and vocalizes spontaneously to mother on reunion	8.8
Child looks to mother for assurance when wary	8.7
Mother and child share positive feelings during play	8.5
Child expresses enjoyment at achieving and accomplishing in play	8.3
Child's predominant mood is happy	8.3
Child returns to mother spontaneously after play	8.3
Child visually and vocally checks in with mother during play	8.3
Transitions from proximity to mother to play are executed smoothly	8.3
Transitions from play to proximity to mother are executed smoothly	8.0
Child solicits and enjoys playful physical contact with mother	8.0

Uncharacteristic of Security with Rank	
Child avoids mother on reunion	1.2
Child ignores mother on reunion	1.3
Child becomes angry at mother on reunion	1.3
Child does not actively solicit comforting from mother when distressed	1.5
Child easily becomes angry at mother	2.0
Over the course of the day child is generally unaware of mother's location	2.2
Child is object-oriented to the exclusion of the social world	2.2
Child does not approach mother to interact	2.2
Child does not accept parent's assurances when wary	2.3
Child stays with mother in adjacent room	2.3

A criterion Q-sort profile was established by having three attachment researchers and three child-care professionals who were familiar with attachment theory and the routine at the Toddler Center complete the Q-sort based
on how they thought an ideal securely attached child would behave during the
first month of the toddler play group. Interrater reliability among the six
raters, calculated using the Spearman-Brown formula, was .96. As is the
practice in deriving scores on constructs from Q-sort data (Block 1978;
Waters & Deane 1985), each child's Q-sort profile was then correlated with
this criterion profile. This resulted in a single measure of the child's security
of attachment at Time 2, which ranged from -1.00 to $+1.00$. Examples of
items which ranked high and low in the security profile are presented in table 4.
(The full Q-sort deck as well as the security score weightings are available
from the authors upon request.)

As table 4 indicates, both researchers and service professionals describe
secure toddlers as smiling and vocalizing to mother on reunion, looking to
mother for assurances when wary, both sharing positive feelings with and visually checking in with mother during play, expressing enjoyment at achieving in play, and returning to parent spontaneously after play. They describe
insecure toddlers as avoiding and/or ignoring the mother on reunion, not actively soliciting comfort from mother when distressed, easily becoming angry

with mother, being unaware of mother's location over the course of the day, and being object-oriented to the exclusion of social interaction.

Time 3. Rating scales (adapted by Goldberg & Easterbrooks 1984 from Matas et al. 1978) were further adapted to measure the child's task orientation and positive affect and enthusiasm during the two problem-solving tasks. Each scale ranged from one to five. A score of one indicated the minimum amount of the behavior being measured, and a score of five indicated the maximum amount of a behavior being measured. Judgments were made for the first three minutes, the last three minutes, and overall for both the easy and the hard tasks.

Each year two different teams of research assistants conducted and videotaped the attachment and problem-solving assessments. Two additional independent teams of assistants subsequently coded the attachment and problem-solving data from videotapes. All teams were blind to any other information about the children. Interrater reliability, calculated as percentage of agreement with an expert and the coding team, exceeded 85%.

Interrater reliability for the Q-sorts was determined by calculating Spearman-Brown correlations among each set of three sorters for each child. The average for all sets of three sorters was .71, the percentage of children for whom the raters' reliability exceeded .60 was 87%.

Results

We reviewed all the tapes of children scoring $-.5$ or less on the secure communication variable in order to determine which of them could be considered insecurely attached-resistant. The tapes of the children scoring in the bottom 33% of the scores were thus examined, which we presumed would include most of the insecurely attached children in our sample. Using normal populations, most attachment research has found approximately one-third of the sample to be insecure (Ainsworth et al. 1978). From those tapes, four children were determined to be insecure-resistant. There were not enough resistant children to treat them as a separate group for data analysis purposes, and given the possibility that including them with the avoidant children might obscure some findings we decided to exclude them from data analysis.

Demographic Variables. Preliminary analyses were conducted in order to examine the effect of gender and age on the four composite attachment variables, the Q-sort attachment variable, and the two autonomy measures of child task orientation and child affect/enthusiasm.

Results revealed only two (of seven possible) significant effects for gender: on the flexible attention-deployment variable, girls (mean = 5.68, s.d. = 2.3) had significantly higher mean scores than the boys (mean = 3.83, s.d. = 2.3), $t(56) = 2.97$, $p < .005$. Gender differences were also found in security scores from the Q-sort measure with girls (mean = .46, s.d. = .25) having significantly higher scores than the boys (mean = .18, s.d. = .28), $t(22)$ = 2.48), $p < .05$. No gender differences were found on the other three attachment composite measures, task orientation, or affect/enthusiasm.

Analyses were then conducted to examine the relationship between age in months and the four attachment components, first for all the subjects and then by gender. Results revealed that, when all the subjects are combined, age is positively correlated with flexible attention-deployment strategy ($r = .27$, $p < .01$). The same pattern emerged when correlations were conducted separately for boys and girls. There were no significant correlations between age in months and the Q-sort attachment variable either for all subjects or by gender. There were also no significant associations between age and either task orientation or affect/enthusiasm when all subjects were combined or when analyzed by gender.

Relationships among the Four Attachment Components. Four Pearson product-moment correlations were computed in order to examine the interrelationships among the four Time 1 attachment variables. The results are presented in table 5.

They indicated that secure communication was significantly positively correlated with a flexible attention deployment strategy and significantly negatively correlated with both separation insecurity and reunion rejection. Similarly, reunion rejection was negatively correlated with flexible attention deployment and positively correlated with separation insecurity. Separation insecurity and reunion rejection were themselves significantly positively correlated.

The Relationship between Time 1 and Time 2 Attachment. Next, four Pearson correlations were conducted to examine the relationship between each child's correlation with the criterion attachment Q-sort and the four attachment variables from the Time 1 attachment assessment, first for all subjects combined and then separately by gender (see table 6). These results reveal that the Q-sort measure of attachment was significantly positively correlated with both secure communication ($r = .50$) and flexible attention-deployment strategy ($r = .53$), and negatively but not significantly correlated with both separation insecurity ($r = -.23$) and reunion rejection ($r = -.25$). This pattern was consistent across gender and was unchanged by partialing out the effects of age.

The Relationship between Attachment at Time 1 and Autonomy at Time 3.[5] Pearson correlations were computed to test the hypotheses of significant rela-

---

5. Although analyses of relations between Q-sort at Time 2 and indices of child autonomy at Time 3 would increase confidence in the Q-sort measure, our sample is not yet large enough to do that.

TABLE 5. ZERO-ORDER CORRELATIONS AMONG THE
FOUR ATTACHMENT VARIABLES ($n = 58$)

	Secure Communication	Attention Deployment	Separation Insecurity	Reunion Rejection
Secure Communication		.56***	−.25*	−.30*
Attention Deployment			−.19	−.25*
Separation Insecurity				.36*

*$p < .05$.
***$p < .001$.

TABLE 6. ZERO-ORDER CORRELATIONS BETWEEN ATTACHMENT
AT TIME 1 AND ATTACHMENT AT TIME 2 ($n = 24$)

	Secure Communication	Attention Deployment	Separation Insecurity	Reunion Rejection
Q-sort	.50**	53**	−.23	−.25

*$p < .05$.
**$p < .01$.

TABLE 7. ZERO-ORDER CORRELATIONS FROM ATTACHMENT
AT TIME 1 TO AUTONOMY AT TIME 3

	Secure Communication	Attention Deployment	Separation Insecurity	Reunion Rejection
All Subjects ($n = 45$)				
Task orientation	.12	.25*	−.13	−.07
Affect/enthusiasm	.07	.16	−.30*	−.02
Males Only ($n = 20$)				
Task orientation	−.28	.00	−.16	.00
Affect/enthusiasm	−.38*	.12	.12	.23
Females Only ($n = 22$)				
Task orientation	.38**	.33*	−.11	−.17
Affect/enthusiasm	.27	.13	−.51**	−.17

NOTE: Partial correlations were computed, partialing out the effects of age and gender, which
were substantially the same; therefore, the zero-order correlations are presented.
*$p < .05$.
**$p < .01$.

tionships between the four Time 1 measures of security and the Time 3 measures of child affect/enthusiasm and child-task orientation during the difficult
problem-solving task, for all subjects together and separately by gender. This
series of correlations are presented in table 7.

These analyses suggest that the relationship between earlier attachment and later autonomy may differ for boys and girls. Although there are two of eight possible significant correlations, the pattern of relationships between the two sets of variables is obscured when boys and girls are analyzed as one group. The weak (.25) correlation between attention deployment and task orientation is actually composed of a stronger correlation for the girls and a lack of association for the boys. The same holds true for the relationship between separation insecurity and affect/enthusiasm, which is weak and positive for the boys and moderate and negative for the girls. Additionally, the lack of association between secure communication and either task orientation or affect/enthusiasm when all subjects are analyzed together, in fact represents two contrasting sets of relationships. For the boys, secure communication is negatively associated with both autonomy indices, while for the girls it is positively associated with both indices. The same pattern of correlations was found after partialing out the effects of age.

Discussion

Our efforts to adapt and begin to validate two measures of security of attachment for use with toddlers in the context of a service program have met with some initial success. Our adaptation of the Ainsworth Strange Situation (Ainsworth et al. 1978) for use as an intake interview allowed us to code reliably four theoretically meaningful components of the attachment system in toddlerhood: the child's secure communication with mother, flexible attention deployment between the mother and the environment, behaviors during separation that indicate insecurity, and behaviors during reunion that indicate rejection of the mother. These four components are interrelated as would be predicted by attachment theory: for example, toddlers high in secure communication are also high in flexibility of attention deployment and low in both separation insecurity and reunion rejection; children high in separation insecurity are also high in reunion rejection.

Similarly, our adaptation of the Waters and Deane (1985) home-based Q-sort technique has been used by student teachers to reliably describe the child's attachment behaviors based on observations of mother-child interaction patterns over the first eight sessions of a toddler developmental play group. The fact that we were able to collect interrater reliable and internally consistent scientific data via procedures designed to meet service (intake interview) and educational (teacher observation) goals is quite encouraging, given our larger goal of closing the gap between service and research. But, of course, in addition to reliability, the scientific value of our modified assessment procedures requires data supporting their validity as well.

We believe that the strongest and clearest validity data reported in this chapter are the correlations between the four components of the attachment system in toddlerhood assessed via the intake interview and the security score measured independently via the Q-sort observations of mother-child interactions during the first month of a toddler play group. Secure communication and flexibility of attention deployment on intake were positively associated with toddler security in a play group six to eight months later (r's $= .51$ and .53). Similarly, for boys and girls, there was a trend for separation insecurity and reunion rejection on intake to be negatively associated with toddler security.

Less clear, but perhaps more interesting, are the data on the longitudinal relationships between the four components of toddler attachment assessed at intake and the two indices of toddler autonomy, namely, their task orientation and positive affect/enthusiasm during a difficult parent-assisted problem-solving task. For boys and girls combined, we report two of a possible eight weak but significant associations between toddler attachment and later autonomy. Specifically, toddlers who are able to flexibly deploy attention between their mothers and the environment during the intake interview are significantly more task oriented in a problem-solving task one year later. Similarly, toddlers who exhibit more separation insecurity on intake appear significantly less positive in affect and enthusiasm one year later. Curiously, even though secure communication is highly correlated with flexibility of attention deployment during intake, it is unrelated to either measure of toddler autonomy when boys and girls were examined together.

These initial findings, however, must be qualified by the follow-up analyses which examined the same relationships between attachment and autonomy separately by gender. From these analyses, we discovered that the two reported significant relationships between (1) flexible attention deployment and later task orientation, and (2) separation insecurity and later positive affect/enthusiasm were restricted to girls (r's $= .33$ and $-.51$) and not boys (r's $= .00$ and $.12$). In addition, the lack of relationship between secure communication and toddler autonomy from analyses that combined boys and girls appears to obscure opposite patterns of association for boys and girls when considered separately. That is, secure communication is positively associated with both task orientation and positive affect/enthusiasm for girls (r's $= .38$ and $.27$) but negatively associated with both for boys (r's $= -.28$ and $-.38$). In light of both the small number of subjects available for these gender-specific analyses, and the general absence of such findings in the literature on correlates of security of attachment, these gender-different patterns must be interpreted with caution. If replicated, they would suggest the discriminant validity of our measures of components of the attachment system in toddlerhood and the need to expand attachment theory to account for such gender differences.

The general pattern of our longitudinal findings derived from our modified attachment paradigms highlights two major themes concerning the conceptualization and measurement of attachment after infancy.

The Role of Across-Episode Attentional and Communicative Processes in Assessing Security of Attachment during Toddlerhood. First, our data add further support to the work of a variety of investigators (Bretherton 1985, 1987;

Grossmann & Grossmann 1984; Main et al. 1985) which focuses on stage- and context-specific manifestations of children's (and adult's) internal working models of self-in-relation-to-others. Following Bowlby ([1969] 1982, 1973, 1980), these investigators viewed the notion of an internal working model as the guiding concept behind life-span attachment theory and research. In infancy, the key feature of an internal working model of self and other relevant to security of attachment is the representation of the caretaker as accessible and predictably responsive versus inaccessible, rejecting and unpredictable, and the complementary representation of self as worthy of love and competent versus unworthy and incompetent. Thus, infant's reunion behaviors in the Strange Situation can be viewed from this perspective as a stage- and context-specific reflection of an infant's internal working model of self and caretaker inasmuch as it can be "read" as a reflection of the infant's expectation of caretaker availability and responsiveness.

The implication of this conceptualization for cross-stage attachment theory becomes clearer when Main et al. (1985) remind us, "Internal working models direct not only feelings and behavior, but also attention, memory and cognitions, insofar as they directly or indirectly relate to attachment. Individual differences in these working models will therefore be related not only to individual patterns in nonverbal behavior, but also to patterns of language and structures of mind" (p. 67).

Thus, a key task for life-span researchers of attachment is to find stage- and context-specific reflections of internal working models, or as Bretherton (1985) calls them, "useful windows into internal working models." Previous theory and research suggest examining not only behaviors and affect in the context of separation/reunion but also attentional and communicational processes and patterns across a variety of attachment-relevant situations (Bretherton, 1987; Grossmann & Grossmann 1984; Grossmann, Grossmann, & Schwan, in press; Main et al. 1985).

Consistent with this, our attachment paradigm/intake interview indicated that secure communication and flexibility of attention deployment were more powerfully related to later teacher Q-sort ratings of attachment and indices of autonomous functioning in a parent-assisted problem-solving paradigm than were separation and reunion behaviors and affect. Although we cannot be sure whether the differences between our findings and those derived from infants in the Strange Situation are attributable to differences in age (19–24-month-olds vs. 12–18-month-olds), context (one vs. two separations), or variables coded (communication and attention vs. proximity seeking, etc.), we can tentatively conclude that a toddler's "secure communication" and "flexibility of attention deployment" in a novel, moderately stressful environment appear to be useful windows into the toddler's internal working model of self-in-relation-to-caretaker.

It is also important to recognize and interpret why separation insecurity and reunion rejection were only weakly predictive of later attachment and autonomy. This pattern may be attributable to a variety of measurement factors. For example, both measures are coded in only one episode as opposed to secure communication and flexible attention-deployment strategy being coded across the entire paradigm. Additionally, both measures are derived from variables coded during the first (and only) separation/reunion episode and not the second as is traditionally done (Ainsworth et al. 1978).

At a theoretical level, the relative lack of power of reunion rejection in particular may be due to developmental advances taking place at around 18 months which influence the form and/or meaning of the child's rejection of the mother. As has been widely reported, with the onset of the "terrible twos," toddlers become increasingly preoccupied with and motivated by autonomy concerns (Sroufe 1979). Thus, normal, phase-specific concerns about autonomous functioning may change the meaning of separation/reunion behaviors during toddlerhood. For example, some toddlers may seem avoidant of their caretakers on reunion when they are really motivated by a healthy, normal desire to establish their independence. This difficulty in discerning nonoptimal avoidance from normative autonomy concerns may be reflected in our code and hence serve to weaken the predictive value of separation/reunion behaviors in our study. Further work both at the coding level (e.g., attempting to identify subtle cues which distinguish autonomy from true avoidance on reunion) and at the data analysis level (e.g., looking at pattern scores which distinguish high reunion rejection with and without high secure communication) is needed to clarify these issues.

Gender Differences in the Organization of the Attachment System in Toddlerhood. The second theme highlighted by our findings involves the pattern of gender differences. To briefly summarize, we found differences between girls and boys in mean levels on two (of five) indices of security: girls scored significantly higher than boys in flexibility of attention deployment (in the intake interview) and on security (rated via teacher Q-sorts). We found no gender differences in mean levels of indices of autonomy (task orientation and affect/enthusiasm), but we did find gender differences in the pattern of relationships between indices of security (at Time 1) and indices of autonomy (at Time 3). In short, the girl toddlers in our study demonstrated patterns of relationships between early indices of security of attachment and later indices of autonomy consistent with previous findings from attachment research with infants (Goldberg & Easterbrooks 1984; Matas et al. 1978). The boy toddlers, however, showed either the opposite pattern or no pattern at all. What are we to make of these preliminary findings of gender differences?

The importance of gender as an organizer and/or determinant of social experience has been a topic of debate for decades. But gender has not been a focus of concern for attachment theorists and researchers. It has been argued

that the attachment system is so important to the survival and future adaptation of human infants that the evolution of the basic features of the attachment
system shuld be gender nonspecific (Ainsworth et al. 1978). Empirically, few
gender differences in the postdictive, concurrent, and predictive validity of
attachment classifications have been reported (presumably because they don't
exist, but perhaps because they haven't been examined).

Yet gender differences have been found in other areas of early social and
emotional development and mother-child interactions (e.g., Clarke-Stewart &
Hevey 1981; Haviland & Malatesta 1981; Martin 1981). Also, gender differences in later attachment-related attitudes (e.g., valuing of intimacy and relatedness) and behaviors (e.g., of child-care responsibilities and behaviors)
frequently have been reported in the adult literature on personality and social
development. In addition, a few investigators have begun to specify relationships between infant attachment and such independent variables as maternal
employment and such dependent variables as child psychopathology, which
are gender-specific (Chase-Lansdale & Owen 1987; Lewis, Feiring, McGuffog, & Jaskir 1984).

In the spirit of beginning to consider gender differences seriously, we will
briefly discuss and then offer several alternative explanations for our patterns
of gender differences.

First, our findings that girls score higher than boys on flexibility of attention deployment is consistent with other findings that girls in general are more
responsive to social stimuli. For example, across age and situations, girls exhibited less gaze aversion and a higher frequency and longer duration of eye
contact than boys and are more responsive to realistic social stimuli than boys
(Haviland & Malatesta 1981). Thus, the fact that girls are more likely to deploy attention to mothers as well as the environment in the intake interview is
consistent with the general pattern found elsewhere.

Second, the fact that girls were rated as more secure than boys on entry
into the play group may be explained by boys and girls experiencing different
histories of socialization of affect. It appears that girls (as compared to boys)
are encouraged to seek comfort when distressed and are discouraged from expressing anger when frustrated (Haviland & Malatesta 1981). Those familiar
with attachment coding will recognize the theoretical relevance of these findings to infant behavior from which security of attachment is inferred.

This socialization of affect hypothesis is supported by the Q-sort data. As
table 2 made evident, items such as "not actively soliciting comfort from
mother when distressed" and "easily becomes angry at mother" are considered key indices of insecurity on the center-based Q-sort. Indeed, half of these
items rated as most characteristic of insecurity relate to turning to the parent
for comfort/reassurance and/or expressions of anger. (Perhaps similar judgments are being made in coding toddler attachment behaviors related to "secure communication" such as "using mother as a secure base" and "positive

affect toward mother"). In short, perhaps girls are rated as more secure than boys on entry to a toddler play group because they are encouraged to seek comfort and discouraged from expressing anger. This may be explained in at least two ways. First, different socialization histories may encourage boys to develop different display rules to express attachment-related behaviors and affects associated with similar internal working models. For example, girls may seek comfort when distressed while boys may express anger. On the other hand, these different histories may lead boys to experience the attachment relationship itself differently, such that the underlying internal working models are different, not just the expressions of behavior and affect.

Third, regarding the gender-specific pattern of association between attachment and autonomy, other theoretical notions may eventually help clarify these findings. As reported by a number of investigators, boys seem to derive something different from "sensitive caretaking" than do girls (Clarke-Stewart & Hevey 1981; Martin 1981). It is possible that high scores on secure communication mean something different for boys than girls and therefore have a different set of predictive correlates. In short, we are raising the possibility that the definition of maternal sensitivity may become increasingly gender-specific with development.

Finally, none of these interpretations are mutually exclusive. Rather they could act in a complex interactive fashion (as proposed by Haviland & Malatesta 1981) all in the context of the (difficult to tease out) gender asymmetry of early mother-child relationships. This asymmetry could take a number of different forms. For example, mothers may differentially respond to the same behavior or affect depending upon the gender of the child (Moss 1974), or boys and girls may respond to the same maternal behavior differently either because of different biological dispositions (Zaslow & Hayes 1986), or because it is experienced in the context of the mother being either the same or a different sex as the child (Chodorow 1978).

IMPLICATIONS

Theoretical/Scientific

One general theoretical implication of our efforts concerns the potential of studying attachment in childhood in modified or nonlaboratory "natural" environments. Certainly, a number of attachment researchers have done this in the home (Ainsworth et al. 1978; Belsky, Rovine, & Taylor 1984; Waters & Deane 1985) and in the preschool (LaFreniere & Sroufe 1985; Sroufe 1983; Sroufe, Fox, & Pancake 1983). As attachment theory becomes increasingly relevant to clinical, program, and policy issues (Aber & Slade 1987; Aber & Allen 1987; Belsky 1986; Cicchetti & Toth 1987; Lyons-Ruth et al. 1987; Phillips, McCartney, Scarr, & Howes 1987), an increasing number of scientists and service providers may want or need attachment-oriented research to be conducted in (their) service settings. On the basis of our experience, we tentatively conclude that conducting scientifically sound, clinically, and programmatically relevant research in service settings is possible. Through our efforts, we have become impressed by both the host of difficulties associated with adapting standard lab paradigms for use in studies conducted in "real-world" settings, and by the potential benefits of such activities. Two sets of advantages/disadvantages have particular relevance for our work to date: the issue of sample size, and the issue of the relationship between theory and measurement.

Sample Size. One disadvantage associated with our model is the limitation of small numbers. Our small sample size all but precludes convincing analyses of the effects of gender on attachment processes using our data set for several more years. However, this disadvantage is offset in two important ways. First, when conducting longitudinal studies, the curse of a small sample size may be offset by the blessing of a devoted, trusting subject population. We suspect that most parents are more willing to return to a valued alma mater in which follow-up research visits are publicized and integrated with a class reunion. Indeed, we are conducting a short-term longitudinal follow-up study of our toddlers in the preschool years based on the strength of our families' loyalties to the Toddler Center (our return rate after two years is approximately 80%).

Second, our "service and research" model includes the opportunity to be "close to the phenomenon of interest," and to employ the service setting as a resource for the generation of hypotheses and of alternative research strategies. Sometimes all this can work hand in hand in rather elegant fashion. For example, through running parent groups at the Toddler Center, Berger and Aber (1986) became fascinated by what they discerned as identifiable individual differences in parent separation/reunion behaviors. Without the opportunity to work extensively with parents in the Center, we may never even have focused on the phenomenon. Now, primarily because of integrating our scientific research with our service efforts, we are developing a developmental theory of "security-promoting parenting" which takes parent's (as well as child's) stage-salient tasks into account.

Theory and Measurement. The second set of advantages/disadvantages centers around the issue of the relationship between measurement and theory. It should be noted that the modifications in our measurement strategy, partially determined by our service goals, qualify the interpretation of our results. Changing the standard Ainsworth Strange-Situation assessment procedure, no matter how advisable, does limit our ability to interpret our findings. Indeed, it might very well have been that the assessment and coding procedures themselves "caused" the findings to differ from what is usually found with younger children in the standard paradigm rather than reflecting real differences in the older children.

However, resolutions to this problem can be addressed in future research through further validation of our assessment and coding procedures. Three such projects are currently underway in our lab. First we are examining group differences on our new measures of toddler attachment between the normal children and the children of depressed mothers. Second, we are using Crittenden's care index (Crittenden 1988) to test the relationship between maternal sensitivity, control, and unresponsiveness in our intake interview and our new measures of toddler attachment. Third, by assessing 12–18-month-olds in our paradigm we are comparing the pattern of correlations found between the attachment components and the two autonomy measures for the 19–24-month-olds with that of younger children. Thus, we are directly testing the hypotheses that gender-specific maternal behavior or developmental progressions account for our present findings (Baker 1989).

Although our efforts to adapt attachment research paradigms for use in service settings partly qualifies the interpretation of results and creates a burden of proof of the validity of the modifications, we believe that it simultaneously has a beneficial impact on theory development in two ways. First, employing modified attachment procedures with older children may lead to the discovery of new features of the attachment system in toddlerhood which may not have otherwise emerged. Two such features have been suggested by our findings: the increasing role of across-episode attentional and communicative processes and the increasing gender specificity of the relationship between attachment and autonomy. Second, conducting attachment research in a service setting eventually will allow us to examine some key issues in attachment theory which either are best addressed or can only be addressed by intervention studies. For instance, Bowlby contends that childrens' internal working models of self-in-relation-to-other becomes increasingly resistant to change with development. We suspect that systematic interventions aimed at helping children at various stages of development to rework insecure internal working models are among the few ways possible to test this key feature of life-span attachment theory.

Clinical/Practical

Finally, we wish to turn to several implications and advantages and disadvantages of our "service and research" model for our service provision. What clinical, educational, and/or practical value do we see in conducting a program of research on attachment processes in the context of a toddler center?

In general, we believe that the principal advantages of our research for services are derived primarily through its effects on the quality of the staff/child interactions in our Center.

At present, evidence is beginning to mount that (1) the effects of nonparental child care and early education on child development are dependent in part on the quality of the child care/early education program (Phillips, Mc-Cartney, & Scarr 1987); and (2) the quality of a child care/early education program is determined in part by the quality of direct training in child care, not the child-care provider's general level of education or amount of previous child-care experience (Clarke-Stewart & Gruber 1984; Howes 1983; Ruopp, Travers, Glantz, & Coelen 1979).

We believe that our education of student teachers through exposure to attachment theory, to the direct observation of attachment-relevant child behavior (via the Q-sort technique on entry to the toddler play group), and to individual differences in patterns of attachment is an effective form of direct training in child care. We believe that this type of training may help improve the quality of staff/child interaction in three important ways.

Basic Needs of Children. Attachment theory starts with the premise that every child has certain needs for assurance when wary, comfort when feeling insecure, etc. Familiarizing student teachers with these assumptions about the child's needs allows them to compare and understand different patterns of parent-child interactions. For instance, to a teacher unfamiliar with attachment theory, an avoidant child may be interpreted as not feeling scared or anxious and as not having needs for comfort and reassurance from the parent. In contrast, a teacher familiar with this basic premise of attachment theory can interpret avoidance of the mother as one particular pattern of expressing these needs. At the same time, we also teach that what makes for good care by parents is basically the same as good care by providers. Thus, student–service-provider training in, and analyses of, good parent-child interactions also teaches them good caretaker-child interactions.

Attachment Status as History. Second, teaching child-care providers to recognize and understand both attachment-relevant behaviors and the basic patterns of the organization of the attachment system (secure, avoidant, resistant, disorganized) allows providers to learn from the children about children. This is because the attachment organization can be "read" or "interpreted" by staff as a very condensed version of the child's earlier relationship history (Sroufe 1979; Sroufe & Fleeson 1986). In addition, it may enable providers to more reliably elaborate on parent descriptions of their children and their direct observations of the children, thereby giving toddlers a "voice" in their own care.

Two significant dangers to this approach of using attachment theory and research to guide early caretaking interactions with infants and toddlers are the twin dangers of "labeling" and "the self-fulfilling-prophecy." Some evidence exists to indicate that children labeled as "atypical" or "avoidant" might be treated differently by caretakers. However, we emphasize in our training several safeguards against these dangers. For example, we talk extensively about how different toddlers "push different buttons in different caregivers." We also emphasize the plasticity of early development, noting that discontinuities in development are as important to recognize and be open to as continuities. Finally, and perhaps more important, we urge our student teachers to treat their formulations of children's attachment status as clinical hypotheses that must remain open to new evidence and reformulation.

Attachment Status as a Likely Developmental Pathway. And finally, just as children's attachment status can be treated as a series of clinical hypotheses about their past relationship history, it can also be used to generate a series of hypotheses about their likely future adaptational history. Scientific data exists to responsibly conclude that insecurity of attachment may place an infant or toddler at risk for problems in early peer relationships, ego-resiliency/impulse control/aggressivity and a poor quality of relationships with nonparental adults (Sroufe 1983). Because these projections entail all the risks of labeling and self-fulfilling prophecies described above, a major challenge for the future will be to devise ways to draw upon the emerging data and theoretical knowledge derived from attachment research to help design early childhood programs and individual service plans for children while avoiding these dangers. In the meantime, we can at least draw on such data to prepare ourselves to respond sensitively and creatively (not in a rote, uninformed fashion) to some of the "expectable" conflicts insecure children may develop.

CONCLUSION

In this chapter, we have presented two procedures to measure indices of security of attachment in toddlerhood. These procedures were adapted from existing research with the belief that they could simultaneously serve our Center's service, research, and educational goals. While the reliability and initial validity of these procedures encourage us about their scientific potential, we are equally encouraged by their clinical and practical import. As attachment theory and research continues to grow and to be refined, we expect that its potential to help guide the design and evaluation of services for young children and their families also will increase. We hope that attachment researchers will continue to modify both theory and research techniques to help close the gap between the development of knowledge about attachment relationships and the application of that knowledge to improve services and policies for young children and their families.

REFERENCES

Aber, L., & Allen, J. (1987). Effects of maltreatment on young children's socioemotional development: An attachment theory perspective. *Developmental Psychology* 23, 406–414.

Aber, L., & Slade, A. (1987, January 10). Attachment theory and research: A framework for clinical interventions. Paper presented at the Regional Scientific Meeting of the Division for Psychoanalysis, Section on Childhood and Adolescence, American Psychological Association, New York.

Aber, L.; Slade, A.; Berger, B.; Bresgi, I.; & Kaplan, M. (1985). *The parent development interview*. Manual and administration procedures. Department of Psychology, Barnard College, Columbia University.

Ainsworth, M. D. S.; Blehar, M. C.; Waters, E.; & Wall, S. (1978). *Patterns of attachment: A psychological study of the strange situation*. Hillside, N.J.: Erlbaum.

Baker, A. J. L. (1989). The child's attachment to the mother in infancy and toddlerhood: A comparative study. Unpublished doctoral dissertation, Teachers College, Columbia University.

Barglow, P.; Vaughn, B.; & Molitor, N. (1987). Effects of maternal absence due to employment on the quality of infant-mother attachment in a low-risk sample. *Child Development* 58, 945–954.

Belsky, J. (1986). Infant day care: A cause for concern? *Zero to Three* 6, 22–24.

Belsky, J., & Nezworski, T. (eds.), (1988). *Clinical implications of attachment*. Hillsdale, N.J.: Erlbaum.

Belsky, J.; Rovine, M.; & Taylor, D. (1984). The Pennsylvania infant and family project: III. The origins of individual differences in infant mother attachment: Maternal and infant contributions. *Child Development* 55, 718–728.

Berger, B., & Aber, J. L. (1986). Maternal autonomy in separation: A new measure of mother's negotiating ability during separation. Paper presented at the International Conference on Infancy Studies, Los Angeles.

Block, J. (1978). *The q-sort method in personality assessment and psychiatric research*. Palo Alto, Calif.: Consulting Psychology Press.

Bowlby, J. ([1969] 1982). *Attachment and loss: Vol. 1. Attachment*. New York: Basic Books.

Bowlby, J. (1973). *Attachment and loss: Vol. 2. Separation*. New York: Basic Books.

Bowlby, J. (1980). *Attachment and loss: Vol. 3. Loss, sadness and depression*. New York: Basic Books.

Bretherton, I. (1985). Attachment theory: Retrospect and prospect. In I. Bretherton & E. Waters (eds.), *Growing Points in attachment theory and research*. *Monographs of the Society for Research in Child Development* 50 (1–2, Serial No. 209), 3–35.

Bretherton, I. (1987). New perspectives on attachment relations: Security, communication and internal working models. In J. Osofsky (ed.), *Handbook of infant psychology* (2 ed., pp. 1061–1100). New York: Wiley.

Chase-Lansdale, L., & Owen, M. (1987). Maternal employment in a family context: Effects on infant-mother and infant-father attachments. *Child Development* 58, 1505–1512.

Chodorow, N. (1978). *The reproduction of mothering: Psychoanalysis and the sociology of gender*. Berkeley and Los Angeles: University of California Press.

Cicchetti, D., & Toth, S. (1987). The application of a transactional risk to intervention with multi-risk maltreating families. *Zero To Three* 7, 1–8.

Clarke-Stewart, A., & Gruber, C. (1984). Daycare forms and features. In R. C. Ainslie (eds.), *Quality variations in day care*. New York: Prager.

Clarke-Stewart, K. A., & Hevey, C. M. (1981). Longitudinal relations in repeated observations of mother-child interaction from 1 to 2½ years. *Developmental Psychology* 17, 127–145.

Crittenden, P. (1988). Relationships at risk. In J. Belsky & T. Nezworski (eds.), *Clinical implications of attachment*. Hillsdale, N.J.: Erlbaum.

Easterbrooks, A., & Goldberg, W. (1984). Toddler development in the family: Impact of father involvement and parenting characteristics. *Child Development* 55, 74–752.

Erikson, E. (1950). *Childhood and society*. New York: Basic Books.

Freud, S. (1905). Three essays on sexuality. *The complete psychological works of Sigmund Freud* (Standard Ed., vol. 7). London: Hogarth.

Goldberg, W. A., & Easterbrooks, M. A. (1984). Role of marital quality in toddler development. *Developmental Psychology* 20, 504–514.

Greenberg, M. (1984). Working paper on attachment beyond infancy. Unpublished manuscript, Department of Psychology, University of Washington.

Greenberg, M. T., & Marvin, R. S. (1979). Attachment patterns in profoundly deaf preschool children. *Merril-Palmer Quarterly* 25, 265–279.

Greenspan, S. (1981). *Psychopathology and adaptation in infancy and early childhood*. New York: International University Press.

Grossmann, K. E., & Grossmann, K. (1984). The development of conversational styles in the first year of life and its relationship to maternal sensitivity and attachment quality between mother and child. Paper presented at the Congress of the German Society for Psychology, Vienna, Austria.

Grossmann, K. E.; Grossmann, K.; & Schwan, A. (in press). Capturing the wider view of attachment: A reanalysis of Ainsworth's strange situation. In C. E. Izard & P. B. Read (eds.), *Measuring emotions in infants and children*. New York: Cambridge University Press.

Haviland, J. J., & Malatesta, C. Z. (1981). The development of sex differences in nonverbal signals: Fallacies, facts and fantasies. In C. Mayo & N. M. Henley (eds.), *Gender and nonverbal behavior*. New York: Springer-Verlag.

Howes, C. (1983). Caregiver behavior in center and family day care. *Journal of Applied Developmental Psychology* 4, 99–107.

Kagan, J. (1981). *The second year of life: The emergence of self-awareness*. Cambridge, Mass.: Harvard University Press.

Kobak, R., & Shaver, P. (1987). Strategies for maintaining felt security: A theoretical analysis of continuity and change in styles of social adaptation. Paper presented for the conference in honor of John Bowlby's eightieth birthday, London.

LaFreniere, P., & Sroufe, L. A. (1985). Profiles of peer competence: Interrelations between measures, influence of social ecology, and relation to attachment history. *Developmental Psychology* 21, 56–58.

Lewis, M.; Feiring, C.; McGuffog, C.; & Jaskir, J. (1984). Predicting psychopathology in six year olds from early social relations. *Child Development* 55, 123–136.

Lieberman, A. F. (1977). Preschooler's competence with a peer: Relations with attachment and peer experience. *Child Development* 48, 1277–1287.

Loevinger, (1957). Objective tests as instruments of psychological theory. *Psychological Reports* 3, 635–694.

Lyons-Ruth, K.; Connell, D.; Zoll, D.; & Stahl, J. (1987). Infants at social risk: Relations among infant maltreatment, maternal behavior and infant attachment behavior. *Developmental Psychology* 23, 223–232.

Maccoby, E. E., & Feldman, S. S. (1972). *Mother-attachment and stranger-reactions in the third year of life. Monographs for the Society for Research in Child Development* 37 (1, Serial No. 146), 1–85.

Mahler, M. S.; Pine, F.; & Bergman, A. (1975). *The psychological birth of the human infant*. New York: Basic Books.

Main, M., & Goldwyn, R. (1984). Predicting rejection of her infant from mother's representation of her own experiences: A preliminary report. *International Journal of Child Abuse and Neglect* 8, 203–217.

Main, M.; Kaplan, N.; & Cassidy, J. (1985). Security of attachment in infancy, childhood and adulthood: A move to the level of representation. In I. Bretherton & E. Waters (eds.), *Growing points in attachment theory and Research. Monographs for Society for Research in Child Development* 50 (1–2, Serial No. 209), 66–104.

Main, M., & Weston, D. (1981). The quality of the child's relationship to mother and father: related to conflict behavior and the readiness to establish new relationships. *Child Development* 52, 932–940.

Martin, J. A. (1981). *A longitudinal study of the consequences of early mother-infant interaction: A microanalytic approach. Monographs for the Society for Research in Child Development* 46(3), 1–58.

Marvin, R. S. (1977). An ethological-cognitive model for the attenuation of mother-child attachment behavior. In T. M. Alloway; L. Kramer; & P. Pliner (eds.), *Advances in the study of communication and affect: Vol. 3. The development of social attachments*. New York: Plenum.

Matas, L.; Arend, R. A.; & Sroufe, L. A. (1978). Continuity of adaptation in the second year: The relationship between quality of attachment and later competence. *Child Development* 49, 547–556.

Moss, H. (1974). Early sex differences and mother-infant interaction. In R. Friedman, R. Richart, & R. Vande Wiele (eds.), *Sex differences in behavior*. New York: Wiley.

Pastor, D. (1981). The quality of mother-infant attachment and its relationship to toddlers' initial sociability with peers. *Developmental Psychology* 17, 326–335.

Phillips, D.; McCartney, K.; & Scarr, S. (1987). Child care quality and childrens' social development. *Child Development* 23, 537–543.

Phillips, D.; McCartney, K.; Scarr, S.; & Howes, C. (1987). Selective review of infant daycare research: A cause for concern. *Zero to Three* 7, 8–21.

Piaget, J. (1936). *The origins of intelligence in the child.* New York: Harcourt & Brace.

Radke-Yarrow, M.; Cummings, M. E.; Kuczynski, L.; & Chapman, M. (1985). Patterns of attachment in two and three year olds in normal families and families with parental depression. *Child Development* 56, 884–893.

Ruopp, R.; Travers, J.; Glantz, F.; & Coelen, C. (1979). *Children at the center: Final report of the National Day Care Study.* Cambridge, Mass.: Abt Associates.

Schachter, F.; Cooper, A.; & Gordet, R. (1968). *A method for assessing personality development for follow-up evaluations of the preschool child. Monographs of the Society for Research in Child Development* 33 (3, Serial No. 119).

Schneider-Rosen, K.; Braunwald, K.; Carlson, V.; & Cicchetti, D. (1985). Current perspectives in attachment theory: Illustrations from the study of maltreated infants. In I. Bretherton & E. Waters (eds.), *Growing points in attachment research. Monographs of the Society for Research in Child Development* 50 (1–2, Serial No. 209), 194–210.

Slade, A., & Aber, L. (1986, April). The internal experience of parenting toddlers: Toward an analysis of individual and developmental differences. Paper presented at the fifth bienniel International Conference on Infancy Studies, Los Angeles.

Sroufe, L. A. (1979). The coherence of individual development: Early care, attachment and subsequent developmental issues. *American Psychologist* 34, 834–841.

Sroufe, L. A. (1983). Infant-caregiver attachment and patterns of adaptation in the preschool: The roots of maladaptation and competence. In M. Perlmutter (ed.), *Minnesota Symposium on Child Psychology* (vol. 16, pp. 41–83) Hillsdale, N.J.: Erlbaum.

Sroufe, L. A., & Fleeson, J. (1986). Attachment and the construction of relationships. In W. Hartrup & Z. Rubin (eds.), *The nature of relationships.* Hillsdale, N.J.: Erlbaum.

Sroufe, L. A.; Fox, N.; & Pancake, V. (1983). Attachment and dependency in developmental perspective. *Child Development* 54, 1615–1627.

Sroufe, L. A., & Waters, E. (1977). Attachment as an organizational construct. *Child Development* 48, 1184–1199.

Waters, E., & Deane, K. (1985). Defining and assessing individual differences in attachment relationships: Q-methodology and the organization of behavior in infancy and early childhood. In E. Waters & I. Bretherton (eds.), *Growing points in attachment theory and research. Monographs for the Society for Research in Child Development* 50 (1–2, Serial No. 209), 41–65.

Waters, E.; Wippman, J.; & Sroufe, L. A. (1979). Attachment, positive affect and competence in the peer group: Two studies in construct validation. *Child Development* 50, 821–829.

Zaslow, M., & Hayes, C. (1986). Sex differences in childrens' responses to psychosocial stress: Toward a cross-context analysis. In M. Lamb, A. Brown, & B. Rogoff (eds.), *Advances in developmental psychology* (vol. 4, pp. 285–337). Hillsdale, N.Y.: Erlbaum.

PART FIVE

Epilogue

Epilogue

Some Considerations Regarding Theory and Assessment Relevant to Attachments Beyond Infancy

Mary D. Salter Ainsworth

HE WHO WRITES an epilogue may choose to deal with each contribution in turn, commenting on the virtues and/or faults in each. I, however, choose to confine myself to two major topics—theory and assessment—in my commentary about this volume, leaving undiscussed any other issues raised in reports of specific research or in the contributions dealing with developmental psychopathology and intervention.

This approach does not seem inappropriate, because virtually every contribution is heavily weighted with theory, and for most of them issues relating to assessment are of direct or indirect relevance. Furthermore, since this volume is concerned with extending attachment research beyond infancy, which has been much explored, into the later preschool years, it is concerned both with expansion of attachment theory and with devising new age-appropriate approaches to the assessment of attachment.

Attachment theory as originated by John Bowlby (see esp. [1969] 1982, 1973, 1980) is an open-ended theory—open to extension, revision, and refinement through research. It seems important, however, that research into the relatively unexplored territory represented by the years beyond infancy be guided by the principles implicit in attachment theory—as indeed is suggested by Cicchetti, Cummings, Greenberg, and Marvin (this vol.). Otherwise, it would not be clear whether the findings of such research provide grounds for refining or redefining attachment theory, or whether they would merely confirm ad hoc hypotheses that themselves are not implicit in attachment theory. Therefore, this commentary is chiefly concerned with a restatement of some concepts of attachment theory that are relevant to the investigation of the years beyond infancy and yet perhaps were not previously stated explicitly enough to avoid misunderstandings. Among the concepts that are considered are the concept of continuity within change (or, if you prefer, change within continuity); the concept of attachment as a behavioral system, comprehending both observable behavior and internal processes and organization; interactions among behavioral systems; distinctions between attachment and attachment relationships; and the issue of the interface between attachment theory and other theories of personality development.

The success of the Strange-Situation assessment procedure (see Ainsworth, Blehar, Waters, & Wall 1978) has been a mixed blessing for attachment research. To be sure, having such a robust procedure has greatly facilitated research into attachment in infancy. Its very success discouraged a search for other procedures. Doubts about the appropriateness of the Strange-Situation procedure to assess attachment beyond infancy, and the lack of alternative procedures, retarded efforts to extend attachment research to other points in the life span—but fortunately did not discourage them altogether—as the contributors to this volume bear witness.

It is no simple matter, however, to find alternative procedures that validly assess attachment, and the difficulty is compounded by three interlocking considerations. First, one needs to have some adequate basis for knowing how attachments manifest themselves beyond infancy. Thus, second, there must be relevant research into how attachments manifest themselves at the age level at issue. But, third, such research is difficult in the absence of a valid assessment procedure. There is no doubt that astute application of theory helps in this difficult enterprise. Furthermore, the lessons to be learned from attachment research to date can help us to avoid pitfalls. It is with such issues that the second section of this commentary will be concerned.

THEORY

Cicchetti, Cummings, Greenberg, and Marvin (this vol.) point out the need of a theoretical framework for the guidance of research. They assert that attachment theory, which was formulated by John Bowlby ([1969] 1982, 1973, 1980) as spanning the life cycle, constitutes an appropriate theoretical framework for guiding research beyond infancy—even though its heuristic value was first demonstrated in the impressive volume of research into the attachment of infant to parent. This view is shared by the other contributors, who expound the facets of attachment theory believed to be most relevant to their work. It is especially gratifying that so many of them reflect three of the facets that Cicchetti et al. emphasize as major—organization of behavior in context, working models, and the secure-base concept. Relatively few, however, emphasize the other three facets. Thus, few contributions reflect the importance of keeping an evolutionary perspective or emphasize the development of a goal-corrected partnership, both of which are essential to Bowlby's view. And only Marvin and Stewart (this vol.) deal with a family systems' perspective, which is in general harmony with Bowlby's theory.

CONTINUITY AND CHANGE:[1] THREE APPROACHES TO THE
DEVELOPMENT OF ATTACHMENT BEYOND INFANCY

Let us begin our discussion of theory with what has already been accomplished in research into attachment in the years beyond infancy. These accomplishments reflect three distinct approaches to an understanding of the development of attachments and each of these represents a different view of the issue of continuity and change: (1) a view that specifies that the organization of attachments to parent figures in infancy influences the way in which the individual responds to the central tasks of each major phase of later development, (2) a view focusing on the thread of continuity in the organization of attachment from infancy to later points in the life span, and (3) an approach that is concerned with the developmental changes that occur in the nature of attachment itself. Let us consider each of these in turn.

1. The first approach implies that the way attachment becomes organized toward primary attachment figures in infancy influences subsequent development, manifesting itself in individual differences in response to the challenges of later phase-specific tasks. Thus, for example, positing that the second major phase of development is one of establishment of autonomy, this approach implies that the way in which a child copes with the task of integrating autonomy with attachment to the parent figure is what we should focus on in the period of transition from infancy to childhood. From this perspective Sroufe and his associates have pioneered valuable research that demonstrates a striking thread of "coherence" between infant patterns of attachment and development to various later points in the preschool years (e.g., Erickson, Sroufe, & Egeland 1985; Matas, Arend, & Sroufe 1978; Sroufe 1983; Sroufe & Waters 1977; Waters, Wippman, & Sroufe 1979). Defining continuity or coherence of infant attachment patterns and their later behavioral correlates also has some limitations and dangers.

One set of dangers lies in the identification of subsequent phases of development and the central developmental tasks implicit in each. Sroufe appears to rely on Erikson's (1959) account of phases of development, of which only the first phase of "basic trust" has clear overlap with phases of development of attachment, corresponding with Bowlby's first three phases. Erikson's sec-

1. Change here refers primarily to expectable developmental change that tends to occur similarly in individuals in a species-characteristic way in an environment not too different from that to which the species is adapted (in the evolutionary sense). There is also change that is attributable to variations in the environment in which the individual is developing. Continuity here refers to aspects of the individual's structure or behavior that remain recognizably similar over time, regardless of either developmental or environmental change. Patterns of attachment to certain specific figures are hypothesized to remain recognizably similar over time despite developmental change, including change in the way attachment manifests itself in behavior. This is not to say that patterns of attachment are totally resistant to changes attributable to major changes in the environment—and all of the researchers cited in this section hold to this position.

ond phase of development is "autonomy." Although there is little doubt that autonomy increases after infancy is past, there is also a gradual increase of autonomy throughout infancy, as implicit in the concept of the infant becoming able to use his attachment figure as a secure base from which to explore. Bowlby (e.g., 1973) suggests that one of the conditions of secure attachment through childhood and adolescence is the parents' "timely encouragement" of the growth of self-reliance. As far as attachment theory is concerned, the interplay between the attachment system and other behavioral systems (such as the exploratory system) is what is relevant here, and this issue continues through still later phases of the life cycle—as does the issue of attachment (trust) itself. It is indeed useful to consider phases of development as having central tasks, but to be optimally useful in guiding attachment research we should base our phase constructs on empirical examination of developmental changes in order to identify those of most relevance to the way in which attachments and attachment behavior develop.

It seems reasonable to suppose that one such change is the expansion of a preschool child's world to encompass a variety of persons outside the home and encountered when unaccompanied by parents. Therefore, it is appropriate that Sroufe and his associates have as one set of correlates of attachment patterns the way in which the child organizes his behavior toward other children in nursery school and toward the nursery school teachers. Thus, this approach has two focuses: identification of developmental tasks the performance of which correlate with infant patterns of attachment, and a focus on individual differences. It is not designed to inform us of the way in which attachment itself develops.

2. The second approach perhaps began with investigations establishing that, at least in middle-class samples, there is a high degree of stability in the patterns of attachment manifested by individuals at different points in the life span. (The earliest studies dealt only with stability from 12 to 18 months of age [Connell 1974; Main & Weston 1981; Waters 1978]; for stability over wider time spans see Main and Hesse, this vol.) This approach is thus concerned with the continuity in attachment from one age level to another in terms of the persistent similarity in the way attachment is organized across time. Thus, Main and Hesse (this vol.) have drawn attention to the fact that the strategies developed by infants for dealing with attachment-relevant situations (which may be inferred from the pattern of attachment developed in the first year of life) are similarly reflected in the patterns of attachment manifest in the sixth year, and even in adulthood—and therefore presumably also in the preschool years beyond infancy. This approach focuses on attachment itself rather than its correlates, but like approach 1 it also focuses on individual differences. Its obvious limitation is that by itself it does not tell us how attachment itself changes in its nature as development proceeds.

3. The approach that is concerned with the developmental changes that

occur in the nature of attachment itself so far has focused on the shift from Bowlby's third phase in the development of attachment to the fourth phase that is characterized by the development of goal-corrected partnerships, which he believed to begin in the preschool years (Bowlby [1969] 1982). He suggested that this was made possible by cognitive advances—the development of language as a mode of communication, by the development of the ability to take another's perspective, and the ability to negotiate shared plans of action. Marvin (1972, 1977; Marvin & Greenberg 1982) promptly initiated research confirming and expanding Bowlby's views.

It is useful in this connection to consider the shift from Phase II in the development of attachment (when the infant gradually comes to discriminate among familiar figures and to manifest attachment behavior differentially) and Phase III. At about the same time a "package" of changes take place, including acquisition of locomotion, onset of separation distress, onset of intentional or goal-directed behavior (which Bowlby, following general systems theory, calls goal-corrected), and the beginning of clear-cut attachment. It is easy to comprehend this package in evolutionary terms. With the onset of locomotion the infant can move away from the mother to explore the more distant world around him, and at this point the proximity maintenance that is necessary for survival demands not only signals of separation distress to activate his mother's caregiving behavior but also a goal-corrected homeostatic mechanism that leads him actively to seek to maintain a tolerable degree of proximity.

Marvin (who suggested the term "package" to me) perceives that the transition from Phase III to Phase IV also involves a "package" of interrelated developmental changes that are also easily viewed in evolutionary terms. These changes include not only the cognitive changes already mentioned but also ability to tolerate separation from attachment figures for a longer time with less distress, contentment upon reunion with mere presence of and interaction with an attachment figure rather than requiring close bodily contact, and advances in locomotion that enable the child to venture farther away from home base to explore the world and to link up with playmates. Indeed, he reports that neurological advances in myelinization make possible the advances in locomotor ability and thus are also part of the package (Marvin 1977).

Another outstanding developmental change takes place with the onset of adolescence, ushered in by hormonal changes, that leads the young person to begin a search for a goal-corrected partnership with an age peer, usually of the opposite sex—a relationship in which the reproductive system and the caregiving system as well as the attachment system are involved. This does not mean that this partnership, when found, necessitates the cessation of attachments to parents, although it does imply a change in such attachments in that they no longer penetrate as many aspects of the person's life as they did before.

In short, to understand the development of attachments from one age level to another, it is necessary to explore and to understand these changes in the context of other developmental changes and how these in turn interlock with how the environment impinges on the developing individual. Developmental stage theories—such as Erikson's or Piaget's—may give attachment researchers leads, but other areas of developmental research ought not to be neglected.

This approach thus focuses on our need to know how attachments themselves change in their nature over time as a consequence of developmental changes, even though—as approach 2 has it—there is a thread of similarity in the strategies represented by different patterns of attachment over time. Although this third approach is essentially normative, it seems clear that it is not incompatible with the investigation of individual differences as Marvin and Greenberg (1982) demonstrate.

Regardless of whether the focus is upon normative development or individual differences, it would perhaps also be appropriate to consider what family systems theorists (see Marvin & Stewart, this vol.) refer to as "crises of transition"—such as the birth of a younger sibling, parental separation or divorce, change of maternal employment, change in child-care arrangements, beginning school, loss of attachment figure, severe illness, and/or any other critical situation entailing major separation from the principal attachment figure. Such events may temporarily affect the security-insecurity of a child's bond to an attachment figure (or figures), and under some circumstances this change might be lasting. (Easterbrooks & Goldberg, this vol., suggest that account should be taken of the effects of events of this kind.) Some of these events occur so inevitably in almost any family that they might well be considered as influences on normal phases of development; others occur less commonly and yet frequently enough that their effects should be explored.

All three of these approaches have demonstrated their usefulness. However, it is clear that the most apposite to the development of attachment per se is the third; it has been the least explored and should be given more attention. So far it has been usually explored in laboratory/experimental situations; now it ought be investigated more often in the child's natural environments—certainly with observations of child-parent interaction in the home environment but also, where pertinent, with observations of behavior of child with parent(s) and/or parent surrogates in day-care settings or nursery school. It is perhaps easy to forget that intensive observation of behavior in the real-life environment is the chief mode of validation of inferences from theory, controlled experiment, or test. More important, direct observation in the natural environment constitutes a major method of discovery, and thus itself contributes directly to the formulation, extension, and/or refinement of theory. It is gratifying that so many of the contributors to this volume acknowledged the need for observational studies in the natural environments of the preschool child.

Behavioral versus Other Indices of Attachment

Bowlby ([1969] 1982) talked of behavioral homeostasis when discussing the young child's tendency to maintain a certain degree of proximity to an attachment figure, that degree—the set-goal of the attachment system—varying from time to time according to circumstances. Although he did not restrict this concept to infancy, somehow the notion seems to have taken hold among some of the contributors to this volume that attachment during infancy is entirely behavioral, whereas in the later preschool period it becomes increasingly a matter of cognitive and affective processes. Undoubtedly the fact that the Strange-Situation procedure for the assessment of attachment is based on behavioral criteria has contributed to this notion. To be sure, during infancy it is only from behavior that we can infer what processes are going on inside. However, Bowlby's ([1969] 1982) concept of the behavioral system included not only an externally observable aspect (behavior) but also an internal organization ultimately to be understood in terms of the functioning of the central nervous system. The initial inner organization is provided by species-characteristic and individual genetic endowment. But in the course of development the system becomes further organized, and among the inner processes therein involved are cognitive and affective processes. This developmental organization is conceived to hold for the attachment system as for all other "instinctive" behavior systems.

Cognition and affect do not suddenly emerge in the transition period between infancy and childhood, having been absent in infancy. Cognitive and affective processes are intimately interlocked with attachment throughout the life span. It is a mistake to think of attachment entirely in behavioral terms at any stage of development. Attachment is organized within the individual, and we must infer its nature from whatever clues that are available to us, whether these be how the individual behaves or what he says about what he is thinking, feeling, or intending. To be sure, once language emerges we have more clues than before, but it would be naive to believe that language necessarily provides more dependable clues than behavior. Indeed, as the person acquires control over what he does and what he says and to the extent that defensive processes have become established the clues may well become more difficult to read even though they are more numerous.

"A move to the level of representation." This is how Main, Kaplan, and Cassidy (1985) characterized their approach to child-parent attachment in the preschool years. They focused on the working models of attachment figures that the child has developed throughout the history of interaction he or she has had with these figures. These working models may be inferred from the child's performance in a variety of attachment-related tasks undertaken in the absence of the attachment figure, including making a drawing of the family, responding to a photograph of the family, and telling stories about a standard set of drawings that portray separation from a parent or parents. Thus, the essential feature of this approach is the inference about an aspect of the internal organization—the working models—not simply the fact that the inference is made from representations such as drawings or verbal behavior rather than from nonverbal, nonrepresentational behavior. Indeed, even with children in their sixth year, they considered it also appropriate to infer the working model of a parent from the child's behavior upon reunion with that parent after separation.

In fact, to an expert eye, similar inferences can be made from infant behavior either in the Strange Situation or at home. Inner organization of attachments is by no means lacking in infancy. Bowlby ([1969] 1982) described working models as developing in infancy, at least from the beginning of Phase III. Ainsworth (e.g., Bell & Ainsworth 1972; Ainsworth et al. 1978) implied a working model when she spoke of the infant having built up a set of expectations about how mother was likely to respond to him on the basis of how she had responded to him in past situations. This raises the issue of *how* inner representations change during the course of development, an issue so far not addressed.

By "a move to the level of representation" Main and her associates did not mean that cognitive ability for the construction of working models was lacking in infancy. They meant to emphasize the importance of paying more attention to inferences about inner organization in moving to the years beyond infancy, whether these inferences came from nonverbal behavior or verbal or other representations.

Feelings. Just as the notion that attachment is behavioral in infancy implies that cognitive processes are not involved in infant attachment, it implies the same for affective processes. On the contrary, Bowlby (e.g., [1969] 1982, 1977) has clearly emphasized the affective processes implicit in attachments throughout life, beginning in infancy. Thus in 1977/1979 he wrote:

> Many of the most intense emotions arise during the formation, the maintenance, the disruption, and the renewal of attachment relationships. The formation of a bond is described as falling in love, maintaining a bond as loving someone, and losing a partner as grieving over someone. Similarly, threat of loss arouses anxiety, and actual loss gives rise to sorrow; whilst each of these situations is likely to arouse anger. The unchallenged maintenance of a bond is experienced as a source of security, and the renewal of a bond as a source of joy. (Bowlby 1979, p. 130.)

Those who believe that attachment theory has neglected affect, either in infancy or later on, are clearly mistaken. The difficulty is, perhaps, that the discussion of affect in Bowlby's theory is either unfamiliar and/or uncongenial.

Bowlby ([1969] 1982) discussed feelings (affective processes) as involved in the process of "appraising and selecting" rather than as motivations in themselves. Thus:

> . . . affects, feelings, and emotions are phases of an individual's intuitive appraisals either of his own organic states and urges to act or of the succession of environmental situations in which he finds himself . . . it is the appraising processes rather than the feeling and the emotion that require first attention. (Bowlby [1969] 1982, pp. 104–105)

Bowlby conceived of appraising processes as having three roles: (1) appraising sensory input, whether from within the organism or from the environment, including feedback from the organism's own actions, and thus playing an important role in the control of behavior; (2) providing a monitoring service regarding the individual's own states, motivations, and situations; and (3) because the appraising processes are usually accompanied by "distinctive facial expressions, bodily postures, and incipient movements" conveying information to others. Appraising processes may be experienced as feelings or, better, "as felt," but except in their monitoring role they are often not felt—which is to say they may operate either at the level of conscious appraising or below it. Bowlby suggests that this "provides a clue to understanding the ambiguous but clinically useful concept of 'unconscious feeling.'"

Always concerned with accurate and consistent terminology, Bowlby uses the term "feeling" to cover a wide range of "feeling experience," just as the term "affect" has been used traditionally. He confines the term "emotion" to feelings that are "inherently connected with one or another form of action, such as loving, hating, being frightened or hungry." In any case, it is clear that affective processes are not neglected in Bowlby's approach, nor are they conceived as negligible in any phase of development.

Motivation

To Bowlby, motivation is implicit in any behavioral system, of which attachment, caregiving, obtaining food, exploration, and reproduction are examples. Presumably, he would also have to include aggression and wariness as behavioral systems, since they are forms of action "inherently connected" with the emotions of anger and fear, respectively. This latter provides some connection between Bowlby's view and that of many clinicians, who hold that emotions are the mainsprings of action. According to Bowlby, however, motivation refers to the causes of a behavioral system becoming active (chap. 6 of the first volume of *Attachment and Loss* [1969] 1982). These causes are complex and interacting, including a specific environmental stimulus, the way the behavioral system is organized in the central nervous system, hormonal state of the organism, general state of arousal of the organism, and general background level of stimulation. (Of these, present-day psychology has given most emphasis to the specific environmental stimulus. Attachment theory gives equal weight to the inner organization of the behavioral system—but also acknowledges the other three factors as contextual factors that indeed sometimes may have overriding importance.) An emotion felt at the time, however, is a feeling associated with activation of a behavioral system but itself is not the cause of the ensuing behavior.

Interaction among Behavioral Systems

From the beginning, attachment theory has acknowledged that the attachment system is only one among what Bowlby termed "instinctive behavioral systems." He used the term "instinctive" to imply "genetically rooted" and "species-characteristic," presumably to distinguish them from other systems that are, in a broad sense, derived from one or more of the instinctive systems, that are acquired in the course of development and which may be described as having become "functionally autonomous."

These systems interact with one another. Thus, attachment behavior and exploratory behavior are antithetical, in the sense that, when attachment behavior is strongly activated, exploratory behavior tends to be overriden, and vice versa. Some systems often act in synchrony; thus, situations activating fearful/wary behavior likewise tend to intensify attachment behavior; increasing distance from the fear-arousing stimulus and increasing proximity to the attachment figure are usually not antithetical. Sometimes behavioral systems may conflict, as when the intensity of activation of each is approximately equal and simultaneous, but the action prompted by one is antithetical to that prompted by the other. Such conflict is well-known to students of animal behavior and may have a variety of outcomes (Bowlby [1969] 1982). (Bretherton & Ainsworth 1974; Cicchetti & Serafica 1981; and Marvin & Greenberg 1982 both provide discussions of interaction among behavioral systems. Main & Hesse, this vol., suggest that the behavior of a disorganized/disoriented infant is an outcome of an attachment-related conflict situation.)

Attachment theory and research has been concerned chiefly with attachment behavior and with the behavior associated with the parental caregiving system, whereas other behavioral systems have not been elaborated. This is unfortunate, for example, in the case of exploratory behavior—and this was brought to mind by the discussion of the interface between "mastery-motivation" theory and attachment theory discussed by Maslin and Spieker (this vol.). It seems clear that attachment theory is in synchrony with Robert White's (1963) classic discussion of "feelings of effectance." His major point, as I understand it, is that the feedback experienced by an infant (when something has happened as a result of his own action) gives him a "feeling of effectance," which when repeated consistently enough gives him a "sense of competence," which may be interpreted as motivation for further exploration to see what he can make happen. The motivation for this exploration is not derived from some other basic drive, be it sex or hunger; as attachment theory would have it, it is implicit in the exploratory system.

The exploratory system is particularly important in attachment theory because of the concept of the "secure base" and because of our introduction of the notion of the "attachment-exploration balance" (Ainsworth, Bell, & Stayton 1971). We conceive of the exploratory system as not only comprehending an infant's interest in investigating the world around him through all modalities, but also extending to any individual's interest in gaining knowledge about the environment and the people in it, in gaining skills of all kinds in the course of learning to cope with or control what is out there, and generally learning to understand how things work in the world as it is salient to him.

Two features characteristic of the mastery-motivation approach are reported to be (1) motivation autonomous of other motives and systems (already discussed), and (2) goal-directed behavior. Attachment theory would hold that these features are characteristic of *any* behavioral system (not only of mastery motivation), although it would hold that goal-directed behavior is dependent upon cognitive advances occurring in the human about the middle of the first year—and Bowlby ([1969] 1982) prefers the term "goal-corrected."

As attachment theory and research extend their scope and begin to fill in the picture of development over the life cycle, it will become increasingly important to consider other behavioral systems and how they interact with the attachment system. Such considerations should help us avoid confusions of one system with another.

Security

Security may be identified as a feeling—a feeling that reflects a positive evaluation that "all is OK; there is no basis for wariness, alarm, hesitation, or reserve." It is a feeling that gives a "go-ahead" kind of evaluation. Bowlby (1987, personal communication) holds that "the feeling of security is best regarded as a personal signal that all is well and that no further action is required at the moment, in other words can relax." Thus security is a comfortable but not necessarily an intense feeling.

Although attachment theory and research have led us to think of an attachment as the source of secure feeling, there is no reason to believe that being able to rely upon an attachment figure is the only source of feeling secure, important as that clearly is. An individual's appraisal of sensory input may yield the interpretation that "I know how to handle this situation" and thus a secure feeling, directly reflecting self-reliance, and only indirectly reflecting reliance on an attachment figure who may have fostered the growth of self-reliance.

These considerations lead to uneasiness about the suggestion of Sroufe and Waters (1977)—apparently adopted by several contributors to this volume—that beyond infancy the set-goal of the attachment system becomes security rather than proximity to an attachment figure. Their implication is that the child plans how to become secure rather than planning for conditions that, as it turns out, make him secure—which seems beyond the capacity of a young child. On the other hand, one can point to the fact that cognitive development transforms the meaning of proximity, such that longer and longer periods apart from the attachment figure can be tolerated without the bond being threatened. Meanwhile, representational processes make it possible to maintain the model of the attachment figure as being responsive, accessible, and understanding—and a source of security. Thus maintenance of proximity can still be conceived as the set-goal of the attachment system, given that the definition of "closeness" is extended by cognitive development. Bowlby (personal communication 1987) holds that "availability of the attachment figure is the set-goal of the attachment system in older children and adults." This, he says, "turns on cognitive processes: (*a*) belief that lines of communication with the attachment figure are open, (*b*) that physical accessibility exists, and (*c*) that the attachment figure will respond if called upon for help."

Attachment and Attachment Relationships

In the attachment literature, the terms "attachment" and "attachment relationship" have often been used as though they were synonymous—but they are not. When we say that a child is attached to a parent, we mean that the child has organized his attachment behavioral system, with its associated thoughts and feelings, in such a way that he seeks to maintain a degree of proximity to that parent, whom he either finds a source of security or at least wishes to do so. The parent may be identified as an attachment figure for this child, but essentially the attachment is the child's. The child's relationship with the parent may be identified as an attachment relationship—implying simply that it is a relationship with an attachment figure, not that attachment is the only component of the relationship.

According to Hinde (1976), the nature of a relationship between two individuals reflects the whole history of their interaction with each other. Although the most salient role a parent can play in interaction with a child is the role of caregiver providing protection and nurturance, in other interactions that also define the relationship the parent may play other roles, for example, playmate, teacher, disciplinarian, and so on. According to attachment theory, the attachment component of the relationship would be most influenced by interaction with the parent as caregiver. But this component constitutes only part of the relationship. The relevance of these considerations to the assessment of quality of attachment will be discussed later.

In the meantime, it would seem a good idea to specify a child's attachment to a particular parent as being secure (or insecure, as the case may be) rather than specifying the attachment relationship as secure (or otherwise). One partner in the relationship may rely on the other as a source of security, but this may well not be reciprocal—as indeed is the usual case in the relationship between a parent and a young child, for the parent does not normally view the child as a source of security.

Working Models

Of all the possible working models, the model of a child's principal attachment figure (the "mother figure") has attracted most interest. The basis for this model is the real-life experience a child has had in interaction with this figure over time. To be sure, day-to-day experiences may have some inconsistencies, but these normally can be integrated together into a coherent model. However, when the inconsistencies are too great to be integrated—as, for example, when what the mother tells the child to believe (or that the child senses that she wants him to believe) is too much at variance with his actual experiences with her—he may form two or more models of the same figure. One of these tends to be easily accessible to conscious processing. The other(s) are normally not accessible, having been cognitively disconnected, but may nevertheless continue to affect feelings and behavior (Bowlby 1980).

Because working models, whether or not accessible to highest-level (i.e., conscious) processing, influence the way the person construes his experience and hence how he behaves, they may act as self-fulfilling prophecies and hence are difficult to alter once established. Nevertheless, Bowlby acknowledges, they can change with changing experiences. Indeed, his fundamental principle of therapy is that the therapist become an attachment figure to the patient, building up the trust that enables the patient to use him as a secure base from which he can reexamine his working models of attachment figures and of self, reevaluate them in the light of subsequent experience, and revise them if they are perceived as no longer being pertinent to his present circumstances (Bowlby [1977] 1979).

However, as Bretherton, Ridgeway, and Cassidy (this vol.) point out, Bowlby's account of working models leaves much still to be accounted for. The child is conceived as having separate working models for each attachment figure, and these may well have different implications for the way he construes situations and for his resultant action. How are these possible disparities managed? Can they be combined together into one complex but integrated model, and if so how? Main (1985) found different patterns of responding by adults to her Adult Attachment Interview (George, Kaplan, & Main 1985) that tended to match up with their children's pattern of attachment to them. She concluded that some kind of generalized view of attachment figures had been formed, which she refers to as "a state of mind with respect to attachments." This model guides adults' interaction with other people, including their caregiving interactions with their children. How is such a generalized view arrived at?

Bowlby also proposed that, complementary to his working model of an attachment figure, a child forms a working model of the self. As Cassidy

(1988, and this vol.) points out, this notion is not out of line with much previous theorizing about the nature and origin of a person's concept of himself. Although seemingly testable, this proposition has been recalcitrant to research, largely because the self-concept has proven to be very difficult to assess, especially in the case of children. Cassidy succeeded in demonstrating a significant match between the pattern of attachment of 6-year-olds to the mother and positive versus negative self-esteem, although further work on the procedures for assessing self-esteem at this age is probably required to sharpen up the distinctions. However, her study leaves unanswered a major set of questions: whether the working models of the self complementary to the working models of secondary or supplementary attachment figures are overriden by the working model of self complementary to that of the principal attachment figure, or whether all are combined in some way, and if so how? And, indeed, since it is reasonable to suppose that working models of persons other than attachment figures may be constructed, can these also have influence on the working model of the self?

Although Bowlby ([1969] 1982) talked of a child forming working models of his environment, of attachment figures, and of self, there is no reason to believe he meant that no other working models could be formed. Indeed, it seems likely that a person can form a working model of essentially anything. Marvin and Stewart (this vol.) suggest that each member of a family may construct his or her own working model of the family and how it operates, based on his or her perceptions of family interactions. Growing out of her work with maltreating families, Crittenden (in press a; in press b) inferred the characteristics of the working models maltreating mothers had of relationships with other people generally—inferring distinctive models for mothers who were abusing, or neglecting, or both abusing and neglecting, or marginally maltreating, or indeed adequate. She inferred these models from observations of the mother's interaction with her children, the pattern of the target child's attachment to her, her relationship with her partner, what she said about her relationship with her own parents, with friends, and other members of her social network, and how "professionals" responded to their interactions with her. This seems to be a most useful kind of distillation—just as Marvin and Stewart's suggestion seems as potentially very useful.

The Interface of Attachment Theory with Other Theories

Bowlby has made it quite clear that his theory is eclectic in its origins. His genius, however, lies in the way he has integrated a diversity of concepts together to form a coherent and comprehensive theory that is still open-ended and subject to revision and/or extension through the research to which it has provided a useful guide. As such, it is understandable that attachment theory has stimulated many who are working within its general framework to attempt to assimilate other theories to it, or at least to look outside of attachment theory for other concepts useful to their work. Thus, as already mentioned, Sroufe and his associates have looked elsewhere for understanding of the central developmental tasks facing a child in each major phase of development, and Marvin and Stewart (this vol.) have sought to assimilate into attachment theory the family systems theory espoused by the Minuchins (e.g., S. Minuchin 1974; P. Minuchin 1985). Maslin and Spieker (this vol.) have dealt with attachment theory in relation to the theory associated with "mastery motivation."

Yet it is difficult to achieve even a limited consensus between adherents of two quite divergent theoretical paradigms. Each tries to translate the principles of the other paradigm into concepts assimilable into the paradigm that has shaped his own understanding—usually with the result that neither is content with the other's efforts. Nevertheless, there is often something to be gained, be it only borrowing from the alien paradigm in a limited way—thus, for example, the good use Bowlby (1973) made of Bandura's research into deconditioning fears. In this volume, Speltz has successfully translated certain procedures used in behavior modification into procedures consonant with attachment theory. Lieberman and Pawl (this vol.), conducting clinical intervention research with young children at very high risk, have combined principles from attachment theory and principles from object-relations theory in such a harmonious way that their findings are comprehensible to adherents of each. One could easily point out that attachment theory attributes to real-life experience that which most object-relations theorists attribute to phantasy, and that the former roots motivation in the behavioral systems whereas many of the latter consider emotions the motivational mainsprings. But Lieberman and Pawl emphasize the common ground between the two approaches.

To the extent that there is common ground between two theories, it is helpful to both to point it out. In general, however, if one adheres to attachment theory, it seems best to try to translate as much as one can into attachment theory, benefiting from the other perspective and not attempting to do so with what is unassimilable. To my way of thinking, it does not work to deal simultaneously with two theoretical paradigms without an attempt to assimilate one to the other; the result is likely to be intellectual confusion, with terminology in one theory having different connotations in the other. Thus, for example, when proceeding from a basis of attachment theory it is confusing to use the term "separation" as Mahlerian theory does—as denoting turning interest toward objects and away from mother rather than denoting physical separation from the attachment figure and thus inaccessibility of that figure.

Assessment

Scattered through this volume are discussions related to assessment. Although these are closely connected to theoretical issues discussed earlier, it seems useful to draw considerations of assessment together in a separate section. Let us indeed speak of "assessment," since "measurement" implies a linear scale—and our most useful assessments of attachments, so far, have been categorical (i.e., classificatory) rather than linear.

Classification of Patterns versus Linear Scales

So far, it has not been feasible to think of attachment as a continuum. Initially, Schaffer and Emerson (1964) attempted to measure the strength of attachment in terms of the intensity of an infant's attachment behavior. However, not only does the intensity of the attachment behavior manifested by any infant depend on the situation in which he is observed, but also it is clearly affected by the extent to which he or she is securely versus insecurely attached to the figure in question, with those who are insecurely attached generally displaying more intense attachment behavior than those who are securely attached—at least in the natural environment of the home.

Instead of measurement in terms of one or more continua, it has proved to be useful to assess individual differences in attachment in terms of patterns of behavior, from which we can infer differences in the way in which the attachment system is internally organized. Assessment through identification of patterns is well suited to the complexity of the cause-effect relationships with which we are dealing. Increasingly, it is recognized that the "causes" with which we are concerned consist of a multiplicity of interacting variables, and that developmental outcomes—"effects"—are equally complex. Instances of linear cause-effect relationships in psychological studies of development are indeed scarce.

The Strange-Situation assessment procedure is essentially a classification procedure that yields identification of three main classificatory categories—the A/B/C categories—which are so well known that familiarity with them is assumed. Now Main has identified a fourth category—first identified as "unclassified" (Main & Weston 1981) and later as "disorganized/disoriented" (Main & Solomon, this vol.). This classificatory system is not a typology, for it does not relate to traits of individuals but rather to the nature of the individual's attachment to a specific figure, and this can differ from one attachment figure to another. It is open-ended, in the sense that subcategories may be distinguished within each of the main categories—as many as seem useful and can be supported by validation research.

The Strange-Situation procedure did provide for supplementary scales (constructed by a modification of Thurstone's scaling procedure) measuring strength of several kinds of Strange-Situation behavior that seemed pertinent to the classificatory system. Although these scales proved useful in multivariate statistical analyses, they are no substitute for the classificatory patterns—nor indeed may the patterns be inferred solely from scale scores. Main and Cassidy (1988), when constructing a procedure for classifying patterns of child-parent attachment in 6-year-olds on the basis of a laboratory reunion situation, also offered scales for measuring avoidance and security-insecurity. The avoidance scale, as in the case of the comparable Strange-Situation avoidance scale, was designed to help the assessor to identify behavior that operated as avoidance. The secure half of the security-insecurity scale also is helpful to the assessor in identifying different degrees of security—but the insecure half is less helpful, for it depends on the assessor having already made a classification of the pattern of behavior into one or other of the insecure subgroups. It certainly cannot substitute for the classifications themselves, except as may be useful for parametric statistics. Indeed, Main et al. (1985) for statistical purposes transformed infant classifications into a simple four-point magnitudinal ordering of groups and subgroups. Cummings (this vol.) proposes a four-point security-insecurity scale that seems to have similar drawbacks and advantages.

"Felt security" and Defensive Processes. A major difficulty with linear scales of security-insecurity is the issue of the effect of defensive processes on feelings of security and insecurity. This issue requires some explanation. As Bowlby (1980) points out, current situations are usually appraised in the light of previous experience carried "in storage," but if the current situation activates conflicts that are too painful to be faced, this previous experience may become disconnected and thus not drawn upon. Memories, thoughts, and feelings previously experienced thus are not brought to bear in interpretation of the present situation; they may well continue to have an influence on behavior, however, even though not "felt" currently. They provide information that is processed at a level below the highest (conscious) level of information processing. And since insecure feelings can be disconnected from conscious processing, as indeed they are when defensive processes such as avoidance are brought into play, the individual may indeed *feel* secure (to the extent that his defense is working), but this security is an undependable security that may veer into insecurity according to circumstance, or it is brittle, sometimes breaking down completely under intense stress. It may be assumed that underlying consciously felt security lurk unconscious feelings of insecurity that may still betray themselves by influencing behavior and/or physiological processes. Furthermore, in some situations the unconscious feelings of insecurity may clearly manifest themselves, such as with projective techniques. Thus avoidant 6-year-olds in the Hansburg Separation Anxiety Test clearly manifested anxious feelings (Kaplan 1987). These issues obviously present a conceptual problem for a scale purporting to measure felt security-insecurity. Which kind of security are we dealing with? That at the conscious level or the unconscious level of processing? At least if we stick to classificatory categories we at least can assume that the category specified as employing strong

defense is likely to show signs of felt security—as well as having unfelt insecurity.

As we proceed with assessment in later ages, the problem of differentiation between the two kinds of security does not disappear. Cassidy (this vol., and 1988), using a self-report interview technique to assess self-esteem, found that 6-year-olds classified as insecure-avoidant tended to report themselves as "perfect" and without shortcomings or flaws. (Unfortunately, so did some securely attached children, who were likely to have had experience better justifying such high self-esteem.) On the other hand, Main, in assessing how the adults in her Berkeley sample thought about attachments on the basis of their experience using the Adult Attachment Interview (AAI), did not have to take at face value the content of the statements yielded in the interview, but as in a clinical interview could identify defensive processes such as detachment. Kobak and Sceery's (1988) research with first-year college students used the Adult Attachment Interview, and compared the classificatory attachment findings with (a) the findings of several self-report inventories and (b) a personality Q-sort assessment undertaken by age peers (Block & Block 1978). It emerged that those classified by the AAI as dismissing of attachment (i.e., detached and defensive) could not be distinguished through self-report from those securely attached, except for lacking of adequate parental support, whereas the personality Q-sort supported an inference of insecurity masked by defensive processes. In summary, it is clear that any assessment of the quality of attachment, presumably at any age, must take defensive processes into account—and this highlights the importance of the assessment differentiating among patterns of organization.

The Disorganized/Disoriented Category. The Strange-Situation classificatory procedure was always intended to be open-ended, for it seemed unreasonable to assume that two small samples of infants from white, middle-class Baltimore families could comprehend all patterns of behavior that could occur in the Strange Situation. Indeed, it is surprising that the three main patterns that had been identified sufficed researchers for so long. As Main and Solomon (this vol.) point out, however, almost from the beginning there were a few infants whose behavior did not precisely fit into the classificatory system, and this was especially the case when "at risk" samples were assessed, such as children of depressed or maltreating parents.

Therefore, it is acceptable to consider adding to the *A/B/C* categories the fourth, *D*, category that Main has identified as disorganized or disoriented, and also to acknowledge her provision of an unclassified (*U*) category for other patterns of behavior that are not classifiable even with this extended system. Now that so much careful work has been done to explore the ramifications of this new category, it may be accepted as a valuable extension of the Strange-Situation classificatory system. No more will be said about this extension here, since the chapters in this volume by Main and Solomon and Main and Hesse provide comprehensive coverage.

Subgroups. Because many investigations using Strange-Situation assessments employed small samples, the size of the subgroups was too small to yield statistically significant discriminations using usual statistical measures. Consequently, many investigators have come to ignore subgroups. This is unfortunate, for these variations on the three main patterns of attachment were in Ainsworth's longitudinal sample related to clear-cut differences in maternal caregiving behavior (Ainsworth et al. 1971). Furthermore, Main and Cassidy (1988) report that their 6-year reunion procedure shows significant subgroup match between two assessments a month apart. And Main (1985) found that the cross-generational match between parents' Adult Attachment Interview subgroup classifications and those of their 1-year-olds proved to be significant.

Of all the major classifications, we have perhaps most difficulty with the anxious-ambivalent (or *C*) pattern—perhaps because it is seen so infrequently in most samples that have been studied. Even in Ainsworth's original longitudinal sample, it seemed to yield a more miscellaneous group than either the *A* or *B* patterns did. Nevertheless, the highly anxious and angry C_1s and the passive C_2s had experienced clearly different antecedent maternal behavior. In the Strange Situation, the C_2s betrayed their anger in being slow to be soothed as well as in subtly resistant behavior such as a little kick when being picked up, even though they were less flamboyant in their angry resistance than the C_1s. Schneider-Rosen (this vol.) apparently overlooked the C_1s altogether when extending the Strange-Situation classificatory procedure to apply to the 18–24-month-old period, for her descriptions of *C*s focused on passivity— and indeed she ignored subgroup distinctions altogether, which is a pity. We need to learn a lot more about the *C* patterns, whether in the 1-year-old or later on.

One last word about subgroups—the identification of *D*s has made obsolete the definition of B_4s given by Ainsworth et al. (1978). The specification of stereotypies and other odd behaviors now suggests disorganization or disorientation—a *D* classification—and should be omitted from the B_4 specifications.

Searching for New Assessment Procedures

It now seems essential to search for new procedures for assessing quality of attachment. Not only is it desirable to find procedures well adapted to different developmental levels, but at any level it seems to me to be desirable to have more than one procedure available. This would perhaps have become evident sooner had not the Strange-Situation procedure for 1-year-olds provided such a robust method. It is not yet clear that any single one of the new procedures available for childhood beyond infancy are similarly robust. Main and her associates have set us a good example in providing several procedures at the level of the sixth year (see Main, Kaplan, & Cassidy 1985) that suggest multiple assessments. The high degree of match among the findings of these procedures yields confidence in their convergent validity, but they seem not to be entirely interchangeable, which implies that greater eventual depth of understanding is to be obtained through their combined use.

Components of Relationships. Researchers in search of new methods of assessing attachment beyond infancy will not find it all clear sailing even if they eschew self-report measures and rely on observation of the individual's interaction with an attachment figure as a basis for the assessment. Some seem to have assumed that any kind of significant interaction with an attachment figure reflects the quality of attachment. Thus, an assessment situation may consist of a mother being instructed to play with her child or to teach her child how to perform some task. To be sure, such situations may tell us something significant about the mother-child relationship, and certainly about the mother's input to the relationship, but not in all cases do they yield significant information about quality of attachment of child to mother.

Although mothers whose sensitive responsiveness to a child's communications fosters secure attachment may also be engaging playmates, or supportive teachers, or skillful disciplinarians, this is not necessarily so. (I remember that the mothers of Ganda babies who were securely attached to them almost never played with them, even though they were highly sensitive caregivers.) Therefore, it is not surprising if investigators find that assessments based on interaction in play, teaching situations, or disciplinary situations show less than desirable match to current or earlier assessments that more directly reflect organization of behavior toward mother in a protective, caregiving role.

Correlated measures. Sroufe and his associates have conducted—and inspired—much research that examines the relationship (degree of coherence) between assessments of attachment at 12 and/or 18 months and performance in a variety of later age-appropriate developmental tasks. Performance on these later tasks correlates with assessments of attachment sometimes impressively, sometimes modestly, and sometimes to no significant extent at all. Some researchers seeking a procedure for assessing attachment at an age at which the Strange-Situation procedure has been deemed to be inappropriate have chosen one of these tasks. These tasks do not constitute procedures for assessing attachment, nor were they so intended by Sroufe and his associates.

Although Sroufe (e.g., 1983) found that infant attachment classifications differentiate different patterns and degrees of social competence with peers in nursery school, this is not to say that all measures of social competence are strongly correlated to the quality of child-mother attachment. Thus, Cohn (1988) did not establish a close connection between child-mother attachment classifications at age 6 with state-of-the-art sociometric measures as used by social psychologists. A surprising proportion of those identified as "popular" sociometrically were classed as anxious-avoidant rather than as securely attached to their mothers. Most of those identified as "neglected" (or perhaps overlooked by their classmates) sociometrically had been identified as securely attached. About half of those identified as "rejected" sociometrically—the more extreme half—had been classed as anxious-avoidant, but the other half had been classed as securely attached. On close examination, these findings were quite understandable, and the study was certainly worth doing—both to discover more about the age group in question and to elucidate that different ways of assessing social competence with peers can yield findings with different theoretical implications.

Stability of Assessments Over Time

Attachment theory holds that there tends to be continuity despite changes in the course of development—or, if you prefer, change despite continuity. Two factors make for continuity in child-parent attachment: (1) an environment that is relatively stable in the quality of age-appropriate interaction between attachment figure and child, and (2) the fact that the way a child has internally organized his attachment behavior with that figure tends to be resistant to change. Although attachment researchers themselves have certainly acknowledged that major environmental changes can be connected with significant changes in attachment quality, critics of attachment theorists claim that we believe that the quality of attachment is set in infancy—for all time. Attachment researchers deny this belief attributed to them, but most of them would insist that the environmental changes that are effective in changing quality of attachment are those that change its internal organization, either because they change the nature of the interaction the attachment figure has with the child, or because they change the child's perception of the responsiveness and accessibility of that figure. In the meantime, it is quite clear that the child's inner organization of attachments serves to guide his behavior. Thus, in the Strange-Situation, in which the behavior of the parent is at least partially controlled, it may be seen that the child is influenced by his inner organization and not solely by the way the parent is currently behaving. Later, somehow, the way the child has organized his attachments to primary figures influences his behavior in situations in which the primary figures are not present. We must conclude that both factors interact in making for continuity of attachment quality—with the inner organization tending to resist change and assimilating new experiences to the organization, and yet being capable of accommodating to changing circumstances.

Assuming that this is so, it is little wonder that, if one wishes to highlight developmental changes in the nature of attachment between different ages, one draws a sample from a population in which major environmental changes are relatively unlikely—for example, from intact families in a white, middle-class American sample, although with the great increase in maternal employment currently such a sample would probably have more such changes than it would have had twenty years ago. If one wishes to study factors that lead to changes in security-insecurity of attachment, one would draw one's sample from a population in which discontinuity and change were likely to be frequent—for example, from a low SES population, or from one of children already judged to be "at risk." Both kinds of enterprise are laudable and necessary.

With the kind of sample likely to minimize change in attachment assessment over time, it has been found that the match of major attachment classification from 12 to 18 months has tended to be about 80%. Having established this, it is reasonable to anchor a later assessment on an earlier assessment considered valid, so that one can recognize developmental transformations of attachment and the way they manifest themselves. This is a major criterion Main and her associates used in devising and checking the validity of their assessments of children in their sixth year and, through cross-generational match, the Adult Attachment Interview classification procedure. This is also one of the criteria in which the 3-year attachment procedure currently under construction is anchored (Cassidy & Marvin with collaboration of the MacArthur Working Group on Attachment, 1989). Inferences from attachment theory provide another criterion, and so do inferences from the child's behavior in the assessment situation, aided by familiarity with attachment-related behavior observed (or reported from) elsewhere. A fourth and very important criterion comes from observation of the child's and the attachment figure's behavior in the natural environment. Although theory and home observation were all that was available to Ainsworth when formulating the Strange-Situation procedure, this is not so with more recent assessment procedures. And, therefore, one need not insist that research with a new procedure need await validation against behavior in the natural environment. Indeed, a partially validated new procedure is likely to stimulate research that we hope, in due course, will yield results promising enough to encourage the great labor (and expense) of adequate naturalistic observations.

Causes of Instability of Assessments. The most obvious causes of change in quality of attachment were mentioned earlier and include (1) events such as prolonged or depriving separation from an attachment figure or permanent loss of that figure through death or desertion; or (2) a substantial alteration of the nature of the caregiving behavior provided by the attachment figure in question, whatever its cause—whether change of caregiving arrangements occasioned by change in maternal employment, marital disharmony, spousal abuse, parental separation or divorce, or, indeed, any change in degree of stress impinging on the attachment figure. So far, the effects of separation and loss have been most studied, and although the short-term effects tend to be predictably adverse research has shown that more long-term effects are very much affected by a variety of other factors. So far, our knowledge of even the short-term effects of the second set of circumstances is inadequately known. They certainly should be researched—and shifts of attachment classification from one age to another are a major point of entry into such investigation.

Other causes of instability in classification may well be very temporary. We attempt to avoid those that seem predictable—thus trying to insure that the child brought in for assessment is neither too fatigued, nor hungry, nor ill, nor having recently experienced a disturbing event, such as a separation of several days or more. In regard to the Strange Situation (and perhaps also other attachment assessment procedures designed for developmental levels beyond infancy), it is a good rule that *no* other procedure should come before it. Other tasks or procedures that themselves introduce stress, or familiarization procedures that either make the child too much at ease or too absorbed to wish to be interrupted, may quite invalidate the assessment procedure being used.

Having worked primarily with infants, perhaps we have paid too little attention to what the family-systems theorists have called "crises of transition," such as the recent birth of a younger sibling, or a move of family residence away from familiar surroundings and friends. Whether or not we can identify such potential sources of change in advance and defer the assessment, in retrospect they may be identified as factors in terms of which change can be accounted for. Some "crises of transition," such as the birth of a younger sibling, may occur so commonly as to constitute normal developmental challenges to be coped with, whereas others, such as a move of family residence, occur more randomly. A child who is securely attached to his caregivers may temporarily be made insecure by such crises, and thus assessments made close to the unsettling event may be misleading. In some cases, however, they may sufficiently alter either the nature of the child's interaction with attachment figures, or his working models of attachment figures and/or self to shift the course of development in a more lasting way. In either case, delay of assessment so that it does not follow too closely upon such a critical event seems advisable, when possible.

Stress. In the Strange Situation, stress was deliberately and progressively introduced—in terms of the unfamiliarity of the situation, the introduction of a stranger, and by two brief separations from the accompanying attachment figure, in the second of which the infant was at first left quite alone. These increasing stresses did indeed heighten attachment behavior—although they were intended to approximate the kind and degree of stresses that middle-class children in Western society have occasionally encountered in real life, and not sufficiently severe as to have any but a very short-term carry-over, or as to make all subjects so distressed as to eliminate individual differences. Although for Ainsworth's longitudinal sample there had been extensive observational records of behavior at home throughout the first year, individual differences in attachment-related behavior with all their day-to-day variations were not as sharply distinguished as they were in the Strange Situation. The stress-induced intensification of the attachment behavioral system greatly facilitated the perception of different patterns of organization of behavior relevant to the attachment figure.

A chief misgiving about using the Strange Situation in assessing attachment much beyond the 12-month level was that, with increasing age, the degree of stress in the situation was increasiingly less, as the child became more accustomed to everyday separations of greater length, and better able to cope with unfamiliar environments and unfamiliar people, even without the presence of an attachmment figure. It is now realized that the Strange Situation offers enough stress even for the assessment of a 3- or 4-year-old, but the criteria for classification must be different in order to accommodate the procedure to age changes, as Marvin proposed as long ago as 1972.

Nevertheless, it seems likely that some degree of appropriate stress helps to highlight the behavior from which we infer differences in patterns of attachment. It tends to smooth out the effects of day-to-day variability in circumstances that affect feelings about attachment figures and attachment-related issues. Indeed, the recently developed assessment procedures are not lacking in stress. Thus, in all of Main's 6-year procedures, there is an hour-long separation from parents, and most of that time is spent in tasks having some relation to family, attachment, or separation issues—all of which appear to occasion some stress. One could not predict that an hour spent in wholly congenial play would occasion the same stress, or that reunion after a much shorter separation would yield the same differentiations that the Main and Cassidy reunion procedure does. Meanwhile, the parents separately have been undergoing the Adult Attachment Interview, which itself has undoubted impact—surprising the subject with its directness in demanding an account of early relationships or, as Main has said, "surprising the unconscious." Different degrees of stress—whether too much or too little—might make a difference in the validity of the inferences the standard procedures call for. On the other hand, both older children and adults have learned pretty well to cope with the everyday kinds of stresses they have been used to encountering. To expose them to a kind or degree of stress that they would not have already learned somehow to cope with probably would be extreme enough or bizarre enough to defeat its own purpose, and furthermore be interpreted by others as unethical.

Conclusion

In conclusion, let us congratulate the contributors to this volume for work that is serving to advance the horizons of our understanding of attachments across the life cycle. Although they tend to have deliberately limited themselves to the preschool years beyond infancy, this is a highly significant period of development. Increased understanding of attachment during this period will provide an important stepping-stone to later periods. Even though some have had substantial success in leaping from infancy to later periods (even adulthood), there is no doubt that investigation of the period immediately beyond infancy is useful—indeed essential. Since agencies supporting research have lost faith in the ambitious long-term longitudinal projects, such as those begun in the 1920s and 1930s, the best hope of longitudinal research is to proceed in a leap-frogging sort of operation. Thus, what we know of the manifestations of attachment in infancy can serve as a basis for leaping to a somewhat older period. Having established a base of knowledge there, we can leap forward for a few years, without having to begin all over again in infancy, and so on. Let us build up a firm base of knowledge of attachment in the preschool years beyond infancy as a basis of another leap. On this basis, longitudinal research becomes feasible.

REFERENCES

Ainsworth, M. D. S.; Bell, S. M.; & Stayton, D. J. (1971). Individual differences in strange-situation behavior of one-year-olds (pp. 17–57). In H. R. Schaffer (ed.), *The origins of human social relations*. New York: Academic Press.

Ainsworth, M. D. S.; Blehar, M. C.; Waters, E.; & Wall, S. (1978). *Patterns of attachment: A study of the strange situation*. Hillsdale, N.J.: Erlbaum.

Bell, S. M., & Ainsworth, M. D. S. (1972). Infant crying and maternal responsiveness. *Child Development* 43, 1171–1190.

Block, J. H., & Block, J. (1978). *The Q-sort method of personality assessment and psychiatric research*. Palo Alto: Consulting Psychologists Press.

Bowlby, J. ([1969] 1982). *Attachment and loss: Vol. 1. Attachment*. New York: Basic Books.

Bowlby, J. (1973). *Attachment and loss: Vol. 2. Separation: Anxiety and anger*. New York: Basic Books.

Bowlby, J. ([1977] 1979). The making and breaking of affectional bonds. *British Journal of Psychiatry* 130, 201–210, and 421–431. Reprinted in J. Bowlby, *The making and breaking of affectional bonds* (pp. 126–160). London: Tavistock.

Bowlby, J. (1980). *Attachment and loss: Vol. 3. Loss: Sadness and depression*. New York: Basic Books.

Bretherton, I., & Ainsworth, M. D. S. (1974). Responses of one-year-olds to a stranger in a strange situation. In M. Lewis, L. A. Rosenblum (eds.), *The origin of fear* (pp. 131–164). New York: Wiley.

Cassidy, J. (1988). Child-mother attachment and the self in six-year-olds. *Child Development* 59, 121–134.

Cassidy, J., & Marvin, R. S.; with the MacArthur Working Group on Attachment Network on the Transition from Infancy to Early Childhood (1989). Attachment organization in three- and four-year-olds: A classification system. Unpublished manuscript, University of Virginia and Pennsylvania State University.

Cicchetti, D., & Serafica, F. C. (1981). The interplay among behavioral systems: Illustration from the study of attachment, affiliation, and wariness in young Down's syndrome children. *Developmental Psychology, 17*, 36–49.

Cohn, D. A. (1988). Security of attachment at 6 years of age and peer social competence in first grade. Unpublished Ph.D. dissertation, University of Virginia.

Crittenden, P. M. (in press a). Distorted patterns of relationship in maltreating families: The role of internal representational models. *Journal of Reproductive and Infant Psychology*.

Crittenden, P. M. (in press b). Dyadic and family patterns of functioning in maltreating families. In K. Browne, C. Davies, & P. Stratton (eds.), *Early prediction and prevention of child abuse*. New York: Wiley.

Connell, D. B. (1974). Individual differences in infant attachment related to a redundant stimulus. Unpublished master's thesis, Syracuse University.

Erickson, M. F.; Sroufe, L. A.; & Egeland, B. (1985). The relationship between quality of attachment and behavior problems in preschool in a high-risk sample. In I. Bretherton & E. Waters (eds.) *Growing points of attachment theory and research. Monographs of the Society for Research in Child Development* 50(1–2, Serial No. 209), 147–166.

Erikson, E. H. (1959). Identity and the life cycle. *Psychological Issues.* Monograph No. 1. New York: International Universities Press.

George, C.; Kaplan, N.; & Main, M. (1985). The Berkeley Adult Attachment Interview. Unpublished protocol, Department of Psychology, University of California, Berkeley.

Greenberg, M. T., & Marvin, R. S. (1982). Reactions of preschool children to an adult stranger: A behavioral systems approach. *Child Development* 55, 481–490.

Hinde, R. A. (1976). On describing relationships. *Journal of Child Psychology and Psychiatry* 17, 1–19.

Kaplan, N. (1987). Individual differences in six-year-old's thoughts about separation: Predicted from attachment to mother at one year. Unpublished Ph.D. dissertation, University of California, Berkeley.

Kobak, R. R., & Sceery, A. (1988). Attachment in late adolescence: Working models, affect regulation, and representations of self and others. *Child Development* 59, 135–146.

Main, M. (1985). An adult attachment classification system: Its relation to infant-parent attachment. In M. Main, Attachment: A move to the level of representation. Symposium conducted at the biennial meeting of the Society for Research in Child Development, Toronto.

Main, M., & Cassidy, J. (1988). Categories of response with the parent at age six: Predicted from infant attachment classifications and stable over a one month period. *Developmental Psychology* 24, 415–426.

Main, M.; Kaplan, N.; & Cassidy, J. (1985). Security in infancy, childhood and adulthood: A move to the level of representation. In I. Bretherton & E. Waters (eds.), *Growing points in attachment theory and research. Monographs of the Society for Research in Child Development* 50(1–2, Serial No. 209), 66–104.

Main, M., & Weston, D. (1981). The quality of the toddler's relationship to mother and to father: Related to conflict behavior and the readiness to establish new relationships. *Child Development* 52, 932–940.

Marvin, R. S. (1972). Attachment-, exploratory- and communicative behavior in 2-, 3-, and 4-year-old children. Unpublished doctoral dissertation, University of Chicago.

Marvin, R. S. (1977). An ethological-cognitive model for the attenuation of mother-child attachment behavior. In T. Alloway, L. Krames, & P. Pliner (eds.), *Advances in the study of communication and affect: Vol. 3. Attachment behavior.* New York: Plenum.

Marvin, R. S., & Greenberg, M. T. (1982). Preschoolers' changing conceptions of their mothers: A social-cognitive study of mother-child attachment. In D. Forbes & M. T. Greenberg (eds.), *New directions in child development: Children's planning strategies* (vol. 18). San Francisco: Jossey-Bass.

Matas, L.; Arend, R. A.; & Sroufe, L. A. (1978). Continuity of adaptation in the second year: The relation between quality of attachment and later competence. *Child Development* 49, 547–556.

Minuchin, P. (1985). Families and individual development: Provocations from the field of family therapy. *Child Development* 56, 289–302.

Minuchin, S. (1974). *Families and family therapy.* Cambridge, Mass.: Harvard University Press.

Schaffer, H. R., & Emerson, P. E. (1964). The development of social attachments in infancy. *Monographs of the Society for Research in Child Development* 29, (3, Serial No. 94).

Sroufe, L. A. (1983). Infant-caregiver attachment and patterns of adaptation in preschool: The roots of maladaptation and competence. In M. Perlmutter (ed.), *Minnesota Symposium on Child Psychology* (vol. 16, pp. 41–81). Hillsdale, N.J.: Erlbaum.

Sroufe, L. A., & Waters, E. (1977). Attachment as an organizational construct. *Child Development* 48, 1184–1199.

Waters, E. (1978). The reliability and stability of individual differences in infant-mother attachment. *Child Development* 49, 483–494.

Waters, E.; Wippman, J.; & Sroufe, L. A. (1979). Attachment, positive affect, and competence in the peer group: Two studies in construct validation. *Child Development* 50, 821–829.

White, R. W. (1963). *Ego and reality in psychoanalytic theory.* New York: International Universities Press.

Index

Pages on which tables appear are designated with *t*